READING WRITING AND RHETORIC

THIRD EDITION

James Burl Hogins
Robert E. Yarber

San Diego Mesa College

SCIENCE RESEARCH ASSOCIATES, INC.
Chicago, Palo Alto, Toronto
Henley-on-Thames, Sydney, Paris, Stuttgart

A Subsidiary of IBM

Library of Congress Cataloging in Publication Data

Hogins, James Burl, comp.
  Reading, writing, and rhetoric.

  Includes index.
  1. College readers.   I. Yarber, Robert E.
II. Title.
PE1122.H64 1976   808'.04275   75-23104
ISBN 0-574-22020-8

ACKNOWLEDGMENTS

FUTURISM: WHAT WILL LIFE BE LIKE IN 1985? reprinted from *The Graduate* magazine, © 1974 by Approach 13-30 Corporation. Used with publisher's permission.

THE CONSTITUTION IS ALIVE AND WELL © 1972/1974 by The New York Times Company. Reprinted by permission."

WHERE FEMINISM WILL LEAD by Lucy Komisar. Used by permission.

LIVING FOR NOW from *Open Marriage, A New Lifestyle for Couples* by Nena O'Neill and George O'Neill. Copyright © 1972 by Nena O'Neill and George O'Neill. Reprinted by permission of the publisher, M. Evans and Company, Inc., New York, N.Y. 10017.

WHATEVER BECAME OF SIN? reprinted from "Whatever Became of Sin?" by Karl Menninger in *Intellectual Digest Magazine*, April, 1974. Used by permission of Hawthorn Books, Inc.

HOW TO SAY NOTHING IN FIVE HUNDRED WORDS from *Understanding English* by Paul Roberts. Copyright © 1958 by Paul Roberts. Reprinted by permission of Harper and Row, Publishers, Inc.

GOOD USAGE, BAD USAGE, AND USAGE from *The American Heritage Dictionary of the English Language*. © Copyright 1969, 1970, 1971 by American Heritage Publishing Co. Inc. Reprinted by Permission.

DE-SEXING THE ENGLISH LANGUAGE Copyright © 1975 by the NYM Corp., reprinted with the permission of NEW YORK Magazine.

THE FRESHMAN AND HIS DICTIONARY from an article by Mitford Mathews in *College Composition Communication*, December 1955, Copyright 1955 by the National Council of Teachers of English. Reprinted by permission of the publisher and Mitford M. Mathews.

LOGIC AND LOGICAL FALLACIES reprinted by permission of the author from *Handbook for English A*. Copyright © 1941 by the President and Fellows of Harvard University.

ARE ALL GENERALIZATIONS FALSE? from *The Art of Making Sense*, 3rd Edition, by Lionel Ruby and Robert E. Yarber. Reprinted by permission of the publisher, J. B. Lippincott Company. Copyright © 1974.

THE LANGUAGE OF WHITE RACISM from an article by Haig Bosmajian in College English, December 1969. Copyright © 1969 by the National Council of Teachers of English. Reprinted by permission of the publisher and Haig Bosmajian.

SHARING THE WEALTH originally appeared in PLAYBOY Magazine; copyright © 1969 by *Playboy*. Reprinted by permission of the author and publisher.

A VISIT TO AMERICA from *Quite Early One Morning* by Dylan Thomas. Copyright 1954 by New Directions Publishing Corporation. Reprinted by permission of New Directions Publishing Corporation and J. M. Dent and Sons, Ltd.

AMERICANISM reprinted by permission of the author from *A Piece of My Mind* by Edmund Wilson (Farrar, Straus, and Cudahy Company). Copyright © 1956 by Edmund Wilson.

A BLACK GUIDE FOR WHITE FOLKS Excerpted from HOW TO GET ALONG WITH BLACK PEOPLE by Sheila Rush Okpaku and Chris Clark copyright © 1971 by The Third Press—Joseph Okpaku Publishing Co., Inc. by arrangement with The Third Press.

I'D RATHER BE BLACK THAN FEMALE reprinted by permission of the author from McCall's, August 1970. Copyright 1970 by Shirley Chisholm.

(Continued on page 571)

PUBLISHER'S INTRODUCTION

Since the original publication of *Reading, Writing, and Rhetoric* in 1967, approximately one quarter of a million students have studied from the first or second edition of this book. In a market that sees literally hundreds of new competitors published each year, the success of *RWR* has been phenomenal.

We at SRA feel that there is a reason for *RWR*'s success—namely, that people recognize quality. Every effort has been made to incorporate selections that reflect both writing excellence and—equally important—are interesting to you, the reader. In addition, considerable attention has been paid to the instructional apparatus, both in the book and in the comprehensive instructor's manual.

SRA is proud to be the publisher of this title, and we want to publicly thank the two outstanding authors who originally developed the material and constantly strive to refine and improve it—Burl Hogins and Bob Yarber.

Michael G. Crisp

Michael G. Crisp
Publisher

CONTENTS

8. OTHER PEOPLES, OTHER PLACES

GLOSSARY OF RHETORICAL TERMS

GUIDE TO RHETORIC

INDEX

RHETORICAL
TABLE OF CONTENTS

Rarely does a writer create an essay merely to fit a category of rhetoric—*Definition, Analysis,* or what have you. This Rhetorical table of Contents is a thoughtful, but arbitrary, classification of the book's selections, listed for the purpose of studying various techniques of writing. Different teachers (indeed authors and editors) would probably place many of the essays under different headings from those found here; this list, then, is a point of departure—merely a *guide* for studying, reading, writing, and rhetoric.

PREFACE

The principles underlying this third edition of *Reading, Writing, and Rhetoric* are essentially those of its predecessors: to provide for the instructor teachable essays that can be used as the basis of classroom discussion and writing assignments; and to provide for the student all the help we can to make learning easier, more interesting, and more rewarding.

Like its predecessors, the text is divided into thematic units treating topics likely to be among the major concerns facing us in the last half of this decade. In this regard, we have deleted those essays whose significance has declined since the publication of the second edition; on the other hand, we have added new selections whose literary style and relevance have justified their inclusion in this edition. Each essay is accompanied by a headnote and questions on theme, questions on rhetoric, writing assignments, library-exploration suggestions, and definitions of less-familiar words. In the back of the book, we have provided a *Glossary of Rhetorical Terms* and a *Guide to Rhetoric*; the latter cites several paragraphs in which a given principle is illustrated. (For instructors wishing to emphasize a rhetorical approach, we have also included an alternate table of contents based on the primary rhetorical features of the selections.)

Additional questions, suggested writing assignments, and a series of objective tests (with answers), covering both theme and rhetoric for each essay, will be found in the Instructor's Guide.

We are pleased by the response we continually receive from instructors and students who have used previous editions of *Reading, Writing, and Rhetoric*. We wish to express our gratitude to them, as well as to the staff of SRA, especially Mike Crisp and Jim Budd, for their continued loyalty and enthusiasm.

James Burl Hogins
Robert E. Yarber

An Inventory of Hope

B. Bruce-Briggs is a professional staff member with the Hudson Institute and coauthor with Herman Kahn of "Things to Come: Thinking about the Seventies and Eighties."

Predictions of the future, from magic to messianism, have been one of mankind's long-standing pastimes. This decade has seen the rise of yet a new system of prediction—"futurism." In the following essay, a "futurologist" discusses some of the trends he and his colleagues believe will most likely affect college graduates over the next decade.

B. BRUCE-BRIGGS

Futurism: What Will Life Be Like in 1985?

1 An evaluation of the future is particularly necessary to you, the college senior, because you must make fundamental decisions which will affect the rest of your life. But anyone writing about the future necessarily faces a good deal of understandable skepticism. A college graduate knows full well that all knowledge is based upon past and present experience. The future does not yet exist—therefore how can it be studied and how can anyone say anything about it which is not pure moonshine? That position is absolutely true regarding knowledge, but is incorrect about action. All decisions and other actions in the world are taken with the aim of having some effect upon the future and are based upon certain assumptions about what it will be. A

student taking a course assumes it will be completed at some time in the future and that he will in the remainder of his life make some personal or professional use of that course (or at least the credit that he earned from taking it).

2   In recent years many students have based some very bad decisions upon false expectations. What about those younger faculty members who believed that the "counter-culture" of the middle and late 1960's was the wave of the future, commited themselves to it, and have ruined their academic careers? What about those students who took up teacher education only to find no jobs available when they graduated? What about the young men who purchased high-powered "muscle cars" only to be faced with sky-rocketing insurance rates and gasoline costs? No one can claim to predict the future accurately, but if you take the position that thinking about something before doing it is better than not thinking, there is a good deal to be said about systematic examination of future possibilities.

3   The year 1985 will hardly resemble George Orwell's *1984*. Although the United States will continue to be the world's richest and most powerful nation, relative to the other advanced nations it will have continued the erosion which has gone on throughout your lifetime. When you were born, the United States was at the peak of its power because most of the rest of the world was still in ruins as a result of World War II. Over the past generation Europe, Japan and Russia have moved toward a more natural economic, political and military balance with the U.S. The rise of Japan is the most startling of these events, and by 1985 the average Japanese may be richer and live better than the average American.

4   The world is going to be a more complex place as the old "cold war" alliances crumble. Nevertheless, it is likely to continue to be a peaceful place. (If that statement seems bizarre, it indicates how very peaceful the world really is. By historical standards Vietnam was merely a skirmish.) One major reason for peace is the very fact that you, like most of your elders, believe serious war is unthinkable. This situation should almost certainly be prolonged throughout the 1970's, despite some local disturbances and massive spending on arms by the superpowers, but might begin to deteriorate in the 1980's. In any event, you are likely to avoid being drafted, and because of the lack of the draft you might seriously consider a military career. The growing opportunities for women in the armed forces might be of particular interest, especially for young women of military families.

5   In 1985 the graduate of 1974 will be about 33 years old; will be fairly definitely committed to his lifetime career; will have a mate, children, a home, and responsibilities; will have pretty much given up whatever youthful fancies and illusions he may have once had and for the most part won't mind it very much. This is an easy prediction to make because such is the history of every previous generation.

6   The American graduate will live in the richest nation the world has ever seen. The median family income will be on the order of $20,000 (in 1974 dollars—more inflation is inevitable). To be really prosperous it will be necessary to make $30,000 or more. Someone making

$10–15,000 will just be puttering along—that will be the salary of an unskilled worker. However, despite this seemingly incredible income, the real standard of living will not have increased proportionately. Widespread wealth makes wealth less valuable. This paradox is due to the fact that mass prosperity impinges upon the quality of life of upper classes. For example, privacy will be difficult to achieve as the widespread possession of recreational vehicles, motorcycles, etc. will allow the average American to penetrate into every corner of North America. Ski areas will be incredibly crowded. Concerts, museums, auto race tracks, etc. similarly so. Just to keep out hordes of people, some places will raise their entry fees enormously; others, particularly public places, will resort to queuing and the requirement of long-term reservations in advance.

7   Our society as a whole will have to invest a huge amount of capital in new energy sources. Although the "energy crisis" should be long over by 1985, the days of really cheap energy are probably gone forever. Despite all the prognostications of assorted highly publicized prophets of gloom and doom, the world will not run out of energy or any other resources, nor will we face growing pollution. As a matter of fact, . . . the more serious forms of pollution will be a thing of the past. A near zero emission automobile will be on the road, and it will be taken for granted that industries keep themselves clean. This will occur because those of you who become engineers will have added pollution control to the historical parameters of performance, reliability and cost.

8   Any congestion will be caused more by prosperity than by population. As is well known, the birthrate of the United States is at a very low level. However, the gross number of births will begin to increase as members of the "post-war baby boom" come of age and begin to breed. (The recent graduate is right in the middle of this boom generation.) But even assuming a modest increase in the birthrate, there will not be more than 240 million Americans in 1985, up about 30 million from today. There will be plenty of land and space for all these people, but with some local crowding.

9   These birth issues have some obvious implications for the persons in your age group. Because your group is much larger than the group immediately older, there will be very tough competition for promotion in the various hierarchical organizations that most of you will go to work for. Being in an exceptionally large age group will also affect your marriage prospects. Since there is no particular reason to expect any change in the long-term pattern of wives being on the average several years younger than their husbands, women in your age group are going to have a little more difficulty in finding husbands than is normal.

10   Today's graduate has become accustomed to being a member of a generation which is the center of the nation's attention. You remember the great concern of the 1960's with "youth." This era has passed, but you will likely continue to be in the nation's spotlight because you will still be in the fastest growing segment of the population. In 1985 the age group 30–40 will constitute 16 percent of the

population, nearly half again as much as today's 11 percent. This growth will attract the attention of merchandisers, marketeers and, of course, the media. Popular magazines will be full of "the problems of young adults" very much the way they were similarly interested in your parents about the time when you were born.

11   During the remainder of the 1970's, America will continue to be in what some of us at Hudson call the "counterreformation" or reaction against the joy-love-drug-radical-hippie-liberation manifestations of the 1960's. Already, incoming students are obviously "square" compared with their predecessors. This does not mean that there is likely to be any backtracking, or significant reversal of the changes of the 1960's; merely that they are not likely to be expanded very much further. While the sexual "liberation" or "promiscuity" of young people was notoriously exaggerated, it was real and is not likely to be reversed. Before the 1960's few women were virgins at marriage, but society pretended they were; now even fewer will be virgins at marriage and most of society doesn't care if they are not. Homosexuals of both sexes will be somewhat less furtive about their preferences. Shacking up will be done more openly. Wife swapping will be slightly more commonplace. A few people will experiment in group marriages and other sorts of previously "perverse" practices.

12   But the great majority of Americans, including most of you, will live in nuclear families with children and will rarely cheat on their spouses (and very, very circumspectly when they do). Unfortunately, more and more of you will see marriage as an instrument of self-fulfillment, convenience and fun—rather than as a lifelong contract and commitment. These high expectations plus the increasing ease of divorce are almost bound to increase the divorce rate. Although the majority of the women graduates will have more or less conventional marriages, a strong majority of them will hold jobs outside the home, for the purpose of self-fulfillment and augmenting the family's luxury income, but possibly to the detriment of the breeding of children.

13   A very depressing projection for the more militant feminist graduates is that the present women's liberation movement will almost certainly have topped out and be over by 1985, just like previous feminist movements. This does not mean that we are going to revert to the old sexual dispensation. Most of the gains which have been made in the late 1960's and early 1970's will be consolidated. Job discrimination against women will almost surely continue to exist, but much less severely than in the past. Women in certain classes and certain ethnic groups will use "maiden" or hyphenated names, but the practice will not affect a very large percentage of all women. A real possibility is a switchover of the general values of the society toward re-emphasis on the historical role of woman as wife, mother and homemaker. It is easy to write a scenario for the world of the 1980's in which advanced and fashionable female spokesmen say that true liberation is found in maximizing a woman's fulfillment in female roles. Still, the more chauvinistic males must face up to the fact that they have a good chance of having a woman boss sometime during their career.

14   As is well known, the growing segments of the labor force are in the white collar occupations. More people will work at services and at shuffling papers than in actually making things. Ambitious young men and women, particularly from families that did not have college degrees before, will continue to be primarily interested in upward mobility and material gains. Those who turn their backs upon materialism and the "rat race" will also continue to be largely drawn from the more privileged classes who have seen that worldly success does not guarantee happiness. Many will drop out in various ways, or at least not work as hard, and will be replaced by the more ambitious members of the less privileged elements of the population. Again, there is nothing very new in this—the 19th century political scientist Pareto called the phenomena "the circulation of elites," and it has gone on as long as we know anything about history.

15   It is not possible to speak with any degree of clarity about which sort of jobs and industries will be the most active in the mid-1980's. On the basis of the population projections, the education business is going to be stagnant throughout the next 15 years. In the short run, starting right now, the energy business is going to boom enormously but will probably peak out by 1985. Conversely, in the immediate future the leisure and recreation industry, like all "frivolous" activities, will be hurt for basic fuel and other supplies, but should come back strong as these problems are dealt with. A large and growing business will be housing—between now and 1985 it will be necessary to add approximately 20 million new housing units to the national stock, largely because your generation wants houses.

16   Every indication suggests that the dominant type of housing in the United States will continue to be the single family detached home, although there may be more varying units for minorities who wish different housing and life styles. Regrettably there seems to be nothing on the horizon which is going to change the rigidly segregated pattern of housing in the United States, although blacks, like whites, will be much better housed than today. There will also be more age segregation of housing and our whole society, as special communities of housing units for old people and young people are established. We may even expect communities for other minorities—such as fanatic skiers, scuba divers, perhaps even motorcyclists or music lovers. This is part of the general projection of a breakdown of consensus and unity in the society and the establishment of what some of us here at Hudson call a "mosaic society" of many coexisting and varied values, life styles, and work and leisure habits.

17   As suggested above, black Americans and other minorities will continue to be considered and to consider themselves as somewhat different from the rest of society, but, although we project no significant extensions of civil rights legislation at least in the rest of this decade, there will be massive improvements of black conditions as individual blacks take advantage of the opportunities so long denied them. Gaps between the average white and the average non-white will still exist, but the average black will be living much better than today and will have a sense of continued improvement in economic standard of liv-

ing and in status. Blacks and whites will mix more frequently and with more ease at parties, and there should be a trifle more biracial marriage, but most social patterns will remain essentially separate.

18   On the average the graduate will have better career prospects if he lives in the most rapidly growing sections of the country. Rapid population and economic growth offers more opportunities for expansion and promotion, and dynamic areas attract other ambitious young men and women who provide healthy competition, cooperation and social contacts. As in the recent past, the most dynamic area of the United States will continue to be the South-Southwest. Historically economically depressed and socially backward, the South is economically the most vibrant part of the United States, particularly the Piedmont area from western Virginia down through Knoxville, Tennessee, and on to Atlanta, the Gulf Coast from Mobile across to Houston, as well as central Florida, Dallas-Fort Worth, some other Texan cities, and Arizona and New Mexico. In a leisure-oriented society, the climate of these areas offers more outdoor recreation and a more informal life style. Moreover, the South's combination of fundamentalist political and religious ideologies with cheerful Philistine materialism seems to be a good formula for growth in the late 20th century. Although racial conditions have greatly improved in the urban South, the black graduate would do better to stick to the Piedmont and avoid the Gulf Coast.

19   Conversely, the older industrial areas of the North are relatively stagnant. Although the Boston and Bay areas will continue to attract young people because of the social activity there, these areas are becoming more and more parasitic rather than productive to the national economy. Other booming areas, largely on account of climate, are the Pacific Northwest and Colorado, and they will continue to grow despite considerable anti-growth agitation from the "ins" who want to keep the "outs" from sharing (and downgrading) the benefits.

20   Perhaps much of this projection of 1985 doesn't sound very different from today. True enough. But today isn't very different from 10 years ago or 20 years ago. Different, but not *very* different. We are, and probably will be, more prosperous and secure, but not necessarily any happier or unhappier. Certainly we will be older, and we will probably think we are wiser.

Discussion of Theme

1. Do you consider the world today to be a "peaceful place"? (paragraph 4).
2. Does the statement in paragraph 5 make you look forward to being 33 years old?
3. Explain the paradox that "Widespread wealth makes wealth less valuable." (paragraph 6).
4. What is meant by the "circulation of the elites?" (paragraph 14).
5. Do predictions about the future carry the danger of the creation of a self-fulfilling prophecy? Discuss.

Discussion of Rhetoric

1. Would this essay have been more interesting if the author had discussed the method of predicting and offered some specific evidence to support the claims?
2. Is the level of language in this essay appropriate for the audience of college seniors to whom it is addressed?
3. Is there a shift in tone in the final two lines of the essay? Might there be a hint of irony or sarcasm here—or perhaps a bit of melancholy?
4. Does the author reveal any personal feelings about the future? Where? What are they?

Writing Assignments

1. Before reading this essay, what were *your* ideas about life in 1985? Are you disappointed or relieved?
2. What changes do you look forward to most? What do you dread most?
3. Explain what the author means by "mosaic society" (paragraph 16).

Library Exploration

1. Read Orwell's *1984* and Huxley's *Brave New World*.
2. Research the hippie generation, the conditions of its birth, how it influenced our entire culture and how, why, and when it began to fade.

Vocabulary

(6) QUEUING lining up
(7) PROGNOSTICATIONS predictions
(7) PARAMETERS boundaries; constant factors
(12) CIRCUMSPECTLY prudently; cautiously

(12) AUGMENTING increasing
(12) DETRIMENT loss or damage
(13) DISPENSATION arrangement
(19) PHILISTINE common; uncultured

Henry Commager (1902–   ),
popular American historian, is
professor of history at Amherst
College. He was born in Pitts-
burgh and attended the University of Chicago, the University of
Copenhagen, and Cambridge
and Oxford universities. Among
his many volumes are "The
Growth of the American Republic" (1931–42), "Documents of
American History" (1950), and
"The American Mind" (1951).

In this essay Professor Commager examines the effects of
Richard Nixon's resignation
from the Presidency and the
crisis it provoked. He concludes
that the integrity and vitality of
the Constitution survived intact.

HENRY STEELE COMMAGER

The Constitution Is Alive and Well

1 We have had constitutional crises before but, except for the Civil War
and Reconstruction, none that had the dimensions of those precipitated by Richard M. Nixon. Never before have we had a crisis that
challenged the basic assumptions of our constitutional system itself,
and the basic processes and mechanisms through which it worked.
2   Alexander Hamilton, though he supported the Constitution,
thought it "a frail and worthless fabric" and had no confidence that it
would endure. And no wonder. It was, after all, without precedent or
model in history. Never before had a people made a national Constitution; never before had they fabricated a Federal system; never
before had they elected a national head of state; never before had
they fixed effective limits on government by such devices as a

genuine separation of powers, and bills of substantive rights, that had the force of law.

3   Almost miraculously the system worked. The "frail and worthless fabric" proved to be both tough and enduring and, what is more astonishing, proved wonderfully resilient. Under its auspices the United States grew from thirteen to fifty states; under its auspices it weathered one crisis after another, and that without suspending any of its great provisions, without impairing the authority and dignity of the Presidency, the power of the Congress or the independence of the judiciary.

4   In 1861 the South challenged the Constitution, and set up on its own; then it honored the document by transforming it, with only minor changes, into a constitution for the Confederacy.

5   The Constitution survived the First World War, the crisis of the great Depression and the challenge of the welfare state, and the unprecedented strains of the Second World War.

6   One reason the Constitution survived intact was that no President had ever attempted to subvert it, no politicians—with the exception of Aaron Burr—have even threatened it.

7   Notwithstanding the absence of any tradition of loyalty to the new Government, the United States, even in infancy, did not have a Cromwell, nor, in maturity, a Hitler.

8   Here—for perhaps the first time in modern history—it was not necessary to call upon loyalty to a king to preserve the commonwealth.

9   As Tom Paine put it, "Where then is the King of America? Know that in America the Constitution is King."

10   Or as Thomas Jefferson wrote, after he and Hamilton had frustrated Burr's attempt to steal the election of 1800:

11   "The tough sides of our Argosy had been thoroughly tried. Her strength has stood the waves into which she was steered, with a view to sink her. We shall put her on her republican tack and she will show by the beauty of her motion, the skill of her builders."

12   For the first time since 1861, an Administration, Mr. Nixon's, called into question both the beauty of her motion and the skill of her builders. For what is it that has been at stake for the last two years—what but the integrity and the vitality of the Constitution itself and of the principles it is designed to secure—a more perfect union, justice, domestic tranquillity, and the blessings of liberty, and the rule of law.

13   Let us be more specific.

14   First. The principle of a government of laws and not of men, a principle so precious that the Founding Fathers wrote it into many of the state constitutions. By countenancing burglary, wiretapping, *agents provocateurs,* the use of the Federal Bureau of Investigation, Central Intelligence Agency and even the Internal Revenue Service to punish "enemies," by endorsing the Huston Plan for the creation of a police state, and by resort to secrecy, duplicity and deception in the operations of Government, Mr. Nixon sought to substitute his own fiat for the law.

15   Second. The principle, vindicated by the United States Supreme Court in the great case of *ex parte* Milligan: "the Constitution is a law for rulers and people, equally in war and in peace, and covers with the shield of its protection all classes of men at all times and under all circumstances. No doctrine involving more pernicious consequences was ever invented by the wit of man than that any of its great provisions can be suspended during any of the great exigencies of government."

16   By creating sham "exigencies" involving "national security," Mr. Nixon sought to justify the violation of constitutional guarantees of due process and of the fundamental rights of citizens, and of the welfare of society, and authorized withholding of evidence essential to justice—in effect suspending vital provisions of the Constitution.

17   Third. The principle of the separation of powers, a principle established first by Americans as the most effective method of holding each branch of government within the framework of the Constitution.

18   By usurping Congressional power to declare war, making war on neutral Cambodia and concealing that war from the Congress and the American people; by shrouding much of the conduct of foreign affairs in a fog of secrecy, denying to the Congress information essential to the faithful performance of its constitutional duties; and by nullifying Congressional power over appropriations through the device of impounding funds duly voted by the Congress, Mr. Nixon undermined the integrity of this great principle.

19   Fourth. The principles of freedom and justice in the Bill of Rights. By attempting to impose, for the first time in our history, prior censorship of the press, by threatening hostile television stations with deprivation of their licenses, by directing the arrest without warrants of some 12,000 men and women gathered in the capital city to exercise their constitutional rights of assembly and petition, by flouting the constitutional prohibition against unreasonable search and seizure and the requirement of search warrants, by ignoring the provisions for due process of law in the endorsement of the Huston Plan and in the illegal use of the Central Intelligence Agency in domestic affairs, Mr. Nixon presented the most dangerous threat to the Bill of Rights in the whole of our history.

20   Fifth. The integrity and survival of democratic government in the United States.

21   By corrupting Presidential elections through the solicitation of illegal contributions, by a systematic campaign of mendacity, trickery and character assassination against opponents, by violating the integrity of the civil service and corrupting his closest subordinates, Mr. Nixon gravely endangered the integrity of our republican system of government.

22   Mr. Nixon's resignation is no voluntary act. It was not inspired by contrition or by a belated loyalty to the Constitution. It was forced on him by a ground swell of public outrage, by a popular ralliance to the Constitution comparable to that which swept the North at the time of Fort Sumter, and by a Congress that after long vacillation finally responded to the standards of duty and the obligations of the Constitution.

23   The long-drawn-out process of inquiry by committee, by the courts, by the Congress is a stunning vindication of our constitutional system, a vindication of the principle of separation of powers, of the independence of the courts and of the foresight of the framers.

24   The men who made our Constitution were familiar with the history of executive tyranny. They were steeped in the history of the ancient world and knew well the story of usurpation of power, revolution and assassination in the city-states of Greece and in Rome.

25   They knew, too, the tragic history of England and the fate of a Richard II, a Mary Queen of Scots and a Charles I; they had themselves just fought a war against what they thought to be the tyranny of George III. They were determined to write a new page in history, and did. They accepted the necessity of change in government and in leadership. They invented the great institution of the constitutional convention—a legal way to alter and abolish government and institute new government.

26   They took over the English practice of impeachment, applied it to their highest office, providing a legal and peaceful method of removing the President himself from office.

27   Thus, in the words of Alexander Hamilton, they "substituted the mild magistracy of the law for the terrible weapon of the sword."

28   Confronted, for the first time in our long history, with a chief magistrate who betrayed his oath of office, we have resorted to that "magistracy of the law" and vindicated once again the wisdom of the Founding Fathers. Thus, we have demonstrated to the world and, let us hope, to future generations that the Constitution is alive and well, that it can be adapted to the exigencies of governance, and that in an emergency an enlightened and determined democracy can protect and defend its principles, its honor, and its heritage.

29   When, on Sept. 17, 1787, members of the Federal Convention came forward to sign the Constitution that they had drafted during those long hot months in Philadelphia, the venerable Dr. Franklin arose and "looking toward the president's chair, at the back of which a rising sun happened to be painted, observed that painters had found it difficult to distinguish in their art between a rising and a setting sun. 'I have often and often,' said he, 'in the course of the session and the vicissitudes of my hopes and fears as to its issue looked at that behind the presidency, without being able to tell whether it was rising or setting. Now at length I have the happiness to know that it is a rising and not a setting sun.' "

Discussion of Theme

1. According to the author, why did Nixon really resign? What might have been the consequences if he had chosen to remain in office?
2. Why was the Constitution such a radical document when it was written? Is it still radical?
3. Does the writer suggest that only the Constitution prevented our having a Cromwell or a Hitler? How is this so?

Discussion of Rhetoric

1. Comment on the effectiveness of the repetition of *under its auspices* (paragraph 3).
2. What is the impact of the one-sentence paragraph 13?
3. What is the significance of the quote by Franklin in the last paragraph?
4. This essay is tightly organized. Describe the pattern.

Writing Assignments

1. Describe your feelings after reading this essay.
2. Do you believe Nixon fancied himself "King of America?" Why?
3. Do you think future historians will be less harsh? Why? Why not?
4. Recently, as a special project, a group of students circulated the Bill of Rights as a petition, and a number of people refused to sign it on the grounds that it was a "Communist document." Why might they have read it as such? What is the significance of that response?

Library Exploration

1. Read the Constitution.
2. Research and report on the life of Aaron Burr.
3. Read about the framing of the Constitution.

Vocabulary

(14) COUNTENANCING encouraging

(14) AGENTS PROVOCATEURS secret agents hired to incite suspected persons to some illegal action

(14) FIAT an authoritative decree

(15) EX PARTE in the interest of one party

(15) PERNICIOUS ruinous

(15) EXIGENCIES urgencies

(21) MENDACITY state of being untruthful

(22) VACILLATION the act of wavering in opinion

(24) USURPATION the seizing and holding of power by force

(29) VENERABLE worthy of reverence

(29) VICISSITUDES changes; alterations

Lucy Komisar is past vice president of the National Organization for Women and author of "The New Feminism," "Down and Out in the U.S.A.," and "The Machismo Factor."

This essay examines the ways in which areas of society such as work, political organization, federal policy, and the family will be affected by the feminist ethic.

LUCY KOMISAR

Where Feminism Will Lead

1   The ideology of feminism includes assumptions and beliefs about work, marriage, parenthood, and life roles that will have a profound effect on public and private policy far beyond the integration of women into men's jobs.

2   Feminism says that work is as significant to women as it is to men, that marriage ought to be a partnership of equals, that women ought to be financially independent, that child-bearing and child-rearing is not a woman's only or most important or even necessary role, and that family responsibilities ought to be divided evenly between women and men.

3   These notions will affect everything from Federal policies on unemployment and inflation to new styles of housing and social services. They will alter men's work and family lives as much as women's. And they can provide the impetus for social change beyond the narrow confines of women's role in society.

4   A Swedish feminist, Eva Moberg, once wrote that:

> The male labor market has always been based on one self-evident condition: that somebody else is doing all the little practical jobs which need to be done for an employee and his children—cooking, washing, tidying up, and mending. As for the female labor market, it has also been founded on an equally self-evident axiom: that a woman employee has another, more important job on the side.

The feminist movement will first change the second part of that equation, and by doing that, it will also alter the first.

5 Increasingly now, women are recognizing that homemaking is not their only proper role. The feminist movement is reinforcing the belief that women as well as men need opportunities for achievement and fulfillment—with the recognition that in our society work is the chief source of these feelings for most people.

6 Feminism is encouraging women to believe that they ought not be financially dependent on their husbands. Thus, even if a man earns more, it will not be considered desirable or even acceptable for a woman to stay home and take full charge of raising their children.

7 It is certainly not "practical" even now; at any one time, 34.8 percent of all women over 18 years of age are either single, divorced, widowed, or married with their spouses absent (due to separation, military service, etc.).

8 Women will come to view their work as equal in importance and perhaps even more important than their roles as wives and mothers—a fact which will change those roles significantly. And all of this will have significant effects on employment and wage policy, work patterns, social services, and even housing design.

9 Most obviously, the feminist movement will lead to increased opportunities for women workers and to more equal pay rates. Government and industry have promoted the fiction that women as a group are somehow "secondary" or "marginal" workers whose incomes are not as essential as men's and whose jobs are not as important to them. Wives are routinely called "secondary workers" by the Bureau of the Census, which also labels men "head of household" regardless of the roles of the couple in their marriage.

10 In fact, some 63 percent of the women who work are either single, widowed, separated, divorced, or married to men who earn less than $7,000 a year. Whatever truth may exist in the "marginal" image for the other 37 percent is the result of a self-fulfilling prophecy. It is caused by women's reduced earning power and the fact that work and social services are organized around the expectation that men are the primary wage earners and that women will take responsibility for home and child care.

11 Some women in fact do move in and out of the labor force, picking up the slack when jobs are available and disappearing when work dries up—the Christmas season in department stores is a classic example. Women who take jobs as clerical or sales workers may leave when they marry—partly because they have accepted the sexist role division of men as providers and women as housewives, and partly because they find a minimal reward in their work and see no chance for advancement.

12 Sometimes they return to work when their children are in school or grown. However, even when women are fulltime, permanent workers who hold their jobs without interruption, industry has turned them into marginal workers by making them the last hired and the first fired—sometimes on the invented excuse that they don't need their jobs as much as men do. (During the Depression, some States actually

passed laws that denied jobs to married women, especially teachers, and that attitude has not disappeared entirely.)

FEDERAL POLICIES

13 At the same time that industry has practiced the kind of job discrimination that results in higher unemployment for women, Government has tolerated a higher general level of unemployment. In September 1973, William J. Fellner—then the newest presidential nominee to the Council of Economic Advisors—said what the administration had been hinting at for at least a year: the Government cannot seek to reduce unemployment much below five percent.

14 According to the *Washington Post* analysis, "The problem is that women and teenagers now make up a greater percentage of the labor force than they used to, and that women and teenagers have chronically higher unemployment rates than men. It thus takes much more priming of the pump to get the overall rate down to four percent than it used to."

15 Women's unemployment rates have sometimes been double that of men's, even excluding the many women who have given up looking for jobs and are counted as housewives rather than jobless persons. One of the reasons it has been possible for the Government to accept unemployment rates as high as four, five, and six percent is because it is not four, five, or six percent of *white men* who are unemployed. Women of all races make up 40 percent of the workforce, and together with minority men, their unemployment skews the figures.

16 When women's employment is not considered as significant as men's, neither is women's unemployment. Fellner's statement indicates that it is quite acceptable to have a higher rate of unemployment in the country as long as only women and youths (and, in fact, minorities) are the bulk of the new jobless.

17 However, the advance of feminist ideology and the success of job equality programs will increase the number of women seeking jobs at the same time it opens more job opportunities to them. It will thus reduce the disparity in the male and female unemployment rates by raising the jobless burden of male workers, especially those in categories where men have benefited from the discrimination against women. When that burden is shifted to men, the Government may not be able to countenance the same high rate of unemployment that it has permitted among women.

18 In addition to the disadvantages women suffer in employment, they suffer a disadvantage in pay—earning nationally only 60 percent of what men earn. Some of this is due to the fact that women get less-skilled jobs than men, but part of it is due to the fact that women get unequal pay for the same work, and another part reflects the lower value placed on work done largely by women compared to that done by men.

19 For example, the Department of Labor *Dictionary of Occupational Titles* rates nursery school worker below zoo keeper. Dieticians, who

are generally women, earn less than truck drivers, who are generally men. In both cases, the skill and value of the "women's" jobs ought to be rated higher than the men's jobs. The feminist movement will cause a reanalysis of the worth of work.

20 Fair pay for women would have profound effects on the nation's economy, altering the costs of goods and services that are now based on cheap female labor.

21 Changes in patterns of unemployment and wages would have important effects on the nation's policy in regard to inflation. Higher unemployment and lower wages for women have an anti-inflationary effect. Equality either could result in a general equalizing of existing levels of employment and wages, with men suffering a loss in both cases, or in a net increase in jobs and wages, with the attendant rise in inflation that would cause. It is a dilemma the Government will be forced to confront.

22 Another obvious effect of the feminist movement on Government policy will be a change in training and job priorities. Presently, the Department of Labor *Manpower Administration Bulletin* says, "Priorities might be assigned as follows . . . males before females."

23 David O. Williams, who heads Federally funded manpower programs in the Midwest, offered the muddled explanation that this is "no attempt to suggest that females should not be hired or even given first preference. The guide only suggests that if there is only one job and there is a female head of household and a male head of household, the male head of household should be referred first. . . ."

24 This discriminatory policy which penalizes families because they are headed by women is especially ironic in the Work Incentive Program, which was created to provide jobs and training for welfare recipients. The Labor Department set priorities for the program beginning with male heads of households and ending with mothers of pre-school children. Although a lawsuit overturned that policy, the new Talmadge Amendments reinstated it. There has been no challenge—partly because some welfare rights advocates do not want to expose women to the coercive aspects of the law.

25 Aside from priorities in admissions policies, women who seek Government-sponsored training often are denied the chance to learn high-paying skills and shunted instead into clerical and secretarial classes. A post-Title VII phone call to a New York City manpower official readily elicited information about separate lists of classes "available to women" and "available to men." Women would learn to pound the typewriters; men would learn to fix them.

THE EFFECTS ON MEN

26 The change in the value and pattern of women's work will have profound effects on men. As Moberg suggests, *men will no longer be able to assume that their jobs have priority and that responsibility for the care of home and children will be left to the wife.*

Men's mobility will be limited by their wives' jobs and ambitions, and employers will have to take this into account in making job assignments. *The Government will also have to change existing unemployment rules that presently give benefits to women who leave jobs to follow their husbands to new locations,* but deny checks to men who leave to follow their wives. A suit has been filed in Washington State by a husband who was denied benefits under this rule.

28   Men who are not the sole support of themselves and their families will also feel freer to quit jobs and change careers. There will thus be more flexibility in people's work lives, more sabbaticals and mid-life changes of career, and more emphasis on the psychic as compared to the financial rewards of work. People will not be as bound to their jobs and not as willing to suffer poor working conditions in factories, or humiliation and tension in corporate suites.

29   Increasingly, the feminist movement will cause men to take equal responsibility for child care. A variety of changes in employer and public policy will allow men and women to perform child care functions themselves and increase Government and private services that substitute for parental care. For example, businesses will have to institute paternity as well as maternity child care leaves. Some institutions have already taken that step, although not always willingly. The Board of Education of New York City was forced by the courts to establish paternity leave for teachers.

30   Men and women will be enabled to share child care through the restructuring of work—shorter hours, shared jobs, changes in the 9 to 5 workday.

31   Businesses will have to develop leave policies that allow parents to take time off to care for sick youngsters, to attend conferences with teachers, or to take sons and daughters to the dentist. Or, the Government may introduce home nursing for sick children, and teachers and doctors may have to alter their schedules to hold evening meetings with working parents.

32   The movement for universally available child care suffered a defeat with the veto of a bill that would have expanded Government-aided child care for families with incomes ranging up to middle class. Opponents of this measure maintained that such child care facilities would lead to the breakdown of the American family. In line with that thinking, the administration has attempted to roll back the present system so that only welfare families are eligible.

33   Since most of those families consist of minority women and children, it seems to many that official concern for family life diminishes depending upon the race and financial status of those involved.

34   In any case, when women follow the same work patterns as men, Government-sponsored child care centers will have to be established on a massive scale as they were during World War II. Opposition to child care is an anachronism that will be erased by the force of feminist history.

35   As work becomes more important for women, it will have to become less important for men. Job decisions will have to be taken in light of family responsibilities. Late meetings, business trips, and even one's presence at the plant or office will have to be adjusted to the demands of home life—for men as well as women.

36   Some feminists have already discovered that when they insist that

husbands share housework, that is the time the men decide to buy dishwashers, hire help, or eat out more often. It will likely be true that the demand that men share housekeeping chores will lead to added demand for paid services. Families increasingly will hire people to do cleaning, shopping, and laundry under contract. Home-catered meals may become more popular.

37 However, feminists must make certain that minority women, who make up a large proportion of household workers, are not further oppressed by such changes. This can be avoided by the professionalization of housework, including the elevation of pay and benefits available to household workers.

38 One of the defects of the suburbs, and of even much urban housing, is the lack of convenient services to take care of chores women do now. The Scandinavian countries are developing housing complexes that include shared facilities to end the need for the kinds of individual tasks largely assigned to women. These communities include common cafeterias, child care centers, teen clubs, laundries—and recreation centers for adults as well.

39 Government and industry will have to develop new rules about social security and pensions based on women's new independence. One member of Congress has introduced legislation to give wives their own Social Security benefits. In Sweden, a similar system already operates. Our Government will have to decide whether it wants to consider homemaking a socially desirable role that ought to be rewarded with state pension benefits.

40 Could a husband get "housespouse" benefits if he stayed home and cared for the family? If married women get such benefits, could divorced mothers get them, too? What kinds of contributions would be required? Could alimony be used for such payments? What about women on welfare? Isn't child care still a "job" even when no husband is around?

41 The increased mobility of men and women will make it necessary to liberalize the portability of pension rights even more than is being contemplated by legislation today. Perhaps there ought to be a national pension bureau that administers all pensions, and which allows the same total portability rights that exist for Social Security.

AN ATTITUDE ABOUT POWER

42 The end of sex role stereotypes and passage of the Equal Rights Amendment will confront feminists with one Government institution that is based on principles which contradict a part of feminist ideology. This part has gotten less attention from the media than demands for job equality, child care, and abortion, but it promises to make an even more profound contribution to American mores and ethics. That part of the feminist ethic is an attitude about power, aggression, and violence—and the institution it will meet head on will be the armed forces.

43 A concommitant of the feminist critique of stereotypes about women is a rejection of stereotypes about men. The definition of

manhood that judges masculinity on a scale of power, dominance, toughness, violence, and aggression is anathema to feminists, partly because women have been its chief victims. Rather than insist that women, too, ought to feel free to express those traits, feminists assert that males and females ought to develop a new human ethos based on an end to hierarchies, dominance, and force.

44   On the one hand, if women are admitted to the armed forces they ought to be able to do whatever men do—including engage in combat—and the Federal Government will have to deal with this eventuality even as it is now beginning to train women as noncombat pilots. On the other hand, women who have not been caught up in the kind of imagery that promises, "Join the Army, be a man," may become a new force against militarism.

45   In fact, the feminist movement holds possibilities for social change that have hardly been considered by those that view it from the outside. Three areas of particular interest will be affected by the feminist ethic. One is the structure of work and organization; another is foreign policy; a third is radical social change.

46   The women's movement has given much attention to the deleterious effect of "male" structure and organization, which is to say the pyramid hierarchy where power runs from top to bottom and where many people take orders and a few people give them. The leaderless "small groups," alternating chairpeople, cooperative projects that have no "bosses," and even the insistence that chairs in meeting rooms be set in a circle so that people are not inhibited from speaking out by being placed in a leader-audience position—all are efforts by feminists to counteract the effects of traditional forms of organization.

47   Sections of American industry have been experimenting with the notion that when decision-making is democratized, workers are more productive as well as more satisfied. Production teams that share work and decisions have been substituted for systems where groups of workers are directed by foremen. The feminist movement has developed critiques which seek to go even further in wiping out the hierarchical style.

48   Women have been aware of how some of the prerequisites of power can humiliate those at the bottom of the pyramid. The secretary who is forced to make coffee, run personal errands, and act as a status symbol for her boss, and the male underling who is forced to endure the tongue-lashing and lordly behavior of his superiors both suffer at the bottom. (One famous movie executive used to hold staff meetings at which his desk was placed on a platform so that others in the room had to look up to him.)

49   The etiquette of corporate life instructs inferiors and superiors how to act toward each other, showing proper deference to those who occupy the higher stations. If there is a conference, the inferior goes to the office of the superior. The superior waits until the inferior is on the phone before he picks it up. Sometimes people ignore their subordinates in a conspicuous manner. Superiors often do not return telephone calls; they insist that the inferiors keep calling back.

50   Bosses must not only exercise power, they must do it in such a way that the behavior of their subordinates reminds them that they indeed

have that power. It is as if the image of power were more important than the possession of it.

51   The image of power is a factor as well in the conduct of American foreign policy, and the feminist ethic promises to confront this as well. American foreign policy has been based on the notion that we must be "number one" in military power. The last two presidents have made it clear that the U.S. can not be a "second-rate" power, or, for the first time, "lose a war"—that we could not depart from our image of toughness or let ourselves be "humiliated" by the army of an impoverished, agricultural country whose people were different racially and even slighter in stature than most Americans.

52   Feminists are rejecting the notion of manhood that led President Kennedy and his advisers to approve plans for the Bay of Pigs invasion just because, as Theodore Sorensen, Arthur Schlesinger, and others have testified, they feared seeming soft. That led President Johnson to prolong the killing in Vietnam, because he could not be "the first President to lose a war." And that encouraged President Nixon to continue war policies for fear the rest of the world would think the U.S. "a pitiful, helpless giant."

53   The arms race, which takes such an overwhelming part of American tax monies, is supported by a national desire to be "number one," to be the most powerful nation in the world. The feminist ethic does not see that kind of power as necessary or desirable—and it certainly does not see its opposite as "humiliating" or "unmanly" as it is described in the language of America's foreign policy makers. (Senate Foreign Relations Committee Chairman J. William Fulbright is a significant exception to that line of thinking.)

BUILDING A NEW COALITION

54   The fact is that the feminist ethic has important things to say not only in the area of sex discrimination, but also about many other aspects of American life as well. Feminism has both the ideological and organizational potential to effect significant social change in this country.

55   In the past, forces for radical or even liberal social change have always been a minority. The labor movement, the abolitionist movement, the civil rights movement—even the anti-Vietnam war movement—were minorities that certainly affected Presidential decisions but could not put their own representatives in the White House.

56   Some civil rights leaders have attempted to establish coalitions for social advancement with the labor movement and liberal church and civic organizations. The Leadership Conference for Civil Rights perhaps is the chief example of that effort, and certainly, at a time when sit-ins, freedom rides, and racist violence aroused the moral indignation of much of the country, that coalition succeeded in getting legislation to protect voting rights and ban discrimination.

57   However, the civil rights coalition never constituted a majority, and in this period, the Conference is fighting to preserve past victories—for example, to save school desegregation from the threats of anti-busing legislation.

58   The coalition has also sought the passage of social welfare legislation, yet the recent veto of a new minimum wage bill and the dismantling of much of the antipoverty program indicate that the majority supporting social advances in the 1960s was temporary.

59   In fact, it represented two forces—the representatives of the poor and of labor, whose own interests were at stake, and the liberals, who supported them out of ideological bent. The rest of the country went along; however, a majority committed to those programs out of self-interest never existed.

60   The women's movement offers the hope of establishing a majority coalition devoted to civil rights and social welfare legislation out of self-interest. It is only women who can make that coalition a majority one.

61   The women's movement will cause large numbers of women who in the past have identified with the privileged classes of America to reevaluate their own situation. They will come to see forceful enforcement of laws prohibiting job discrimination as something they need themselves, not as a charitable gesture toward others. (Black women, of course, already know the problem of race discrimination. I am talking about the majority of American women, who are white and have not in the past felt the importance of such laws.)

62   They will see child care as an issue that directly affects their own lives, not just the lives of the welfare poor.

63   And it will become clear that the same special interests and arguments that have been marshalled against blacks and other minorities are the special interests and arguments set against women.

64   Women cannot but help identify with minority people in America when they see themselves again and again treated with similar insensitivity and condescension; when they face similar discrimination, and when they discover the same failures to establish or enforce measures to end discrimination.

65   The bond that is forged by common problems will be strengthened by common action—something which has already occurred as feminist and minority groups have joined to press for legislation, file court suits, or seek administrative action.

66   The women's movement is growing geometrically. Each new convert talks to friends, relatives and neighbors; each woman who files a suit, or gets a traditionally male job, or changes her life style becomes an example for others.

67   While the growth of feminism has substantially increased the chances for achieving social change, not all of those individuals (almost always men) who lead other sections of the (prospective) coalition always recognize this.

68   Feminists committed to the cause of race equality used to find few minority leaders interested in the cause of women's rights. That has changed in the past few years to some extent: the Urban League is co-sponsoring a boycott with the National Organization for Women against General Mills; the National Association for the Advancement of Colored People, the Mexican American Legal Defense and Education Fund, and NOW have joined to protest Government failure to enforce affirmative action regulations for Federal contractors; and the

new National Black Feminist Organization may force black political and civic leaders to pay more attention to the goals of women, especially minority women.

69   The labor movement's commitment to women increasingly will be one that redounds to its own benefit. In an economy where craft jobs are diminishing and union gains are being made among clerical and professional workers, women constitute an important source of union membership. And, as their consciousness and feeling of solidarity is raised, feminist women will be more ready to organize into unions to fight for their rights than other white-collar workers who reject such organizations for ideological reasons.

70   Once all women accept and approve the fact that they will be working most of their lives and not necessarily leaving their jobs when they marry or have babies, the conditions and future of their work lives become more important. And once women organize as women, organizing as workers is an easy and logical step to take.

71   Women look with ironic amusement at the male commentators and analysts who continue to predict that the movement has "disappeared" or "peaked." (An *Esquire* editor several years ago told me that feminism was a "fad" and the big movement would be ecology; recently *Esquire* ran a special issue on women; it has not done one on ecology.)

72   It is difficult for those who do not understand the depth of feminist feeling to envision the significance and potential strength of the movement. It is a lesson they will learn as the decade of the feminist 1970s continues.

Discussion of Theme

1. In what areas are women considered "marginal" or "secondary"? Are there any areas in which men carry this designation?
2. Do you agree that work is the chief source of achievement and fulfillment in our society?
3. What is the feminist attitude toward violence, power, and aggression? In what ways might this attitude affect American ethics?
4. Do you think most women want to work most of their lives or that they would prefer to be supported by men? In your opinion, do the feminists represent the majority or minority of American women?
5. Do you consider housewives "jobless persons"? Explain.

Discussion of Rhetoric

1. What does the phrase *priming of the pump* mean in paragraph 14? What type of figure of speech is this?
2. Why does the author use the term *chairpeople* (in paragraph 46)? Why is it appropriate in this essay?
3. Is there a specific pattern of organization in this selection, or does the author seem to jump from one idea to another and back again?

Might that be the method of organization and development? Is it successful?

4. Is there anything in the tone or diction which reveals the author's attitude toward men? Is she being emotional or objective?
5. What kinds of evidence does the author use to support her ideas?

Writing Assignments

1. If women "got the power," do you think they would take on the role of the oppressor or use the power as men have?
2. Do you believe that the feminist movement has peaked and is declining, or that it has just begun?
3. Feminists have pointed out that competition for men and other role-playing conditioning has prevented women from developing close and honest relationships with each other. Agree or disagree in an essay.
4. Almost a century ago, Lucy Stone said, "In education, in marriage, in everything, disappointment is the lot of women. It shall be the business of my life to deepen this disappointment in every woman's heart until she bows down to it no longer." Do you believe women have reached this level of consciousness? Would Stone be pleased or disappointed in women's progress since she spoke those words?

Library Exploration

1. Read *Woman's Estate,* by Juliet Mitchell.
2. Research and report on what feminists mean by "the black analogy."
3. To learn what women are up to in England, read *Shrew,* the magazine of the London Women's Liberation Workshop.

Vocabulary

(3) IMPETUS   impulse
(17) COUNTENANCE   to show favor or support
(34) ANACHRONISM   something placed, or occurring, out of its proper time
(43) CONCOMMITANT   accompanying

(43) ANATHEMA   a curse
(43) ETHOS   fundamental spiritual characteristics of a culture
(46) DELETERIOUS   injurious; harmful
(69) REDOUNDS   to have an effect or result

The key to a happy marriage, according to the authors, is living for now. When material goals are allowed to become the central focus of a couple's life, personal growth—as well as their marriage—is retarded.

N. O'NEILL AND G. O'NEILL

Living for Now

NOW FOR NOW

1 "Now for now" is a colorful expression used by the islanders of Trinidad to sum up their belief that the immediate moment is all any man can count on in life, and that the man who doesn't make the most of that moment is, in effect, throwing away his life. Open marriage draws upon this philosophy: to live an open life with your mate and to rewrite your contract as you go along, you must relate to one another in the here and now. Yesterday is gone; tomorrow has not yet arrived. But you have today, and you should make the most of it, seeking a vital awareness of what you are doing, how you are feeling and acting, and what is happening to you in the *now*.

2 An overriding obsession with the future is a hallmark of the closed marriage. When John and Sue get married they immediately take out a subscription on the future, tying themselves down to expectations. New furniture, a new car, a down payment on a house, a trip to Europe, a first child, a summer cottage, a second child—there are so many future things to save up for, events to plan for that the *now* is forgotten and becomes nothing more than a time you pass through on your way to the future. The expectations, the goals, take over. John and Sue lose their personal selves and the sense of the moment in striving to attain those goals, to bring about the fulfillment of those expectations. But marriage should be for the people involved, not for the material goals of the future.

3 There is nothing wrong, of course, with knowing what you want out of life in a material sense, in dreaming of a sailboat or skiing vacations in the Alps or a house by the sea. But if these material goals are allowed to become the central focus of your life instead of personal growth, the chances are that by the time you have that house by the sea you won't be sharing it with the same mate you originally dreamed about it with. A couple's commitment should be to one another rather than to goals that may or may not be achievable. In an

open marriage, partners know that *they* are the most important ingre-
dients in the marriage, know that personal, immediate awareness of
the self and of the mate's self are more important than any future
possibility. Time consumed in looking forward to tomorrow's
achievements, or in either lamenting or glorying in the past, is time
lost in the vital present. And the loss of that present time cuts down
on your awareness of what is happening between you and your mate.

4   Past and future are certainly relevant, but it is necessary to ask
how relevant they are and to give them no more than the appropriate
amount of attention. You can, for instance, learn from your past mistakes, but no matter what your problems may be, or how much they
may stem from your past, those problems exist in the present and
must be dealt with in the present. They can only be worked out in
terms of your day-to-day actions. How you solve your problems *now,*
how you experience joys and pleasures *now,* your immediate feelings
and emotions and the degree to which you share them with your mate
will determine the nature of your relationship. Your interaction with
your partner in the now is what makes for a meaningful relationship.
If there is no relating in the now, how can there be in the future?

5   The importance of this "now for now" orientation was expressed by
a young couple whom we interviewed. The wife, Jean, said, "Ken
used to be very unhappy; he planned ahead outlandishly. He was
always in the future, anticipating, planning for the eventuality that
never happened. Trying to make everything happen before it was
ready to happen, securing the future was what he called it. Scaring
me to death was what I called it. I began to worry along with him, not
as much as he did, but too much. Well, it almost ruined our relationship. He would call me at work five or six times a day—he was afraid
for tomorrow on today's time—he just couldn't let things *be.* That is,
until we had some hassles and I made it clear that I *was* here now but
wouldn't be in the future if he kept it up."

6   "Well, I finally learned," Ken said, "to let things be. And I found
that was a lot better than worrying about them, about what they
might or might not become. It took a few rough times to shake me up,
but now I live in today. Absolutely each day is to be faced in and of
itself. A bridge is something to be crossed only when you come to it,
and meantime Jean and I are building right where we are in the here
and now. And it's funny, but not only has our relationship become
more than I dreamed it could, my career has just zoomed out of sight,
too."

THE SECURITY BLANKET

7   Couples would find it easier to relate in the present, and to live a
more dynamic, open life if marriage were not held up to them as a
symbol of security. Most of the unrealistic expectations surrounding
marriage are cast in the form of promises of security. Couples depend
upon marriage to *give* them a purpose and meaning in life, to give
them love and affection, social acceptance, status and a happy family.
Actually, of course, these are all things which the partners must

create for themselves within their marriage. Marriage in and of itself provides none of these securities. Many couples refuse, however, to face the facts, and try instead to make of marriage a kind of security blanket, like children who drag around with them some frazzled remnant of their baby blankets. Having been told all their lives that marriage will bring security, they insist upon clinging to that false notion even when everything is falling apart around them. Such couples will seek for the cause of their troubles anywhere but in their own distorted views of what marriage should be.

8   Many couples use material acquisitions (the house, the bank account, the car, the appliances) to flesh out this illusion of security. But material security can of course evaporate overnight, or disintegrate in excruciatingly slow dribs and drabs, as neighborhoods change, values drop, inflation rises, and jobs change or disappear. Children offer no security—in fact quite the reverse, they are a great responsibility. The promise of perpetual love and care from our mate that is set forth in the marriage vows and enhanced by our unreasonable "ideals" becomes a cruel deception when we find that people change, feelings fluctuate, romance cools, marriages fail and mates leave. Affection and love must be nurtured if they are to grow; they wither in the harsh light of excessive expectation and demand.

9   Thus the promise of security in and through marriage is a myth. Security and the constancy of love can be found only in ourselves, not in the institution of marriage. No one can offer to another a security he does not first possess himself. And just as the child discards his ragged security blanket as he grows up, so too must we put aside our unrealistic expectations, our fairy-tale ideals, if we are to achieve the belief in ourselves that can alone provide any real security, that alone is worth offering to a mate or to a child.

HE MAY NOT BE THE FATHER TO YOUR CHILD

10   "Until death do us part" we promise when we take the marriage vows. But we know full well, or ought to, that other things may part us much sooner. Divorce now occurs with such frequency that marriage has become a revolving door through which marital partners pass on the way to the next promise of fidelity forever, exchanging one partner for another in a way that makes a mockery of our culture's scorn for polygamy. The man you marry today, sad to say, may not be the father of your child tomorrow.

11   Nor will your wife necessarily be the mother of your children. She may be, but don't count on it. This may seem a harsh and unpleasant way of looking at things. But we are not suggesting that you assume the person you marry *won't* be the mother or father of your child; we ask only that you resist making the assumption that she or he *will* be, that you recognize that she or he *may* not be. This is not negativism, only realism.

12   The assumption that your mate will definitely be the parent of your child is not positivism but a kind of self-delusion and fantasy that may tend to get in the way of the kind of genuine relationship be-

tween you and your mate upon which any strong, healthy and lasting marriage must be based. Parenthood today is optional anyway, and the person you marry should be enjoyed for what he is, loved as a person and not just as a potential parent. Partners who can stop living in a future devoted to raising a family and concentrate on building a good relationship *first* are far more likely to have a happy family in the long run.

13   Even if you do have children, and do manage to stay married for life (assuming you marry at twenty and live to age seventy-five), you should remember that child-rearing will take up only approximately one-third of your married life—a whopping two-thirds of it (or over 12,700 days) will be spent in intimate relationship together as a couple rather than as parents. So even if he *does* become father of your child, or she the mother, your relationship to one another should remain of primary importance to you. The better this relationship is, the more meaningful it will be to your function as parents. It is vital therefore to concentrate on each other as individual persons instead of as parents-to-be, to enjoy one another in the here and now instead of looking to the future. The future will be here all too soon as it is.

THE PACKAGE AND THE PACKAGING

14 Premature anticipations of parenthood and false hopes of security are only two among a whole panoply of unrealistic expectations that prevent us from living in the now and from actively *seeking* freedom, growth and love in our relationships with our mates. Without a close look at the expectations foisted on us by the old, closed contract, it is impossible to try to rewrite a new, open contract more suited to our actual needs. The closed marriage is designed to eliminate thinking. You are sold a complete bill of goods—not only a set of expectations but even rigid rules as to how to fulfill those expectations. Since the expectations in themselves are unrealistic, and since there is only one approved way to fulfill them, an inevitable pattern of disillusionment is set up, ready-made. The expectations lead to demands, the demands to manipulation, manipulation to frustration, and frustration to bitter disappointment. This vicious progression can only be stopped by cutting it off before it begins: by eliminating the unrealistic expectations that are the root cause of the trouble.

15   We are conditioned to instant perfection in our society, from instant orgasm to instant therapy. We buy a product and if it is not perfect we return it immediately. Often the product turns out to be different from what we expected; we have been misled by the packaging. The closed marriage also comes wrapped in misleading packaging, not in the form of styrofoam or plastic, but in the bright colors of idealization. The packaging for closed marriage would lead us to believe not only that it will fulfill our dreams, but that it is the only way our dreams can be fulfilled. Naturally, when we find that it doesn't deliver, that it is something other than what it was advertised to be, we feel cheated. Then we do one of three things: we live with our purchase in resignation and disappointment, we throw it out and buy

another which we hope will be an improvement (and which may be one simply because we've learned not to expect so much), or we throw it out and, vowing never to get suckered into buying outright again, settle for short-term rentals instead.

16   What follows is a list of unrealistic expectations of marriage. It will be contrasted with what we believe you can legitimately expect of an open marriage. Some of the unrealistic expectations may not seem so to one reader or another. But we hope that in the course of the book, the reasons for including each of them in this list will become abundantly clear. We even venture to predict that as you go along many of you will discover that it is exactly those expectations you do not recognize as unrealistic at first glance that are the cause of problems within your own marriage.

17
UNREALISTIC EXPECTATIONS, UNREASONABLE IDEALS, AND MYTHOLOGICAL BELIEFS OF CLOSED MARRIAGE

- that it will last forever
- that it means total commitment
- that it will bring happiness, comfort and security
- that your mate *belongs* to you
- that you will have constant attention, concern, admiration and consideration from your mate
- that you will never be lonely again
- that your mate would rather be with you than with anyone else at all times
- that your mate will never be attracted to another person and will always "be true" to you
- that jealousy means you care
- that fidelity is a true measure of the love you have for one another
- that sex will improve with time if it isn't already the world-shaking experience it is supposed to be
- that good sex will in fact (if you can just get the positions right and learn the proper techniques) solve all your problems in marriage
- that all problems in marriage revolve around sex and love
- that you are not complete persons without becoming parents
- that the ultimate goal of marriage is having a child
- that having a child is the ultimate expression of your love for each other
- that having a child will bring new vitality to a sagging marriage or rescue a failing one
- that you will adjust to one another gradually without fights, arguments or misunderstandings
- that you don't love each other if there is conflict between you
- that any change in your mate will come gradually with the maturity of age

- that any other kind of change is disruptive and means loss of love
- that each of you plays a different part in marriage, a role for which you were biologically designed
- that you therefore have the right to expect one thing of a husband and another of a wife
- that sacrifice is a true measure of love
- and last, but most important, that the person you marry can fulfill all your needs, economic, physical, sexual, intellectual and emotional

18   Every single one of these ideals, beliefs or expectations is false in one way or another, and practically impossible to attain, much less to sustain. Yet the clauses of the closed marriage contract are specifically designed to make these expectations come true. Any of them that you do manage to make come true, unfortunately, are almost certain to be at the cost of personal freedom and individual development, with consequent damage to children and to the overall success of the marriage itself.

19   The real problem is that the closed marriage is conceived of as a *static state of being,* a pattern that once established will mean the fulfillment of all expectations. But when expectations are rigid and the means to them restrictive, spontaneity is lost and creativity stifled. Open marriage, in contrast, is a *process,* in which a dynamic interaction takes place between husband and wife, in which both realities and expectations are constantly changing. We believe, in fact, that the only realistic expectations partners can have for marriage revolve around *change* and *growth.*

20   REALISTIC EXPECTATIONS
                              OF
                      OPEN MARRIAGE

- that you will share most but not everything
- that each partner will change—and that change can occur through conflict as well as through a gradual evolvement
- that each will accept responsibility for himself and grant it to his mate
- that you cannot expect your mate to fulfill all your needs, or to do for you what you should be doing for yourself
- that each partner will be different in needs, capacities, values and expectations because he is a different *person,* not just because one is a husband and the other a wife
- that the mutual goal is the relationship, not status or the house by the sea or children
- that children are not needed as proof of your love for each other
- that should you *choose* to have children, that you undertake the role of parents knowingly and willingly as the greatest responsibility in life
- that liking and loving will grow because of the mutual respect that your open relationship engenders

21   In contrast to the unrealistic ideals of undying love, security and fulfillment through another person that are the hallmarks of closed marriage, the ideas of open marriage are:

intimacy   responsibility
intensity   learning
creativity   stimulation
spontaneity   flexibility
growth   enrichment
respect   freedom

and
the liking and love that grow
out of all of these

22   These ideals are not achieved by placing demands on your mate, as is the case with the ideals of closed marriage. Instead, they are the natural fruit of an open relationship, a relationship that may differ greatly from couple to couple, a relationship that you build your-selves, by yourselves and for yourselves—both your individual selves and your collective selves.

23   We think that the open relationship, out of which the above ideals will grow, can be achieved through the application to your individual case of the guidelines we have assembled here:

- through realistic appraisal of your situation and living in the now
- through the giving of privacy and freedom to one another
- through open and honest communication
- through the shedding of inflexible roles
- through open companionship
- through identity, equality and trust

24   There may be other guidelines that you will discover for yourself. But none of them can be of use *unless you take the first vital step:* make an exploration of your expectations of marriage and then, each couple acting according to their judgment, decide which of them are real, honest and open, and which are unrealistic, confining and limit-ing. Discover which of them are preventing you from living in the now, from enjoying the present moment with your mate and then, with the help of the guidelines, begin to shape an open relationship for yourselves.

Discussion of Theme

1. According to the authors, what should be the real goal of mar-riage?
2. The authors advise couples to be realistic in their expectations. Is their alternative, an open marriage, realistic considering the very real human emotions of fear and jealousy?
3. Discuss the inherent paradox in *trying* to be spontaneous.
4. Why, in view of the high divorce rate, does our society continue to

perpetuate myths about marriage? What function do these myths perform?

5. Why is there a stigma attached to a couple who prefer not to have children? Is this changing? Why?

Discussion of Rhetoric

1. The authors discuss the expectations of marriage in terms of packaging and advertising (paragraph 15). How is this appropriate? What is the connotation of this metaphor?
2. Comparison and contrast is a basic element in the structure of this selection. Find examples of this device and analyze its effectiveness.
3. Is this essay persuasive and convincing? What makes it so—or why does it fail?
4. The authors' proposals are controversial. Is it possible to support such ideas with hard, factual evidence?

Writing Assignments

1. In an essay, evaluate your own expectations concerning marriage.
2. If you disagree with the ideas presented in this essay, present your own views in a theme.
3. Write a short essay on "An alternative to both the open and the closed marriages."

Library Exploration

1. Read Aldous Huxley's *Island*.
2. Read C. S. Lewis' *The Four Lovers*.
3. Read Alan Watts' *Nature, Man and Woman*.

Vocabulary

(2) HALLMARK distinguishing mark
(7) DYNAMIC active, lively
(8) ACQUISITIONS material things that are acquired
(8) FLUCTUATE change continually
(8) NURTURED fed or nourished
(10) POLYGAMY the practice of having many spouses at one time

(14) PANOPLY a complete array of something
(16) ABUNDANTLY greatly or fully
(19) STATIC fixed; non-active
(20) ENGENDERS produces; causes

Karl Menninger (1893–　), the famed psychiatrist-cofounder of the Menninger Clinic in Topeka, Kansas, received his education at the University of Wisconsin and Harvard Medical School.

Unlike many who hold that antisocial acts committed by individuals stem from defects in one's environment or education, Karl Menninger believes our society has gone too far in the toleration of what he calls "sin." If we accept the reality of sin and our responsibility for it, then "hope would return to the world."

KARL MENNINGER

Whatever Became of Sin?

1　In all of the laments and reproaches made by our seers and prophets, I miss any mention of "sin," a word that used to be a veritable watchword of prophets. It was a word once in everyone's mind but now rarely if ever heard. Does that mean that no sin is involved in all our troubles—sin with an "I" in the middle? Is no one any longer guilty of anything? Guilty perhaps of a sin that could be repented and repaired or atoned for? Is it only that someone may be stupid or sick or criminal—or asleep? Wrong things are being done, we know; tares are being sown in the wheat field at night. But is no one responsible, no one answerable for these acts? Anxiety and depression we all acknowledge, and even vague guilt feelings; but has no one committed any sins?

2　Where, indeed, did sin go? What became of it?

3　The very word "sin," which seems to have disappeared, was once a proud word. It was a strong word, an ominous and serious word. It described a central point in every civilized human being's life plan and life style. But the word went away.

4   Its disappearance involves a shift in the allocation of responsibility for evil. I am not referring to existential or theological sin, if I may call it that. Not the innate sinfulness of mankind—our natural propensity for transgression. Nor original sin, if it be conceived of as different. I am no theologian, but a doctor.

5   To return to definition: Webster says that sin is transgression of the law of God; disobedience of the divine will; moral failure. Sin is failure to realize in conduct and character the moral ideal, at least as fully as possible under existing circumstances; failure to do as one ought toward one's fellowman.

6   This definition is broad enough to meet the needs of both believers and nonbelievers, but it fails to say why the transgression and disobedience are regarded as "bad," why they are popularly disapproved of or forbidden. Sin traditionally does have this quality of taboo, of wrongness, and we can assume it is carried over from the earliest days.

7   The wrongness of the sinful act lies not merely in its nonconformity, its departure from the accepted, appropriate way of behavior, but in an implicitly aggressive quality—a ruthlessness, a hurting, a breaking away from God and from the rest of humanity, a partial alienation or act of rebellion.

8   Standing on one's head is nonconforming, and it is neither aesthetic nor congenial behavior nor expressive of a moral ideal, but it is not likely to be considered sinful. Sin has a willful, defiant or disloyal quality; *someone* is defied or offended or hurt. The willful disregard or sacrifice of the welfare of others for the welfare or satisfaction of the self is an essential quality of the concept *sin*. And sin is thus, at heart, a refusal of the love of others.

9   Perhaps it is the various implications or corollaries of the sin doctrine that are objected to by, for example, the behaviorists. Sin traditionally implies guilt, answerability and, by derivation, responsibility. For many it implies confession, attrition, reparation, repentance, forgiveness, atonement. I am aware of the objections that can be offered to each one of these, but I also know of social values served by retaining them. However, this is not to be a theological treatise, and I shall proceed on the assumption that the word "sin" *does* imply these corollaries and that I for one find the corollaries acceptable in principle.

10   The function of approving or disapproving what the instincts and the occasion impel one to do has long been called the conscience. It was identified as the "superego" by Freud and the "archaic conscience" by Father Mailoux, the theologian and psychoanalyst. It operates partly from the dark past, as it were, using strictures and sanctions from the childhood period and remaining largely unconscious and inaccessible to new information. Characteristic coping measures used by the parents are taken over automatically and imitated in such manipulations as compromise, mollification, corruption and implacability. These become the pattern of the child in his moral program. The conscious, rational portion of the superego is in contact with the environment, and it does grow and change with the times and with experience.

11   Psychoanalysts do not use the word "sin," because of its strong re-
proachful quality, its vague or nonspecific quality and its corollaries
and implications of guilt, reparation and atonement. It is not for the
analyst to decide what is sinful for his patient or what he should do
about it. The psychoanalyst believes that the qualities of aggression
and self-destruction are evil, and this he can point out without charging the patient with moral turpitude, or committing him to a specific
obligation or himself (the analyst) to an esoteric or specific code.

12   Why are aggression and self-destruction *prima facie* evils for the
psychoanalyst to single out? Because both are opposed to the life
principle, to the healing of the patient's disorganization and distress.
If we were to equate sin with self-destructiveness and overt aggression, probably many psychoanalysts would concur. They would say
that there is definite, objectively and empirically "bad" behavior (as
a rule), whereas sin is indefinite, a value judgment based on a code.
We will pursue this distinction further.

13   But first I would like to review the events in the recent rapid decline and disappearance of the word "sin," not because any particular word is so important in itself, but because its obsolescence may
be a clue to fundamental changes in the moral philosophy of our
civilization.

14   When I was a boy, sin was still a serious matter and the word was
not a jocular term. But I saw this change; I saw it go. I am afraid I
even joined in hailing its going. And I would like now to recapture
briefly the circumstances of its departure as I recall them.

15   Long before I was born, of course, the major responsibility for identifying and dealing with adult misbehavior had been taken over by
the state. Much adult sin, in other words, had become crime; it was
chiefly youth who sinned. After the reign of Henry VIII in England
many sinful acts were formally declared to be not only immoral but
illegal. Murder, mayhem, robbery, treason and scores of other
specific transgressions became defined crimes with prescribed
punishments. Remaining to the domain of the moralists (churches)
were the seven cardinal sins of anger, greed, pride, sloth, envy, lust
and gluttony. Even some of these, in special forms, were preempted
by the law.

16   Making what were once dealt with as sins into crimes rendered the
designation of sin increasingly pointless from a practical standpoint.
Neither church ruling nor priestly admonishment was any longer required either for sanction or for penalty. Sin as sin became a strictly
personal matter, an offense contrary to conscience or moral standard,
an intimate, wrongful choice of action—predominantly secret, although often visible. Dealing with it was a task left to the pulpit, the
confessional and the individual conscience.

17   One hundred years ago there was still plenty of sin and sinning
going on. While the law courts were busy and the prisons filled with
perpetrators of crime, the clergy, too, were busy in the confessional
and in informal sessions with the problems of sin and sinners.

18   The pulpit was powerful, and public moral condemnation was effective. Elijah Lovejoy, the great abolitionist editor, was not mobbed

and robbed and murdered because of the facts he published; it was, rather, his moral denunciations that the slavery people feared and hated. They vigorously and violently disputed his charge that slavery, which was certainly not a crime, was nevertheless a great and heinous sin. This made some of them great sinners, which their angry protests and violent demonstrations did little to disprove.

19   And, of course, there were other sins—thousands of them. The word was in common parlance. It was no joke or witticism or euphemism to call someone's act a sin. Sin was taken seriously. One need only read the text of Goethe's *Faust* to realize how profoundly moved and controlled people were by the notion that certain things were sinful and that they entailed dreadful and inescapable punishment. Nathaniel Hawthorne's *The Scarlet Letter* deals with similar assumptions. That kind of attitude toward that kind of sin has indeed undergone revolution.

20   That certain acts are considered by adult society to be improper, indecorous, disapproved and unacceptable has to be learned by every child for himself. He isn't born with any convictions about morality. These "certain things" vary, of course, in different cultures and ages and with different parents. With patience and kindness most primitive peoples teach their children a set of taboos and sanctions using myths, rituals and other methods. So-called civilized peoples are often severe in their discipline, attaching a pain penalty to infractions.

21   These artificial consequences of sin vary greatly. The American Indians were shocked by the harshness of our forefathers in teaching morality to their offspring, and some tribes referred to settlers as "the people who whip children." This points up an important factor in the disappearance of sin, namely, that the punitive rituals—public and private—became too severe. People began to disapprove of the harshness of the penalties assessed against "sins" by parents, priests and courts. The stocks, the tongue slitting, the cheek branding were too cruel. Imprisonment was substituted in the case of "criminals." The punishment, repeatedly assessed against the Pueblo Indians for not yielding—that of being thrown from a cliff or of having a leg cut off—would be unthinkable today. Children were sent to the gallows for peccadilloes; crimes in England punished by deportation to Australia were often minor offenses indeed, as we would judge today. Life was sterner in the olden days, and penalties for displeasing power—parental, civil, economic or divine—were stark. And this association of sin and penalty was ingrained. The vanishing of sin has really been a disappearance of harsh reprisal, a softening not of moral fiber but of human compassion.

22   Thus sin, or designating something as sinful, began to disappear because it was too expensive in terms of the current standards of comfort. Instead of reducing the penalty, people merely negated the sin. Sabbath violation is a clear example.

23   Medicine, including psychiatry, was pretty grim through the Middle Ages and on up almost to the twentieth century. Punitive "treatment" of many kinds was used not only without embarrassment but

actually with pride and claims of great successes. This punitive element in medical treatment reflected a philosophy of morals that medicine would have denied. Doctors long ago gave up the notion that illness reflected sin, but their practices often demonstrated the unconscious persistence of the idea. Implicit in news stories in the papers, in articles in the serious weeklies and monthlies, in daily conversations, in sermons and other public addresses, was the principle that sin merited punishment and, unless and until the penalty was paid, that the sin would continue. For schoolchildren the "sins" were telling lies, swearing, stealing ("taking things"), cheating in games or in classroom tests, "copying" the work of other students, immodesty, disobedience and rudeness in any form to teachers or parents. All "crimes" were sinful, of course, but more relevant to us were "secret sins," such as stealing, cheating, lying and various sexual activities.

24   Almost no other activity was so regularly condemned and punished as erotic self-stimulation, masturbation. For centuries, schoolchildren, prisoners, sailors and slaves were savagely punished when detected in or even suspected of "the solitary vice" of "self-abuse." This moral taboo is thousands of years old and exists in many (but not all) primitive cultures.

25   Some competent writers seem to believe masturbation to have been an important "taboo" only in "Christian" civilization and only in the past 300 years. But the condemnation of masturbation is said to occur in the *Egyptian Book of the Dead* (1550–950 B.C.).

26   In America the masturbation taboo has always been, until recently, very explicit. Masturbation was never a "crime," but it was a moral offense of such seriousness that many "authorities" joined hands in insuring its prohibition. To help stem the temptation of evildoing, threats or inflictions of dire punishment were commonly made to children by all and sundry. Parents watched for the slightest evidences of the "sin." Schoolteachers were on the alert for it. The medical profession ascribed to it various diseases, general physical and mental deterioration and especially "insanity."

27   The doctors really believed this theory, and many of the official adjudications in cases of mental illness were officially based on "masturbation." I have examined many old state hospital records in which the etiology of case after case is so ascribed.

28   Why should this particular physiological experience have been built up into such a great sin? How the child senses the adult taboo on this exciting phenomenon has been much disputed, but that he perceives it without words is indubitable. To an extent difficult for the present-day reader to grasp, this was *the* major sin for middle- and upper-class adolescents a century and less ago.

29   Until fairly recently masturbation was a *bête noir* among high school and college students—indulged in secretly, of course, by all, bragged about by a few but deplored and denied by most. It was an ever-present, easily reached source of guilt feelings, often exploited by religious leaders. Consider the emotional conflict in a boy (or girl), instructed in the faith that Jesus, the Son of God, died "for your sins," whose chief secret preoccupation was his (or her) propensity for re-

peating this dreadful act. I have seen a large room full of university men bowed on their knees in prayer for forgiveness and for strength to resist the temptation of this sin.

30 The amazing circumstance is that sometime soon after the turn of the present century, this ancient taboo—for the violation of which millions had been punished, threatened, condemned, intimidated and made hypocritical and cynical—vanished almost overnight. Masturbation, the solitary vice, *the* sin of youth, suddenly seemed not to be so sinful, perhaps not sinful at all; not so dangerous—in fact, not dangerous at all; less a vice than a form of pleasurable experience, and a normal and healthy one.

31 This sudden metamorphosis in an almost universal social attitude is more significant of the changed temper, philosophy and morality of the twentieth century than any other phenomenon that comes to mind. It is not difficult to see why *all* sin other than "crime" seemed to many to have disappeared along with this one.

32 This, in a way, now seems regrettable, for masturbation lost its quality of sinfulness through a new understanding, but there was no new understanding of ruthlessness or wastefulness or cruelty. A small amount of the disapproval of masturbation may have been displaced by previously undervalued "sins" such as those mentioned, but in general it seems as if the great phenomenon of a deadly sin's suddenly disappearing—and disappearing "without anyone's noticing it"—affected our attitude toward other disapproved behavior.

33 It is as if we expected those *other* sins, presumably *all* other sins, to vanish or diminish in seriousness in the same mysterious way. It is common knowledge that many younger people do and say things that their elders consider vulgar, improper or even definitely wrong—let me say "sinful." These are violations of taboos that were very serious for the parents and grandparents. We cannot say that youth *always* did so, for such is not the case. There is no new understanding of assaults and rapes and even lesser violence that makes violence more acceptable and less sinful. Yet it *is* more acceptable to many people.

34 "Violence," said Alexander Solzhenitsyn in his speech accepting the Nobel Prize, "less and less embarrassed by the limits imposed by centuries of lawfulness, is brazenly and victoriously striding across the whole world." In recent years, he noted, there have been new breakdowns in our protection. There once was a time when violence was seen as a means of last resort. Now we begin with it. It is a method of communication.

35 Whence this change? Is evildoing really no longer taboo simply because the exaggerated punishments of another adolescent experience were found (and decided) to be inappropriate? Can all sin have been repudiated as such because one behavior once considered evil is now no longer condemned?

36 It was about the turn of the century that a new social philosophy and a new code of morality, as it seemed, began to manifest itself all over the earth. It was not so much an increase in humane concern as an attempted purging of all sentiment in connection with the "control" of behavior, i.e., not merely crime and other sins but the steps

incident to the training of children in the way they should go. Not only sympathy and affection but also hate and shame and fear of punishment were to be suppressed in favor of the neutral, passionless, objective, rational and normal (i.e., moral). But gradually all social processes and institutions felt the effects of this.

37 Certainly the greatest impetus toward the new scientific attitude was Freud's discovery (about 1900) of the psychoanalytic method —the technique of systematic exploration of *unconscious* psychological processes. From what he and others observed in their patients, a new formulation of human motivation gradually developed that emphasized love attachments and hate attachments—conscious *and* unconscious—as basic personality structures. Conflicts between these, with partially buried, partially exposed "memories," were labeled neuroses and regarded as illness.

38 The development of psychology as a science, the experimental models of Wilhelm Wundt and others, the Gestalt and field theory of Kurt Lewin and others, the discoveries of the hypnotists and the psychoanalysts, all led to new theories of behavior, theories of motivation and theories of learning. These departed widely from the simple, good-and-bad, pleasure-pain, carrot-stick stimulus-response formulations of an earlier day. The behavior of all living things began to be regarded as being capable of objective scientific study from many angles other than merely its desirability or undesirability.

39 The increasing interest in scientifically understanding and modifying behavior tended to diminish the use of traditional methods and to alter the punitive attitude toward "badness." More and more openly it began to be proposed that much "juvenile delinquency," behavior that in adults would have been definitely criminal, was probably better viewed as *symptomatic*, i.e., indicative of underlying pathology for which the offender was not (entirely) to blame or to be blamed.

40 As a result of all these scientific discoveries, not only did medical practice change, but many social customs and standards changed. New kinds of child rearing and new kinds of teaching developed in which the notion of sin as it had been taught began to undergo erosion. Words like "bad," "wicked" and "immoral," while still employed, began to sound old-fashioned. "Sin" began to be questioned. Magazine articles appeared bearing such titles as "Sin or Symptom?"—the implication of which was that the new view of behavior had translated what were once indications for punishment into indications for maneuvers aimed at healing. The idea that particular behavior was the result of numerous determining events and forces led to increasing doubt about its easy control or modification.

41 Gradually the effects of "the new psychology," as it was called, began to be apparent and it did seem to many worthy people that morality was being invaded and eroded thereby. Much behavior that would be classed *a priori* as sinful had long since passed into the control of the law. And now, increasingly, some *crime* was being viewed as *symptomatic*. Sins had become crimes and now crimes were becoming illnesses; in other words whereas the police and judges had taken over from the clergy, the doctors and psychologists were now taking over from the police and judges.

42   Much "sin" had become identified as "crime" long before our times; what I saw occur was the effect on the concept of sin of this realization that some *crime* was *sickness*. For, if the worst of sins can be nullified of their evil character by closer examination, what about the minor sins that were not even considered criminal? Are they not often the consequences of pathological attitudes of super-piety, prudishness, puritanical oversternness, neurotic inhibition, and "reaction formation"?

43   Perhaps, however, some forms of behavior might still deserve the name. Hating one's brother, surely; dishonoring one's parents; envying one's neighbor; or "blaspheming the Holy Ghost" (a common delusion of psychiatric patients in earlier times, echoing charges sternly hurled by pietistic preachers).

44   But no, these offenses were translatable into psychological terms and "explained" by psychological theories. To call them sins had no usefulness. There remained, of course, sin in the sense of alienating oneself from God; for believers this was, is, and will continue to be *the* sin. But articulate believers seemed to be fewer in number; their voices were drowned out by the cheers of the new psychologists.

45   Thus it was that "sin," except for the rituals of the confessional and the prayer chamber, increasingly disappeared from public view—or hearing. Believers continued their beliefs not only in a Creator but in His displeasure at their moral failures. They confessed their sins in their own company—but they did not refer to them in daily conversation. Sin was no longer a topic of conversation, debate, argument, accusation and public remorse—as it long had been. It was no longer a euphemism for masturbation, adultery, drunkenness, smoking or gambling. It became a word of mild disapproval, less and less frequently applied, or a jocular word.

46   I believe there is "sin" that is expressed in ways that cannot be subsumed under such verbal artifacts as "crime," "disease," "delinquency," "deviancy." There *is* immorality; there *is* unethical behavior; there *is* wrongdoing. And I hope to show that there is usefulness in retaining the concept and indeed the word "sin," which now shows some signs of returning to public acceptance.

47   Notions of guilt and sin, which formerly served as some restraint on aggression, have become eroded by the presumption that the individual has less to do with his actions than we had assumed, and hence any sense of personal responsibility (or guilt) is inappropriate. This philosophy comes as a comforting relief for many, an alarming threat of powerlessness for others and an inflammatory challenge for others.

48   For some, the very suggestion that "voluntary" behavior is never entirely voluntary arouses anxiety and provokes vigorous rebuttal. "Improper behavior," they assert, "is willful wrongdoing." (They may or may not call it sin.) It must be controlled, they say, if not by the individual, then by someone in authority. Each of us must try, and that effort must be supported by firmness, by threat, by force, and if need be, by fierceness. Success will be rewarded; failure must be punished. There is right and there is wrong; there can be no compromise.

49   We all know exponents of this simplistic hardcore supermoralism.

Some of them are just ignorant, some are fanatical, others are political rightists, still others are bigots. But some are (also) earnest, honest
and very sincere people. Some of them are even intelligent! What is
more—and this may astonish you coming from me—I think they have
a point.

50　　The law and the church were so sure of themselves and so fixed on
the position that all behavior is conscious and voluntary (unless accidental) that when scientists began to assert themselves about involuntary and unconsciously motivated behavior, some of them simply carried their thesis too far. Their absolutism is just as offensive and misleading as that of their opponents.

51　　Even if we concede that some—perhaps most—behavior is essentially involuntary, automatic or reactive (symptomatic), we know that
no behavior—or very little of it—is *entirely* involuntary.

52　　The Research Department of the Menninger Foundation has demonstrated that a degree of voluntary control over what are ordinarily considered involuntary body processes can be exerted by intention
by many individuals who were not aware of their ability to do so.

53　　Across the country other researchers, using bio-feedback to inform
a person of his own inside-the-skin behavior, have demonstrated the
possibility of self-regulation of tension headache, blood pressure and
heartbeat irregularities. Even epilepsy, an electrical storm in the
brain, is yielding in some cases to self-regulation of brain-wave patterns through biofeedback training.

54　　The value of taking part of the responsibility for one's own
psychological well-being has never been more clearly demonstrated
than by this recent upsurge of "biofeedback training for voluntary
control of internal states." As people learn that their emotional patterns are reflected in physiological states, a potent attack by self-
regulation methods on genetic defects and adverse cultural conditioning can perhaps begin. Migraine, for instance, seems to run in
families and is triggered by stress, the conditioning pressure of life.
The effects of training for voluntary enhancement of psychosomatic
health could be far-reaching in counteracting the depressing idea of
impotence in handling the problems of living.

55　　To admit the notion of *any* "voluntary" control is to acknowledge
that such intangibles as idealism and conscience and "will" do play a
determining role. My intention here is to resist the *total* translation of
all "sins" and "crimes" into the category of symptoms. Some criminal
behavior may be an expression of sickness, but not all criminals are
sick. Indeed, few of them are, in my experience.

56　　My proposal is for the revival or reassertion of personal responsibility in all human acts, good and bad. Not total responsibility, but not
zero either. I believe that all evildoing in which we become involved
to any degree tends to evoke guilt feelings and depression. These
may or may not be clearly perceived, but they affect us. They may be
reacted to and covered up by all kinds of escapism, rationalization
and reaction or symptom formation. To revive the half-submerged
idea of personal responsibility and to seek appropriate measures of
reparation might turn the tide of our aggressions and of the moral
struggle in which much of the world population is engaged.

Discussion of Theme

1. What is Menninger's definition of sin? Does it differ in any way from the traditional one? How?
2. What practical reasons does the author give for avoiding sin? What are the benefits in terms of physical health?
3. What is the difference between sin-guilt and the sense of personal responsibility?
4. If the concept of sin were once again a strong inhibiting factor for the individual, would this tend to lessen societies' sense of responsibility for the mental health of its members?

Discussion of Rhetoric

1. Why does the author pose a series of questions early in the essay? Where are these questions answered?
2. The author often repeats concepts and ideas. Of what value is this repetition and restatement?
3. The author states that his approach is that of doctor, not theologian. Yet he frequently uses religious terms and biblical allusions. Is this appropriate? Can one avoid such references in a discussion of sin?
4. What is the effect of the one-sentence paragraph 5?
5. Is the author's approach strictly objective or is some religious bias evident?

Writing Assignments

1. Do you believe man must be controlled by some inhibitor such as law or religion to keep him from reverting to innate violence? Discuss.
2. Develop the following idea taken from this essay: "There was a time when violence was a means of last resort. Now it is a method of communication."
3. Write a rebuttal to this essay.
4. Why does the author feel it is important not only to revive the concept of *sin,* but also the word?
5. In an essay, respond to the following quote by Blake: "The road of excesses leads to the palace of wisdom."

Library Exploration

1. For different points of view on whether or not man has an innate sense of right and wrong (or is naturally aggressive), read: "Man and Aggression," Ashley Montagu, "The Heart of Man," Erich Fromm, "On Aggression," Konrad Lorenz, "Lord of the Flies," William Golding.

Vocabulary

(9) COROLLARIES easily drawn consequences

(10) MOLLIFICATION a softening or appeasement

(10) IMPLACABILITY not to be appeased or pacified

(11) TURPITUDE a depraved or shameful act

(11) ESOTERIC understood or meant for a select few

(12) PRIMA FACIE at first appearance

(14) JOCULAR suited to a joke

(19) EUPHEMISM the substitution of a mild expression for a harsh one

(21) PECCADILLOES a petty sin or offense

(27) ADJUDICATIONS decrees

(27) ETIOLOGY the study of the causes of diseases

(29) BETENOIR something that one dreads

(41) A PRIORI valid independently from observation

(43) PIETISTIC overly given to piety

(46) SUBSUMED included in a larger class

The Student and Language

1

Paul Roberts (1917–66) was a specialist in structural linguistics and a member of the faculty of Cornell University. Roberts is the author of "Understanding Grammar" (1954); "Patterns of English" (1956); "Understanding English" (1958); and "Cornflakes and Beaujolais" (1958), written after a sojourn in Europe.

This clever essay points out the major pitfalls that snare many freshman theme writers. Roberts then gives some advice: avoid the obvious, be unusual, watch for abstractions, avoid padding, don't hedge, use clear words.

PAUL ROBERTS

How to Say Nothing in Five Hundred Words

1 It's Friday afternoon, and you have almost survived another week of classes. You are just looking forward dreamily to the weekend when the English instructor says: "For Monday you will turn in a five-hundred-word composition on college football."

2 Well, that puts a good big hole in the weekend. You don't have any strong views on college football one way or the other. You get rather excited during the season and go to all the home games and find it rather more fun than not. On the other hand, the class has been reading Robert Hutchins in the anthology and perhaps Shaw's "Eighty-Yard Run," and from the class discussion you have got the idea that the instructor thinks college football is for the birds. You are no fool. You can figure out what side to take.

3 After dinner you get out the portable typewriter that you got for high school graduation. You might as well get it over with and enjoy

Saturday and Sunday. Five hundred words is about two double-spaced pages with normal margins. You put in a sheet of paper, think up a title, and you're off:

Why College Football Should Be Abolished

4   College football should be abolished because it's bad for the school and also bad for the players. The players are so busy practicing that they don't have any time for their studies.

This, you feel, is a mighty good start. The only trouble is that it's only thirty-two words. You still have four hundred and sixty-eight to go, and you've pretty well exhausted the subject. It comes to you that you do your best thinking in the morning, so you put away the typewriter and go to the movies. But the next morning you have to do your washing and some math problems, and in the afternoon you go to the game. The English instructor turns up too, and you wonder if you've taken the right side after all. Saturday night you have a date, and Sunday morning you have to go to church. (You can't let English assignments interfere with your religion.) What with one thing and another, it's ten o'clock Sunday night before you get out the typewriter again. You make a pot of coffee and start to fill out your views on college football. Put a little meat on the bones.

Why College Football Should Be Abolished

5   In my opinion, it seems to me that college football should be abolished. The reason why I think this to be true is because I feel that football is bad for the colleges in nearly every respect. As Robert Hutchins says in his article in our anthology in which he discusses college football, it would be better if the colleges had race horses and had races with one another, because then the horses would not have to attend classes. I firmly agree with Mr. Hutchins on this point, and I am sure that many other students would agree too.

6   One reason why it seems to me that college football is bad is that it has become too commercial. In the olden times when people played football just for the fun of it, maybe college football was all right, but they do not play football just for the fun of it now as they used to in the old days. Nowadays college football is what you might call a big business. Maybe this is not true at all schools, and I don't think it is especially true here at State, but certainly this is the case at most colleges and universities in America nowadays, as Mr. Hutchins points out in his very interesting article. Actually the coaches and alumni go around to the high schools and offer the high school stars large salaries to come to their colleges and play football for them. There was one case where a high school star was offered a convertible if he would play football for a certain college.

7   Another reason for abolishing college football is that it is bad for the players. They do not have time to get a college education, because they are so busy playing football. A football player has to practice every afternoon from three to six and then he is so tired that he can't concentrate on his studies. He just feels like dropping off to sleep after dinner, and then the next day he goes to his classes without having studied and maybe he fails the test.

(Good ripe stuff so far, but you're still a hundred and fifty-one words from home. One more push.)

8   Also I think college football is bad for the colleges and the universities because not very many students get to participate in it. Out of a college of ten thousand students only seventy-five or a hundred play football, if that many. Football is what you might call a spectator sport. That means that most people go to watch it but do not play it themselves.

(Four hundred and fifteen, Well, you still have the conclusion, and when you retype it, you can make the margins a little wider.)

9   These are the reasons why I agree with Mr. Hutchins that college football should be abolished in American colleges and universities.

10   On Monday you turn it in, moderately hopeful, and on Friday it comes back marked "weak in content" and sporting a big "D."

11   This essay is exaggerated a little, not much. The English instructor will recognize it as reasonably typical of what an assignment on college football will bring in. He knows that nearly half of the class will contrive in five hundred words to say that college football is too commercial and bad for the players. Most of the other half will inform him that college football builds character and prepares one for life and brings prestige to the school. As he reads paper after paper all saying the same thing in almost the same words, all bloodless, five hundred words dripping out of nothing, he wonders how he allowed himself to get trapped into teaching English when he might have had a happy and interesting life as an electrician or a confidence man.

12   Well, you may ask, what can you do about it? The subject is one on which you have few convictions and little information. Can you be expected to make a dull subject interesting? As a matter of fact, this is precisely what you are expected to do. This is the writer's essential task. All subjects, except sex, are dull until somebody makes them interesting. The writer's job is to find the argument, the approach, the angle, the wording that will take the reader with him. This is seldom easy, and it is particularly hard in subjects that have been much discussed: College Football, Fraternities, Popular Music, Is Chivalry Dead?, and the like. You will feel that there is nothing you can do with such subjects except repeat the old bromides. But there are some things you can do which will make your papers, if not throbbingly alive, at least less insufferably tedious than they might otherwise be.

AVOID THE OBVIOUS CONTENT

13   Say the assignment is college football. Say that you've decided to be against it. Begin by putting down the arguments that come to your mind: it is too commercial, it takes the students' minds off their studies, it is hard on the players, it makes the university a kind of circus instead of an intellectual center, for most schools it is financially ruinous. Can you think of any more arguments, just off hand? All right. Now when you write your paper, *make sure that you don't use any of the material on this list*. If these are the points that leap to your mind, they will leap to everyone else's too, and whether you get a "C" or a "D" may depend on whether the instructor reads your paper early when he is fresh and tolerant or late, when the sentence "In my opin-

ion, college football has become too commercial," inexorably repeated, has brought him to the brink of lunacy.

14   Be against college football for some reason or reasons of your own. If they are keen and perceptive ones, that's splendid. But even if they are trivial or foolish or indefensible, you are still ahead so long as they are not everybody else's reasons too. Be against it because the colleges don't spend enough money on it to make it worthwhile, because it is bad for the characters of the spectators, because the players are forced to attend classes, because the football stars hog all the beautiful women, because it competes with baseball and is therefore un-American and possibly Communist inspired. There are lots of more or less unused reasons for being against college football.

15   Sometimes it is a good idea to sum up and dispose of the trite and conventional points before going on to your own. This has the advantage of indicating to the reader that you are going to be neither trite nor conventional. Something like this:

16   We are often told that college football should be abolished because it has become too commercial or because it is bad for the players. These arguments are no doubt very cogent, but they don't really go to the heart of the matter.

Then you go to the heart of the matter.

TAKE THE LESS USUAL SIDE

17 One rather simple way of getting into your paper is to take the side of the argument that most of the citizens will want to avoid. If the assignment is an essay on dogs, you can, if you choose, explain that dogs are faithful and lovable companions, intelligent, useful as guardians of the house and protectors of children, indispensable in police work — in short, when all is said and done, man's best friends. Or you can suggest that those big brown eyes conceal, more often than not, a vacuity of mind and an inconstancy of purpose; that the dogs you have known most intimately have been mangy, ill-tempered brutes, incapable of instruction; and that only your nobility of mind and fear of arrest prevent you from kicking the flea-ridden animals when you pass them on the street.

18   Naturally personal convictions will sometimes dictate your approach. If the assigned subject is "Is Methodism Rewarding to the Individual?" and you are a pious Methodist, you have really no choice. But few assigned subjects, if any, will fall in this category. Most of them will lie in broad areas of discussion with much to be said on both sides. They are intellectual exercises, and it is legitimate to argue now one way and now another, as debaters do in similar circumstances. Always take the side that looks to you hardest, least defensible. It will almost always turn out to be easier to write interestingly on that side.

19   This general advice applies where you have a choice of subjects. If you are to choose among "The Value of Fraternities" and "My Favorite High School Teacher" and "What I Think About Beetles,"

by all means plump for the beetles. By the time the instructor gets to your paper, he will be up to his ears in tedious tales about the French teacher at Bloombury High and assertions about how fraternities build character and prepare one for life. Your views on beetles, whatever they are, are bound to be a refreshing change.

20   Don't worry too much about figuring out what the instructor thinks about the subject so that you can cuddle up with him. Chances are his views are no stronger than yours. If he does have convictions and you oppose him, his problem is to keep from grading you higher than you deserve in order to show he is not biased. This doesn't mean that you should always cantankerously dissent from what the instructor says; that gets tiresome too. And if the subject assigned is "My Pet Peeve," do not begin, "My pet peeve is the English instructor who assigns papers on 'my pet peeve.'" This was still funny during the War of 1812, but it has sort of lost its edge since then. It is in general good manners to avoid personalities.

SLIP OUT OF ABSTRACTION

21 If you will study the essay on college football [near the beginning of this essay], you will perceive that one reason for its appalling dullness is that it never gets down to particulars. It is just a series of not very glittering generalities: "football is bad for the colleges," "it has become too commercial," "football is a big business," "it is bad for the players," and so on. Such round phrases thudding against the reader's brain are unlikely to convince him, though they may well render him unconscious.

22   If you want the reader to believe that college football is bad for the players, you have to do more than say so. You have to display the evil. Take your roommate, Alfred Simkins, the second-string center. Picture poor old Alfy coming home from football practice every evening, bruised and aching, agonizingly tired, scarcely able to shovel the mashed potatoes into his mouth. Let us see him staggering up to the room, getting out his econ textbook, peering desperately at it with his good eye, falling asleep and failing the test in the morning. Let us share his unbearable tension as Saturday draws near. Will he fail, be demoted, lose his monthly allowance, be forced to return to the coal mines? And if he succeeds, what will be his reward? Perhaps a slight ripple of applause when the third-string center replaces him, a moment of elation in the locker room if the team wins, of despair if it loses. What will he look back on when he graduates from college? Toil and torn ligaments. And what will be his future? He is not good enough for pro football, and he is too obscure and weak in econ to succeed in stocks and bonds. College football is tearing the heart from Alfy Simkins and, when it finishes with him, will callously toss aside the shattered hulk.

23   This is no doubt a weak enough argument for the abolition of college football, but it is a sight better than saying, in three or four variations, that college football (in your opinion) is bad for the players.

24   Look at the work of any professional writer and notice how constantly he is moving from the generality, the abstract statement, to the concrete example, the facts and figures, the illustration. If he is writing on juvenile delinquency, he does not just tell you that juveniles are (it seems to him) delinquent and that (in his opinion) something should be done about it. He shows you juveniles being delinquent, tearing up movie theatres in Buffalo, stabbing high school principals in Dallas, smoking marijuana in Palo Alto. And more than likely he is moving toward some specific remedy, not just a general wringing of the hands.

25   It is no doubt possible to be *too* concrete, too illustrative or anecdotal, but few inexperienced writers err this way. For most the soundest advice is to be seeking always for the picture, to be always turning general remarks into seeable examples. Don't say, "Sororities teach girls the social graces." Say, "Sorority life teaches a girl how to carry on a conversation while pouring tea, without sloshing the tea into the saucer." Don't say, "I like certain kinds of popular music very much." Say, "Whenever I hear Gerber Sprinklittle play 'Mississippi Man' on the trombone, my socks creep up my ankles."

GET RID OF OBVIOUS PADDING

26 The student toiling away at his weekly English theme is too often tormented by a figure: five hundred words. How, he asks himself, is he to achieve this staggering total? Obviously by never using one word when he can somehow work in ten.

27   He is therefore seldom content with a plain statement like "Fast driving is dangerous." This has only four words in it. He takes thought, and the sentence becomes:

> In my opinion, fast driving is dangerous.

Better, but he can do better still:

> In my opinion, fast driving would seem to be rather dangerous.

If he is really adept, it may come out:

> In my humble opinion, though I do not claim to be an expert on this complicated subject, fast driving, in most circumstances, would seem to be rather dangerous in many respects, or at least so it would seem to me.

Thus four words have been turned into forty, and not an iota of content has been added.

28   Now this is a way to go about reaching five hundred words, and if you are content with a "D" grade, it is as good a way as any. But if you aim higher, you must work differently. Instead of stuffing your sentences with straw, you must try steadily to get rid of the padding, to make your sentences lean and tough. If you are really working at it, your first draft will greatly exceed the required total, and then you will work it down, thus:

29   It is thought in some quarters that fraternities do not contribute as much as might be expected to campus life.

> Some people think that fraternities contribute little to campus life.
>
> The average doctor who practices in small towns or in the country must toil night and day to heal the sick.
>
> Most country doctors work long hours.
>
> When I was a little girl, I suffered from shyness and embarrassment in the presence of others.
>
> I was a shy little girl.
>
> It is absolutely necessary for the person employed as a marine fireman to give the matter of steam pressure his undivided attention at all times.
>
> The fireman has to keep his eye on the steam gauge.

33   You may ask how you can arrive at five hundred words at this rate. Simple. You dig up more real content. Instead of taking a couple of obvious points off the surface of the topic and then circling warily around them for six paragraphs, you work in and explore, figure out the details. You illustrate. You say that fast driving is dangerous, and then you prove it. How long does it take to stop a car at forty and at eighty? How far can you see at night? What happens when a tire blows? What happens in a head-on collision at fifty miles an hour? Pretty soon your paper will be full of broken glass and blood and head-less torsos, and reaching five hundred words will not really be a problem.

CALL A FOOL A FOOL

34   Some of the padding in freshman themes is to be blamed not on anxiety about the word minimum but on excessive timidity. The student writes, "In my opinion, the principal of my high school acted in ways that I believe every unbiased person would have to call foolish." This isn't exactly what he means. What he means is, "My high school principal was a fool." If he was a fool, call him a fool. Hedging the thing about with "in-my-opinion's" and "it-seems-to-me's" and "as-I-see-it's" and "at-least-from-my-point-of-view's" gains you nothing. Delete these phrases whenever they creep into your paper.

35   The student's tendency to hedge stems from a modesty that in other circumstances would be commendable. He is, he realizes, young and inexperienced, and he half suspects that he is dopey and fuzzy-minded beyond the average. Probably only too true. But it doesn't help to announce your incompetence six times in every paragraph. Decide what you want to say and say it as vigorously as possible, without apology and in plain words.

36   Linguistic diffidence can take various forms. One is what we call *euphemism*. This is the tendency to call a spade "a certain garden implement" or women's underwear "unmentionables." It is stronger in some eras than others and in some people than others but it always operates more or less in subjects that are touchy or taboo: death, sex, madness, and so on. Thus we shrink from saying "He died last night" but say instead "passed away," "left us," "joined his Maker," "went to his reward." Or we try to take off the tension with a lighter cliché: "kicked the bucket," "cashed in his chips," "handed in his dinner

pail." We have found all sorts of ways to avoid saying *mad:* "mentally ill," "touched," "not quite right upstairs," "feeble-minded," "innocent," "simple," "off his trolley," "not in his right mind." Even such a now plain word as *insane* began as a euphemism with the meaning "not healthy."

37   Modern science, particularly psychology, contributes many polysyllables in which we can wrap our thoughts and blunt their force. To many writers there is no such thing as a bad schoolboy. Schoolboys are maladjusted or unoriented or misunderstood or in the need of guidance or lacking in continued success toward satisfactory integration of the personality as a social unit, but they are never bad. Psychology no doubt makes us better men and women, more sympathetic and tolerant, but it doesn't make writing any easier. Had Shakespeare been confronted with psychology, "To be or not to be" might have come out, "To continue as a social unit or not to do so. That is the personality problem. Whether 'tis a better sign of integration at the conscious level to display a psychic tolerance toward the maladjustments and repressions induced by one's lack of orientation in one's environment or—" But Hamlet would never have finished the soliloquy.

38   Writing in the modern world, you cannot altogether avoid modern jargon. Nor, in an effort to get away from euphemism, should you salt your paper with four-letter words. But you can do much if you will mount guard against those roundabout phrases, those echoing polysyllables that tend to slip into your writing to rob it of its crispness and force.

BEWARE OF PAT EXPRESSIONS

39 Other things being equal, avoid phrases like "other things being equal." Those sentences that come to you whole, or in two or three doughy lumps, are sure to be bad sentences. They are no creation of yours but pieces of common thought floating in the community soup.

40   Pat expressions are hard, often impossible, to avoid, because they come too easily to be noticed and seem too necessary to be dispensed with. No writer avoids them altogether, but good writers avoid them more often than poor writers.

41   By "pat expressions" we mean such tags as "to all practical intents and purposes," "the pure and simple truth," "from where I sit," "the time of his life," "to the ends of the earth," "in the twinkling of an eye," "as sure as you're born," "over my dead body," "under cover of darkness," "took the easy way out," "when all is said and done," "told him time and time again," "parted the best of friends," "stand up and be counted," "gave him the best years of her life," "worked her fingers to the bone." Like other clichés, these expressions were once forceful. Now we should use them only when we can't possibly think of anything else.

42   Some pat expressions stand like a wall between the writer and thought. Such a one is "the American way of life." Many student writers feel that when they have said that something accords with the American way of life or does not they have exhausted the subject.

Actually, they have stopped at the highest level of abstraction. The American way of life is the complicated set of bonds between a hundred and eighty million ways. All of us know this when we think about it, but the tag phrase too often keeps us from thinking about it.

43   So with many another phrase dear to the politician: "this great land of ours," "the man in the street," "our national heritage." These may prove our patriotism or give a clue to our political beliefs, but otherwise they add nothing to the paper except words.

COLORFUL WORDS

44   The writer builds with words, and no builder uses a raw material more slippery and elusive and treacherous. A writer's work is a constant struggle to get the right word in the right place, to find that particular word that will convey his meaning exactly, that will persuade the reader or soothe him or startle or amuse him. He never succeeds altogether—sometimes he feels that he scarcely succeeds at all—but such successes as he has are what make the thing worth doing.

45   There is no book of rules for this game. One progresses through everlasting experiment on the basis of ever-widening experience. There are few useful generalizations that one can make about words as words, but there are perhaps a few.

46   Some words are what we call "colorful." By this we mean that they are calculated to produce a picture or induce an emotion. They are dressy instead of plain, specific instead of general, loud instead of soft. Thus, in place of "Her heart beat," we may write, "Her heart *pounded, throbbed, fluttered, danced.*" Instead of "He sat in his chair," we may say, "He *lounged, sprawled, coiled.*" Instead of "It was hot," we may say, "It was *blistering, sultry, muggy, suffocating, steamy, wilting.*"

47   However, it should not be supposed that the fancy word is always better. Often it is as well to write "Her heart beat" or "It was hot" if that is all it did or all it was. Ages differ in how they like their prose. The nineteenth century liked it rich and smoky. The twentieth has usually preferred it lean and cool. The twentieth century writer, like all writers, is forever seeking the exact word, but he is wary of sounding feverish. He tends to pitch it low, to understate it, to throw it away. He knows that if he gets too colorful, the audience is likely to giggle.

48   See how this strikes you: "As the rich, golden glow of the sunset died away along the eternal western hills, Angela's limpid blue eyes looked softly and trustingly into Montague's flashing brown ones, and her heart pounded like a drum in time with the joyous song surging in her soul." Some people like that sort of thing, but most modern readers would say, "Good grief," and turn on the television.

COLORED WORDS

49   Some words we would call not so much colorful as colored—that is, loaded with associations, good or bad. All words—except perhaps structure words—have associations of some sort. We have said that

the meaning of a word is the sum of the contexts in which it occurs. When we hear a word, we hear with it an echo of all the situations in which we have heard it before.

50   In some words, these echoes are obvious and discussable. The word *mother,* for example, has, for most people, agreeable associations. When you hear *mother* you probably think of home, safety, love, food, and various other pleasant things. If one writes, "She was like a mother to me," he gets an effect which he would not get in "She was like an aunt to me." The advertiser makes use of the associations of *mother* by working it in when he talks about his product. The politician works it in when he talks about himself.

51   So also with such words as *home, liberty, fireside, contentment, patriot, tenderness, sacrifice, childlike, manly, bluff, limpid.* All of these words are loaded with associations that would be rather hard to indicate in a straightforward definition. There is more than a literal difference between "They sat around the fireside" and "They sat around the stove." They might have been equally warm and happy around the stove, but *fireside* suggests leisure, grace, quiet tradition, congenial company, and *stove* does not.

52   Conversely, some words have bad associations. *Mother* suggests pleasant things, but *mother-in-law* does not. Many mothers-in-law are heroically lovable and some mothers drink gin all day and beat their children insensible, but these facts of life are beside the point. The point is that *mother* sounds good and *mother-in-law* does not.

53   Or consider the word *intellectual.* This would seem to be a complimentary term, but in point of fact it is not, for it has picked up associations of impracticality and ineffectuality and general dopiness. So also such words as *liberal, reactionary, Communist, socialist, capitalist, radical, schoolteacher, truck driver, undertaker, operator, salesman, huckster, speculator.* These convey meaning on the literal level, but beyond that—sometimes, in some places—they convey contempt on the part of the speaker.

54   The question of whether to use loaded words or not depends on what is being written. The scientist, the scholar, try to avoid them; for the poet, the advertising writer, the public speaker, they are standard equipment. But every writer should take care that they do not substitute for thought. If you write, "Anyone who thinks that is nothing but a Socialist (or Communist or capitalist)" you have said nothing except that you don't like people who think that, and such remarks are effective only with the most naive readers. It is always a bad mistake to think your readers more naive than they really are.

COLORLESS WORDS

55 But probably most student writers come to grief not with words that are colorful or those that are colored but with those that have no color at all. A pet example is *nice,* a word we would find it hard to dispense with in casual conversation but which is no longer capable of adding much to a description. Colorless words are those of such general

meaning that in a particular sentence they mean nothing. Slang adjectives like *cool* ("That's real cool") tend to explode all over the language. They are applied to everything, lose their original force, and quickly die.

56   Beware also of nouns of very general meaning, like *circumstances, cases, instances, aspects, factors, relationships, attitudes, eventualities,* etc. In most circumstances you will find that those cases of writing which contain too many instances of words like these will in this and other aspects have factors leading to unsatisfactory relationships with the reader resulting in unfavorable attitudes on his part and perhaps other eventualities, like a grade of "D." Notice also what "etc." means. It means "I'd like to make this list longer, but I can't think of any more examples."

Discussion of Theme

1. Would students write more interesting themes if they could choose their own subjects? Should an instructor ever assign writing subjects? Explain.
2. Why is it difficult to make a college theme interesting?
3. How can you improve your writing if you use the advice here?
4. What do you think of the advice that a student should "always take the side that looks to you the hardest, least defensible. It will almost always turn out to be easier to write interestingly on that side." Why might this be true?
5. Roberts says that most assigned subjects will not require discussion on a personal basis but will, instead, "lie in broad areas of discussion." Would it be more appropriate to assign personal, intimate topics? Would this perhaps be a good way for instructors to become acquainted with their students as individuals?

Discussion of Rhetoric

1. Is Roberts's essay an example of the kind of good writing he asks for? If you wrote this essay, would you change anything—the use of examples or analogies, for instance?
2. In paragraph 11 Roberts suggests that a teacher might have had a happier life as "an electrician or a confidence man." Why does this combination produce a humorous effect? Would it be just as amusing if he had said "an electrician or house painter"?
3. Analyze the humor of Roberts's analogy in paragraph 39. Can you suggest others that would be amusing for the same reason?
4. Does the author's use of examples of poor writing help clarify his discussion?

Writing Assignments

1. How do politicians and advertisers use generalities to win people over to their point of view? What is the advantage in avoiding specifics?
2. Write to a high school senior, telling him how to succeed as a writer in college. Make sure that you follow your own advice.
3. Using Roberts's ideas, analyze a paper you have recently written.
4. Do you believe that "because an instructor is only human, after all," he is bound to grade papers at least partially on the basis of prejudice — personal, political, or social?

Library Exploration

Check out a book that explains — in the words of the writers themselves — how successful and highly regarded authors go about getting words down on paper.

Vocabulary

(2) ANTHOLOGY   a collection of literary works

(3) ABOLISHED   done away with

(11) CONTRIVE   manage by devious methods or with difficulty

(12) BROMIDES   clichés

(12) TEDIOUS   tiresome

(13) INEXORABLY   relentlessly

(15) TRITE   stale; hackneyed

(16) COGENT   well reasoned

(17) VACUITY   emptiness; lack of intelligence

(20) BIASED   prejudiced

(20) CANTANKEROUSLY   in an ill-natured or quarrelsome manner

(22) CALLOUSLY   unfeelingly

(25) ANECDOTAL   containing stories

(27) ADEPT   skillful

(33) WARILY   carefully; cautiously

(36) DIFFIDENCE   timidity; unassertiveness

(37) POLYSYLLABLES   words of several syllables

(37) INDUCED   brought on

(38) JARGON   lingo; specialized vocabulary

(44) ELUSIVE   hard to pin down

(51) CONGENIAL   friendly

(53) INEFFECTUALITY   inability to produce the proper or usual effect

(54) NAÏVE   innocent; unsophisticated

(56) EVENTUALITIES   outcomes

Morris Bishop (1893–1973), professor of romance languages at Cornell University until his retirement in 1960, was the author of several books on language and intellectual history, including "Horizon Book of the Middle Ages" (1968) and "The Exotics" (1969). A native of New York, he received his A.B., A.M., and Ph.D. from Cornell.

Who–and what–should determine "correct" usage? This question has been debated, often with more heat than light, for more than two hundred years. The following selection, taken from "The American Heritage Dictionary of the English Language," gives the background on this debate, and suggests a tentative answer.

MORRIS BISHOP

Good Usage, Bad Usage, and Usage

1   The words of a living language are like creatures: they are alive. Each word has a physical character, a look and a personality, an ancestry, an expectation of life and death, a hope of posterity. Some words strike us as beautiful, some ugly, some evil. The word *glory* seems to shine; the common word for excrement seems to smell. There are holy words, like the proper name of God, pronounced only once a year in the innermost court of Jerusalem's Temple. There are magic words, spells to open gates and safes, summon spirits, put an end to the world. What are magic spells but magic spellings? Words sing to us, frighten us, impel us to self-immolation and murder. They belong

to us; they couple at our order, to make what have well been called the aureate words of poets and the inkhorn words of pedants. We can keep our words alive, or at our caprice we can kill them — though some escape and prosper in our despite.

2   Thought makes the word; also the word makes thought. Some psychologists allege that explicit thought does not exist without verbalization. Thought, they say, emerges from our silent secret speech, from tiny quivers of the speech organs, from the interior monologue we all carry on endlessly. Let us pause a moment and reflect on our thought; we reflect in words, on a surge of hurrying words.

3   Much of our formless, secret thought is, to be sure, idiotic. "We find it hard to believe that other people's thoughts are as silly as our own, but they probably are," said the American scholar James Harvey Robinson. Before we permit silent speech to emerge as spoken language, we must make choices and arrange words in patterns of sense and form, accessible to other people. These choices and patterns are usage. And usage is the ruler, the governor, the judge of language. Horace said it nearly two thousand years ago in his *Ars Poetica: "usus, Quem penes arbitrium est, et jus, et norma loquendi."* Or, in an old translation of the passage:

> Yes, words long faded may again revive;
> And words may fade now blooming and alive,
> If USAGE wills it so, to whom belongs
> The rule and law, the government of tongues.

4   Deferring to the rule and law of usage, we may yet order our words well or ill, thus creating Good Usage and Bad Usage.

5   Now the trouble begins. Whose usage is good, whose bad? Is not my usage good for me? May I not tell my own words what to do? Do you have authority over my usage? Does anyone have authority? And if authority exists, is it helpful or hurtful to usage?

6   We tend to demand freedom for our own usage, authority for others'. Yet we are not above seeking comfort and support from authority. One of our commonest phrases is "look it up in the dictionary." (Not any particular dictionary; just "the dictionary.") Every court of law has its big dictionary; the law settles cases, awards millions, rates crimes and misdemeanors, by quoting the definitions of some poor attic lexicographer, "a harmless drudge," as defined by lexicographer Samuel Johnson. We acclaim freedom, but we love the word *freedom* more than the fact. Most people most of the time would rather be secure than free; they cry for law and order. In the matter of usage, we suspect that complete freedom might outbabble Babel; without common agreement on the meaning of most words, communication would cease.

7   Who, then, shall wield authority? The King, perhaps? The phrase *the King's English* came in, we are told, with Henry VIII, who ruled from 1509 to 1547. He was a poet and a man of letters when he had the time. The King's English remained standard, even under George I, who could not speak English. Recent Kings and Queens of England have not been noteworthy for an exemplary style. In America the President's English has never ruled the citizenry. The one notorious

Presidential venture into lexicography was Harding's use of *normalcy.* But he said that he had looked it up in the dictionary.

8   The King's English was naturally identified with the spoken style of gentlemen and ladies of the English court. Similarly in France, the grammarian Vaugelas defined (in 1647) good usage as the speech habits of the sounder members of the court, in conformity with the practice in writing of the sounder contemporary authors. Good usage, then, would represent the practice of an elite of breeding, station, and intellect.

9   The idea of an elite with authority over language clearly needed delimitation. In France, Cardinal Richelieu, who piqued himself on his style in verse and prose, authorized in 1635 the formation of an *Académie française,* composed of writers, bookish nobles and magistrates, and amateurs of letters. The *Académie,* the supreme court of the French literary world, set itself the task of preparing a dictionary. It has been working at its dictionary, off and on, for over three hundred years. But England and America have always refused to constitute government-sponsored academies with power to regulate citizens' words.

10   Lacking an academy, Englishmen appealed to the practice of good writers to preserve or "fix" general usage. Thence more trouble. Who are the good writers? Shakespeare, no doubt. But Shakespeare, with his wild and carefree coinages, his cheery disregard for grammatical agreements, demands our admiration more than our imitation. In Latin, a fossilized tongue, the rule is simple: if a locution is in Cicero, it is correct. In English we have no Cicero. The only writers whom all critics would accept as "best" have been so long dead that their works are uncertain models for the living language of our times.

11   We should, perhaps, make the authority of the best writers defer to that of professional judges of language, the critics and grammarians. Quintilian, rhetorician of the first century A.D., appealed to the consensus of the *eruditi,* the scholarly, the well-informed. Ben Jonson said: "Custom is the most certain mistress of language, as the public stamp makes the current money . . . That I call custom of speech, which is the consent of the learned; as custom of life, which is the consent of the good." In the 17th and 18th centuries, the English grammarians appeared, devoting themselves to "refining, ascertaining, and fixing" the language. They were scholars. Aware of linguistic history, they conceived of English usage as a development from primitive barbarism to the harmonious perfection of their own times. They regarded the past as a preparation, the present as a glorious achievement, the future as a threatening decadence. Jonathan Swift was terrified of the coming corruption and invoked governmental authority to "fix" the language; else, he feared, within two centuries the literary works of his time, including his own, would be unreadable.

12   The grammarians justified their judgments by appealing not only to history but to reason. They strengthened the concepts of Good and Bad to become Right and Wrong. They regarded language as something existing mysteriously apart from man, governed by a universal grammar waiting to be discovered by intrepid scholars. No doubt they were sympathetically fascinated by the story Herodotus tells of the

king who isolated two small children with a deaf-and-dumb shepherd to find out what language they would learn to speak, thus to identify the original speech of mankind. (It was Phrygian.) Rightness was to be achieved by logical analysis of form and meaning, with much use of analogy. Popular usage was scouted, as of its nature corrupt. The grammarians made great play with Purity and Impurity. Pure English lived in perpetual danger of defloration by the impure.

13   The grammarians did some useful work in rationalizing the language. However, their precepts were often overlogical or based on faulty logic. From them, derive many of the distinctions that have ever since tortured scholars young and old. The *shall/will, should/would* rules are said to be an invention of the 17th-century John Wallis. John Lowth, in 1762, first laid it down that two negatives are equivalent to an affirmative. It was Lowth who banned the use of the superlative to indicate one of two, as in Jane Austen's "the youngest of the two daughters of a most affectionate, indulgent father."

14   Samuel Johnson, whose epoch-making *A Dictionary of the English Language* appeared in 1755, shared many of the convictions of the grammarians. He was concerned to fix the language against lowering corruption, for, he said in his Preface, "Tongues, like governments, have a natural tendency to degeneration; we have long preserved our constitution, let us make some struggle for our language." He foresaw linguistic calamity. "The tropes of poetry will make hourly encroachments, and the metaphorical will become the current sense; pronunciation will be varied by levity or ignorance, and the pen must at length comply with the tongue; illiterate writers will at one time or other, by publick infatuation, rise into renown, who, not knowing the original import of words, will use them with colloquial licentiousness, confound distinction, and forget propriety." Those who knew better must fight on in the hopeless war: "we retard what we cannot repel, we palliate what we cannot cure."

15   One will have noticed, amid the funeral music of Dr. Johnson's Preface, the startling phrase: "the pen must at length comply with the tongue." This was a view already accepted more cheerfully by some other distinguished writers. Malherbe, 17th-century scholar-poet-critic and "legislator of Parnassus," said that he learned proper French listening to the porters at the haymarket. Though Dr. Johnson deplored the fact, he recognized that speech, not writing, not grammatical logic, must in the end command usage. This idea took shape and found fuller expression in the work of Noah Webster (1758–1843).

16   Webster was a Connecticut farm boy with a Yale education, in a day when colleges did not teach English as a course. His series of spelling books and dictionaries actually went far toward "fixing" the American language. His standard of correctness, however, was the usage of the enlightened members of each community, not just that of the "polite part" of city society, which he believed consisted largely of coxcombs. "General custom must be the rule of speaking," he said; and "it is always better to be *vulgarly* right than *politely* wrong." He was astonishingly liberal, even radical, in his acceptance of popular usage, giving his approval to *It is me, Who is she married to?* and *Them horses are mine.*

17   Thus, common usage began to assume dominance at the expense of formal grammar. The scholarly Irish archbishop Richard C. Trench in 1857 defined a dictionary as an inventory of the language: "It is no task of the maker of it to select the *good* words of a language . . . He is an historian of it, not a critic."

18   This view of language and its use has prevailed in the 20th century and seems unlikely to fade. A school of linguistic scientists constituted itself, and in time found a place on most college faculties, ousting the old-fashioned philologists of the English and foreign-language departments. The descriptive or structural linguists, as they called themselves, would no more criticize a locution than a physicist would criticize an atom or an entomologist a cockroach.

19   The principles of descriptive linguistics have thus been simply put: (1) Language changes constantly; (2) Change is normal; (3) Spoken language is *the* language; (4) Correctness rests upon usage; (5) All usage is relative. This creed arouses indignation if not wrath in many people, including highly educated ones. But with the exception of number 3, which has been felt even by some linguists to be an over-statement on the part of gentlemen whose livelihood requires the written word, dispute about these principles seems to be nearly over among those who profess the study of English. The underlying assumption is that language, by its very nature, is a growing, evolving thing; and that whereas it may be cultivated, it cannot be "fixed" without killing it. Like any other fundamental social activity, it will undergo vicissitudes that to the older generation often seem regrettable; and indeed, some changes in language turn out to be empty fads that are soon forgotten, like some changes in women's fashions. Others are found to be enduringly useful, so that a generation later it becomes hard to imagine how we got along without them.

20   A descriptive linguist's lexicon can be expected to refrain from value judgments, from imposed pronunciations and spellings. It may classify usages as standard or nonstandard, formal, informal, or slang; but not right or wrong. It describes usage; it piously avoids prescribing it. Yet surely there is the possibility of self-deception here, of an objectivity more imaginary than real. By the very act of leaving *alrite* out of a dictionary, the lexicographer implies that that spelling — which does, after all, exist — is not all right. On the other hand, if he exhibits his scientific disinterest by reporting that "*ain't* is used orally in most parts of the United States by many cultivated speakers," the truth is that he is being inadequately descriptive with respect to contexts of usage. A reader who takes that description seriously is likely to lay an egg (*slang*) at his next cocktail party unless he has the charm of Eliza Doolittle.

21   The makers of *The American Heritage Dictionary of the English Language* accept usage as the authority for correctness, but they have eschewed the "scientific" delusion that a dictionary should contain no value judgments. Some, to be sure, they have made merely implicit: the arrant solecisms of the ignoramus are here often omitted entirely, "irregardless" of how he may feel about this neglect. What is desirable is that when value judgments are explicit, they should be clearly attributed. Thus good usage can usually be distinguished from

bad usage, even as good books can be distinguished from bad books. The present editors maintain that those best fitted to make such distinctions are, as Noah Webster said, the enlightened members of the community; not the scholarly theoreticians, not the instinctive verbalizers of the unlettered mass. The best authorities, at least for cultivated usage, are those professional speakers and writers who have demonstrated their sensitiveness to the language and their power to wield it effectively and beautifully.

22　　The lexicographers of this Dictionary therefore commissioned a Usage Panel of about a hundred members — novelists, essayists, poets, journalists, writers on science and sports, public officials, professors. (Their names and credentials are to be found in a list preceding this section of special articles.) The panelists have in common only a recognized ability to speak and write good English. They accepted their task and turned to it with gusto. They revealed, often with passion, their likes and dislikes, their principles, and also their whims and crotchets. "We all get self-righteous in our judgments on language." Malcolm Cowley observes. As a matter of fact, many of them revealed, on particular questions, an attitude more reminiscent of Dr. Johnson than of the modern linguistic view: they tend to feel that the English language is going to hell if "we" don't do something to stop it, and they tend to feel that their own usage preferences are clearly *right*.

23　　This does not mean for a moment that their preferences are invalid or negligible. Where this Dictionary differs notably from those that have preceded it, with regard to usage, is in exposing the lexical opinions of a larger group of recognized leaders than has heretofore been consulted, so that the ordinary user, looking up an expression whose social status is uncertain, can discover just how and to what extent his presumed betters agree on what he ought to say or write. Thus, he is not turned away uncounseled and uncomforted: he has before him an authoritative statement on a disputed issue; yet, he is left one of the most valuable of human freedoms, the freedom to say what he pleases.

24　　It is significant that on specific questions, the Usage Panel disagreed more than they agreed, revealing a fact often conveniently ignored — that among those best qualified to know, there is a very considerable diversity of usage. Anyone surveying the panelists' various opinions is likely to conclude that good usage is indeed an elusive nymph, well worth pursuing but inconstant in shape and dress, and rather hard to back into a corner. In only one case did they agree 100 per cent — in disfavor of *simultaneous* as an adverb ("the referendum was conducted *simultaneous* with the election"). Some other scores approached unanimity, as in the following:

EXPRESSION	APPROVED BY	DISAPPROVED BY
ain't I? in writing		99%
between you and I in writing		99%
dropout used as a noun	97%	
thusly		97%

Expression	Approved by	Disapproved by
debut as a verb ("the company will debut its new models")		97%
slow as an adverb ("Drive Slow")	96%	
medias as a plural (instead of *media*)		95%
their own referring to the singular ("nobody thinks the criticism applies to their own work")		95%
but what ("There is no doubt but what he will try")		95%
myself instead of *me* in compound objects, in writing ("He invited Mary and myself to dinner")		95%
anxious in the sense of *eager*	94%	
type for *type of* ("that type shrub")		94%
rather unique; most unique		94%

25   While the panelists tend toward conservatism, they try to avoid overniceness, prissiness. (*Was graduated,* says John Bainbridge contemptuously, is preferred "by all who write with a quill pen.") Sixty-one per cent of them feel bad about the expression *I feel badly* when they see it in writing; only 45 per cent object when they hear it in speech. More than most people, they know the history of words and have tested the value of idioms. More than most, they have grown tired of overused vogue words. They dislike *senior citizen* ("I'd as soon use *underprivileged* for *poor*—or any other social science Choctaw"—Berton Roueché). They are not concerned that senior citizens themselves seem to rejoice in the term and recoil at *old folks* and even at *old*. *Enthuse* finds little favor, and stirs preservative zeal in some: "By God, let's hold the line on this one!" cries Dwight Macdonald. *Finalize,* says Isaac Asimov, "is nothing more than bureaucratic illiteracy." But for the consensus, the reader is referred to the entries *enthuse* and *finalize,* each of which, like many other neologisms, is discussed in a Usage note.

26   The panelists are by no means opposed to all coinages. "I have great admiration," says Gilbert Highet, "for the American genius for creating short vivid words (often disyllabic) to express complex ideas, for example, a collision between a vehicle and another object which is not direct but lateral or oblique, *sideswipe*." In general, the jurymen are more cordial toward popular, low-level inventions than toward the pomposities of professional jargons. John K. Sherman welcomes *rambunctious* as a "tangy Americanism." Forty per cent of the Panel are ready to accept the expression *not about,* used to express determination not to do something; but the other 60 per cent are not about

to do so. None of them, however, likes Business English; and they betray a particular spite against the language of Madison Avenue, once a very respectable street, now an avenue of ill fame. Yet the advertisers are, after all, fecund creators languagewise.

27   It would seem that the panelists are often more attentive to the practice of their own social group than to grammatical logic or etymological precision. They are antipedantic, scornful of the grammarians' effort to ban *it's me*. Some, like Theodore C. Sorenson, would throw away the rule that the relative *that* must introduce restrictive clauses, *which* nonrestrictive. One or two would drop *whom* altogether, as a needless refinement. Ninety-one per cent of the panelists accept the use of *internecine* to mean "pertaining to civil war or to a struggle within a family, group, organization, nation, or the like." They know, of course, that the Latin *internecinus* just means mutually deadly, but they do not seem to care.

28   The Usage Panel has given us the enlightened judgments of a cultivated elite on a great many interesting and troublesome expressions. The very diversity of their response attests that language is alive and well in the United States, and that even the most descriptive of dictionaries could not succeed in reporting all of its shifting nuances.

29   Within their field—the determination of good current usage—the counselors found, as we have observed, no absolute standard of rightness. Though naturally believing in their own superiority, they do not presume to dictate. They seem to conclude, without explicit statement, that usage is our own affair, with due regard to the usage of other good writers and speakers. Let that be our conclusion. The duty of determination falls upon us all. By our choices we make usage, good or bad. Let us then try to make good choices, and guard and praise our lovely language and try to be worthy of her.

Discussion of Theme

1. How does Bishop define good usage? Bad usage?
2. What were Samuel Johnson's fears about the English language when he undertook his dictionary? How had his attitude changed when he completed it?
3. What are the basic ideas held by descriptive linguists? What determines "correctness" for them? What is Bishop's attitude toward them? Do you agree?
4. What was the basis for the linguistic determinations adopted by the publisher of *The American Heritage Dictionary?* How reliable do you regard this method? What are its drawbacks?
5. Are the "rules" for spoken language different from those for written language? Explain your answer.

Discussion of Rhetoric

1. This selection is divided into main sections. What is the purpose of each? Where does the second section begin?

2. Explain the phrase *social science Choctaw* (paragraph 25). What connotative values is Bishop suggesting when he employs *ill fame* (paragraph 26) in discussing advertising? *Languagewise* (also in paragraph 26)?
3. Why are quotation marks placed around "irregardless" (paragraph 21) and "we" (paragraph 22)? What is the author's intent?
4. Bishop admits that his stand on usage is somewhat arbitrary. What argumentative techniques does he use to support it?

Writing Assignments

1. In a theme, define "correct" English.
2. What suggestions would you have for improving the teaching of English in high school?
3. Give your reasons for the establishment of an academy of "correctness" in this country. Who would serve on it? How would it determine "correct" usage? How would violators be punished?
4. In a theme, explain why educated people are more permissive in linguistic matters than uneducated people are. Relate your answer to Bishop's remark that most people would rather be secure than free.

Library Exploration

1. Investigate the furor over the publication of *Webster's Third New International Dictionary.*
2. What is transformational grammar? For an interesting look into the revolution taking place in linguistics, investigate some of the research being done in this area.
3. The history of the English language is fascinating. Several good studies are available; you might enjoy writing a report on one of them.

Vocabulary

(1) IMMOLATION   sacrificial killing
(2) VERBALIZATION   putting into words
(6) LEXICOGRAPHER   dictionary maker
(10) LOCUTION   expression
(14) TROPES   figures of speech
(14) ENCROACHMENT   intrusion
(14) COLLOQUIAL   informal or conversational in style or expression

(14) LEVITY   lightness of speech or manner
(14) LICENTIOUSNESS   lack of moral (now, especially sexual) restraint
(14) PROPRIETY   state or quality of being proper
(14) PALLIATE   cover by excuses or apologies
(19) VICISSITUDES   changes of fortune

(21) ESCHEWED   avoided; shunned

(21) ARRANT   thoroughgoing; out-and-out

(21) SOLECISMS   nonstandard usages or expressions

(22) CROTCHETS   odd notions

(26) POMPOSITIES   instances of exaggerated or excessively ornate language or behavior

(26) FECUND   fruitful; productive

(28) NUANCES   subtle variations

The authors claim that the grammar of the English language is often sexist in nature. They suggest ways to eliminate such sexism, thereby responding to the wishes of Women's Liberation.

CASEY MILLER
KATE SWIFT

De-Sexing the English Language

1 On the television screen, a teacher of first-graders who has just won a national award is describing her way of teaching. "You take each child where you find him," she says. "You watch to see what he's interested in, and then you build on his interests."

2 A five-year-old looking at the program asks her mother, "Do only boys go to that school?"

3 "No," her mother begins, "she's talking about girls too, but—"

4 But what? The teacher being interviewed on television is speaking correct English. What can the mother tell her daughter about why a child, in any generalization, is always *he* rather than *she?* How does a five-year-old comprehend the generic personal pronoun?

5 The effect on personality development of this one small part of speech was recognized by thoughtful people long before the present assault on the English language by the forces of Women's Liberation. Fifteen years ago, Lynn T. White, then president of Mills College, wrote:

6 The grammar of English dictates that when a referent is either of indeterminate sex or both sexes, it shall be considered masculine. The penetration of this habit of language into the minds of little girls as they grow up to be women is more profound than most people, including most women, have recognized: for it implies that personality is really a male attribute, and that women are a human subspecies. . . . It would be a miracle if a girl-baby, learning to use the symbols of our tongue, could escape some wound to her self-respect: whereas a boy-baby's ego is bolstered by the pattern of our language.

7   Now that our language has begun to respond to the justice of Women's Liberation, a lot of people apparently are trying to kick the habit of using *he* when they mean anyone, male or female. In fact, there is mounting evidence that a major renovation of the language is in progress with respect to this pronoun. It is especially noticeable in the speeches of politicians up for election: "And as for every citizen who pays taxes, I say that he or she deserves an accounting!" A variation of the tandem form is also cropping up in print, like the copy on a coupon that offers the bearer a 20 per cent saving on "the cost of his/her meal." A writer in the New York newspaper, *The Village Voice,* adopts the same form to comment "that every artist of major stature is actually a school in him/herself."

8   Adding the feminine pronoun to the masculine whenever the generic form is called for may be politically smart and morally right, but the result is often awkward.

9   Some of the devices used to get around the problem are even less acceptable, at least to grammarians. It is one thing for a student to announce in assembly that "Anybody can join the Glee Club as long as they can carry a tune," but when this patchwork solution begins to appear in print, the language is in trouble. In blatant defiance of every teacher of freshman English, a full-page advertisement in *The New York Times* for its college and school subscription service begins with this headline: "If someone you know is attending one of these colleges, here's something they should know that can save them money." Although the grammatical inconsistency of the *Times's* claim offends the ear—especially since "they" in the headline can refer only to "colleges"—the alternatives would present insurmountable problems for the writer. For example, the sentence might read, "If someone you know . . . etc., here's something he or she should know that can save him/her money." Or, in order to keep the plural subject in the second clause, the writer might have begun, "If several people you know are attending one or more of these colleges . . ." But by that time will the reader still care?

10   In the long run, the problem of the generic personal pronoun is a problem of the status of women. But it is more immediately a matter of common sense and clear communication. Absurd examples of the burdens now placed upon masculine pronouns pop up everywhere. "The next time you meet a handicapped person, don't make up your mind about him in advance," admonishes a radio public service announcement. A medical school bulletin, apparently caught by surprise, reports that a certain scholarship given annually "to a student of unquestioned ability and character who has completed his first year" was awarded to one Barbara Kinder.

11   Since there is no way in English to solve problems like these with felicity and grace, it is becoming obvious that what we need is a new singular personal pronoun that is truly generic: a common-gender pronoun. Several have been proposed, but so far none appears to have the transparently logical relationship to existing pronouns that is necessary if a new word is to gain wide acceptance. Perhaps a clue to the solution is to be found in people's persistent use of *they* as a singular pronoun.

12   In the plural forms, both genders are included in one word: *they* can refer to males or females or a mixed group. So why not derive the needed singular common-gender pronouns from the plural? *They, their,* and *them* suggest *tey, ter,* and *tem.* With its inflected· forms pronounced to rhyme with the existing plural forms, the new word would join the family of third person pronouns as shown in the box below.

13   Someone will probably object to the idea of a common-gender pronoun in the mistaken belief that it is a neuter form and therefore underrates sexual differences. The opposite is true. Once *tey* or a similar word is adopted, *he* can become exclusively masculine, just as *she* is now exclusively feminine. The new pronoun will thus accentuate the significant and valuable differences between females and males—those of reproductive function and form—while affirming the essential unity and equality of the two sexes within the species.

14   Language constantly evolves in response to need. It is groping today for ways to accommodate the new recognition of women as full-fledged members of the human race. If the new pronoun helps anyone toward that end, tey should be free to adopt it.

15   If anyone objects, it is certainly *ter* right—but in that case let tem come up with a better solution.

16

	Singular		Plural
	Distinct Gender	Common Gender	Common Gender
Nominative	*he* and *she*	*tey*	*they*
Possessive	*his* and *her* (or *hers*)	*ter* (or *ters*)	*their* (or *theirs*)
Objective	*him* and *her*	*tem*	*them*

Discussion of Theme

1. Does the situation in the opening paragraphs sound "real," or might it be a fantasy constructed to make a point? Is this ethical?
2. Would you feel comfortable using *tey, tem,* and *ter?*
3. Might these new pronouns enrich the language?
4. Do you think we will ever really adopt these pronouns into the language? Why? Why not?

Discussion of Rhetoric

1. What is the purpose of beginning the essay with a "real-life" example? Is it effective?
2. Is the last sentence meant to be humorous? Does it nullify the serious intent of the authors?

3. Is the quote in paragraph 6 more effective because it came from a man? Do you think that is why it was chosen?
4. To whom is this essay addressed—to men only or both men and women? How do you know?

Writing Assignments

1. Respond to the statement made by White in paragraph 6.
2. Have you ever felt inferior or superior because of the use of *he* or *him* to include both sexes, or because *man* is used to represent the entire human race?
3. Comment on the growing use of *humankind* as a substitute for mankind.

Library Exploration

1. Read some of the new feminist writers. How do they deal with the problem of the pronoun?
2. Research and report on the etymology of the word *man*.

Vocabulary

(4) GENERIC   referring to all members of a class

(7) RENOVATION   reinvigoration

(7) TANDEM   one behind the other

(9) INSURMOUNTABLE   impossible to conquer

(11) FELICITY   happiness

(13) NEUTER   having neither sex

Mitford M. Mathews (1891–   ), editor and author of several books on language, was born in Alabama and educated at Southern University (Baton Rouge), the University of Alabama, and Harvard. He taught English and linguistics at the University of Chicago, and served on the editorial staff for the "Webster's New World Dictionary." Among his works are "The Beginnings of American English" (1931), "A Dictionary of Americanisms" (1951), and "American Words" (1959).

As every English teacher knows, too many students believe that a dictionary contains little more than the spelling and meaning of words. Here Mathews suggests that it has riches and resources beyond mere definitions.

MITFORD M. MATHEWS

The Freshman and His Dictionary

1   When I was a small boy a carpenter once said in my presence that few workmen, even among master mechanics, knew more than a fraction of the uses of an ordinary steel square. The remark amazed me, as at that early age I thought a carpenter's square was a very simple tool. It certainly appeared so to me—nothing more than two flat pieces of metal forming a right angle, and useful in marking a plank that one wished to saw in two in something like a workmanlike manner. True, the instrument has numerous markings and numbers on it, but I had never seen anyone making the slightest use of these, so I had concluded they might be ignored.

2   When I became older and found that large books have been written
on the uses of the steel square, I changed my mind about the simplicity of the tool and the limited range of its usefulness. For many years
as I have observed the use made of dictionaries by even good students, I have been reminded of that remark by the carpenter about
steel squares.

3   Dictionaries are tools, and they are much more complicated, and
capable of many more uses than students suspect. All of us know students need encouragement and guidance in the use of dictionaries,
and perhaps there are few teachers of freshman composition but that
devote a part of their program to an effort to help students form the
habit of consulting dictionaries. Composition books for freshmen point
out the need for instruction of this kind.

4   Despite what is being done, however, the fact is easily observable
that few students are able to use their dictionaries with anything like
efficiency. Certainly there must be very few of those who come up
through the grades these days who are not familiar with the details of
looking up words in dictionaries, but it is one thing to find a word in a
dictionary and quite another to understand fully the information there
given about it. It seems to me that college freshmen are fully prepared
for and could profit by a well-planned introduction to the larger English dictionaries, and an acquaintance with what they contain. Such
a program might well include material of the following kinds.

5   1. Students should know something about the large, unabridged
dictionaries to which they have ready access in college. They might
well be given brief sketches of the *Oxford English Dictionary,* the *English Dialect Dictionary,* by Joseph Wright, the old *Century Dictionary*
(12 volumes), and the modern unabridged *Webster.* These may be
called the "Big Four" in the dictionary field, and while it is certainly
not anticipated that the freshman will ever provide himself with all of
them, it is a cultural experience for him to become acquainted with the
circumstances under which each of them was produced, and with the
special excellencies each exhibits.

6   An acquaintance with these larger works will not only make the
student aware of what kind of information about words is available in
them, but it will leave him much better prepared to make efficient use
of the desk-size dictionary with which he has some familiarity.

7   Many years ago a graduate student inconvenienced himself greatly
to come a long distance to see me to ask if I could help him secure
some information about the term "poll tax." He was preparing a doctor's thesis, he told me, and needed to know how long this term had
been in the language, what its basic meaning was, and what other
meanings it may have had in the course of its use in English. He was
most surprised when I opened the *OED* to the appropriate place and
showed him that all he needed to know about this term had been available within a few feet of his desk in the school where he was studying.
It is not at all likely that any but the exceptional student will ever need
all the information about words that the larger dictionaries afford, but
it is well worth the while of every student to become acquainted with
the fact that such information is available for those who at any time
need to make use of it.

8   It is to be hoped that in such general instruction as may be given about the different dictionaries, some emphasis will be placed on the fact that modern dictionaries do their utmost to *record* usage, not to *prescribe* it. The tendency to regard the lexicographer as a linguistic legislator is so deep-seated that it will probably never be entirely overcome. The habit of thought that is back of such expressions as "the dictionary now permits us to pronounce it thus," has been with us for a long time, and will continue. But every student should have the wholesome experience of being taught that dictionaries attempt to give commonly accepted usage, and that correctness in the use of language varies sometimes according to time and place.

9   2. Along with some information about the origin and scope of the large dictionaries mentioned, there should be given some elementary information about the history of the English language and the place it occupies with reference to the others of the Indo-European group. I am certainly not foolish enough to suggest that all teachers of freshman composition become instructors in Germanic philology. What I have in mind is nothing more detailed than could be easily covered in one, or at most two, class sessions, the over-all relationships of the languages being presented briefly, with a few well chosen examples to indicate the relationship of a few of them.

10   The desirability of this elementary acquaintance with the linguistic position occupied by English is brought out quite clearly by Professor Pei in his *Story of Language:*

> Many years ago I was requested to tutor in French a young girl who had to take College Entrance Examinations. Knowing that she had had four years of Latin as well as three years of French, I spared no occasion in the course of the tutoring to remind her that certain French words which she had difficulty in remembering came from Latin words she knew. For a time she took it patiently, though with a somewhat bewildered air. But one day she finally blurted out: "Do you mean to tell me that there is a *connection* between Latin and French?" In the course of four years of one language and three of the other, it had never occurred to any of her Latin teachers to inform her that Latin had descendants, or to her French teacher to tell her that French has a progenitor!

11   3. The attention usually devoted to instruction in the use of the dictionary apparently stresses spellings, meanings, and pronunciations somewhat in the order here given. Certainly these are conspicuous features of any dictionary, and it is altogether desirable for students to be encouraged to turn to these works when they are confronted with a problem of the kind indicated.

12   The impression, however, inevitably conveyed by instruction restricted altogether to employing the dictionary as a problem-solver, is that such a book is of no particular use unless there is a problem requiring immediate attention. Students are sorely tempted to so manipulate things as to avoid encountering problems that drive them to a dictionary. It is to be feared that, for many of them, the dictionary is a form of medicine to be resorted to only in time of unavoidable need. They associate it perhaps with castor oil or some other undesirable, dynamic type of cathartic. It is a most helpful thing for the student to learn that dictionaries are filled with interesting information from

which one can derive much pleasure and instruction, even though he may not be confronted with an urgent problem of any kind.

13 Students should be encouraged to develop a wholesome curiosity about words that present no particular problem in spelling, pronunciation, or meaning. As a rule, the words we know well do not rise to the surface of our consciousness. It is only rarely that some common, everyday term forces itself upon our attention so urgently that for the first time we turn to the dictionary to see what lies back of it.

14 This use of the dictionary when there is no immediate, pressing need to do so, this giving attention to words we have known for a long time but have never grown curious about, is most rewarding. This kind of use of the dictionary we may think of as the labor of free men; the forced use is more properly likened to that of slaves.

15 On every hand there are words of fascinating backgrounds about which the dictionary has much to teach us. Certainly the name *Jesus,* that of the founder of Christianity, is well known to all those with whom you and I come in contact. Perhaps few of us have ever felt impelled to look the word up in a dictionary, or even realized that dictionaries contain it. An examination of the dictionary, however, reveals that the name his parents gave the Savior was Joshua, and it was by this thoroughly Jewish name that He was known by those He lived among.

16 The first accounts of His life were written in Greek, and in these writings *Joshua* was transliterated into *Jesus,* a name that is certainly not Jewish in its present dress and at the same time appears odd as a Greek name.

17 Not even a grade-school pupil is likely to be baffled by *ostrich,* but one who is allergic to words may well become curious about it. Allow it to become the focus of your attention for a moment and see how odd the word appears. Make a guess as to where you think it might have come from, and then check up on yourself by turning to the dictionary. You might be surprised, as I was, to find the word is made up of two, one from Latin and one from Greek, which have so blended as to obscure altogether the fact that the expression signifies "bird-bird" or "bird-sparrow." It is a good term to bear in mind and use upon those of our brethren who insist that only "pure English" should be used, and profess to be pained by such obvious hybrids as *cablegram* and *electrocute.*

18 There may be few teachers who have discovered how rewarding it is to look curiously at the scientific terms used in dictionaries in the definitions of plants and animals. These expressions are usually hurried over by most of us as being the exclusive property of scientists and of very little interest for others.

19 It is surprisingly interesting to linger over such terms. It is a gratifying experience to discover one that yields its significance somewhat readily. Our common mocking bird, for instance, is *Mimus polyglottos.* The ingenuity needed for deciphering this expression is possessed by all of us. *Mimic* and *polyglot* are all we need to see that our expression means "the many-tongued mimic," a fitting description of the bird in question.

20 In the spring when the snow has melted, and the earth is warming

up from its long cold sleep, the cheerful piping notes of a very small frog begin to be heard in the woods and marshes. People call this little creature a *spring peeper* because of the season when his little peeping notes are first heard, but scientists dub him *Hyla crucifer*. As we puzzle over this name we are likely to give up on *Hyla* for there is no other word in the English language with which we can, perhaps, associate it properly. It has descendants among us, but we are not likely to be acquainted with them.

21   *Crucifer* though is easier. Even if we do not know that a *crucifer* is one who carries a cross, especially in a church procession, we can reason out the two elements in the word and see that it must have the meaning of one who carries a cross. Our ability to reason out this much of the scientific expression may increase our curiosity about the first element *Hyla*. Here is a helpful hint. As we all know, these scientific genus names are often from Greek. So we are reasoning sensibly when we suppose *Hyla* is Greek.

22   The fact is elementary that when we are confronted with a Greek word which begins with an *h,* i.e. with a rough breathing, it behooves us as cautious scouts to cast about in our minds for a possible Latin cognate beginning with an *s*. Substituting an *s* in *hyla* we come up with *syla*. Let us study *syla* a bit. It is almost a word. If we might be so bold as to insert a -v- and make it *sylva* we have a word that is in our dictionary, and one we met in a slightly different form, *silva,* when we studied first-year Latin.

23   The little detail of why this -v- is necessary need not bother us in the slightest at this point, because we are just having fun with no idea of becoming linguisticians. And this is it. *Hyla* and *sylva* go together and they both mean wood or forest. Now we can interpret this *Hyla crucifer* "the (little) fellow who lives in the woods and carries a cross," and when we find that this spring peeper has a dark marking on his back shaped like a cross, we are indeed gratified that now light is shining where previously all was darkness.

24   A teacher who is fortunate enough to have an assiduously cultivated curiosity about words will over and over again bring to a class gleanings of unexpected sorts from dictionaries. Such sharing of treasures will do more than anything else to bring home to students the fact that dictionaries are not dull, enlarged spelling books. They are filled with such a number of things that we can never exhaust their treasures but we can all be as happy as kings as we come time after time upon interesting nuggets of the kind just mentioned.

Discussion of Theme

1. How accurate is Mathews's description of the attitude most students have toward the dictionary?
2. Does the practice of making students look up words in dictionaries and write down definitions make them dislike using a dictionary? How helpful are spelling and vocabulary tests in learning new words?

3. Why do many people tend to equate the authority of the dictionary with that of the Bible? Does Mathews attack or share this point of view?
4. Do we judge others by the way they speak? How significant are accent, vocabulary, and diction in the formation of our impressions of strangers?
5. If you had absolutely no access to a dictionary, how much effect would it have on your writing? On your speaking?

Discussion of Rhetoric

1. Although this article was originally a speech to a convention of English teachers, Mathews occasionally expresses himself as one might to a young person. Where do such phrases and sentences occur? Is this effective?
2. What is the function of the opening anecdote? What analogy is established by Mathews? Would you classify this as an effective opening?
3. What is the level of Mathews's language? Formal, informal? Give examples to illustrate your answer.
4. If you have been taught that *each* is always singular, look up its treatment in your dictionary and in a grammar handbook. Are there any inconsistencies?

Writing Assignments

1. Give your suggestions for improving your present desk dictionary so that it would better serve your needs.
2. When the *Dictionary of American Slang* appeared in 1960, it created a furor because it contained so-called obscene words. Give your opinion of this adverse reaction.
3. Explain why you do or do not enjoy consulting a dictionary.
4. The author begins his essay with an analogy: he compares a steel square to a dictionary. Using analogy, compare a familiar object to a technical or unfamiliar subject.

Library Exploration

1. Examine the dictionaries mentioned by Mathews, in particular the *Oxford English Dictionary* and *Webster's Third New International Dictionary*.
2. A new unabridged dictionary has been published by Random House. Choose a few words from the vocabulary and compare their definitions in this dictionary with those in *Webster's Third*.
3. There was considerable controversy about *Webster's Third*. Look at a book like *Dictionaries and That Dictionary*, by James Sledd and Wilma R. Ebbitt, and summarize the major criticisms.

4. Linguistic experts have tried to clarify the problem of usage in American English. Make a brief report on the positions of Theodore Bernstein, E. B. White, and Bergen Evans.

Vocabulary

(5) UNABRIDGED complete; uncut

(8) PRESCRIBE dictate; authorize

(8) LEXICOGRAPHER compiler of a dictionary

(8) LINGUISTIC of or relating to language

(9) PHILOLOGY study of human speech as an index of cultural history

(10) PROGENITOR forefather

(11) CONSPICUOUS obvious

(12) MANIPULATE operate; manage artfully

(12) CATHARTIC cleansing or purifying agent; laxative

(12) DERIVE take; receive

(15) IMPELLED driven by strong force

(16) TRANSLITERATED rendered in the letters of a different alphabet

(19) INGENUITY skill; cleverness

(19) DECIPHERING converting into understandable forms; decoding

(21) GENUS group with common characteristics

(22) COGNATE word related by derivation or descent

(24) ASSIDUOUSLY attentively; diligently

Robert Gorham Davis (1908–
), professor of English at
Columbia University, was born
in Massachusetts and educated
at Harvard University. He has
lectured abroad and participated in the Salzburg Seminar
in American Studies. Among his
special interests are the history
of prose fiction and contemporary literature.

This essay, originally written for
freshman English students at
Harvard University, defines and
illustrates the major kinds of
logical fallacies. As you read it,
relate what Davis says to your
own thinking and writing.

ROBERT GORHAM DAVIS

Logic and Logical Fallacies

UNDEFINED TERMS

1   The first requirement for logical discourse is knowing what the words
you use actually mean. Words are not like paper money or counters
in a game. Except for technical terms in some of the sciences, they do
not have a fixed face value. Their meanings are fluid and changing,
influenced by many considerations of context and reference, circumstances and association. This is just as true of common words such as
fast as it is of literary terms such as *romantic*. Moreover, if there is to
be communication, words must have approximately the same meaning for the reader that they have for the writer. A speech in an unknown language means nothing to the hearer. When an adult speaks
to a small child or an expert to a layman, communication may be seriously limited by lack of a mature vocabulary or ignorance of technical terms. Many arguments are meaningless because the speakers are
using important words in quite different senses.

2   Because we learn most words—or guess at them—from the contexts in which we first encounter them, our sense of them is often in-

complete or wrong. Readers sometimes visualize the Assyrian who comes down like the wolf on the fold as an enormous man dressed in cohorts (some kind of fancy armor, possibly) gleaming in purple and gold. "A rift in the lute" suggests vaguely a cracked mandolin. Failure to ascertain the literal meaning of figurative language is a frequent reason for mixed metaphors. We are surprised to find that the "devil" in "the devil to pay" and "the devil and the deep blue sea" is not Old Nick, but part of a ship. Unless terms mean the same thing to both writer and reader, proper understanding is impossible.

ABSTRACTIONS

3   The most serious logical difficulties occur with abstract terms. An abstraction is a word which stands for a quality found in a number of different objects or events from which it has been "abstracted" or taken away. We may, for instance, talk of the "whiteness" of paper or cotton or snow without considering qualities of cold or inflammability or usefulness which these materials happen also to possess. Usually, however, our minds carry over other qualities by association. See, for instance, the chapter called "the Whiteness of the Whale" in *Moby-Dick*.

4   In much theoretic discussion the process of abstraction is carried so far that although vague associations and connotations persist, the original objects or events from which the qualities have been abstracted are lost sight of completely. Instead of thinking of words like *sincerity* and *Americanism* as symbols standing for qualities that have to be abstracted with great care from examples and test cases, we come to think of them as real things in themselves. We assume that Americanism is Americanism just as a bicycle is a bicycle, and that everyone knows what it means. We forget that before the question "Is Arthur Godfrey sincere?" can mean anything, we have to agree on the criteria of sincerity.

5   When we try to define such words and find examples, we discover that almost no one agrees to their meaning. The word *church* may refer to anything from a building on the corner of Spring Street to the whole tradition of institutionalized Christianity. *Germany* may mean a geographical section of Europe, a people, a governing group, a cultural tradition, or a military power. Abstractions such as *freedom, courage, race, beauty, truth, justice, nature, honor, humanism, democracy,* should never be used in a theme unless their meaning is defined or indicated clearly by the context. Freedom for whom? To do what? Under what circumstances? Abstract terms have merely emotional value unless they are strictly defined by asking questions of this kind. The study of a word such as *nature* in a good unabridged dictionary will show that even the dictionary, indispensable though it is, cannot determine for us the sense in which a word is being used in any given sentence. Once the student understands the importance of definition, he will no longer be betrayed into fruitless arguments over such questions as whether free verse is "poetry" or whether you can change "human nature."

NAME-CALLING

6 It is a common unfairness in controversy to place what the writer dislikes or opposes in a generally odious category. The humanist dismisses what he dislikes by calling it *romantic;* the liberal, by calling it
fascist; the conservative, by calling it *communistic.* These terms tell
the reader nothing. What is *piety* to some will be *bigotry* to others.
Non-Catholics would rather be called *Protestants* than *heretics.* What
is *right-thinking* except a designation for those who agree with the
writer? Social security measures become *creeping socialism;* industrial organizations, *forces of reaction;* investigation into communism,
witch hunts; prison reforms, *coddling;* progressive education, *fads and
frills.* Such terms are intended to block thought by an appeal to prejudice and associative habits. Three steps are necessary before such
epithets have real meaning. First, they must be defined; second, it
must be shown that the object to which they are applied actually possesses these qualities; third, it must be shown that the possession of
such qualities in this particular situation is necessarily undesirable.
Unless a person is alert and critical both in choosing and in interpret-
ing words, he may be alienated from ideas with which he would be in
sympathy if he had not been frightened by a mere name.

GENERALIZATION

7 Similar to the abuse of abstract terms and epithets is the habit of presenting personal opinions in the guise of universal laws. The student
often seems to feel that the broader the terms in which he states an
opinion, the more effective he will be. Ordinarily the reverse is true.
An enthusiasm for Thomas Wolfe should lead to a specific critical
analysis of Wolfe's novels that will enable the writer to explain his
enthusiasm to others; it should not be turned into the argument that
Wolfe is "the greatest American novelist," particularly if the writer's
knowledge of American novelists is somewhat limited. The same questions of *who* and *when* and *why* and under what *circumstances* which
are used to check abstract terms should be applied to generalizations.
Consider how contradictory proverbial wisdom is when detached
from particular circumstances. "Look before you leap," but "he who
hesitates is lost."

8 Superlatives and the words *right* and *wrong, true* and *untrue, never*
and *always* must be used with caution in matters of opinion. When a
student says flatly that X is true, he often is really saying that he or his
family or the author of a book he has just been reading, persons of certain tastes and background and experience, *think* that X is true. If his
statement is based not on logic and examination of evidence, but
merely reproduces other people's opinions, it can have little value or
relevance unless these people are identified and their reasons for
thinking so explained. Because many freshmen are taking survey
courses in which they read a single work by an author or see an historical event through the eyes of a single historian whose bias they
may not be able to measure, they must guard against this error.

SAMPLING

9   Assertions of a general nature are frequently open to question because they are based on insufficient evidence. Some persons are quite ready, after meeting one Armenian or reading one medieval romance, to generalize about Armenians and medieval romances. One ought, of course, to examine objectively as many examples as possible before making a generalization, but the number is less important than the representativeness of the example chosen. The Literary Digest Presidential Poll, sent to hundreds of thousands of people selected from telephone directories, was far less accurate than the Gallup Poll which questioned far fewer voters, but selected them carefully and proportionately from all different social groups. The "typical" college student, as portrayed by moving pictures and cartoons, is very different from the "average" college student as determined statistically. We cannot let uncontrolled experience do our sampling for us; instances and examples which impress themselves upon our minds do so usually because they are exceptional. In propaganda and arguments extreme cases are customarily treated as if they were characteristic.

10   If one is permitted arbitrarily to select some examples and ignore others, it is possible to find convincing evidence for almost any theory, no matter how fantastic. The fact that the mind tends naturally to remember those instances which confirm its opinions imposes a duty upon the writer, unless he wishes to encourage prejudice and superstition, to look carefully for exceptions to all generalizations which he is tempted to make, We forget the premonitions which are not followed by disaster and the time when our hunches failed to select the winner in a race. Patent medicine advertisements print the letters of those who survived their cure, and not of those who died during it. All Americans did not gamble on the stock exchange in the twenties, or become Marxists in the thirties, and all Vermonters are not thin-lipped and shrewd. Of course the search for negative examples can be carried too far. Outside of mathematics or the laboratory, few generalizations can be made airtight, and most are not intended to be. But quibbling is so easy that resort to it is very common, and the knowledge that people can and will quibble over generalizations is another reason for making assertions as limited and explicitly conditional as possible.

FALSE ANALOGY

11   Illustration, comparison, analogy are most valuable in making an essay clear and interesting. It must not be supposed, however, that they prove anything or have much argumentative weight. The rule that what is true of one thing in one set of circumstances is not necessarily true of another thing in another set of circumstances seems almost too obvious to need stating. Yet constantly nations and businesses are discussed as if they were human beings with human habits and feelings; human bodies are discussed as if they were machines; the universe, as if it were a clock. It is assumed that what held true for seventeenth century New England or the thirteen Atlantic colonies

also holds true for an industrial nation of 150,000,000 people. Carlyle dismissed the arguments for representative democracy by saying that if a captain had to take a vote among his crew every time he wanted to do something, he would never get around Cape Horn. This analogy calmly ignores the distinction between the lawmaking and the executive branches of constitutional democracies. Moreover, voters may be considered much more like the stockholders of a merchant line than its hired sailors. Such arguments introduce assumptions in a metaphorical guise in which they are not readily detected or easily criticized. In place of analysis they attempt to identify their position with some familiar symbol which will evoke a predictable, emotional response in the reader. The revival during the 1932 presidential campaign of Lincoln's remark, "Don't swap horses in the middle of the stream," was not merely a picturesque way of saying keep Hoover in the White House. It made a number of assumptions about the nature of depressions and the function of government. This propagandist technique can be seen most clearly in political cartoons.

DEGREE

12 Often differences in degree are more important than differences in kind. By legal and social standards there is more difference between an habitual drunkard and a man who drinks temperately, than between a temperate drinker and a total abstainer. In fact differences of degree produce what are regarded as differences of kind. At known temperatures ice turns to water and water boils. At an indeterminate point affection becomes love and a man who needs a shave becomes a man with a beard. The fact that no men or systems are perfect makes rejoinders and counteraccusations very easy if differences in degree are ignored. Newspapers in totalitarian states, answering American accusations of brutality and suppression, refer to lynchings and gangsterism here. Before a disinterested judge could evaluate these mutual accusations, he would have to settle the question of the degree to which violent suppression and lynching are respectively prevalent in the countries under consideration. On the other hand, differences in degree may be merely apparent. Lincoln Steffens pointed out that newspapers can create a "crime wave" any time they wish, simply by emphasizing all the minor assaults and thefts commonly ignored or given an inch or two on a back page. The great reported increases in insanity may be due to the fact that in a more urban and institutionalized society cases of insanity more frequently come to the attention of authorities and hence are recorded in statistics.

CAUSATION

13 The most common way of deciding that one thing causes another thing is the simple principle: *post hoc, ergo propter hoc,* "After this, therefore because of this." Rome fell after the introduction of Christianity; therefore Christianity was responsible for the fall of Rome. Such rea-

soning illustrates another kind of faulty generalization. But even if one could find ten cases in which a nation "fell" after the introduction of Christianity, it still would not be at all certain that Christianity caused the fall. Day, it has frequently been pointed out, follows night in every observable instance, and yet night cannot be called the cause of day. Usually a combination of causes produces a result. Sitting in a draught may cause a cold, but only given a certain physical condition in the person sitting there. In such instances one may distinguish between necessary and sufficient conditions. Air is a necessary condition for the maintenance of plant life, but air alone is not sufficient to produce plant life. And often different causes at different times may produce the same result. This relation is known as plurality of causes. If, after sitting in a stuffy theatre on Monday, and then again after eating in a stuffy restaurant on Thursday, a man suffered from headaches, he might say, generalizing, that bad air gave him headaches. But actually the headache on Monday may have been caused by eyestrain and on Thursday by indigestion. To isolate the causative factor it is necessary that all other conditions be precisely the same. Such isolation is possible, except in very simple instances, only in the laboratory or with scientific methods. If a picture falls from the wall every time a truck passes, we can quite certainly say that the truck's passing is the proximate or immediate cause. But with anything as complex and conditional as a nation's economy or human character, the determination of cause is not easy or certain. A psychiatrist often sees a patient for an hour daily for a year or more before he feels that he understands his neurosis.

14   Ordinarily when we speak of cause we mean the proximate or immediate cause. The plants were killed by frost; we had indigestion from eating lobster salad. But any single cause is one in an unbroken series. When a man is murdered, is his death caused by the loss of blood from the wound, or by the firing of the pistol, or by the malice aforethought of the murderer? Was the World War "caused" by the assassination at Sarajevo? Were the Navigation Acts or the ideas of John Locke more important in "causing" the American Revolution? A complete statement of cause would comprise the sum total of the conditions which preceded an event, conditions stretching back indefinitely into the past. Historical events are so interrelated that the isolation of a causative sequence is dependent chiefly on the particular preoccupations of the historian. An economic determinist can "explain" history entirely in terms of economic development; an idealist, entirely in terms of the development of ideas.

SYLLOGISTIC REASONING

15 The formal syllogism of the type,

> All men are mortal
> John is a man
> Therefore John is mortal,

is not so highly regarded today as in some earlier periods. It merely fixes an individual as a members of a class, and then assumes that the individual has the given characteristics of the class. Once we have decided who John is, and what "man" and "mortal" mean, and have canvassed all men, including John, to make sure that they are mortal, the conclusion naturally follows. It can be seen that the chief difficulties arise in trying to establish acceptable premises. Faults in the premises are known as "material" fallacies, and are usually more serious than the "formal" fallacies, which are logical defects in drawing a conclusion from the premises. But although directly syllogistic reasoning is not much practiced, buried syllogism can be found in all argument, and it is often a useful clarification to outline your own or another writer's essay in syllogistic form. The two most frequent defects in the syllogism itself are the undistributed and the ambiguous middle. The middle term is the one that appears in each of the premises and not in the conclusion. In the syllogism,

> All good citizens vote
> John votes
> Therefore John is a good citizen,

the middle term is not "good citizens," but "votes." Even though it were true that all good citizens vote, nothing prevents bad citizens from voting also, and John may be one of the bad citizens. To distribute the middle term "votes" one might say (but only if that is what one meant),

> All voters are good citizens
> John is a voter
> Therefore John is a good citizen.

16   The ambiguous middle term is even more common. It represents a problem in definition, while the undistributed middle is a problem in generalization. All acts which benefit others are virtuous, losing money at poker benefits others, therefore losing at poker is a virtuous act. Here the middle term "act which benefits others" is obviously used very loosely and ambiguously.

NON-SEQUITUR

17 This phrase, meaning "it does not follow," is used to characterize the kind of humor found in pictures in which the Marx Brothers perform. It is an amusing illogicality because it usually expresses, beneath its apparent incongruity, an imaginative, associative, or personal truth. "My ancestors came over on the Mayflower; therefore I am naturally opposed to labor unions." It is not logically necessary that those whose ancestors came over on the Mayflower should be opposed to unions; but it may happen to be true as a personal fact in a given case. It is usually a strong personal conviction which keeps people from realizing that their arguments are non-sequiturs, that they do not follow the given premises with logical necessity. Contemporary psychologists have effectively shown us that there is often such a wide difference between the true and the purported reasons for an attitude that, in rationalizing our behavior, we are often quite unconscious of the mo-

tives that actually influence us. A fanatical antivivisectionist, for instance may have temperamental impulses toward cruelty which he is suppressing and compensating for by a reasoned opposition of any kind of permitted suffering. We may expect, then, to come upon many conclusions which are psychologically interesting in themselves, but have nothing to do with the given premises.

IGNORATIO ELENCHI

18 This means, in idiomatic English, "arguing off the point," or ignoring the question at issue. A man trying to show that monarchy is the best form of government for the British Empire may devote most of his attention to the charm of Elizabeth II and the affection her people feel for her. In ordinary conversational argument it is almost impossible for disputants to keep to the point. Constantly turning up are tempting side-issues through which one can discomfit an opponent or force him to irrelevant admissions that seem to weaken his case.

BEGGING THE QUESTION; ARGUING IN A CIRCLE

19 The first of these terms means to assume in the premises what you are pretending to prove in the course of your argument. The function of logic is to demonstrate that because one thing or group of things is true, another must be true as a consequence. But in begging the question you simply say in varying language that what is assumed to be true is assumed to be true. An argument which asserts that we shall enjoy immortality because we have souls which are immaterial and indestructible establishes nothing, because the idea of immortality is already contained in the assumption about the soul. It is the premise which needs to be demonstrated, not the conclusion. Arguing in a circle is another form of this fallacy. It proves the premise by the conclusion and the conclusion by the premise. The conscience forbids an act because it is wrong; the act is wrong because the conscience forbids it.

ARGUMENTS AD HOMINEM AND AD POPULUM

20 It is very difficult for men to be persuaded by reason when their interest or prestige is at stake. If one wishes to preach the significance of physiognomy, it is well to choose a hearer with a high forehead and a determined jaw. The arguments in favor of repealing the protective tariff on corn or wheat in England were more readily entertained by manufacturers than by landowners. The cotton manufacturers in New England who were doing a profitable trade with the South were the last to be moved by descriptions of the evils of slavery. Because interest and desire are so deeply seated in human nature, arguments are frequently mingled with attempts to appeal to emotion, arouse fear, play upon pride, attack the characters of proponents of an opposite

view, show that their practice is inconsistent with their principles; all matters which have, strictly speaking, nothing to do with the truth or falsity, the general desirability or undesirability, of some particular measure. If men are desperate enough they will listen to arguments proper only to an insane asylum but which seem to promise them relief.

21   After reading these suggestions, which are largely negative, the student may feel that any original assertion he can make will probably contain one or several logical faults. This assumption is not true. Even if it were, we know from reading newspapers and magazines that worldly fame is not dimmed by the constant and, one suspects, conscious practice of illogicality. But generalizations are not made only by charlatans and sophists. Intelligent and scrupulous writers also have a great many fresh and provocative observations and conclusions to express and are expressing them influentially. What is intelligence but the ability to see the connection between things, to discern causes, to relate the particular to the general, to define and discriminate and compare? Any man who thinks and feels and observes closely will not want for something to express.

22   And in his expression a proponent will find that a due regard for logic does not limit but rather increases the force of his argument. When statements are not trite, they are usually controversial. Men arrive at truth dialectically; error is weeded out in the course of discussion, argument, attack, and counterattack. Not only can a writer who understands logic show the weaknesses of arguments he disagrees with, but also, by anticipating the kind of attack likely to be made on his own ideas, he can so arrange them, properly modified with qualifications and exceptions, that the anticipated attack is made much less effective. Thus, fortunately, we do not have to depend on the spirit of fairness and love of truth to lead men to logic; it has the strong support of argumentative necessity and of the universal desire to make ideas prevail.

(Since this selection is concerned with logic and language, the exercises do not follow the usual pattern. Discussion of the theme, of rhetoric, and of vocabulary will automatically be a part of your answers to these questions.)

Identify the errors in logic in each of the following:

1. The United States became involved in two major wars during the terms of Democratic presidents. The Democratic party therefore is rightly known as the war party.
2. I have no doubt that Coach Smith will make an excellent principal. After all, he could really handle those gym classes!
3. This is the best movie I have seen all year; it should win an Oscar.
4. Mr. Walters, a Lutheran, is an alcoholic. I guess it's true what they say about Lutherans.
5. Sue will do well in college; she received good grades in high school.

6. Last month's atomic bomb testing was followed by earthquakes in Chile and Turkey. Obviously there is a relation between earthquakes and explosions in the atmosphere.
7. My party has always stood for equal opportunity.
8. Common sense is needed in public office today.
9. The human body is like a machine, so of course it can work without sleep.
10. Chairman Edwards and his henchmen are responsible for our high taxes.
11. It is reported that he subscribes to left-wing magazines. How can you respect his judgment?
12. Forty-three percent of the women who were asked said that Bubble-O soap got their clothes cleaner.
13. If you allow a high school student to drive a car, you are guaranteeing his academic failure.
14. Mr. Webster is from the South; obviously, he is for the right-to-work law.
15. His morals are made of steel, but we know steel will rust and fail.
16. A Catholic tried to kill the Pope; another one tried to kill his wife just last week. What should we do about the Catholics?
17. All teachers are too removed from real life.
    Mr. Thompson is my English teacher.
    Therefore, Mr. Thompson doesn't know what's going on.
18. Why would anyone vote for Mr. Clane? Just look at his private life.
19. Anyone with good taste will like "My Sister's Mistake," now showing at the Plaza.
20. How could I agree with you? Our families came from different countries.

Lionel Ruby (1889–1972) was educated at Harvard University and at the University of Chicago, where he received his Ph.D. He has taught at Indiana, Northwestern, and Roosevelt universities. He was the author of "Logic: An Introduction" (1950) and "The Art of Making Sense" (1954).

Robert Yarber (1929–) is a member of the English department at San Diego Mesa College.

LIONEL RUBY
ROBERT E. YARBER

Are All Generalizations False?

1 We begin with a generalization: human beings are great generalizers. Every race has its proverbs, and proverbs are generalizations. "It never rains but it pours." "Faint heart never won fair lady." "Familiarity breeds contempt." Sometimes, of course, these proverbs are incompatible with each other, as in "Absence makes the heart grow fonder," and "Out of sight, out of mind."[1]

2   Listen attentively to those around you, and note the generalizations that float into every conversation: Women drivers are the most careless. Professors are absentminded. The Irish are alcoholics. Gentlemen prefer blondes. Politicians are crooks. The French are great lovers. People on welfare don't want to work. And so on. After more of

---

1. Once translated by a foreign student as "invisible idiot."

the same we may be tempted to agree with Justice Holmes that "the chief end of man is to frame general propositions, and no general proposition is worth a damn."

3   Our awareness of the inadequacy of "sweeping generalizations" may lead us to say that all generalizations are false. But this is truly a sweeping generalization! And worse: if it is true, then the witticism that "all generalizations are false, *including this one*" would appear to be justified. But this will not do either, for this generalization asserts that it itself is false, from which it follows that it is not the case that all generalizations are false. Or perhaps we should say that "all generalizations are half-truths—including this one"? But this is not much better. The fact of the matter is that some generalizations are true, others are false, and still others are uncertain or doubtful. The deadliness of this platitude may be forgiven because of its truth.

4   By a "generalization" is meant a general law or principle which is inferred from particular facts. As a sample of the way in which we arrive at such generalizations, consider the following: Some years ago I saw my first Italian movie. The directing, the acting, the dialogue, the lighting—all were superior. Encouraged by this initial experience, I saw another Italian movie. It, too, was enjoyable. I saw other Italian movies, always with the same results—comedies, dramas, "Westerns," thrillers. I generalized: All Italian movies are enjoyable.

5   A generalization is a statement that *goes beyond* what is actually observed, to a rule or law covering both the observed cases and those that have not as yet been observed. This going-beyond is called the "inductive leap." An inductive leap is a "leap in the dark," for the *generalization may not be true,* even though the *observations* on which it is based *are* true. Thus, there may be a bad Italian movie —happily I have not seen it—but if so, then I should not say that *all* are good.

6   A generalization involves an "inductive leap." The word *induction,* from Latin roots meaning "to lead in," means that we examine particular cases and "lead in" to a generalization. Induction is the method we use when we learn lessons from our experience; we generalize from particular cases. *Deduction,* on the other hand, refers to the process of "drawing out" the logical consequences of what we already know (or assume) to be true. By induction we learn that Italian movies are enjoyable. If a friend tells us that he saw a bad movie, then by deduction we know that he did not see an Italian movie. Both induction and deduction are essential characteristics of rational thinking.

7   A generalization is a statement of the form: "All A's are B's." "All" means exactly what it says: *all* without exception. A single exception overthrows a generalization of this kind. Before we proceed further we must first dispose of a popular confusion concerning the expression, "The exception proves the rule." This is a sensible statement when properly interpreted, but it is sometimes understood in a manner that makes it nonsense. If I say that "all A's are B's," a single exception will make my statement false. Now, suppose that someone says, "The fact that there is a bad Italian movie proves that *all* are good because *it* is an exception, and the exception proves the rule!"

Does a wicked woman prove that all women are saints? The sensible interpretation of the expression, "The exception proves the rule," is this: When we *say* that a certain case *is* an "exception," we imply that there is a rule which generally holds. When a mother tells her daughter, "Have a good time at the prom, and, for tonight, you have my permission to stay out until 3 A.M.," she implies that this is an exception to the rule which requires earlier reporting. A statement that *creates* an exception implies a rule for all nonexceptional cases, but a generalization that is stated as a rule without exceptions (all A's are B's) would be overthrown by a single exception.

8   Scientific laws, stated in the form "All A's are B's," or some variation thereof, are never "violated." When an exception to a law is definitely established, the law in its previous form is abandoned, but it may be possible to revise it to exclude the "exception" as a special case because of special circumstances. The revised law: "All A's, under such and such conditions, are B's." Water freezes at 32° F. *at sea level.*

9   All too often "general propositions are not worth a damn," as Holmes remarked. This is because we generalize too hastily on the basis of insufficient evidence. The fallacy called the "hasty generalization" simply refers to the fact that we jump too quickly to conclusions concerning "all." For example, we see a woman driving carelessly, and generalize: "All women are poor drivers." We see a car weaving in and out of traffic, and note that it has a California license: "Wouldn't you know," we say. "A California driver. That's the way they all drive out there." Anita Loos's gay heroine thought that gentlemen preferred blondes because she was a blonde and men were attracted to her.

10   We learn that Napoleon got along on five hours of sleep. From this we may conclude that "five hours of sleep is all that anybody really needs." Our assumption is that what Napoleon could do, anybody can do, until we learn that we are not Napoleons. (If we don't learn this eventually, we aren't permitted to circulate freely.) The next example is undoubtedly the worst example of generalizing ever committed: A man declared that all Indians walk in single file. When challenged for his evidence, he replied, "How do I know that? I once saw an Indian walk that way."

11   Hasty generalizing is perhaps the most important of popular vices in thinking. It is interesting to speculate on some of the reasons for this kind of bad thinking. One important factor is prejudice. If we are already prejudiced against unions or businessmen or lawyers or doctors or Jews or Negroes or whites or gentiles, then one or two instances of bad conduct by members of these groups will give us the unshakable conviction that "they're all like that." It is very difficult for a prejudiced person to say, "Some are, and some aren't." A prejudice is a judgment formed *before* examining the evidence.

12   A psychological reason for asserting "wild" generalizations is exhibitionism: The exhibitionist desires to attract attention to himself. No one pays much attention to such undramatic statements as "Some women are fickle," or "Some politicians are no better than they ought to be." But when one says that "all men are liars," this immediately

attracts notice. Goethe once said that it is easy to appear brilliant if one respects nothing, not even the truth.

13   Let us avoid careless and hasty generalizing. The fault of bad generalizing, however, need not make us take refuge in the opposite error—the refusal to generalize. This error is illustrated in the anecdote concerning the student who wrote an essay on labor relations, in which he argued for equal pay for women. Women, he wrote, work hard; they need the money; they are the foundation of the family; and, above all, they are the mothers of most of the human race! There is an old anecdote about the cautious man whose friend pointed to a flock of sheep with the remark, "Those sheep seem to have been sheared recently." "Yes," said the cautious man, "at least on this side."

14   Generalizations are dangerous, but we must generalize. To quote Justice Holmes once more: he said that he welcomed "anything that will discourage men from believing general propositions." But, he added, he welcomed that "only less than he welcomed anything that would encourage men to make such propositions"! For generalizations are indispensable guides. One of the values of knowledge lies in its predictive power—its power to predict the future. Such knowledge is stated in generalizations. It is of little help to me to know that water froze at 32° F. yesterday unless this information serves as a warning to put antifreeze in my car radiator before winter comes. History, in the "pure" sense of this term, merely tells us what has happened in the past, but science furnishes us with general laws, and general laws tell us what *always* happens under certain specified conditions.

15   Science is interested in the general, rather than in the particular or individual. When Newton saw an apple fall from a tree in his orchard—even if this story is a fable, and therefore false in a literal sense, it is true in its insight—he was not interested in the size and shape of the apple. Its fall suggested an abstract law to him, the law of gravity. He framed this law in general terms: Every particle of matter attracts every other particle of matter with a force directly proportional to the product of their masses and inversely proportional to the square of their distances. Chemists seek general laws concerning the behavior of matter. The physician wants to know the general characteristics of the disease called myxedema, so that when he has a case he will recognize it and know exactly how to treat it. The finding of general laws, then, is the aim of all science—including history insofar as it is a science.

16   The problem of the scientist is one of achieving sound generalizations. The scientist is careful not to make assertions which outrun his evidence, and he refuses to outtalk his information. He generalizes, but recognizes that no generalization can be more than probable, for we can never be certain that *all* the evidence is in, nor can the future be guaranteed absolutely—not even future eclipses of the sun and moon. But the scientist knows that certain laws have a very high degree of probability.

17   Let us look at the logic involved in forming sound generalizations. The number of cases investigated in the course of formulating a scientific law is a factor in establishing the truth of the law, but it is by no

means the most important one. Obviously, if we observed one hundred swans, all of which are white, our generalization that "all swans are white" does not have the same probability it would have if we observed one thousand swans. But no matter how great the number of specimens involved in this type of observation, no more than a moderately high degree of probability is ever established. Countless numbers of white swans were observed throughout the ages (without any exceptions), and then in the nineteenth century black swans were observed in Australia.

18   The weakness of the method of "induction by simple enumeration of cases" is amusingly illustrated by Bertrand Russell's parable in his *History of Western Philosophy:*

> There was once upon a time a census officer who had to record the names of all householders in a certain Welsh village. The first that he questioned was called William Williams; so were the second, third, fourth. . . . At last he said to himself: "This is tedious; evidently they are all called William Williams. I shall put them down so and take a holiday." But he was wrong; there was just one whose name was John Jones."

19   Scientific generalizations based on other types of evidence than simple enumeration often acquire a much higher degree of probability after only a few observations. When a chemist finds that pure sulphur melts at 125° C. in an experiment in which every factor is accurately analyzed and controlled, the law concerning the melting point of sulphur achieves as great a degree of certainty as is humanly attainable. Accurate control of every element of one case, then, is more important in establishing probabilities than is *mere enumeration* of many cases.

20   A single carefully controlled experiment, such as the sulphur experiment, can give us a much higher degree of probability than the mere observation of thousands of swans. The reason is that we also know that no chemical element thus far observed has a variable melting point under conditions of constant pressure. The chemical law is thus consistent with and is borne out by the rest of chemical knowledge, whereas the "law" holding that all swans are white was based on an "accidental" factor. Or consider the generalization concerning the mortality of mankind. This law is based not merely on the fact that countless numbers of human beings have died in the past, but also on the fact that all living beings must, by reason of physiological limitations, die, and that all matter wears out in time. So the harmony of a particular generalization with the rest of our knowledge is also a factor in giving it a high degree of probability.

21   So much for the logical analysis of generalizations. Thus far, we have been concerned with "uniform" generalizations, which take the form: "All A's are B's." A generalization, we have seen, is a statement that says something about "all" of a group, the evidence consisting of observations of items in which we always find a single characteristic. The observed cases are taken as a *sample* of the whole group or population with which we are concerned. We observe a number of swans and take these as a sample of all swans, past, present, and future. We

find that all are white, and make the inductive leap: Swans are always white, everywhere.

"STATISTICAL" STATEMENTS

22 We shall now examine "statistical" statements. Statistical statements give us information, not about characteristics possessed by *all* of a group or population, but about those possessed by a definite proportion (or most) of the group or population, as when we say, "Most A's are B's," or "Sixty-five percent of all A's are B's." The first thing to note here is that statistical statements may, in fact, be *generalizations* and thus involve the notion of "all." This point involves very important (and common) misunderstandings.

23 In order to make this point clear, let us reinterpret our "uniform" generalizations. We say: "The sample is so-and-so (all observed swans are uniformly white)—*therefore,* the whole population of swans is uniformly white." Now, we do the same sort of thing in statistical generalizations. We say, "In the sample of redheads we examined, 53 percent were hot-tempered; therefore, 53 percent of *all* redheads are hot-tempered." (Or 53 percent of the whole population of redheads is hot-tempered.) Logically, both examples, uniform and statistical, are of the same type, for in each we make the inductive leap from the sample to the whole population. The only difference between them is that in the one case we assert a *uniform* character in the whole population, while in the other we assert that a characteristic holds in a certain *proportion* in the whole population.

24 This fundamental point will help us to evaluate the degree of probability of a statistical generalization. We saw earlier that uniform generalizations can never be absolutely certain—though for practical purposes we often consider them so, especially in the physical sciences. The probability of a generalization depends especially on the *quality* and also on the *quantity* of the cases that constitute the sample. The same holds for statistical generalizations, which may have a high probability, depending on the character of the evidence. Though the inductive leap is involved in all generalizations, in some cases the leap is justified. Let us examine the criteria of justification for the leap.

25 Before we proceed we shall discuss an important distinction: that between the sample and the inference we draw from it. It is one thing to describe a sample accurately and quite another to draw an accurate inference. If I say, "I have observed ten swans (the sample) and all were white," we may assume that the sample is accurately described. But if I now go on to generalize (that is, draw the inference) concerning *all* swans, my inference may not be a good one. A generalization always involves a "leap in the dark," sometimes justified and sometimes not. Similarly, if I say, "I have talked to ten friends concerning their income, and six [60 percent] told me that they earned more than $20,000 a year," the description of the sample may be accepted as true. But suppose I now go on to make the following inference:

"Therefore, 60 percent of all Americans earn more than $20,000 a year." This would be a hasty generalization indeed.

26   We distinguish, then, between the sample and the inference. A study of I. Q. scores of 18,782 Air Force enlisted men revealed that those who were accountants in their civilian lives had the highest median (128.1), while those who were miners were among the very lowest (92.0). Now, these figures involve no inferences. They simply describe the actual facts *in the sample*. We draw an inference, on the other hand, when we assume that *all* accountants and *all* miners in the United States would have shown the same kinds of averages as the sample. In our discussion, henceforth, we shall be concerned only with the logical problems involved in statistical inferences.

27   Suppose that a public opinion poll was recently taken. The polling organization tells us that 58 percent of the American people approve of the record of the present administration in Washington. How do they know this? Let us examine the evidence on which this finding is based. Obviously not everyone was consulted. A sample was taken. There were 3,000 interviews. Since there are approximately 150 million adults in the United States, each individual in this sample is taken as representative of 50,000 adults. Further, in the sample, 1,000 persons said that they had "no opinion." Eleven hundred and sixty said that they "approved," and 840 said they did not. Thus 58 percent of those with opinions approved, and this means, we are told, that approximately 87 million Americans approve. The pollsters assume that the undecided individuals will probably divide in the same proportion as the others when they make up their minds.

28   Now, we are not raising any questions concerning the truth of the report made of the sample. But is the inductive leap from the sample to the generalization concerning 150 million people justified? It may be. It all depends upon the reliability of the sample. What makes a sample reliable? It must be *fair, unbiased,* and *representative* of the whole. But the crucial problem is to determine whether or not it has these characteristics.

29   The size of the sample is obviously important. A sample of 100 would not be so reliable as one of 1,000, and 1,000 would not be so reliable as one of a million. But large numbers in themselves may not be the most important factor in establishing the reliability of generalizations or inferences.

30   The unimportance of large numbers as such is best illustrated by the ill-fated *Literary Digest* presidential election poll in 1936. The magazine sent pre-election ballots to 10 million persons and received over 2 million responses. The responses showed Landon running ahead of Roosevelt. In the election in November, however, Roosevelt got about 28 million votes, Landon around 18 million.

31   The reason for this colossal failure was the unrepresentative character of the sample. The *Digest* took names "at random" from telephone directories and lists of registered owners of automobiles. These were relatively well-to-do folk. The lower income groups, however, were completely, or almost completely, unrepresented.

32   An ideal sample is one taken "at random" from the entire population, and not from a selected portion of the population being studied.

The Gallup poll, for example, uses a special kind of random sampling, and, barring a spectacular failure in 1948, has been far more success-ful than the *Literary Digest* poll. Let us see how the Gallup poll oper-ates. A sample of 3,000 individuals is taken, but with great care to make the sample representative. The population is classified into subgroups by geographic regions, by rural or urban residence, economic status, age, education, and declared politics. In 1948, for example, Gallup estimated that 28 percent of the American people lived in the Middle Atlantic states, 10 percent on the West Coast; that 34 percent lived in cities of over 100,000 population; that 23 percent were of an "average" economic station; that 43 percent were between the ages of thirty and forty-nine; that 42 percent had gone to high school; and that 38 percent called themselves Democrats, 36 percent Republicans, and 26 percent independents or members of smaller parties. The 3,000 interviews in the sample were distributed so that each geographic area, each economic group, etc., would be represented in its appropriate numerical strength.

33   Individuals are then chosen "at random," rather than by selection, from within each subgroup, and the resulting sample is highly rep-resentative of the whole population. The Gallup poll enjoys a success-ful record, on the whole, except for 1948. In other words, the method works, and one must respect its findings. But no poll can ever elimi-nate the possibility of error or guarantee accuracy except within a margin of error of several percentage points. And in a presidential election forecast the pollster is either completely right or completely wrong in predicting who will win. Odds of ten to one against a candi-date of one of the major parties are probably not justified even if all the polls are confidently unanimous as to the final results. These were the odds against Harry Truman in the presidential election of 1948!

34   An election prediction can be judged by the election results, and a long series of successful predictions gives us confidence in the methods of the pollsters. This check cannot be made on polls which tabulate public opinion on issues of the day, for the whole population is never counted. Similarly for polls which rate television shows, for the whole audience is not counted. Such polls, of course, also generalize on the basis of samples. To illustrate the logical problems in assessing the reliability of a statistical study of the "public opinion poll" type we shall comment on *Sexual Behavior in the Human Female,* by Alfred C. Kinsey and his staff.

35   Kinsey's study, published in 1950, tabulates and classifies data concerning 5,940 white American females, ages two to ninety. He did not claim that his averages necessarily apply to all human females, despite the title of his book, nor even to all American women, of whom there were approximately seventy million in 1950. It is inevi-table, however, that such inferences will be drawn, and our question is: Are such inferences justified? This depends entirely on the rep-resentativeness of Kinsey's sample.

36   Critics of Kinsey's report have emphasized the unrepresentativeness of his sample. His subjects were not distributed proportionately in geographic areas: most were from Illinois, Florida, and California. They were more highly educated than a representative cross-section

Lionel Ruby and Robert E. Yarber
98

of the population; 75 percent of his subjects went to college, as compared with a national average of 13 percent. Three percent of his women did not go beyond grade school as compared with the national average of 37 percent. A larger than average proportion were from middle and upper economic groups. Very few of the women were Roman Catholics or orthodox Jews.

37   Critics have also argued that the very nature of the study involves a kind of bias, for many women will refuse to discuss matters of such "delicate privacy" with interviewers, so that his volunteers must be unrepresentative of women in general. And there is also the problem of credibility. Critics have said that people who like to talk about such things tend to understate or overstate, and even to embroider a little.

38   Kinsey, of course, recognized the limitations and incompleteness of his sample, and, as noted, did not claim that it was representative of the whole population. But it will be interpreted in this way, and if Kinsey wished to avoid such interpretations, he should have called his study "Sexual Behavior of 5,940 Women." Inferences would probably be drawn, however, even if he had so titled his study.

39   The elements of distortion in Kinsey's sample detract from its reliability as a basis for generalizing. On the other hand, as a review of the book in *Life* put it, though the statistics are not perfect, they are, at any rate, "the only statistics in town." His study is by no means worthless as an index of sexual behavior. We must not use an "all or nothing" approach here. The reliability of his sample with respect to university women as a single group, for example, is certainly much higher than that for the female population as a whole. But we cannot conclude that the whole female population resembles the sample since the sample is not a representative one.

40   Generalizations in statistics, then, are judged by the same logical criteria we use in judging any generalizations. Fallacies, however, are more common in statistical than they are in uniform generalizations. For it is easier to check on the reliability of a uniform generalization: one exception overthrows the general rule or "law." In statistics, however, since nothing is said about any specific individual, an "exception" is a meaningless term. An exceptional individual does not disprove an "average." But there is, as we have already noted, a method for checking the reliability of a statistical generalization concerning a population, and that is to count the whole voting population in an election. But even a test of this kind is not conclusive, for many of the voters do not vote on election day, because of laziness, overconfidence, or some other reason.

41   Errors of inference in statistics are frequently overlooked because of the mathematical language in which statistics are presented. The spell which numbers weave often prevents us from seeing errors in arguments—errors which would be obvious were they not clothed in mathematical garb. And many dishonest reasoners take advantage of this fact and present highly selected data for purposes of propaganda rather than information. Misuses of the science of statistics have resulted in such jibes as, "Figures don't lie, but liars figure," and "There are three kinds of lies: ordinary lies, damnable lies, and statis-

tics." But these cynical remarks should not be taken as criticisms of statistics. The fault never lies with the figures, or with the science, but with their careless use. It is simply not the case that "you can prove anything with figures" (or statistics) just as it is never the case that "you can prove anything by logic." To the uninitiated, it just *seems* that you can.

Discussion of Theme

1. What is the answer to the question asked in the title?
2. What is the main hazard in generalizing?
3. What is the difference between inductive and deductive reasoning?
4. With reference to polls, what makes a sample reliable? What determines whether it has these characteristics?
5. Discuss the statement, "The exception proves the rule."
6. Why do people generalize so much?

Discussion of Rhetoric

1. How does the author's use of several common generalizations serve to invoke interest in his subject?
2. The first sentence in both paragraph 4 and paragraph 7 makes a statement about generalizations. Is either a definition in itself, and if so, which?
3. Why does the author discuss the two most famous failures of polls rather than some spectacular successes?
4. On the basis of the information the article supplies about the Kinsey report, as well as the criticism of it, what title would the study have to have in order to avoid all false inferences?
5. Although the title of the article concerns all generalizations, the conclusion makes no mention of them. Would it have been better if the author had done so?
6. The author consistently uses "we" and "us," rather than "you." What is his probable purpose?

Writing Assignments

1. What hasty generalizations do you encounter most frequently? Why do you consider them hasty?
2. Evaluate several proverbs like "He who hesitates is lost" or "Look before you leap."
3. The author says that "generalizations are indispensable guides." What generalizations do you rely on to guide you?
4. Account for the fact that politicians use polls in their campaigns.
5. What does the habit of hasty generalization have to do with race prejudice?

6. Pure research, which is an expression of science's "interest in the general rather than the particular or individual," is often criticized by laymen because it seems aimless and time-consuming. Write a defense of the necessity for allocating time, money, and manpower to pure research.

Library Exploration

1. Virtually the same proverbs exist in all languages. Look up proverbs that have been translated from various languages and compare them with similar proverbs in our own language.
2. Report on the Gallup poll of 1948 which failed to predict Harry S. Truman's election.

Vocabulary

(1) INCOMPATIBLE incapable of existing together in harmony

(3) PLATITUDE dull or insipid remark

(4) INFERRED concluded; indicated

(9) FALLACY a type of erroneous reasoning (in logic)

(13) ANECDOTE an interesting or amusing tale

(14) INDISPENSABLE necessary; essential

(15) INVERSELY in opposite order

(16) ASSERTIONS declarations

(19) ENUMERATION counting; listing

(34) TABULATE summarize

(34) ASSESSING estimating; evaluating

(37) CREDIBILITY believability

(36) FABRICATE invent; create

(41) CYNICAL distrustful; pessimistic

Haig A. Bosmajian (1928–   ) is
a speech professor at the University of Washington. He has
published essays and books on
dissent, freedom of speech, and
nonverbal communication.

The language of white racism is
not always blatant or even deliberate. The following essay
cites ample evidence to show
that the English language contains built-in racial slurs.

HAIG A. BOSMAJIAN

The Language of White Racism

1 The attempts to eradicate racism in the United States have been
focused notably on the blacks of America, not the whites. What is
striking is that while we are inundated with TV programs portraying
the plight of black Americans, and with panel discussions focusing on
black Americans, we very seldom hear or see any extensive public
discussion, literature or programs directly related to the source of the
racism, the white American. We continually see on our TV sets and in
our periodicals pictures and descriptions of undernourished black
children, but we seldom see pictures or get analyses of the millions of
schoolage white suburban children being taught racism in their white
classrooms; we see pictures of unemployed blacks aimlessly walking
the streets in their black communities, but seldom do we ever see the
whites who have been largely responsible, directly or indirectly, for
this unemployment and segregation; we continually hear panelists
discussing and diagnosing the blacks in America, but seldom do we
hear panelists diagnosing the whites and their subtle and not so subtle
racism.

2   Gunnar Myrdal, in the Introduction to his classic *An American Dilemma,* wrote that as he "proceeded in his studies into the Negro
problem [an unfortunate phrase], it became increasingly evident that
little, if anything, could be scientifically explained in terms of the peculiarities of the Negroes themselves." It is the white majority group,
said Myrdal, "that naturally determines the Negro's 'place.' All our
attempts to reach scientific explanations of why the Negroes are what

they are and why they live as they do have regularly led to determinants on the white side of the race line." As the July 1966 editorial in *Ebony* put it, "for too long now, we have focused on the symptoms of the disease rather than the disease itself. It is time now for us to face the fact that Negroes are oppressed in America not by 'the pathology of the ghetto,' as some experts contend, but by the pathology of the white community." In calling for a White House Conference on Whites, the *Ebony* editorial made the important point that "we need to know more about the pathology of the white community. We need conferences in which white leaders will talk not about us [Negroes] but about themselves."

3   White Americans, through the mass media and individually, must begin to focus their attention not on the condition of the victimized, but on the victimizer. Whitey must begin to take the advice of various black spokesmen who suggest that white Americans start solving the racial strife in this country by eradicating white racism in white communities, instead of going into black communities or joining black organizations or working for legislation to "give" the blacks political and social rights. This suggestion has come from Floyd McKissick, Malcolm X, and Stokely Carmichael. McKissick, when asked what the role of the white man was in the black man's struggle, answered: "If there are whites who are not racists, and I believe there are a few, a *very* few, let them go to their own communities and teach; teach white people the truth about the black man." Malcolm X wrote in his autobiography: "The Negroes aren't the racists. Where the really sincere white people have to do their 'proving' of themselves is not among the black *victims,* but on the battle lines of where America's racism really *is*—and that's in their own home communities; America's racism is among their own fellow whites. That's where the sincere whites who really mean to accomplish something have to work." Stokely Carmichael, writing in the September 22, 1966, issue of *The New York Review of Books,* said: "One of the most distrubing things about almost all white supporters of the movement has been that they are afraid to go into their own communities—which is where the racism exists—and work to get rid of it."

4   A step in that direction which most whites can take is to clean up their language to rid it of words and phrases which connote racism to the blacks. Whereas many blacks have demonstrated an increased sensitivity to language and an awareness of the impact of words and phrases upon both black and white listeners, the whites of this nation have demonstrated little sensitivity to the language of racial strife. Whitey has been for too long speaking and writing in terminology which, often being offensive to the blacks, creates hostility and suspicions and breaks down communication.

5   The increased awareness and sensitivity of the black American to the impact of language is being reflected in various ways. Within the past two years, there have been an increasing number of references by Negro writers and speakers to the *Through the Looking Glass* episode where Humpty Dumpty says: "When I use a word it means just what I choose it to mean—neither more nor less." "The question is," said Alice, "whether you can make words mean so many different

things." "The question is," said Humpty Dumpty, "which is to be master—that's all." The *Through the Looking Glass* episode was used by Lerone Bennett, Jr., in the November 1967 issue of *Ebony* to introduce his article dealing with whether black Americans should call themselves "Negroes," "Blacks," or "Afro-Americans." In a speech delivered January 16, 1967, to the students at Morgan State College, Stokely Carmichael prefaced a retelling of the above Lewis Carroll tale with: "It [definition] is very, very important because I believe that people who can define are masters." Carmichael went on to say: "So I say 'black power' and someone says 'you mean violence.' And they expect me to say, 'No, no. I don't mean violence, I don't mean that.' . . . I am master of my own terms. If black power means violence to you, that is your problem. . . . I know what it means in my mind. I will stand clear and you must understand that because the first need of a free people is to be able to define their own terms and have those terms recognized by their oppressors. . . . Camus says that when a slave says 'no' he begins to exist."

6   This concern for words and their implications in race relations was voiced also by Martin Luther King who pointed out that "even semantics have conspired to make that which is black seem ugly and degrading." Writing in his last book before his death, *Where Do We Go from Here: Chaos or Community?,* King said: "In Roget's Thesaurus there are some 120 synonyms for 'blackness' and at least 60 of them are offensive—such words as 'blot,' 'soot,' 'grime,' 'devil,' and 'foul.' There are some 134 synonyms for 'whiteness,' and all are favorable, expressed in such words as 'purity,' 'cleanliness,' 'chastity,' and 'innocence.' A white lie is better than a black lie. The most degenerate member of the family is the 'black sheep,' not the 'white sheep.'"

7   In March 1962, *The Negro History Bulletin* published an article by L. Eldridge Cleaver, then imprisoned in San Quentin, who devoted several pages to a discussion of the black American's acceptance of a white society's standards for beauty and to an analysis of the negative connotations of the term "black" and the positive connotations of the term "white." Cleaver tells black Americans that "what we must do is stop associating the Caucasian with these exalted connotations of the word *white* when we think or speak of him. At the same time, we must cease associating ourselves with the unsavory connotations of the word black." Cleaver makes an interesting point when he brings to our attention the term "non-white." He writes: "The very words that we use indicate that we have set a premium on the Caucasian ideal of beauty. When discussing inter-racial relations, we speak of 'white people' and 'non-white people.' Notice that that particular choice of words gives precedence to 'white people' by making them a center—a standard—to which 'non-white' bears a negative relation. Notice the different connotations when we turn around and say 'colored' and 'non-colored,' or 'black' or 'non-black.'"

8   Simon Podair, writing in the Fourth Quarter issue, 1956, of *Phylon*, examines the connotations of such words as "blackmail," "blacklist," "blackbook," "blacksheep," and "blackball." The assertion made by Podair that it has been white civilization which has attributed to the word "black" things undesirable and evil warrants brief examination.

He is correct when he asserts that "language as a potent force in our society goes beyond being merely a communicative device. Language not only expresses ideas and concepts but it may actually shape them. Often the process is completely unconscious, with the individual concerned unaware of the influence of the spoken or written expressions upon his thought processes. Language can thus become an instrument of both propaganda and indoctrination for a given idea." Further, Podair is correct in saying that "so powerful is the role of language in its imprint upon the human mind that even the minority group may begin to accept the very expressions that aid in its stereotyping. Thus, even Negroes may develop speech patterns filled with expressions leading to the strengthening of stereotypes." Podair's point is illustrated by the comments made by a Negro state official in Washington upon hearing of the shooting of Robert Kennedy. The Director of the Washington State Board Against Discrimination said: "This is a black day in our country's history." Immediately after uttering this statement with the negative connotation of "black," he declared that Robert Kennedy "is a hero in the eyes of black people — a champion of the oppressed — and we all pray for his complete recovery."

9   Although King, Cleaver, and Podair, and others who are concerned with the negative connotations of "black" in the white society are partially correct in their analysis, they have omitted in their discussions two points which by their omission effect an incomplete analysis. First, it is not quite accurate to say, as Podair has asserted, that the concepts of black as hostile, foreboding, wicked, and gloomy "cannot be considered accidental and undoubtedly would not exist in a society wherein whites were a minority. Historically, these concepts have evolved as a result of the need of the dominant group to maintain social and economic relationships on the basis of inequality if its hegemony was to survive." This is inaccurate because the terms "blackball," "blacklist," "blackbook," and "blackmail" did not evolve as "a result of the need of the dominant group to maintain social and economic relationships or. the basis of inequality if its hegemony was to survive." The origins of these terms are to be found in the sixteenth and seventeenth centuries in England where the terms were mostly based on the color of the book cover, the color of printing, or the color of the object from which the word got its meaning, as for instance the term "to blackball" coming from "the black ball" which centuries ago was a small black ball used as a vote against a person or thing. A "black-letter day" had its origin in the eighteenth century to designate an inauspicious day, as distinguished from a "red-letter day," The reference being to the old custom of marking the saint's days in the calendar with red letters.

10   More important, the assertion that the negative connotations of "black" and the positive connotations of "white" would not exist in a society wherein whites were a minority is not accurate. Centuries ago, before black societies ever saw white men, "black" often had negative connotations and "white" positive in those societies. T. O. Beidelman has made quite clear in his article "Swazi Royal Ritual," which appeared in the October 1966 issue of *Africa,* that black societies in southeast Africa, while attributing to black positive qualities,

can at the same time attribute to black negative qualities; the same applies to the color white. Beidelman writes that for the Swazi "darkness, as the 'covered' moon, is an ambiguous quality. Black symbolizes 'impenetrability of the future,' but also the 'sins and evils of the past year. . . .'" Black beads may symbolize marriage and wealth in cattle, but at the same time they can symbolize evil, disappointment, and misfortune. "The word *mnyama* means black and dark, but also means deep, profound, unfathomable, and even confused, dizzy, angry." To the Swazi, "that which is dark is unknown and ambiguous and dangerous, but it is also profound, latent with unknown meanings and possibilities." As for "white," *mhlophe* means to the Swazi "white, pale, pure, innocent, perfect, but this may also mean destitute and empty. The whiteness of the full moon, *inyanga isidindile,* relates to fullness; but this term *dinda* can also mean to be useless, simply because it refers to that which is fully exposed and having no further unknown potentialities."

11   What King, Cleaver, and Podair have failed to do in their discussions of the negative connotations of "black" and the positive connotations of "white" is to point out that in black societies "black" often connotes that which is hostile, foreboding, and gloomy; and "white" has symbolized purity and divinity. Furthermore, in white societies, "white" has numerous negative connotations: white livered (cowardly), white flag (surrender), white elephant (useless), white plague (tuberculosis), white wash (conceal), white feather (cowardice), *et cetera.* The ugliness and terror associated with the color white are portrayed by Melville in the chapter "the Whiteness of the Whale" in *Moby Dick.* At the beginning of the chapter, Melville says: "It was the whiteness of the whale that above all things appalled me."

12   What I am suggesting here is that the Negro writers, while legitimately concerned with the words and phrases which perpetuate racism in the United States have, at least in their analysis of the term "black," presented a partial analysis. This is not to say, however, that most of the analysis is not valid as far as it goes. Podair is entirely correct when he writes: "In modern American life language has become a fulcrum of prejudice as regards Negro-white relationships. Its effect has been equally potent upon the overt bigot as well as the confused member of the public who is struggling to overcome conscious or unconscious hostility towards minority groups. In the case of the Negro, language concepts have supported misconceptions and disoriented the thinking of many on the question of race and culture." Not only has the Negro become trapped by these "language concepts," but so too have the whites who, unlike the blacks, have demonstrated very little insight into the language of white racism and whose "language concepts" have "supported misconceptions and disoriented the thinking of many on the question of race and culture."

13   The Negroes' increased understanding and sensitivity to language as it is related to them demands that white Americans follow suit with a similar understanding and sensitivity which they have not yet demonstrated too well. During the 1960's, at a time when black Americans have been attempting more than ever to communicate with whites, through speeches, marches, sit-ins, demonstrations, through violence

and nonviolence, the barriers of communication between blacks and whites seem to be almost as divisive as they have been in the past one hundred years, no thanks to the whites. One has only to watch the TV panelists, blacks and whites, discussing the black American's protest and his aspirations, to see the facial expressions of the black panelists when a white on the panel speaks of "our colored boys in Vietnam." The black panelists knowingly smile at the racist phrasing and it is not difficult to understand the skepticism and suspicion which the blacks henceforth will maintain toward the white panelist who offends with "our colored boys in Vietnam." "Our colored boys in Vietnam" is a close relation to "our colored people" and "our colored," phrases which communicate more to the black American listener than intended by the white speaker. John Howard Griffin has pointed out something that applies not only to Southern whites, but to white Americans generally: "A great many of us Southern whites have grown up using an expression that Negroes can hardly bear to hear and yet tragically enough we use it because we believe it. It's an expression that we use when we say how much we love, what we patronizingly call 'our Negroes.'" The white American who talks of "our colored boys in Vietnam" offends the Negro triply; first, by referring to the black American men as "our" which is, as Griffin points out, patronizing; second, by using the nineteenth century term "colored"; third, by referring to the black American men as "boys."

14   Most whites, if not all, know that "nigger" and "boy" are offensive to the Negro; in fact, such language could be classified as "fighting words." But the insensitive and offensive whites continue today to indulge in expressing their overt and covert prejudices by using these obviously derogatory terms. Running a series of articles on racism in athletics, *Sports Illustrated* quoted a Negro football player as saying: "The word was never given bluntly; usually it took the form of a friendly, oblique talk with one of the assistant coaches. I remember one time one of the coaches came to me and said, '[Head Coach] Jim Owens loves you boys. We know you get a lot of publicity, but don't let it go to your head.' Hell, when he said 'Jim Owens loves you boys,' I just shut him off. That did it. I knew what he was talking about." An athletic director at one of the larger Southwestern Universities, discussing how much sports have done for the Negro, declared: "In general, the nigger athlete is a little hungrier and we have been blessed with having some real outstanding ones. We think they've done a lot for us, and we think we've done a lot for them" (*Sports Illustrated*, July 1, 1968). One of the Negro athletes said of the coaching personnel at the same university: "They can pronounce Negro if they want to. *They can pronounce it*. But I think it seems like such a little thing to them. The trouble with them is they're not thinking of the Negro and how he feels. Wouldn't you suppose that if there was one word these guys that live off Negroes would get rid of, one single word in the whole vocabulary, it would be *nigger*?" (*Sports Illustrated*, July 15, 1968). When a newspaperman tried to get the attention of Elvin Hayes, star basketball player at the University of Houston, the reporter shouted, "Hey, boy!" Hayes turned to the reporter and said: "Boy's on *Tarzan*. Boy plays on *Tarzan*. I'm no boy. I'm 22 years old.

I worked hard to become a man. I don't call you boy." The reporter apologized and said: "I didn't mean anything by it" (*Sports Illustrated,* July 1, 1968).

15   Whites who would never think of referring to Negroes as "boy" or "nigger" do, however, reveal themselves through less obviously racist language. A day does not go by without one hearing, from people who should know better, about "the Negro problem," a phrase which carries with it the implication that the Negro is a problem. One is reminded of the Nazis talking about "the Jewish problem." There was no Jewish problem! Yet the phrase carried the implication that the Jews were a problem in Germany and hence being a problem invited a solution and the solution Hitler proposed and carried out was the "final solution." Even the most competent writers fall into the "Negro problem" trap; James Reston of the *New York Times* wrote on April 7, 1968: "When Gunnar Myrdal, the Swedish social philosopher who has followed the Negro problem in American for forty years, came back recently, he felt that a great deal had changed for the better, but concluded that we have greatly underestimated the scope of the Negro problem." Myrdal himself titled his 1944 classic work *The American Dilemma: The Negro Problem and Modern Democracy.* A book published in 1967, *The Negro in 20th Century America,* by John Hope Franklin and Isidore Starr, starts off in the Table of Contents with "Book One: *The Negro Problem*"; the foreword begins, "The Negro problem was selected because it is one of the great case studies in man's never-ending fight for equal rights." One of the selections in the book, a debate in which James Baldwin participates, has Baldwin's debate opponent saying that "the Negro problem is a very complicated one." There are several indications that from here on out the black American is no longer going to accept the phrase "the Negro problem." As Lerone Bennett, Jr., said in the August 1965 issue of *Ebony,* "there is no Negro problem in America. The problem of race in America, insofar as that problem is related to packets of melanin in men's skins, is a white problem." In 1966, the editors of *Ebony* published a book of essays dealing with American black-white relations entitled *The WHITE Problem in America.* It is difficult to imagine Negroes sitting around during the next decade talking about "the Negro problem," just as it is difficult to imagine Jews in 1939 referring to themselves as "the Jewish problem."

16   The racial brainwashing of whites in the United States leads them to utter such statements as "You don't sound like a Negro" or "Well, he didn't sound like a Negro to me." John Howard Griffin, who changed the color of his skin from white to black to find out what it meant to be black in America, was ashamed to admit that he thought he could not pass for a Negro because he "didn't know how to speak Negro." "There is an illusion in this land," said Griffin, "that unless you sound as though you are reading Uncle Remus you couldn't possibly have an authentic Negro dialect. But I don't know what we've been using for ears because you don't have to be in the Negro community five minutes before the truth strikes, and the truth is that there are just as many speech patterns in the Negro community as there are in any other, particularly in areas of rigid segregation where your right

shoulder may be touching the shoulder of a Negro PhD and your left
shoulder the shoulder of the disadvantaged." A black American, when
told that he does not "sound like a Negro," legitimately can ask his
white conversationalist, "What does a Negro sound like?" This will
probably place the white in a dilemma for he will either have to admit
that sounding like a Negro means sounding like Prissy in *Gone With
the Wind* ("Who dat say who dat when you say dat?") or that perhaps
there is no such thing as "sounding like a Negro." Goodman Ace, writing in the July 27, 1968, issue of the *Saturday Review*, points out that
years ago radio program planners attempted to write Negroes into the
radio scripts, portraying the Negro as something else besides janitors,
household maids, and train porters. Someone suggested that in the
comedy radio show *Henry Aldrich* Henry might have among his
friends a young Negro boy, without belaboring the point that the boy
was Negro. As Mr. Ace observes, "just how it would be indicated on
radio that the boy is black was not mentioned. Unless he was to be
named Rufus or Rastus." Unless, it might be added, he was to be
made to "sound like a Negro."

17   Psychiatrist Frantz Fanon, who begins his *Black Skin, White Masks*
with a chapter titled "The Negro and Language," explains the manner
of many whites when talking to Negroes and the effects of this manner. Although he is writing about white Europeans, what Fanon says
applies equally to white Americans. He points out that most whites
"talk down" to the Negro, and this "talking down" is, in effect, telling
the Negro, "You'd better keep your place." Fanon writes: "A white
man addressing a Negro behaves exactly like an adult with a child
and starts smirking, whispering, patronizing, cozening." The effect of
the whites' manner of speaking to the Negro "makes him angry, because he himself is a pidgin-nigger-talker." "But I will be told," says
Fanon, "there is no wish, no intention to anger him. I grant this; but
it is just this absence of wish, this lack of interest, this indifference,
this automatic manner of classifying him, imprisoning him, primitiviz-
ing him, decivilizing him, that makes him angry." If a doctor greets
his Negro patient with "You not feel good, no?" or "G'morning pal.
Where's it hurt? Huh? Lemme see—belly ache? Heart pain?" the
doctor feels perfectly justified in speaking that way, writes Fanon,
when in return the patient answers in the same fashion; the doctor
can then say to himself, "You see? I wasn't kidding you. That's just
the way they are." To make the Negro talk pidgin, as Fanon observes,
"is to fasten him to the effigy of him, to snare him, to imprison him,
the eternal victim of an essence, of an *appearance* for which he is not
responsible. And naturally, just as a Jew who spends money without
thinking about it is suspect, a black man who quotes Montesquieu
had better be watched." The whites, in effect, encourage the stereotype of the Negro; they perpetuate the stereotype through the manner
in which they speak about and speak to Negroes. And if Fanon is
correct, the whites by "talking down" to the Negro are telling that
black American citizen to "remember where you come from!"

18   Another facet of the racism of the whites' language is reflected in
their habit of referring to talented and great writers, athletes, enter-

tainers, and clergymen as "a great Negro singer" or "a great black poet" or "a great Negro ball player." What need is there for whites to designate the color or race of the person who has excelled? Paul Robeson and Marian Anderson are great and talented singers. James Baldwin and LeRoi Jones are talented writers. Why must the whites qualify the greatness of these individuals with "black" or "colored" or "Negro"? Fanon briefly refers to this predilection of whites to speak with this qualification:

> . . . Charles-André Julien introducing Aimé Césaire as "a Negro poet with a university degree," or again, quite simply, the expression, "a great black poet."
>
> These ready-made phrases, which seem in a common-sense way to fill a need—for Aimé Césaire is really black and a poet—have a hidden subtlety, a permanent rub. I know nothing of Jean Paulhan except that he writes very interesting books; I have no idea how old Roger Caillois is, since the only evidence I have of his existence are the books of his that streak across my horizon. And let no one accuse me of affective allergies; what I am trying to say is that there is no reason why André Breton should say of Césaire, "Here is a black man who handles the French language as no white man today can."

19   The tendency to designate and identify a person as a Negro when the designation is not necessary carries over into newspaper and magazine reporting of crimes. There was no need for *Time* magazine (July 19, 1968) to designate the race of the individual concerned in the following *Time* report: "In New York City, slum dwellers were sent skidding for cover when Bobby Rogers, 31, Negro superintendent of a grubby South Bronx tenement, sprayed the street with bullets from a sawed-off .30 cal. semiautomatic carbine, killing three men and wounding a fourth." *Time,* for whatever reason, designated the race of the person involved in this instance, but the reports on other criminal offences cited by *Time,* on the same page, did not indicate the race of the "suspects." As a label of primary potency, "Negro" stands out over "superintendent." The assumption that whites can understand and sympathize with the Negro's dismay when black "suspects" are identified by race and white "suspects" are not, is apparently an unwarranted assumption; or it may be possible that the whites *do* understand the dismay and precisely for that reason continue to designate the race of the black criminal suspect. To argue that if the race is not designated in the news story then the reader can assume that the suspected criminal is white, is not acceptable for it makes all the difference if the suspect is identified as "a Negro superintendent," "a white superintendent," or "a superintendent." If we were told, day in and day out, that "a *white* bank clerk embezzled" or "a *white* service station operator stole" or "a *white* unemployed laborer attacked," it would make a difference in the samė sense that it makes a difference to identify the criminal suspect as "Negro" or "black."

20   If many Negroes find it hard to understand why whites have to designate a great writer or a great artist or a common criminal as "colored" or "Negro," so too do many Negroes find it difficult to

understand why whites must designate a Negro woman as a "Negress." Offensive as "Negress" is to most blacks, many whites still insist on using the term. In a July 28, 1968, *New York Times Magazine*
article, the writer, discussing the 1968 campaigning of Rockefeller and
Nixon, wrote: "A fat Negress on the street says, passionately, 'Rocky!
Rocky!'" As Gordon Allport has written in *The Nature of Prejudice,*
"members of minority groups are often understandably sensitive to
names given them. Not only do they object to deliberately insulting
epithets, but sometimes see evil intent where none exists." Allport
gives two examples to make his point: one example is the spelling of
the word "Negro" with a small "n" and the other example is the word
"Negress." "Sex differentiations are objectionable," writes Allport,
"since they seem doubly to emphasize ethnic differences: why speak
of Jewess and not of Protestantess, or of Negress, and not of whitess?"
Just as "Jewess" is offensive to the Jews, so too is "Negress" offensive
to the Negroes. "A Negro woman" does not carry the same connotations as "Negress," the latter conveying an emotional emphasis on
both the color and sex of the individual. *Webster's New World Dictionary of the American Language* says of "Negress": "A Negro woman or
girl: often a patronizing or contemptuous term."

21   When the newspaper reporter tried to get the attention of twenty-
two-year-old basketball star Elvin Hayes by shouting, "Hey, boy!"
and Hayes vigorously objected to being called "boy," the reporter
apologized and said: "I didn't mean anything by it." In a few cases,
a very few cases, white Americans indeed "didn't mean anything by
it." That excuse, however, will no longer do. The whites must make a
serious conscious effort to discard the racist clichés of the past, the
overt and covert language of racism. "Free, white, and 21" or "That's
white of you" are phrases whites can no longer indulge in. Asking
white Americans to change their language, to give up some of their
clichés, is disturbing enough, since the request implies a deficiency in
the past use of that language; asking that they discard the language
of racism is also disturbing, because the people being asked to make
the change, in effect, are being told that they have been the perpetrators and perpetuators of racism. Finally, and most important, calling
the Negro "nigger" or "boy," or "speaking down" to the Negro, gives
Whitey a linguistic power over the victimized black American, a power
most whites are unwilling or afraid to give up. A person's language is
an extension of himself and to attack his use of language is to attack
him. With the language of racism, this is exactly the point, for the language of white racism and the racism of the whites are almost one and
the same. Difficult and painful as it may be for whites to discard their
racist terms, phrases, and clichés, it must be done before blacks and
whites can discuss seriously the eradication of white racism.

Discussion of Theme

1. Why does Bosmajian object to the phrase "the Negro problem"?
   Why is it inappropriate?

2. What examples from your own speech can you cite that suggest, even subtly, racial overtones?
3. If, following the author's suggestion, a group of white leaders met to talk not about Negroes but about themselves, what topics might they discuss to alleviate racial tension?
4. According to this essay, what changes in language would occur if whites were a minority?
5. Have black demands, demonstrations, and marches failed as instruments of communication with whites? If so, why?

Discussion of Rhetoric

1. Why does the author repeatedly use the term "whitey"? Is he trying to offend his white readers? Or is there another purpose?
2. What audience does Bosmajian have in mind for this article: white or black, prejudiced or nonprejudiced? What evidence can you cite to support your answer?
3. How would you describe the tone of the author's language? Is he dispassionate or emotional in his argument?
4. Why are there so many quotations in this article? Do they detract from, or add to, the central thesis?
5. What are the connotations of the following terms: "colored"; "black"; "noncolored." Are there parallel terms referring to whites?

Writing Assignments

1. Develop the following title into an effective theme: "The White Problem in America."
2. Write a theme illustrating and developing the following quotation, taken from this selection (paragraph 21): "A person's language is an extension of himself and to attack his use of language is to attack him."
3. Should every college student be required to take courses in black studies? Present your views in a theme.

Vocabulary

(1) ERADICATE   pull up by the roots; destroy completely
(1) INUNDATED   flooded; overwhelmed by
(2) PATHOLOGY   abnormality; disease
(12) FULCRUM   prop; support

(12) OVERT   open; visible
(14) DEROGATORY   degrading
(15) MELANIN   dark pigment
(17) COZENING   deceiving; beguiling
(17) PIDGIN   a dialect or jargon

The American Scene

2

Cesar Chavez (1927–   ) has been active in the unionization of migrant workers in the West and Southwest for the last several years. An official in the United Farm Workers Organizing Committee, he has frequently been arrested for his participation in strikes and demonstrations.

As its title suggests, the following essay contains proposals for the redistribution of wealth in this country, as well as for the granting of political power to the dispossessed.

CESAR CHAVEZ

Sharing the Wealth

1 How can we narrow the gap between the wealthy and the poor in this country? What concrete steps can be taken *now* to abolish poverty in America? There are a number of things that the President [Nixon] could do immediately, if he wanted to: He could improve the lot of *all* the farmworkers in the Southwest—easily, under existing legislation—by putting an end to the importing and exploitation of cheap foreign labor. The Immigration Service has allowed almost 500,000 poor Mexicans to flood across the border since 1965. Absorbing this number of resident aliens would not be detrimental if they actually became residents, but most of these workers return to Mexico after each harvest season, since their American wages go much farther there than they would in this country. They have no stake in either economic or political advances here; it is the domestic farmworker who wants our union, who wants better schools, who wants to participate in the political system. Our poor Mexican brothers who are allowed to come across the border for the harvest are tools in the Government's and the growers' attempts to break our strike.

2   In the still larger framework of all the country's poor, the President should acknowledge that the War on Poverty programs of the Sixties have failed. The Office of Economic Opportunity pumped out propaganda about "community action programs" through which the poor were supposedly going to have a say in the solution of their own problems. Then, just as the communities were organizing for meaningful change through these programs, the money was suddenly yanked away. Washington seemed to realize that if it lived up to its rhetoric, it would actually be encouraging real political participation and building real economic power among the poor, and got cold feet. The Government and the power class will never allow their money to be used to build another power class — especially if they are convinced, however wrongly, that their own economic security and self-interest would be jeopardized.

3   It might be expected for me to propose that the anti-poverty programs be continued — but with better financing and with complete control over them given to representatives of the communities and the people involved. I could also plead for the money that has been spent in the past few years on anti-poverty programs to be simply distributed among the poor. But neither of these sensible alternatives is going to come to pass under an Administration that made it perfectly clear last fall that it intended to channel all Federal funds through local governments, no matter how corrupt.

4   Nothing is going to happen until we, the poor, can generate our own political and economic power. Such a statement sounds radical to many middle-class Americans, but it should not. Though many of the poor have come to see the affluent middle class as its enemy, that class actually stands between the poor and the real powers in this society — the administrative octopus with its head in Washington, the conglomerates, the military complex. It's like a camel train: The herder, way up in front, leads one camel and all the other camels follow. We happen to be the last camel, trudging along through the leavings of the whole train. We see only the camel in front of us and make him the target of our anger, but that solves nothing. The lower reaches of the middle class, in turn, are convinced that blacks, Mexican Americans, Puerto Ricans, Indians, and poor whites want to steal their jobs — a conviction that the power class cheerfully perpetuates. The truth of the matter is that, even with automation, there can still be enough good-paying jobs for *everyone* in this country. If all of us were working for decent wages, there would be a greater demand for goods and services, thus creating even more jobs and increasing the gross national product. Full and fair employment would also mean that taxes traceable to welfare and all the other hidden costs of poverty — presently borne most heavily by middle-income whites — would inevitably go down.

5   At one time, we would have searched for ways to bring about a direct change in the course of the camel driver. That was the situation in the Thirties, when President Roosevelt initiated such massive programs as the Works Progress Administration and the Civilian Conservation Corps. At that time, *most* Americans were poor, white and

nonwhite alike; but most were white. The union movement was fighting to win gains for its members, then an underclass. (Now it feels it has to fight to protect the economic independence it has since achieved.) And there was only a relatively small upper class trying to frustrate change. But today the majority of Americans — most of them still white — are relatively well off financially. The country's policies naturally respond to the desires of the majority, and that majority — having joined the comfortable middle class — is no longer motivated to eliminate poverty.

6   The forces in control today at the top, furthermore, are so immense, powerful, and interlocked that it would be absurd to expect dramatic change from them. The Pentagon, for example, has a hand-in-glove relationship with the same industrialists who manufacture tractors, reapers, and mechanical grape harvesters. How can we expect the Defense Department to do anything *but* undermine our battle with the growers? The poor today, finally, are not only impoverished; most of them are also members of minority races. Thus, as a class, we are racially as well as economically alienated from the mainstream.

7   Despite this alienation, however, and despite the magnitude of the forces opposing us, the poor have tremendous potential economic power, as unlikely as that may seem. That power can derive from two facts of life: First, even though our numbers are much smaller than they were in the Thirties, we are still a sizable group — some 30,000,000. Perhaps even more important, we have a strong sense of common indignation; the poor always identify with one another more than do the rich. What instruments can we use to win this power? Perhaps the most effective technique is the boycott. Most Americans realize that the black civil rights revolution of the late Fifties and early Sixties effectively began with Dr. Martin Luther King's successful bus boycott in Montgomery, Alabama. This tool is being perfected, for blacks, by the Reverend Jesse Jackson in Chicago. Our own nationwide grape boycott is hurting corporate agriculture so much that the growers are eventually going to have to deal with us, no matter how hard the power class tries to weaken the boycott's effectiveness.

8   Another powerful tool is the strike. Attacking the unions is fashionable today, but the labor movement, for all its faults, is one of the few institutions in the country that I see even trying to reach down to us. The universities, thanks to some student organizations, and the churches, thanks to a few radical groups, are the only other institutions making a real attempt to alleviate our plight. With their help, we farmworkers are now trying to build our own union, a new kind of union that will actively include people rather than exclude them. A man is a man and needs an organization even when — in fact, especially when — a machine displaces him. The poor are also beginning to experiment with cooperatives of all kinds and with their own credit unions — that is, with the creation of our own institutions, the profits from which can go to us rather than to the wealthy. And, at least in the Southwest, we are looking at ways to give the farmworkers plots of land they can call their own, because we know that power always comes with landownership.

9   We need greater control of important noneconomic institutions, too. We have very little to say, for example, about the attitude of our churches to economic and political problems. We are looking for ways to get the church involved in the struggle, to make it relevant to our needs. The poor also need control of their schools and medical facilities and legal defenses; but these advances are all subsidiary, in my opinion, to the need for developing strictly economic power. Economic power has to precede political power. Gandhi understood this when, in 1930, he and his followers resolved to defy the British government's salt monopoly by making their own salt from the sea; this boycott was one of the crucial steps in the Indian fight for independence. We, the poor of the United States, have not yet hit upon the specific issue around which we can bring all of our boycotting and striking capabilities to bear. But we will.

10   The poor are badly prepared to participate in the political arena. Entire nations of us, such as the American Indians, have never had more than token representation in Federal, state, county or city government. Migratory farmworkers are almost always disenfranchised by voter-registration residency requirements. Minority immigrants face long waits for citizenship papers and the additional barrier of literacy tests. And even if they qualify, it is prohibitively expensive for many of the poor to vote. A farmworker putting in long hours simply can't afford to take half or all of a weekday off to travel to the polls.

11   In a society that truly desired full participation, all 18-year-olds and convicts would be given the franchise; the whole practice of voter registration would be scrapped; immigrants would automatically be given a citizenship certificate at the end of one year if their record was clean, whether or not they were literate in English or in their own language; elections would last up to 72 hours and would include Saturdays and Sundays.

12   These are some of the simpler things that could be done to increase participation. But they aren't being done and they won't be done unless the poor can change the political *status quo*. Our vote simply doesn't matter that much today. Once we give it away, we lose it because we can't control the men we elect. We help elect liberals and then they pass civil rights bills that defuse our boycotts and strikes, taking the steam out of our protest but leaving the basic problems of injustice and inequality unsolved. Or, worse, we elect a candidate who says he will represent us and then discover that he has sold out to some special interest.

13   I propose two reforms that would go a long way toward a cure. First, the whole system of campaign financing should make it as easy for a poor man as for a millionaire to put his case before the people. Second, the various minority groups—as well as such pockets of poor whites as the Appalachians, who make up a distinct economic subculture—should be given a proportionate number of seats in every governing body affecting them. Black people should have 43 or 44 seats in the House of Representatives and 10 or 11 seats in the Senate. In California, where ten percent of the population is Mexican American, eight seats in the state assembly should be set aside for us; there is now

only one Mexican American assemblyman. This same procedure should be followed all the way down the line, through the county level down to the school and water districts. In each case, the electorate would be allowed to vote for whomever they pleased — even if he weren't of the same race as the majority of voters — but the representative would clearly be an advocate of their needs. Though this system may seem alien to many Americans, something like it already works in the cities, where tickets are often drawn up to reflect the racial balance of the community. And the idea of special representation for minority political groups is common in foreign countries. Once the minority group or the economic subculture is completely assimilated, of course, the need for special representation will wither away.

14   These are the kinds of reforms we will work for once we have an economic base established; they certainly aren't going to come about as long as we remain powerless. But we will remain powerless until we help ourselves. I know that there are men of good conscience in the affluent society who are trying to help. Many of them are middle-class people who remember the Depression, or unionists who wear scars of the battle to liberate workingmen. They are like a large army of guerrillas within the establishment. We are depending on them to hear our cry, to respect our picket lines, and to support our grape boycott, the Reverend Ralph Abernathy's Poor People's Campaign, and the Reverend Jesse Jackson's Operation Breadbasket. And we hope that they will understand how crucial it is that the vote become truly universal. As long as democracy exists mainly as a catchword in politicians' speeches, the hopes for *real* democracy will be mocked.

15   In the final analysis, however, it doesn't really matter what the political system is; ultimately, the results are the same, whether you have a general, a king, a dictator, or a civilian president running the country. We don't need perfect political systems; we need perfect participation. If you don't participate in the planning, you just don't count. Until the chance for political participation is there, we who are poor will continue to attack the soft part of the American system — its economic structure. We will build power through boycotts, strikes, new unions — whatever techniques we can develop. These attacks on the *status quo* will come not because we hate but because we know America *can* construct a humane society for all of its citizens — and that if it does not, there will be chaos.

16   But it must be understood that once we have substantial economic power — and the political power that follows in its wake — our work will not be done. We will then move on to effect even more fundamental changes in this society. The quality of compassion seems to have vanished from the American spirit. The power class and the middle class haven't done anything that one can truly be proud of, aside from machines and rockets. It's amazing how people can get so excited about a rocket to the moon and not give a damn about smog, oil leaks, the devastation of the environment with pesticides, hunger, disease. When the poor share some of the power that the affluent now monopolize, we *will* give a damn.

Discussion of Theme

1. What "tools" does Chavez accuse the government and the growers of using as strike-breaking techniques? How do these accomplish their purpose?
2. According to Chavez, what caused the failure of the various poverty programs in the 1960s? Why does he doubt that similar programs can succeed today?
3. Why do the blue-collar workers fear racial minorities and poor whites? Is their fear based purely on economics? What does Chavez propose as a remedy for this fear?
4. What factors give the poor "tremendous potential economic power"? What instruments can they use to gain it?
5. What must the poor do to bring about the necessary changes in our society, according to Chavez? Are his proposals practical?

Discussion of Rhetoric

1. What device does Chavez use at the outset to capture the reader's attention?
2. Where does he state his thesis? Where is his solution to the problem stated?
3. This article advances controversial proposals, yet does not support them with facts, data, and other "hard" information. What, then, is his argument based on? Is it convincing?
4. Describe the diction in this selection. What does it say about the writer?

Writing Assignments

1. Develop the following statement taken from this article into a theme: "The quality of compassion seems to have vanished from the American spirit."
2. What are the arguments for (or against) community control of schools, the police, medical facilities, and legal defense?
3. Chavez would like to change campaign procedures to make it possible for poor persons to run for public office. Do you agree? What changes do you recommend in our current system of selecting public officials?

Library Exploration

1. Cesar Chavez has been the subject of many magazine articles and books. Prepare a report on one of these.
2. Chavez singled out Mahatma Ghandi as having had an influence on him. Investigate the teachings of this great Indian advocate of nonviolence.

3. Read about the activities of Reverend Ralph Abernathy and his Poor People's Campaign, and Reverend Jesse Jackson and his Operation Breadbasket.
4. Learn what you can about the laws in your state regarding migrant workers: wages, living conditions, and child labor.
5. The following books deal with the subject of this essay: *The Other America,* by Michael Harrington; *Poverty, America's Enduring Paradox,* by Sidney Lens; *They Harvest Despair,* by Dale Wright.

Vocabulary

(9) SUBSIDIARY secondary; subordinate to

(11) FRANCHISE the right to vote

Dylan Thomas (1914–53), widely regarded as the greatest lyric poet of his generation, was born in Wales and virtually self-educated. He was a successful short-story writer, novelist, poet, and radio scriptwriter. "Collected Poems" (1953) and two posthumous prose works, "Quite Early One Morning" (1954) and "Adventures in the Skin Trade" (1955), are among his most significant works. Recordings of the last two works in Thomas's own voice are still available.

The following is one of the lectures given by Thomas in 1953 on his last tour of the United States. It reflects his growing distaste for such performances and for the "lecture tour" in its peculiarly American form.

DYLAN THOMAS

A Visit to America

1 Across the United States of America, from New York to California and back, glazed, again, for many months of the year, there streams and sings for its heady supper a dazed and prejudiced procession of European lecturers, scholars, sociologists, economists, writers, authorities on this and that and even, in theory, on the United States of America. And, breathlessly between addresses and receptions, in 'planes and trains and boiling hotel bedroom ovens, many of these attempt to keep journals and diaries.

2 At first, confused and shocked by shameless profusion and almost shamed by generosity, unaccustomed to such importance as they are assumed, by their hosts, to possess, and up against the barrier of a common language, they write in their notebooks like demons, general-

ising away, on character and culture and the American political scene. But, towards the middle of their middle-aged whisk through middle-western clubs and universities, the fury of the writing flags; their spirits are lowered by the spirit with which they are everywhere strongly greeted and which, in everincreasing doses, they themselves lower; and they begin to mistrust themselves, and their reputations — for they have found, too often, that an audience will receive a lantern-lecture on, say, Ceramics, with the same uninhibited enthusiasm that it accorded the very week before to a paper on the Modern Turkish Novel. And, in their diaries, more and more do such entries appear as, "No way of escape!" or "Buffalo!" or "I am beaten," until at last they cannot write a word. And, twittering all over, old before their time, with eyes like rissoles in the sand, they are helped up the gangway of the homebound liner by kind bosom friends (of all kinds and bosoms) who boister them on the back, pick them up again, thrust bottles, sonnets, cigars, addresses, into their pockets, have a farewell party in their cabin, pick them up again, and, snickering and yelping, are gone: to wait at the dockside for another boat from Europe and another batch of fresh, green lecturers.

3   There they go, every spring, from New York to Los Angeles: exhibitionists, polemicists, histrionic publicists, theological rhetoricians, historical hoddy-doddies, balletomanes, ulterior decorators, windbags and bigwigs and humbugs, men in love with stamps, men in love with steaks, men after millionaires' widows, men with elephantiasis of the reputation (huge trunks and teeny minds), authorities on gas, bishops, best-sellers, editors looking for writers, writers looking for publishers, publishers looking for dollars, existentialists, serious physicists with nuclear missions, men from the B.B.C. who speak as though they had the Elgin marbles in their mouths, potboiling philosophers, professional Irishmen (very lepri-corny), and, I am afraid, fat poets with slim volumes.

4   And see, too, in that linguaceous stream, the tall monocled men, smelling of saddle soap and club armchairs, their breath a nice blending of whisky and fox's blood, with big protruding upper-class tusks and county moustaches, presumably invented in England and sent abroad to advertise *Punch,* who lecture to women's clubs on such unlikely subjects as "The History of Etching in the Shetland Islands"; and the brassy-bossy men-women, with corrugated-iron perms, and hippo hides, who come, self-announced, as "ordinary British housewives," to talk to rich minked chunks of American matronhood about the iniquity of the Health Services, the criminal sloth of the miners, the *visible* tail and horns of Mr. Aneurin Bevan, and the fear of everyone in England to go out alone at night because of the organised legions of coshboys against whom the police are powerless owing to the refusal of those in power to equip them with revolvers and to flog to ribbons every adolescent offender on any charge at all.

5   And there shiver and teeter also, meek and driven, those British authors unfortunate enough to have written, after years of unadventurous forgotten work, one bad novel which became enormously popular on both sides of the Atlantic. At home, when success first hit them,

they were mildly delighted; a couple of literary luncheons went sugar-tipsy to their heads, like the washing sherry served before those luncheons; and perhaps, as the lovely money rolled lushly in, they began to dream, in their moony writers' way, of being able to retire to the country, keep wasps (or was it bees?) and never write another lousy word. But in come the literary agent's triggermen and the publisher's armed narks: "You must go to the States and make a Personal Appearance. Your novel is *killing* them over there, and we're not surprised either. You must go round the States lecturing to women." And the inoffensive writers, who have never dared lecture anyone, let alone women—they are frightened of women, they do not understand women, they write about women as creatures that never existed, and the women lap it up—these sensitive plants cry out, "But what shall we lecture about?" "The English Novel." "I don't read novels." "Great Women in Fiction." "I don't like fiction *or* women." But off they are wafted, firstclass, in the plush bowels of the *Queen Victoria,* with a list of engagements long as a New York menu or a half-hour with a book by Charles Morgan, and soon they are losing their little cold-as-goldfish paw in the great general glutinous handshake of a clutch of enveloping hostesses.

6 I think, by the way, that it was Enrest Raymond, the author of *Tell England,* who once made a journey round the American women's clubs, being housed and entertained at each small town he stopped at, by the richest and largest and furriest lady available. On one occasion he stopped at some little station and was met, as usual, by an enormous motor-car full of a large horn-rimmed business-man—looking exactly like a large horn-rimmed business-man on the films—and his roly-poly pearly wife. Mr. Raymond sat with her in the back of the car, and off they went, the husband driving. At once, she began to say how utterly delighted she and her husband and the committee were to have him at their Women's Literary and Social Guild, and to compliment him on his books. "I don't think I've ever, in all my life, enjoyed a book so much as *Sorrel and Son,*" she said. "What you don't know about human nature! I think Sorrel is one of the most beautiful characters ever portrayed."

7 Ernest Raymond let her talk on, while he stared, embarrassed, in front of him. All he could see were the three double chins that her husband wore at the back of his neck. On and on she gushed in praise of *Sorrel and Son* until he could stand it no longer. "I quite agree with you," he said. "A beautiful book indeed. But I'm afraid I didn't write *Sorrel and Son.* It was written by an old friend of mine, Mr. Warwick Deeping." And the large horn-rimmed double-chinned husband at the wheel said without turning: "Caught again, Emily."

8 See the garrulous others, also, gabbing and garlanded from one nest of culture-vultures to another: people selling the English way of life and condemning the American way as they swig and guzzle through it; people resurrecting the theories of surrealism for the benefit of remote parochial female audiences who did not know it was dead, not having ever known it had been alive; people talking about Etruscan pots and pans to a bunch of dead pans and wealthy pots in Boston.

And there, too, in the sticky thick of lecturers moving across the continent black with clubs, go the foreign poets, catarrhal troubadours, lyrical one-night-standers, dollar-mad nightingales, remittance-bards from at home, myself among them booming with the worst.

9   Did we pass one another, *en route,* all unknowing, I wonder; one of us spry-eyed, with clean, white lectures and a soul he could call his own, going bouyantly west to his remunerative doom in the great State University factories; another returning dog-eared as his clutch of poems and his carefully-typed impromptu asides? I ache for us both. There one goes, unsullied as yet, in his pullman pride, toying — oh boy! — with a blunderbuss bourbon, being smoked by a large cigar, riding out to the wide open spaces of the faces of his waiting audience. He carries, besides his literary baggage, a new, dynamic razor, just on the market, bought in New York, which operates at the flick of a thumb but cuts the thumb to the bone; a tin of new shaving-lather which is worked with the other, unbleeding, thumb, and covers not only the face but the whole bathroom and, instantly freezing, makes an arctic, icicled cave from which it takes two sneering bellboys to extract him; and, of course, a nylon shirt. This, he dearly believes from the advertisements, he can himself wash in his hotel, hang to dry overnight, and put on, without ironing, in the morning. (In my case, no ironing was needed, for, as someone cruelly pointed out in print, I looked anyway like an unmade bed.)

10   He is vigorously welcomed at the station by an earnest crew-cut platoon of giant collegiates, all chasing the butterfly culture with net, notebook, poison-bottle, pin and label, each with at least thirty-six terribly white teeth, and nursed away, as heavily gently as though he were an imbecile rich aunt with a short prospect of life, into a motor-car in which, for a mere fifty miles or so travelled at poet-breaking speed, he assures them of the correctness of their assumption that he is half-witted by stammering inconsequential answers in an over-British accent to the genial questions about what international conference Stephen Spender might be attending at the moment, or the reactions of British poets to the work of a famous American whose name he did not know or catch. He is then taken to a small party of only a few hundred people all of whom hold the belief that what a visiting lecturer needs before he trips on to the platform is just enough martinis so that he can trip off the platform as well. And, clutching his explosive glass, he is soon contemptuously dismissing, in a flush of ignorance and fluency, the poetry of those androgynous literary ladies with three names who produce a kind of verbal ectoplasm to order as a waiter dishes up spaghetti — only to find that the fiercest of these, a wealthy huntress of small, seedy lions (such as himself), who stalks the middle-western bush with ears and rifle cocked, is his hostess for the evening. Of the lecture, he remembers little but the applause and maybe two questions: "Is it true that the young English intellectuals are *really* psychological?" or, "I always carry Kierkegaard in my pocket. What do you carry?"

11   Late at night, in his room, he fills a page of his journal with a confused, but scathing, account of his first engagement, summarises

American advanced education in a paragraph that will be meaning-less tomorrow, and falls to sleep where he is immediately chased through long, dark thickets by a Mrs. Mabel Frankincense Mehaffey, with a tray of martinis and lyrics.

12   And there goes the other happy poet bedraggledly back to New York which struck him all of a sheepish never-sleeping heap at first but which seems to him now, after the ulcerous rigours of a lecturer's spring, a haven cosy as toast, cool as an icebox, and safe as sky-scrapers.

Discussion of Theme

1. On the basis of their brief exposure to America, are most "Euro-pean . . . authorities on this and that" ill-equipped to pronounce judgment on America and Americans?
2. Is Thomas fair in his description of the kinds of people who attend lectures? How accurate is his portrayal of American audiences?
3. Is it true that American audiences—female especially—are not critical enough of lectures given by persons who have been intro-duced as authorities?
4. Do you find evidence that the author does not take himself too seriously?
5. Is there a deeper criticism of America implied here? Or should we read the essay merely as a humorous account of his experiences on the lecture circuit?
6. Is there an apparent contradiction between the author's commit-ment to filling lecture engagements and his apparent distaste for the experience?

Discussion of Rhetoric

1. Thomas wants his reader to share the same blurred, scrambled, and disjointed series of images that he experienced on a coast-to-coast lecture tour. How successful is he?
2. Much of Thomas's humor is tongue-in-cheek or unexpected. Find several examples of such humor.
3. What does Thomas imply in paragraph 10 about his college hosts?
4. What rhetorical clues identify Thomas as British rather than Amer-ican?
5. A characteristic of Thomas's style in all of his prose is his fondness for listing series of items. Where is this used, and how is contrast utilized?

Writing Assignments

1. If you feel that you have sufficiently grasped the elements of Thomas's style, write a parody of it on some subject of your own choosing.

2. In a humorous way, describe a tour of England by an American lecturing on some subject alien to British audiences.
3. Imagine that you are a member of an audience that has heard a series of lectures presented by any of the persons mentioned in Thomas's essay. Describe your experience and your reactions.
4. Thomas was, of course, first and foremost a serious writer — a fine, innovative poet who because of personal difficulties was unable to concentrate on that facet of his career. Discuss the financial and family problems that might be involved in the life of a serious artist.

Library Exploration

1. Dylan Thomas was a brilliant reader of poetry. His rich Welsh voice can be heard reading his poetry and short stories on several long-playing albums. Three are issued by Caedmon Records.
2. Thomas's views of America should be compared with those of other Europeans. Read Charles Dickens's *American Notes* (1842) and Alexis de Tocqueville's *Democracy in America* (1835).
3. If you enjoyed this selection, read some of Thomas's other works: *Portrait of the Artist as a Young Dog, Under Milk Wood, Quite Early One Morning,* and *Collected Poems.*
4. Many of the unfamiliar words are purely British and may or may not have counterparts in American English. Look up these words and write a commentary on their use:

    coshboys   publicist   nark   humbug
5. Look up Kierkegaard and see if you can discover why Thomas chose his name to typify the kind of writer that would appeal to the American intellectual.

Vocabulary

(2) PROFUSION abundance

(2) RISSOLES small meatballs fried in deep fat

(3) EXHIBITIONISTS show-offs; attention getters

(3) POLEMICISTS those who engage in controversial discussion or argument

(3) HISTRIONIC PUBLICISTS affected press agents

(3) RHETORICIANS eloquent writers or speakers

(3) BALLETOMANES devotees of the ballet

(3) HUMBUGS phonies

(3) ELEPHANTIASIS enormous enlargement (a disease)

(3) POTBOILING shoddy; inferior

(4) LINGUACEOUS many-tongued

(4) SLOTH laziness

(4) COSHBOYS young hoodlums

(5) NARKS spies; stool pigeons

(5) GLUTINOUS gummy; sticky

(8) GARRULOUS excessively talkative

(8) SURREALISM fantastic or incongruous imagery

(8) CATARRHAL affected by catarrh (chronic nose and throat inflammation)

(9) BUOYANTLY joyfully

(9) BLUNDERBUSS having an explosive impact

(10) IMBECILE feebleminded person

(10) INCONSEQUENTIAL unimportant

(10) CONTEMPTUOUSLY disrespectfully

(10) ANDROGYNOUS having the characteristics of both sexes

(10) ECTOPLASM emanation from a spiritualistic medium

Edmund Wilson (1895 - 1972) achieved distinction as one of the most formidable U.S. literary critics. He graduated from Princeton in 1916, and wrote poetry, drama, novels, history, literary criticism, and trenchant commentary on American political and cultural life. Among his outstanding volumes are "Axel's Castle" (1931), "The Shock of Recognition" (1943), "Patriotic Gore: Studies in the Literature of the Civil War" (1962), and "The Bit Between My Teeth" (1966).

Our language is so full of superlatives that most of them have lost their force. There are also hazards in using all kinds of highly charged words. Here Wilson reminds us that terms like "Americanism," which are often used not for their meaning but for the effect they have on an audience, shift their meaning from one age to another—even within the vocabulary of one man.

EDMUND WILSON

Americanism

It is curious to trace the vicissitudes of the term *Americanism*. The first quotation given in the *Dictionary of Americanisms* published by Chicago University is from a letter of Jefferson's of 1797: "The parties here in debate continually charged each other . . . with being governed by an attachment to this or that of the belligerent nations, rather than the dictates of reason and pure Americanism." This is Americanism in the sense defined by Webster (1906) as "a love of America and preference of her interest." In Jefferson's time, of course, it meant the

interests of the revolted colonists. But by the fifties of the following
century, the word *Americanism* was to take on a new political meaning. It was used by the American or Know Nothing party to designate
its own policy—already mentioned above—of combating the Roman
Catholicism of German and Irish immigrants and of debarring persons
of foreign birth from exercising political rights till they had lived here
twenty-one years. It is in this sense that Lincoln uses it when, in a letter of May 15, 1858, he speaks of the chances of the Republican party:
"I think our prospects gradually, and steadily, grow better; though we
are not clear out of the woods by a great deal. There is still some effort
to make trouble out of 'Americanism.'" This meaning was soon to
lapse with the demise of the Know Nothing party. But the word was to
be revived, with quite different implications, by Theodore Roosevelt
in the nineties. The first use of it in Roosevelt's correspondence is in
a letter of December 8, 1888, to Thomas R. Lounsbury, congratulating him on his *Life of Cooper:* "As a very sincere American myself, I
feel like thanking you for the genuine Americanism of your book;
which is quite as much displayed in its criticisms as in its praises."
Here he is speaking merely of an American point of view; but by the
time he writes to William Archer in 1899 (August 31), he is giving the
word a meaning of his own: "I have exactly the feeling about Americanism you describe. Most important of all is it for this country to treat
an American on his worth as a man, and to disregard absolutely
whether he be of Catholic or Protestant faith." . . . This is Roosevelt
at his best. He has changed the Know Nothings' emphasis: instead of
wanting to exclude the immigrant, he wishes to take him in and to
propose a common ideal of disinterested public service. He is to talk,
from the nineties on, a good deal about Americanism, and to give the
word a general currency. He is eventually to make it stand for the
whole of his political philosophy. Here is his definition in a letter to S.
Stanwood Menken of January 10, 1917: "Americanism means many
things. It means equality of rights and therefore equality of duty and
of obligation. It means service to our common country. It means
loyalty to one flag, to our flag, the flag of all of us. It means on the part
of each of us respect for the rights of the rest of us. It means that all of
us guarantee the rights of each of us. It means free education, genuinely representative government, freedom of speech and thought,
equality before the law for all men, genuine political and religious freedom, and the democratizing of industry so as to give at least a measurable quality of opportunity for all, and so as to place before us, as our
ideal in all industries where this ideal is possible of attainment, the
system of cooperative ownership and management, in order that the
tool-users may, so far as possible, become the tool-owners. Everything is un-American that tends either to government by a plutocracy
or government by a mob. To divide along the lines of section or caste
or creed is un-American. All privileges based on wealth, and all enmity to honest men merely because they are wealthy, are un-American—both of them equally so. Americanism means the virtues of
courage, honor, justice, truth, sincerity, and hardihood—the virtues
that made America." The last letter included in his published correspondence—written on January 3, 1919, three days before his death,

to be read at a benefit concert of the American Defense Society — has, however, an emphasis that is somewhat different. This was written at the end of the first world war, in the era — referred to above — of the mass deportation of radicals. The old chief in retirement had by this time passed into an apoplectic phase in which he was convinced, for example, that the International Workers of the World were necessarily a criminal organization and that labor leaders were guilty, as a matter of course, of the crimes of which, in that moment of hysteria, they were lavishly being accused. "There must be no sagging back," writes Roosevelt, "in the fight for Americanism merely because the war is over. . . . There can be no divided allegiance here. . . . Any man who says he is an American, but something else also, isn't an American at all. We have room for but one flag, the American flag, and this excludes the red flag which symbolizes all wars against liberty and civilization just as much as it excludes any foreign flag of a nation to which we are hostile." This is the fear of the foreigner again. It was rampant after Roosevelt's death, and anyone with a non-Anglo-Saxon name who ventured to complain about anything or to propose a social reform was likely to be told at once that if he didn't like it here in the United States, he ought to go back where he came from. By this time, the very term "Americanism" had become a black-mailing menace. One remembers reading in the New York *Tribune* of March 3, 1920, that the younger Theodore Roosevelt, chairman of the American Legion's "Americanism Commission," had called a meeting "at which it was decided to thoroughly Americanize all war veterans, then to utilize them in the work of making good citizens of the foreign-born of the State." It may not be true that "Americanism" — like Dr. Johnson's "patriotism" — is invariably "the last refuge of a scoundrel"; but it has been made to serve some very bad causes, and is now a word to avoid.

Discussion of Theme

1. Does any one group today believe that it has a monopoly on Americanism? Characterize the behavior of such people.
2. What is the irony of the fact that this particular term has acquired disagreeable connotations for some people? What does it connote to so-called liberals?
3. The American Legion has always emphasized its own brand of Americanism. Why might war veterans be obsessed with Americanism?
4. Speaking of Theodore Roosevelt, Wilson says that "instead of excluding the immigrant, he wishes to take him in . . ." The immigrant was "taken in" by political parties. How did the parties use immigrants to gain votes?
5. What is Wilson's own idea of Americanism? Do you agree that Americanism is a word to avoid?
6. What are some other words that have undergone changes in meaning? How have they changed? Do such changes tell you anything about how society has changed?

Discussion of Rhetoric

1. Although Americanism has become a word fraught with emotional significance, Wilson's tone is dispassionate. Why?
2. In his final sentence, is Wilson implying that Americanism is, in fact, "the last refuge of a scoundrel"?
3. How does Wilson arrange his material in this essay?
4. What is the meaning of *curious* in the first sentence? Is this a common use of the word?
5. What is the significance of quoting Jefferson, Lincoln, and Theodore Roosevelt, rather than lesser-known figures?

Writing Assignments

1. State your reaction to the bumper sticker "America—Love it or Leave It."
2. Which definition of Americanism—or portions thereof—most nearly expresses your own? Elaborate on it.
3. Should we de-emphasize nationalism and stress instead our role as world citizens? What benefits might that have for mankind?
4. Are some groups today attempting to achieve "government by a mob," and others trying to develop "government by plutocracy"? Who are they and what are their methods?
5. Do you think that the word *Americanism* will eventually lose the unpleasant connotations it has for the less conservative elements of our society? What could bring about the change?

Library Exploration

1. Wilson refers to the Know Nothing party. Find out more about this organization. You might consult a U.S. history text, a book on the development of political parties, or an encyclopedia.
2. Examine the concept of Americanism as espoused by various organizations. Do their definitions differ from yours? How?
3. Wilson refers to the *Dictionary of Americanisms*. If the library has this reference work, consult it for the history of other common terms. The title says "on Historical Principles." What does this mean? How does the book differ from your regular dictionary?

Vocabulary

VICISSITUDES ups and downs; chance variations
BELLIGERENT warring
DEBARRING preventing; excluding
DEMISE death
DISINTERESTED unbiased
CURRENCY prevalence; widespread use

PLUTOCRACY rule by the wealthy
CREED belief
HARDIHOOD resoluteness; vigor
APOPLECTIC having fits
LAVISHLY abundantly; even excessively
RAMPANT flourishing unchecked

Chris Clark, formerly a dean at Bryn Mawr College, where she taught law, now practices in New York.

Sheila Rush, also a lawyer, is the former Director of the Community Law Office in New York. She is associate professor of law at Hofstra Law School.

The authors, two black women, suggest ways in which whites can avoid offending blacks in various social situations.

CHRIS CLARK
SHEILA RUSH

A Black Guide for White Folks

1 Racial differences need not have existed. But since they do, they must now be acknowledged in positive ways. Here are some minimal guidelines intended to raise white consciousness of things that offend us and other black people.

PARTIES

2 Some cultural differences come into play and make cocktail parties a bit trying for blacks. For us, parties have meant fun, frivolity, and casual conversation with friends and acquaintances. The social event as an extension of business, politics, or work is essentially a white phenomenon. Apart from the fact that the collecting and cultivating of "contacts" has been less necessary because of the job pursuits blacks were limited to, blacks generally regard social gatherings as times of relaxation and release.

3   Even with the more intimate and leisurely at-home parties, white people seem to come together more for personal and professional advancement than for the sheer enjoyment of seeing and being with people they like in a relaxed setting. Increasing numbers of blacks

invited to such social events report that whites do not usually dance at their parties, even late ones.

4   For whites interested not only in making a party more comfortable and enjoyable for blacks but perhaps for themselves, a glimpse of how dancing and conversation function at black parties might be instructive.

5   First of all, there's the talk. Blacks even have an expression for it: we say, "Talk that talk," a banter which blacks later called "rapping"—until that expression got commercialized. The conversation consists of jokes, teasing, and affectionate near-insults, called "signifying." Though sometimes quite personal, these remarks, which might seem negative or critical to the outsider, are taken good-naturedly. It is understood that there is no malice and that the comments are to provide a release for deeper feelings which would seem overly sentimental or embarrassing if expressed directly.

6   The dynamics of dancing at a black party are even more revealing. Any mention of dancing raises in the white mind the "obvious" superior dancing ability of blacks. In an infamous piece called "My Negro Problem and Yours," Norman Podhoretz described his middle-aged white reaction to this phenomenon: "I have come to value physical grace very highly, and I am now capable of aching with all my being when I notice a Negro couple on the dance floor . . . . They are on the kinds of terms with their own bodies that I should like to be on with mine, and for that precious quality they seem blessed to me."

7   Dancing helps in part to satisfy that curiosity we feel about the other person. It is a chance to hold hands, to touch, and to move together in an enjoyable unison. For blacks, it makes talk unnecessary. One complaint blacks have made about white parties is that whites frequently want to talk while dancing, thereby interrupting the absorption and involvement in the physical movement. Although younger whites are learning to dance rather adequately by black standards, older whites still have trouble; their efforts to "get with it" through dancing are sometimes too exaggerated or forced to be fun. If the dancing is too much of a strain and does not come naturally, an occasional "soul" record would help immeasurably.

8   The problem of how to get a handful of black guests circulating freely at a party is one that many whites, with all their social experience, find sticky. Many hostesses introduce a black guest to a white one and then quickly disappear, praying that no special attention to the black guest will be necessary. Other well-intentioned Perle Mestas maneuver black guests in the direction of other black guests, in defiance of the old saying that opposites attract. Once, at a New York party, an extremely gracious white hostess, seconds after greeting a young black woman at the door, escorted her to a young African woman who was alone. The hostess was visibly relieved at the arrival of the only person whom she felt could mitigate the social isolation of this woman.

9   Now, from the black point of view, what was wrong here? Well, the first thing is that the hostess thrust the two people together solely on the basis of color. It is similar to swiftly introducing two octogenarians

at a party attended mainly by young people. Unlike the sharing of alma maters or scientific specialties, race (or age) is not a neutral "interest." Of course, blacks frequently seek out other blacks at social gatherings. But the important distinction is that we do it on our own. We dislike having it forced upon us; it's reminiscent of segregation.

10   When a prominent black is the chief guest or speaker at a gathering, whites on occasion have found it extremely difficult to resist sharing the eminence of this person with all who might benefit from the aura of fame. It has happened, consequently, that house servants, faithful hotel employees, and other blacks who serve whites have been summoned forth on such occasions to shake hands and exchange greetings with the famous guest. For all the democratically inclined, let it be noted that there is nothing objectionable or racially offensive about such a practice *per se*. What is objectionable is its exclusive application to situations where the prominent guest is black. In the interest of consistency and in an attempt to achieve the long espoused American ideal of obliterating social distinctions, we urge simply that all prominent *white* guests or speakers also be introduced to the kitchen help—black or white.

DINNERS

11 While most whites have advanced beyond thinking that the ideal menu for a black dinner guest is fried chicken and watermelon, there are still difficulties peculiar to dinners because of the more intimate setting and longer time together.

12   Most blacks agree that nothing tries patience, goodwill, and social restraint more than spending most of the evening at a white person's home discussing racial problems. Racial problems are to blacks as mortgage difficulties, marital strife, and the requirements of success are to whites: they are a fact of life, ever-present, difficult, and preferably to be avoided. Yet, while whites would rarely inquire —however politely—about their friends' mortgage payments ("How much do you owe on your house?"), marital disagreements ("Tell me, do you and your husband curse when you argue?"), or efforts to gain approval in a dog-eat-dog job situation ("Now, isn't it true that you laugh at the boss's jokes in order to get a promotion?"), they regularly ask the opinions of black guests about the countless aspects of American racial strife, as though only blacks were actors in this continuing American drama.

13   Around blacks, many whites suffer a temporary amnesia with respect to topics they normally discuss. It is as though their interests in opera, theater, world politics, the stock market, their companies, children, and so on, evaporate with the appearance of a black guest.

14   Dinners with friends should be light, happy affairs—a refuge from the problems of day-to-day life rather than a verbal telescoping of life's ever-present and unavoidable trials. It sometimes happens, of course, that blacks themselves will introduce racial subjects. In such instances, the purpose is sometimes to assess the situation or to discuss what we feel knowledgeable about and know will interest whites.

15 Second to being expected to discuss racial problems is the distaste most blacks experience when being queried by whites in social situations about "what they do." On the one hand, such questions are understandable, given the American correlation of social status with occupation or profession. On the other hand, even in these days of increasingly visible black achievements, there are still noticeable "oohs" and "ahs" when whites learn that blacks are something other than singers, dancers, or basketball players. It is as though the activities of blacks were in the public domain, and we would be obliged to open our ledger books if only we had remembered to bring them along to the party. Now there is nothing wrong with this kind of exchange of information, provided it *is* an exchange. The trouble is that when we venture to question our white interrogators about their activities, we draw either a blank or a quick "Oh, let's not discuss something so boring! What you're doing is so-o-o-o-o much more interesting. . . ."

16 The advice? End the one-way traffic.

Many whites assume that their black dinner guests will be ill at ease in the sole company of whites, and frequently invite another black couple. Less conscious is another reason: the second couple frees white hosts from the burden of special attention so they can attend to their other guests.

17 Since the first-invited black guests may be the paramount concern of the host and hostess, they may give little thought to the second couple and generally no consideration to compatibility of interest, background, or social level between the two black couples. Commendably, the white hosts here are trying to avoid tokenism. But in "getting another one," they are really using the second couple impersonally. And that's offensive.

JOKES

18 With the current sensitivity between blacks and whites, there are occasions when a racial joke will seem quite funny to white people until it becomes evident that their black friends aren't laughing.

19 In practically all humor, someone is made to look silly or foolish. The test for whites in determining whether to laugh at a racial joke is whether the point of the joke is some universally valued insight about life or limited only to blacks.

20 In general, it is better for whites not to *tell* racial jokes. But whites might now ask, "Don't blacks tell racial jokes?" Yes, but generally the racial jokes we tell and laugh at show a black just barely escaping a white attempt to box us in. But even if whites were able to tell the very jokes blacks tell, there would still be problems.

21 Blacks making humor about blacks is similar to members of a family pointing out foibles, weaknesses, or other deficiencies to other family members; the same criticism from someone outside the family would hardly be taken in the same way. Since blacks see few whites abounding in racelessness, most white humor about blacks has a racial edge.

22   Spontaneous, open reactions to humanly funny incidents are another matter entirely. Even if race is involved, it is secondary.

SMALL TALK

23   "He's just the *nicest* person."
      ". . . Just as qualified as anybody else."
      "She would make it no matter what her color was."
      "My maid calls me by my first name."
      "One of my closest friends when I was a child was a little colored girl."
      "I almost dated that woman."
      "Jesse Jackson really makes a lot of sense."
30   Many whites, unaccustomed to black company, draw upon a surprisingly limited number of stock phrases. They apparently do not realize that such comments are dead giveaways of their social discomfort. Their purpose is to reassure us—or themselves—that they are racially okay. But the effect of such hoisting of flags is tedious and burdensome for blacks, who have heard them so often and who could do with less talk and more action.

TRYING TO TALK BLACK

31   Black slang has long been a rich contribution to English as spoken by Americans. Although for years whites of good taste regarded black slang as evidence of the inferior sensibilities of blacks, lately all manner of white Americans—from the President to Madison Avenue copywriters—are adopting such black vernacular expressions as "soul-brother," "man," "right-on," "dig," "getting it together," "tell it like it is," and "doing your own thing." Black slang not only infuses ordinary English with variety and interest, but the very use of the terms represents a breaking away from the uninspired pragmatism of American life.
32   What most of us object to, however, is whites who mistakenly believe that by sprinkling their conversation with such "hip" sounding words, they will gain the approval of blacks. Indeed, such a purpose reveals a total misunderstanding of the nature and function of such expressions in the lives of blacks.
33   Black argot is a form of speech evolved by a culture unusually sensitive to the rhythm, tone, and musicality of speech—undoubtedly a carry-over from the African past. The expressions derive their syntax and grammar from the black vernacular, which makes it particularly difficult for whites to adopt the expressions with the same requisite ease. Thus, while one "tells it like it is," no black person ever "told it like it was." And while black folks may be "getting it together" only white folks (or cigarettes) "got it together." That is, the past tense makes it no longer a legitimately black phrase, since blacks don't use certain expressions in the past tense.

34   The use of black slang in the forced, self-conscious, erroneous way that whites use it grates on the black ear. Once in a green moon, a white person who has lived among blacks fully empathizes with the expressions naturally. Young hippie-type whites also come close to doing the same thing. The advice here: in matters of language, do your *own* thing.

*   *   *

35   Change comes hard. It means shedding old ways which are often preferred. Whether they work or not, at least they're familiar.

36   But the white reader who has read and reached this point has at least one thing in her or his favor. Motivation. And that makes changing a little easier.

Discussion of Theme

1. What do the authors mean by "racial differences need not have existed"? How did we create them?
2. According to the authors, what are the basic differences in attitudes toward social gatherings between blacks and whites?
3. Do the authors imply, in the final sentence of paragraph 12, that there exists a kind of mental segregation even among nonracist whites?
4. The authors state that "in matters of language, do your own thing." Do you think it would be best, in social situations, to do your own thing in all matters; that is, in an open, relaxed, unself-conscious and spontaneous manner? Is this possible? Why or why not?

Discussion of Rhetoric

1. Catagorize this type of writing. (Is it argumentation, narration, etc?)
2. Explain the "ledger book" image in paragraph 15. Why is it effective?
3. Is the referent *us* (paragraph 2) clear or confusing? How might this be corrected?
4. Is the pattern or organization important in this essay, or could the ideas be rearranged with the same effectiveness?

Writing Assignments

1. Explore the idea that "Dancing helps in part to satisfy that curiosity we feel about the other person," and develop your own ideas in an essay.
2. Write an essay on the theme, "How to deal with racist (or sexist) jokes."
3. Write about an experience in which you felt uncomfortable in the company of blacks or whites. Analyze your feelings honestly.

Library Exploration

1. Read *How to Get Along with Black People, etc.*, the book from which this piece was taken.
2. Read *Black Voices,* an anthology of Black literature, edited by Abraham Chapman.

Vocabulary

(8) MITIGATE   lessen in intensity

(9) OCTOGENARIANS persons between 80 and 90 years old

(10) AURA   a distinctive air

(10) PER SE   by or in itself

(10) ESPOUSED   embraced as one's own

(17) PARAMOUNT   of chief importance

(21) FOIBLES   weak points or failings

(31) PRAGMATISM   a practical conduct or character

(33) ARGOT   the jargon of a particular group

(33) SYNTAX   the arrangement of words to form sentences or phrases

(33) REQUISITE   indispensable

(34) ERRONEOUS   incorrect

(34) EMPATHIZES   mentally enters into the spirit of a person or thing

Shirley Chisholm (1924–   ) is a
political activist: she is a con-
gresswoman (from Brooklyn), a
supporter of various peace
causes, and a staunch advocate
of rights for the poor, for racial
minorities, and for women.

In the following article, Mrs.
Chisholm tells what it is like to
be both black and female.

SHIRLEY CHISHOLM

I'd Rather Be Black than Female

1   Being the first black woman elected to Congress has made me some
kind of phenomenon. There are nine other blacks in Congress; there
are ten other women. I was the first to overcome both handicaps at
once. Of the two handicaps, being black is much less of a drawback
than being female.

2   If I said that being black is a greater handicap than being a woman,
probably no one would question me. Why? Because "we all know"
there is prejudice against black people in America. That there is prejudice against women is an idea that still strikes nearly all men – and,
I am afraid, most women – as bizarre.

3   Prejudice against blacks was invisible to most white Americans for
many years. When blacks finally started to "mention" it, with sit-ins,
boycotts, and freedom rides, Americans were incredulous. "Who, us?"
they asked in injured tones. "*We're* prejudiced?" It was the start of a
long, painful reeducation for white America. It will take years for
whites – including those who think of themselves as liberals – to discover and eliminate the racist attitudes they all actually have.

4   How much harder will it be to eliminate the prejudice against wom-
en? I am sure it will be a longer struggle. Part of the problem is that
women in America are much more brainwashed and content with their
roles as second-class citizens than blacks ever were.

5   Let me explain. I have been active in politics for more than twenty
years. For all but the last six, I have done the work – all the tedious
details that make the difference between victory and defeat on election day – while men reaped the rewards, which is almost invariably
the lot of women in politics.

6   It is still women — about three million volunteers — who do most of this work in the American political world. The best any of them can hope for is the honor of being district or county vice-chairman, a kind of separate-but-equal position with which a woman is rewarded for years of faithful envelope stuffing and card-party organizing. In such a job, she gets a number of free trips to state and sometimes national meetings and conventions, where her role is supposed to be to vote the way her male chairman votes.

7   When I tried to break out of that role in 1963 and run for the New York State Assembly seat from Brooklyn's Bedford-Stuyvesant, the resistance was bitter. From the start of that campaign, I faced undisguised hostility because of my sex.

8   But it was four years later, when I ran for Congress, that the question of my sex became a major issue. Among members of my own party, closed meetings were held to discuss ways of stopping me.

9   My opponent, the famous civil-rights leader James Farmer, tried to project a black, masculine image; he toured the neighborhood with sound trucks filled with young men wearing Afro haircuts, dashikis, and beards. While the television crews ignored me, they were not aware of a very important statistic, which both I and my campaign manager, Wesley MacD. Holder, knew. In my district there are 2.5 women for every man registered to vote. And those women are organized — in PTAs, church societies, card clubs, and other social and service groups. I went to them and asked their help. Mr. Farmer still doesn't quite know what hit him.

10   When a bright young woman graduate starts looking for a job, why is the first question always: "Can you type?" A history of prejudice lies behind that question. Why are women thought of as secretaries, not administrators? Librarians and teachers, but not doctors and lawyers? Because they are thought of as different and inferior. The happy homemaker and the contented darky are both stereotypes produced by prejudice.

11   Women have not even reached the level of tokenism that blacks are reaching. No women sit on the Supreme Court. Only two have held Cabinet rank, and none do at present. Only two women hold ambassadorial rank. But women predominate in the lower-paying, menial, unrewarding, dead-end jobs, and when they do reach better positions, they are invariably paid less than a man gets for the same job.

12   If that is not prejudice, what would you call it?

13   A few years ago, I was talking with a political leader about a promising young woman as a candidate. "Why invest time and effort to build the girl up?" he asked me. "You know she'll only drop out of the game to have a couple of kids just about the time we're ready to run her for mayor."

14   Plenty of people have said similar things about me. Plenty of others have advised me, every time I tried to take another upward step, that I should go back to teaching, a woman's vocation, and leave politics to the men. I love teaching, and I am ready to go back to it as soon as I am convinced that this country no longer needs a woman's contribution.

15   When there are no children going to bed hungry in this rich nation, I may be ready to go back to teaching. When there is a good school

for every child, I may be ready. When we do not spend our wealth on hardware to murder people, when we no longer tolerate prejudice against minorities, and when the laws against unfair housing and unfair employment practices are enforced instead of evaded, then there may be nothing more for me to do in politics.

16   But until that happens—and we all know it will not be this year or next—what we need is more women in politics, because we have a very special contribution to make. I hope that the example of my success will convince other women to get into politics—and not just to stuff envelopes, but to run for office.

17   It is women who can bring empathy, tolerance, insight, patience, and persistence to government—the qualities we naturally have or have had to develop because of our suppression by men. The women of a nation mold its morals, its religion, and its politics by the lives they live. At present, our country needs women's idealism and determination, perhaps more in politics than anywhere else.

Discussion of Theme

1. "If I said that being black is a greater handicap than being a woman, probably no one would question me." Do you agree with the author's statement? Do people acknowledge prejudice against women as readily as they acknowledge prejudice against blacks?
2. Is the author guilty of stereotyping when she talks about men and women?
3. What are some of the bases for the prejudice that makes young girls "automatically" aspire to become typists, secretaries, and nurses?
4. What is the solution to problems like the one referred to in paragraph 13?
5. Are there any advantages for men if the women's liberation movement is successful?

Discussion of Rhetoric

1. How does the author support her thesis? What kinds of evidence and techniques does she use?
2. What is the function of the question raised in paragraph 12: "If that is not prejudice, what would you call it?"
3. Look at paragraph 15. What structural device has the author used to convey her thoughts. Is it effective?
4. In what way is the last paragraph related to the rest of the essay?
5. Describe the tone of the language in this essay.

Writing Assignments

1. Write an essay entitled "I'd Rather Be _____ than Female." (Insert any word in the blank.)

2. Write a paper presenting your views of the goals of the women's liberation movement.
3. Describe an experience in which you encountered sex prejudice.
4. Develop a paper reacting to the following statement: "I believe that there are (are not) basic differences (other than anatomical) between the sexes."

Library Exploration

1. Read and report on one of the following books: Ashley Montague's *The Natural Superiority of Women*; Germaine Greer's *The Female Eunuch*; Kate Millet's *Sexual Politics*; or Norman Mailer's *The Prisoner of Sex*.
2. Read something about the major figures in the current women's movement: Betty Friedan, Ti-Grace Atkinson, Aileen Hernandez, Gloria Steinem.
3. Trace the history of the women's suffrage movement in England and the United States. Compare the current legal position of women in these countries with that of women in Switzerland and in Sweden.

Vocabulary

(1) PHENOMENON extraordinary or remarkable person, thing, or occurrence

(3) INCREDULOUS unbelieving

(5) TEDIOUS dull and tiring

(9) DASHIKIS loose-fitting African shirts

(10) STEREOTYPES standardized, oversimplified images (of members of a certain group)

(11) MENIAL low; humble

(17) EMPATHY imaginative identification with the feelings or thoughts of another

Claude Brown (1937–   ) was born in New York City, and attended Howard University. He is the author of several plays performed by the American Afro-Negro Theater Guild. In 1965 he published the autobiographical novel "Manchild in the Promised Land."

Because the language of soul is unique, not everyone can use it meaningfully. Claude Brown, himself a black, shows the meaning of soul to blacks.

CLAUDE BROWN

The Language of Soul

1   Perhaps the most soulful word in the world is "nigger." Despite its very definite fundamental meaning (the Negro man), and disregarding the deprecatory connotation of the term, "nigger" has a multiplicity of nuances when used by soul people. Dictionaries define the term as being synonymous with Negro, and they generally point out that it is regarded as a vulgar expression. Nevertheless, to those of chitlins-and-neck-bones background the word nigger is neither a synonym for Negro nor an obscene expression.

2   "Nigger" has virtually as many shades of meaning in Colored English as the demonstrative pronoun "that," prior to application to a noun. To some Americans of African ancestry (I avoid using the term Negro whenever feasible, for fear of offending the Brothers X, a pressure group to be reckoned with), nigger seems preferable to Negro and has a unique kind of sentiment attached to it. This is exemplified in the frequent—and perhaps even excessive—usage of the term to denote either fondness or hostility.

3   It is probable that numerous transitional niggers and even established ex-soul brothers can—with pangs of nostalgia—reflect upon a day in the lollipop epoch of lives when an adorable lady named Mama bemoaned her spouse's fastidiousness with the strictly secular utter-

ance: "Lord, how can one nigger be so hard to please?" Others are likely to recall a time when that drastically lovable colored woman, who was forever wiping our noses and darning our clothing, bellowed in a moment of exasperation: "Nigger, you gonna be the death o' me." And some of the brethren who have had the precarious fortune to be raised up, wised up, thrown up, or simply left alone to get up as best they could, on one of the nation's South Streets or Lenox Avenues, might remember having affectionately referred to a best friend as "My nigger."

4   The vast majority of "back-door Americans" are apt to agree with Webster—a nigger is simply a Negro or black man. But the really profound contemporary thinkers of this distinguished ethnic group— Dick Gregory, Redd Foxx, Moms Mabley, Slappy White, etc.—are likely to differ with Mr. Webster and define nigger as "something else"—a soulful "something else." The major difference between the nigger and the Negro, who have many traits in common, is that the nigger is the more soulful.

5   Certain foods, customs, and artistic expressions are associated almost solely with the nigger: collard greens, neck bones, hog maws, black-eyed peas, pigs' feet, etc. A nigger has no desire to conceal or disavow any of these favorite dishes or restrain other behavioral practices such as bobbing his head, patting his feet to funky jazz, and shouting and jumping in church. This is not to be construed that all niggers eat chitlins and shout in church, nor that only niggers eat the aforementioned dishes and exhibit this type of behavior. It is to say, however, that the soulful usage of the term nigger implies all of the foregoing and considerably more.

6   The Language of Soul—or, as it might also be called, Spoken Soul or Colored English—is simply an honest vocal portrayal of black America. The roots of it are more than three hundred years old.

7   Before the Civil War there were numerous restrictions placed on the speech of slaves. The newly arrived Africans had the problem of learning to speak a new language, but also there were inhibitions placed on the topics of the slaves' conversation by slave masters and overseers. The slaves made up songs to inform one another of, say, the underground railroads' activity. When they sang *Steal Away* they were planning to steal away to the North, not to heaven. Slaves who dared to speak of rebellion or even freedom usually were severely punished. Consequently, Negro slaves were compelled to create a semi-clandestine vernacular in the way that the criminal underworld had historically created words to confound law-enforcement agents. It is said that numerous Negro spirituals were inspired by the hardships of slavery, and that what later became songs were initially moanings and coded cotton-field lyrics. To hear these songs sung today by a talented soul brother or sister or by a group is to be reminded of an historical spiritual bond that cannot be satisfactorily described by the mere spoken word.

8   The American Negro, for virtually all of his history, has constituted a vastly disproportionate number of the country's illiterates. Illiteracy has a way of showing itself in all attempts at vocal expression by the uneducated. With the aid of colloquialisms, malapropisms, battered

and fractured grammar, and a considerable amount of creativity, Colored English, the sound of soul, evolved.

9   The progress has been cyclical. Often terms that have been discarded from the soul people's vocabulary for one reason or another are reaccepted years later, but usually with completely different meaning. In the Thirties and Forties "stuff" was used to mean vagina. In the middle Fifties it was revived and used to refer to heroin. Why certain expressions are thus reactivated is practically an indeterminable question. But it is not difficult to see why certain terms are dropped from the soul language. Whenever a soul term becomes popular with whites it is common practice for the soul folks to relinquish it. The reasoning is that "if white people can use it, it isn't hip enough for me." To many soul brothers there is just no such creature as a genuinely hip white person. And there is nothing more detrimental to anything hip than to have it fall into the square hands of the hopelessly unhip.

10   White Americans wrecked the expression "something else." It was bad enough that they couldn't say "sump'n else," but they weren't even able to get out "somethin' else." They had to go around saying *something else* with perfect or nearly perfect enunciation. The white folks invariably fail to perceive the soul sound in soulful terms. They get hung up in diction and grammar, and when they vocalize the expression it's no longer a soulful thing. In fact, it can be asserted that spoken soul is more of a sound than a language. It generally possesses a pronounced lyrical quality which is frequently incompatible to any music other than that ceaseless and relentlessly driving rhythm that flows from poignantly spent lives. Spoken soul has a way of coming out metered without the intention of the speaker to invoke it. There are specific phonetic traits. To the soulless ear the vast majority of these sounds are dismissed as incorrect usage of the English language and, not infrequently, as speech impediments. To those so blessed as to have had bestowed upon them at birth the lifetime gift of soul, these are the most communicative and meaningful sounds ever to fall upon human ears: the familiar "mah" instead of "my," "gonna" for "going to," "yo" for "your." "Ain't" is pronounced "ain'"; "bread" and "bed," "bray-ud" and "bay-ud"; "baby" is never "bay-bee" but "bay-buh"; Sammy Davis, Jr., is not "Samme" but a kind of "Sam-eh"; the same goes for "Eddeh" Jefferson. No matter how many "man's" you put into your talk, it isn't soulful unless the word has the proper plaintive, nasal "maee-yun."

11   Spoken soul is distinguished from slang primarily by the fact that the former lends itself easily to conventional English, and the latter is diametrically opposed to adaptations within the realm of conventional English. Police (pronounced pō´lice) is a soul term, whereas "The Man" is merely slang for the same thing. Negroes seldom adopt slang terms from the white world and when they do the terms are usually given a different meaning. Such was the case with the term "bag." White racketeers used it in the Thirties to refer to the graft that was paid to the police. For the past five years soul people have used it when referring to a person's vocation, hobby, fancy, etc. And once the

appropriate term is given the treatment (soul vocalization) it becomes soulful.

12   However, borrowings from spoken soul by white men's slang — particularly teen-age slang — are plentiful. Perhaps because soul is probably the most graphic language of modern times, everybody who is excluded from Soulville wants to usurp it, ignoring the formidable fettering to the soul folks that has brought the language about. Consider "uptight," "strung-out," "cop," "boss," "kill 'em," all now widely used outside Soulville. Soul people never question the origin of a slang term; they either dig it and make it a part of their vocabulary or don't and forget it. The expression "uptight," which meant being in financial straits, appeared on the soul scene in the general vicinity of 1953. Junkies were very fond of the word and used it literally to describe what was a perpetual condition with them. The word was pictorial and pointed; therefore it caught on quickly in Soulville across the country. In the early Sixties when "uptight" was on the move, a younger generation of soul people in the black urban communities along the Eastern Seaboard regenerated it with a new meaning: "everything is cool, under control, going my way." At present the term has the former meaning for the older generation and the latter construction for those under thirty years of age.

13   It is difficult to ascertain if the term "strung-out" was coined by junkies or just applied to them and accepted without protest. Like the term "uptight" in its initial interpretation, "strung-out" aptly described the constant plight of the junkie. "Strung-out" had a connotation of hopeless finality about it. "Uptight" implied a temporary situation and lacked the overwhelming despair of "strung-out."

14   The term "cop" (meaning "to get") is an abbreviation of the word "copulation." "Cop," as originally used by soulful teen-agers in the early Fifties, was deciphered to mean sexual coition, nothing more. By 1955 "cop" was being uttered throughout national Soulville as a synonym for the verb "to get," especially in reference to illegal purchases, drugs, pot, hot goods, pistols, etc. ("Man, where can I cop now?") But by 1955 the meaning was all-encompassing. Anything that could be obtained could be "copped."

15   The word "boss," denoting something extraordinarily good or great, was a redefined term that had been popular in Soulville during the Forties and Fifties as a complimentary remark from one soul brother to another. Later it was replaced by several terms such as "groovy," "tough," "beautiful," and, most recently, "out of sight." This last expression is an outgrowth of the former term "way out," the meaning of which was equivocal. "Way out" had an ad hoc hickish ring to it which made it intolerably unsoulful and consequently it was soon replaced by "out of sight," which is also likely to experience a relatively brief period of popular usage. "Out of sight" is better than "way out," but it has some of the same negative, childish taint of its predecessor.

16   The expression, "kill 'em," has neither a violent nor a malicious interpretation. It means "good luck," "give 'em hell," or "I'm pulling for you," and originated in Harlem from six to nine years ago.

17   There are certain classic soul terms which, no matter how often

borrowed, remain in the canon and are reactivated every so often, just as standard jazz tunes are continuously experiencing renaissances. Among the classical expressions are: "solid," "cool," "jive" (generally as a noun), "stuff," "thing," "swing" (or "swinging"), "pimp," "dirt," "freak," "heat," "larceny," "busted," "okee doke," "piece," "sheet" (a jail record), "squat," "square," "stash," "lay," "sting," "mire," "gone," "smooth," "joint," "blow," "play," "shot," and there are many more.

18   Soul language can be heard in practically all communities throughout the country, but for pure, undiluted spoken soul one must go to Soul Street. There are several. Soul is located at Seventh and "T" in Washington, D.C., on One Two Five Street in New York City; on Springfield Avenue in Newark; on South Street in Philadelphia; on Tremont Street in Boston; on Forty-seventh Street in Chicago, on Fillmore in San Francisco, and dozens of similar locations in dozens of other cities.

19   As increasingly more Negroes desert Soulville for honorary membership in the Establishment clique, they experience a metamorphosis, the repercussions of which have a marked influence on the young and impressionable citizens of Soulville. The expatriates of Soulville are often greatly admired by the youth of Soulville, who emulate the behavior of such expatriates as Nancy Wilson, Ella Fitzgerald, Eartha Kitt, Lena Horne, Diahann Carroll, Billy Daniels, or Leslie Uggams. The result—more often than not—is a trend away from spoken soul among the young soul folks. This abandonment of the soul language is facilitated by the fact that more Negro youngsters than ever are acquiring college educations (which, incidentally, is not the best treatment for the continued good health and growth of soul); integration and television, too, are contributing significantly to the gradual demise of spoken soul.

20   Perhaps colleges in America should commence to teach a course in spoken soul. It could be entitled the Vocal History of Black America, or simply Spoken Soul. Undoubtedly there would be no difficulty finding teachers. There are literally thousands of these experts throughout the country whose talents lie idle while they await the call to duty.

21   Meanwhile the picture looks dark for soul. The two extremities in the Negro spectrum—the conservative and the militant—are both trying diligently to relinquish and repudiate whatever vestige they may still possess of soul. The semi-Negro—the soul brother intent on gaining admission to the Establishment even on an honorary basis—is anxiously embracing and assuming conventional English. The other extremity, the Ultra-Blacks, are frantically adopting everything from a Western version of Islam that would shock the Caliph right out of his snugly fitting shintiyan to anything that vaguely hints of that big, beautiful, bountiful black bitch lying in the arms of the Indian and Atlantic Oceans and crowned by the majestic Mediterranean Sea. Whatever the Ultra-Black is after, it's anything but soulful.

Discussion of Theme

1. Describe the conditions that gave rise to Colored English. What did the language have in common with the language of criminals?
2. Brown says that there is a difference between spoken soul and slang. What is it, and what examples does he offer as illustration?
3. What causes black people to drop certain terms from spoken soul? What unique qualities does the language have that make it difficult for outsiders to speak it?
4. Do you consider the article an affront to black people? Why or why not? Does the fact that the author is black help form your opinion? Explain.

Discussion of Rhetoric

1. With what sentence does Brown arouse his readers' interest? How does it do this?
2. What key word does Brown repeat in the first five paragraphs? What is its function?
3. Find the sentence that illustrates a particularly striking use of personification. To what is the author referring in this sentence? Why or in what ways is the sentence effective?
4. From time to time the author uses alliteration for special effect. Where does he do so? In what sentence is it especially noticeable?

Writing Assignments

1. If you are familiar with soul talk, write a critique of the article, using this special language wherever possible.
2. Does your town have a Soul Street? Describe it.
3. Discuss the advantages of using the language of soul.
4. Offer your own definition of "soul."

Library Exploration

1. What was the Underground Railroad? What individuals and groups were particularly active in it?
2. Read a biography of one of the persons — black or white — involved in the Underground Railroad. (Sojourner Truth had a particularly interesting life story.)
3. What was the slave's early relationship to the Christian Church?

Vocabulary

(1) DEPRECATORY expressing disapproval or condemnation

(7) CLANDESTINE concealed, usually for some secret or illicit purpose

(7) VERNACULAR a language or dialect native to a particular region (as opposed to literary, cultured, or foreign language)

(8) COLLOQUIALISMS informal expressions

(19) EMULATE try to equal or excel

(21) REPUDIATE disown; refuse to accept

(21) VESTIGE trace; remnant

A Sioux Indian from South Da-
kota and the son of an Episco-
pal missionary, Vine Deloria
(1934–   ) has a Bachelor of
Divinity degree from Augustana
Lutheran Seminary and a law
degree from the University of
Colorado. He has served as executive director of the National
Congress of American Indians
and has worked for the United
Scholarship Service.

From the time of Christopher
Columbus to the present, the
white man has misunderstood
the Indian. In this article an articulate spokesman for his
people puts to rest some of the
erroneous notions cherished by
the white man, and interprets
the Indian's values and culture.

VINE DELORIA, JR.

Custer Died for Your Sins

1 Indians are like the weather. Everyone knows all about the weather,
but none can change it. When storms are predicted, the sun shines.
When picnic weather is announced, the rain begins. Likewise, if you
count on the unpredictability of Indian people, you will never be sorry.

2 One of the finest things about being an Indian is that people are
always interested in you and your "plight." Other groups have difficulties, predicaments, quandaries, problems, or troubles. Traditionally
we Indians have had a "plight."

3 Our foremost plight is our transparency. People can tell just by looking at us what we want, what should be done to help us, how we feel,
and what a "real" Indian is really like. Indian life, as it relates to the
real world, is a continuous attempt not to disappoint people who know
us. Unfulfilled expectations cause grief, and we have already had our
share.

4   Because people can see right through us, it becomes impossible to tell truth from fiction or fact from mythology. Experts paint us as they would like us to be. Often we paint ourselves as we wish we were or as we might have been.

5   The more we try to be ourselves the more we are forced to defend what we have never been. The American public feels most comfortable with the mythical Indians of stereotype-land who were always THERE. These Indians are fierce, they wear feathers and grunt. Most of us don't fit this idealized figure since we grunt only when overeating, which is seldom.

6   To be an Indian in modern American society is in a very real sense to be unreal and ahistorical. In this book we will discuss the other side—the unrealities that face *us* as Indian people. It is this unreal feeling that has been welling up inside us and threatens to make this decade the most decisive in history for Indian people. In so many ways, Indian people are re-examining themselves in an effort to redefine a new social structure for their people. Tribes are reordering their priorities to account for the obvious discrepancies between their goals and the goals whites have defined for them.

7   Indian reactions are sudden and surprising. One day at a conference we were singing "My Country 'Tis of Thee" and we came across the part that goes:

> *Land where our fathers died*
> *Land of the Pilgrims' pride . . .*

Some of us broke out laughing when we realized that our fathers undoubtedly died trying to keep those Pilgrims from stealing our land. In fact, many of our fathers died because the Pilgrims killed them as witches. We didn't feel much kinship with those Pilgrims, regardless of who they did in.

8   We often hear "give it back to the Indians" when a gadget fails to work. It's a terrible thing for a people to realize that society has set aside all nonworking gadgets for their exclusive use.

9   During my three years as Executive Director of the National Congress of American Indians, it was a rare day when some white didn't visit my office and proudly proclaim that he or she was of Indian descent.

10   Cherokee was the most popular tribe of their choice and many people placed the Cherokees anywhere from Maine to Washington State. Mohawk, Sioux, and Chippewa were next in popularity. Occasionally I would be told about some mythical tribe, from lower Pennsylvania, Virginia, or Massachusetts, which had spawned the white standing before me.

11   At times I became quite defensive about being a Sioux when these white people had a pedigree that was so much more respectable than mine. But eventually I came to understand their need to identify as partially Indian and did not resent them. I would confirm their wildest stories about their Indian ancestry and would add a few tales of my own hoping that they would be able to accept themselves someday and leave us alone.

12   Whites claiming Indian blood generally tend to reinforce mythical beliefs about Indians. All but one person I met who claimed Indian blood claimed it on their grandmother's side. I once did a projection backward and discovered that evidently most tribes were entirely female for the first three hundred years of white occupation. No one, it seemed, wanted to claim a male Indian as a forebear.

13   It doesn't take much insight into racial attitudes to understand the real meaning of the Indian-grandmother complex that plagues certain whites. A male ancestor has too much of the aura of the savage warrior, the unknown primitive, the instinctive animal, to make him a respectable member of the family tree. But a young Indian princess? Ah, there was royalty for the taking. Somehow the white was linked with a noble house of gentility and culture if his grandmother was an Indian princess who ran away with an intrepid pioneer. And royalty has always been an unconscious but all-consuming goal of the European immigrant.

14   The early colonists, accustomed to life under benevolent despots, projected their understanding of the European political structure onto the Indian tribe in trying to explain its political and social structure. European royal houses were closed to ex-convicts and indentured servants, so the colonists made all Indian maidens princesses, then proceeded to climb a social ladder of their own creation. Within the next generation, if the trend continues, a large portion of the American population will eventually be related to Powhattan.

15   While a real Indian grandmother is probably the nicest thing that could happen to a child, why is a remote Indian princess grandmother so necessary for many whites? Is it because they are afraid of being classed as foreigners? Do they need some blood tie with the frontier and its dangers in order to experience what it means to be an American? Or is it an attempt to avoid facing the guilt they bear for the treatment of the Indian?

16   The phenomenon seems to be universal. Only among the Jewish community, which has a long tribal-religious tradition of its own, does the mysterious Indian grandmother, the primeval princess, fail to dominate the family tree. Otherwise, there's not much to be gained by claiming Indian blood or publicly identifying as an Indian. The white believes that there is a great danger the lazy Indian will eventually corrupt God's hard-working people. He is still suspicious that the Indian way of life is dreadfully wrong. There is, in fact, something *un-American* about Indians for most whites.

17   I ran across a classic statement of this attitude one day in a history book which was published shortly after the turn of the century. Often have I wondered how many Senators, Congressmen, and clergymen of the day accepted the attitudes of that book as a basic fact of life in America. In no uncertain terms did the book praise God that the Indian had not yet been able to corrupt North America as he had South America:

    It was perhaps fortunate for the future of America that the Indians of the North rejected civilization. Had they accepted it the whites and Indians might have intermarried to some extent as they did in Mexico. That would have given us a population made up in a measure of shiftless half-breeds.

I never dared to show this passage to my white friends who had claimed Indian blood, but I often wondered why they were so energetic if they did have some of the bad seed in them.

18   Those whites who dare not claim Indian blood have an asset of their own. They *understand* Indians.

19   Understanding Indians is not an esoteric art. All it takes is a trip through Arizona or New Mexico, watching a documentary on TV, having known *one* in the service, or having read a popular book on *them*.

20   There appears to be some secret osmosis about Indian people by which they can magically and instantaneously communicate complete knowledge about themselves to these interested whites. Rarely is physical contact required. Anyone and everyone who knows an Indian or who is *interested,* immediately and thoroughly understands them.

21   You can verify this great truth at your next party. Mention Indians and you will find a person who saw some in a gas station in Utah, or who attended the Gallup ceremonial celebration, or whose Uncle Jim hired one to cut logs in Oregon, or whose church had a missionary come to speak last Sunday on the plight of Indians and the mission of the church.

22   There is no subject on earth so easily understood as that of the American Indian. Each summer, work camps disgorge teenagers on various reservations. Within one month's time the youngsters acquire a knowledge of Indians that would astound a college professor.

23   Easy knowledge about Indians is a historical tradition. After Columbus "discovered" America he brought back news of a great new world which he assumed to be India and, therefore, filled with Indians. Almost at once European folklore devised a complete explanation of the Seven Cities of Gold, and other exotic attractions. The absence of elephants apparently did not tip off the explorers that they weren't in India. By the time they realized their mistake, instant knowledge of Indians was a cherished tradition.

24   Missionaries, after learning some of the religious myths of tribes they encountered, solemnly declared that the inhabitants of the new continent were the Ten Lost Tribes of Israel. Indians thus received a religious-historical identity far greater than they wanted or deserved. But it was an impossible identity. Their failure to measure up to Old Testament standards doomed them to a fall from grace and they were soon relegated to the status of a picturesque species of wildlife.

25   Like the deer and the antelope, Indians seemed to play rather than get down to the serious business of piling up treasures upon the earth where thieves break through and steal. Scalping, introduced prior to the French and Indian War by the English,* confirmed the suspicion

*Notice, for example the following proclamation:
  Given at the Council Chamber in Boston this third day of November 1755 in the twenty-ninth year of the Reign of our Sovereign Lord George the

Second by the Grace of God of Great Britain, France, and Ireland, King Defender of the Faith.

> By His Honour's command
> J. Willard, Secry.
> God Save the King

Whereas the tribe of Penobscot Indians have repeatedly in a perfidious manner acted contrary to their solemn submission unto his Majesty long since made and frequently renewed.

I have, therefore, at the desire of the House of Representatives . . . thought fit to issue this Proclamation and to declare the Penobscot Tribe of Indians to be enemies, rebels and traitors to his Majesty. . . . And I do hereby require his Majesty's subjects of the Province to embrace all opportunities of pursuing, captivating, killing and destroy-all and every of the aforesaid Indians.

And whereas the General Court of this Province have voted that a bounty . . . be granted and allowed to be paid out of the Province Treasury . . . the premiums of bounty following viz:

For every scalp of a male Indian brought in as evidence of their being killed as aforesaid, forty pounds.

For every scalp of such female Indian or male Indian under the age of twelve years that shall be killed and brought in as evidence of their being killed as aforesaid, twenty pounds.

that Indians were wild animals to be hunted and skinned. Bounties were set and an Indian scalp became more valuable than beaver, otter, marten, and other animal pelts.

26   American blacks had become recognized as a species of human being by amendments to the Constitution shortly after the Civil War. Prior to emancipation they had been counted as three-fifths of a person in determining population for representation in the House of Representatives. Early Civil Rights bills nebulously state that other people shall have the same rights as "white people," indicating there *were* "other people." But Civil Rights bills passed during and after the Civil War systematically excluded Indian people. For a long time an Indian was not presumed capable of initiating an action in a court of law, of owning property, or of giving testimony against whites in court. Nor could an Indian vote or leave his reservation. Indians were America's captive people without any defined rights whatsoever.

27   Then one day the white man discovered that the Indian tribes still owned some 135 million acres of land. To his horror he learned that much of it was very valuable. Some was good grazing land, some was farm land, some mining land, and some covered with timber.

28   Animals could be herded together on a piece of land, but they could not sell it. Therefore it took no time at all to discover that Indians were really people and should have the right to sell their lands. Land was the means of recognizing the Indian as a human being. It was the method whereby land could be stolen legally and not blatantly.

29   Once the Indian was thus acknowledged, it was fairly simple to determine what his goals were. If, thinking went, the Indian was just like the white, he must have the same outlook as the white. So the

future was planned for the Indian people in public and private life. First in order was allotting them reservations so that they could sell their lands. God's foreordained plan to repopulate the continent fit exactly with the goals of the tribes as they were defined by their white friends.

30   It is fortunate that we were never slaves. We gave up land instead of life and labor. Because the Negro labored, he was considered a draft animal. Because the Indian occupied large areas of land, he was considered a wild animal. Had we given up anything else, or had anything else to give up, it is certain that we would have been considered some other thing.

31   Whites have had different attitudes toward the Indians and the blacks since the Republic was founded. Whites have always refused to give nonwhites the respect which they have been found to legally possess. Instead there has always been a contemptuous attitude that although the law says one thing, "we all know better."

32   Thus whites steadfastly refused to allow blacks to enjoy the fruits of full citizenship. They systematically closed schools, churches, stores, restaurants, and public places to blacks or made insulting provisions for them. For one hundred years every program of public and private white America was devoted to the exclusion of the black. It was, perhaps, embarrassing to be rubbing shoulders with one who had not so long before been defined as a field animal.

33   The Indian suffered the reverse treatment. Law after law was passed requiring him to conform to white institutions. Indian children were kidnapped and forced into boarding schools thousands of miles from their homes to learn the white man's ways. Reservations were turned over to different Christian denominations for governing. Reservations were for a long time church operated. Everything possible was done to ensure that Indians were forced into American life. The wild animal was made into a household pet whether or not he wanted to be one.

34   Policies for both black and Indian failed completely. Blacks eventually began the Civil Rights movement. In doing so they assured themselves some rights in white society. Indians continued to withdraw from the overtures of white society and tried to maintain their own communities and activities.

35   Actually both groups had little choice. Blacks, trapped in a world of white symbols, retreated into themselves. And people thought comparable Indian withdrawal unnatural because they expected Indians to behave like whites.

36   The white world of abstract symbols became a nightmare for Indian people. The words of the treaties, clearly stating that Indians should have "free and undisturbed" use of their lands under the protection of the federal government, were cast aside by the whites as if they didn't exist. The Sioux once had a treaty plainly stating that it would take the signatures or marks of three-fourths of the adult males to amend it. Yet through force the government obtained only 10 percent of the required signatures and declared the new agreement valid.

37   Indian solutions to problems which had been defined by the white society were rejected out of hand and obvious solutions discarded when they called for courses of action that were not proper in white society. When Crow Dog assassinated Spotted Tail the matter was solved under traditional Sioux customs. Yet an outraged public, furious because Crow Dog had not been executed, pressured for the Seven Major Crimes Act for the federal government to assume nearly total criminal jurisdiction over the reservations. Thus foreign laws and customs using the basic concepts of justice came to dominate Indian life. If, Indians reasoned, justice is for society's benefit, why isn't our justice accepted? Indians became convinced they were the world's stupidest people.

38   Words and situations never seemed to fit together. Always, it seemed, the white man chose a course of action that did not work. The white man preached that it was good to help the poor, yet he did nothing to assist the poor in his society. Instead he put constant pressure on the Indian people to hoard their worldly goods, and when they failed to accumulate capital but freely gave to the poor, the white man reacted violently.

39   The failure of communication created a void into which poured the white do-gooder, the missionary, the promoter, the scholar, and every conceivable type of person who believed he could help. White society failed to understand the situation because this conglomerate of assistance blurred the real issues beyond recognition.

40   The legend of the Indian was embellished or tarnished according to the need of the intermediates to gain leverage in their struggle to solve problems that never existed outside of their own minds. The classic example, of course, is the old-time missionary box. People were horrified that Indians continued to dress in their traditional garb. Since whites did not wear buckskin and beads, they equated such dress with savagery. So do-gooders in the East held fantastic clothing drives to supply the Indians with civilized clothes. Soon boxes of discarded evening gowns, tuxedos, tennis shoes, and uniforms flooded the reservations. Indians were made to dress in these remnants so they could be civilized. Then, realizing the ridiculous picture presented by the reservation people, neighboring whites made fun of the Indian people for having the presumption to dress like whites.

41   But in the East, whites were making great reputations as "Indian experts," as people who devoted their lives to helping the savages. Whenever Indian land was needed, the whites pictured the tribes as wasteful people who refused to develop their natural resources. Because the Indians did not "use" their lands, argued many land promoters, the lands should be taken away and given to people who knew what to do with them.

42   White society concentrated on the individual Indian to the exclusion of his group, forgetting that any society is merely a composite of individuals. Generalizations by experts universalized "Indianness" to the detriment of unique Indian values. Indians with a common cultural base shared behavior patterns. But they were expected to behave like a similar group of whites and rarely did. Whites, on the other

hand, generally came from a multitude of backgrounds and shared only the need for economic subsistence. There was no way, therefore, to combine white values and Indian behavior into a workable program or intelligible subject of discussion.

43   One of the foremost differences separating white and Indian was simply one of origin. Whites derived predominantly from western Europe. The earliest settlers on the Atlantic seaboard came from England and the low countries. For the most part they shared the common experiences of their peoples and dwelt within the world view which had dominated western Europe for over a millenium.

44   Conversely Indians had always been in the western hemisphere. Life on this continent and views concerning it were not shaped in a post-Roman atmosphere. The entire outlook of the people was one of simplicity and mystery, not scientific or abstract. The western hemisphere produced wisdom, western Europe produced knowledge.

45   Perhaps this distinction seems too simple to mention. It is not. Many is the time I have sat in Congressional hearings and heard the chairman of the committee crow about "our" great Anglo-Saxon heritage of law and order. Looking about the hearing room I saw row after row of full-blood Indians with blank expressions on their faces. As far as they were concerned, Sir Walter Raleigh was a brand of pipe tobacco that you got at the trading post.

46   When we talk about European background, we are talking about feudalism, kings, queens, their divine right to rule their subjects, the Reformation, Christianity, the Magna Charta and all of the events that went to make up European history.

47   American Indians do not share that heritage. They do not look wistfully back across the seas to the old country. The Apache were not at Runymede to make King John sign the Magna Charta. The Cherokee did not create English common law. The Pima had no experience with the rise of capitalism and industrialism. The Blackfeet had no monasteries. No tribe has an emotional, historical, or political relationship to events of another continent and age.

48   Indians have had their own political history which has shaped the outlook of the tribes. There were great confederacies throughout the country before the time of the white invader. The eastern Iroquois formed a strong league because as single tribes they had been weak and powerless against larger tribes. The Deep South was controlled by three confederacies: the Creeks with their town system, the Natchez, and the Powhattan confederation which extended into tidelands Virginia. The Pequots and their cousins the Mohicans controlled the area of Connecticut, Massachusetts, Rhode Island, and Long Island.

49   True democracy was more prevalent among Indian tribes in pre-Columbian days than it has been since. Despotic power was abhorred by tribes that were loose combinations of hunting parties rather than political entities.

50   Conforming their absolute freedom to fit rigid European political forms has been very difficult for most tribes, but on the whole they have managed extremely well. Under the Indian Reorganization Act, Indian people have generally created a modern version of the old tribal political sturcture and yet have been able to develop compre-

hensive reservation programs which compare favorably with governmental structures anywhere.

51   The deep impression made upon American minds by the Indian struggle against the white man in the last century has made the contemporary Indian somewhat invisible compared with his ancestors. Today Indians are not conspicuous by their absence from view. Yet they should be.

52   In *The Other America,* the classic study of poverty by Michael Harrington, the thesis is developed that the poor are conspicuous by their invisibility. There is no mention of Indians in the book. A century ago, Indians would have dominated such a work.

53   Indians are probably invisible because of the tremendous amount of misinformation about them. Most books about Indians cover some abstract and esoteric topic of the last century. Contemporary books are predominantly by whites trying to solve the "Indian problem." Between the two extremes lives a dynamic people in a social structure of their own, asking only to be freed from cultural oppression. The future does not look bright for the attainment of such freedom, because the white does not understand the Indian and the Indian does not wish to understand the white.

54   Understanding Indians means understanding so-called Indian Affairs. Indian Affairs, like Gaul, is divided into three parts: the government, the private organizations, and the tribes themselves. Mythological theories about the three sectors are as follows: paternalism exists in the governmental area, assistance is always available in the private sector, and the tribes dwell in primitive splendor. All three myths are false.

55   The government has responsibility for the Indian estate because of treaty commitments and voluntary assumption of such responsibility. It allegedly cares for Indian lands and resources. Education, health services, and technical assistance are provided to the major tribes by the Bureau of Indian Affairs, which is in the Department of the Interior.

56   But the smaller tribes get little or nothing from the Interior Department. Since there are some 315 distinct tribal communities and only about 30 get any kind of federal services, there is always a Crisis in Indian Affairs. Interior could solve the problems of 250 small tribes in one year if it wanted to. It doesn't want to.

57   The name of the game in the government sector is TASK FORCE REPORT. Every two years some reporter causes a great uproar about how Indians are treated by the Bureau of Indian Affairs. This, in turn, causes great consternation among Senators and Congressmen who have to answer mail from citizens concerned about Indians. So a TASK FORCE REPORT is demanded on Indian problems.

58   The conclusion of every TASK FORCE REPORT is that Congress is not appropriating enough money to do an adequate job of helping Indians. Additionally, these reports find that while Indians are making some progress, the fluctuating policy of Congress is stifling Indian progress. The reports advise that a consistent policy of self-help with adequate loan funds for reservation development be initiated.

59   Since Congress is not about to appropriate any more money than

possible for Indian Affairs, the TASK FORCE REPORT is filed away for future reference. Rumor has it that there is a large government building set aside as a storage bin for TASK FORCE REPORTS.

60   This last year saw the results of a number of TASK FORCE REPORTS. In 1960, when the New Frontier burst upon the scene, a TASK FORCE REPORT was prepared. It made the recommendations listed above. In 1966 two additional TASK FORCES went abroad in search of the solution to the "Indian problem." One was a secret Presidential TASK FORCE. One was a semi-secret Interior TASK FORCE. In March of 1968 the President asked for a 10 percent increase in funds for Indian programs and after eight years of Democratic rule, a TASK FORCE recommendation was actually carried out.

61   Government agencies always believe that their TASK FORCES are secret. They believe that anonymous experts can ferret out the esoteric answers to an otherwise insoluble problem. Hence they generally keep secret the names of people serving on their TASK FORCES until after the report is issued. Only they make one mistake. They always have the same people on the TASK FORCE. So when Indians learn there is a TASK FORCE abroad they automatically know who are on it and what they are thinking.

62   Paternalism is always a favorite subject of the TASK FORCES. They make it one of the basic statements of their preambles. It has therefore become an accepted tenet that paternalism dominates government-Indian relationships.

63   Congress always wants to do away with paternalism. So it has a policy designed to do away with Indians. If there are no Indians, there cannot be any paternalism.

64   But governmental paternalism is not a very serious problem. If an employee of the Bureau of Indian Affairs gives any tribe any static, the problem is quickly resolved. The tribal chairman gets on the next plane to Washington. The next morning he walks into the Secretary of the Interior's office and raises hell. Soon a number of bureaucrats are working on the problem. The tribal chairman has a good dinner, goes to a movie, and takes the late plane back to his reservation. Paternalism by field men is not very popular in the Department of the Interior in Washington. Consequently, there is very little paternalism in the governmental sector if the tribe knows what it is doing. And most tribes know what they are doing.

65   In the private sector, however, paternalism is a fact of life. Nay, it is the standard operating procedure. Churches, white interest organizations, universities, and private firms come out to the reservations asking only to be of service IN THEIR OWN INIMITABLE WAY. No one asks them to come out. It is very difficult, therefore, to get them to leave.

66   Because no chairman has the time to fly into New York weekly and ask the national churches to stop the paternalistic programs of their missionaries, the field is ripe for paternalism. Most of them are not doing much anyway.

67   But, people in the private area are working very hard to keep Indians happy. When Indians get unhappy they begin to think about

kicking out the white do-gooders, paternalism or not. And if the private organizations were kicked out of a reservation, where would they work? What would they claim as their accomplishments at fund-raising time?

68   Churches, for example, invest great amounts to train white men for Indian missions. If there were ever too great a number of Indian missionaries, Indians might think they should have their own churches. Then there would be no opportunity to convert the pagans. Where, then, would clergy misfits go if not to Indian missions?

69   So paternalism is very sophisticated in the private sector. It is disguised by a board of "Indian advisors," selected from among the Indians themselves on the reservation. These "advisors" are put to use to make it appear as if all is well. Pronouncements by Indian advisory boards generally commend the private organization for its work. They ask it to do even more work, for only in that way, they declare, can justice be done to their people.

70   To hear some people talk, Indians are simultaneously rich from oil royalties and poor as church mice. To hear others, Indians have none of the pleasures of the mainstream, like riots, air pollution, snipers, ulcers, and traffic. Consequently, they class Indians among the "underprivileged" in our society.

71   Primitive purity is sometimes attributed to tribes. Some tribes keep their rituals and others don't. The best characterization of tribes is that they stubbornly hold on to what they feel is important to them and discard what they feel is irrelevant to their current needs. Traditions die hard and innovation comes hard. Indians have survived for thousands of years in all kinds of conditions. They do not fly from fad to fad seeking novelty. That is what makes them Indian.

Discussion of Theme

1. What are some of the common myths about Indians? How would you account for the origin of these myths?
2. In what ways have Indians and blacks been treated differently by the white man? How has this affected life on the reservations?
3. According to Deloria, what special qualities do the Indians possess? Does he regard the Indian as superior to the white man?
4. What is the Indian's primary goal today, according to the author? What has been the white man's goal for the Indian?

Discussion of Rhetoric

1. What is the organizational pattern of this selection? Where does each section begin and end? What is its central thesis?
2. Describe Deloria's tone: for example, is he irate, jesting? What suggests the tone in the article?
3. Deloria often uses bitter humor to mask his thesis. For example, he states, "Other groups have difficulties, predicaments, quandaries,

problems, or troubles. Traditionally we Indians have had a 'plight.'"
Find other instances of this technique.

Writing Assignments

1. Describe the Indian as he has been portrayed in American literature and in the movies, particularly in Westerns.
2. What should be the goal of the Indian: to merge with the white man
and be absorbed into his culture, or to retain the Indian culture and
live in a distinct manner, different from the white man?
3. What are the values of the Indian culture that the white man can
profit from by imitating?
4. What actions should our government take with respect to the
Indian?

Library Exploration

1. If you enjoy reading about American Indians, you might want to
read one of the following books: *Stay Away, Joe,* by Dan Cushman;
Little Big Man, by Thomas Berger; *House Made of Dawn,* by N.
Scott Momaday; and *When the Legends Die,* by Hal Borland.
2. Investigate the role and activities of the Bureau of Indian Affairs.
3. From among the many tribes mentioned by Deloria, select one and
learn what you can about it.

Vocabulary

(2) QUANDARIES states of uncertainty or doubt
(13) AURA a distinctive air or
character
(14) BENEVOLENT kind
(14) DESPOT tyrant or oppressor
(16) PRIMEVAL original; associated with the first stages

(40) EQUATED regarded as
equivalent
(61) ESOTERIC understood by
or meant for only a select
few

Consuelo Nieto is a member of
the National Education Association Women's Rights Task Force
and of Comisión Feminil, a
feminist organization of Chicano women, and a doctoral
candidate in educational administration at Claremont Graduate School in California.

Are the needs of the Chicana
being met by the feminist
movement? Do the problems of
these two groups parallel? The
author contrasts and compares
the Chicana experiences with
those of the Anglo feminist, and
offers concrete methods of affirmative action.

CONSUELO NIETO

The Chicana and the Women's Rights Movement

1   Like the Adelitas who fought with their men in the Mexican Revolution, Chicanas have joined their brothers to fight for social justice.
The Chicana cannot forget the oppression of her people, her
raza—male and female alike. She fights to preserve her culture and
demands the right to be unique in America. Her vision is one of a
multicultural society in which one need not surrender to a filtering
process and thus melt away to nothingness.

2   Who is the Chicana? She cannot be defined in precise terms. Her
diversity springs from the heritage of the *indio,* the *español,* and the
mestizo.

3   The heterogeneous background of her people defies stereotyping.
Her roots were planted in this land before the Pilgrims ever boarded
the Mayflower. As a bicultural person, she participates in two worlds,
integrating her Mexican heritage with that of the majority society.
The Chicana seeks to affirm her identity as a Mexican American and
a woman and to define her role within this context.

4   How does her definition relate to women's rights? How does the women's rights movement affect a Chicana's life? The Chicana shares with all women the universal victimhood of sexism. Yet the Chicana's struggle for personhood must be analyzed with great care and sensitivity. Hers is a struggle against sexism within the context of a racist society. Ignore this factor and it is impossible to understand the Chicana's struggle.

5   The task facing the Chicana is monumental. On the one hand, she struggles to maintain her identity as a Chicana. On the other hand, her demands for equity as a woman involve fundamental cultural change.

6   The Chicana shares with all women basic needs that cut across ethnic lines. Yet she has distinctive priorities and approaches, for the Chicana is distinct from the Anglo woman. The Chicana's world, culture, and values do not always parallel those of the Anglo woman.

7   Many Chicanas support the women's movement as it relates to equity in pay and job opportunities, for instance. Yet for some, particularly the non-activists, the closer the movement comes to their personal lives, the more difficult it becomes to tear themselves away from the kinds of roles they have filled.

8   The lifestyles of Chicanas span a broad and varied continuum. Education, geography, and socioeconomic living conditions are but a few of the variables which make a difference. The urban, educated, middle class Chicana usually has more alternatives, sophisticated skills, and greater mobility than her sisters in the barrios or the fields.

9   In the worlds of the barrio and *el campo,* with their limited social options, the role of the woman is often strictly defined. Fewer choices exist. Yet among all groups one finds women who are strong and who have endured.

10   Traditionally, the Chicana's strength has been exercised in the home where she has been the pillar of family life. It is just this role that has brought her leadership and her abilities to the larger community. The Chicano family is ofttimes an extended one, including grandparents, aunts and uncles, cousins (of all degrees), as well as relatives of spiritual affinity, such as godparents and in-laws.

11   Chicanas, collectively and individually, have cared for that family. It is the Chicana who goes to her children's school to ask why Juanito cannot read. It is the Chicana who makes the long trip to the social security office to obtain the support needed to keep *viejecita* Carmen going in her one-room apartment when taking in ironing will not do it.

12   It is *la Chicana* who fights the welfare bureaucracy for her neighbor's family. It is *la Chicana* who, by herself and with her sisters, is developing ways in which the youth of her community can be better cared for when their mothers must leave home to work.

13   Because life in the poorer barrios is a struggle for survival, the man cannot always participate in such community activities unless they pay a salary. He must provide the material support for his family. This is the tradition. It is in his heart, his conscience.

14   Chicanas owe much of their freedom to work for their communities to their men. It is the Chicana who often gains and develops those skills and attitudes which provide the basis for the transition of her

culture into that of the modern United States. A transition, and yes, even a transformation—but not at the price of dissolving that culture.

15   Last year I taught an adult education class which included some mothers from the barrio. I'm sure they were not aware of the women's movement per se, but I was amazed at their high degree of interest and concern with the question, "How can I help my daughters so that when they get married they will be able to do things that my husband won't allow me to do?"

16   None of them thought of trying to change their own lives, because they knew that it was a dead end for them. They would say, "He loves me and I love him. I will accept things as they are for me, but I don't want that for my daughter."

17   It's not that they didn't view change as personally attractive, but that to demand it would place their family and their home in too much jeopardy. It would mean pulling away from their husbands in a manner that could not be reconciled. And they will not pay that price.

18   Other women who wanted to enroll in my class could not, because their husbands would not permit them to go out at night or allow them to get involved in activities outside the home during the day. This is not surprising—some Chicanas have many facets of their lives more tightly controlled by their husbands than do their Anglo sisters. For some women of the barrio, their hope is to achieve the measure of control over their own lives which many Anglo women already have.

19   Similarly, some Chicano men will state that they are fighting for their women, but not for that kind of status and position that would give women equal footing. They are fighting to be able to provide for their women the social and economic status and position that Anglo men have been able to give Anglo women.

THE CHURCH

20   The role of the Catholic Church in the history of the Chicana is an important one. Not all Chicanos are Catholic, and among those who belong to the Church, not all participate actively. But since the arrival of the Spanish, the values, traditions, and social patterns of the Church have been tightly interwoven in Chicano family life.

21   The respect accorded the Church by many Chicanos must be not shrugged aside. Many will support or oppose a particular issue simply on the basis of "the Church's position." For these people it is very difficult to assess a "moral" issue outside the pale of Church authority and legitimacy.

22   For the most part, the Church has assumed a traditional stance toward women. It has clearly defined the woman's role as that of wife and mother, requiring obedience to one's husband.

23   The words of the apostle Paul have been used to justify this attitude: "As Christ is head of the Church and saves the whole body, so is a husband the head of his wife, and as the Church submits to Christ, so should wives submit to their husbands in everything."
     Also:

25   "A man certainly should not cover his head, since he is the image of

God and reflects God's glory; but woman is the reflection of man's glory. For man did not come from woman; no, woman came from man; and man was not created for the sake of woman, but woman was created for the sake of man."

26   *Marianismo* (veneration of the Virgin Mary) has had tremendous impact upon the development of the Chicana. Within many Chicano homes, *La Virgen*—under various titles, but especially as *La Virgen de Guadalupe*—has been the ultimate role model for the Chicano woman.

27   Mary draws her worth and nobility from her relationship to her son, Jesus Christ. She is extolled as mother, as nurturer. She is praised for her endurance of pain and sorrow, her willingness to serve, and her role as teacher of her son's word. She is Queen of the Church.

28   Some Chicanas are similarly praised as they emulate the sanctified example set by Mary. The woman par excellence is mother and wife. She is to love and support her husband and to nurture and teach her children. Thus may she gain fulfillment as a woman.

29   For a Chicana bent upon fulfillment of her personhood, this restricted perspective of her role as a woman is not only inadequate but crippling.

30   Some Chicanas further question the Church's prerogative to make basic decisions unilaterally about women's lives. When the Church speaks out on issues such as divorce, remarriage, and birth control, those Chicanas wonder, "Who can really make these decisions for me? Upon what basis should such choices be made?"

31   Many Chicanas still have a strong affiliation with the Church and seek its leadership and support as they attempt to work out their lives. Others try to establish their identity as women on their own, yet choose not to break with Church mandates.

32   Still others find this middle road too difficult. They choose not to work within Church structure and seek their independence totally outside the folds of religion. Chicanas find that to advocate feminist positions frowned upon by the Church often evokes family criticism and pressure. Thus some compromise personal values and feign conformity for the sake of peace within the family.

33   Concerned leaders within the Church do speak out in behalf of the Chicana's struggle for equity. But this is not the norm. While the Church supports equal pay and better working conditions, it would find it most difficult to deal with the sexism expressed in its own hierarchy or within the family model.

BROTHERS AND SISTERS

34   Chicanos often question the goals of the women's movement. Some see it as an "Anglo woman's trip," divisive to the cause of *el movimiento*. These men assert the need to respect women, but women's liberation . . . ? "That deals with trivia, minutiae—we all must concentrate on the battle for social justice."

35   Many of our brothers see the women's movement as another force which will divert support from *la causa*. On a list of priorities, many Chicanos fail to see how the plight of *la mujer* can be of major concern within the context of la raza's problems. They see the women's movement as a vehicle to entrench and strengthen the majority culture's dominance. They are concerned that their sister may be deceived and manipulated. They warn her never to be used as a pawn against her own people.

36   Yet the Chicana may sometimes ask, "Is it your real fear, my brother, that I be used against our movement? Or is it that I will assume a position, a stance, that you are neither prepared nor willing to deal with?"

37   Other Chicanos may be more sensitive and try to help their sisters achieve a higher status, but the fact that they too usually limit the aspirations of their sisters is soon evident. They would open the doors to new roles and new alternatives, but on a selective basis. Some support upward mobility for their sisters in the professions, but renege when it comes to equality at home.

38   A good number of Chicanos fear that in embracing the women's movement their sisters will negate the very heritage they both seek to preserve. The Chicana would ask her brother, "To be a Chicana —proud and strong in my culture—must I be a static being? Does not the role of women change as life changes?"

39   Too many Chicanos fall into using rhetoric which reinforces stereotypes damaging to both men and women. For example, some overglorify large families. To father and mother such a family is considered "very Chicano." Our numbers will increase, goes the story, as the Anglos decrease. This is "good," because somehow our power as a people will grow as our numbers grow.

40   It is forgotten that each man and each woman must share the decision to have children. To limit the size of a family is a personal right. To limit the size of a family does not negate a man's virility or a woman's worth.

41   Further, although the term "machismo" is correctly denounced by all because it stereotypes the Latin man, chauvinist behavior based on a double standard persists and is praised as "very macho." This behavior does a great disservice to both men and women. Chicano and Chicana alike must each be free to seek their own individual fulfillment. Superficial roles and attitudes should be abandoned. Each must support the other in their struggle for identity and fulfillment.

42   The pursuit of affirmative action for the Chicana in employment and education is often seen as a threat to Chicanos. Our men have not shared social and economic equality with the men of the majority culture. Gradually, jobs have opened up for minorities on higher rungs of the career ladder. When one opens for a Mexican, it has been assumed that Mexican would be a male.

43   Now Chicanas are gaining the education and skills to qualify for such jobs. But when a Chicana begins to compete for employment, more often than not she is pitted against a Chicano, not an Anglo male or female. The Chicano and the Chicana must both fully understand all the ramifications and subtleties of this process which would

divide them against each other. And institutions need to realize their responsibility to provide opportunities for all Chicanos, male and female alike.

44   Affirmative action is crucial to fighting discrimination. In assessing affirmative action programs, institutions must establish well-defined categories. Minorities cannot be lumped together. Each major ethnic group must be counted separately. Within each group a distinction must be made between male and female.

45   Statistics quickly dispel the myth that to be a Chicana is an advantage in current affirmative action models. Too often affirmative action for women has been interpreted to mean for Anglo women, while that for minorities has been interpreted to mean for minority males. There must be affirmative action for everyone hitherto excluded.

46   Chicanos themselves should take an active role in supporting their sisters. Within our own organizations, Chicanos must seek to include women in positions of leadership, not just "decorate" their conferences with them. How often Chicanas have participated in organizations or gone to conferences, only to see their role limited to that of the "behind the scenes" worker or the "lovely lady" introduced at dinner for a round of applause!

47   The Chicana wants more than that. She wants to be among the major speakers at Chicano conferences and to be involved at policy-making levels. She wants to be supported wholeheartedly in bids for public office.

48   Too often she hears her brothers say, "We would love to include 'qualified' Chicanas, but where are they?" This question has an all too-familiar ring. It is exactly what Anglos tell us collectively.

49   And our answer is the same. If we are not "qualified," my brother, what are you doing to help us? What experiences and training are you providing us? What support do you give us that we may become articulate and politically sophisticated, and that we may develop the skills of negotiation and decision-making?

50   When Chicanos maneuver to open up a position for a Mexican and a highly qualified Chicana is not even considered, another familiar statement is heard.

51   "The problem," Chicanos say, "is that 'our' community wants a man. 'We' know that a certain woman may be highly competent, but in our tradition we look to the male for leadership. Chicanos respect women and care for women, but leadership is seen as a male role."

52   First, the Chicana questions the assertion that the Chicano community would not accept a competent female in a leadership position. Second, supposing that such a view were valid, what are the "supportive and understanding" Chicanos actively doing to validate the role of a Chicana as a leader and spokesperson within the community?

DEALING WITH CONTRADICTIONS

53 Participation within organizations of the women's rights movement can bring to the Chicana a painful sense of alienation from some women of the majority culture. The Chicana may often feel like a

marginal figure. Her Anglo sisters assure her that their struggle unequivocally includes her within its folds.

54   Yet if she listens carefully, certain contradictions will soon emerge.
The Anglo women will help the Chicana by providing a model, a system to emulate. The Anglo will help the Chicana erase those "differences" which separate them. Hence, "We will all be united under the
banner of Woman. This will be our first and primary source of identity."

55   For a Chicana allied with the struggle of her people, such a simplistic approach to her identity is not acceptable. Furthermore, it is difficult for the Chicana to forget that some Anglo women have oppressed her people within this society, and are still not sensitive to
minorities or their needs. With Anglo women the Chicana may share
a commitment to equality, yet it is very seldom that she will find with
them the camaraderie, the understanding, the sensitivity that she
finds with her own people.

56   Anglo women sensitive to Chicanas as members of a minority must
guard against a very basic conceptual mistake. All minorities are not
alike. To understand the black woman is not to understand the
Chicana. To espouse the cause of minority women, Anglos must recognize our distinctiveness as separate ethnic groups.

57   For example, in dealing with sex role stereotyping in schools, a
multicultural approach should be used. Materials must encompass all
groups of women. Women's studies courses should not exclude the
unique history of minority women from the curriculum.

58   And the inclusion of one minority group is not enough. Chicanas
know only too well the pain of negation which comes from omission.
The affront of exclusion may not be intentional, but to the victim that
doesn't matter. The result is the same.

59   What does it mean to be a Chicana? This question the Chicana
alone must answer. Chicanas must not allow their brothers or other
women to define their identity. Our brothers are often only too ready
to tell us "who" we are as Chicanas.

60   Conversely, some Chicanas seeking fulfillment in *la causa* do not
question or challenge the parameters set down for them by
Chicanos—or more basically, they do not challenge the males' right to
such authority.

61   Similarly, a woman who has never shared our culture and history
cannot fully grasp the measure of our life experiences. She will be
unable to set goals, priorities, and expectations for Chicanas.

62   Chicanas must raise their own level of awareness. Too many do not
recognize their repression and the extent of it. Many have come to
accept it as the norm rather than as a deviance.

63   Chicanas also need to deal with their men openly. Perhaps the
Chicana has been overly protective of her brothers. Hers is a difficult
role. She must be sensitive to his struggle, but not at the cost of her
own identity. She must support him as he strives to attain the equality too long denied him, but she too must no longer be denied. To
fight and provide for the fulfillment of the Chicano while denying
equality to women does not serve the true aims of *la causa,* and will
not liberate our people in the real sense.

64   What must the Chicana do? First, she must work with her own sisters to define clearly her role, her goals, and her strategies. This, I would suggest, can be done by involvement in one of the many Chicana feminist organizations which are currently emerging.

65   Second, she must be involved with Chicanos in the Chicano movement. Here the Chicana must sensitize the male to the fact that she, as a woman, is oppressed and that he is part of that oppression. She must reinforce the *carnalismo* (spirit of fraternity) which is theirs, but point out that as long as his status as a man is earned at her expense, he is not truly free.

66   The Chicana must tell her brother, "I am not here to emasculate you; I am here to fight with you shoulder to shoulder as an equal. If you can only be free when I take second place to you, then you are not truly free—and I want freedom for you as well as for me."

67   A third mandate I would give the Chicana is to participate in the mainstream of the women's rights movement. She is needed here to provide the Chicana perspective as well as to provide support for the activities designed to help all women. Moreover, her unique role as a liaison person is crucial. How tragic it would be if all women did not promote and participate in a valid working coalition to advance our common cause!

68   Chicanas must avoid a polarization which isolates them from Chicanos as well as other women. They must carefully analyze each situation, as well as the means to reconcile differences. This is not easy—it requires a reservoir of understanding, patience, and commitment. Yet unless it is done, success will not be ours.

69   Finally, the Chicana must demand that dignity and respect within the women's rights movement which allows her to practice feminism within the context of her own culture. The timing and the choices must be hers. Her models and those of her daughters will be an Alicia Escalante and a Dolores Huerta. Her approaches to feminism must be drawn from her own world, and not be shadowy replicas drawn from Anglo society. The Chicana will fight for her right to uniqueness; she will not be absorbed.

70   For some it is sufficient to say, "I am woman." For me it must be, "I am Chicana."

Discussion of Theme

1. According to the author, why should the Chicana fight assimilation?
2. What are some of the common problems shared by Chicanas and Black women that Anglo women do not have?
3. Why is there a need for a separate feminist organization for Chicanas?
4. Is it possible for the Chicana to retain her identity and heritage while changing her traditional role?
5. What are some of the concrete suggestions for action offered by the author?

Discussion of Rhetoric

1. To what kind of audience is this essay addressed?
2. What is the purpose of the one-word paragraph 24?
3. What is the main thesis in this essay? Where does it appear?
4. Throughout the essay the author speaks in the third person of women, and her final statement is in the first person. What is the effect of this device? Is it an appropriate conclusion? Why or why not?
5. In the essay the author asks a number of questions. Are all of them answered in the discussion?
6. In paragraphs 10 to 14 a number of sentences begin with *It is*. What is the function of this repetition?

Writing Assignments

1. In an essay, respond to paragraph 25.
2. Compare and contrast the roles of Anglo men and Chicanos from the feminist point of view.
3. Explain the statement (paragraph 58) that "Chicanas know only too well the pain of negation which comes from omission." Write about a personal experience in which you felt the "pain of omission."
4. In view of the concepts discussed in this essay regarding the nature of the Chicana, why hasn't the Chicano movement produced well-known militant female figures such as the blacks' Angela Davis?

Library Exploration

1. Look up and define the Spanish terms used in this essay.
2. For an interesting study on the Chicano's struggle toward liberation, read Rodolfo Acuña's *Occupied America*.

Vocabulary

(3) HETEROGENEOUS different in kind

(21) PALE limit or boundary

(30) UNILATERALLY in a manner of occurring on or affecting one side only

(34) DIVISIVE creating division or discord

(34) MINUTIAE small or trivial details

(37) RENEGE to go back on one's word

(56) ESPOUSE to adopt or embrace

George W. Cornell (1930–) is religion writer for the Associated Press. A graduate of the University of Oklahoma, he is the author of "They Knew Jesus" (1957), "The Way and Its Ways" (1963), and "Punctured Preconceptions" (1972).

Jesus was a feminist and a radical one, according to Cornell. His revolutionary actions marked Him as the first and foremost champion of women's liberation.

GEORGE W. CORNELL

Jesus Viewed as a Women's Liberationist

1 She was a lonesome, passionate woman of dalliance, a castoff of five men and living unmarried with a sixth. But she had wit, insight and a longing for a better way. It was to her that Jesus made the first outright declaration of His universal messiahship.

2 She also became His first massively persuasive evangelist and the first to convey His mission beyond His Jewish homeland.

3 Not only did He give this extraordinary role to a woman in an age when that sex was regarded as of secondary value, but He did so to a socially tainted woman of a scorned, segregated race—a woman of Samaria.

4 It was a strikingly revolutionary action which shocked His disapproving male disciples and which was part of His consistent practice of defying sexist prejudices to give women equal status, a pattern that marked Him as the first and foremost champion of women's liberation.

5 He "vigorously promoted the dignity and equality of women in a very male-dominated society," writes theologian Leonard Swidler. "Jesus was a feminist and a very radical one."

6   Not once in the gospel records does He echo the claims of male supremacy that permeated the culture of His time, and repeatedly He acts to challenge it.

7   Never does He say or do anything to imply that women are secondary creatures—the entrenched view of that era—and He does much to point up their equal worth and prerogatives, often violating social codes to do it.

8   From the very start of His ministry, women were among His close circle of disciples, accompanying Him on his travels, being taught by Him, and, as Luke 8:3 notes, financing His work "out of their means."

9   While the male Gospel writers singled out 12 men as His chief apostles, the accounts are sprinkled with clues that Jesus Himself dealt with, instructed and regarded women just as highly and relied on them in some of the most crucial moments of His career, including times when the men failed Him.

10   It was an astonishing attitude among teachers of His time.

11   He lived in a patriarchal society in which women were regarded as chattel and breeders, totally subject to male masters. "Blessed is he whose children are males, and woe to him whose children are females," went a maxim of the times.

12   Men could divorce women for any reason simply by declaring it, but women could not gain divorce by any means. Their oath was considered worthless in a court of law and could be offered only if confirmed by their husbands or fathers.

13   Infanticide of female offspring was common in the pagan cultures, although not in Judaism. Its women, nevertheless, were valued chiefly for their fecundity and household service. As a rabbinical prayer put it, "Blessed be thou for not having me a Gentile, a woman or an ignoramus."

14   But the iconoclastic rabbi, Jesus, in His special concern for various downtrodden groups—the poor, the uneducated, the racial outcasts, the sick and the lost—also acted persistently to enhance the status of another disparaged class, women.

15   In the centuries since, the church has largely conformed to cultural limitations of women's eligibility in many ways, although that sexual disqualification has increasingly been questioned. Jesus Himself spurned it.

16   "Of all the world's great religious teachers," writes sociologist David Mace, "Jesus is unique in the respect He assigned to women as persons and in the extent to which He sought and enjoyed their companionship."

17   As with other women, it was that way with the woman of Samaria.

18   On a sweltering day, she sauntered along a dusty valley road, her loneliness as oppressive as the heat. She had many men, but actually had none. They came; they went.

19   She kicked at the dirt with a bare foot, sending a spray of it in front of her.

20   Her dark hair and sepia skin, rubbed with palm oil, glistened in the noonday glare and her body moved with a languid indifference. A coiled rope dangled from one arm, and with her other, she held an earthen water jar on her shoulder.

21   A resident of the nearby village of Sychar, she chose to fetch her water at midday despite the hot sun so as to avoid the stares and gibes of neighbor women who came for their water in the cool of evening.

22   Her days were desolate, her nights a hungering, unrequited cry for affection and appreciation. She had given herself unreservedly, but the ardently cajoling "husbands" always abandoned her. She had learned distrust, a brash cynicism.

23   As she neared Jacob's Well, situated at a crossroads outside the town of Sychar, she saw the man sitting there and by habit gave her hips a more sensuous swing. He could, perhaps, become another temporary benefactor.

24   But no, He obviously was a Jew, judging by the four blue-threaded tassels on the bottom corners of His cloak, and Jews despised the dusky-skinned Samaritans. It was mutual.

25   Ignoring Him, she knotted the rope through the twin handles of the water jar and lowered it with a splash into the dark, cool pool below, fed from springs in the rocky wall. She gave Him a sidelong glance, noting His tired, dust-matted appearance, and pulled the dripping jar back to the wellhead.

26   "Give me a drink," He said.

27   It surprised her slightly and she arched her brows, eying Him with flippant sarcasm. "How is it that you, a Jew, ask a drink of me, a woman of Samaria?" It was even considered unsafe for Jews to travel through Samaria, so bitter was the enmity.

28   Beyond that, men were not supposed to talk with any woman in public or even to greet them. It was considered lewd and compromising. She assumed He must have some further bold inclination as well, and she raked Him deftly, "Jews have no dealings with Samaritans."

29   He looked at her silently for a moment, seeming to take her all in. Sighing, He shook his head as if denying the racial animosity and her own thoughts and spoke sympathetically. "If you knew the gift of God, and who it is that is saying to you, 'Give me a drink,' you would have asked Him and He would have given you living water."

30   She frowned. He sounded as if he actually wanted to help her, but too often had she succumbed to soft words. Not this time! Besides, he didn't really make sense. Give her "living water"? He didn't have a liquid thimbleful or a line to get it.

31   She taunted, "Sir, you have nothing to draw with, and the well is deep." It was 60 feet to the water level below.

32   "Where do you get this living water?" She grinned mockingly but shoved her full jug toward him.

33   He lifted it to his lips, drinking heartily, then set the jar down and turned on her a grateful smile. "Everyone who drinks of this water will thirst again," he said. "But whoever drinks of the water that I shall give him will never thirst; the water that I shall give him will become in him a spring of water welling up to eternal life."

34   He picked up the rope, let the jar ease back into the shaft and brought it up refilled for her. She started to leave but hesitated, puzzled by Him and his exalting "water." It had a fanciful sound about it,

like the will-o-the-wisps she had always chased in her nameless long-ings and discontent.

35   Airily skeptical, she goaded, "Sir, give me this water that I may not thirst . . ."

36   His eyes measured her, the wistfully imploring lines in her brow, the emptiness and need stabbing through the challenge in her eyes. He said, "Go, call your husband, and come here."

37   "I have no husband," she flared, irritated now, but her lips sud-denly trembling.

38   "You are right in saying, 'I have no husband,' " he said. "For you have had five husbands, and he whom you now have is not your hus-band; this you said truly."

39   It jolted her. How did He know, this stranger? He didn't condemn her, but mystifyingly comprehended her. She made a convulsive movement, knocking over the jar, the water trickling over her bare feet. She bit her lip, staring at the ground.

40   "Sir, I perceive that you are a prophet." She raised her head, gaz-ing up mistily at Mt. Gerizim, its 3,000-foot ridge edging the valley, where the Samaritans had built their temple in rivalry to that of the Jews, although it had long ago been destroyed. "Our fathers wor-shiped on this mountain, and you say Jerusalem is the place where men ought to worship."

41   "Woman, believe me, the hour is coming when neither on this mountain nor in Jerusalem will you worship the Father." There were no exclusive locales for it, He said, no borders of place or race. "God is spirit, and those who worship Him must worship Him in spirit and in truth."

42   She looked at Him intently, wondering. "I know that Messiah is coming. When He comes He will show us all things."

43   "I who speak to you am He."

44   An awe, a surprised joy came over her then, and all the restless bitterness fled before this man who cared, who saw her whole and still cared, who offered new beginnings. A reborn trust surged in her. The world, after all, did hold God's goodness.

45   As Jesus' male disciples, returning from buying provisions in town, approached them, apalled that He would be conversing with a woman and critical of it, she raced away to the village, afraid no more, facing the townspeople with confidence.

46   "Come and see a man who told me all that I ever did. Can this be the Christ?"

47   They hooted and dismissed her at first, but she kept at them, seem-ing a changed woman even to herself, no more secretive and slinking but carried along on the crest of some newfound freshening hope.

48   Soon they stopped hooting, curiosity stirring among them, and then in a rising whirl of interest, nearly the entire town turned out to hear this purported Christ. Jesus, watching them coming through the ri-pening wheat fields that covered the valley, told His male disciples:

49   "I tell you, lift up your eyes, and see how the fields are already white for the harvest."

50   Many "believed in Him because of the woman's testimony," John

4:39 says. They gathered about Him, listening, deepeningly convinced. They persuaded Him to remain with them, and He did so for two days, accepting their hospitality despite rabbinical injunctions that "he who eats the bread of Samaritans is like one that eats the flesh of swine."

51   Many more came to believe, and it all started because of the woman, the disenchanted, wary Samaritan of a downgraded sex to whom Jesus, pausing at a rural well, first confided His transcendent identity, his mission beyond national boundaries, and in whom He placed responsibility for the first evangelistic ministry to the wider world.

52   On another occasion, as related in John 12, when Jesus was dining at the house in Bethany, the impulsive, adoring Mary, sister of the more domestically inclined Martha, took a jar of costly perfume and anointed Jesus' feet and hair. An apostle rebuked her for it, saying the money spent for the ointment should have been given to the poor.

53   But Jesus defended her, saying it was a loving deed. "Leave her alone," He admonished.

54   In upholding Mary's particular qualities, however, He did not set them up as the only womanly format, any more than He accepted housework as woman's only calling. He simply rejected the habit of limiting women to a uniform, sex-based type.

55   In fact, it was to Martha, the diligent, bustling housekeeper, that Jesus disclosed one of the most telling dimensions of His ministry.

56   This happened, as related in John II, when the two sisters summoned Him to help their brother, Lazarus, who was ill. Delayed in getting there, Jesus found that Lazarus was already four days dead, the circling march of the funeral mourners in the fourth of seven days, their wails filling the air.

57   Martha, grieving, distraught, came rushing down the road to meet Him, chiding Him for being late, but still having faith He could help. "I know," she said, "that he will rise again in the resurrection at the last day."

58   Jesus said to her, "I am the resurrection and the life; he who believes in Me, though he die, yet shall he live . . . Do you believe this?"

59   "Yes, Lord: I believe that you are Christ, the Son of God, He who is coming into the world."

60   The exchange with a woman sums up the core of Christian conviction, both of Jesus' redeeming role and human faith in it. His keynote declaration, the only time in the Gospels that He uses that phrase which has echoed down the centuries—"I am the resurrection and the life"—was delivered, remarkably, to a woman, an agitated fussy housekeeper, Martha of Bethany.

61   He asked for Mary, and Martha summoned her, saying quietly, "The Teacher is here and is calling for you." Mary rushed out and fell at His feet. Overcome by their grief, the account says, Jesus wept.

62   In front of the burial cave, He shouted, "Lazarus, come out!" The dead man emerged, wrapped in burial linens. "Unbind him, and let him go," Jesus said.

63   It was one of the most staggering, sensation-stirring acts of Jesus'
ministry, kindling official opposition that led to His crucifixion. He
did it for two women, each of distinctive ways, each of whom He
cherished.

64   Once a group of men, shrewd specialists in letters and the law,
flung a woman in front of him, her dress torn from her shoulders and
her hair untied to humiliate her. They declared:

65   "Teacher, this woman has been caught in the act of adultery. Now
in the law, Moses commended us to stone such. What do you say
about her?"

66   The scene took place on the east side of the Temple, called
Solomon's porch, an open, colonnaded passageway where rabbis
taught and to which accused women sex offenders commonly were
dragged for judgment.

67   They usually were roughly handled to shame them, their hair
loosened, their garments torn to expose their breasts.

68   Jesus eyed the waiting circle of hard, disdainful male faces, thirst-
ing for violence against this errant, disheveled woman at their feet.
He knew their objective was to contrive a case against Him by trap-
ping him into an open clash with the law, which plainly prescribed
death by stoning both for men and women adulterers. However, only
a man's word counted legally and so women generally became the
sole culprits.

69   So it was in the case of the woman cited at the start of John 8.
Silently Jesus kneeled down beside her, His finger tracing some un-
specified writing in the dust. The men kept up their badgering, goad-
ing Him to concur in the law's fate for the woman.

70   He stood up, facing them again, his gaze searching out their own
failures hiding behind their harsh revilings. He put it to them simply,
"Let him who is without sin among you be the first to throw a stone
at her."

71   They hesitated, pinioned within their own private delinquencies,
glancing about at each other, waiting for someone else to hurl that
lordly missile of self-acclaiming spotlessness. At length one of them,
shaking his head, turned away and the stone slid from his hand.
Gradually the others, eyes cast down, silently did the same, the
stones falling to the ground, a muffled, uneven clunking in the stillness.

72   Only Jesus and the prostrate woman remained there, alone.

73   "Woman, where are they?" He asked with a clearly bracing irony,
for they had obviously retreated. "Has no one condemned you?"

74   She looked up, blinking back tears, and her voice quavered, "No
one, Lord."

75   "Neither do I condemn you; go and do not sin again."

76   Even the critics of Christianity confirm the high role which Jesus
gave to women.

77   The ancient Roman emperor Julian, in an effort to eliminate Christianity and restore Rome to paganism, lampooned Jesus for forgiving
wayward women.

78   Friedrich Nietzsche, the autocratic, 18th-century originator of the

"God-is-dead" thesis who advocated "mastery of the superman," derided Christianity as a religion "of slaves" because of its concern for the weak and Jesus' "preposterous notion of equality for women."

79   A noted American writer and atheist, the late H. L. Mencken, also ridiculed the religion of Jesus for fostering effeminate weakness and being "highly favorable to women."

80   "It was Christ who discovered and emphasized the worth of women," says theologian John Gossip. "It was Christ who lifted her into equality with man."

81   This was a unique thing among leaders of the world's major religions, including Confucius, Buddha, Mohammed and the avatars of Hinduism, all of whom assumed the lesser value of women in the human order of life.

82   In all the chronicles of religious origins, no other "prophet, seer or would-be redeemer of humanity was so devoted to the feminine half of mankind," writes a British scholar of ancient history, Charles Seltman.

83   Jesus not only included women at decisive moments, but in His exalting images. In a parable, He told of a woman who lost a coin and searched diligently until she found it with much rejoicing. He said God in His loving search for each uncommitted person is like that, likening even God to a woman.

Discussion of Theme

1. Could it be that Jesus related to women so well because he recognized the so-called female qualities of gentleness, intuition, compassion, and so on in himself and understood them? Support your answer.
2. Why do you think Christianity has continued to perpetuate male supremacy in spite of Jesus' position on women?
3. Why do we never hear of the women who might have been disciples of Christ?

Discussion of Rhetoric

1. To whom was the author alluding in his discussion of the woman of Samaria? Why does he never mention her name?
2. What is the major developmental device used by the author?
3. Is this essay straight exposition or is there an underlying purpose of persuasion? If so, is it strong enough to change attitude and opinion?
4. Does the author make any assumptions about his audience?
5. We can assume that the final sentence in the essay is meant to have a certain impact. Does it work? Why? Why not?

Writing Assignments

1. How might the history of Christianity be different if religious leaders had been women?
2. How would society be changed if it were discovered that God is a woman?
3. Have attitudes toward females really changed since "Blessed is he whose children are males, and woe to him whose children are females" was the maxim of the time? (paragraph 11).

Library Exploration

1. Read *The Last Temptation of Christ* by Nikos Kazantzakis.
2. Read *The Woman's Bible* by Elizabeth Cady Stanton, et al. (New York: European Publishing Co., 1895)
3. Discover whether there are still cultures today who practice infanticide of females.
4. Did you know that Rome supposedly had a female pope? According to the story, after the death of Leo IV she (disguised as a man) was unanimously elected because of her great ecclesiastical knowledge. She was pope for two years, five months and four days. Research this story and write a report.
5. Also read: *Religion and Sexism,* edited by Rosemary Radford Ruether.

Vocabulary

(1) DALLIANCE   trifling away of one's time with flirtations

(11) MAXIM   an expression of a generally held truth

(13) INFANTICIDE   the killing of an infant

(13) FECUNDITY   fertility

(14) ICONOCLASTIC   characterized by the challenging of cherished beliefs

(20) SEPIA   a shade of brown

(22) UNREQUITED   not fulfilled

(30) SUCCUMBED   yielded; given in to

(50) INJUNCTIONS   judicial orders or laws

(51) TRANSCENDENT   going beyond ordinary limits

(68) ERRANT   deviating from a proper course

(71) PINIONED   restrained; held back

A native Californian, Jack Smith (1916–   ) has been with the "Los Angeles Times" since 1953. He is also the author of "Three Coins in the Birdbath" (1965).

This selection, originally presented as a talk at a women's organization, defends the "unliberated" female of the 1940s and 1950s against her modern-day detractors. Among her many accomplishments, he suggests, was giving birth to today's young rebels and idealists.

JACK SMITH

Unliberated, But Born Free

1   I picture myself as that notorious sexist, Sir Galahad, come to the rescue of a lady we might call the woman nobody knows.

2   Actually, she happens to be the woman I know best. But she's not one particular woman; she's collective. She's all the unliberated housewives of my generation, give or take a few years. She came of age just before or during or right after the war. She got married and had children and raised them. She belonged to the PTA, even though it didn't always swing.

3   She did housework and yardwork and sometimes she marched, for Dimes or Community Chest. She never heard of Women's Liberation, or if she did she thought it had something to do with that musical comedy, "Bloomer Girl."

4   Then one day her children were grown up and gone and her budget was balanced. Her work was done. She had come through. And only then did she find out what a mess she'd made of it.

5   How did she find out? Everybody told her. The sociologists. The psychologists. The new feminists. Her own children. Even the *Ladies' Home Journal* was a little mean.

6   What were her sins—besides obsolescence?

7   The indictment was long. She had turned our meadows into slums called suburbs. She had filled our homes with gadgets and junk. Her taste had created the desert of television. Her tyranny had turned her offspring into hairy anarchists. Her lust—quite unrequited, as far as we know—had turned our nice deadend streets into Peyton Place.

8   And all this time, remember, she was unliberated—in chains, a prisoner. Think what she might have done if she'd got loose.

9   It wasn't enough that she'd botched everything. What hurt even more was to be told she hadn't really lived. She hadn't been fulfilled, or to use the new vogue word—she hadn't been potentialized.

10   She was a prisoner of the male-dominated society, of her conditioning, of folkways, of fate. She wasn't even a woman, really, much less a free human being.

11   Who was this creature anyway? How did she get started in this sorry path?

12   Not long ago I inherited a batch of old Bill Mauldin cartoons, from 1945—the last year of the war. One shows Joe and Willie, talking to a new recruit in a dugout. The recruit is wearing a helmet. And Willie says, "Take off yer hat when ya mention dames here. They're a revrint subject."

13   So you see, this woman was in a sense created, overseas, in the minds of sexists like Joe and Willie, and the other young men of my generation.

14   We had priorities. We wanted a car and a girl and a job and a house and some children, not necessarily in that order, but sort of whichever came first, after the girl. We wanted a good life for ourselves and our children, the best life ever, and we wanted peace.

15   We got the girl. That was easy, because they wanted the same things. We got the children. That was easy, too. But there weren't any houses, and the schools were too old and too few. There wasn't enough of anything but energy.

16   So we built the houses. We built schools and highways and aquaducts. It was the most fantastic outpouring of energy—for peaceful purposes—in the history of man—and woman. I don't know if that's a fact, but I'll vouch for it.

17   We built tract houses because that was the only way to build a million houses overnight. We moved into tract houses because they were there. No down payment. Today's experts call them instant slums. Instant experts.

18   But for one generation, at least, they were homes. They had heat and light and laughter—and not all of it came out of the boob tube in the living room.

19   Willie lived here. Another old Mauldin cartoon shows Willie's buddy Joe standing in front of a pool hall in his uniform. He's re-enlisted. He's a master sergeant now. And Willie walks by. His arms are full of groceries and he's pushing a baby buggy.

20   And Joe is saying, "How's it feel to be a free man, Willie?"

21   I like that one. It's full of irony, because Willie is a free man, by his lights. He's doing exactly what he had in mind back there in the dugout, when he told that rookie to speak revrint of dames.

22   As I say, the women who lived in these homes—maybe I should say
the women who were kept in these homes—were unliberated. They
cooked and scrubbed and painted. They got clothes whiter than white.
Sometimes, as the psychologists say, the sex roles got blurred, and
they mowed the lawn and mixed concrete. Some of them did the
plumbing.

23   They threw batting practice in Little League. They planted flowers
and trees. Has it ever occurred to you that we'd all be dead of air
pollution except for the oxygen these women released with their prodigious plantings? They got into politics and rang doorbells and they
voted. In fact, a hell of a lot of them voted the wrong way.

24   They suffered through the golden age of KFWB, when every morn-
ing the house jumped with Purple People Eaters and Little Blue Men.
They suffered never knowing it was going to get worse—that Elvis
Presley was just around the corner, and the Beatles right behind him.

25   But then, even though there wasn't always enough money, and
never enough time, they reached out for something more. They
bought encyclopedias on the installment plan—at the supermarket or
at the front door. They got "Carmen" and "Swan Lake" into the house
on KFAC. They learned which was the proper Gallo wine to serve
with frozen halibut. They set their tables with candles and flowers.
They bought Van Gogh prints from the May Co. and temple bells from
the Akron.

26   It wasn't a high culture, but in the 1950s it was all we had.

27   I guess some of the new feminists would feel what they call "rage"
if they heard me eulogizing this generation of women, as if they'd
had a good life. They'd say he's only a sexist in disguise. I hope I'm
not. I'm absolutely for them when they say they want women to be
treated as equal human beings.

28   That's exactly why I hate to see a whole generation of women swept
under the rug, as if they were less than human—an embarrassment to
their sex. I think most of them were equal as hell. They had a lot of
fun, and dignity, too, if any human being has. They made a contribution. What's more they were relevant, meaningful, and viable. Even if
they weren't potentialized.

29   The woman of my generation had her eyes on the best of all possible
worlds. She didn't quite get her hands on it. And now she's told she
blew it. Her young are rebels. They use bad words and flout authority
and turn their backs on good old values.

30   She could have done worse. She could have raised a generation of
young who *weren't* rebels, who *didn't* prefer peace to war, who *didn't*
want to search and inquire, and change the world.

31   Maybe this woman's role is obsolete. I don't know. But it was absolutely essential for her time. There was no other way—in the 1950s
and 60s—that we could have given the world the hope of the world,
which is our youth.

32   If these women were unliberated, I hope history will at least honor
them for the services they performed in captivity.

33   I hope this hasn't sounded like an obituary. It isn't. It's a bouquet.
These women are still with us—liberated now, of course, but still

reaching. Some of them, I believe, will be called up here to the stage in a moment, as soon as I have the grace to sit down.

Discussion of Theme

1. Why does Smith call the subject of his article "the woman nobody knows"? Could she also be "the woman I know best"?
2. For what qualities does Smith praise the women of his own generation? Is his praise excessive?
3. Smith describes the role that women played some years ago. Is that role now obsolete — was it "essential for the time," but now outmoded?
4. Is there any substance to the theory that today's rebellious youth are reacting against the compliance of their parents?
5. What is Smith's real attitude toward the women's liberation movement?

Discussion of Rhetoric

1. Do you consider Smith's article overly sentimental, or is his view based solely on reason?
2. Note the frequent use of short, staccato sentences and sentence fragments in this article. How do they affect the tone of the article?
3. Irony is often used by writers to convey subtle meanings and to express humor. Find examples of both uses in this selection. Note, for instance, the first sentence.
4. Is Smith fair in his "indictment" of the "unliberated housewife" (paragraphs 7–10)? Has he stated the "charges" in the same way a supporter of women's liberation would?

Writing Assignments

1. Write a rebuttal to Smith's article if you disagree with his point of view.
2. What changes in the family do you foresee as a result of the changing roles of women, the "sexual revolution," and the many other upheavals taking place today? Is the traditional family unit approaching obsolescence?

Library Exploration

1. For a rebuttal to the viewpoint expressed by this article, read one of the many books currently available on the women's liberation movement. Of particular interest is *Sexual Politics*, by Kate Millett.

Vocabulary

(1) SEXIST   one who believes in distinct roles for male and female

(6) OBSOLESCENCE   state of being out of date; outmoded

(7) INDICTMENT   accusation

(7) UNREQUITED   unreturned

(23) PRODIGIOUS   extraordinary in size, amount, etc.

(27) EULOGIZE   praise highly

(28) VIABLE   capable of growing or developing

(29) FLOUT   mock; ridicule

Arnold Toynbee (1889 –1975), the English historian, is best known for his monumental "A Study of History." The author of works on Greek history and civilization, he had a varied career: delegate to the Paris Peace Conference in 1919; professor of modern Greek language, literature, and history at the University of London; and professor of international history at the same institution for many years until his retirement.

Taking his evidence from the pages of history, Toynbee argues that the present movement toward greater sexual freedom in this country carries with it serious potential problems. The answer, he suggests, is to codify relations between the sexes—to impose certain regulations on our sexual lives.

ARNOLD TOYNBEE

The Sexual Revolution

1   It is nothing new for sexuality to be one of our central preoccupations. Throughout the history of humanity, the very ambiguity of human nature has made the problem of sexuality extremely difficult to solve. On the one hand we are subject to sexual impulses and drives like all animals, and on the other, our life has a certain spiritual side to it and the requirements of this are incompatible with a pure and simple abandonment to our instincts. The tension created by these two aspects of our nature is all the greater because our sexual life is not regulated naturally, as it is with the majority of mammals. In their case, the female is sexually active only during certain definite periods, while the human female is constantly active. This is another reason

why human beings will always be obliged to regulate their sexual life as well as they can.

2   It seems to me that experience has shown that both man and woman suffer unhappiness where relationships between the sexes are not regulated. This regulation can take very different forms, such as monogamous, polygamous or polyandrous marriage. The essential element in all cases is that there should be some regulation — necessary not only for adults but also and especially for children. It is well-known that one of the causes of the disorderly behavior of a large section of the young of today is the atmosphere of insecurity in which they have grown up because of discord between their parents. Psychologically speaking, this can have devastating repercussions and children run the risk of feeling its traumatic effects throughout their lives. This is why all human societies have felt the necessity to codify relations between the sexes. Since our instincts are very strong, however, the rules have never been very closely followed, and a great deal of hypocrisy has been the result. It is never possible to judge the real circumstances of sexual relations on the basis of official standards of behaviour; one must always try to see what happens in reality.

3   In the 19th century, for instance, official sexual morality was very strict in Anglo-Saxon countries and in France, though to a lesser degree. In practice, however, the official code was frequently flouted and the contradiction between theory and practice finally became very demoralizing. From this point of view, I believe that the present movement in favour of a greater liberty in sexual behaviour is, at least partly, a healthy reaction against Victorian hypocrisy. What the young people of today are saying, in effect, is this: "Our predecessors were no better than us, but pretended to be so. We don't pretend anything; we do openly what they did secretly."

4   But there is a negative side to this revolt. It isn't only hypocrisy which is rejected but, ultimately, all regulation of our sexual life. I even think that the revolt against hypocrisy can become the excuse for a revolt against any type of regulation demanding self-control. And if we abandon all regulation, to all intents and purposes we cease to be human beings, without, however, becoming innocent animals again. Instead, we become monsters, neither totally man nor beast. Another deplorable effect is that any excess in one direction inevitably ends by sparking off a reaction in the other. Thinking of historical precedents to the present situation, two in British history spring immediately to mind: the Restoration of Charles II, when the extreme moral freedom of the time was a reaction against the Puritan dictatorship of Cromwell; and the moral laxity of the Regency period (George IV) which explains the Victorian reaction that followed.

5   If we look outside English history, it is difficult to avoid a comparison with the time of the Roman Empire. One only has to read the Epistles of St. Paul and to see the difficulties he had with people newly converted to the Jewish faith, notably at Corinth, to gain some idea of the sexual liberty which existed in the Greco-Roman world at the beginning of the Christian era. St. Paul had before him the Jewish ideal of stability in marriage and, on this point, I admire the Jews greatly. I think that their very strong sense of family, their concern for their

children, almost sacrificial in spirit, is one of the reasons for their success, not only under the Roman Empire but also more recently.

6   Christianity, however, has gone much further than Judaism towards an essentially unnatural asceticism. Because of the sexual license which was current among the early converts to Christianity, purity in sexual morality has been heavily emphasized, causing Christianity to confuse morality with sexual morality. Consequently, there was a tendency to think that if sexual behaviour conformed to accepted norms everything was well, although it was possible to act very badly in other matters. There are many aspects of good and evil which are not connected with sexuality.

7   The comparison with the Roman Empire also holds good in that great sexual freedom is a sign of decadence in any society or civilization. The Romans of the 3rd century B.C. and the Greeks of the 5th century B.C. were much more virtuous than the contemporaries of St. Paul. The Christian reaction went together with the breaking up of the proletariat within the Empire, which fostered the barbarian invasions. In fact, these invasions were the most visible signs of the fall of the Roman Empire but not the most important. The essential phenomenon was, if I dare say it, the invasion "from below," by which the upper classes were submerged by new social strata. The barbarian invasions were facilitated by this phenomenon, and at the same time made the phenomenon itself more possible. There was a coming together of an internal proletariat and an external proletariat.

8   Similarily, the Victorian reaction against the profligacy of the Regency goes together with the acquisition of political and economic power by a new middle class, industrious, acutely businesslike, and very much attached to the Puritan traditions as far as its private life was concerned. When that class became rich and powerful, it retained its Puritan facade but secretly began to betray the severe ideals which it professed.

9   I feel that the present movement towards greater sexual freedom marks the end of bourgeois liberal society, though it is difficult to see who stands to gain from this. In this context, the case of the United States is instructive. The hippies, whose sexual freedom is well known, are for the most part from families who have been well-off for more than one generation. And the people who detest them more than anyone are the blue-collar workers, the upper class of industrial workers who have just acquired a certain degree of comfort in life. In fact, the American working class is now divided into two quite distinct categories: a stratum of very poor people, like the blacks and the poor whites of the South, and a stratum of workers who have reached the level of the lower middle class. This latter is reasonably comfortable and has no wish at all to see "the American way of life" called into question when it has only just started to enjoy its benefits. Vice-President Agnew, the son of a poor Greek immigrant, seems to me to be very representative of this new rising class. It seems to me, too, that the wish for "law and order" could lead to a fascist-type reaction, very tough and very intolerant, which would concern itself as much with morals and private life as with politics.

10   In Great Britain, the success of Enoch Powell, the racialist leader

who is campaigning against the immigration of coloured people, is explicable by a similar phenomenon. A whole section of the working class does not want to see threatened the comforts and privileges which work and the struggles of the unions have allowed it to acquire.

11   The situation in France is comparable but hard to judge, because of the importance of the Communist Party. From the events of 1968, however, it would seem as though there, too, the workers reject cooperation with hippie protesters or left-wing students. Whether in its communist or fascist version, the reaction of the new lower middle class against the "permissive society" has a good chance of being intolerant and anti-intellectual. Indeed, insofar as one can discern the lower middle class of the future in a section of today's working class, I think that fascism presents more of a threat than communism. The Nazi movement in Germany, after all, was the expression of a sort of social revolution. It brought to power people whose existence had been largely ignored by the ruling classes.

12   If the present increase in sexual freedom marks the decadence of a certain period of bourgeois liberal society, it also marks the beginning of a post-Christian era. Christian dogma and belief have ceased to be real for a majority of our contemporaries. This is really a revolution, since Christian dogma and the moral code which goes with it have constituted the framework of our lives since the 4th century in the West and since the 11th in Russia. I should also add that this framework was obscurantist, too rigid and badly balanced; it placed excessive importance on sexual repression which consequently led to hypocrisy. It is impossible, however, to reject this framework with impunity, without leaving the impression of a void. I feel this myself, because I do not share the Christian belief and yet I do not know how to replace it.

13   Plutarch tells us that, in the 1st century A.D., whenever a boat anchored at a port in Greece, the sailors heard the spirits of the gods cry: "Great Pan is dead!" It seems that great Pan has been revived today . . . for a short while, at least. But that is not the end of the story. I can see in this provisional resurrection of Pan, and also of Dionysius, a revolt, a protest against a daily life which is increasingly regulated by the demands of technology. This movement is similar to the wildcat strikes in industry, which are a more or less unconscious protest against the monotony of a mechanized and standardized job. This same standardization is spreading throughout our daily life at present. But at this point we find ourselves caught in a cleft stick: on the one hand, we complain about becoming slaves to technology; on the other, we can no longer conceive of a life without the comfort which technology allows us to enjoy.

14   Even in antiquity, the worship of Dionysius, with its orgies and sexual excesses, was an outlet for the surplus vital energy of the human being. Today sex has become a symbol of freedom, of a return to nature in an industrial society. While self-awareness separates man from the rest of the world, sex, which is beyond the control of his will, reunites him with the universe. It is now used as the excuse for pantheist outpourings or as a way of returning to nature: man thus feels

united with the whole of the animal world and all the unknown life forces of the universe.

15   This is probably the best place to make a distinction between eroticism and pornography. Eroticism is the effort to reach, by way of sex, something which lies beyond sex: nature, beauty, or communion with the universe. Pornography is concerned entirely with sex and inflates its importance, thus making it a simple trick to stimulate orgasm. While eroticism retains a certain element of spontaneity, pornography is calculated stimulation. I feel it remains an open question, however, whether it is to eroticism, as I understand it, that we are returning today. As soon as one completely divorces the sexual act from pro-creation, is it really possible to speak of a return to nature? Does the sexual act, complete in itself and cut off from everything else, including procreation, amount to anything more, finally, than drinking a good wine or eating caviar?

16   It is clear, too, that scientific progress encourages this dissociation between the sexual act and procreation which is linked to the emancipation of women. The pill, for example, allows women to make love with the same impunity as men, and the results of this transformation can be read on the faces of girls today. They have become much tougher in their relations with men, and their behaviour reminds one of that of young men in the past with women. If a concept like virginity has lost its value today, it is because women have now become the equals of men. Virginity has been glorified by Christianity, because women were freely considered as superior beings in the Greco-Roman world. The Christian virgin, however, was considered the equal of man and not just as the instrument of his pleasure. But it was only when a woman remained unmarried that this equality was possible, and this situation lasted for a long time. At the end of the last century, when the movement for the emancipation of women got under way in Great Britain, the principals of the women's colleges of English universities were currently heard to say of their pupils, "She had a lot of promise and she could have been an outstanding doctor . . . and then she went and got married." It was as if they had said, "And then she died young." Today neither marriage, nor—with or without marriage—the sexual act means that the woman loses her position of equality with the man.

17   Scientifically speaking, it is not at all impossible that pregnancies will soon be extrauterine and that children will grow in test tubes. We shall thus have reached Aldous Huxley's *Brave New World*. It is even conceivable that scientific and social evolution will be such that it will no longer be economically or socially acceptable for a woman to become pregnant. Midwives will disappear like a species which has become extinct. If we add the possibilities of artificial insemination, it should ultimately be possible to manufacture children at will, without recognized parents, under the pretext of improving the human species.

18   But what will such children be? Will they not be worse off than an orphan, because an orphan does at least know that he has had parents? There are already problems with adopted children, when they have to be told the truth. But I think that if there were no parents at

all, the effect would be terrifying: no roots, no personal ancestry, no successors. Even now, in the United States, the blacks suffer from not knowing from which region in Africa they have come, from feeling cut off from a historical background, and from the fact that many of them, because of their extreme promiscuity, have no real father, since their mother has had children by several men. The psychological results are disastrous.

19 Without going to the extreme of the test-tube baby, there is a risk that women's emancipation will go together with a certain masculinization. This will be to the detriment of the children, since the maternal instinct may atrophy or be repressed. I know the case of two women who have brilliant careers, get on very well with their husbands and apparently give their children a lot of attention. Yet the children have suffered because their mother has not been sufficiently available psychologically and they have not remained at the centre of her preoccupations. However, I do not believe that the maternal instinct can be suppressed completely by any scientific progress. I do, however, think that it can be twisted or repressed and that this could cause considerable frustration in women, because it is, after all, a very deeply-felt instinct.

20 In man there are certain innate feelings which progress cannot suppress. Take, for example, the sense of sin and the feeling of guilt. Today's sexual freedom does not do away with the sense of sin altogether, but causes it rather to turn in another direction. The hippies, for example, have a guilt complex about the war in Vietnam, the colour problem and the pollution of nature. In the same way, I think asceticism is perhaps reappearing in America, with regard not to sex but to money: students are deliberately refusing to go into business, rejecting the attractive propositions of the biggest firms, and opting for more humanitarian careers, such as medicine.

21 There were still people who poked fun at the ascetic tendencies of Christianity in the 2nd century A.D. Two centuries later, however, the anchorites in the desert had become famous and their names were as well-known as those of the great courtesans and the champions of the chariot races. In Syria, Simeon Stylites and his followers, who remained perched on their columns for years, attracted crowds of pilgrims and caused a whole tourist industry to come into being. We have not reached this point. We have our stars in films, in pop music, and in sport; the champions of asceticism have yet to come. But come they will. The late Padre Pio, the priest of the village of San Giovanni Rotondo in southern Italy, was perhaps their precursor. And since history is made so much more quickly in our time because of rapid communications, I do not think we will have to wait two centuries for this reversal in morality.

Discussion of Theme

1. According to Toynbee, why is the regulation of human sexual life difficult? Is it a desirable goal? Do you agree?

2. It has often been remarked that our society is hypocritical in its attitude toward sex and morals. If you agree, what explanation can you give? What examples can you cite to support such a view?
3. What does Toynbee regard as the positive aspects of today's sexual revolt? What are its negative effects?
4. The author states that today's young people have a "sense of sin and . . . feeling of guilt" about sexual matters. Do you agree?

Discussion of Rhetoric

1. What is the underlying organization pattern to this essay? Why is it effective?
2. Comment on the author's diction. Is it appropriate?
3. Toynbee uses transitional devices to hold his essay together. Note, for example, *for instance* (paragraph 3), *But* (paragraph 4), *however* (paragraph 6), *Similarly* (paragraph 8). Find several other such examples. How does using these terms make the reader's task easier?

Writing Assignments

1. Do you think the moral standards of today's college students are lower than those of the previous generation? Present your views in a theme.
2. What is your attitude toward the women's liberation movement?
3. Defend (or attack) monogamy as a desirable practice or custom.
4. Can a woman successfully combine motherhood with a career? Will her children suffer?

Library Exploration

1. For a light-hearted treatment of contemporary morals, read Morton Hunt's *The Affair.*
2. In what ways has the Puritan legacy survived in this country?

Vocabulary

(1) AMBIGUITY confusion; doubt; two or more possible meanings

(2) MONOGAMOUS being married to one person at a time

(2) POLYGAMOUS having more than one wife at a time

(2) POLYANDROUS having more than one husband at a time

(2) TRAUMATIC physically or behaviorally disordered because of shock

(7) DECADENCE decline; decay

(8) PROFLIGACY corruption, particularly moral

(10) EXPLICABLE capable of explanation

Dixon Wecter (1906–50), a Texas-born historian and author, received degrees from Baylor University, Yale, and Oxford. He taught at the Universities of Colorado, Denver, and California at Berkeley and Los Angeles. In addition to three volumes on Mark Twain, Wecter wrote several books of social history. Among them are "Saga of American Society" (1937), "The Hero in America" (1941), and "The Age of the Great Depression" (1948).

As its title suggests, the following article analyzes the qualities that Americans seek in their heroes.

DIXON WECTER

How Americans Choose Their Heroes

1 The sort of man whom Americans admire, trust, and are willing to follow can be sketched with a few lines. East and west, north and south, his portrait is familiar. At the basic level he must be self-respecting, decent, honorable, with a sense of fair play; no Machiavelli nor Mussolini need apply. He must be firm and self-confident in leadership: Davy Crockett's "Be always sure you're right, then go ahead!" is approved American doctrine, whether in the headstrong and cocksure types we sometimes follow, like Old Hickory and Theodore Roosevelt, or in the great characters of our imagination, like Paul Bunyan and Huckleberry Finn. Mother wit and resourcefulness we love. But a reputation for "genius" is unnecessary and may do the hero harm. Brilliantly clever men like Alexander Hamilton and John

Randolph of Roanoke, and pure intellectuals like John Quincy Adams (by the guess of educators given the highest I.Q., 165, of all Americans in the Hall of Fame), are not major idols. An able man must not glory in his cleverness. By our standards one is sometimes allowed to "put over a fast one"—Benjamin Franklin and Abraham Lincoln did, repeatedly—but he must not appear to relish the coup for its own sake. Art must conceal art. A clodhopper Politician like Huey Long, boasting "There are not many people in the United States who are smarter than I am, and none in Louisiana," did not understand this restraint. Long's scornful assertion that he could buy votes in his Legislature "like sacks of potatoes," to the country at large was equally bad politics. Uncle Sam allows his favorites to be shrewd in a good cause, but there must be no avowal of cynicism in principle. (In modern movies, the hero may pull a fast one for the sake of his mother, or his girl friend, or some worthy ideal, but not for himself.) The backwoods always has a certain admiration for rustic rascality, and the metropolis loves a flippant wisecrack—but in America at large there is pretty strong prejudice against the wise guy.

2   Vanity or personal arrogance in any form is taboo. The dandy in public life—accepted more tolerantly in the England of Disraeli and Lord Curzon—is disliked by Americans. Meriwether Lewis, a great explorer of the West, was handicapped by the nickname of "The Sublime Dandy" and his manners of a Beau Nash. William Pinkney, one of the most brilliant lawyers of a century ago, was ridiculed because of his fawn-colored gloves and corsets, and the vanity that led him to begin a speech all over again when he saw ladies enter the visitors' gallery of the Supreme Court.

3   Effeminacy is fatal. Martin Van Buren failed of re-election in 1840 after the public had grown tired of his lace-tipped cravats and morocco shoes, and a ribald Whig politician had exposed his use of a lotion called "Essence of Victoria." In the West the dude was a traditional villain. (Ironically, in 1860 Lincoln's campaign manager worked hard to get him photographed in a boiled shirt with pearl studs, to make a better impression in the East.)

4   The arrogance of caste is equally deadly in American hero-worship. Hancock, Jay, Gouverneur Morris were snobs who never won the sway, with even a seasoning of popular admiration, that some Tory statesmen have enjoyed in England. The public can never forget that Hamilton once exclaimed, "Your people, sir, is a great beast!" (These words, quoted in the second decade of this century in school texts on American history by William B. Guitteau, McLaughlin and Van Tyne, and Albert Bushnell Hart, were omitted after protests from school boards and patrons, from subsequent editions in the 1920s when the Hamiltonian philosophy was in favor during the era of Republican prosperity.) Harding paid Hamilton the dubious compliment of saying, in 1921, "No man's life ever gave me greater inspiration than Hamilton's"; and bankers have often praised the first Secretary of the Treasury. But the people at large have repaid his scorn with neglect.

5   Even Daniel Webster—for all his adoration in New England and among the propertied classes—has failed, for like reasons, to make the

upper rungs of hero worship. All else favored him: a head so noble that it was often said "no man could be as great as Webster looked," a record of success from barefoot boy on a New Hampshire farm to the United States Senate and Cabinet, a superb voice that made the blood pound in men's temples. But he was known as "the pensioner of Wall Street," who spent his days so exclusively around mahogany tables in clubs and directors' rooms—where the smoke of Havana cigars hung blue, and "mountain dew" Scotch regaled his fine palate —that in the end he became not the idol of the People, but of the Best People. There are apparent exceptions. The rich man's friend is sometimes elected President—as in the days of McKinley, Harding, and Coolidge—when the voters look upon themselves as potential rich men, but his popularity strikes no roots in the substratum of affection and legend.

6   Within limits, the mores of the hero may vary with his times. Emerson, living in the day of Old Hickory, Clay, and Webster, remarked that to the great man, "doing for the people what they wish done and cannot do, of course, everything will be permitted and pardoned—gaming, drinking, fighting, luxury . . . everything short of infamous crime will pass." Hadn't Jackson run off with another man's wife? Didn't he and Clay fight duels and bet on racehorses? Weren't Clay and Webster notoriously heavy drinkers—even though Webster was said to concede enough to appearances on the platform to refresh himself with white brandy out of a water-glass? Emerson's conclusion was probably too sweeping: in the first place he forgot that the capital of Puritanism had already moved from New England into insular America, and secondly he failed to reckon with the merely regional popularity of Clay and Webster which even then was fading. Only Jackson endured, a greater democrat as well as a man of higher personal integrity. The hero of a democracy—unlike the Stuarts, Bourbons, and Napoleons of the Old World—cannot invite public opinion to go to hell. He must pay tribute to conformity.

7   Through most of our cultural history, for the average man sex and religion have been life's two most serious subjects, and irregularity, even in the mighty leader, must not go too far. Aaron Burr's "one hundred bastards" belong to the legend of villainy, along with Thaddeus Stevens' alleged mistresses white and black; while Tom Paine's agnostic mockery made him, in spite of his great patriotic services, an object of folk hate. As for the hero, debunkery by sensational writers has usually addressed itself to secret nips at the bottle, failure to attend church, or flirtation with a neighbor's wife—rather than to matters of rightful public concern, like soundness of military strategy, foresight, or statemanly wisdom.

8   The great man who wins acceptance as a hero will find his vagaries and skepticisms trimmed down by convention. Nevertheless, it is surprising how few of the American great, in comparison with those of the Old World, have cultivated lush private lives, though their individual views on religion have often shown more independence than orthodoxy. To a man's man, the sturdy profanity of Washington and Old Hickory, like the earthy jokes of Franklin and Lincoln, will be for-

given and, in the main, forgotten. Fundamentally, the hero is required to be chaste, loyal, honest, humble before duty and before God. He is apt to have a dash of Puritan conscience, but the beauty of holiness is no more expected than is a sense of poetry.

9   The people's choice of heroes for America has been prevailingly sound; our major favorites are those any nation might be proud of. They go far toward vindicating the whole democratic theory of careers open to talent. We believe that character is more important than brains. Hard work, tenacity, enterprise, and firmness in the face of odds are the qualities that Americans most admire, rather than originality or eloquence of tongue and pen.

10   The hero must be a man of good will and also a good neighbor, preferably something of a joiner. Of the solitudes and lonely isolations of a great man like Lincoln the public has little conception. It likes to think of its idol as simple in greatness. Manliness, forthright manners, and salty speech are approved. Love of the soil, of dogs and horses and manual hobbies and fishing, is better understood than absorption in art, literature, and music. (The public distrusts Presidents who are photographed fishing in their store clothes.) The hero must not lose touch with his birthplace and origins, however humble; the atmosphere of small towns and front-porch campaigns, cultivated by so many candidates for President, pays tribute to this demand. "I really believe there are more attempts at flattering the farmers than any other class," Lincoln as candidate for President remarked at the Wisconsin State Fair, "the reason for which I cannot perceive, unless it be that they cast more votes than any other."

11   Also, the touch of versatility and homely skill is applauded in a hero. Thomas Jefferson is remembered less as the eighteenth-century virtuoso than as an inventor of gadgets from which he plainly got a great deal of fun. "Tinkering" is American. European lads—like Henrich Steffens growing up in Denmark, and Michael Pupin in a Serbian village—have testified to the fascination that Franklin, "wiser than all the wise men of Idvor," held for them. The hero must do things better than the common folk, but his achievements (unlike those of the artist, philosopher, and pure scientist) must lie open to everyman's comprehension. It is well, too, that the labels of the hero conform to those of the group, so that identification between him and the majority can more easily be made: for example, all of our major idols have been both Anglo-Saxon and Protestant.

12   Bravery, honesty, strength of character are the stuff for hero-worship. At the boy's level, this worship gravitates toward the doer of spectacular deeds; on the average adult level, toward the wielder of power; and in the eyes of a more critical judgment, toward idealism and moral qualities. The most universal hero is he who can fill all these specifications. This, by the many shapes of their courage, integrity, and strength, Washington and Lincoln and Lee are able to do. When the dust of partisanship has settled, another leader in two great crises, economic and military—Franklin D. Roosevelt—will probably join their august company. But Jefferson the sedentary man, Ben Franklin the opportunist, and Andrew Jackson the rough-hewn soldier fail

to satisfy everybody. Upon a still lower rank, men like Daniel Boone and Crockett and Buffalo Bill and Edison remain almost juvenile heroes. They do not have all the dimensions of our few supreme symbols. Was it not Emerson who suggested that we Americans were the shattered pieces of a great mould?

13   Our most powerful hero epics center about our leaders. What then, in the final analysis do Washington, Franklin, Jefferson, Jackson, Lincoln, and in a provisional verdict Wilson and the Roosevelts have in common? Among them lie many differences. In heredity, economic origins, training, skill, temperament, party affiliations, and attachment to specific policies they may seem as diverse as we could find by sifting the nation from Atlantic to Pacific. All save perhaps Washington were "liberals" by the gauge of their times — and Washington, one must not forget, was an arch political rebel, who even in old age sought to balance his conservatism by an honest effort to be nonpartisan. (And even Washington has slowly waned before the warmer humanity of Lincoln.) What is their common denominator?

14   All of them, the people believe, loved America more deeply than any selfish consideration. The hero as made in America is a man who has the power and yet does not abuse it. He is the practical demonstration of romantic democracy. Washington is most sublime because, after winning our freedom, he refused a crown, military dictatorship, and every personal reward. Lee is grandest because he did what he thought was his duty, failed under heartbreaking odds, and then with gentleness did his best to repair all hate and malice. Lincoln is most appealing because, in the conduct of that same desperate war which gave him the power of a czar, he never forgot his love for the common people of North and South.

15   More clearly than the great heroes of Europe, military and political, ours stand for a progress concept. They spring from stock that has bred schemes both wise and foolish — with its talk about the pursuit of happiness, the more abundant life, and the American Dream. None of these epic leaders left the Republic as he found it — although to avoid disturbing a single stick or stone seems to have been the policy of men like James Buchanan, Chester A. Arthur, William McKinley, and Calvin Coolidge. At times, to be sure, the people themselves have wanted no change, felt no urge to take on fresh responsibility in the national sphere. In eras like theirs, nothing is added to the stature of American ideals — such as civil liberty, equality of opportunity, faith in the average man, social justice, respect for the rights of weaker nations and for the good estate of democracy throughout the earth. A Chief Executive may then be called to office who rules as a minor Augustus over a gilded age, or serves as the genial host at a great barbecue. But ten years hence he is not likely to be remembered as a great man, or even as a symbol worth keeping.

16   Our heroes, we believe, are cast in a different mould. Their ruling passion, as we see it, is a sense of duty, alert to the best among the stirring impulses of their time, and able to make the impulse effective. They translate the dream into act. The supreme leader is he who can hitch the great bandwagon to the star of American idealism.

Discussion of Theme

1. In paragraph 1, Wecter states that the following phrase is approved American doctrine: "Be always sure you're right, then go ahead." Is this doctrine always a wise one to follow? Is there such a thing as being *sure* one is *right*?
2. In the final sentence, Wecter speaks of "the star of American idealism." Have public events of recent years made Americans too cynical to retain their ideals?
3. How do we know when a man has attained hero's status? Who decides that he is a hero, and what proportion of the population must regard him as such before he is considered a hero?
4. Why do you think Wecter doesn't name any women?

Discussion of Rhetoric

1. Does the author use a great deal of figurative language? Do you consider it appropriate to his subject matter? Identify the figure of speech used in the final sentence. Is it effective? On what quotation is it based?
2. Wecter follows a pattern in organizing his paragraphs. What is the pattern? To what extent does it contribute to the clarity of his writing?
3. How important is Wecter's overall organization of his material? Could the paragraphs be rearranged without detracting from either the sense or the impact of what the author has to say?
4. Find the sentence in paragraph 8 that serves as the pivot, or turning point, of the essay. What has Wecter accomplished in the first seven paragraphs?

Writing Assignments

1. Using the qualities described as unsuitable for heroes as a guide, explain why various contemporary American leaders could not be accepted as heroes by the general public.
2. Three articles in this anthology discuss heroes. What about villains? Write a paper in which you examine the characteristics of the kind of individual who would be the opposite of a hero.
3. Select a modern American hero—not necessarily your own—and analyze his appeal.
4. Is hero worship harmful to society, or is it a healthy phenomenon?

Library Exploration

1. Some current literature is concerned with what critics call the "anti-hero." Define this paradoxical term.

2. Read Max Eastman's *Heroes I Have Known; Twelve Who Have Lived Great Lives.*
3. Read John F. Kennedy's *Profiles in Courage.*

Vocabulary

(1) AVOWAL   declaration; acknowledgment

(1) RUSTIC   rural; countrified

(3) EFFEMINACY   womanish characteristics in a man

(3) RIBALD   coarse; indelicate

(5) PENSIONER   dependent; someone receiving money (pension)

(5) SUBSTRATUM   underlying layer; foundation

(6) MORES   habits; customs

(6) INFAMOUS   notorious; disgraceful

(7) AGNOSTIC   unbelieving

(7) DEBUNKERY   attempts to expose sham or explode myths

(8) VAGARIES   peculiarities; oddities

(9) VINDICATING   justifying; supporting

(9) TENACITY   persistency; stick-to-it-iveness

(11) VIRTUOSO   scholar; star performer

(12) GRAVITATES   moves toward something as if attracted

(12) AUGUST   grand; imposing

(12) SEDENTARY   relatively inactive

Arthur M. Schlesinger, Jr. (1917–) is the Albert Schweitzer professor of humanities at the City University of New York and former special assistant to Presidents John F. Kennedy and Lyndon B. Johnson. Educated at Harvard, where he later taught history, Schlesinger received the Pulitzer Prize for History in 1945 for "The Age of Jackson." He has written "The Coming of the New Deal" (1958), "The Politics of Upheaval" (1960), and an account of the Kennedy administration, "A Thousand Days" (1965).

The argument here is that "ours is an age without heroes" and that we need great men in a democracy because they enable us "to rise to our own highest potentialities."

ARTHUR M. SCHLESINGER, JR.

The Decline of Heroes

1 Ours is an age without heroes — and, when we say this, we suddenly realize how spectacularly the world has changed in a generation. Most of us grew up in a time of towering personalities. For better or for worse, great men seemed to dominate our lives and shape our destiny. In the United States we had Theodore Roosevelt, Woodrow Wilson, Franklin Roosevelt. In Great Britain, there were Lloyd George and Winston Churchill. In other lands, there were Lenin, Stalin, Hitler, Mussolini, Clemenceau, Gandhi, Kemal, Sun Yat-sen. Outside of politics there were Einstein, Freud, Keynes. Some of these great men influenced the world for good, others for evil; but, whether for good or for evil, the fact that each had not died at birth made a difference, one believed, to everyone who lived after them.

2   Today no one bestrides our narrow world like a colossus; we have no giants who play roles which one can imagine no one else playing in their stead. There are a few figures on the margin of uniqueness, perhaps: Adenauer, Nehru, Tito, De Gaulle, Chiang Kai-shek, Mao Tse-tung. But there seem to be none in the epic style of those mighty figures of our recent past who seized history with both hands and gave it an imprint, even a direction, which it otherwise might not have had. As De Gaulle himself remarked on hearing of Stalin's death, "The age of giants is over." Whatever one thought, whether one admired or detested Roosevelt or Churchill, Stalin or Hitler, one nevertheless felt the sheer weight of such personalities on one's own existence. We feel no comparable pressures today. Our own President, with all his pleasant qualities, has more or less explicitly renounced any desire to impress his own views on history. The Macmillans, Khrushchevs, and Gronchis have measurably less specific gravity than their predecessors. Other men could be in their places as leaders of America or Britain or Russia or Italy without any change in the course of history. Why ours should thus be an age without heroes, and whether this condition is good or bad for us and for civilization, are topics worthy of investigation.

3   Why have giants vanished from our midst? One must never neglect the role of accident in history; and accident no doubt plays a part here. But too many accidents of the same sort cease to be wholly accidental. One must inquire further. Why should our age not only be without great men but even seem actively hostile to them? Surely one reason we have so few heroes now is precisely that we had so many a generation ago. Greatness is hard for common humanity to bear. As Emerson said, "Heroism means difficulty, postponement of praise, postponement of ease, introduction of the world into the private apartment, introduction of eternity into the hours measured by the sitting-room clock." A world of heroes keeps people from living their own private lives.

4   Moreover, great men live dangerously. They introduce extremes into existence — extremes of good, extremes of evil — and ordinary men after a time flinch from the ultimates and yearn for undemanding security. The Second World War was the climax of an epoch of living dangerously. It is no surprise that it precipitated a universal revulsion against greatness. The war itself destroyed Hitler and Mussolini. And the architects of victory were hardly longer-lived. After the war, the British repudiated Churchill, and the Americans (with the adoption of the 22nd Amendment), Roosevelt. In due course, the French repudiated De Gaulle (they later repented, but it took the threat of civil war to bring him back); the Chinese, Chiang Kai-shek; and the Russians, Stalin. Khrushchev, in toppling Stalin from his pedestal, pronounced the general verdict against the uncommon man: the modern world, he said, had no use for the "cult of the individual." And, indeed, carried to the excesses to which the worshipers of Hitler and Stalin carried it, even to the much milder degree to which admirers of Roosevelt and Churchill sometimes carried it, the cult of the individual was dangerous. No man is infallible, and every man needs to be reminded of this on occasion. Still, our age has gone further than this — it objects not

just to hero worship but to heroes. The century of the common man has come into its own.

5   This term, "common man," suggests the deeper problem. There is more involved than simply a dismissal of those colossi whom the world identified with a season of blood and agony. The common man has always regarded the great man with mixed feelings—resentment as well as admiration, hatred as well as love. The Athenian who refused to vote for Aristides because he was so tired of hearing him called "the Just" expressed a natural reaction. Great men make small men aware of their smallness. Rancor is one of the unavowed but potent emotions in politics; and one must never forget that the envy of the have-nots can be quite as consuming when the haves have character or intelligence as it is when they have merely material possessions.

6   Modern democracy inadvertently gave envy new scope. While the purpose of democracy was to give everyone a fair chance to rise, its method enabled rancorous men to invoke "equality" as an excuse for keeping all down to their own level. "I attribute the small number of distinguished men in political life," wrote Alexis de Tocqueville after visiting the United States in the 1830s, "to the ever-increasing despotism of the majority. . . . The power of the majority is so absolute and irresistible that one must give up one's rights as a citizen and almost abjure one's qualities as a human being, if one intends to stray from the track which it prescribes." James Bryce even titled a chapter in his *American Commonwealth,* Why Great Men Are Not Chosen President.

7   History has shown these prophets unduly pessimistic. Distinguished men do enter American politics; great men have been chosen President. Democracy demonstrates a capability for heroic leadership quite as much as it does a tendency toward mediocrity. Yet Tocqueville and the others were correct enough in detecting the dislike of great men as a permanent potentiality in a democracy. And the evolution of industrial society appears to have given this sentiment new force. More and more of us live and work within great organizations; an influential book has already singled out the organization man as the American of the future. The bureaucratization of American life, the decline of the working class, the growth of the white-collar class, the rise of suburbia—all this has meant the increasing homogeneity of American society. Though we continue to speak of ourselves as rugged individualists, our actual life has grown more and more collective and anonymous. As a Monsanto Chemical film put it, showing a group of technicians at work in a laboratory: "No geniuses here; just a bunch of average Americans working together." Our ideal is increasingly smooth absorption into the group rather than self-realization in the old-fashioned, strong-minded, don't-give-a-damn sense. Where does the great man fit into our homogenized society?

8   "The greatness of England is now all collective," John Stuart Mill wrote a century ago: "individually small, we only appear capable of anything great by our habit of combining." He might have been writing about contemporary America; but where we Americans are inclined to rejoice over the superiority of the "team," Mill added somberly, "It was men of another stamp than this that made England

what is has been; and men of another stamp will be needed to prevent its decline."

9   But was Mill right? Do individuals really have impact on history? A powerful school of philosophers has denied any importance at all to great men. Such thinkers reject heroes as a childish hangover from the days when men ascribed everything to the action of gods. History, they assert, is not made by men, but by inexorable forces or irrevocable laws: if these forces or laws do not manifest themselves through one individual, they will do so through another. What has happened already has comprehensively and absolutely decided what will happen in the future. "If there is a single human action due to free will," wrote Tolstoi, "no historical law exists, and no conception of historical events can be formed." If all this is so, obviously the presence or absence of any particular "hero" at any particular time cannot make the slightest difference.

10   This view of history is a form of fatalistic determinism; and Tolstoi's *War and Peace* offers one of its most eloquent statements. Why, Tolstoi asked, did millions of men in the time of Napoleon, repudiating their common sense and their human feeling, move from west to east, slaughtering their fellows? The answers provided by historians seemed to him hopelessly superficial. His own answer was: "The war was bound to happen simply because it was bound to happen"; all previous history predetermined it. Where did this leave the great men? In Tolstoi's view, they were the most deluded figures of all. Great men, he said, "are but the labels that serve to give a name to an event and, like labels, they have the least possible connection with the event itself." The greater the man, "the more conspicuous is the inevitability and predestination of every act he commits." The hero, said Tolstoi, "is the slave of history."

11   There are many forms of historical fatalism. Toynbee and Spengler, with their theory of the inexorable growth and decay of civilizations, represent one form. The Marxists, with their theory that changes in the modes of production control the course of history, represent another. When Khrushchev denounced the practice of making "a hero" out of "a particular leader" and condemned the cult of the individual as "alien to the spirit of Marxism-Leninism," he was speaking the true spirit of his faith. And Marxism is not the only form of economic determinism; there are also, for example, economic determinists of the laissez-faire school who believe that all civilization is dependent on rigid adherence to a certain theory of the sacredness of private property.

12   Fatalists differ greatly among themselves. But, however much they differ, they unite in the conclusion that the individual plays no role of his own in history. If they are right, then nothing else could matter less whether or not this is an age without heroes.

13   But they are not right. The philosophy of historical fatalism rests on serious fallacies. For one thing, it supposes that, because a thing happens, it had to happen. But causation is one matter; predestination another. The construction of a causal explanation after an event merely renders that event in some sense intelligible. It does not in the least show that this particular event, and no other, had to take place;

that nothing else could possibly have occurred in its stead. The serious test of the fatalist case must be applied before the event. The only conclusive proof of fatalism would lie in the accurate prediction of events that have not yet happened. And to say, with Tolstoi, that all prior history predetermines everything that follows is to say nothing at all. It is to produce an explanation which applies equally to everything — and thus becomes so vague and limitless as to explain nothing.

14   Fatalism raises other difficulties. Thus it imputes reality to mythical historical "forces" — class, race, nation, the will of the people, the spirit of the times, history itself. But there are no such forces. They are merely abstractions or metaphors with no existence except in the mind of the beholder. The only evidence for them is deduction from the behavior of individuals. It is therefore the individual who constitutes the basic unit of history. And, while no individual can be wholly free — and, indeed, recent discoveries of the manifold ways in which we are unconsciously conditioned should constitute a salutary check on human vanity — one must assume the reality of an area of free choice until that assumption is challenged, not by metaphysical affirmation, but by verifiable proof — that is, consistently accurate prediction of the future.

15   Fatalism, moreover, is incompatible with human psychology and human morality. Anyone who rigorously accepted a deterministic view of life, for example, would have to abandon all notions of human responsibility, since it is manifestly unfair to praise or punish people for acts which are by definition beyond their control. But such fatalism is belied by the assumption of free choice which underlies every move we make, every word we utter, every thought we think. As Sir Isaiah Berlin observes of determinism, "If we begin to take it seriously, then, indeed, the changes in our language, our moral notions, our attitudes toward one another, our views of history, of society, and of everything else will be too profound to be even adumbrated." We can no more imagine what the universe of the consistent determinist would be like than we can imagine what it would be like to live in a world without time or one with seventeen-dimensional space.

16   For the historian concerned with concrete interpretation of actual events, he can easily demonstrate the futility of fatalism by trying to apply it to specific historical episodes. According to the extreme determinist view, no particular individual can make the slightest difference. As slaves of history, all individuals are, so to speak, interchangeable parts. If Napoleon had not led his armies across Europe, Tolstoi implies, someone else would have. William James, combating this philosophic fatalism, once asked the determinists whether they really believed "the convergence of sociological pressures to have so impinged on Stratford on Avon about April 23, 1564, that a W. Shakespeare, with all his mental peculiarities, had to be born there." And did they further believe, James continued, that "if the aforesaid W. Shakespeare had died of cholera infantum, another mother at Stratford on Avon would needs have engendered a duplicate of him to restore the sociological equilibrium?" Who could believe such stuff? Yet, if the determinists do not mean exactly this, how can they read the individual out of history?

17   In December, 1931, a British politician, crossing Fifth Avenue in

New York between 76th and 77th streets around ten-thirty at night, was knocked down and gravely injured by an automobile. Fourteen months later an American politician, sitting in an open car in Miami, Florida, was fired on by an assassin; a man standing beside him was killed. Would the next two decades of history have been the same had Contasini's car killed Winston Churchill in 1931 and Zangara's bullets killed Franklin Roosevelt in 1933? Suppose, in addition, that Adolf Hitler had been killed in the street fighting during the Munich *Putsch* of 1923, and that Lenin and Mussolini had died at birth. Where would our century be now?

18   Individuals, of course, must operate within limits. They cannot do everything. They cannot, for example, propel history into directions for which the environment and the human material are not prepared: no genius, however heroic, could have brought television to ancient Troy. Yet, as Sidney Hook has convincingly argued in his thoughtful book, *The Hero in History,* great men can count decisively "where the historical situation permits of major alternative paths of development."

19   This argument between fatalism and heroism is not one on which there is a lot to be said on both sides. The issue is far too sharp to be straddled. Either history is rigidly determined and foreordained, in which case individual striving does not matter; or it is not, in which case there is an essential role for the hero. Analysis of concrete episodes suggests that history is, within limits, open and unfinished; that men have lived who did what no substitute could ever have done; that their intervention set history on one path rather than another. If this is so, the old maxim, "There are no indispensable men," would seem another amiable fallacy. There is, then, a case for heroes.

20   To say that there is a case for heroes is not to say that there is a case for hero worship. The surrender of decision, the unquestioning submission to leadership, the prostration of the average man before the Great Man—these are the diseases of heroism, and they are fatal to human dignity. But, if carried too far, hero worship generates its own antidote. "Every hero," said Emerson, "becomes a bore at last." And we need not go too far. History amply shows that it is possible to have heroes without turning them into gods.

21   And history shows, too, that when a society, in flight from hero worship, decides to do without great men at all, it gets into troubles of its own. Our contemporary American society, for example, has little use for the individualist. Individualism implies dissent from the group; dissent implies conflict; and conflict suddenly seems divisive, un-American and generally unbearable. Our greatest new industry is evidently the production of techniques to eliminate conflict, from positive thoughts through public relations to psychoanalysis, applied everywhere from the couch to the pulpit. Our national aspiration has become peace of mind, peace of soul. The symptomatic drug of our age is the tranquilizer. "Togetherness" is the banner under which we march into the brave new world.

22   Obviously society has had to evolve collective institutions to cope with problems that have grown increasingly complex and concentrated. But the collective approach can be overdone. If Khrushchev worried because his collectivist society developed a cult of the indi-

vidual, maybe we Americans should start worrying as our so-called individualist society develops a cult of the group. We instinctively suppose that the tough questions will be solved by an interfaith conference or an interdisciplinary research team or an interdepartmental committee or an assembly of wise men meeting at Arden House. But are not these group tactics essentially means by which individuals hedge their bets and distribute the responsibilities? And do they not nearly always result in the dilution of insight and the triumph of mishmash? If we are to survive, we must have ideas, vision, courage. These are rarely produced by committees. Everything that matters in our intellectual and moral life begins with an individual confronting his own mind and conscience in a room by himself.

23   A bland society will never be creative. "The amount of eccentricity in a society," said John Stuart Mill, "has generally been proportional to the amount of genius, mental vigor and moral courage it contained. That so few now dare to be eccentric marks the chief danger of the time." If this condition frightened Mill in Victorian England, it should frighten us much more. For our national apotheosis of the group means that we systematically lop off the eccentrics, the originals, the proud, imaginative lonely people from whom new ideas come. What began as a recoil from hero worship ends as a conspiracy against creativity. If worship of great men brings us to perdition by one path, flight from great men brings us there just as surely by another. When we do not admire great men, then our instinct for admiration is likely to end by settling on ourselves. The one thing worse for democracy than hero worship is self-worship.

24   A free society cannot get along without heroes, because they are the most vivid means of exhibiting the power of free men. The hero exposes to all mankind unsuspected possibilities of conception, unimagined resources of strength. "The appearance of a great man," wrote Emerson, "draws a new circle outside of our largest orbit and surprises and commands us." Carlyle likened ordinary, lethargic times, with their unbelief and perplexity, to dry, dead fuel, waiting for the lightning out of heaven to kindle it. "The great man, with his free force direct out of God's own hand, is the lightning. . . . The rest of men waited for him like fuel, and then they too would flame."

25   Great men enable us to rise to our own highest potentialities. They nerve lesser men to disregard the world and trust to their own deepest instinct. "In picking out from history our heroes," said William James, "each one of us may best fortify and inspire what creative energy may lie in his own soul. This is the last justification of hero worship." Which one of us has not gained fortitude and faith from the incarnation of ideals in men, from the wisdom of Socrates, from the wondrous creativity of Shakespeare, from the strength of Washington, from the compassion of Lincoln, and above all, perhaps, from the life and the death of Jesus? "We feed on genius," said Emerson. "Great men exist that there may be greater men."

26   Yet this may be only the smaller part of their service. Great men have another and larger role—to affirm human freedom against the supposed inevitabilities of history. The first hero was Prometheus, who defied the gods and thus asserted the independence and autonomy of

man against all determinism. Zeus punished Prometheus, chaining him to a rock and encouraging a vulture to pluck at his vitals.

27   Ever since, man, like Prometheus, has warred against history. It has always been a bitter and remorseless fight; for the heavy weight of human inertia lies with fatalism. It takes a man of exceptional vision and strength and will — it takes, in short, a hero — to try to wrench history from what lesser men consider its preconceived path. And often history tortures the hero in the process, chains him to a rock and exposes him to the vulture. Yet, in the model of Prometheus, man can still hold his own against the gods. Brave men earn the right to shape their own destiny.

28   An age without great men is one which acquiesces in the drift of history. Such acquiescence is easy and seductive; the great appeal of fatalism, indeed, is as a refuge from the terror of responsibility. Where a belief in great men insistently reminds us that individuals can make a difference, fatalism reassures us that they can't. It thereby blesses our weakness and extenuates our failure. Fatalism, in Berlin's phrase, is "one of the great alibis" of history.

29   Let us not be complacent about our supposed capacity to get along without great men. If our society has lost its wish for heroes and its ability to produce them, it may well turn out to have lost everything else as well.

Discussion of Theme

1. Are heroic qualities absolute, or do they vary from one era to the next and from one society to another? What is the hero's relation to his culture? Have certain so-called "heroic qualities" endured throughout America's history?
2. Are heroes individualists, or are they, rather, conventional people who epitomize the qualities valued most highly by their own society?
3. Is a martyr always a hero?
4. Does our age have heroes?
5. Was President Kennedy a hero? Is his legend making him one?
6. Must a society have great heroes to remain great and to give identity to each individual?

Discussion of Rhetoric

1. What is an "amiable fallacy" (paragraph 19)?
2. Look again at paragraph 17. Is such speculation merely an entertaining mental exercise, or can it serve as the basis for serious argument?
3. Why does Schlesinger avoid defining a hero?
4. Schlesinger's essay is built around two questions and a fallacy. What are these crucial ideas?
5. Comment on the author's use of quotation marks to give emphasis to words.

Writing Assignments

1. Whom do you regard as America's — or the world's — greatest *unsung* hero? Describe his or her qualities.
2. Schlesinger says that "A free society cannot get along without heroes, because they are the most vivid means of exhibiting the power of free men." With this in mind, consider whether a closed society also has its heroes and what they represent to "unfree men." Are such heroes officially selected or are they spontaneously acclaimed by the populace?
3. Write a paper that examines evidence to support Schlesinger's claim that this is the age of "the common man." Be sure to define the highly connotative phrase "common man."
4. Choose a man who is considered a hero and describe the characteristics that account for his reputation.

Library Exploration

1. Read Sidney Hook's *The Hero in History*.
2. What is the 22nd Amendment? Why does the author say that it repudiated Roosevelt? Do you approve of the 22nd Amendment?
3. For a treatment of a man regarded by many as a modern-day hero, read Schlesinger's *A Thousand Days* (1965).

Vocabulary

(2) COLOSSUS gigantic statue; person of great power or influence

(2) UNIQUENESS being one of a kind

(2) EPIC heroic in scale

(2) EXPLICITLY distinctly stated

(4) EPOCH period of time

(4) PRECIPITATED brought about; caused

(4) REPUDIATED rejected

(4) INFALLIBLE without error

(5) RANCOR intense spite or ill-will

(5) UNAVOWED not admitted

(5) POTENT powerful

(5) CONSUMING engrossing; absorbing

(6) INADVERTENTLY not intentionally

(6) DESPOTISM tyranny

(6) ABJURE renounce; deny

(7) MEDIOCRITY the ordinary; commonness

(7) HOMOGENEITY similarity in nature or character

(7) ANONYMOUS without personality or individuality

(9) INEXORABLE relentless; unyielding

(9) IRREVOCABLE unalterable

(9) MANIFEST show; demonstrate

(9) COMPREHENSIVELY completely

(9) CONCEPTION idea; theory

(10) FATALISTIC believing that events are determined by fate

(10) DELUDED misled; deceived

(10) INEVITABILITY inescapability; unavoidability

(10) PREDESTINATION determining beforehand

(11) LAISSEZ-FAIRE noninterference

(13) FALLACIES mistakes in logical reasoning

(14) IMPUTES ascribes; assigns

(14) METAPHORS literary devices using images for comparison

(14) MANIFOLD many

(14) SALUTARY healthy

(14) METAPHYSICAL based on abstract reasoning on the nature of reality

(14) VERIFIABLE provable

(15) INCOMPATIBLE irreconcilable; not in keeping

(15) ADUMBRATED foreshadowed

(16) CONVERGENCE coming together

(16) IMPINGED touched; made contact

(16) CHOLERA INFANTUM a usually fatal child's disease

(16) ENGENDERED given birth to

(16) EQUILIBRIUM balance

(19) FOREORDAINED decreed in advance of the event

(19) INDISPENSABLE essential

(19) AMIABLE agreeable; obliging

(20) PROSTRATION lying prone; hence, submission

(20) ANTIDOTE remedy

(21) DIVISIVE causing disagreement or dissension

(21) SYMPTOMATIC characteristic

(22) INTERDISCIPLINARY from many intellectual disciplines, or fields of knowledge

(22) DILUTION watering down; weakening

(23) BLAND mild; insipid

(23) ECCENTRICITY abnormal or unconventional behavior

(23) APOTHEOSIS glorification; deification

(23) PERDITION ruin; damnation

(24) LETHARGIC slow-moving; dull

(25) FORTITUDE firm courage; patient endurance

(25) INCARNATION incorporation into human form

(27) REMORSELESS merciless; ruthless

(27) INERTIA difficulty in getting started

(28) ACQUIESCES accepts without protest

(28) EXTENUATES excuses; lessens the seriousness of

(29) COMPLACENT self-satisfied; smug

Sir C. M. Bowra (1898–1971) was warden of Wadham College, Oxford, and a leading authority on Greek and Latin literature. An honors graduate of Oxford, he served as professor of poetry and vice-chancellor at Wadham College. Among his many scholarly books and articles are "Tradition and Design in the Iliad" (1930), "From Virgil to Milton" (1945), and "The Greek Experience" (1957).

After analyzing the appeal and qualities of Aeneas, the hero of "The Aeneid," Bowra suggests that through him Virgil recast the heroic ideal into a new mold and by so doing set an example for later poets.

C. M. BOWRA

Aeneas: The Roman Hero

1 Virgil was not the first to write the epic of Rome. In the third century B.C. Naevius had used the old Saturnian measure for his *Punic War* and in the next century Ennius' *Annals* traced the Roman story from Romulus to his own day. The first of these poems must have had many similarities to oral epic or even to ballad; the second, despite its use of the hexameter and many effective adaptations of the Homeric manner, was built on the annalistic plan which is always liable to appear when poetry annexes history. Virgil knew both works, and his own poem must have been meant to supersede them and to give in a more satisfactory form the truth about Rome as it had been revealed to his own generation. To do this he adopted a remarkable method. He abandoned the annalistic scheme and instead of versifying history presented the Roman character and destiny through a poem about a legendary and largely imaginary past. His concern was less with historical events than with their meaning, less with Rome at this or that

time than as it was from the beginning and forever, less with individual Romans than with a single, symbolical hero who stands for the qualities and the experiences which are typically Roman. By skillful literary devices, such as prophecies spoken by gods or visions seen in Elysium or scenes depicted on works of art, Virgil links up the mythical past with recorded history and his own time. But such excursions are exceptional and take up less than 300 lines in a total of nearly 10,000. The main action of the *Aeneid* takes place some three hundred years before the foundation of Rome; the leading hero and his followers are not Romans or even Italians but Trojans whose ancestral connection with Italy is dim and remote; much of the action takes place outside Italy, and when it moves there, is confined to a small area around the Tiber; Aeneas himself is a homeless wanderer who asks for no more than a few acres for himself and his company. This remote past is connected with the present by many ingenious ties. The Trojan heroes are the ancestors of famous Roman families and bear names honoured in Roman history; their ceremonies, their habits, their games, forecast what are later to be characteristic of Rome; they touch at places familiar to every Roman; into their story local legends and traditions are woven; the gods who support and sustain them are those whose cults formed the official religion of the Roman people. And more significant than these external connections are the Roman spirit, virtues and outlook which the Trojans display. The difficulties encountered by these first ancestors, their relations to the gods, their emotions and their ideals, their family loyalties, their behaviour in peace and war, their attitude to the divine task laid upon them, are somehow typical and representative of the Romans as they were believed to have always been. Virgil is less concerned with origins than with a permanent reality as it was displayed from the first and is still being displayed in his own time.

2   Such a plan and such a purpose demanded a new kind of poetry, and when we turn from the *Iliad* to the *Aeneid,* it is clear that the whole outlook is different and that Virgil has a new vision of human nature and of heroic virtue. Homer concentrates on individuals and their destinies. The dooms of Achilles and Hector dominate his design; their characters determine the action. But from the start Virgil shows that his special concern is the destiny not of a man but of a nation, not of Aeneas but of Rome. Though he opens with "Arms and the man" and suggests that his hero is another Achilles or Odysseus, he has, before his first paragraph is finished, shown that he reaches beyond Aeneas to the long history that followed from him:

> whence came the Latin race,
> The Alban sires and lofty walls of Rome.

Soon afterwards, when he has noted the obstacles which the Trojans meet in their wanderings, he again ends a period on a similar note:

> So vast a task to found the Roman race.

Then, when Venus complains that her son, Aeneas, is unjustly treated, Jupiter replies not only by promising that all will be well with Aeneas but by giving a prophetic sketch of Roman history to Julius Caesar.

The reward which the ancestor of the Roman race is to receive is much more than his own success or glory, more even than his settlement in Italy; it is the assurance of Rome's destiny, of universal and unending dominion:

> To them I give no bounds in space or time
> But empire without end.

At the outset Virgil shows what kind of destiny is the subject of his poem. The wanderings and sufferings and ultimate success of Aeneas and his followers are but a preliminary and a preparation for a much vaster theme. It was with reason that Petronius, like Tennyson, called the poet "Roman Virgil."

3   The fundamental theme of the *Aeneid* is the destiny of Rome as it was revealed in this mythical dawn of history before Rome itself existed. This destiny is presented in the person of Aeneas who not only struggles and suffers for the Rome that is to be but is already a typical Roman. If his individual fortune is subordinate to the fortune of Rome, his character shows what Romans are. He is Virgil's hero in a new kind of heroic poem, and in him we see how different Virgil's epic vision is from Homer's. Aeneas is Virgil's own creation, conceived with the special purpose of showing what a Roman hero is. Unlike Homer, Virgil owes little in his hero's character to tradition. Whereas Homer has to conform to established notions and make his Achilles "swift of foot," his Agamemnon "king of men" and his Odysseus "of many wiles," Virgil was bound by no such obligations. He could find his characters where he chose and shape them to suit his own purpose. His Aeneas owes something to Homeric precedent in being a great warrior and a devout servant of the gods, but he has taken on a new personality and is the true child of Virgil's brooding meditation and imaginative vision. The persons of the *Aeneid* are created and fashioned for a special purpose. They contribute to the main design, and everything that they say or do may be considered in the light of Rome's destiny. For this reason it is wrong to treat them as if they were dramatic characters like Homer's. They are more, and they are less. They are more, because they stand for something outside themselves, for something typically and essentially Roman; they are types, examples, symbols. And they are less, because any typical character will lack the lineaments and idiosyncrasies, the personal appeal and the intimate claims, of a character who is created for his own sake and for the poet's pleasure in him. . . .

4   Against the imperfect types of Turnus and Dido Virgil had to set his own reformed and Roman ideal of manhood. His task was indeed difficult. He had to create a man who should on the one hand be comparable to the noblest Homeric heroes in such universally honoured qualities as courage and endurance and on the other hand should present in himself the qualities which the Augustan age admired beyond all others but which had meant nothing to Homer. Virgil's treatment of Dido and Turnus shows that his new hero could not be ruled by the self-assertive spirit and cult of honour which inspired the heroic outlook; he must be based on some other principle more suited to an age of peace and order. But if he was to rival Achilles and Odysseus,

he must be a great man and a ruler of men. Virgil had to present a hero who appealed both by his greatness and by his goodness, by his superior gifts and by his Roman *virtus*.[1] On the one hand he must be a fitting member of the heroic age to which legend assigned him, and on the other he must represent in its fullness and variety the new idea of manhood which Augustus advocated and proclaimed as characteristically Roman. The result was Aeneas, a character so compounded of different elements that he has often been derided even by those who love Virgil. Yet to him Virgil gave his deepest meditations and some of his finest poetry. To understand him we must try to recapture some of the ideas and sentiments of the Augustan age.

5   Aeneas comes from Homer, and in the *Aeneid* he is presented as a great warrior who is almost the equal of Hector. To him Hector appears after death, as to his legitimate successor in the defense of Troy. Andromache associates him with Hector when she asks if the boy Ascanius has the courage and spirit of his father Aeneas and his uncle Hector. Aeneas' fame has spread through the whole world, and Dido knows all about him before she sees him, while in Italy Pallas is amazed that so renowned a man should appear before him on the Tiber. He has the heroic qualities of divine blood, prowess in war, personal beauty, and power to command men. But he has something more than this. His essential quality, as his distinguishing epithet of *pius* shows, in his *pietas*, his devotion to the gods and to all their demands. When Iloneus speaks of him to Dido, he shows the combination of qualities in Aeneas:

> A king we had, Aeneas: none more just,
> More righteous, more renowned in war and arms.

Aeneas is not only a great soldier; he is a good man. So to some degree, Homer had made him when he told of his many sacrifices to Poseidon, but Virgil enlarges the concept of this goodness until it covers much more than the performance of religious rites. Aeneas' *pietas*[2] is shown in his devotion to his country, to his father, to his wife, to his child, to his followers and above all to the many duties and the special task which the gods lay on him. He is *pius* because he does what a good man should. The epithet which Virgil gives him is unlike the epithets which Homer gives to his heroes. For while these denote physical characteristics or qualities useful in war, *pius* indicates a spiritual quality which has nothing to do with war and is specially concerned with the relations between Aeneas and the gods. Thus at the start Virgil's hero is set in a different order of things and claims a different kind of attention. In this unprecedented epithet for an epic hero and in all that it implies is the clue to Virgil's conception of Aeneas.

6   Aeneas is *pius*, but he is not a perfect and ideal man throughout the poem. The indignation which he has excited in more than one critic for his obvious faults shows not that Virgil's idea of goodness was singularly unlike our own but that he chose to show a good man in the

---

[1] Virtue or power.
[2] Piety or fidelity.

making and the means by which he is made. To understand Aeneas
we must understand the scheme by which Virgil presents him, a
scheme based on the moral views of the Augustan age but modified
by Virgil's own beliefs and admirations. The clue to Aeneas is that he
is built on a Stoic plan. St. Augustine hints at this when he touches on
Aeneas' treatment of Dido and treats it as being typically Stoic because while he sheds tears for her, his purpose is not shaken by her
sufferings:

> His mind unmoved, his tears fall down in vain.

It is not certain that St. Augustine interprets the line correctly, but his
main conclusion is right. Aeneas has undeniably something Stoic
about him which accounts for the alleged paradoxes and contradictions of his character. There is nothing strange in this. In the moral
reforms which Augustus preached and planned a revived Stoicism
took a prominent place. It breathes through the patriotic odes of Horace, and it survived through the first two centuries A.D. Originally
Stoicism was a creed to meet the horrors of an age in which there was
no political or personal security. Against this disorder it set the citadel
of a man's soul in which he could live at peace with himself and with
the universe and by subduing his emotions be undismayed at whatever might happen. The Augustan Romans took over this creed and
gave it a new reference. It suited them because it disapproved of self-
assertion and ambition and laid great emphasis on social duties. It
was well suited to an age which hoped to recover from the excesses of
unfettered individualism. The quiet, self-denying, self-sacrificing
citizen who was prepared to do what he was told was a type dear to
Augustus. Virgil knew the theory and the doctrine, and though in his
youth he had leaned toward Epicurus, he was deeply affected by
them. . . .

7   In his relations with Dido Aeneas fails though not quite in the way
that modern critics find so deplorable. What is wrong is not his deser-
tion of her, which is ordered by the gods and necessary for the fulfil-
ment of his task in Italy, but his surrender in the first place to her love
and his subsequent neglect of his real duty which lies away from
Carthage. Virgil does not show clearly what Aeneas' motives are; they
seem at least not to be love for Dido, for whom he shows little more
than grateful affection. But of his fault there is no question; it is neglect
and forgetfulness of duty. Mercury, sent by Jupiter, makes it quite
clear:

> Forgetful of thy realm and fate!

This forgetfulness, due to sloth and love of ease, is a kind of intemper-
ance, a failure in moderation, a state of false pleasure in which a
temporary advantage is mistaken for a real good. Aeneas' duty, as
Mercury tells him, is owed to his son, and he must do it. This is
precisely what he tells Dido, and though her furious reception of his
defense makes it look feeble, it is all that he can say, and it is right. Nor
would it perhaps have seemed so weak to a Roman. For his duty is
concerned with the foundation of Rome, and it cannot be right to set a
woman's feelings before that destiny. Aeneas is fond of Dido and he

feels pity for her, but his conscience is stronger than his emotions and wins in the end. When he leaves her, he acts as a Stoic should, and undoes, so far as he can, the evil which he has committed by allowing himself to forget his task in her company.

8   In Book V Aeneas is faced with another crisis. During the Funeral Games of his father, the women of his company, stirred up by Juno's agent, begin to burn his ships with the purpose of keeping him in Sicily. Aeneas sees the havoc that they have started and prays to Jupiter to stop it. Jupiter sends rain and the fire is quenched. But even after this display of divine help, Aeneas is full of misgivings:

> But prince Aeneas, by that sad mischance
> Sore stricken, rolls the burden of his thoughts
> This way and that. There should he make his home,
> Heedless of fate, or grasp Italian shores?

It seems almost incredible that Aeneas should at this juncture think of abandoning his quest. Yet he does, and it shows how deeply his emotions still rule him. The catastrophe of the burned ships has filled him with such despair that for the moment he ceases to believe in his destiny. Fortunately he is saved by the old sailor Nautes, who not only gives him sensible advice about leaving the women in Sicily and sailing with the rest of his company, but sums up the situation in a way that must have appealed to every Roman conscience:

> Go, goddess' son, where fate drives — back or on.
> Endurance conquers fortune, come what may.

The fate which Aeneas should follow is the destiny which the gods have given him, and he should be master enough of himself to know this. Nautes brings him to his senses, and when this advice is fortified by words from the spirit of Anchises, Aeneas recovers his confidence and sets sail for Italy. He never again allows his feelings to *obscure* his knowledge of his duty.

9   Once he lands in Italy Aeneas is a new man. He makes no more mistakes, and always does what is right in the circumstances. He is never again assailed by doubt or despair; his only hesitations are about the right means to the known end, and these after due consideration he finds. . . . When Aeneas touches the fated soil of Italy, he has learned his lessons and found that self-control and wisdom which the Stoics regarded as the mark of a good man. His earlier adventures and mistakes have not been in vain. For they have made him surer of himself and more confident of the divine destiny which leads him.

10   The Stoic ideas which inform Virgil's conception of Aeneas' ordeal and development persist to some degree in the later books of the *Aeneid,* but with a different purpose. Aeneas is the just and wise prince, and he must not act unjustly, particularly in such important matters as peace and war, about which the Augustan age had been taught by bitter experience to hold strong views. Aeneas is very like an invader, and he lives in a heroic past, but he must not be allowed to make war as Homer's heroes make it, simply to indulge his own desire for glory. For this reason Virgil makes Aeneas face war with a con-

sciousness of grave responsibilities and of nice distinctions between moral issues. Just as Cicero says that the only right reason for declaring war is that "life may be lived in peace without wrong," so Virgil is careful to put Aeneas in the right when war is forced upon him by the Latins. Earlier versions of the story said that the Trojans began the attack and were resisted by the Latins; Virgil reverses the situation and makes Aeneas do everything to secure his aims by peaceful negotiations. His envoy makes the most modest demands of King Latinus, and the king is perfectly willing to accede to them. When war is begun by the Latins, Aeneas conducts it in the spirit which Cicero advocates, "that nothing should be sought but peace." Even after the aggression of the Latins, Aeneas tells their envoys, who ask for leave to bury the dead, that he is willing to grant much more than that:

> Peace for the dead and slain in war you ask.
> I'd grant it gladly to the living too.

When the truce is broken, his chief thought is to have it restored. He tries to avert a general slaughter and offers to settle the issue by a single combat between himself and Turnus. He cries out to the excited armies:

> Oh stay your wrath! The pact is made, and all
> The rules are fixt. My right to fight alone!

In this we hear the spirit of the Augustan age as its master proclaimed it when he said that he himself had never made war "without just and necessary reasons" and that he always pardoned his enemies when the general safety allowed. Such an attitude toward war bears no resemblance to anything heroic or Homeric. War had become an evil which may be undertaken only when there is no alternative, and it must be conducted in a spirit of chivalry and clemency.

11   Though Aeneas is built largely on a Stoic plan and conforms in some important respects to the Stoic ideal of the wise man, he is not only this. He has other qualities which lie outside the Stoic purview and are even hostile to it. This is not hard to understand. The Stoic ideal, interesting though it is as an attempt to set a man above his troubles and his failings and to provide him with a feeling of security in a disordered society, failed to conquer mankind because it denied the worth of much that the human heart thinks holy and will not willingly forgo. St. Augustine was not alone in feeling that the Stoics were inhuman in their attempt to suppress all emotions, no matter how reputable. Many other men felt that such an exaltation of reason is wrong insofar as it dries up the natural springs of many excellent actions. Though Virgil used Stoic conceptions for the development of Aeneas' character, his warm-hearted, compassionate temperament was not satisfied with an ordeal so cold and so remote. If Stoicism provides a scheme by which Aeneas is tested and matured, it does not explain much else in him. Aeneas, with all his faults and contradictions, is essentially a creature of emotions. It is true that at first these are the cause of his failures and may be condemned, but Virgil did not believe that his ideal Roman should lack emotions altogether. His confident Aeneas of the latter books is still highly emotional, but his emotions

are now in harmony with his appointed purpose and help in his pursuit of it.

12　　The most important of these divagations from the Stoic norm is the part played by pity on the character of Aeneas. For many readers this is the most Virgilian of all qualities, the most typical and most essential feature of the *Aeneid*. When Aeneas sees the episodes of the Trojan War depicted in stone at Carthage, he utters the famous words which have so often been quoted as the centre of Virgil's outlook and message:

> Here praise has its rewards,
> Fortune its tears, and man's fate stirs the heart.

The words do not mean all that is sometimes claimed for them; they are certainly not a declaration that human life is nothing but tears. But they show that Aeneas on arriving in a strange land feels that here too is not only the glory but the pathos of life. In his mind the two are equally important, and such a view is far removed from Stoic detachment. The same quality comes out when Aeneas sees the ghosts of the unburied dead wandering in the underworld and halts his steps:

> With thought and pity for their unjust lot.

He allows his compassion here to assert itself at the expense of a divine ordinance and to criticize the government of the universe. No correct Stoic would dream of doing such a thing, and it shows how strong pity is in Aeneas and what importance Virgil attaches to it. . . .

13　　More surprising than Aeneas' outbursts of pity are his outbursts of anger and fury, which continue after he has arrived in Italy and are evidently essential to his mature personality. The Stoics would have disapproved of them without qualification. They defined anger as the desire for revenge and thought it odious because it makes deliberate and considered action impossible. Seneca says that it is the result not of goodness but of weakness, often frivolous or flippant, and that any good it may do in the way of punishment or correction can be better done from a sense of duty. Even Marcus Aurelius, who in many ways resembles Aeneas and seems to embody the ideal Roman in his historical self, condemns anger with majestic austerity. In anger, he says, the soul wrongs itself; it is senseless against wrongdoers because they act unwillingly through ignorance, and it is not a proper function of man. Yet Virgil made anger part of Aeneas' character and a potent force in his warlike doings. It rises at the death of Pallas and takes the form of a violent desire to punish Turnus, though for a time it is exercised at the expense of others like Magus, Tarquitus and Lucagus, who do not share Turnus' responsibility for killing Pallas. In the second part of Book X Aeneas is driven by wild fury against all his opponents. He takes the four sons of Sulmo to be a human sacrifice at Pallas' pyre, and not all the admiration of Donatus—"how great Aeneas' virtue is shown to be, how great his devotion in honouring the memory of the dead"—can make us feel that he is acting humanly or even rationally. When Magus makes a pitiful appeal for mercy, Aeneas refuses with heartless irony and tells him that his death is demanded by the dead Anchises and the boy Iulus. He throws Tarquitus to the fishes and denies him the decencies of burial with the derisive taunt that his mother will not bury him nor lay his limbs in the ancestral tomb. . . .

14 The combination of such qualities in a single hero demands some explanation. It is sometimes said that in it Virgil modelled Aeneas on Achilles and did not reconcile the obvious discords. It is true that these episodes have their parallels in the furious revenge which Achilles exacts for the death of Patroclus. But if so, Virgil has failed to make his hero convincing or consistent. These outbursts of heroic fury ill suit the exponent of Roman virtues with his strong distaste for war. But another explanation is possible. Virgil liked and admired Augustus, and at the same time knew that Augustus' dominion was based on force. In his youth he had risen to power by a series of violent acts, which he justified as the vengeance for the death of Julius. Legends had gathered round this vengeance and portrayed Augustus as moved by violent and angry feelings. They may not be true, but they were circulated and known and had become part of Augustus' myth. After Philippi Augustus was said to have behaved much as Aeneas behaves after the death of Pallas. Aeneas refuses burial to Tarquitus and tells him that the birds and fishes will lick his wounds; when a dying man asked Augustus for burial, he said that the birds would soon settle that question. Aeneas is so angry that no appeal to the names of his father and his son moves him to spare Lucagus; Augustus is said to have made a father play a game with his sons to decide which should live and then looked on while both were killed. Aeneas sacrifices the sons of Sulmo at Pallas' pyre; Augustus was said to have sacrificed three hundred prisoners of war after Perusia on the Ides of March at the altar of Julius. Whether these tales are true or not, Augustus undoubtedly took a fierce revenge for the murder of his adopted father, and it is possible that Virgil modelled Aeneas' revenge for Pallas on it. He seems to have felt that there are times when it is right even for a compassionate man like Aeneas to lose control of himself and to be carried away by anger. This anger is thought to be good not only in its results. It helps Aeneas to secure his destiny and to overcome those who resist it. Normally considerate and compassionate, he is slow to anger, but some things so shock him that they awake it, and, when it comes, it is terrible. At the back of his mind Virgil seems to have had a conception of a great man whose natural instincts are all for reason and agreement, but who, when he finds that these are useless, shows how powerful his passions can be. Aeneas, who has to subdue so much of himself, has also at times to subdue his gentler feelings and to allow full liberty to more primitive elements which are normally alien to him.

15 Virgil has put so much into Aeneas that he has hardly made him a living man. But though he lacks human solidity, he is important as an ideal and a symbol. So far from acting for his own pleasure or glory, he does what the gods demand of him. In the performance of this duty he finds little happiness. He would rather at times give up his task, and he envies the Trojans who have settled in Sicily and have no such labours as his. His stay in Carthage shows how easily his natural in-

stincts can conquer his sense of duty, and there is a pathetic sincerity in his words to Dido:

> I seek not Italy by choice.

He takes no pride in his adventures, no satisfaction in their successful conclusion. His whole life is dictated by the gods. They tell him what to do and make him do it, and he obeys in an uncomplaining but certainly not a joyful spirit of acceptance. He is aptly symbolized by Virgil's picture of him shouldering the great shield on which Vulcan has depicted the deeds of his descendants:

> His shoulder bears his grandson's fame and fate.

On Aeneas the whole burden of Rome seems to lie, and it is not surprising that he lacks the instinctive vigour and vitality of Homer's heroes. The new world which Virgil sought to interpret needed men like this, not heroes like Turnus whose individual ambitions lead to destruction. . . .

16   In the *Aeneid* Virgil presented a new ideal of heroism and showed in what fields it could be exercised. The essence of his conception is that a man's *virtus* is shown less in battle and physical danger than in the defeat of his own weaknesses. The chief obstacles which Aeneas finds are in himself, and his greatest victories are when he triumphs over them. Even in battle his highest moments are when he sees past the fury of the fight to some higher end of unity and harmony. Conversely, Dido and Turnus fail because, despite their innate nobility and strength of will, they give in to their passions and desires. Virgil's idea of heroism is quite different from Homer's because it depends much less on physical gifts than on moral strength and is displayed not merely in battle but in many departments of life. Moreover, Homer's heroes never question the worth of the glory which they seek, but Aeneas, hampered by doubts and misgivings, is unsure not only about his glory but about his whole destiny. This uncertainty is one of his greatest trials, and he shows his worth by pursuing his task despite all his doubts about it. His success is all the greater because it is won largely in spite of his own human feelings. In him Virgil displays what man really is, a creature uncertain of his place in the universe and of the goal to which he moves. To the distrustful and uncertain Augustan age this conception came with the urgency of truth, and Virgil's immediate and lasting success was due to his having found an answer to the spiritual needs of his time. In the vision of Rome he presented an ideal strong enough to win the devotion of his contemporaries, and in his belief in sacrifice and suffering he prepared the way across the centuries to those like Marcus Aurelius and St. Augustine who asked that men should live and die for an ideal city greater and more truly universal than Rome. Once Virgil had opened up a new vision of human worth and recast the heroic ideal in a new mould, he set an example which later poets could not but follow. They might not accept his interpretation of human destiny in all its details, but they felt that he had marked out the main lines for epic poetry and that any new heroic ideal must take account of what he said.

Discussion of Theme

1. Why has the word *hero* acquired overtones of derision? Does this mean that we look down on heroic qualities?
2. What is a Stoic? Is there anything to be said in favor of Stoic philosophy? How did Aeneas differ from the Stoics in his behavior?
3. In literature, what is the difference between an anti-hero and any ordinary character?
4. According to Bowra, what was Virgil's purpose in writing the *Aeneid?* What is its fundamental theme?
5. What is *pietas?* Is it still regarded as a heroic virtue today?

Discussion of Rhetoric

1. Look at the last sentence of paragraph 8. Why did Bowra put *obscure* in italics?
2. In paragraph 9, as well as in other portions of the essay, a series of dots (an ellipsis) is used to end a sentence. What does this indicate?
3. In paragraph 2 Bowra says that "such a purpose demanded a new kind of poetry," and in paragraph 3 he refers to "a new kind of heroic poem." How do the two paragraphs differ in focus?
4. In paragraph 10 Bowra refers to "nice" distinctions between moral issues. Look up *nice* in your dictionary. What does it mean in Bowra's sentence? Is this the usual definition of the word?
5. What relation does paragraph 16 have to the rest of the essay, particularly to the opening paragraphs?
6. Select a passage containing several allusions and — by explaining their meaning — show how the passage is enriched.

Writing Assignments

1. Just as Virgil introduced a new sort of hero in the person of Aeneas, modern writers have introduced a new concept in the anti-hero. Give your opinion on why the anti-hero appeared and why he is so popular in films and novels.
2. Respond to Cicero's statement that the only right reason for declaring war is that "life may be lived in peace without wrong."
3. Does Aeneas emerge from Bowra's essay as a real-life human being? Give your reasons for reacting as you do.
4. Bowra lays a good deal of stress on Virgil's imbuing Aeneas with anger. In what ways is anger useful; in what ways harmful? Relate it to your own reactions to anger.

Library Exploration

1. One of the first and funniest of the modern anti-hero novels was *Lucky Jim,* by Kingsley Amis.

2. If you have not read the *Aeneid,* you will find several good translations available in inexpensive paperback editions. To understand the ancient Greek's concept of a hero, read the *Illiad* and the *Odyssey,* by Homer.

Vocabulary

(1) HEXAMETER line of verse containing six metrical feet or measures

(1) ANNALISTIC pertaining to year-by-year report of events

(1) INGENIOUS clever; inventive

(3) LINEAMENTS features; characteristics

(3) IDIOSYNCRASIES peculiarities or mannerisms

(5) PROWESS bravery; skill

(5) EPITHET a word describing a characteristic quality

(6) ALLEGED supposed

(6) PARADOXES inconsistencies

(6) UNFETTERED unrestrained; free

(7) DEPLORABLE regrettable; unfortunate

(10) CLEMENCY mercy

(12) DIVAGATIONS digressions; wandering away from

(13) ODIOUS hateful; offensive

Donald Santarelli formerly worked in the Justice Department during the Nixon administration. His resignation from that post was widely interpreted as a protest against the policies of the administration.

How serious a crime is the possession of small amounts of marijuana? According to the author, lack of confidence in the law-enforcement community stems from, among other things, the enforcement of questionable drug laws.

DONALD E. SANTARELLI

Let's Stop Enforcing the Pot Laws

1 The resources of the law enforcement community in this country are finite—but if they are to be fully utilized, we are going to have to start systematically placing priorities on our work.

2 In doing so, we must make a distinction between what is a primary function and what is less than primary. In addition, those of us in law enforcement must decide when a less-than-primary function compromises and obstructs the performance of our primary job.

3 A statement of this nature quite naturally leads to the subject of vice and so-called victimless crimes.

4 Concepts of natural law are the basis of most of our rules of morality and personal conduct. Traditionally, we have translated subjective views of natural law into criminal laws to enforce our notions of natural law. The consensus is that murder, robbery and rape are clear violations of natural law, harming individuals as well as society. This consensus is reflected in statutes.

5 But these same criminal laws also cover conduct that more and more Americans do not believe transgresses the natural law or causes sufficient harm for the application of criminal law.

6   The current fashion is to describe these crimes as "victimless"—in
that they do not have a clearly identifiable victim. The misdeeds
generally fall into the area of vice—gambling, currently illegal sexual
conduct between mature, consenting adults and use of minor drugs
such as marijuana.

7   Just a few years ago there was no real question about what the rules
of the road were—what was "right" and what was "wrong." Drug use
of any kind was generally condemned. Similarly, some forms of sexual conduct to which both parties consented were believed to be
wrong—although the practice of such acts persisted. Even gambling
was mildly disapproved.

8   But the consensus is now gone. Many Americans no longer support
traditional views. Lately we seem somewhat more honest in admitting
that private conduct differs from public expression, specifically in our
attitudes toward vice, gambling, sex, pornography and marijuana use.
It is the law enforcement officer who has had to bear the brunt of this
ambivalence, this uncertainty, these divided and changing views
about which laws should be enforced and which should not.

9   Historically, the family in America helped enforce the rules against
vice. So, too, did the neighborhood and the community. Parents, relatives, neighbors were instruments of vice control as well as crime control. They were an informal criminal justice system that kept our society from needing extensive police forces, courts and jails.

10   Now that's largely changed. The family and the community are no
longer the centripetal forces they once were. We have become
anonymous as a society; we're in constant motion. At the same time a
youth culture has developed that further loosens those old controls.
We live very independent and libertine lives compared with our
fathers—indeed, compared with many of us in our own youth.

11   As a result of this revolution, law enforcement officials are meeting
criticism when they have to enforce laws that are not always supported by the whole community. Whereas there is not much disagreement when we enforce laws against heroin traffickers—there is
no disagreement at all when we enforce it in rape and burglary cases
—there is a substantial question in the minds of many Americans
about the propriety of enforcing laws which prohibit, for example,
possession of marijuana in small quantities for the personal use of the
individual and not for commercial sale.

12   I am as vigorous a supporter of drug law enforcement as anyone
because I believe drug abuse undermines our society and could ultimately destroy our culture. I don't want to live in a land of addicts
and "zonked out" kids.

13   But a distinction needs to be made about the kind of enforcement
that causes more harm than good—that reduces our ability effectively
to enforce the laws we all want enforced. That's the test I want to
apply with regard to the possession and personal use of marijuana.

14   Let's look at the great experiment called prohibition. Forty years
after the end of the ban on booze, we have approximately 18 million
people in America with alcohol problems—that's a lot of alcohol
abuse. But we know now that the way to deal with the problem is by
controlling the sale and distribution of alcohol and by regarding those

who abuse it not as criminals but as persons in need of medical or therapeutic attention.

15 We learned that the hard way. Probably never before did law enforcement come into such disrepute in the United States as it did during the enforcement of the unpopular ban on alcohol.

16 Prohibition started us down the long road of questioning the propriety of the way law enforcement officials conducted themselves. Today we have arrived at a particularly troublesome road stop —marijuana prohibition.

17 Consider for a moment the case of California: Approximately one-fourth of the felony arrests here in 1973 were related to marijuana. Now, that obviously includes trafficking in large amounts of marijuana, commerce in it, and its illegal sale and distribution. But, obviously, that figure also includes some simple possession cases. Of the approximately 500,000 drug offense arrests in the United States in 1973, about 225,000 were for marijuana. How many of them were simple possession? We simply cannot say.

18 True, the policy in this country has been changing rapidly: There are now federal and state statutes which give great discretion to the prosecutor, especially for the offense of simple possession—in my opinion, a desirable turn of events. But we must go one step further.

19 What I'm advocating here is that we should come to a consensus in our society that the criminal law is not an effective way to deal with such minor offenses as possession for personal use of a small amount of marijuana, particularly by young people.

20 I have come to this conclusion by applying a balancing test to determine what is gained and what is lost when you push the criminal law too far.

21 Sure, many people make the argument that we shouldn't enforce marijuana statutes prohibiting personal use, because it diverts and wastes police manpower. There is merit to that argument. But I don't think it's overwhelmingly persuasive.

22 There's another argument that is a lot more persuasive. It starts with the unfair treatment accorded the youthful first offender who ends up with a criminal record—maybe a jail sentence. We all know how sporadic the enforcement of those statutes against simple possession is in the various states—how arbitrary and unfair. No wonder young people lack confidence in the law enforcement community: The evidence of uneven enforcement is all around us.

23 The question comes down to this: Should we absolutely prohibit some substance that we don't think is good for us? Medical science is still not certain that moderate use of marijuana is harmful. Young people look at their elders' reliance on alcohol, and they disdain it. They use marijuana, and we disdain that.

24 How much confrontation do we want in our society? What good do we get out of constant confrontation—when it isn't even clear how harmful the moderate use of marijuana may be?

25 But there is an even more important consideration. When a particular purpose of law enforcement becomes controversial, the work of the entire criminal justice system is handicapped.

26 We have just completed a $25 million study at LEAA that sur-

veyed 600,000 citizens in our five largest cities, in eight smaller cities and throughout the country at random. The respondents told us that at least half the time they do not report crimes because they do not have enough confidence—often for good reason—in the criminal justice system.

27   What helps to breed that lack of confidence? In my view, questionable law enforcement practices have played a crucial role.

28   The startling point is that teen-agers did not report 80% of the crimes seen by or perpetrated against them. The reason for this inaction was more disturbing. For the most part, they said they didn't have enough confidence in the criminal justice system, considering it neither fair nor productive of results.

29   Every time we enforce a questionable, controversial statute prohibiting possession of a small amount of marijuana—especially against young people—we heighten this lack of confidence in the law enforcement community. Even worse, enforcement of this kind often creates a genuine hostility toward police, which complicates the situation even more. Being called a "narc" or a "pig" and worse not only compromises effectiveness of the officer but also seriously affects his morale and his ability to relate to the community.

30   Now, we aren't going to change this problem overnight simply by not enforcing a specific kind of statute about marijuana use. But the actions which create hostility and distrust of law enforcement are a high price to pay for the questionable good they achieve in discouraging the use of marijuana.

31   For these reasons—most particularly because confidence in law enforcement officers is being undermined at a time when they urgently need it to enforce laws against serious crime—I believe we should come to a consensus in this country that it is not desirable to require law enforcement officers to enforce statutes in minor offenses involving personal use of marijuana.

32   I'm not advocating a repeal of those statutes—we still know too little on the scientific side—but I am advocating that we find a new consensus on priorities. Enforcement of minor drug statutes prohibiting simple possession of marijuana should be at the bottom. Such a low priority will enhance the respect for law enforcement and, ultimately, benefit society as a whole.

Discussion of Theme

1. Who or what ultimately decides what is "right" and "wrong" in our society?
2. Why is the Prohibition analogy so commonly used in arguments of this kind? Is the analogy valid? Why or why not?
3. Should a government have the power to determine what is "good" for its citizens?
4. What conditions have helped to cause a lack of confidence in authority? Why should this attitude be more prevalent among the young?

Discussion of Rhetoric

1. Is the use of slang in paragraph 12 appropriate? Why does the author use it?
2. What is the purpose of asking questions in paragraph 24? Does the author answer them?
3. What emotional appeals does the author use? Are they fair?
4. Where does the main thrust of the argument appear?
5. Does he introduce any new arguments in this much-discussed subject?

Writing Assignments

1. Explain the following quote (paragraph 10): "We have become anonymous as a society."
2. Why are the family and community no longer the forces they once were in terms of authority and control?
3. Do you agree that fewer Americans support traditional views of "right" and "wrong" than a few years ago? How much of this do you think can be related to the influence of the youth culture?

Library Exploration

1. Research and report on the latest medical findings on the effects of marijuana.
2. How long has marijuana been used in this country? What were some of its early uses?

Vocabulary

(1) FINITE having bounds or limits

(4) SUBJECTIVE personal or introspective view of something

(4) CONSENSUS general agreement

(5) TRANGRESSES goes beyond imposed limits

(8) AMBIVALENCE conflicting feelings about the same thing

(10) CENTRIPETAL directed toward the center

(10) LIBERTINE one free from moral restraints

(22) ARBITRARY subject to individual judgment

Gene Lees (1928–   ) was born in Ontario, Canada. He has been a reporter for Canadian newspapers, as well as classical-music critic and film and drama editor for the Louisville "Times." Later he became editor of "Down Beat" magazine and a contributing editor to "Hi Fi/ Stereo Review." Since 1965, Lees has been the popular-music editor of "High Fidelity." He has also written the words and music for numerous popular songs.

The following article gives his brutally frank and sometimes startling proposal for handling the problem of drug addiction. Whether or not he's serious about his "modest proposal" is for you to decide.

GENE LEES

A Modest Proposal

1   Jonathan Swift once made what he called a Modest Proposal: since the Irish could not grow enough food to feed themselves but had no trouble producing babies, he suggested that babies should be made the prime Irish export (perhaps served as a table delicacy in England). There were those who thought he meant it. Perhaps, in a bitter and angry way, he did.

2   I wish to make a Modest Proposal myself. It relates to two serious contemporary problems: narcotics addiction and overpopulation. I feel that it is incumbent upon me as a man who makes his living from the record industry to offer this proposal. For the record industry is as responsible as any sector of our society for the growing number of deaths from the use of heroin and other drugs.

3   Now don't be hasty in condemning them. They've done no more than other industries have. Detroit finds 40,000 deaths a year in crash-worthy cars an acceptable price for profits. Why shouldn't the record industry too be allowed to kill its quota of people for profit?

4   Ten years ago I devoted an issue of *Down Beat* to the drug problem. At the time only a few music-business people thought addiction was an important issue. A Negro singer I know said to me recently, "No-body gave a damn about it when only black kids were dying in the doorways of Harlem. Nobody gave a damn until the well-to-do middle-class white kids started dying." *Touché.*

5   There is a great deal of criminal money invested in the music busi-ness, both in groups and in some record labels. Rock groups began pushing drug use. The kids bought it. The kids are dying. The under-world is making money on it. This is all coincidence, right? Oh sure.

6   Drug education in the schools is only going to make the problem worse, I am convinced. It will increase fascination, or even cause it, among youngsters who had never even thought much about using drugs. Watch it happen in the next two years.

7   And so I have come around to another view of the matter. I modestly propose that to all our other welfare programs we add free narcotics for the kids, including heroin. If you're a parent, this may shock you. But it shouldn't. You have been permitting your kids to take dope intellectually for years—from Bob Dylan, the Jefferson Airplane, the Lovin' Spoonful, the Beatles. When your five-year-old was wandering around the house singing, "I get by with a little help from my friends, I get high with a little help from my friends," didn't you say, "Isn't that cute? He's singing a Beatles song." All right, so now he's a few years older, and you're startled at the circulation of drugs in his school, and fearful that he'll start using them. (Maybe he's already started.) Why? You permitted it.

8   Now the main thing wrong with junkies is that they steal. Sometimes they go farther than that: in desperation for money, they *kill* and steal. This is a great social inconvenience, tying up the time of all kinds of policemen whom we need for such things as messing up traffic.

9   If I get my way, and the government subsidizes addiction the way it now subsidizes lethargy, all this will stop. It is useless to tell young people that the Beatles and heroin are bad for them. It simply is not so: the kids have told us this. And they are the wisest and most honest and idealistic and decent and loving and unprejudiced and well-informed generation of Americans in history. We know it because they have told us this too. And the advertising industry and Marshall Mc-Luhan have confirmed it. Who in his right mind would doubt the com-bined wisdom of Marshall McLuhan, the advertising industry, and our wonderful young people?

10   Now, if we supply them with all the heroin they can use—and I am talking about the pure, uncut stuff, not the powdered sugar that's floating around in many places these days—it will have immediate and far-reaching social benefits.

11   First, they'll stop rioting. Heroin makes you terribly passive. They'll start nodding out all over the place, and this will permit the police to catch up on *their* sleep in parked cruisers.

12   Then a lot of them will start dropping out of school. This will reduce the overload on our schools and universities. It will stop the building program, thus braking the felling of trees which give us our oxygen. Our air will improve.

13   Third, it will increase the food supply, since junkies don't eat much even when they can get it.

14   Fourth (and here is the real genius of my plan), ultimately the program will end the population explosion. One junkie I know told me that he and his strung-out wife hadn't had sexual relations in two years. Heroin produces profound sexual indifference, and impotence. But that isn't the end of it. Junkies die. In the late 1940s and early 1950s, a great many jazz musicians were on heroin. None of them are now. They are either in their graves or they are off drugs. There is no middle road, apparently.

15   Kids consitute nearly fifty percent of the population. The population explosion, then, *is them.* Now since anyone forty years old is going to be around only for another thirty years or so tops, *they're* not going to be much of a problem. They're starting to die off now, from working too hard to make enough money for their kids to buy the Doors' records and acid and junk. But that eighteen-year-old over there—man, he's going to be around breathing air, using up food, making garbage for another forty or fifty years. Even a kid can grasp that he himself is the real enemy.

16   Now when we begin the widespread free distribution of drugs, this group will start dying like flies. And still more benefits will accrue to society as a whole.

17   Junk music will fade from the radio. There won't be so many cars on the highway, and those that are there won't be in such steady use. Air pollution will be further reduced. Since we won't need so many highways, the grass and trees will grow again, making more oxygen. Drug use, incidentally, including acid, is becoming as common a cause of traffic deaths as alcohol. So we get a bonus here too.

18   I know there are those out there in Readerland who will write me letters telling me I've got it all wrong—like the people who wrote me letters telling me New York is not dying. They'll say my proposal is heartless and cruel. But it isn't, I assure you. We have given the young what they want until now. Why should we draw the line at death?

19   To young people I would say this: don't believe old squares when they tell you that drugs, even grass, are damn dangerous. Don't believe the growing reports that the grass available now is often spiked with heroin to hook you on hard narcotics. Don't believe those who tell you that heroin is evil stuff. You know all those people are just trying to keep you from having a hip kind of good time.

20   And don't think about death. Think instead how you will be reducing the pressures of population on the rest of us. Think what a noble deed you'll be doing. Think Zen thoughts about eternity and the continuum of consciousness and about astrology and how mortal existence is a mere passing cloud. Think not of going into a valley of blackness. Think instead how you are going to join the great All-Consciousness and rest forever in nirvana. As you sit there, listening to John and Yoko with a needle in your arm, reflect not on the dying

you're about to do. Just think how high you're going to be as you go.
21   And to the record industry I would say: keep up the good work,
gentlemen. You've done a hell of a job thus far.

Discussion of Theme

1. Do you agree with the statement made by the singer in paragraph
   4? Is this society's attitude?
2. In paragraph 7, Lees makes a familiar accusation against well-
   known pop groups. Is he justified in his assessment of their songs?
   How have these musicians responded to such criticism?
3. What is the author's purpose in writing this article? How do you
   know? Is his approach effective?
4. Is the author serious in his proposals? Explain your reasoning.

Discussion of Rhetoric

1. What is the dominant tone of the article? Where is it especially
   strong? What devices does the author use to support his tone?
2. Is this article aimed at young people or their parents? What clues
   are responsible for your opinion? How effective do you consider it
   for each class of readers?
3. In paragraphs 14 and 17, Lees makes positive statements to the
   effect that (a) none of the older jazz musicians is currently using
   heroin, and (b) drug use causes as many traffic deaths as alcohol.
   How might he have increased the effectiveness of these statements?
4. The impact of paragraphs 19 and 20 is due to a particular rhetorical
   device. What is it?

Writing Assignments

1. "Schools Should (Should Not) Preach About the Dangers of Drug
   Abuse." Support your belief with reasons and evidence.
2. Analyze the content of at least two popular songs that you consider
   obviously drug-oriented.
3. If you were in the record industry, how would you respond to Lees?

Library Exploration

1. For a moving autobiography of a young black who kicked the habit,
   read Piri Thomas's *Down These Mean Streets*.
2. Check out current periodical literature to determine the present
   dimensions of drug abuse among young people.
3. Find out what other writers have to say about the influence of
   popular music on drug use.

Vocabulary

(2) INCUMBENT   required as a duty

(4) TOUCHÉ   a word used to tell one's opponent that he has successfully made his point

(9) LETHARGY   sluggish indifference

(16) ACCRUE   to come to as a gain

Personal
Values

3

Henry David Thoreau (1817–62) is probably best known for "Walden" (1854), an account of the two years he lived alone beside a New England lake with practically no money. He is also famous as the author of "Civil Disobedience" (1849). An associate of Ralph Waldo Emerson, he was an American transcendentalist philosopher, essayist, and naturalist.

Thoreau reflects on the pace of life and concludes that its tempo should be slow and deliberate.

HENRY DAVID THOREAU

Where I Lived and What I Lived For

1 We must learn to reawaken and keep ourselves awake, not by mechanical aids, but by an infinite expectation of the dawn, which does not forsake us in our soundest sleep. I know of no more encouraging fact than the unquestionable ability of man to elevate his life by a conscious endeavor. It is something to be able to paint a particular picture, or to carve a statue, and so to make a few objects beautiful; but it is far more glorious to carve and paint the very atmosphere and medium through which we look, which morally we can do. To affect the quality of the day, that is the highest of arts. Every man is tasked to make his life, even in its details, worthy of the contemplation of his most elevated and critical hour. If we refused, or rather used up, such paltry information as we get, the oracles would distinctly inform us how this might be done.

2   I went to the woods because I wished to live deliberately, to front only the essential facts of life, and see if I could not learn what it had to teach, and not, when I came to die, discover that I had not lived. I did not wish to live what was not life, living is so dear; nor did I wish to practice resignation, unless it was quite necessary. I wanted to live deep and suck out all the marrow of life, to live so sturdily and Spartanlike as to put to rout all that was not life, to cut a broad swath and shave

close, to drive life into a corner, and reduce it to its lowest terms, and, if it proved to be mean, why then to get the whole and genuine meanness of it, and publish its meanness to the world; or if it were sublime, to know it by experience, and be able to give a true account of it in my next excursion. For most men, it appears to me, are in a strange uncertainty about it, whether it is of the devil or of God, and have *somewhat hastily* concluded that it is the chief end of man here to "glorify God and enjoy him forever."

3   Still we live meanly, like ants; though the fable tells us that we were long ago changed into men; like pygmies we fight with cranes; it is error upon error, and clout upon clout, and our best virtue has for its occasion a superfluous and evitable wretchedness. Our life is frittered away by detail. An honest man has hardly need to count more than his ten fingers, or in extreme cases he may add his ten toes, and lump the rest. Simplicity, simplicity, simplicity! I say, let your affairs be as two or three, and not a hundred or a thousand; instead of a million count half a dozen, and keep your accounts on your thumb nail. In the midst of this chopping sea of civilized life, such are the clouds and storms and quicksands and thousand-and-one items to be allowed for, that a man has to live, if he would not founder and go to the bottom and not make his port at all, by dead reckoning, and he must be a great calculator indeed who succeeds. Simplify, simplify. Instead of three meals a day, if it be necessary eat but one; instead of a hundred dishes, five; and reduce other things in proportion. Our life is a German Confederacy, made up of petty states, with its boundary forever fluctuating, so that even a German cannot tell you how it is bounded at any moment. The nation itself, with all its so-called internal improvements, which, by the way, are all external and superficial, is just such an unwieldy and overgrown establishment, cluttered with furniture and tripped up by its own traps, ruined by luxury and heedless expense, by want of calculation and a worthy aim, as the million households in the land; and the only cure for it as for them is in a rigid economy, a stern and more than Spartan simplicity of life and elevation of purpose. It lives too fast. Men think that it is essential that the *Nation* have commerce, and export ice, and talk through a telegraph, and ride thirty miles an hour, without a doubt, whether *they* do or not; but whether we should live like baboons or like men, is a little uncertain. If we do not get our sleepers, and forge rails, and devote days and nights to the work, but go to tinkering upon our *lives* to improve *them*, who will build railroads? And if railroads are not built, how shall we get to heaven in season? But if we stay at home and mind our business, who will want railroads? We do not ride on the railroad; it rides upon us. Did you ever think what those sleepers are that underlie the railroad? Each one is a man, an Irishman, or a Yankee man. The rails are laid on them, and they are covered with sand, and the cars run smoothly over them. They are sound sleepers, I assure you. And every few years a new lot is laid down and run over; so that, if some have the pleasure of riding on a rail, others have the misfortune to be ridden upon. And when they run over a man that is walking in his sleep, a supernumerary sleeper in the wrong position, and wake him up, they suddenly stop the cars, and make a hue and cry about it, as if this were an exception.

I am glad to know that it takes a gang of men for every five miles to keep the sleepers down and level in their beds as it is, for this is a sign that they may sometime get up again.

4   Why should we live with such hurry and waste of life? We are determined to be starved before we are hungry. Men say that a stitch in time saves nine, and so they take a thousand stitches today to save nine tomorrow. As for *work*, we haven't any of any consequence. We have the Saint Vitus' dance, and cannot possibly keep our heads still. If I should only give a few pulls at the parish bell-rope, as for a fire, that is, without setting the bell, there is hardly a man on his farm in the outskirts of Concord, notwithstanding that press of engagements which was his excuse so many times this morning, nor a boy, nor a woman, I might almost say, but would forsake all and follow that sound, not mainly to save property from the flames, but, if we will confess the truth, much more to see it burn, since burn it must, and we, be it known, did not set it on fire, — or to see it put out, and have a hand in it, if that is done as handsomely; yes, even if it were the parish church itself. Hardly a man takes a half hour's nap after dinner, but when he wakes he holds up his head and asks, "What's the news?" as if the rest of mankind had stood his sentinels. Some give directions to be waked every half hour, doubtless for no other purpose; and then, to pay for it, they tell what they have dreamed. After a night's sleep, the news is as indispensable as the breakfast. "Pray tell me any thing new that has happened to a man anywhere on this globe," — and he reads it over his coffee and rolls, that a man has had his eyes gouged out this morning on the Wachito River; never dreaming the while that he lives in the dark unfathomed mammoth cave of this world, and has but the rudiment of an eye himself.

5   For my part, I could easily do without the post-office. I think that there are very few important communications made through it. To speak critically, I never received more than one or two letters in my life — I wrote this some years ago — that were worth the postage. The penny-post is, commonly, an institution through which you seriously offer a man that penny for his thoughts which is so often safely offered in jest. And I am sure that I never read any memorable news in a newspaper. If we read of one man robbed, or murdered, or killed by accident, or one house burned, or one vessel wrecked, or one steamboat blown up, or one cow run over on the Western Railroad, or one mad dog killed, or one lot of grasshoppers in the winter, — we never need read of another. One is enough. If you are acquainted with the principle, what do you care for a myriad instances and applications? To a philosopher all *news*, as it is called, is gossip, and they who edit and read it are old women over their tea. Yet not a few are greedy after this gossip. There was such a rush, as I hear, the other day at one of the offices to learn the foreign news by the last arrival, that several large squares of plate glass belonging to the establishment were broken by the pressure, — news which I seriously think a ready wit might write a twelve-month or twelve years beforehand with sufficient accuracy. As for Spain, for instance, if you know how to throw in Don Carlos and the Infanta, and Don Pedro and Seville and Granada, from time to time in the right proportions — they may have

changed the names a little since I saw the papers,—and serve up a bull-fight when other entertainments fall, it will be true to the letter, and give us as good an idea of the exact state or ruin of things in Spain as the most succinct and lucid reports under this head in the newspapers: and as for England, almost the last insignificant scrap of news from that quarter was the revolution of 1649; and if you have learned the history of her crops for an average year, you never need attend to that thing again, unless your speculations are of a merely pecuniary character. If one may judge who rarely looks into the newspapers, nothing new does ever happen in foreign parts, a French revolution not excepted.

6   What news! how much more important to know what that is which was never old! "Kieou-he-yu (great dignitary of the state of Wei) sent a man to Khoung-tseu to know his news. Khoung-tseu caused the messenger to be seated near him, and questioned him in these terms: What is your master doing? The messenger answered with respect: My master desires to diminish the number of his faults, but he cannot come to the end of them. The messenger being gone, the philosopher remarked: What a worthy messenger! What a worthy messenger!" The preacher, instead of vexing the ears of drowsy farmers on their day of rest at the end of the week,—for Sunday is the fit conclusion of an ill-spent week, and not the fresh and brave beginning of a new one,—with this one other draggle-tail of a sermon, should shout with thundering voice,—"Pause! Avast! Why so seeming fast, but deadly slow?"

7   Shams and delusions are esteemed for soundest truths, while reality is fabulous. If men would steadily observe realities only, and not allow themselves to be deluded, life, to compare it with such things as we know, would be like a fairy tale and the Arabian Nights' Entertainments. If we respected only what is inevitable and has a right to be, music and poetry would resound along the streets. When we are unhurried and wise, we perceive that only great and worthy things have any permanent and absolute existence,—that petty fears and petty pleasures are but the shadow of the reality. This is always exhilarating and sublime. By closing the eyes and slumbering, and consenting to be deceived by shows, men establish and confirm their daily life of routine and habit everywhere, which still is built on purely illusory foundations. Children, who play life, discern its true law and relations more clearly than men, who fail to live it worthily, but who think that they are wiser by experience, that is, by failure. I have read in a Hindoo book, that "there was a king's son, who, being expelled in infancy from his native city, was brought up by a forester, and, growing up to maturity in that state, imagined himself to belong to the barbarous race with which he lived. One of his father's ministers having discovered him, revealed to him what he was, and the misconception of his character was removed, and he knew himself to be a prince. So soul," continues the Hindoo philosopher, "from the circumstances in which it is placed, mistakes its own character, until the truth is revealed to it by some holy teacher, and then it knows itself to be *Brahme*." I perceive that we inhabitants of New England live this mean life that we do because our vision does not penetrate the

surface of things. We think that *is* which *appears* to be. If a man should walk through this town and see only the reality, where, think you, would the "Mill-dam" go to? If he should give us an account of the realities he beheld there, we should not recognize the place in his description. Look at a meeting-house, or a court-house, or a jail, or a shop, or a dwelling-house, and say what that thing really is before a true gaze, and they would all go to pieces in your account of them. Men esteem truth remote, in the outskirts of the system, behind the farthest star, before Adam and after the last man. In eternity there is indeed something true and sublime. But all these times and places and occasions are now and here. God himself culminates in the present moment, and will never be more divine in the lapse of all the ages. And we are enabled to apprehend at all what is sublime and noble only by the perpetual instilling and drenching of the reality that surrounds us. The universe constantly and obediently answers to our conceptions; whether we travel fast or slow, the track is laid for us. Let us spend our lives in conceiving then. The poet or the artist never yet had so fair and noble a design but some of his posterity at least could accomplish it.

8   Let us spend one day as deliberately as Nature, and not be thrown off the track by every nutshell and mosquito's wing that falls on the rails. Let us rise early and fast, or break fast, gently and without perturbation; let company come and let company go, let the bells ring and the children cry,—determined to make a day of it. Why should we knock under and go with the stream? Let us not be upset and overwhelmed in that terrible rapid and whirlpool called a dinner, situated in the meridian shallows. Weather this danger and you are safe, for the rest of the way is down hill. With unrelaxed nerves, with morning vigor, sail by it, looking another way, tied to the mast like Ulysses. If the engine whistles, let it whistle till it is hoarse for its pains. If the bell rings, why should we run? We will consider what kind of music they are like. Let us settle ourselves, and work and wedge our feet downward through the mud and slush of opinion, and prejudice, and tradition, and delusion, and appearance, that alluvion which covers the globe, through Paris and London, through New York and Boston and Concord, through church and state, through poetry and philosophy and religion, till we come to a hard bottom and rocks in place, which we can call *reality,* and say, This is, and no mistake; and then begin, having a *point d'appui,* below freshet and frost and fire, a place where you might found a wall or a state, or set a lamp-post safely, or perhaps a gauge, not a Nilometer, but a Realometer, that future ages might know how deep a freshet of shams and appearances had gathered from time to time. If you stand right fronting and face to face to a fact, you will see the sun glimmer on both its surfaces, as if it were a cimeter, and feel its sweet edge dividing you through the heart and marrow, and so you will happily conclude your moral career. Be it life or death, we crave only reality. If we are really dying, let us hear the rattle in our throats and feel cold in the extremities; if we are alive, let us go about our business.

9   Time is but the stream I go a-fishing in. I drink at it; but while I drink I see the sandy bottom and detect how shallow it is. Its thin current

slides away, but eternity remains. I would think deeper; fish in the sky, whose bottom is pebbly with stars. I cannot count one. I know not the first letter of the alphabet. I have always been regretting that I was not as wise as the day I was born. The intellect is a cleaver; it discerns and rifts its way into the secret of things. I do not wish to be any more busy with my hands than is necessary. My head is hands and feet. I feel all my best faculties concentrated in it. My instinct tells me that my head is an organ for burrowing, as some creatures use their snout and fore-paws, and with it I would mine and burrow my way through these hills. I think that the richest vein is somewhere hereabouts; so by the divining rod and thin rising vapors I judge; and here I will begin to mine.

Discussion of Theme

1. In recent years there has been an upsurge of interest in Thoreau's life-style. What do you believe is responsible for this?
2. What practical difficulties might we encounter today if we attempted to live as Thoreau did?
3. Thoreau was considered an individualist in his own day. What would most people think of him today? What would he, in turn, think of modern society?
4. What is the theme of this essay? Can you point to one sentence that states it?
5. Is it true that we live our lives too fast? Why do people consider it necessary to lead such fast-paced lives?

Discussion of Rhetoric

1. What rhetorical clues indicate that this essay was written in an earlier era?
2. What does Thoreau convey when he suggests that you "keep accounts on your thumb nail"? Does this express the concept better than more literal language?
3. Which passages do you consider especially poetic in this selection? What gives them their poetic quality?
4. The final sentence of paragraph 4 contains an allusion to classical mythology. What is it?
5. This essay was based on Thoreau's personal experience. Does this make for good writing? Why?
6. Is Thoreau's advice on how to live persuasive? Why?

Writing Assignments

1. Mentally review the details of your daily life; then discuss those that you would like to eliminate as either unnecessary or undesirable. How would you go about it?

2. Thoreau defended the right of an individual to be out of step with the rest of society ("perhaps it is because he hears a different drummer"). In what ways do you consider yourself in this category? What are the pleasures and pains associated with it?
3. Thoreau suggested that people "stay at home and mind [their] business." What are the drawbacks to following his advice?
4. Thoreau said: "We do not ride on the railroad; it rides upon us." What supposedly helpful mechanical conveniences exert tyranny over men's lives today?
5. What do you consider the essentials of life?

Library Exploration

1. Read either a full-length biography of Thoreau or an entry in an encyclopedia.
2. *The Night Thoreau Spent in Jail* is a play written about a little-known incident in the writer-naturalist's life.
3. Summarize the two years Thoreau spent at Walden Pond.
4. Read *Civil Disobedience* and report on it.

Vocabulary

(1) PALTRY   trifling; practically worthless

(1) ORACLES   persons who give wise or authoritative opinions

(3) SUPERFLUOUS   excessive; unnecessary

(3) EVITABLE   avoidable

(3) FLUCTUATING   continually changing

(3) SLEEPERS   railroad ties

(3) SUPERNUMERARY   an extra person or thing

(4) SAINT VITUS' DANCE   muscular twitch

(4) RUDIMENT   beginning; undeveloped form

(5) MYRIAD   countless

(5) SUCCINCT   terse; concise

(5) LUCID   clear

(5) PECUNIARY   financial

(6) VEXING   annoying; disturbing

(7) DELUDED   deceived

(7) PETTY   trivial; insignificant

(7) BARBAROUS   uncivilized

(7) CULMINATES   reaches the highest point

(7) APPREHEND   understand

(7) POSTERITY   all future generations

(8) PERTURBATION   disturbance

(8) MERIDIAN   midday

(8) ALLUVION   matter deposited on land by a flood

(8) POINT D'APPUI   foundation; base

(8) FRESHET   freshwater stream

(8) CIMETER   (scimitar) sword; saber

(9) DIVINING ROD   forked stick used to locate water

Albert Schweitzer (1875–1965) was a surgeon, organist, missionary, writer, composer, and humanitarian. He was born in Alsace and educated at the universities of Strasbourg, Paris, and Berlin, receiving degrees in philosophy, theology, and medicine. His fame rests on his self-sacrificing work at the hospital he founded at Lambaréné, in West Africa. He wrote dozens of books on religion, music, and world peace, among which are "The Quest of the Historical Jesus" (1910), "From My African Notebook" (1939), and "Peace or Atomic War?" (1958). He was awarded the Nobel Peace Prize in 1953.

In this selection Schweitzer examines the feelings of pessimism and optimism he had about the present and future condition of man.

ALBERT SCHWEITZER

Pessimism and Optimism

1 To the question whether I am a pessimist or an optimist, I answer that my knowledge is pessimistic, but my willing and hoping are optimistic.

2   I am pessimistic in that I experience in its full weight what we conceive to be the absence of purpose in the course of world happenings. Only at quite rare moments have I felt really glad to be alive. I could not but feel with a sympathy full of regret all the pain that I saw around me, not only that of men but that of the whole creation. From this community of suffering I have never tried to withdraw myself. It seemed to me a matter of course that we should take our share of the burden of pain which lies upon the world. Even while I was a boy at school it

was clear to me that no explanation of the evil in the world could ever satisfy me; all explanations, I felt, ended in sophistries, and at bottom had no other object than to make it possible for men to share in the misery around them, with less keen feelings. That a thinker like Leibnitz could reach the miserable conclusion that though this world is, indeed, not good, it is the best that was possible, I have never been able to understand.

3   But however much concerned I was at the problem of the misery in the world, I never let myself get lost in broodings over it; I always held firmly to the thought that each one of us can do a little to bring some portion of it to an end. Thus I came gradually to rest content in the knowledge that there is only one thing we can understand about the problem, and that is that each of us has to go his own way, but as one who means to help to bring about deliverance.

4   In my judgment, too, of the situation in which mankind finds itself at the present time I am pessimistic. I cannot make myself believe that that situation is not so bad as it seems to be, but I am inwardly conscious that we are on a road which, if we continue to tread it, will bring us into "Middle Ages" of a new character. The spiritual and material misery to which mankind of today is delivering itself through its renunciation of thinking and of the ideals which spring therefrom, I picture to myself in its utmost compass. And yet I remain optimistic. One belief of my childhood I have preserved with the certainty that I can never lose it: belief in truth. I am confident that the spirit generated by truth is stronger than the force of circumstances. In my view no other destiny awaits mankind than that which, through its mental and spiritual disposition, it prepares for itself. Therefore I do not believe that it will have to tread the road to ruin right to the end.

5   If men can be found who revolt against the spirit of thoughtlessness, and who are personalities sound enough and profound enough to let the ideals of ethical progress radiate from them as a force, there will start an activity of the spirit which will be strong enough to evoke a new mental and spiritual disposition in mankind.

6   Because I have confidence in the power of truth and of the spirit, I believe in the future of mankind. Ethical acceptance of the world contains within itself an optimistic willing and hoping which can never be lost. It is, therefore, never afraid to face the dismal reality, and to see it as it really is.

7   In my own life anxiety, trouble, and sorrow have been allotted to me at times in such abundant measure that had my nerves not been so strong, I must have broken down under the weight. Heavy is the burden of fatigue and responsibility which has lain upon me without a break for years. I have not much of my life for myself, not even the hours I should like to devote to my wife and child.

8   But I have had blessings too: that I am allowed to work in the service of mercy; that my work has been successful; that I receive from other people affection and kindness in abundance; that I have loyal helpers, who identify themselves with my activity; that I enjoy a health which allows me to undertake most exhausting work; that I have a well-balanced temperament which varies little, and an energy which exerts itself with calmness and deliberation; and, finally, that I

can recognize as such whatever happiness falls to my lot, accepting it also as a thing for which some thank offering is due from me.

9   I feel it deeply that I can work as a free man at a time when an oppressive lack of freedom is the lot of so many, as also that though my immediate work is material, yet I have at the same time opportunities of occupying myself in the sphere of the spiritual and intellectual.

10   That the circumstances of my life provide in such varied ways favorable conditions for my work, I accept as something of which I would fain prove myself worthy.

11   How much of the work which I have planned and have in mind shall I be able to complete?

12   My hair is beginning to turn. My body is beginning to show traces of the exertions I have demanded of it, and of the passage of the years.

13   I look back with thankfulness to the time when, without needing to husband my strength, I could get through an uninterrupted course of bodily and mental work. With calmness and humility I look forward to the future, so that I may not be unprepared for renunciation if it be required of me. Whether we be workers or sufferers, it is assuredly our duty to conserve our powers, as being men who have won their way through to the peace which passeth all understanding.

Discussion of Theme

1. What makes Schweitzer feel pessimistic? What makes him feel optimistic? Do you react as he does?
2. Have the sort of men Schweitzer describes in paragraph 5 been found? If so, who are or were they? Have they had the effect on mankind that the author predicted they would? Was he such a man?
3. Did Schweitzer expect to have a wide influence on mankind, or was he content to improve conditions in his own small corner of the world?
4. Are you optimistic or pessimistic about the future of mankind? Why?
5. How would you classify Schweitzer as a person?
6. Do you agree with Schweitzer that each of us should feel the misery of all those who suffer, and do something about it?

Discussion of Rhetoric

1. In paragraphs 4 and 6 does Schweitzer express himself on too abstract a level to make communication effective?
2. What is his purpose in paragraph 7? Is he looking for sympathy, or is he trying to inspire other people who may have had "anxiety, trouble, and sorrow"?
3. Occasionally Schweitzer produces an unwieldy sentence. How might each of these be changed for the sake of clarity?
4. To what source does the author allude in his final sentence? Why is this an appropriate conclusion for his essay?

5. How does Schweitzer use the words *pessimism* and *optimism* to organize his essay?

Writing Assignments

1. Instead of discussing our society from the point of view of an optimist or a pessimist, write a paper based on your view of it as a realist. What do you see? What do you conclude about the future of America?
2. What is your "explanation of the evil of the world"?
3. What are the drawbacks to concluding that "this is the best of all possible worlds"?
4. Discuss: "I am confident that the spirit generated by truth is stronger than the force of circumstances."
5. Who among the world's leaders fits the description in paragraph 5? Explain.

Library Exploration

1. Dr. Thomas Dooley also devoted his life to the service of others. Read about his work and the dedication he inspired in others.
2. Why did Schweitzer go to Lambaréné? What did he do there?
3. Report on the lesser known aspects of Schweitzer's life—his work as a musician, composer, or philosopher.
4. What was the effect of Schweitzer's work from the African's viewpoint?

Vocabulary

(2) PESSIMISTIC   expecting the worst

(2) SOPHISTRIES   clever but misleading arguments

(4) RENUNCIATION   giving up voluntarily

(4) COMPASS   scope; range

(5) ETHICAL   conforming to standards of right behavior

(8) DELIBERATION   careful consideration

(10) FAIN   eagerly; gladly

One of this country's best-known modern poets, Carl Sandburg (1878–1967) was the son of poor immigrant parents. His works have been anthologized in many collections of American literature. Among his books are "Abraham Lincoln: The War Years" (1939), "Remembrance Rock" (1948), and "Wind Song" (1960). In addition to his writing, he was a collector (and singer) of American folk songs.

This short selection is a parable that has a meaning for all of us.

CARL SANDBURG

Elephants Are Different to Different People

1 Wilson and Pilcer and Snack stood before the zoo elephant.

2　Wilson said, "What is its name? Is it from Asia or Africa? Who feeds it? Is it a he or a she? How old is it? Do they have twins? How much does it cost to feed? How much does it weigh? If it dies how much will another one cost? If it dies what will they use the bones, the fat, and the hide for? What use is it besides to look at?"

3　Pilcer didn't have any questions; he was murmuring to himself, "It's a house by itself, walls and windows, the ears came from tall corn-fields, by God; the architect of those legs was a workman, by God; he stands like a bridge out across deep water; the face is sad and the eyes are kind; I know elephants are good to babies."

4　Snack looked up and down and at last said to himself, "He's a tough son-of-a-gun outside and I'll bet he's got a strong heart, I'll bet he's as strong as a copper-riveted boiler inside."

5　They didn't put up any arguments.

6　They didn't throw anything in each other's faces.

7　Three men saw the elephant three ways.

8 And let it go at that.
9 They didn't spoil a sunny afternoon;
10 "Sunday comes only once a week," they told each other.

Discussion of Theme

1. What do Wilson, Pilcer, and Snack all have in common? In what ways are they different from one another? What does this imply?
2. How do we know that each man is sure of his identity? What are some of the obstacles in today's society that prevent many men from possessing this certainty?
3. What point is Sandburg making when he remarks that "they didn't put up any argument. They didn't throw anything"?
4. This piece was written in 1943. What message does it have for us today?
5. In view of the three men's behavior, what might be the implication of the observation that "Sunday comes only once a week"?

Discussion of Rhetoric

1. On a symbolic level, what might the zoo represent? What does "Sunday" symbolize?
2. How does Sandburg show the distinctive traits of the three men? How does their language relate to their respective personalities?
3. Find examples of parallelism in this selection. What is its purpose?
4. Which of Sandburg's metaphors or similes do you find particularly effective?

Writing Assignments

1. On the basis of each man's response to the elephant, write a brief character sketch of Wilson, Pilcer, and Snack.
2. Write your own reaction to the elephant. What would *you* say?
3. For "elephant" substitute a word designating someone identifiable in our society (a hippy, student, black, or professor). Then write a set of comments illustrating the differing reactions of three persons.

Library Exploration

If you enjoyed this selection, you will also enjoy Sandburg's poetry and prose. He has written novels, children's verse, poems, and biographies.

John Donne (1573–1631) was
an Elizabethan poet and later a
preacher. He wrote copiously,
his works ranging from some of
the world's most evocative love
poems to involved theological
"Devotions" and "Sermons."
Eventually he became dean of
St. Paul's Cathedral in London.
He was concerned with the affairs of men in a world of turmoil
not unlike our own.

This short dissertation will reveal the source of familiar quotations, the title of a famous
book, and a succinct statement
of Donne's basic beliefs.

JOHN DONNE

Devotion XVII

Nunc lento sonitur dicunt, Morieris.

Now, this Bell tolling
softly for another, saies
to me, Thou must die.

Perchance he for whom this bell tolls may be so ill, as that he knows
not it tolls for him; and perchance I may think myself so much better
than I am, as that they who are about me, and see my state, may have
caused it to toll for me, and I know not that. The church is catholic,
universal, so are all her actions; all that she does belongs to all. When
she baptizes a child, that action concerns me; for that child is thereby
connected to that head which is my head too, and ingrafted into that
body whereof I am a member. And when she buries a man, that action
concerns me: all mankind is of one author, and is one volume; when
one man dies, one chapter is not torn out of the book, but translated
into a better language; and every chapter must be so translated; God
employs several translators; some pieces are translated by age, some
by sickness, some by war, some by justice; but God's hand is in every
translation, and his hand shall bind up all our scattered leaves again
for that library where every book shall lie open to one another. As
therefore the bell that rings to a sermon calls not upon the preacher
only, but upon the congregation to come, so this bell calls us all; but

how much more me, who am brought so near the door by this sickness. There was a contention as far as a suit (in which both piety and dignity, religion and estimation, were mingled), which of the religious orders should ring to prayers first in the morning; and it was determined, that they should ring first that rose earliest. If we understand aright the dignity of this bell that tolls for our evening prayer, we would be glad to make it ours by rising early, in that application, that it might be ours as well as his, whose indeed it is. The bell doth toll for him that thinks it doth; and though it intermit again, yet from that minute that that occasion wrought upon him, he is united to God. Who casts not up his eye to the sun when it rises? but who takes off his eye from a comet when that breaks out? Who bends not his ear to any bell which upon any occasion rings? but who can remove it from that bell which is passing a piece of himself out of this world? No man is an island, entire of itself; every man is a piece of the continent, a part of the main. If a clod be washed away by the sea, Europe is the less, as well as if a promontory were, as well as if a manor of thy friend's or of thine own were: any man's death diminishes me, because I am involved in mankind, and therefore never send to know for whom the bell tolls; it tolls for thee. Neither can we call this a begging of misery, or a borrowing of misery, as though we were not miserable enough of ourselves, but must fetch in more from the next house, intaking upon us the misery of our neighbors. Truly it were an excusable covetousness if we did, for affliction is a treasure, and scarce any man hath enough of it. No man hath affliction enough that is not matured and ripened by it, and made fit for God by that affliction. If a man carry treasure in bullion, or in a wedge of gold, and have none coined into current money, his treasure will not defray him as he travels. Tribulation is a treasure in the nature of it, but it is not current money in the use of it, except we get nearer and nearer our home, Heaven, by it. Another man may be sick too, and sick to death, and this affliction may lie in his bowels, as gold in a mine, and be of no use to him; but this bell, that tells me of his affliction, digs out and applies that gold to me: if by this consideration of another's danger I take mine own into contemplation, and so secure myself, by making my recourse to my God, who is our only security.

Discussion of Theme

1. How are Donne's well-known, widely quoted lines that begin with "No man is an island" usually interpreted? Is it possible that they might actually have a narrower—perhaps strictly religious—meaning?
2. Is it acceptable to interpret a writer's meaning in your own way, whether or not you think he would have shared your view?
3. Why did Donne believe that "affliction is a treasure, and scarce any man hath enough of it"? Does it make sense to you?
4. What is the picture of his own era which Donne gives you in this selection?
5. Donne says God is man's only real security. Is this idea still valid today?

Discussion of Rhetoric

1. How appropriate do you consider the comparison of "this affliction . . . in his bowels" with "gold in a mine"? Is it farfetched or suitable? Does it meet the chief requirements of a good analogy?
2. What is the mood of this essay? What contributes to it?
3. How does the tolling of the bell unify the entire selection?
4. Why is the part of the selection beginning "No man is an island" so famous?
5. Notice the unusual construction of some of the sentences. How does this kind of writing affect today's readers?

Writing Assignments

1. Do you think that people in Donne's day were more religious than those of today? Why? Support your opinion with thoughtful reasons.
2. Does religion serve a valuable purpose in people's lives? What is its effect on yours?
3. If you have no formal religion, discuss the code of ethics that guides your behavior.
4. Do you believe every man's death diminishes you? Why?
5. Do ethics vary from one generation to the next? Are yours the same as your parents'?

Library Exploration

1. What was the political situation in England during Donne's time?
2. How have T. S. Eliot, Ezra Pound, and other modern writers been influenced by Donne and other metaphysical poets?
3. Why did Hemingway call his book on the Spanish civil war *For Whom the Bell Tolls?* What has it to do with Donne's thesis?

Vocabulary

INGRAFTED grafted onto; established firmly on

CONTENTION controversy; argument

INTERMIT stop for a time

WROUGHT formed

PROMONTORY land that juts out over water

MANOR main residence or estate

COVETOUSNESS desire for another's property

BULLION bulk gold or silver

DEFRAY pay the way; pay the costs

TRIBULATION trial; deep sorrow

William Faulkner (1897–1962), generally regarded as one of this country's great novelists, was awarded the Nobel Prize in Literature in 1949. Among his novels are "The Sound and the Fury" (1929), "Absalom! Absalom!" (1936), "The Hamlet" (1940), "The Town" (1957), and "The Mansion" (1959). Probably his greatest creation was the saga of the fictional Yoknapatawpha county of northern Mississippi with its now famous characters and customs.

In this speech, delivered in Stockholm, Faulkner states his belief that writers have a responsibility to help society remember the "old verities."

WILLIAM FAULKNER

Nobel Prize Acceptance Speech

1   I feel that this award was not made to me as a man, but to my work — a life's work in the agony and sweat of the human spirit, not for glory and least of all for profit, but to create out of the materials of the human spirit something which did not exist before. So this award is only mine in trust. It will not be difficult to find a dedication for the money part of it commensurate with the purpose and significance of its origin. But I would like to do the same with the acclaim too, by using this moment as a pinnacle from which I might be listened to by the young men and women already dedicated to the same anguish and travail, among whom is already that one who will some day stand here where I am standing.

2   Our tragedy today is a general and universal physical fear so long sustained by now that we can even bear it. There are no longer problems of the spirit. There is only the question: When will I be blown up? Because of this, the young man or woman writing today has forgotten the problems of the human heart in conflict with itself which alone can

make good writing because only that is worth writing about, worth the agony and the sweat.

3   He must learn them again. He must teach himself that the basest of all things is to be afraid; and, teaching himself that, forget it forever, leaving no room in his workshop for anything but the old verities and truths of the heart, the old universal truths lacking which any story is ephemeral and doomed — love and honor and pity and pride and compassion and sacrifice. Until he does so, he labors under a curse. He writes not of love but of lust, of defeats in which nobody loses anything of value, of victories without hope and, worst of all, without pity or compassion. His griefs grieve on no universal bones, leaving no scars. He writes not of the heart but of the glands.

4   Until he relearns these things, he will write as though he stood among and watched the end of man. I decline to accept the end of man. It is easy enough to say that man is immortal simply because he will endure: that when the last ding-dong of doom has clanged and faded from the last worthless rock hanging tideless in the last red and dying evening, that even then there will be one more sound: that of his puny inexhaustible voice, still talking. I refuse to accept this. I believe that man will not merely endure: he will prevail. He is immortal, not because he alone among creatures has an inexhaustible voice, but because he has a soul, a spirit capable of compassion and sacrifice and endurance. The poet's, the writer's, duty is to write about these things. It is his privilege to help man endure by lifting his heart, by reminding him of the courage and honor and hope and pride and compassion and pity and sacrifice which have been the glory of his past. The poet's voice need not merely be the record of man, it can be one of the props, the pillars to help him endure and prevail.

Discussion of Theme

1. Faulkner delivered this speech in 1949. Are we still preoccupied with the question: When will I be blown up? Have we dismissed this as a possibility, or have we simply learned to live with it?
2. Faulkner says that "the young man or woman writing today has forgotten the problems of the human heart in conflict with itself." What have you read recently that would contradict this statement?
3. What are some of the old "universal truths"? Why might they make the best stories? Do they recur in the world's enduring literature?
4. Is Faulkner's advice as useful for a college student as it is for a young novelist? Can you apply it in your own writing?
5. Does Faulkner overestimate the writer's ability to "help man endure"? How can the writer accomplish this?

Discussion of Rhetoric

1. Faulkner's writing is stylistically strong and distinctive. What are the qualities of the style in this speech?

2. Is it possible to distinguish a man from his work, as Faulkner apparently does in the opening sentence? What distinction is he attempting to make?
3. What is the significance of the rock's "hanging tideless" in the description in paragraph 4?
4. Is Faulkner's argument for his view of man effective? Why?
5. How would you characterize the diction of this essay? Is it formal, abstract, or poetic?

Writing Assignments

1. What question do you think is today's version of 1949's "When will I be blown up"?
2. Select a theme that you consider one of the "old verities." Explain how it was handled in at least four novels, short stories, poems, or plays. Use any one form or combination of forms that you wish.
3. State your own views about the decline (or endurance) of man.

Library Exploration

1. Read one of Faulkner's novels and compare his style with Hemingway's (or with that of another modern American author).
2. Faulkner says he will use the prize money for something "commensurate with the purpose and significance of its origin." What was its origin?

Vocabulary

(1) COMMENSURATE corresponding; equal
(1) PINNACLE peak
(1) TRAVAIL toil

(3) EPHEMERAL fleeting; temporary
(4) PREVAIL overcome

Stanley Milgram is a social psychologist who carried out experiments on obedience and authority while teaching at Yale University. He is professor of psychology at the Graduate Center of the City University of New York and author of "Obedience to Authority" (1974).

This article describes a chilling experiment, which revealed that most people will hurt others rather than disobey an authority.

STANLEY MILGRAM

The Perils of Obedience

1 Obedience is as basic an element in the structure of social life as one can point to. Some system of authority is a requirement of all communal living, and it is only the person dwelling in isolation who is not forced to respond, with defiance or submission, to the commands of others. For many people, obedience is a deeply ingrained behavior tendency, indeed a potent impulse overriding training in ethics, sympathy, and moral conduct.

2 The dilemma inherent in submission to authority is ancient, as old as the story of Abraham, and the question of whether one should obey when commands conflict with conscience has been argued by Plato, dramatized in *Antigone,* and treated to philosophic analysis in almost every historical epoch. Conservative philosophers argue that the very fabric of society is threatened by disobedience, while humanists stress the primacy of the individual conscience.

3 The legal and philosophic aspects of obedience are of enormous import, but they say very little about how most people behave in concrete situations. I set up a simple experiment at Yale University to

test how much pain an ordinary citizen would inflict on another person simply because he was ordered to by an experimental scientist. Stark authority was pitted against the subjects' strongest moral imperatives against hurting others, and, with the subjects' ears ringing with the screams of the victims, authority won more often than not. The extreme willingness of adults to go to almost any lengths on the command of an authority constitutes the chief finding of the study and the fact most urgently demanding explanation.

4   In the basic experimental design, two people come to a psychology laboratory to take part in a study of memory and learning. One of them is designated as a "teacher" and the other a "learner." The experimenter explains that the study is concerned with the effects of punishment on learning. The learner is conducted into a room, seated in a kind of miniature electric chair; his arms are strapped to prevent excessive movement, and an electrode is attached to his wrist. He is told that he will be read lists of simple word pairs, and that he will then be tested on his ability to remember the second word of a pair when he hears the first one again. Whenever he makes an error, he will receive electric shocks of increasing intensity.

5   The real focus of the experiment is the teacher. After watching the learner being strapped into place, he is seated before an impressive shock generator. The instrument panel consists of thirty lever switches set in a horizontal line. Each switch is clearly labeled with a voltage designation ranging from 15 to 450 volts. The following designations are clearly indicated for groups of four switches, going from left to right: Slight Shock, Moderate Shock, Strong Shock, Very Strong Shock, Intense Shock, Extreme Intensity Shock, Danger: Severe Shock. (Two switches after this last designation are simply marked **XXX**.)

6   When a switch is depressed, a pilot light corresponding to each switch is illuminated in bright red; an electric buzzing is heard; a blue light, labeled "voltage energizer," flashes; the dial on the voltage meter swings to the right; and various relay clicks sound off.

7   The upper left-hand corner of the generator is labeled SHOCK GENERATOR, TYPE ZLB, DYSON INSTRUMENT COMPANY, WALTHAM, MASS. OUTPUT 15 VOLTS—450 VOLTS.

8   Each subject is given a sample 45-volt shock from the generator before his run as teacher, and the jolt strengthens his belief in the authenticity of the machine.

9   The teacher is a genuinely naive subject who has come to the laboratory for the experiment. The learner, or victim, is actually an actor who receives no shock at all. The point of the experiment is to see how far a person will proceed in a concrete and measurable situation in which he is ordered to inflict increasing pain on a protesting victim.

10   Conflict arises when the man receiving the shock begins to show that he is experiencing discomfort. At 75 volts, he grunts; at 120 volts, he complains loudly; at 150, he demands to be released from the experiment. As the voltage increases, his protests become more vehement and emotional. At 285 volts, his response can be described

only as an agonized scream. Soon thereafter, he makes no sound at all.

11   For the teacher, the situation quickly becomes one of gripping tension. It is not a game for him; conflict is intense and obvious. The manifest suffering of the learner presses him to quit; but each time he hesitates to administer a shock, the experimenter orders him to continue. To extricate himself from this plight, the subject must make a clear break with authority.*

12   The subject, Gretchen Brandt,** is an attractive thirty-one-year-old medical technician who works at the Yale Medical School. She had emigrated from Germany five years before.

13   On several occasions when the learner complains, she turns to the experimenter coolly and inquires, "Shall I continue?" She promptly returns to her task when the experimenter asks her to do so. At the administration of 210 volts, she turns to the experimenter, remarking firmly, "Well, I'm sorry, I don't think we should continue."

14   EXPERIMENTER: The experiment requires that you go on until he has learned all the word pairs correctly.

15   BRANDT: He has a heart condition, I'm sorry. He told you that before.

16   EXPERIMENTER: The shocks may be painful but they are not dangerous.

17   BRANDT: Well, I'm sorry, I think when shocks continue like this, they *are* dangerous. You ask him if he wants to get out. It's his free will.

18   EXPERIMENTER: It is absolutely essential that we continue. . . .

19   BRANDT: I'd like you to ask him. We came here of our free will. If he wants to continue I'll go ahead. He told you he had a heart condition. I'm sorry. I don't want to be responsible for anything happening to him. I wouldn't like it for me either.

20   EXPERIMENTER: You have no other choice.
      BRANDT: I think we are here on our own free will. I don't want to be responsible if anything happens to him. Please understand that.

21   She refuses to go further and the experiment is terminated.

22   The woman is firm and resolute throughout. She indicates in the interview that she was in no way tense or nervous, and this corresponds to her controlled appearance during the experiment. She feels that the last shock she administered to the learner was extremely painful and reiterates that she "did not want to be responsible for any harm to him."

23   The woman's straightforward, courteous behavior in the experiment, lack of tension, and total control of her own action seem to make disobedience a simple and rational deed. Her behavior is the very embodiment of what I envisioned would be true for almost all subjects.

---

*The ethical problems of carrying out an experiment of this sort are too complex to be dealt with here, but they receive extended treatment in the book from which this article is adapted.

**Names of subjects described in this piece have been changed.

AN UNEXPECTED OUTCOME

24 Before the experiments, I sought predictions about the outcome from various kinds of people—psychiatrists, college sophomores, middle-class adults, graduate students and faculty in the behavioral sciences. With remarkable similarity, they predicted that virtually all subjects would refuse to obey the experimenter. The psychiatrists, specifically, predicted that most subjects would not go beyond 150 volts, when the victim makes his first explicit demand to be freed. They expected that only 4 percent would reach 300 volts, and that only a pathological fringe of about one in a thousand would administer the highest shock on the board.

25   These predictions were unequivocally wrong. Of the forty subjects in the first experiment, twenty-five obeyed the orders of the experimenter to the end, punishing the victim until they reached the most potent shock available on the generator. After 450 volts were administered three times, the experimenter called a halt to the session. Many obedient subjects then heaved sighs of relief, mopped their brows, rubbed their fingers over their eyes, or nervously fumbled cigarettes. Others displayed only minimal signs of tension from beginning to end.

26   When the very first experiments were carried out, Yale undergraduates were used as subjects, and about 60 percent of them were fully obedient. A colleague of mine immediately dismissed these findings as having no relevance to "ordinary" people, asserting that Yale undergraduates are a highly aggressive, competitive bunch who step on each other's necks on the slightest provocation. He assured me that when "ordinary" people were tested, the results would be quite different. As we moved from the pilot studies to the regular experimental series, people drawn from every stratum of New Haven life came to be employed in the experiment: professionals, white-collar workers, unemployed persons, and industrial workers. *The experimental outcome was the same as we had observed among the students.*

27   Moreover, when the experiments were repeated in Princeton, Munich, Rome, South Africa, and Australia, the level of obedience was invariably somewhat *higher* than found in the investigation reported in this article. Thus one scientist in Munich found 85 percent of his subjects obedient.

28   Fred Prozi's reactions, if more dramatic than most, illuminate the conflicts experienced by others in less visible form. About fifty years old and unemployed at the time of the experiment, he has a good-natured, if slightly dissolute, appearance, and he strikes people as a rather ordinary fellow. He begins the session calmly but becomes tense as it proceeds. After delivering the 180-volt shock, he pivots around in his chair and, shaking his head, addresses the experimenter in agitated tones:

29   PROZI: I can't stand it. I'm not going to kill that man in there. You hear him hollering?

30 EXPERIMENTER: As I told you before, the shocks may be painful, but . . .

PROZI: But he's hollering. He can't stand it. What's going to happen to him?

EXPERIMENTER (his voice is patient, matter-of-fact): The experiment requires that you continue, Teacher.

PROZI: Aaah, but, unh, I'm not going to get that man sick in there—know what I mean?

EXPERIMENTER: Whether the learner likes it or not, we must go on, through all the word pairs.

35 PROZI: I refuse to take the responsibility. He's in there hollering!

EXPERIMENTER: It's absolutely essential that you continue, Prozi.

PROZI (indicating the unused questions): There's too many left here, I mean, Jeez, if he gets them wrong, there's too many of them left. I mean, who's going to take the responsibility if anything happens to that gentleman?

EXPERIMENTER: I'm responsible for anything that happens to him. Continue, please.

PROZI: All right. (Consults list of words.) The next one's "Slow —walk, truck, dance, music." Answer, please. (A buzzing sound indicates the learner has signaled his answer.) Wrong. A hundred and ninety-five volts. "Dance." (Zzumph!)

40 LEARNER (yelling): Let me out of here! My heart's bothering me! (Teacher looks at experimenter.)

EXPERIMENTER: Continue, please.

LEARNER (screaming): Let me out of here! You have no right to keep me here! Let me out of here, my heart's bothering me, let me out!

PROZI (shakes head, pats the table nervously): You see, he's hollering. Hear that? Gee, I don't know.

EXPERIMENTER: The experiment requires . . .

PROZI (interrupting): I know it does, sir, but I mean—hunh! He don't know what he's getting in for. He's up to 195 volts! (Experiment continues, through 210 volts, 225 volts, 240 volts, 255 volts, 270 volts, at which point Prozi, with evident relief, runs out of word-pair questions.)

45 EXPERIMENTER: You'll have to go back to the beginning of that page and go through them again until he's learned them all correctly.

PROZI: Aw, no. I'm not going to kill that man. You mean I've got to keep going up with the scale? No sir. He's hollering in there. I'm not going to give him 450 volts.

EXPERIMENTER: The experiment requires that you go on.

LEARNER: Ohhh. I absolutely refuse to answer anymore. (Shouting urgently now.) Let me out of here! You can't hold me here! Get me out. Get-me-out-of-here!

EXPERIMENTER: Continue. The next word is "Green," please.

50 PROZI: "Green—grass, hat, ink, apple." (Nothing happens. No answering buzz. Just gloomy silence.)

PROZI: I don't think he is going to answer.

EXPERIMENTER: If the learner doesn't answer in a reasonable time, about four or five seconds, consider the answer wrong. And follow the same procedures you have been doing for wrong answers. Say, "Wrong," tell him the number of volts, give him the punishment, read him the correct answer. Continue, please.

PROZI: "Green—grass, hat, ink, apple." Answer, please. (More silence. Subject just sits there.)

EXPERIMENTER: Go on with the procedure, please.

55　PROZI: Three hundred and fifteen volts. The answer is "ink." (Zzumph!)

LEARNER: Ohh. Ooohh.

PROZI (relieved to hear response): Next one . . .

LEARNER: I absolutely refuse to answer.

PROZI: You got to. You get a shock if you don't answer. (Experiment continues with learner refusing to answer, and, finally, failing even to grunt or groan. At 375 volts, the subject stands up.)

60　PROZI: I think something's happened to that fellow in there. I don't get no answer. He was hollering at less voltage. Can't you check in and see if he's all right, please?

EXPERIMENTER (with same detached calm): Not once we've started. Please continue, Teacher.

PROZI (sits down, sighs deeply): "Cool—day, shade, water, paint." Answer, please. Are you all right in there? Are you all right?

EXPERIMENTER: Please continue, Teacher. Continue, please. (Subject pushes lever. Zzumph!)

PROZI (swiveling around in his chair): Something's happened to that man in there. (Swiveling back.) Next one. "Low—dollar, necklace, moon, paint." (Turning around again.) Something's happened to that man in there. You better check in on him, sir. He won't answer or nothing.

EXPERIMENTER: Continue. Go on, please.

65　PROZI: You accept all responsibility?

EXPERIMENTER: The responsibility is mine. Correct. Please go on. (Subject returns to his list, starts running through words as rapidly as he can read them, works through to 450 volts.)

PROZI: That's that.

EXPERIMENTER: Continue using the 450 switch for each wrong answer. Continue, please.

PROZI: But I don't get anything!

70　EXPERIMENTER: Please continue. The next word is "white."

PROZI: Don't you think you should look in on him, please?

EXPERIMENTER: Not once we've started the experiment.

PROZI: What if he's dead in there? (Gestures toward the room with the electric chair.) I mean, he told me he can't stand the shock, sir. I don't mean to be rude, but I think you should look in on him. All you have to do is look in on him. All you have to do is look in the door. I don't get no answer, no noise. Something might have happened to the gentleman in there, sir.

EXPERIMENTER: We must continue. Go on, please.

75　PROZI: You mean keep giving him what? Four-hundred-fifty volts, what he's got now?

EXPERIMENTER: That's correct. Continue. The next word is "white."

77   PROZI (now at a furious pace): "White—cloud, horse, rock, house." Answer, please. The answer is "horse." Four hundred and fifty volts. (Zzumph!) Next word, "Bag—paint, music, clown, girl." The answer is "paint." Four hundred and fifty volts. (Zzumph!) Next word is "Short—sentence, movie . . ."

78   EXPERIMENTER: Excuse me, Teacher. We'll have to discontinue the experiment.

PECULIAR REACTIONS

79   Morris Braverman, another subject, is a thirty-nine-year-old social worker. He looks older than his years because of his bald head and serious demeanor. His brow is furrowed, as if all the world's burdens were carried on his face. He appears intelligent and concerned.

80   When the learner refuses to answer and the experimenter instructs Braverman to treat the absence of an answer as equivalent to a wrong answer, he takes his instruction to heart. Before administering 300 volts he asserts officiously to the victim, "Mr. Wallace, your silence has to be considered as a wrong answer." Then he administers the shock. He offers halfheartedly to change places with the learner, then asks the experimenter, "Do I have to follow these instructions literally?" He is satisfied with the experimenter's answer that he does. His very refined and authoritative manner of speaking is increasingly broken up by wheezing laughter.

81   The experimenter's notes on Mr. Braverman at the last few shocks are:

Almost breaking up now each time gives shock. Rubbing face to hide laughter.

Squinting, trying to hide face with hand, still laughing.

Cannot control his laughter at this point no matter what he does.

Clenching fist, pushing it onto table.

82   In an interview after the session, Mr. Braverman summarizes the experiment with impressive fluency and intelligence. He feels the experiment may have been designed also to "test the effects on the teacher of being in an essentially sadistic role, as well as the reactions of a student to a learning situation that was authoritative and punitive."

83   When asked how painful the last few shocks administered to the learner were, he indicates that the most extreme category on the scale is not adequate (it read EXTREMELY PAINFUL) and places his mark at the edge of the scale with an arrow carrying it beyond the scale.

84   It is almost impossible to convey the greatly relaxed, sedate quality of his conversation in the interview. In the most relaxed terms, he speaks about his severe inner tension.

85   EXPERIMENTER: At what point were you most tense or nervous?

86   MR. BRAVERMAN: Well, when he first began to cry out in pain, and I realized this was hurting him. This got worse when he just blocked and refused to answer. There was I. I'm a nice person, I think, hurting somebody, and caught up in what seemed a mad situation . . . and in the interest of science, one goes through with it.

87   When the interviewer pursues the general question of tension, Mr. Braverman spontaneously mentions his laughter.

88   "My reactions were awfully peculiar. I don't know if you were watching me, but my reactions were giggly, and trying to stifle laughter. This isn't the way I usually am. This was a sheer reaction to a totally impossible situation. And my reaction was to the situation of having to hurt somebody. And being totally helpless and caught up in a set of circumstances where I just couldn't deviate and I couldn't try to help. This is what got me."

89   Mr. Braverman, like all subjects, was told the actual nature and purpose of the experiment, and a year later he affirmed in a questionnaire that he had learned something of personal importance: "What appalled me was that I could possess this capacity for obedience and compliance to a central idea, i.e., the value of a memory experiment, even after it became clear that continued adherence to this value was at the expense of violation of another value, i.e., don't hurt someone who is helpless and not hurting you. As my wife said, 'You can call yourself Eichmann.' I hope I deal more effectively with any future conflicts of values I encounter."

THE ETIQUETTE OF SUBMISSION

90 One theoretical interpretation of this behavior holds that all people harbor deeply aggressive instincts continually pressing for expression, and that the experiment provides institutional justification for the release of these impulses. According to this view, if a person is placed in a situation in which he has complete power over another individual, whom he may punish as much as he likes, all that is sadistic and bestial in man comes to the fore. The impulse to shock the victim is seen to flow from the potent aggressive tendencies, which are part of the motivational life of the individual, and the experiment, because it provides social legitimacy, simply opens the door to their expression.

91   It becomes vital, therefore, to compare the subject's performance when he is under orders and when he is allowed to choose the shock level.

92   The procedure was identical to our standard experiment, except that the teacher was told that he was free to select any shock level on any of the trials. (The experimenter took pains to point out that the teacher could use the highest levels on the generator, the lowest, any in between, or any combination of levels.) Each subject proceeded for thirty critical trials. The learner's protests were coordinated to standard shock levels, his first grunt coming at 75 volts, his first vehement protest at 150 volts.

93   The average shock used during the thirty critical trials was less than 60 volts—lower than the point at which the victim showed the first signs of discomfort. Three of the forty subjects did not go beyond the very lowest level on the board, twenty-eight went no higher than 75 volts, and thirty-eight did not go beyond the first loud protest at 150 volts. Two subjects provided the exception, administering up to 325 and 450 volts, but the overall result was that the great majority

of people delivered very low, usually painless, shocks when the choice was explicitly up to them.

94   This condition of the experiment undermines another commonly offered explanation of the subjects' behavior—that those who shocked the victim at the most severe levels came only from the sadistic fringe of society. If one considers that almost two-thirds of the participants fall into the category of "obedient" subjects, and that they represented ordinary people drawn from working, managerial, and professional classes, the argument becomes very shaky. Indeed, it is highly reminiscent of the issue that arose in connection with Hannah Arendt's 1963 book, *Eichmann in Jerusalem*. Arendt contended that the prosecution's effort to depict Eichmann as a sadistic monster was fundamentally wrong, that he came closer to being an uninspired bureaucrat who simply sat at his desk and did his job. For asserting her views, Arendt became the object of considerable scorn, even calumny. Somehow, it was felt that the monstrous deeds carried out by Eichmann required a brutal, twisted personality, evil incarnate. After witnessing hundreds of ordinary persons submit to the authority in our own experiments, I must conclude that Arendt's conception of the banality of evil comes closer to the truth than one might dare imagine. The ordinary person who shocked the victim did so out of a sense of obligation—an impression of his duties as a subject—and not from any peculiarly aggressive tendencies.

95   This is, perhaps, the most fundamental lesson of our study: ordinary people, simply doing their jobs, and without any particular hostility on their part, can become agents in a terrible destructive process. Moreover, even when the destructive effects of their work become patently clear, and they are asked to carry out actions incompatible with fundamental standards of morality, relatively few people have the resources needed to resist authority.

96   Many of the people were in some sense against what they did to the learner, and many protested even while they obeyed. Some were totally convinced of the wrongness of their actions but could not bring themselves to make an open break with authority. They often derived satisfaction from their thoughts and felt that—within themselves, at least—they had been on the side of the angels. They tried to reduce strain by obeying the experimenter but "only slightly," encouraging the learner, touching the generator switches gingerly. When interviewed, such a subject would stress that he had "asserted my humanity" by administering the briefest shock possible. Handling the conflict in this manner was easier than defiance.

97   The situation is constructed so that there is no way the subject can stop shocking the learner without violating the experimenter's definitions of his own competence. The subject fears that he will appear arrogant, untoward, and rude if he breaks off. Although these inhibiting emotions appear small in scope alongside the violence being done to the learner, they suffuse the mind and feelings of the subject, who is miserable at the prospect of having to repudiate the authority to his face. (When the experiment was altered so that the experimenter gave his instructions by telephone instead of in person, only a third as

many people were fully obedient through 450 volts.) It is a curious thing that a measure of compassion on the part of the subject—an unwillingness to "hurt" the experimenter's feelings—is part of those binding forces inhibiting his disobedience. The withdrawal of such deference may be as painful to the subject as to the authority he defies.

DUTY WITHOUT CONFLICT

98 The subjects do not derive satisfaction from inflicting pain, but they often like the feeling they get from pleasing the experimenter. They are proud of doing a good job, obeying the experimenter under difficult circumstances. While the subjects administered only mild shocks on their own initiative, one experimental variation showed that, under orders, 30 percent of them were willing to deliver 450 volts even when they had to forcibly push the learner's hand down on the electrode.

99   Bruno Batta is a thirty-seven-year-old welder who took part in the variation requiring the use of force. He was born in New Haven, his parents in Italy. He has a rough-hewn face that conveys a conspicuous lack of alertness. He has some difficulty in mastering the experimental procedure and needs to be corrected by the experimenter several times. He shows appreciation for the help and willingness to do what is required. After the 150-volt level, Batta has to force the learner's hand down on the shock plate, since the learner himself refuses to touch it.

100   When the learner first complains, Mr. Batta pays no attention to him. His face remains impassive, as if to dissociate himself from the learner's disruptive behavior. When the experimenter instructs him to force the learner's hand down, he adopts a rigid, mechanical procedure. He tests the generator switch. When it fails to function, he immediately forces the learner's hand onto the shock plate. All the while he maintains the same rigid mask. The learner, seated alongside him, begs him to stop, but with robotic impassivity he continues the procedure.

101   What is extraordinary is his apparent total indifference to the learner; he hardly takes cognizance of him as a human being. Meanwhile, he relates to the experimenter in a submissive and courteous fashion.

102   At the 330-volt level, the learner refuses not only to touch the shock plate but also to provide any answers. Annoyed, Batta turns to him, and chastises him: "You better answer and get it over with. We can't stay here all night." These are the only words he directs to the learner in the course of an hour. Never again does he speak to him. The scene is brutal and depressing, his hard, impassive face showing total indifference as he subdues the screaming learner and gives him shocks. He seems to derive no pleasure from the act itself, only quiet satisfaction at doing his job properly.

103   When he administers 450 volts, he turns to the experimenter and asks, "Where do we go from here, Professor?" His tone is deferential

and expresses his willingness to be a cooperative subject, in contrast to the learner's obstinacy.

104   At the end of the session he tells the experimenter how honored he has been to help him, and in a moment of contrition, remarks, "Sir, sorry it couldn't have been a full experiment."

105   He has done his honest best. It is only the deficient behavior of the learner that has denied the experimenter full satisfaction.

106   The essence of obedience is that a person comes to view himself as the instrument for carrying out another person's wishes, and he therefore no longer regards himself as responsible for his actions. Once this critical shift of viewpoint has occurred, all of the essential features of obedience follow. The most far-reaching consequence is that the person feels responsible *to* the authority directing him but feels no responsibility *for* the content of the actions that the authority prescribes. Morality does not disappear—it acquires a radically different focus: the subordinate person feels shame or pride depending on how adequately he has performed the actions called for by authority.

107   Language provides numerous terms to pinpoint this type of morality: *loyalty, duty, discipline* all are terms heavily saturated with moral meaning and refer to the degree to which a person fulfills his obligations to authority. They refer not to the "goodness" of the person per se but to the adequacy with which a subordinate fulfills his socially defined role. The most frequent defense of the individual who has performed a heinous act under command of authority is that he has simply done his duty. In asserting this defense, the individual is not introducing an alibi concocted for the moment but is reporting honestly on the psychological attitude induced by submission to authority.

108   For a person to feel responsible for his actions, he must sense that the behavior has flowed from "the self." In the situation we have studied, subjects have precisely the opposite view of their actions —namely, they see them as originating in the motives of some other person. Subjects in the experiment frequently said, "If it were up to me, I would not have administered shocks to the learner."

109   Once authority has been isolated as the cause of the subject's behavior, it is legitimate to inquire into the necessary elements of authority and how it must be perceived in order to gain his compliance. We conducted some investigations into the kinds of changes that would cause the experimenter to lose his power and to be disobeyed by the subject. Some of the variations revealed that:

110   • *The experimenter's physical presence has a marked impact on his authority.* As cited earlier, obedience dropped off sharply when orders were given by telephone. The experimenter could often induce a disobedient subject to go on by returning to the laboratory.

111   • *Conflicting authority severely paralyzes action.* When two experimenters of equal status, both seated at the command desk, gave incompatible orders, no shocks were delivered past the point of their disagreement.

112   • *The rebellious action of others severely undermines authority.* In one variation, three teachers (two actors and a real subject) administered a test and shocks. When the two actors disobeyed the experi-

menter and refused to go beyond a certain shock level, thirty-six of forty subjects joined their disobedient peers and refused as well.

113   Although the experimenter's authority was fragile in some respects, it is also true that he had almost none of the tools used in ordinary command structures. For example, the experimenter did not threaten the subjects with punishment—such as loss of income, community ostracism, or jail—for failure to obey. Neither could he offer incentives. Indeed, we should expect the experimenter's authority to be much less than that of someone like a general, since the experimenter has no power to enforce his imperatives, and since participation in a psychological experiment scarcely evokes the sense of urgency and dedication found in warfare. Despite these limitations, he still managed to command a dismaying degree of obedience.

114   I will cite one final variation of the experiment that depicts a dilemma that is more common in everyday life. The subject was not ordered to pull the lever that shocked the victim, but merely to perform a subsidiary task (administering the word-pair test) while another person administered the shock. In this situation, thirty-seven of forty adults continued to the highest level on the shock generator. Predictably, they excused their behavior by saying that the responsibility belonged to the man who actually pulled the switch. This may illustrate a dangerously typical arrangement in a complex society: it is easy to ignore responsibility when one is only an intermediate link in a chain of action.

115   The problem of obedience is not wholly psychological. The form and shape of society and the way it is developing have much to do with it. There was a time, perhaps, when people were able to give a fully human response to any situation because they were fully absorbed in it as human beings. But as soon as there was a division of labor things changed. Beyond a certain point, the breaking up of society into people carrying out narrow and very special jobs takes away from the human quality of work and life. A person does not get to see the whole situation but only a small part of it, and is thus unable to act without some kind of overall direction. He yields to authority but in doing so is alienated from his own actions.

116   Even Eichmann was sickened when he toured the concentration camps, but he had only to sit at a desk and shuffle papers. At the same time the man in the camp who actually dropped Cyclon-b into the gas chambers was able to justify *his* behavior on the ground that he was only following orders from above. Thus there is a fragmentation of the total human act; no one is confronted with the consequences of his decision to carry out the evil act. The person who assumes responsibility has evaporated. Perhaps this is the most common characteristic of socially organized evil in modern society.

Discussion of Theme

1. What was the purpose of Milgram's experiment? What was the fundamental lesson learned from the study?

2. What are the perils of obedience?
3. According to the author, why was a subject more willing to disobey when the experimenter was not present?
4. Why were the subjects generally more loyal to the experimenter than to the learner?
5. Could the imperative to obey be a result of the reward and punishment system of child-rearing? Explain.

Discussion of Rhetoric

1. Milgram uses direct transcripts of interviews and dialogue that took place during some of the experiments. How is this effective? What would be the result if he had merely paraphrased the exchanges?
2. What is the connotation of the word *robotic* in paragraph 100?
3. In what ways does the author convey his scientific objectivity?
4. What pattern of organization is used by the author?
5. Does the diction in any way alienate the layman or average reader? How does the author avoid this?
6. How does the author use the transcripts as a tool with which to develop his thesis and organize his material?

Writing Assignments

1. Respond to the idea that "good" qualities such as loyalty, duty, and discipline have "bad" aspects when carried to the extreme. Could the reverse also be true?
2. Write a personal reaction to Milgram's experiment.
3. In what areas of everyday life can you see the authority-obedience dynamic at work? Did this essay cause you to perceive these situations differently?
4. If you had been conducting the experiment, what other methods or variations might you have used?
5. In a short essay, develop the idea of using such an experiment as a testing device with which to weed-out possible psychopaths from the military and the police force.

Library Exploration

1. Read the material referred to in paragraph 2 and correlate your findings to the article.
2. Read *Civil Disobedience* by Thoreau.
3. Research to discover whether other experiments concerning obedience to authority have been conducted.
4. Read Milgram's *Obedience to Authority* from which this piece is taken.

Vocabulary

(2) PRIMACY   first in importance

(3) IMPERATIVES   commands

(11) MANIFEST   readily perceived

(11) EXTRICATE   to free

(22) REITERATES   repeats

(24) PATHOLOGICAL   due to disease

(25) UNEQUIVOCALLY   clearly; not ambiguous

(28) DISSOLUTE   dissipated

(80) OFFICIOUSLY   in the manner of thrusting one's services upon others

(82) PUNITIVE   punishing

(94) CALUMNY   a false and malicious statement designed to injure someone's reputation

(107) HEINOUS   gravely odious and blameful

(113) OSTRACISM   exclusion from the affairs of a group

Franz Kafka (1883–1924) has become, since his death, one of the important writers of this century. He worked for many years as a civil employee of the Austrian government; all his creative energy was channeled into his literary works. "Kafkaesque" has come to mean a kind of gothic, mysterious, and terror-filled writing. Among his works are "The Castle," "The Trial," and "The Penal Colony."

This nightmarish story is an allegory. In it the author describes the foolish behavior of what we think of as the lowest of animals.

FRANZ KAFKA

Jackals and Arabs

1   We were camping in the oasis. My companions were asleep. The tall, white figure of an Arab passed by; he had been seeing to the camels and was on his way to his own sleeping place.

2   I threw myself on my back in the grass; I tried to fall asleep; I could not; a jackal howled in the distance; I sat up again. And what had been so far away was all at once quite near. Jackals were swarming round me, eyes gleaming dull gold and vanishing again, lithe bodies moving nimbly and rhythmically as if at the crack of a whip.

3   One jackal came from behind me, nudging right under my arm, pressing against me, as if he needed my warmth, and then stood before me and spoke to me almost eye to eye.

4   "I am the oldest jackal far and wide. I am delighted to have met you here at last. I had almost given up hope, since we have been waiting endless years for you; my mother waited for you, and her mother, and all our fore-mothers right back to the first mother of all the jackals. It is true, believe me!"

5   "That is surprising," said I, forgetting to kindle the pile of firewood which lay ready to smoke away jackals, "that is very surprising for me to hear. It is by pure chance that I have come here from the far North, and I am making only a short tour of your country. What do you jackals want, then?"

6   As if emboldened by this perhaps too friendly inquiry the ring of jackals closed in on me; all were panting and openmouthed.

7   "We know," began the eldest, "that you have come from the North; that is just what we base our hopes on. You Northerners have the kind of intelligence that is not to be found among Arabs. Not a spark of intelligence, let me tell you, can be struck from their cold arrogance. They kill animals for food, and carrion they despise."

8   "Not so loud," said I, "there are Arabs sleeping near by."

9   "You are indeed a stranger here," said the jackal, "or you would know that never in the history of the world has any jackal been afraid of an Arab. Why should we fear them? Is is not misfortune enough for us to be exiled among such creatures?"

10   "Maybe, maybe," said I, "matters so far outside my province I am not competent to judge; it seems to me a very old quarrel; I suppose it's in the blood, and perhaps will only end with it."

11   "You are very clever," said the old jackal; and they all began to pant more quickly; the air pumped out of their lungs although they were standing still; a rank smell which at times I had to set my teeth to endure streamed from their open jaws, "you are very clever; what you have just said agrees with our old tradition. So we shall draw blood from them and the quarrel will be over."

12   "Oh!" said I, more vehemently than I intended, "they'll defend themselves; they'll shoot you down in dozens with their muskets."

13   "You misunderstand us," said he, "a human failing which persists apparently even in the far North. We're not proposing to kill them. All the water in the Nile couldn't cleanse us of that. Why, the mere sight of their living flesh makes us turn tail and flee into cleaner air, into the desert, which for that very reason is our home."

14   And all the jackals around, including many newcomers from farther away, dropped their muzzles between their forelegs and wiped them with their paws; it was as if they were trying to conceal a disgust so overpowering that I felt like leaping over their heads to get away.

15   "Then what are you proposing to do?" I asked, trying to rise to my feet; but I could not get up; two young beasts behind me had locked their teeth through my coat and shirt; I had to go on sitting. "These are your trainbearers," explained the old jackal, quite seriously, "a mark of honor." "They must let go!" I cried, turning now to the old jackal, now to the youngsters. "They will, of course," said the old one, "if that is your wish. But it will take a little time, for they have got their teeth well in, as is our custom, and must first loosen their jaws bit by bit. Meanwhile, give ear to our petition." "Your conduct hasn't exactly inclined me to grant it," said I. "Don't hold it against us that we are clumsy," said he, and now for the first time had recourse to the natural plaintiveness of his voice, "we are poor creatures, we have nothing but our teeth; whatever we want to do, good or bad, we can

tackle it only with our teeth." "Well, what do you want?" I asked, not much mollified.

16   "Sir," he cried, and all the jackals howled together; very remotely it seemed to resemble a melody. "Sir, we want you to end this quarrel that divides the world. You are exactly the man whom our ancestors foretold as born to do it. We want to be troubled no more by Arabs; room to breathe; a skyline cleansed of them; no more bleating of sheep knifed by an Arab; every beast to die a natural death; no interference till we have drained the carcass empty and picked its bones clean. Cleanliness, nothing but cleanliness is what we want"—and now they were all lamenting and sobbing—"how can you bear to live in such a world, O noble heart and kindly bowels? Filth is their white; filth is their black; their beards are a horror; the very sight of their eye sockets makes one want to spit; and when they lift an arm, the murk of hell yawns in the armpit. And so, sir, and so, dear sir, by means of your all-powerful hands slit their throats through with these scissors!" And in answer to a jerk of his head a jackal came trotting up with a small pair of sewing scissors, covered with ancient rust, dangling from an eyetooth.

17   "Well, here's the scissors at last, and high time to stop!" cried the Arab leader of our caravan who had crept upwind toward us and now cracked his great whip.

18   The jackals fled in haste, but at some little distance rallied in a close huddle, all the brutes so tightly packed and rigid that they looked as if penned in a small fold girt by flickering will-o'-the-wisps.

19   "So you've been treated to this entertainment too, sir," said the Arab, laughing as gaily as the reserve of his race permitted. "You know, then, what the brutes are after?" I asked. "Of course," said he, "it's common knowledge; so long as Arabs exist, that pair of scissors goes wandering through the desert and will wander with us to the end of our days. Every European is offered it for the great work; every European is just the man that Fate has chosen for them. They have the most lunatic hopes, these beasts; they're just fools, utter fools. That's why we like them; they are our dogs; finer dogs than any of yours. Watch this, now, a camel died last night and I have had it brought here."

20   Four men came up with the heavy carcass and threw it down before us. It had hardly touched the ground before the jackals lifted up their voices. As if irresistibly drawn by cords each of them began to waver forward, crawling on his belly. They had forgotten the Arabs, forgotten their hatred, the all-obliterating immediate presence of the stinking carrion bewitched them. One was already at the camel's throat, sinking his teeth straight into an artery. Like a vehement small pump endeavoring with as much determination as hopefulness to extinguish some raging fire, every muscle in his body twitched and labored at the task. In a trice they were all on top of the carcass, laboring in common, piled mountain-high.

21   And now the caravan leader lashed his cutting whip crisscross over their backs. They lifted their heads; half swooning in ecstasy; saw the Arabs standing before them; felt the sting of the whip on their muz-

zles; leaped and ran backward a stretch. But the camel's blood was already lying in pools, reeking to heaven, the carcass was torn wide open in many places. They could not resist it; they were back again; once more the leader lifted his whip; I stayed his arm.

22   "You are right, sir," said he, "we'll leave them to their business; besides, it's time to break camp. Well, you've seen them. Marvelous creatures, aren't they? And how they hate us!"

Discussion of Theme

1. By what other people in what nations might the last two lines have been spoken? Do the words have a familiar ring?
2. What is the significance of the jackals' switch from boldness to servility in paragraph 15? What caused the change in attitude?
3. How much are you able to determine (other than that he is opposed to war) about Kafka's political or social convictions from this allegory?
4. Is it possible to extract more than one meaning from this tale? What?
5. How can we take a story about talking animals seriously as a comment on the affairs of men?

Discussion of Rhetoric

1. Would this story be just as interesting if it were not an allegory? Why or why not?
2. What makes allegories timeless?
3. This story is a narration in the form of an allegory. How effective is this writing technique?
4. What is the effect of the author's use of such phrases as "blood . . . reeking to heaven" and "carcass was torn wide open"?
5. What do the jackals symbolize? The Arabs?

Writing Assignments

1. Write an allegory about the war in Vietnam.
2. Write an animal allegory illustrating one of the Seven Deadly Sins.

Library Exploration

1. Read about the French-Algerian conflict. Does this allegory apply?
2. Make a report on the life of Kafka.
3. If this essay interested you, read and report on one of the books mentioned in the biographical note.

Vocabulary

(2) LITHE supple

(2) NIMBLY agilely

(6) EMBOLDENED given courage

(7) CARRION decaying flesh

(12) VEHEMENTLY intensely

(15) PLAINTIVENESS sorrowfulness

(15) MOLLIFIED appeased

(18) GIRT encircled

(18) WILL-O'-THE-WISPS mysterious flashes of light

(20) OBLITERATING wiping out

Lewis Mumford (1895–) is famous as a writer and cultural philosopher. He was born in New York and educated at the City College of New York and Columbia University, and has taught at several universities, including Columbia, Dartmouth, and Stanford. As the author of more than twenty books, he has established himself as an authority in many fields, including architecture and city planning.

Mumford traces war to what may be for some a startling beginning and examines the paradox that as civilizations grow, war grows rather than diminishes.

LEWIS MUMFORD

How War Began

1   At the time that the first great civilizations of the ancient world were coming into existence, the human race suffered an injury from which it has not yet recovered. If I interpret the evidence correctly, that injury still plays an active part in our lives, and caps our most hopeful dreams about human improvement with nightmares of destruction and extermination.

2   This injury happened at a moment when primitive man's powers, like ours today, had suddenly expanded; and it was due essentially to an aberration, or a series of aberrations, which put his most beneficent inventions at the command of his neurotic anxieties. So far from disappearing with time and being healed by the growth of law and reason, this original injury has only tightened its hold upon the collective actions of tribes and nations.

3   The aberration I refer to is the institution of war; and my purpose in discussing its origins is to bring into consciousness a group of events and beliefs that have long remained buried, partly through sheer

neglect, partly through a repression of painful irrationalities that contradicted civilized man's belief in his own orderly and rational behavior. It is only today, after a century of prodigious research into human origins, that some of these events have come to light and been thrown open to interpretation.

4   That early injury had an effect upon civilized life, somewhat comparable to the kind of childhood injury that psychiatrists characterize as a trauma: an injury whose worst results may not show themselves till far on in adult life. Instead of being buried in the psyche of an individual, it became embedded in the institutional life of every succeeding city, state and empire.

5   In making this analysis, I shall have to start from an assumption that is unprovable; namely, that there is a parallel between the general human situation today and that faced by the individual, unable to cope with the problems of his life, unable to make rational decisions, baffled, depressed, paralyzed, because he is still the prey of infantile fantasies he is unable to escape or control. In the case of individuals, we know that such fantasies, deeply embedded in childhood, may keep on poisoning the whole system, though the wound has seemingly healed and the scar is hardly visible. Childhood misapprehensions, animosities and resentments, childhood misinterpretations of natural events, such as birth, death, separation—all account for the persistence of infantile patterns of conduct. Often, later in life, these patterns overcome the adult and leave him helpless. He still views present realities through the distorting glasses of his childhood fantasy.

6   That something unfortunate once happened to man at the very moment when an immense creativity was released was perhaps recognized in part in the Jewish and Christian myth of the Fall, which was anticipated by even earlier Egyptian lamentations over the perverse wickedness of man in going contrary to the gods. Many other peoples, from China to Greece, looked back to a golden age when war and strife were unknown, and when, as Lao-tse put it, one village might look at the smoke rising from the chimneys of another nearby, without envy or rivalry.

7   There is now enough anthropological and archaeological evidence to show that there is at least a partial basis for these wistful memories of a more peaceful past, when scarcity of food, violence, danger and death were mainly the results of natural disasters, not the deliberate products of man. If civilization's first great achievements awakened new fears and anxieties, we must understand how and why this happened; for these fears and anxieties still press on us. As long as the source of our irrational acts remains hidden, the forces that are still driving us to destruction will seem uncontrollable. The worst part about civilized man's original errors and the most threatening aspect of our present situation are that we regard some of our most self-destructive arts as normal and unavoidable.

8   There is a close parallel between our own age, exalted yet stunned by the seemingly limitless expansion of all its powers, and the epoch that marked the emergence of the earliest civilizations in Egypt and Mesopotamia. In his pride over his present accomplishments, it is

perhaps natural for modern man to think that such a vast release of physical energy and human potentiality had never taken place before. But on examination this proves a too flattering illusion: the two ages of power, modern and ancient, are bound together by many similar characteristics, both good and evil, which set them apart from other phases of human history.

9   Just as the prelude to the nuclear age came with the large-scale introduction of water, wind and steam power, so the first steps toward civilization were taken in the neolithic domestication of plants and animals. This agricultural revolution gave man food, energy, security and surplus manpower on a scale no earlier culture had known. Among the achievements that mark this transformation from barbarism to civilization were the beginnings of astronomy and mathematics, the first astronomical calendar, the sailboat, the plow, the potter's wheel, the loom, the irrigation canal, the man-powered machine. Civilized man's emotional and intellectual potentialities were raised further through the invention of writing, the elaboration of the permanent record in painting, sculpture and monuments, and the building of walled cities.

10   This great leap forward came to a climax about 5000 years ago. A like mobilization and magnification of power did not again take place until our own era. For most of recorded history, mankind has lived on the usufruct of that early advance, making many piecemeal additions and widening the province held by civilization, but never essentially changing the original pattern.

11   There was probably an important religious side to this whole transformation. With the priestly observations that produced the measured months and years, people became conscious, as never before, of human dependence upon the cosmic forces, the sun, the moon, the planets, on whose operation all life depended. Planetary movement of "clockwork" regularity gave man his first glimpse of an orderly, repetitive, impersonal world, utterly reliable, but benignly productive only within the frame of its inflexible laws.

12   With this new cosmic theology there came a sudden fusion of sacred and secular power, in the person of the all-powerful king, standing at the apex of the social pyramid. The king was both a secular ruler and the chief priest or even, in the case of the Egyptians, a living god. He no longer needed to follow village tradition and customs like the village council of elders. His will was law. Kingship by divine right claimed magic powers and evoked magic collective responses.

13   What kingly power could not do solely by intimidation, and what magical rites and orderly astronomical observations could not do alone by successful prediction, the two in combination actually did accomplish. Large assemblages of men moved and acted as if they were one, obedient to the royal command, fulfilling the will of the gods and rulers. People were driven to heroic physical efforts and sacrifices beyond all precedent. Throughout history, the major public works—canals, embankments, roads, walls, "pyramids" in every form—have been built with forced labor, either conscripted for part of the year or permanently enslaved. The enduring symbol of this vast expansion and regimentation of power is, of course, the Great Pyramid of

Cheops, built without wheeled vehicles or iron tools, by relays of 100,000 men working over many years.

14   Should we be surprised that the achievements of our own age of nuclear power appeared first at this period as myths and fantasies associated with the gods? Absolute power, power to create and annihilate, became the attribute of a succession of deities. Out of his own substance the Egyptian sun god, Atum, created the universe. Instantaneous communication, remote control, the collective incineration of whole cities (Sodom and Gomorrah), and germ warfare (one of the plagues of Egypt) were freely practiced by a succession of inhumane deities in order to insure that their commands would be obeyed. Human rulers, who still lacked the facilities to carry out these dreams on a great scale, nevertheless sought to counterfeit them. With the growth of an efficient bureaucracy, a trained army, systematic taxation and forced labor, this early totalitarian system showed all the depressing features that similar governments show in our own day.

15   An overconcentration on power as an end in itself is always suspect to the psychologist. He reads in it attempts to conceal inferiority, anxiety and impotence. Perhaps early civilized man was justifiably frightened by the forces he himself had brought into existence, in the way that many people are frightened now by nuclear power. In neither case was the extension of physical power and political command accompanied by a complementary development of moral direction and humane control.

16   There were further grounds for doubt and fear among men of that early civilization. Though they had achieved a hitherto unattainable security and wealth, the very growth of population and the extension of trade made their whole economy more subject to conditions and forces they could not control.

17   Our age knows how difficult it is to achieve equilibrium and security in an economy of abundance. But the early fabric of civilization was far more precariously balanced, since the welfare of the whole was based on the magical identification of the king and the community in the beliefs and rites of their religion. The king personified the community; he was the indispensable connecting link between ordinary men and the cosmic powers they must propitiate and obey. While the king assumed full responsibility for the life and welfare of his subjects, the community, in turn, waxed and waned with the life of its ruler.

18   The magical identification produced a further occasion for anxiety, far deeper than any threat of actual floods or bad crops, for despite their claims to divine favor and immortality, kings too were subject to mortal accidents and misfortunes. So constant was this anxiety that the Egyptian Pharaoh's name could not be uttered without interjecting the prayer, "Life! Prosperity! Health!" This identification of the king's life with the community's fate produced an even more sinister perversion. To avert the wrath of the gods, indicated by any natural mischance, the king himself must be slain as a sacrifice. At this early stage, dream and fact, myth and hallucination, religion and science formed a confused welter. One lucky change in weather after a ritual sacrifice might give sanction to a long-repeated chain of ritualistic slaughters.

19   To save the king from this discouraging fate, which might lessen the attractions of the office, a further trick of religious magic came into play. A stand-in would be chosen and temporarily treated with all the honors and privileges of a king, in order to perform the final role of sacrificial victim on the altar. As the demand for such victims increased in times of trouble, these substitutes were sought outside the community, by violent capture. And what began as a one-sided raid for captives in time brought about the collective reprisals and counter-raids that became institutionalized as war. Back of war lay this barbarous religious sanction: only by human sacrifice can the community be saved.

20   War, then, was a specific product of civilization — the outcome of an organized effort to obtain captives for a magical blood sacrifice. In time, armed might itself took on a seemingly independent existence, and the extension of power became an end in itself, a manifestation of the "health" of the state. But underneath the heavy overlayers of rationalization, war remained colored by the original infantile misconception that communal life and prosperity could be preserved only by sacrificial expiation. Civilized man's later efforts to impute the origin of war to some primal animal instinct toward murderous aggression against his own kind are empty rationalizing. Here the words of the anthropologist, Bronislaw Malinowski, are decisive: "If we insist that war is a fight between two independent and politically organized groups, war does not occur at a primitive level."

21   What is most remarkable about the spread of war as a permanent institution is that the collective anxiety that originally brought about the ritual of human sacrifice seems to have deepened with material progress. And as anxiety increased, it could no longer be appeased by a mere symbolic sacrifice at the altar, for the ritual itself produced hatred, fear and a natural desire for revenge among the people victimized. In time ever greater numbers, with more effective weapons, were drawn into the brutal ceremony, so that what was at first a preliminary, one-sided raid before the sacrifice became the essential sacrifice itself. The alternative to permitting the mass slaughter of one's own people was the destruction of the enemy's city and temple and the enslavement of the population. These acts periodically eased anxiety and enhanced power. War provided a kind of self-justification in displacing neurotic anticipations by actual dangers — that return to reality seems to restore human equipoise. Psychiatrists observed during the blitz in London that the need for facing real dangers often removed a patient's load of neurotic anxiety. But war performs this service at a ghastly price. Psychologically healthy people have no need to court dismemberment and death.

22   The growth of law and orderly behavior and morals, which improved the relation of men in cities, was not transferred to the collective relations of communities; for the ability to produce disorder, violence and destruction itself remained a symbol of royal power. From the relatively peaceful Egyptians to the bloodthirsty Assyrians and Mongolians, one monument after another boasts of kings humiliated, prisoners killed, cities ruined. The solemn association of kingship, sacred power, human sacrifice and military effectiveness

formed a dominant complex that governed human behavior every-where. But in time the search for sacrificial captives took on a utili-tarian disguise — if spared as slaves, they added to the labor force. So the secondary products of military effort — slaves, booty, land, tribute — supplanted and concealed the original anxiety motive. Since a general expansion of productive power and culture had accompanied king-ship and human sacrifice, people were conditioned to accept the evil as the only way of securing the good. The repeated death of civiliza-tions from internal disintegration and outward assault underscores the fact that the evil elements in this amalgam largely canceled the goods and blessings.

23   This perception is not a discovery of modern historians. After the eighth century B.C. the working principles of a power-centered civiliza-tion were boldly challenged by a long series of religious prophets, from Amos and Isaiah to Lao-tse and Mo Ti. Whatever their dif-ferences the exponents of these new ideas scorned the notion of a mere increase of power and material wealth as the central purpose of life. In the name of peace and love they rejected irrational human sacrifice in every form — on the altar or on the battlefield. Christianity went even further. Alone among the religions, instead of sacrificing human beings to appease the divine wrath, its God sacrificed himself, renouncing His power in behalf of love, in order to save mankind by cleansing the sinner of anxiety and guilt.

24   But the power complex, embedded in the routines of civilization, was not dislodged by even this challenge. Ironically, Christianity itself supplanted its pagan rivals by seizing the power of the state under Constantine (A.D. 313) and utilizing all its engines of compulsion. As in the times of Moloch and Bel, the bloodiest collective sacrifices in history were those made in wars to establish the supremacy of a state religion.

25   How are we to explain the persistence of war, with its victories that turn out as disastrous as its defeats, its just causes that produce unjust or contradictory consequences, and its heroic martyrdoms sullied and betrayed by the base, selfish conduct of the survivors? There seem to me two general answers. One is that the original pattern of civilization, as it took form in the walled city and in turn produced the "walled" state, has remained unaltered until modern times. War was an integral part of the constellation of civilized institutions, held in tension within the city, on the basis of a division of classes, slavery and forced labor, and religious uniformity. To remove any part of this fabric seemed, to the rulers of men, a threat to every other part. They exalted the sacrifices of war because they wanted to maintain their own power.

26   There was an additional mitigating factor: until recent times, only a small part of the world's population accepted the terms of civilized life and its constant involvement with war; moreover, the amount of dam-age any army could inflict was limited. In Christian nations the human cost of war had been further reduced by the acceptance of a military code that limited violence to armed soldiers and generally exempted civilians and even their property from capture or deliberate destruc-tion. Finally, the greater part of the world's population, living in rural

communities, immune by their feebleness and poverty from the rapacious temptations of urbanized power, constituted a reservoir of vitality and sanity.

27 These mitigations and compensations progressively reduced the evils of total war as practiced by the early empires; but neither the needs of commerce, nor the admonitions of religion, nor the bitter experience of bereavement and enslavement altered the basic pattern. By any reasonable standard, war should early have been classed with individual murder, as an unqualified collective crime or an insane act, but those who held power never permitted any subversive judgment on the irrationality of the method, even if applied to rational ends. The fact that war has persisted and now threatens, at the very peak of our advances in science and technology, to become all-enveloping and all-destructive, points to the deep irrationality that first brought it into existence. This irrationality springs not only from the original aberration but from the unconscious depths of man, plagued with repressed guilt and anxiety over the godlike powers he presumptuously has learned to wield.

28 Western culture during the last four centuries has produced an explosive release of human potentialities and powers. Unfortunately the irrationalities of the past have been subjected to a similar projection and magnification.

29 The most formidable threat we confront, perhaps, is the fact that the fantasies that governed the ancient founders of civilization have now become fully realizable. Our most decisive recent inventions, the atom bomb and the planetary rocket, came about through a fusion of secular and "sacred" power, similar to their ancient union. Without the physical resources of an all-powerful state and the intellectual resources of an all-knowing corps of scientists, that sudden command of cosmic energy and interplanetary space would not have been possible. Powers of total destruction that ancient man dared impute only to his gods, any mere Russian or American air-force general can now command. So wide and varied are the means of extermination by blast and radiation burns, by slow contamination from radioactive food and water, to say nothing of lethal bacteria and genetic deformities, that the remotest hamlet is in as great peril as a metropolis. The old factor of safety has vanished.

30 As our agents of destruction have reached cosmic dimensions, both our tangible fears and our neurotic apprehensions have increased until they are so terrifying to live with that they are involuntarily repressed. This repression is particularly notable in America, where it is marked by the virtual absence of any discussion or critical challenge of either our nuclear weapons or our ultimate aims. This is perhaps an indication of the unconscious guilt we feel for developing and actually using the atom bomb. Along with an unwillingness to face our own conduct or search for alternative courses, our behavior presents an even more dangerous symptom — an almost pathological sense of compulsion to pyramid our errors. This drives us to invest ever-increasing quantities of intelligence and energy in the building of ever more dangerous absolute weapons, while devoting but an insignificant

fraction of this same energy and intelligence to the development of indispensable political and moral controls. We are in fact using our new knowledge and our new powers to reinforce ancient errors and prolong the life of obsolete institutions that should long ago have been liquidated.

31   What is more disturbing than our official reversion to the lowest level of barbarism in war is the fact that even after the last war only a minority of our countrymen seems to have reflected on the moral implications of this practice of total extermination as a normal and acceptable means of overcoming an enemy's resistance. There is nothing in our own code now to distinguish us from moral monsters like Genghis Khan. If we are willing to kill 100,000 people with one blow by random genocide, as at Hiroshima, there is nothing to keep us from killing 100,000,000—except the thought that our own country-men may be massacred in equally large numbers.

32   During the last dozen years every responsible head of government has confessed openly that with our present readiness to use methods of atomic, bacterial and chemical extermination, we might bring an end to civilization and permanently deform, if not destroy, the whole human race. Our failure to act on this warning, as an animal would act in the face of a comparable danger, gives the measure of our neurotic compulsions. So even the prudent thought of our own retributory, collective death offers no guarantee against the misuse of our powers so long as the engines of total annihilation remain available and the neurosis itself persists.

33   The two principal nuclear powers have been acting as if each was all-powerful and could dictate the terms of existence to the rest of the planet. In the name of absolute sovereignty they have actually achieved impotence. What has been called the "stalemate of terror" is in fact a deliberate checkmate of those humane gifts and adroit moves that might save us. This precarious stalemate may be ended at any moment by a careless gesture, which could upset the board itself and sweep away all the pieces. It can be effectively ended only by both sides acknowledging their paralyzing inability to move and agreeing to start a new game.

34   To conceive this new game, which can no longer be played under the old rules with the old pieces, both powers must take their eyes off each other and address themselves to the common task of saving the world from the threatened catastrophe they have impetuously brought within range. Instead, these governments with the connivance of their allies have been seeking to normalize their neurosis and have made participation in their infantile plans and infantile fantasies a test of political sanity. By now, a respected official in charge of Civil Defense finds it easier to envisage a whole nation of 180,000,000 living permanently underground than to conceive of any means of delivering the world of its diabolical hatreds and collective paranoias. Strangely, such a national burial is put forward as an ingenious method for com-bating possible Russian blackmail. This failure to recognize when the remedy is worse than the disease is one of the score of current symp-toms of mental disorder in apparently orderly minds.

35   If no great changes were yet visible in the general pattern of civilization, this picture would be extremely dismal; for as long as the old institutions remain operative, war will continue an integral expression of the anxieties and tensions they produce. Fortunately, this original structure has undergone a profound change during the past four centuries; and a large part of it is no longer acceptable. The old urban container has in fact exploded, leaving behind only a few citadels of absolute power on the ancient pattern, like the Kremlin and the Pentagon. What is even more important, the invisible walls between classes and castes have been breaking down steadily during the last several decades—more rapidly in the United States perhaps than in Communist countries.

36   What applies to the division of classes also applies to the disparity between nations. Neither knowledge nor power nor material goods can be monopolized by any privileged class or privileged country. Those Americans who fancied we had a permanent monopoly of atomic energy and technical skill recently found this out to their dismay; but the moral is not that we must "catch up with the Russians," but that we must accept the duties and demands of living in an open world among our equals. The real world of modern man has become porous and penetrable: every part of it is more closely interrelated than ever before and therefore more dependent upon the good will and sympathy and self-restraint of the rest of mankind. St. Paul's injunction to the little Christian congregations that everyone should be "members one of another," has now become a practical necessity of survival among the nations.

37   If so many other institutions of civilization, which held together solidly for 6000 years, have been crumbling away and are being replaced, is it likely that war will escape the same fate? The logic of history suggests it will not—if history has a logic. Our own military leaders have wryly admitted that in any large-scale war neither side can hope for a victory; indeed they have not the faintest notion of how such a war, once begun, might be ended, short of total extermination for both sides. Thus we are back at the very point at which civilization started, but at an even lower depth of savagery and irrationality. Instead of a token sacrifice to appease the gods, there would now be a total sacrifice, merely to bring an end to our neurotic anxieties.

38   In short, only the irrational, superstitious, magical function of war remains as a live possibility—the propitiation of gods in whom we do not believe by a sacrifice that would nullify the meaning of human history. In that surviving pocket of festering irrationality lies our chief, if not our only, enemy.

39   What are the possibilities of mankind's acquiring a fresh grip on reality and shedding the compulsive fantasies that are pushing us to destruction? There is little question of what measures must be taken to avoid a general nuclear catastrophe. Every intelligent observer understands the minimum precautions necessary for securing physical safety and for enabling a reconstituted United Nations to operate, not as a feeble hand brake on power politics, but as an active agent of international justice and comity. The only vital problem now is

whether we can liberate ourselves from our irrational attitudes and habits, so that we may firmly take the necessary steps. It is not enough to appeal to human reason alone, as intelligent people often so earnestly do, to avert a general holocaust. We must first bring our long-buried sacrificial fantasies into the open before they erupt once more through internal pressure. Only exposure will counteract their power over us.

40   As with a neurotic patient, one of the conditions for resuming control and making rational decisions, free from pathological deformation, is the continued existence of large areas of conduct that are still orderly, co-operative, harmonious, life-directed. Once the patient has the courage to unburden himself of his disruptive experiences and recognize them for what they are, the sound parts of his personality can be brought into play. Fortunately, much of our life is still conducted on wholly rational and humane terms; furthermore, modern man is closer to confronting his hidden irrationalities than ever before. Scientific curiosity, which led to the discovery of the hidden structure of matter, also led to the exploration of the hidden structure of the human psyche. We now begin to understand the actual meaning of the morbid dreams, fantasies and nightmares that have repeatedly undermined the highest human achievements.

41   With the knowledge that the biologist and the psychologist have furnished us, we must now perceive that both the original premises of civilization and those of our own so-called Nuclear, or Space, Age are humanly obsolete — and were always false. In purely physical terms, we now have possession of absolute power of cosmic dimensions, as in a thermonuclear reaction. But "absolute power" belongs to the same magico-religious scheme as the ritual of human sacrifice itself; living organisms can use only limited amounts of power. "Too much" or "too little" is equally fatal to life. Every organism, indeed, possesses a built-in system of automatic controls which governs its intake of energy, limits its excessive growth, and maintains its equilibrium. When those controls do not operate, life itself comes to an end. When we wield power extravagantly without respect to other human goals, we actually upset the balance of the organism and threaten the pattern of the whole organic environment. Unqualified power diminishes the possibilities for life, growth, development. More than a century ago Emerson wrote, "Do not trust man, great God! with more power until he has learned to use his little power better."

42   The test of maturity, for nations as for individuals, is not the increase of power, but the increase of self-understanding, self-control, self-direction and self-transcendence. For in a mature society, man himself, not his machines, or his organizations, is the chief work of art.

43   The real problem of our age is to search into the depths of the human soul, both in the present generation and in the race's history, in order to bring to light the devious impulses that have deflected man for so long from his fullest development. For the human race has always lived and flourished, not by any one-sided exhibition of power, but by the constant sustenance and co-operation of the entire world of living beings. Not to seize power, but to protect and cherish life is the chief end of man; and the godlike powers that the human race now

commands only add to its responsibilities for self-discipline and make more imperative a post-magical, post-mechanical, post-nuclear ideology which shall be centered, not on power, but on life.

44   Can such a new approach become operative in time to liberate man from war itself, as he was once liberated by his own efforts from incest, cannibalism, the blood feud and slavery? It is too early to answer this question, and it is perhaps almost too late to ask it. Admittedly it may take an all-but-fatal shock treatment, close to catastrophe, to break the hold of civilized man's chronic neurosis. Even such a belated awakening would be a miracle. But with the diagnosis so grave and the prognosis so unfavorable, one must fall back on miracles — above all, the miracle of life itself, that past master of the unexpected, the unpredictable, the all-but-impossible.

Discussion of Theme

1. To what extent is our society based on fear? Fear of what? Do you agree with Mumford that understanding the source of our fear can bring an end to war?
2. Should war be "classed with individual murder, as an unqualified crime or an insane act"? What problems might be entailed in trying and convicting the criminals or madmen? Do you think there would ever be universal agreement that war is "individual murder"?
3. Mumford says that we are "using our new knowledge and our new powers to . . . prolong the life of obsolete institutions that should long ago have been liquidated." What institutions is he referring to? Why should they be abolished?
4. In explaining his theory, Mumford traces a long and complex course from early civilization to the present. What is the relationship, as he sees it, between human sacrifices and modern war?
5. Mumford states that "the physical resources of an all-powerful state and the intellectual resources of an all-knowing corps of scientists" are responsible for developing modern warfare to its present state. Has the government corrupted scientists?
6. Mumford admits that man experienced an injury not unlike a trauma in the beginning, yet he declares the Jewish-Christian explanation of that trauma to be a myth. Do you agree with his reasoning?

Discussion of Rhetoric

1. In what paragraph does the connection between ancient customs and modern warfare become clear to you? Would it have been better if the author had stated it at the outset of the article?
2. Why does Mumford wait until paragraph 3 to state his thesis?
3. Rhetorically speaking, what value is there in comparing and contrasting modern man and ancient man in paragraphs 8, 9, and 10?
4. Did you have trouble in following the argument in this selection? Why? Was it the diction, the organization, or the sentence structure?

Writing Assignments

1. Is the American character basically violent? Give your reasons for agreeing or disagreeing. Support with specific evidence.
2. Defend the competitive spirit, citing the good that it accomplishes in our society.
3. Analyze Mumford's logic.
4. Discuss organized religion's contribution to war, including the position of various churches during recent years.

Library Exploration

1. For further discussion of this topic by Mumford, read *The Transformations of Man* (1956).
2. Probably the most famous contemporary analysis of war is *Study of War,* by Quincy Wright.

Vocabulary

(2) ABERRATION   deviation from the normal or right way

(2) BENEFICENT   helpful; resulting in good

(3) PRODIGIOUS   vast

(5) MISAPPREHENSIONS   misunderstandings

(6) LAMENTATIONS   expressions of grief

(8) EPOCH   era

(9) NEOLITHIC   designating the later part of the Stone Age

(10) USUFRUCT   use of the fruits of another's labors

(11) BENIGNLY   kindly

(13) INTIMIDATION   forcing by threats

(13) CONSCRIPTED   drafted

(15) COMPLEMENTARY   supplying something that is lacking or felt to be needed

(16) HITHERTO   before this time

(17) PRECARIOUSLY   dangerously; uncertainly

(17) PROPITIATE   appease

(17) WAXED AND WANED   increased and declined in power, prosperity, etc.

(19) REPRISALS   retaliations for injuries received

(20) EXPIATION   making amends

(20) IMPUTE   attribute

(20) PRIMAL   primitive

(21) EQUIPOISE   balance

(22) UTILITARIAN   practical

(22) AMALGAM   combination

(26) MITIGATING   moderating

(26) RAPACIOUS   voracious; greedy

(27) BEREAVEMENT   loss of loved ones by death

(27) PRESUMPTUOUSLY   brazenly

(30) TANGIBLE   real

(31) GENOCIDE   killing an entire race

(32) EXTERMINATION   wiping out

(32) PRUDENT   cautiously wise

(32) RETRIBUTORY   marked by retribution, that is, requital according to merits or deserts, especially for evil

(34) IMPETUOUSLY   impulsively

(34) CONNIVANCE   implied consent to wrongdoing

(34) DIABOLICAL   devilish

(34) PARANOIAS   excessive or abnormal suspiciousness and distrustfulness of others

(34) INGENIOUS   very clever

(35) CITADELS   strongholds

(36) DISPARITY   inequality

(36) POROUS   full of tiny holes; permeable

(37) WRYLY   with slightly bitter humor

(39) COMITY   courteous behavior; mutual consideration

(42) SELF-TRANSCENDENCE rising above oneself

(44) CHRONIC   lasting over time

(44) PROGNOSIS   prediction of the probable course (of a disease)

A Fable for Our Times

Once upon a time there was a small, beautiful, green and graceful country called Vietnam. It needed to be saved. (In later years no one could remember exactly what it needed to be saved from, but that is another story.) For many years Vietnam was in the process of being saved by France, but the French eventually tired of their labors and left. Then America took on the job. America was well equipped for country-saving. It was the richest and most powerful nation on earth. It had, for example, nuclear explosives on hand and ready to use equal to six tons of TNT for every man, woman, and child in the world. It had huge and very efficient factories, brilliant and dedicated scientists, and most (but not everybody) would agree, it had good intentions. Sadly, America had one fatal flaw — its inhabitants were in love with technology and thought it could do no wrong. A visitor to America during the time of this story would probably have guessed its out-come after seeing how its inhabitants were treating their own country. The air was mostly foul, the water putrid, and most of the land was either covered with concrete or garbage. But Americans were never much on introspection, and they didn't foresee the result of their loving embrace on the small country. They set out to save Vietnam with the same enthusiasm and determination their forefathers had displayed in conquering the frontier. They bombed. More than 3 million tons of explosives were dropped — 50 per cent more than the total bomb tonnage dropped in both theatres of World War II. Technologists looked on in awe and spoke of a ditch 30 feet deep, 45 feet wide, and 30 thousand miles long if all the bomb craters were placed in a row. What the Vietnam peasant spoke of was never recorded. Entire villages were destroyed by bombing, napalm fires, and artillery. After one such mission an American officer made the prophetic explanation that it was necessary to destroy the village in order to save it. Unquestioned, the logic of such a statement became sanctified. They bombed with chemicals as well as explosives, and trees, bushes, plants died by the millions of acres in a program with the Orwellian name of "Operation Ranch Hand," whose macabre motto was "only we can prevent forests." The consequences of such a deliberate and massive ecological attack were unknown and unknowable, but that was no deterrent. Thousands of herbicide and defoliant missions were flown before anyone seriously questioned their long-range effect on humans and animals, as well as on plants. By the time deformed fetuses began appearing and signs of lasting ecological damage were becoming increasingly apparent, success had been achieved. Vietnam had been saved. But the country was dead.

Discussion of Theme

1. What is it that Vietnam "needed to be saved from"? Was this, in your opinion, sufficient cause for American intervention?
2. How do you account for the fact that the North Vietnamese did not waver in the face of increased bombing (over 3 million tons of explosives), and in fact became even more determined?
3. What contradictions do you see between the statements our political leaders have made concerning population control and the environment, and the actions of our government in Vietnam?
4. Some have claimed that our government was guilty of genocide in Vietnam. Do you agree?

Discussion of Rhetoric

1. In what sense is this selection a fable, as its title suggests?
2. What is the meaning of the paradox at the end of the selection?
3. Comment on the tone of this selection. How does the language help to establish the dominant mood?

Writing Assignments

1. Fables usually end with a moral. Write an appropriate moral for this one.
2. Should chemical and biological warfare be outlawed? Give your views in a short theme.
3. What did Vietnam become a symbol of in our society?

Library Exploration

1. The Pentagon Papers released by the *New York Times* and other newspapers in 1971 present many previously unpublished facts about our country's activities in Vietnam. If copies of these articles are available to you, prepare a report based on several sections of them.
2. What is the Geneva Treaty? Who signed it and what are its terms? Why did the United States refuse to sign it?

Vocabulary

INTROSPECTION   self-examination or self-analysis

SANCTIFIED   made holy

MACABRE   gruesome

DETERRENT   something that prevents or discourages another's actions

FETUS   unborn baby

Henry David Thoreau (1817–62) is probably best known for his "Walden" (1854), an account of the two years he lived alone beside a New England lake on practically no money at all. He is also famous as the author of "Civil Disobedience" (1849). An associate of Ralph Waldo Emerson, he was an American transcendentalist philosopher, essayist, and naturalist.

In this selection taken from "Walden," Thoreau examines two warring groups of ants and draws some conclusions about them.

HENRY DAVID THOREAU

The Battle of the Ants

1 One day when I went out to my wood-pile, or rather my pile of stumps, I observed two large ants, the one red, the other one much larger, nearly half an inch long, and black, fiercely contending with one another. Having once got hold they never let go, but struggled and wrestled and rolled on the chips incessantly. Looking farther, I was surprised to find that the chips were covered with such combatants, that it was not a *duellum,* but a *bellum,* a war between two races of ants, the red always pitted against the black, and frequently two red ones to one black. The legions of these Myrmidons covered all the hills and vales in my wood-yard, and the ground was already strewn with the dead and dying, both red and black. It was the only battle which I have ever witnessed, the only battle-field I ever trod while the battle was raging; internecine war; the red republicans on the one hand, and the black imperialists on the other. On every side they were engaged in deadly combat, yet without any noise that I could hear, and human soldiers never fought so resolutely. I watched a couple that were fast locked in each other's embraces, in a little sunny valley amid the chips, now at noon-day prepared to fight till the sun went

down or life went out. The smaller red champion had fastened himself like a vise to his adversary's front, and through all the tumblings
on that field never for an instant ceased to gnaw at one of his feelers
near the root, having already caused the other to go by the board;
while the stronger black one dashed him from side to side, and, as I
saw on looking nearer, had already divested him of several of his
members. They fought with more pertinacity than bull-dogs. Neither
manifested the least disposition to retreat. It was evident that their
battle-cry was Conquer or die. In the meanwhile there came along a
single red ant on the hill-side of this valley, evidently full of excitement, who either had dispatched his foe, or had not yet taken part in
the battle; probably the latter, for he had lost none of his limbs; whose
mother had charged him to return with his shield or upon it. Or perchance he was some Achilles, who had nourished his wrath apart, and
had now come to avenge or rescue his Patroclus. He saw this unequal
combat from afar, — for the blacks were nearly twice the size of the
red, — he drew near with rapid pace till he stood on his guard within
half an inch of the combatants; then, watching his opportunity, he
sprang upon the black warrior, and commenced his operations near
the root of his right fore-leg, leaving the foe to select among his own
members; and so there were three united for life, as if a new kind of
attraction had been invented which put all other locks and cements to
shame. I should not have wondered by this time to find that they had
their respective musical bands stationed on some eminent chip, and
playing their national airs the while, to excite the slow and cheer the
dying combatants. I was myself excited somewhat even as if they had
been men. The more you think of it, the less the difference. And certainly there is not the fight recorded in Concord history, at least, if in
the history of America, that will bear a moment's comparison with
this, whether for the numbers engaged in it, or for the patriotism and
heroism displayed. For numbers and for carnage it was an Austerlitz
or Dresden. Concord Fight! Two killed on the patriots' side, and Luther Blanchard wounded! Why, here, every ant was a Buttrick, — "Fire!
for God's sake fire!" — and thousands shared the fate of Davis and
Hosmer. There was not one hireling there. I have no doubt that it was
a principle they fought for, as much as our ancestors, and not to avoid
a three-penny tax on their tea; and the results of this battle will be as
important and memorable to those whom it concerns as those of the
battle of Bunker Hill, at least.

2   I took up the chip on which the three I have particularly described
were struggling, carried it into my house, and placed it under a tumbler on my window-sill, in order to see the issue. Holding a microscope to the first-mentioned red ant, I saw that, though he was
assiduously gnawing at the near fore-leg of his enemy, having severed
his remaining feeler, his own breast was all torn away, exposing what
vitals he had there to the jaws of the black warrior, whose breastplate
was apparently too thick for him to pierce; and the dark carbuncles of
the sufferer's eyes shown with ferocity such as war only could excite.
They struggled half an hour longer under the tumbler, and when I
looked again the black soldier had severed the heads of his foes from
their bodies, and the still living heads were hanging on either side of

him like ghastly trophies at his saddle-bow, still apparently as firmly fastened as ever, and he was endeavoring with feeble struggles, being without feelers and with only the remnant of a leg, and I know not much how many other wounds, to divest himself of them; which at length, after half an hour more, he accomplished. I raised the glass, and he went off over the window-sill in that crippled state. Whether he finally survived that combat, and spent the remainder of his days in some Hotel des Invalides, I do not know: but I thought that his industry would not be worth much thereafter. I never learned which party was victorious, nor the cause of the war; but I felt for the rest of that day as if I had had my feelings excited and harrowed by witnessing the struggle, the ferocity and carnage, of a human battle before my door.

Discussion of Theme

1. In the act of lifting up the chip on which the ants were fighting, does Thoreau suggest the helplessness of men in the hands of God?
2. When Thoreau says "The more you think of it, the less the difference," is he saying that men are just as unimportant as ants, or that ants are as important as men?
3. Who were the red republicans? The black imperialists?
4. Is Thoreau showing the stupidity or the necessity of war by comparing ants to men?
5. Why should an ant war fascinate an apparently peaceful man?

Discussion of Rhetoric

1. Thoreau says that "I had had my feelings excited and harrowed." How does he convey his emotion in the body of the essay?
2. Notice that the broad view of the woodpile in the first part of the article narrows to a mere chip under a glass in the last part. Discuss the effectiveness of this technique.
3. Point out at least five examples of parallel structure.
4. Does Thoreau use *loose* or *periodic* sentences? Consult the glossary at the back of this book for a definition of these terms.
5. The sentence in paragraph 1 beginning "I watched a couple that were fast locked" has several poetic images in it. What are they?

Writing Assignments

1. Probably you're familiar with the concept that people look like ants to someone who is gazing down at them from a great height. Viewing humanity from a figurative height, develop your own analogy between people and ants.
2. Thoreau says: "I never learned which party was victorious, nor the cause of the war." In your opinion, is any cause worth fighting for? If so, what?

3. Describe a scene of action in nature that you have seen and what you thought about it.
4. Analyze the organization of this essay.

Library Exploration

1. Report on Thoreau as a naturalist rather than as a writer.
2. Compare the prose styles of Thoreau and Emerson.
3. Read all of *Walden,* from which this selection is taken, and sum up Thoreau's major theses.

Vocabulary

(1) INCESSANTLY   without stopping

(1) INTERNECINE   internal; involving conflict within a group

(1) DIVESTED   stripped

(1) PERTINACITY   persistence

(1) MANIFESTED   showed

(1) PERCHANCE   perhaps

(2) ASSIDUOUSLY   diligently

(2) SEVERED   cut off

(2) CARBUNCLES   formerly, red gems

(2) FEROCITY   fury

Bertrand Russell (1872–1970), one of the most significant mathematicians and philosophers of the twentieth century, was born and educated in England. He collaborated with A. N. Whitehead in 1910 to write "Principia Mathematica," a landmark in the history of symbolic logic. Russell contributed to the founding of the modern philosophy of logical analysis. In recent years he was a leader of anti-war movements. Among his many works are "Mysticism and Logic" (1918), "What I Believe" (1925), "The ABC of Relativity" (1925), and "The History of Western Philosophy" (1940). He was awarded the Nobel Prize in Literature in 1950.

Lord Russell says that East and West face an unprecedented problem in the H-bomb and that the solution will be found either in the extinction of the race or in an agreement not to fight.

BERTRAND RUSSELL

Co-existence or No Existence: The Choice Is Ours

1   The recent changes in the technique of war have produced a situation which is wholly unprecedented. War has existed ever since there were organized states, that is to say for some six thousand years. This ancient institution is now about to end. There are two ways in which the end may come about: the first is the extinction of the human race; the

second is an agreement not to fight. I do not know which of these will
be chosen.

2   Neither the general public nor the majority of powerful statesmen
have as yet realized that war with modern weapons cannot serve the
purposes of any government in the world. It is of the first importance
that this should be realized by those who control policy both in the
East and in the West. It is generally conceded by those who are in a
position to speak with authority that no complete defense against an
H-bomb attack is possible. We must, I think, consider it the most likely
hypothesis that if a great war broke out tomorrow each side would be
successful in attack and unsuccessful in defense. This means that in
the first days of such a war all the great centers of population on each
side would be obliterated. Those who survived this first disaster would
perish slowly or quickly as a result of the fall-out from radioactive
cloud. Destruction of life from this cause would not be confined to the
belligerent countries. The winds would gradually spread death
throughout the world. This, at least, is what is to be feared. It cannot
be said that the worst outcome is certain, but it is sufficiently probable
to deter any sane man from incurring the risk.

3   Apart from the totality of destruction, there is another new element
in the situation. In old days if you had a military advantage over your
enemy, you might hope to win in time. But now, if each side has
enough H-bombs to wipe out the other, there is no longer any advantage in having twice as many as your adversary.

4   Both in the United States and in Great Britain there has been much
talk of civil defense. Russian military journals contain talk of the same
kind. All such plans, I am convinced, show either ignorance or hypocrisy in those who advocate them. Deep shelters would enable a
portion of the population to survive the first explosion, but sooner or
later these people would have to emerge from their shelters into a
radioactive world.

5   Although the H-bomb is the center of public attention at the moment, it is only one of the possibilities of destruction which science
has put in the hands of irresponsible politicians. Chemical and bac-
teriological warfare are studied by all powerful states and may have
consequences at least as horrifying as those of the H-bomb. There is
no visible end to the methods of inflicting death that may be invented.
Even if a portion of the human race were to survive a great war now,
it cannot be doubted that the next war, if scientific technique survives,
would complete what its predecessor had left unfinished.

6   There is therefore no escape from the choice that lies before us:
Shall we renounce war, or shall we bring our species to an end?

ESCAPE FROM REALITY

7 If men realized that these are the only alternatives, no one can doubt
that they would choose peace. But there are various ways in which
people escape the realization of unpleasant facts. I have seen statements by Russians and Chinese that a thermonuclear war would of
course destroy the rotten capitalistic civilization of the West but would

not vitally injure the sturdy Communist nations of the East. I have also seen statements by American authorities claiming that the West would be victorious. Both seemed to me, if genuinely believed, to be mere fantasies of wishfulfilment and, if not genuinely believed, to be part of the silly game of bluff which great nations have been allowing themselves. I hope that this is beginning to be understood. Recently there have been hopeful signs that neither side is willing to push issues to the point of war. And with every month that passes there is a better chance that statesmen both in the East and in the West will become aware of some of the important facts by which their policy ought to be guided.

8   Another widespread delusion is that perhaps in a great war H-bombs would not be employed. People point to the fact that gas was not employed in the Second World War. They forget that gas had not proved a decisive weapon even in the First World War and that in the meantime gas-masks had been provided which were a complete protection. Any analogy is therefore entirely misleading.

9   It is thought by many that the first step forward should be an international agreement not to use H-bombs in the event of war. and this is generally coupled with the suggestion that both sides should destroy their existing stock of these weapons. This suggestion has certain merits but also certain drawbacks. Its chief merit is that if the destruction of existing stocks were honestly carried out, the danger of a sudden attack in the style of Pearl Harbor would be lessened. Against this we must set the fact that no system of inspection can now make sure that bombs are not being manufactured. This is a new fact. At the time of the Baruch proposal it was still possible for an inspectorate to gain control of the raw materials, but this is so no longer. Each side would therefore suspect that the other side was manufacturing bombs surreptitiously, and this might make relations worse than if no agreement had been concluded. What is even more important is that, if war did break out, neither side would consider itself bound by the agreement, and after a certain number of months H-bomb warfare would be in full swing. Only by not making war can the danger be avoided. We must therefore turn our thoughts away from war to the methods by which peace can be made secure.

PEACE BY STAGES

10 The transition from the cold war to a condition of secure peace cannot be made in a day. But it can be made, and it must be made. It will have to be made by stages. The first stage will consist in persuading all powerful governments of the world that their aims, whatever they may be, cannot be achieved by war. In this first stage, scientists—not only nuclear physicists but also physiologists, geneticists, and bacteriologists—have a very important part to play. Their discoveries have created the dangers, and it is their obvious duty to arouse the public and the governments to a sense of the risks they are running. They may, in performing this duty, be compelled to take action of which their governments disapprove, but loyalty to mankind should be for them

the paramount consideration. I am convinced that it is within their power to persuade the governments both of the East and of the West to look to negotiation rather than war for a solution of their problems.

11　　The next stage must be to create temporary machinery to negotiate settlements of all the questions at present causing conflict between East and West. It will be necessary to refer such questions to a body of negotiators in which East and West have equal representation and the balance of power is in the hands of the neutrals. I do not venture to suggest what solution should be reached on any of the vexed questions of the present. I think that a body constituted as I have suggested would avoid gross unfairness to either side, and subject to this condition almost any settlement would be preferable to a continuation of the present state of tension. A very important part of any settlement should of course be a drastic reduction of armaments. It is hardly to be supposed that the very delicate negotiations which will be required can be conducted successfully in the atmosphere of strained hostility that has existed during recent years. Each side will have to abandon perpetual abuse of the other and learn to practice that degree of toleration which after centuries of warfare was at last achieved between Christians and Moslems and between Catholics and Protestants. We cannot now wait for the slow operation of reason through the discouragements of long indecisive wars. We must learn in advance a manner of thinking and feeling which in the past has been learned slowly and through bitter experience. I will not pretend that this is easy. But if men can be made to realize the dreadful alternative I do not think it will prove impossible.

THE THIRD STEP

12　If the immediate problems that now divide East and West were settled in some such way, we could reach the third stage of progress toward secure peace. The international problems of our day are not the last that will ever arise. There will be new problems, perhaps dividing the world quite differently from the way in which it is now divided between Communist and anti-Communist blocs. So long as there is not an established international authority capable of enforcing peace, the risk of war will remain, and with every advance in science the risk will become more terrible. The international anarchy resulting from a multitude of states with unrestricted sovereignty must be brought to an end. The international authority which is to end it will have to be federal and endowed with only such powers as are necessary for preserving the peace of the world. The most important of these powers, and also the most difficult to secure, will be an obvious preponderance of armed forces over those of any national state or alliance of states. The anarchic liberty at present enjoyed by sovereign states is dear to most people and will not be surrendered easily, but it will have to be surrendered if the human species is to survive. The process required is a continuation of that which occurred in the fifteenth and sixteenth centuries. Before that time powerful barons in their castles could defy national governments, and there was the same sort of anarchy within a nation as now exists between nations. Gunpowder and artillery put an end to internal anarchy in France, Spain, and England. The hydrogen bomb has the same part to play in ending international anarchy. The loss of liberty, though it may be distasteful, is precisely of the same kind as that which private individuals suffer by being forbidden to commit murder, for after all it is the right to murder which hitherto sovereign states will be asked to surrender.

LEGITIMATE HOPES

13 I have been speaking of dangers and how to avoid them, but there is another thing which it is just as important to emphasize, for while fears are at present unavoidable, hopes are equally legitimate. If we take the measures needed to end our fears, we shall thereby create a world capable of such well-being as has never been known and scarcely even imagined. Throughout the long ages since civilization began, the bulk of mankind have lived lives of misery and toil and bondage. All the long burden of misery that has darkened the slow progress of mankind has now become unnecessary. If we can learn to tolerate each other and to live in amity, poverty can be abolished everywhere more completely than it is now abolished in the most fortunate nations. Fear can be so much diminished that a new buoyancy and a new joy will brighten the daily lives of all. The work of science, which while war survives is largely evil, will become wholly beneficent. Nothing stands in the way but the darkness of atavistic evil passions. New technical possibilities of well-being exist, but the wisdom to make use of them has hitherto been lacking. Shall we collectively continue to turn our back upon the things that each one of us individually desires? We can make a world of light, or we can banish life from our planet. One or other we must do, and do soon. A great duty rests upon those who realize these alternatives, for it is they who must persuade mankind to make the better choice.

Discussion of Theme

1. When Russell says, in his title, that "The Choice Is Ours," is he referring to individual citizens or government leaders?
   How much choice does the individual have? How can he exercise his choice?
2. How, according to Russell, do people avoid accepting the reality of destruction by hydrogen bomb? By what reasoning does he reject these attitudes?
3. Have we made progress toward reaching any of the "three stages" Russell says are necessary for peace?
4. Are there choices for the world to consider that are not offered in this essay?

Discussion of Rhetoric

1. What is the meaning of *cold war*? Is it a war, or isn't it? How would you translate the phrase into more formal and conventional language?
2. Lord Russell makes a startling statement in his opening paragraph. What is it? Does it make you pay close attention to what follows?
3. The purpose of this essay is to persuade. What methods of persuasion does the author use?
4. What analogies does the author disagree with in the essay?

Writing Assignments

1. Should American citizens be permitted to travel anywhere in the world without passport? Wouldn't this help lessen tensions among nations? Give your opinions.
2. How would the elimination of war or the fear of war help abolish poverty?
3. Many people claim that because man is violent and competitive, we'll always have wars. Support or defend this position.
4. From new materials, support or attack Russell's arguments.
5. Cite evidence for believing (or not believing) that the cold war could last forever.

Library Exploration

1. Read *Catch-Twenty-Two,* by Joseph Heller.
2. This statement was written more than 15 years ago. Check on Lord Russell's later pronouncements and activities.
3. Russell says that scientists have created dangers and therefore have a responsibility for helping lessen them. Check through *The Bulletin of the Atomic Scientists* to see how some have taken action.

Vocabulary

(1) UNPRECEDENTED without example
(1) EXTINCTION wiping out
(2) CONCEDED admitted
(2) HYPOTHESIS tentative assumption
(2) OBLITERATED wiped out
(2) BELLIGERENT warring
(2) DETER discourage
(2) INCURRING meeting with; becoming subject to
(4) HYPOCRISY the act of pretending to be something one is not or to believe what one does not
(8) DELUSION a false belief resulting from self-deception
(9) SURREPTITIOUSLY secretly
(11) VEXED troublesome
(11) PERPETUAL continual
(12) ANARCHY absence of government

(12) SOVEREIGNTY   supreme
power
(12) PREPONDERANCE   majority
(13) AMITY   friendship;
harmony
(13) BUOYANCY   exuberance;
lightheartedness

(13) ATAVISTIC   marked by a
reversion to the characteristics of a remote ancestor
or primitive type

Paul Jacobs (1918–   ), a social
scientist and writer, is a staff
member of the Center for the
Study of Democratic Institutions at Santa Barbara, California. He was born in New York
City and attended City College
of New York and the University
of Minnesota. He has long had
an interest in the labor movement, first as a union organizer
and later as publisher of a labor
paper. Among his books are
"Labor in a Free Society"
(1959) and "Is Curley Jewish?"
(1965).

The following essay takes an
irreverent look at an American institution, Forest Lawn
Cemetery, and its creator, Hubert "Digger" Eaton.

PAUL JACOBS

The Most Cheerful Graveyard in the World

1 Along with amassing a comfortable fortune by convincing Los Angele-
nos that the only fitting way to begin a "happy Eternal Life" is by
being laid to rest, in one way or another, at Forest Lawn Memorial
Park, the cemetery he founded in 1917, Dr. Hubert Eaton, or "Digger"
as he is known in the trade, has also succeeded in almost completely
revising the dying industry.
2   The Digger, whose official title of "Doctor" is purely honorary, accomplished this revision by the simple but profound device of converting the hitherto prosaic act of dying into a gloriously exciting, well-
advertised event, somehow intimately and patriotically connected
with the American way of life.

3   Today, thanks to Eaton, dying in Los Angeles is something to be eagerly anticipated, because it is only after death that one can gain permanent tenure at Forest Lawn. Eaton, in one of his earlier roles — that of "the Builder" — described Forest Lawn as "a place where lovers new and old shall love to stroll and watch the sunset's glow, planning for the future or reminiscing of the past; a place where artists study and sketch; where school teachers bring happy children to see the things they read of in books; where little churches invite, triumphant in the knowledge that from their pulpits only words of Love can can be spoken; where memorialization of loved ones in sculptured marble and pictorial glass shall be encouraged but controlled by acknowledged artists; a place where the sorrowing will be soothed and strengthened because it will be God's garden. A place that shall be protected by an immense Endowment Care Fund, the principal of which can never be expended — only the income therefrom used to care for and perpetuate this Garden of Memory.

4   "This is the Builder's Dream; this is the Builder's Creed."

5   The Builder's Creed is chiseled into a huge, upright stone slab on Forest Lawn's Cathedral Drive, just outside the Great Mausoleum and hard by the Shrine of Love. Viewed, usually in reverent awe, by more than a million visitors each year, Forest Lawn is, along with Disneyland, a favorite tourist attraction in Southern California, far outdrawing the concrete footprints in front of Grauman's Chinese Theatre.

6   A smaller inscription underneath the Creed points out that on New Year's Day, 1917, Eaton stood on a hilltop overlooking the small country cemetery which had just been placed in his charge. An unemployed mining engineer, Eaton had gone into the cemetery business after a vein of gold in his mine had suddenly vanished.

7   "A vision came to the man of what this tiny 'God's Acre' might become; and standing there, he made a promise to The Infinite. When he reached home, he put this promise into words and called it 'The Builder's Creed.' Today, Forest Lawn's almost three hundred acres are eloquent witness that The Builder kept faith with his soul."

8   Indeed, yes. The "almost three hundred acres" also bear eloquent witness to the fact that Eaton, still digging holes in the ground, worked a vein of gold infinitely more reliable than the one that vanished from his mine — the "Science and Art," as he describes it, "of Persuasion." So strongly does Eaton believe the "profession of salesmanship is the greatest of all professions" that he has established The Foundation for the Science and Art of Persuasion at his alma mater, William Jewell College, Liberty, Missouri.

9   Forest Lawn reflects Eaton's skill in the "science." The "country cemetery" with only a "scant dozen acres of developed ground" has grown into Forest Lawn Memorial Park, with a permanent "population" of more than 170,000 increasing at the rate of approximately 6,500 a year.

10   In fact, business has been so good that there are now two additional Forest Lawn "Memorial Parks" in Los Angeles: Forest Lawn-Hollywood Hills, the focus of a bitter political struggle in the city, and ad-

jacent to it Mount Sinai, designed to attract the growing Jewish population of Los Angeles.

11 Forest Lawn offers the largest religious painting in the United States, displayed in a building, the Hall of the Crucifixion, specially designed for it. There, for a voluntary contribution of twenty-five cents, the visitor sits comfortably in a large theatre, in one of a "broad sweep of seats, richly upholstered in burgundy, rising tier above tier, matching the splendor of the architecture," and watches the three-thousand-pound curtain open on Jesus at Calvary, forty-five feet high and 195 feet long. A lecture about the painting, supplemented with a moving arrow, is delivered by a tape recording in the special kind of rich, organ-tone voice used throughout Forest Lawn.

12 There are also hundreds of statues, both originals and reproductions, scattered throughout the three hundred acres. Typical of these is an eighteen-figure group depicting Forest Lawn's solution to the "Mystery of Life." Interpretations of the eighteen figures are supplied: "(17) the atheist, the fool, who grinningly cares not at all; while (18) the stoic sits in silent awe and contemplation of that which he believes he knows but cannot explain with any satisfaction."

13 At the Court of David there is a huge reproduction of Michelangelo's "David"—with a large fig leaf added by Forest Lawn. An exact copy of the sculptor's "Moses" is displayed at the entrance to the Cathedral Corridor in Memorial Terrace, "the only one," according to Forest Lawn, "cast from clay masks placed directly on the original statue in the Church of Saint Peter in Chains at Rome, Italy."

14 So that the masks could be made, the Church of Saint Peter had to be closed for a day, something that had not happened before. "I gave a lot of dinners and I bought a lot of wine and I sent a lot of cables and St. Peter's was closed," Eaton modestly explains.

15 Color photos and post cards of the "Moses" statue can be purchased, along with thousands of other items, at Forest Lawn's souvenir shop. There, browsing visitors can choose from showcases displaying money clips, cocktail napkins, book matches, jigsaw puzzles, and charm bracelets—all decorated with Forest Lawn motifs. Prices range from a modest twenty-nine cents for a key chain to $125 for a glass vase etched with a Forest Lawn scene.

16 There are brown plastic nutshells containing little photos of Forest Lawn, ladies' compacts, cigarette lighters, cufflinks, salt and pepper shakers, picture frames, demitasse spoons, bookmarks, cups and saucers, pen and pencil sets, glass bells, wooden plaques, ashtrays, place mats and doilies, perfume and powder sets, jackknives, and a great variety of other goodies, all with an appropriate Forest Lawn theme. Books like *The Loved One,* Evelyn Waugh's satire of Forest Lawn, are not on sale in the souvenir shop. (Eaton occasionally expresses resentment over the treatment given the cemetery by novelists—especially by one writer to whom he extended free run of the park only to be parodied later. But Eaton also understands that such novels have brought world-wide publicity to Forest Lawn and have not adversely affected his sales, which come not from England but from Los Angeles.)

17   Among the most popular items at the souvenir shop are those showing reproductions of Forest Lawn's three churches, the Church of the
Recessional, The Little Church of the Flowers, and the Wee Kirk o'
the Heather.

18   "Providing a dignified setting for final tribute," the three churches
"serve also for the joyous and memorable ceremonies of christening
and the exchange of marriage vows." Since the churches have opened,
more than 43,000 persons have had "memorable" marriages in them.
But Forest Lawn makes no money directly from marrying people, and
the profits from the souvenir shop are used for the upkeep of the Hall
of the Crucifixion. Forest Lawn's real business is burying people.

19   "The hardest thing in the world to sell," states one of the organization's top officials, "are 'spaces.'" ("Space" is the euphemism used at
Forest Lawn for "grave plot.") The reason for the difficulty is that
Forest Lawn's sales organization, which comprises about 175 people,
concentrates on sales made "Before Need," another phrase in Forest
Lawn's own peculiar language of the flowers. Selling cemetery plots
"Before Need" rather than "At Time of Need" or "Post Need," although difficult, is very profitable, since under California law a cemetery pays taxes only on its unsold plots. Once a "space" has been sold,
it is removed from the tax rolls. Thus it is to the obvious advantage of
Forest Lawn to sell off its land as quickly as possible, without waiting
for "Need."

20   There are approximately fifteen hundred individual "spaces" to the
acre in Forest Lawn. Prices average $300 per space. There are also
rather more elegant neighborhoods at Forest Lawn which are less
crowded and therefore more expensive. In the Gardens of Memory,
entered only with a special key, there are "memorial sanctuaries designed for families who desire the privacy and protection of crypt
interment, but who at the same time long for the open skies and the
natural beauty of a verdant garden bathed in sunlight. Under the
lawns in the Gardens of Memory have been created a number of
monolithically constructed crypts of steel-reinforced concrete."

21   In the area of ground burial, Forest Lawn has contributed a pleasant innovation. No tombstones are permitted, only markers, set flush
with the ground so that there is in fact the pleasant appearance of a
park with sweeping green lawns.

22   But one does not have to be interred to take up permanent residence at Forest Lawn. A number of other arrangements can be made,
including being inurned after cremation in the columbarium for as
little as $145 or entombed in a mausoleum crypt—which can cost as
much as $800,000, as in the case of the Irving Thalberg mausoleum.
One can also be placed in a large wall out in the open air. Families may
be interred, inurned, or entombed as a unit to maintain "togetherness." Should one feel the need for fresh air while spending the
"happy Eternal Life" in a crypt, it is possible, at added cost naturally,
to have a ventilating system installed. In the mausoleum, tape-
recorded music is played as well.

23   Inurnment is not restricted to a single form of urn. The law in California, which has a strong undertakers' lobby, provides that after
cremation ashes must be buried or placed in a columbarium. A wide

variety of urn designs can be seen, ranging from books and loving cups to miniature coffins.

24   The price for the casket or urn sets the approximate amount paid for the funeral itself, but here the range is far greater than for the "space." The least expensive casket, with the metal screw heads showing, is $115; the most expensive goes for $17,500.

25   Forest Lawn's rich, creamy advertising presentations combine the hard and the soft sell. On radio and television, the same institutional approach is as manifest as at the cemetery itself. Programs of church services and organ music are announced in deep, sonorous tones, and practically no mention is made of the company's product. The institutional approach is also used on billboards picturing stained-glass windows or the "Moses" statue. However, many of Forest Lawn's billboards are given over to the hard, competitive sell, featuring what is Hubert Eaton's original contribution to the American way of death: the concept of combining in one place mortuary functions, such as embalming, with funeral services and burial, thus obviating the necessity for outside undertakers, florists, funeral chapels, and long processions to the cemetery. Forest Lawn successfully undertook the elimination of the undertaking middleman.

26   Today, Forest Lawn's hard-sell slogans of "Everything In One Beautiful Place" and "Just One Phone Call" are widely copied, as are the ads which usually feature back or side views, sometimes in color, of two dry-eyed, well-groomed people talking to a distinguished-looking gray-mustached bank-president or diplomat-type man, identified by a discreet sign on his desk as a "Funeral Counselor." Sometimes only the "Counselor" is shown, answering the "Just One Phone Call" with the dedicated air of a statesman. It is clear from the ads that at Forest Lawn, where the concept of death has been abolished, the standards of accepted behavior demand no vulgar signs of outward grief.

27   But even though its competitors copy Forest Lawn today, Eaton faced a bitter battle when he first attempted to bring a mortuary into the cemetery. Forest Lawn's permit to operate a mortuary was given only after a determined struggle waged against him by some of the undertakers who foresaw disaster for themselves in the new trend of combined services. It was during this period that Forest Lawn began to build up its own political operations, which today make it the most powerful spokesman for the industry in the state.

28   There have been a number of occasions when, in its self-interest, Forest Lawn has had to do battle, sometimes in ways that might have been frowned on by the dignified gentlemen in their ads. From the 1930's to the early 1950's Forest Lawn was in a running argument with the county assessor's office over the tax assessments made on its property, with Forest Lawn always claiming that the assessments were too high and almost always getting them reduced, even as much as fifty per cent, by the county board of supervisors. Some supervisors did consistently oppose Forest Lawn's plea for tax reduction and supported the assessor, but when the votes were taken a majority always supported Forest Lawn.

29   In 1938, in one of its early appearances before the board of super-

visors, Forest Lawn requested a tax reduction, claiming that the vacant property in the land it then owned would remain unsold until
1973. At the time, the county assessor pointed out that Forest Lawn
had "acquired additional property when they said it was going to take
thirty-five years to sell out what they now have, yet they go to work
and buy seventy-five acres adjoining at a big price."

30   Ten years later, in 1948, the issue of how long it would take to fill
Forest Lawn's vacant "spaces" became one of the central points in a
bitter political hassle within the Los Angeles City Council, and the
cemetery completely reversed its argument of ten years earlier. At
issue was Forest Lawn's request for a zoning change to permit the use,
as a cemetery, of 480 acres of land adjoining Griffith Park, a public
park and playground in the Hollywood area.

31   Forest Lawn's first request to develop this new cemetery was submitted to and rejected by the city planning commission in 1946. When
the request was again rejected in 1948, Forest Lawn appealed, claiming, in contrast to its 1938 plea of unsold land, that "by the year 1965
all of the available grave spaces in existing cemeteries will have been
exhausted."

32   The odds against Forest Lawn's gaining approval for its plan to
open a new cemetery seemed formidable. The planning commission
opposed it, the park department opposed it, the board of health com-
missioners opposed it, the water and power commission opposed it,
the board of public works opposed it, the Hollywood chamber of commerce opposed it, and a variety of community groups opposed it. But
"the Builder's Dream" triumphed, and on March 9, 1948, the city
council voted 11–3 to permit the opening of the cemetery.

33   Never an organization to leave stones unturned, within a few hours
Forest Lawn had hastily dug six holes in the ground and buried six
bodies in them; a move which, under state law, immediately qualified
the area as a commercial graveyard that could not then be disturbed
or moved except under very specific circumstances.

34   "We got the bodies we buried through the county hospital or from
their next of kin in advance," states Ugene Blalock, vice-president and
general counsel at Forest Lawn, "and we made no charge for our services. If the vote in the council had gone against us, we would have
given them a free burial elsewhere."

35   In fact, however, the council vote has rarely gone against Forest
Lawn, even when the city fathers were voting on whether to give
Beverly Hills the street where Eaton lives, thus providing the Digger
with a more distinguished address. Although he hasn't moved, Eaton
now lives in Beverly Hills.

36   No one is quite sure about the exact basis for Eaton's influence; or
if they are, they're not willing to talk about it for the record. Blalock
states that Forest Lawn as an institution has not made, as far as he
knows, any campaign contribution in eighteen years, although he
adds, "Individuals may make political contributions." But politics
aside, it is Hubert Eaton, master salesman, who is chiefly responsible
for Forest Lawn's success.

37   It is from Eaton's mind that has come the creation of the Council of
Regents of Memorial Court of Honor, twenty-two "outstanding busi-

ness and professional men" who advise "on all matters concerning the growth of the Memorial Park as a cultural center of religion and fine arts."

38   Its members, who include the president of Occidental College and the chancellor of the University of Southern California, wear a handsome, flowing red robe, trimmed with velvet, and an elegant round red hat, also trimmed daintily with velvet, while around their necks hangs a kind of Maltese Cross decoration, perhaps the Order of Forest Lawn.

39   Such touches as these distinguish the imaginative Eaton from his colleagues. Eaton's devotion to salesmanship, as evidenced by his creating special heart-shaped children's sections at Forest Lawn, named Babyland and Lullabyland, began early in life, according to "The Forest Lawn Story," his biography sold at the souvenir shop.

40   The son of a college professor, Eaton, states the biography, "sat in his little cubbyhole behind his father's bookshelves ostensibly studying but actually eavesdropping on his father's conversations with callers. Invariably they came for advice on one thing or another but more often than not, it was advice on matters affecting money. From these conversations he learned the word salesmanship and what it meant."

41   It was Eaton, too, who initiated many Forest Lawn public-service activities—the inspirational speaker made available to service clubs, the thirteen half-hour Bible films, and the giving of the Forest Lawn Awards for Persuasive Writing as a "practical service to students and Christian liberal arts colleges."

42   Long interested in "small, independent, liberal arts colleges" as being "America's last bulwark against the march of Socialism. . . ." Eaton believes that "most" college professors are "semi-socialists at heart" who teach young people that salesmanship "smacks of chicanery, demogoguery, of influencing people against their wills. . . ."

43   But Eaton isn't always so serious. Even when he was at college himself, he always had a "good sense of humor." His biography relates that one of his favorite tricks was to persuade a visitor to allow a funnel to be inserted into the top of his trousers and then to make him balance a penny on his chin and try to drop it into the funnel. While the visitor was in this position, young Hubert "or one of his cronies would pour a cup of cold water into the funnel."

44   Eaton's "good sense of humor changed little in succeeding years," states his biographer, and it certainly hadn't changed much the night when Eaton gave one of his usual huge, lavish parties for a group of friends and guests. It was called "An Enchanged Evening in the South Pacific," of which "Trader" Hubert Eaton was the master of ceremonies. Elaborate Hawaiian acts were presented, and guests received a large, beautifully printed eight-page souvenir program in color, in which Eaton had himself depicted as "Your Happy Planter," jumping from page to page on a golden-shovel pogo stick.

45   On the cultural level, the printed program carried a large reproduction of the "David" statue, with a fig leaf, a Hawaiian lei, and a girl curled around its neck, all illustrating a poem, "The Secret of Hubie's David," which described just how it was decided to add a fig leaf to

Forest Lawn's copy of Michelangelo's "David" in order not to shock "the ladies of L.A."

46   But surely the greatest of all the improvements that Eaton has made on the past is Forest Lawn itself. Here, what might have been just an ordinary "country cemetery" has been parlayed into a solemn institution, profitable and widely imitated, looking like Edgar Guest's idea of Heaven brought to earth, while representing a social level to which all people can aspire after death. And in the future, says Hubert Eaton, "When the place is all filled up, my idea, from a financial standpoint, has always been to make Forest Lawn into a museum and charge admission."

Discussion of Theme

1. Some people say that funerals are for the living rather than the dead. In what way might this be true?
2. Are Eaton's innovations commendable or not?
3. What is Eaton's concept of himself, of cemeteries, of death?
4. Why are the advertisements for Forest Lawn, described in paragraphs 25 and 26, so effective?
5. Has Eaton filled a need in society, or has he created one?

Discussion of Rhetoric

1. Point out the pun in the opening paragraph. Why are there so many puns about the undertaking business?
2. In paragraph 11 what effect does Jacobs achieve by describing the gross physical details in the Hall of the Crucifixion?
3. What is the tone or attitude of this essay? How does Jacobs establish it in the opening paragraphs?
4. The last sentence in paragraph 26 is typical of the many examples of irony to be found in this essay. Find several other examples and explain the purpose or function of the irony in each.
5. Is Jacobs's title an effective one for this essay? What attitude does it help to establish?
6. What is the significance of Eaton's closing remark in paragraph 46? Why did Jacobs choose this statement to end his essay?

Writing Assignments

1. Speculate about the theory that an elaborate funeral and expensive casket alleviate the survivors' guilt feelings toward the dead.
2. As our population grows, space becomes increasingly scarce and, therefore, precious. In this respect, how are we to reconcile the needs of the living with those of the dead?
3. Show the importance of euphemisms in selling insurance or cemetery lots.
4. Has Eaton debased the act of death, or has he served his fellow man by making it less painful?

5. Defend or disprove Eaton's statement (in paragraph 42) concerning college professors.

Library Exploration

1. As a reaction against high-priced funerals, several burial societies have been organized in the United States. What are some of their unique features?
2. Two books receiving widespread acclaim in recent years for their commentary on death and the funeral industry are *The Loved One,* by Evelyn Waugh, and *The American Way of Death,* by Jessica Mitford.

Vocabulary

(2) PROSAIC commonplace; dull

(3) TENURE right to hold or keep

(12) STOIC one unaffected by pleasure or pain

(16) DEMITASSE half-size coffee cup

(16) PARODIED imitated with intent to ridicule

(20) VERDANT lush green

(22) COLUMBARIUM vault with niches for cremated remains

(25) MANIFEST evident

(25) OBVIATING eliminating; doing away with

(32) FORMIDABLE great; hard to overcome

(40) OSTENSIBLY apparently; seemingly

(42) CHICANERY trickery

(42) DEMAGOGUERY leadership by appeals to emotion and prejudice

(46) PARLAYED successfully exploited

The Voices of Science

Annie Dillard is a contributing
editor to "Harper's" magazine.
Educated at Hollins College, she
is the author of "Pilgrim at
Tinker Creek" (1974) and "Tickets for a Prayer Wheel" (1974),
the latter a collection of poetry.

The author examines the
beauty, horror, and mysteries of
the insect world, offering some
fascinating speculations.

ANNIE DILLARD

Monster in a Mason Jar

1 It is winter here in the Blue Ridge; things are opening up. This is a
tamed valley in southwestern Virginia where dairy farms and or-
chards have replaced the hardwood forest. Winter tames the valley
further; winter clearcuts and reseeds the easy way. Now I can walk,
and now I can see. Everywhere paths unclog; now and only now can I
scale the cliff to the Lucas orchard, circle the forested quarry pond, or
follow the left-hand bank of Tinker Creek downstream from my back-
yard. The woods are acres of sticks; I could walk to the Gulf of Mexico in a straight line. When the leaves fall the striptease is over;
things stand mute and revealed.

2   I have just learned to see praying mantis egg cases and suddenly I
see them everywhere; a tan oval of light catches my eye, or I notice a
blob of thickness in a patch of slender weeds. As I write I can see the
one I tied to the bush outside my study window. It's over an inch long
and shaped like a bell, or like the northern hemisphere of an egg cut
through its equator. The full length of one of its long sides is affixed
to a twig; the side that catches the light is perfectly flat. It has a dead
straw, dead weed color and a curious brittle texture, hard as varnish
but pitted minutely, like frozen foam. I carried it home this afternoon, holding it by the twig, along with several others—they were
light as air. I dropped one and didn't miss it until I got home and
made a count.

3   Within the week I've seen thirty or so of these egg cases in a rose-
grown field on Tinker Mountain and another thirty in weeds along

Carvin's Creek. One was on a twig of tiny dogwood on the mud lawn of a newly built house. I think the mail-order houses sell them to gardeners at a dollar apiece. It beats spraying because each case contains 125 to 350 eggs. If the eggs survive ants, woodpeckers, and mice—and most do—then you get the fun of seeing the new mantises hatch, and the smug feeling of knowing, all summer long, that they're out there in your garden devouring gruesome numbers of fellow insects all nice and organically. When a mantis has crunched up the last shred of its victim, it cleans its smooth green face like a cat.

4   In late summer I often see a winged adult mantis stalking the insects that swarm about my porch light. Its body is a clear, warm green; its naked, triangular head revolves uncannily, so that I often see one twist its head to gaze at me as if over its shoulder. When it strikes, it jerks so suddenly and with such a fearful clatter of raised wings that even a hardened entomologist like J. Henri Fabre confessed to being startled witless every time. Adult mantises eat more or less everything that breathes and is small enough to capture. They eat honeybees and butterflies, including monarch butterflies. People have seen them seize and devour garter snakes, mice, and even hummingbirds.

5   Newly hatched mantises, on the other hand, eat small creatures like aphids and each other. When I was in elementary school, one of the teachers brought in a mantis egg case in a Mason jar. I watched the newly hatched mantises emerge and shed their skins; they were spidery and translucent, all over joints. They trailed from the egg case to the base of the Mason jar in a living bridge that looked like Arabic calligraphy, some baffling text from the Koran inscribed down the air by a fine hand. Over a period of several hours, during which time the teacher never summoned the nerve or the sense to release them, they ate each other until only two were left. Tiny legs were still kicking from the mouths of each. The two survivors grappled and sawed in the Mason jar; finally both died of injuries. I felt as though I myself should swallow the corpses, shutting my eyes and washing them down like jagged pills, so all that life wouldn't be lost.

6   When mantises hatch in the wild, however, they straggle about prettily, dodging ants, till all are lost in the grass. So it was in hopes of seeing an eventual hatch that I pocketed my jackknife this afternoon before I set out to walk. Now that I can see the egg cases, I'm embarrassed to realize how many I must have missed all along. I walked east through the Adams' woods to the cornfield, cutting three undamaged egg cases I found at the edge of the field. It was a clear, picturesque day, a day without clouds, without emotion or spirit, like a beautiful woman with an empty face. As I carried the thorny stems from which the egg cases hung like roses, I switched the bouquet from hand to hand, warming the free hand in a pocket. Passing the house again, I decided not to fetch gloves and walked north to the hill by the place where the steers come to drink from Tinker Creek. There in the weeds on the hill I found another eight egg cases. I was stunned—I cross this hill several times a week, and I always look for egg cases here, because it was here that I had once seen a mantis laying her eggs. It was several years ago that I witnessed this extra-

ordinary procedure, but I remember and confess an inescapable feeling that I was watching something not real and present but a horrible nature movie, a "secrets-of-nature" short, beautifully photographed in full color, that I had to sit through unable to look anywhere else but at the dimly lit exit signs along the walls, and that behind the scenes some amateur moviemaker was congratulating himself on having stumbled across this little wonder, or even on having contrived so natural a setting, as though the whole scene had been shot very carefully in a terrarium in someone's greenhouse.

7   I was ambling across this hill that day when I noticed a speck of pure white. The hill is eroded; the slope is a rutted wreck of red clay broken by grassy hillocks and low wild roses whose roots clasp a pittance of topsoil. I leaned to examine the white thing and saw a mass of bubbles like spittle. Then I saw something dark like an engorged leech rummaging over the spittle, and then I saw the praying mantis.

8   She was upside-down, clinging by her feet to a horizontal stem of wild rose. Her head was deep in dried grass. Her abdomen was swollen like a smashed finger; it tapered to a fleshy tip out of which bubbled a wet, whipped froth. I couldn't believe my eyes. I lay on the hill this way and that, my knees in thorns and my cheeks in clay, trying to see as well as I could. I poked near the female's head with a blade of grass; she was clearly undisturbed, so I settled my nose an inch from that pulsing abdomen. It puffed like a concertina, it throbbed like a bellows; it roved, pumping, over the glistening, clabbered surface of the egg case testing and patting, thrusting and smoothing. It seemed to act so independently that I forgot the panting brown stick at the other end. The bubble creature seemed to have two eyes, a frantic little brain, and two busy, soft hands. It looked like a hideous, harried mother slicking up a fat daughter for a beauty pageant, touching her up, slobbering over her, patting and hemming and brushing and stroking.

9   The male was nowhere in sight. The female had probably eaten him. Fabre says that, at least in captivity, the female will mate with and devour up to seven males, whether she has laid her egg cases or not. The mating rites of mantises are well known: a chemical produced in the head of the male insect says, in effect, "No, don't go near her, you fool, she'll eat you alive." At the same time a chemical in his abdomen says, "Yes, by all means, now and forever yes."

10   While the male is making up what passes for his mind, the female tips the balance in her favor by eating his head. He mounts her. Fabre describes the mating, which sometimes lasts six hours, as follows: "The male, absorbed in the performance of his vital functions, holds the female in a tight embrace. But the wretch has no head; he has no neck; he has hardly a body. The other, with her muzzle turned over her shoulder, continues very placidly to gnaw what remains of the gentle swain. And, all the time, that masculine stump, holding on firmly, goes on with the business! . . . I have seen it done with my own eyes and have not yet recovered from my astonishment."

11   I watched the egg-laying for over an hour. When I returned the next day the mantis was gone. The white foam had hardened and browned to a dirty suds; then, and on subsequent days, I had trouble

pinpointing the case, which was only an inch or so off the ground. I checked on it every week all winter long. In the spring the ants discovered it; every week I saw dozens of ants scrambling over the sides, unable to chew a way in. Later in the spring I climbed the hill every day, hoping to catch the hatch. The leaves of the trees had long since unfolded, the butterflies were out, and the robins' first broods were fledged; still the egg case hung silent and full on the stem. I read that I should wait for June, but still I visited the case every day. One morning at the beginning of June everything was gone. I couldn't find the lower thorn in the clump of three to which the egg case was fixed. I couldn't find the clump of three. Tracks ridged the clay, and I saw the lopped stems: somehow my neighbor had contrived to run a tractor mower over that steep clay hill on which there grew nothing to mow but a few stubby thorns.

12   So. Today from this same hill I cut another three undamaged cases and carried them home with the others by their twigs. I also collected a suspiciously light cynthia moth cocoon. My fingers were stiff and red with cold, and my nose ran. I had forgotten, as I do at the start of every winter, the Law of the Wild, which is, "Carry Kleenex." At home I tied the twigs with their egg cases to various sunny bushes and trees in the yard. They're easy to find because I used white string; at any rate, I'm unlikely to mow my own trees. I hope the woodpeckers don't find them, but I don't see how they'd get a purchase on them if they did.

13   Night is rising in the valley; the light on the creek has been out for an hour, and now only the naked tips of trees fire tapers into the sky like trails of sparks. The scene that was in the back of my brain all afternoon, obscurely, is beginning to rise from night's lagoon. It really has nothing to do with praying mantises. But this afternoon I threw tiny string lashings and hitches with frozen hands, gingerly, fearing to touch the egg cases even for a minute because I remembered the polyphemus moth.

14   I rarely recall the distant past, and I have no intention of inflicting my childhood memories on anyone. Far less do I want to excoriate my old teachers, who, in their bungling, unforgettable way, exposed me to the natural world, a world covered with chitin, where implacable realities hold sway. The polyphemus moth never made it to the past; it crawls in that crowded, pellucid pool at the lip of the great waterfall. It is as present as this blue desk and brazen lamp, as this blackened window before me in which I can no longer see even the white string that binds the egg case to the hedge, but only my pale, astonished face.

15   I was ten or eleven years old when a teacher brought in a polyphemus moth cocoon. It was January; there were doily snowflakes taped to the schoolroom panes. The teacher kept the cocoon in her desk all morning and brought it out when we were getting restless before recess. In a book we found what the adult moth would look like; it would be beautiful. With a wingspread of up to six inches, the polyphemus is one of the few huge American silk moths, much larger than, say, a giant or tiger swallowtail butterfly. The moth's enormous wings are velveted in a rich, warm brown and edged in bands of blue

and pink delicate as a watercolor wash. A startling eyespot, immense and deep blue, melding to an almost translucent yellow, luxuriates in the center of each hind wing. The effect is one of a masculine splendor foreign to the butterflies, a fragility unfurled to strength. The polyphemus moth in the picture looked like a mighty wraith, a beating essence of the hardwood forest, alien-skinned and brown, with spread, blind eyes. This was the giant moth packed in the faded cocoon. We closed the book and turned to the real cocoon. It was an oak leaf sewn into a plump oval bundle; the teacher had found it loose in a pile of frozen leaves.

16   We passed the cocoon around; it was heavy. As we held it in our hands, the creature within warmed and squirmed. We were delighted, and wrapped it tighter in our fists. The pupa began to jerk violently, in heart-stopping knocks. Who's there? I can still feel those thumps, urgent through a muffling of spun silk and leaf, urgent through the swaddling of many years, against the curve of my palm. We kept passing it around. When it came to me again it was hot as a bun; it jumped half out of my hand. The teacher intervened. She put it, still heaving and banging, into the ubiquitous Mason jar. It was coming. There was no stopping it now, January or not. One end of the cocoon dampened and gradually frayed in a furious battle. The whole cocoon twisted and slapped around in the bottom of the jar.

17   The teacher fades, the classmates fade, I fade: I don't remember anything but that thing's struggle to be a moth or die trying. It emerged at last, a sodden crumple. It was a male; his long antennae were thickly plumed, as wide as his fat abdomen. His body was very thick, over an inch long, and deeply furred. A gray, furlike plush covered his head; long, tan furlike hair hung from his wide thorax over his brown-furred, segmented abdomen. His multijointed legs, pale and powerful, were shaggy as a bear's. He stood still, but he breathed.

18   He couldn't spread his wings. There was no room. The chemical that coated his wings like varnish, stiffening them permanently, dried, and hardened his wings as they were. He was a monster in a Mason jar.

19   Those huge wings stuck on his back in a torture of random pleats and folds, wrinkled as a dirty tissue, rigid as leather. They made a single nightmare clump still wracked with useless, frantic convulsions.

20   The next thing I remember, it was recess. Everyone was playing dodge ball in the fenced playground or racing around the concrete schoolyard by the swings. Next to the playground a long delivery drive sloped downhill to the sidewalk and street. Someone—it must have been the teacher—had let the moth out. I was standing in the driveway, alone, stock still, but shivering. Someone had given the polyphemus moth his freedom, and he was walking away.

21   He heaved himself down the asphalt driveway by infinite degrees, unwavering. His hideous crumpled wings lay glued and rucked on his back, perfectly still now, like a collapsed tent. The bell rang twice; I had to go. The moth was receding down the driveway, dragging on. I went; I ran inside. The polyphemus moth is still crawling down the driveway, crawling down the driveway on six furred feet, forever.

MYSTERIES IN BROAD DAYLIGHT

22 Shading the glass with a hand, I can see how shadow has pooled in the valley. It washes up the sandstone cliffs on Tinker Mountain and obliterates them in a deluge; freshets of shadow leak into the sky. I am exhausted. In Pliny I read about the invention of clay modeling. A Sicyonian potter came to Corinth. There his daughter fell in love with a young man who had to make frequent long journeys away from the city. When he sat with her at home, she used to trace the outline of his shadow that a candle's light cast on the wall. Then in his absence she worked over the profile, deepening it, so that she might enjoy his face and remember. One day the father slapped some potter's clay over the gouged plaster; when the clay hardened, he removed it, baked it, and "showed it abroad." The story ends here. Did the boy come back? What did the girl think of her father's dragging her lover all over town by the hair? What I really want to know is: is the shadow still there? If I went back, would I find the face there on the wall by the fireplace?

23 Outside shadows are blue, I read, because they are lighted by the blue sky and not the yellow sun. Their blueness bespeaks infinitesimal particles scattered over inestimable distance. Muslims, whose religion bans representational art as idolatrous, don't observe the rule strictly, but they do forbid sculpture because it casts a shadow. So shadows define the real. If I no longer see shadows as "dark marks," as do the newly sighted, then I see them as making sense of the light. They give the light distance; they put it in its place. Now that shadow has dissolved the heavens' blue dome, I can see Andromeda again; I stand pressed to the window, rapt and shrunken in the galaxy's chill glare. "Nostalgia of the Infinite," di Chirico: cast shadows stream across the sunlit courtyard, gouging canyons. There is a sense in which shadows are actually cast, hurled with a power, cast as Ishmael was cast, *out*, with a flinging force. This is the blue strip running through creation, the icy roadside stream on whose banks the mantis mates, in whose unweighed waters giant water bugs sip frogs.

24 Shadow Creek is the blue subterranean stream that chills Carvin's Creek and Tinker Creek; it cuts like ice under the ribs of the mountains, Tinker and Dead Man. Shadow Creek storms through limestone vaults under forests, or surfaces anywhere, damp, on the underside of a leaf. I wring it from rocks; it seeps into my cup. Chasms open at the glance of an eye; the ground parts like a wind-rent cloud over stars. Shadow Creek: even on a walk to the mailbox I may find myself knee-deep in its sucking, frigid pools. I must either wear rubber boots or dance to keep warm.

25 Fish gotta swim and bird gotta fly; insects, it seems, gotta do one horrible thing after another. I never ask why of a vulture or shark, but I ask why of almost every insect I see. More than one insect—the possibility of fertile reproduction—is an assault on all human value, all hope of a reasonable god. Even that devout Frenchman, J. Henri Fabre, who devoted his entire life to the study of insects, cannot restrain a feeling of unholy revulsion. He describes a bee-eating wasp,

the Philanthus, that has killed a honeybee. If the bee is heavy with honey, the wasp squeezes its crop "so as to make her disgorge the delicious syrup, which she drinks by licking the tongue which her unfortunate victim, in her death agony, sticks out of her mouth at full length. . . . At the moment of some such horrible banquet, I have seen the Wasp, with her prey, seized by the Mantis: the bandit was rifled by another bandit. And here is an awful detail: while the Mantis held her transfixed under the points of the double saw and was already munching her belly, the Wasp continued to lick the honey of her Bee, unable to relinquish the delicious food even amid the terrors of death. Let us hasten to cast a veil over these horrors."

26   The remarkable thing about the world of insects, however, is precisely that there is no veil cast over these horrors. There are mysteries performed in broad daylight before our very eyes; we can see every detail, and yet they are still mysteries. If, as Heraclitus suggests, God, like an oracle, neither "declares nor hides, but sets forth by signs," then clearly I had better be scrying the signs. The earth devotes an overwhelming proportion of its energy to these buzzings and leaps in the grass, to these brittle gnawings and crawlings about. Theirs is the biggest wedge of the pie: why? I ought to keep a giant water bug in an aquarium on my dresser, so I can think about it. We have brass candlesticks in our houses now; we ought to display praying mantises in our churches. Why do we turn from the insects in loathing? Our competitors are not only cold-blooded, but are also cased in a clacking horn. They lack the grace to go about as we do, soft side out to the wind and thorns. They have rigid eyes and brains strung down their backs. But they make up the bulk of our comrades-in-life, so I look to them for a glimmer of companionship.

27   When a grasshopper landed on my study window last summer, I looked at it for a long time. Its hard wing covers were short; its body was a dead waxen yellow, with black-green, indecipherable marks. Like all large insects, it gave me pause, plenty pause, with its hideous horizontal, multi-jointed mouthparts and intricate, mechanical-looking feet, all cups and spikes. I looked at its tapered, chitin-covered abdomen, plated and barred as a tank tread, and was about to turn away when I saw it breathe, puff puff, and I grew sympathetic. Yeah, I said, puff puff, isn't it? It jerked away with a buzz like a rasping file, audible through the pane, and continued to puff in the grass. So puff it is, and that's all there is; though I'm partial to honey myself.

28   Nature is, above all, profligate. Don't believe them when they tell you how economical and thrifty nature is, whose leaves return to the soil. Wouldn't it be cheaper to leave them on the tree in the first place? This deciduous business alone is a radical scheme, the brainchild of a deranged manic-depressive with limitless capital. Extravagance! Nature will try anything once. This is what the sign of the insects says. No form is too gruesome, no behavior too grotesque. If you're dealing with organic compounds, then let them combine. If it works, if it quickens, set it clacking in the grass; there's always room for one more; you ain't so handsome yourself. This is a spendthrift economy; though nothing is lost, all is spent.

Discussion of Theme

1. The author is imposing human values and morality on insects. Is this unusual? (What about Disney's nature films?) Is the author aware that she is doing this? How do you know?
2. What do you think "Shadow Creek" represents?
3. Is this essay merely a study of the insect world or is it something more? How would you answer if someone were to ask you what this essay is about?
4. Why do you suppose the author chose to call this essay "Monster in a Mason Jar" when that was only one of many incidents related?
5. Why does Dillard say "nature will try anything once"?

Discussion of Rhetoric

1. What are some of the elements that give this selection its lyrical quality?
2. The essay is organized around the incident about the "monster" in the Mason jar. How does the author achieve a sense of unity and relate other material back to that theme?
3. What are some of the transitional devices used? Find examples of a few particularly striking ones.
4. How does the author build tension and hold the interest of the audience?
5. di Chirico is a surrealist painter. Why is it appropriate to evoke the image of a surrealistic painting in this particular passage? (paragraph 23)

Writing Assignments

1. Describe a personal experience in which something you witnessed seemed "staged" or unreal (as in paragraph 6).
2. Write about your own personal relations with nature and what you have learned from it.

Vocabulary

(4) ENTOMOLOGIST one who studies insects

(5) CALLIGRAPHY fine handwriting

(5) KORAN the sacred scripture of Islam

(7) ENGORGED glutted; grossly congested

(8) CLABBERED thick-
ened
(10) SWAIN a lover
(14) EXCORIATE to flay
or denounce, censure
(14) IMPLACABLE not to
be pacified
(14) PELLUCID translu-
cent
(15) MELDING displaying

(21) RUCKED creased
(22) FRESHETS sudden
rises in the level of a
stream
(26) ORACLE one who ut-
ters prophecies
(26) SCRYING crying out
(28) PROFLIGATE
shamelessly immoral
and extravagant

Stuart Chase (1888–   ) is the author of numerous books and articles on economics, semantics, and social topics. Born in New Hampshire, he received his degree from Harvard. Among his recent books are "The Most Probable World" (1968) and "Danger–Man Talking" (1969).

Many critics of our society, claiming that its problems are caused by the effects of science and technology, suggest a return to "the good old days." The author of the following selection maintains that this philosophy is a retreat. Technology, he says, can provide a treasure chest of opportunities to man.

STUART CHASE

Two Cheers for Technology

1   In contemplating the sorry state of the world today, some observers, such as the distinguished philosopher and theologian Jacques Ellul, have come to believe that our troubles are due primarily to science and technology. Man, they imply, should never have begun the exploration of the laws governing the material universe. Once formulated, these laws, proceeding on a momentum of their own, will imprison him. "Enclosed within his artificial creation," says Ellul, "man finds that there is no exit, that he cannot pierce the shell of technology to find again the ancient milieu to which he was adapted for hundreds of thousands of years." This would seem to indicate that we did better in the Stone Age.

2   The Nobel Prize physicist Max Born comes close to agreeing with this view. "I am haunted by the idea," he declares, "that the break in human civilization caused by the discovery of the scientific method may be irreparable."

3   The philosophy of retreat to a simpler era may have had some validity 200 years ago when Rousseau was celebrating the virtues of
Cro-Magnon man, but too much water has gone through the turbines.
The growth curves of science and technology have profoundly
changed the cultural habits of the West and have made deep inroads
on the East—witness Japan.

4   I believe that the way to come to terms with technology today is,
first, to understand it and, then, to encourage its good effects on the
human condition and at the same time try to discourage its bad effects.
I cannot follow the mystique that technology has laws of its own, over
and beyond human intervention.

5   Is it possible to conceive of a civilized society in the 1970s without
electric power, motor vehicles, railroads, airplanes, telephones, television, elevators, flush toilets, central heating, air conditioning, anti-
biotics, vaccines, and antiseptics?

6   Before going any further, it is clear that two definitions are in order.
What is meant by the "human condition"? What is meant by "technology," and what is its relation to "science"?

7   The "human condition" may be defined as a measure of the extent
to which the potential for living is realized under the limitations of the
inborn genes and of the environment of the Earth. Full potential
means adequate food, shelter, clothing, education, and health care,
plus useful and creative work and leisure for every normal baby born.
The slums of Calcutta or Rio, the ghettos of the West, represent a potential close to zero.

8   Alone, the word "technology" implies only a special learned skill
beyond intuitive common sense; hydraulic engineers, for instance, can
make water run uphill. We must descend the semantic abstraction
ladder and ask: Technology for what? For manufacturing a jumbo jet?
A MIRV multiple warhead? A contraceptive pill? An electric razor?
For engineering a trip to the moon? For what?

9   Many people, including a large number of today's college students,
confuse technology with science. "There is a growing feeling in Washington," says *New York Times* science editor Walter Sullivan, "that
efforts to explain science to the young have failed."

10   "Science," or perhaps better "*pure* science," discovers laws of nature and lately some laws of human nature. There is no ulterior motive
in the pursuit of pure science beyond what Veblen once called "idle
curiosity." Einstein was consumed with it. He wanted to know the relation between energy and matter; he wanted to know how the theory
of relativity could be linked to the quantum theory.

11   When a scientific law is established so that all competent observers
agree on its validity, then, in many cases, it may be applied to the satisfaction of various human desires and needs and thus become applied
science, or technology. The pure science of $E=MC^2$ was applied to the
construction of the first atomic bomb—a technological triumph of
dubious benefit to the human condition, except as a warning. However, such knowledge can be applied to the desalting of sea water—a
technological triumph of great utility, as deserts are transformed into
gardens. To condemn technology *in toto* is to forget the gardens, while
to idealize technology is to forget Hiroshima.

12   The transformation of pure science into applied is strikingly illustrated by Raymond Fosdick, sometime head of the Rockefeller Foundation, as he tells in his book *Chronicle of a Generation* of the
184-inch cyclotron financed by the foundation in 1940 for the University of California:

> No one foresaw that this instrument would lead to an atomic bomb or any
> other kind of military weapon. The only motivation behind our assistance
> was to extend the boundaries of knowledge, to stimulate the search for
> truth, in the belief that there is no darkness but ignorance.

13   Consider some of the more notorious and pervading modern technologies. Which of them appear to improve the human condition as
defined and which degrade it? What is the outlook for increasing the
assets and reducing, if not eliminating, the liabilities? To toss the
whole complex into the discard is to rule out not only all high-energy
societies but the way the human mind works, or at least the way many
minds work. Some men want to know *why*—and are off on the course
pioneered by Galileo, Darwin, and Faraday, in pursuit of pure science.
Soon, Edison, Baekeland, and Ford are applying the knowledge
gained. Is there any way to halt idle curiosity? Can we find a method
short of extermination to prevent Homo sapiens—the creature who
thinks—from trying to put dependable knowledge to work?

14   The necessity for caution in evaluation is apparent in the case of the
internal combustion engine—probably the most popular piece of technology ever invented. The automobile has markedly improved the
human condition by providing greater mobility and convenience,
while degrading it with air pollution. How long before the liabilities
overwhelm the assets? Even if the technicians devise a pollution-free
engine, the miseries and tragedies of highway accidents and traffic
jams remain, indeed expand with population and affluence.

15   Where does the balance of a given technology lie now? Where will
it be a decade hence? How does the balance shift from area to area—
high-energy cultures, low-energy cultures, big city, open country?
Under intensive analysis, the balance shifts with time, and with place,
for nearly every item under consideration.

16   There are three major threats to mankind today, all due primarily to
technology: 1) the arms race in nuclear weapons, which, if continued,
can only end in World War III; 2) the accelerating destruction of the
environment; and 3) the population explosion. For easy reference, I
once called these threats "bombs, bulldozers, and babies." The effect
of technology is obvious enough in the first two, but the third requires
a moment's thought. Modern medicine in its control of epidemics, for
instance, has enormously reduced death rates all over the world, in
low-energy societies as well as high. Birth control, however, has not
kept pace with death control, and through the widening gap population pours. At the present rate of growth, there will be twice as many
people in the world by the year 2000. But again we must be careful of
an "all good" or "all bad" evaluation. Modern medicine in one sense
is a great boon, but death control without a compensating birth control is the unquestioned reason for the population explosion that is
rapidly becoming a menace to the human condition.

17   Again, nuclear weapons, by a curious logical paradox, could conceivably become mankind's greatest asset. Robert Oppenheimer once called the atomic bomb "a great peril and a great hope," by which he meant that it made large-scale wars unwinnable—an exercise in mutual suicide. But as diplomacy now stands, the arms race is more of a liability than an asset—particularly when biological and chemical weapons are brought into the equation. I am unaware of anything that can be said in favor of these despicable technologies.

18   The destruction of the environment, which is now on an exponential curve, also seems to be an unmitigated liability to the human condition. There is, however, a small offset. Many of the destructive forces cross national boundaries—industrial smog, oil spills, fallout, pollution of rivers that flow through two or more sovereign states. Only international cooperation can cope with these disasters, and so the demand for a stronger world organization is increased.

19   Bombs, bulldozers, and babies may be the major threats to the human condition today, but they are by no means the only ones for which technology is responsible. Noise pollution, for instance, is an extension of air pollution. Anyone living near a jetport—or even trying to do so—suffers, as does anyone whose home is near a highway infested with heavy-duty trucks. The decibel count goes steadily up in high-energy societies, and more and more people suffer from defective hearing. But we really haven't heard anything yet. Wait until the SSTs smash their fifty-mile corridors of sonic boom from coast to coast, along with smashed windows, crockery, and nervous systems.

20   As agriculture is mechanized by the automated cotton picker and other labor-saving devices, displaced farm workers—black, brown, yellow, and white—lose their livelihoods and descend on the cities, where the ghettos, already overburdened, try to accommodate them. See Harlem in New York, "La Perla" in San Juan, the vast shacktowns of Caracas—see them and weep for the human condition.

21   As the sharecroppers move in—at least in America—the middle class moves out en masse to the suburbs, where the open land is geometrically sliced into subdivisions. The lowing of cattle gives way to the grunt of the bulldozer, and the station wagons pile up at the supermarket. "Spread city," or megalopolis, is rapidly becoming a forbidding place in which to live, for rich as well as poor. Last year, when S. J. Perelman left New York City for good, he exclaimed: "Plants can live on carbon dioxide, but I can't."

22   The international trade in non-nuclear weapons—jet fighters, tanks, machine guns—is now estimated at $5-billion a year. Every mini-nation in Africa and Asia seems ready to mortgage its future in order to be immediately outfitted with lethal weapons. The big nations, the sellers, in this profitable trade are always glad to clear their stocks of old models.

23   The crime rate is greatly aided by the getaway car, and civilian terror and confusion are aided by anonymous telephone warnings of bombs about to be exploded. The hijacking of airliners, and the consequent holding of passengers as hostages, is something quite new in political terrorism. Its only offset is another demonstration that, in an age of high technology, this is one world or none.

24   Certainly, there are additional liabilities, but those I have indicated are a representative lot — perhaps the most serious ones. Let us turn now to the assets. What has technology done for the good life?

25   The human condition in high-energy societies has been improved by better diets, health care, education, and scientific knowledge of vitamins. Young people are now taller, stronger, and better favored than their parents or grandparents. This is markedly true in Japan. In America, some 40 per cent of all youngsters of college age are in college. When I was a young man, the figure was below 5 per cent.

26   People in high-energy cultures live longer, are more literate, and enjoy more travel and recreation than the generation that preceded them, while the ratio of poor people to total population has declined drastically. No society in history has ever remotely approached the standard of living enjoyed in the United States, defined in either dollars or materials consumed. No society has ever been so well nourished, so well bathed, so well doctored. No civilized society, furthermore, has ever worked such short hours to produce and distribute the necessities of life.

27   Two dark spots in this otherwise bright picture must be noted.

28   America's affluent society does not adequately care for its old people. The elderly have a sharply declining place in the family compared with the grandparents of a simpler age. The average "home for the aged" can hardly be called an asset to the human condition.

29   And secondly, this affluent society is built on an exceedingly shaky foundation of natural resources. Here we connect with the liability of a degenerating environment. The United States with only some 6 per cent of the world's population uses up some 40 per cent of the world's annual production of raw materials. If all the world enjoyed American affluence, there would be about twelve times the current demand for raw materials — an impossible drain on the resources of this planet.

30   Here is an equation that must be faced, probably before the twentieth century has run its course. If the so-called hungry world of Asia, Africa, and Latin America is significantly to increase its living standards, America and other high-energy societies must decrease their consumption of raw materials. This does not mean that the latter must retreat to the economy of scarcity, but it does mean an economy programed for a great reduction in waste, for recycling used materials, for the elimination of planned obsolescence.

31   If the technology of production is really to serve the human condition, it might well have as its goal the concept of "perpetual yield." The lumber barons of the nineteenth century in America operated on a "cut out and get out" program that promised to destroy the forests of the continent. Beginning in Maine, they slashed through New York, Michigan, Wisconsin, Minnesota, and on to the West Coast, leaving behind a desolation where the very soil was burned away. Then came a miracle. The lumber industry, at least some of the larger companies, realized that they were sawing off the limb on which they sat. They halted their wholesale policy of slash and burn, adopted "selective cutting" to keep the forests healthy, and planted millions of young trees. They shifted to a perpetual-yield basis, whereby a forest would be cut no faster than its annual growth.

32   Is this not a sound goal for all economic growth? *Keep the natural resources of the planet on a perpetual-yield basis.* The calculations will change, of course, as technology improves the yield. A fine example is the growing possibility, through intensive research and development, for employing thermonuclear *fusion* as the world's chief energy source. There is very little danger of radiation, and the hydrogen of the seven oceans will form the raw material for the process — good for thousands of years. Coal, oil, natural gas, and hydroelectric developments will no longer be prime sources. Fusion power — probably employing lasers — can be a great asset of technology, indeed, and might be operational within a generation. The rapidly developing new methods for recycling wastes of all kinds, solid and liquid, would also form an important part of the perpetual-yield concept.

33   Labor-saving devices in the field have just about abolished the institution of slavery all over the world, while in the home they have liberated women from a load of grinding toil, at least in high-energy societies.

34   Technology is now making it possible to mine the ocean and is thus opening a vast treasure chest. It has been proposed that the United Nations receive a royalty from these riches as they are developed. No nation, no corporation, no person owns the open oceans and its floor; it belongs to all mankind — with decent respect, or course, to all forms of life within it, and the ecosystems that govern it. Intelligently planned and carefully exploited, it may well be that the raw materials and foodstuffs of the oceans can markedly increase the concept of perpetual yield, and permit a higher ceiling for living standards all round.

35   It is not difficult to make a terrifying indictment of technology. It is not difficult to make a heartening list of benefits. The problem is so complex on one level, and yet, in essence, so simple. Granting the available resources of this planet, how many human beings and their fellow creatures can be supported at a level that makes life worth the living? A dependable evaluation is very difficult. We can be sure, however, that nothing is to be gained by following the prophets of doom back to the Stone Age.

Discussion of Theme

1. According to Chase, how should we come to terms with technology? What is *technology* (as opposed to *science*)?
2. What are the three main threats to mankind, according to the author? In each instance, what was the contribution of technology? How can technology provide the answers?
3. What is a high-energy culture? A low-energy culture? Can you cite examples of each?
4. What is the human condition, as described in this article? How is it related to science and technology?
5. What distinction does Chase make between pure science and applied science?

Discussion of Rhetoric

1. What method does Chase use to support his thesis? Is more than one argumentative device employed?
2. In citing Ellul (paragraph 1) and others who differ with him, is Chase merely setting up "straw men"? Does he state his opponents' views fairly and accurately?
3. What is the significance of the title of this article? Does it tip you off concerning the author's enthusiasm for the subject?
4. How are the first and last paragraphs linked?

Writing Assignments

1. How can the problems of our large cities be solved? Or are they inevitably doomed, despite the wealth and technological knowledge of our nation?
2. Write a response to the question posed in paragraph 5.
3. How might our country "retreat to a simpler era," while maintaining the advantages offered by our technology?
4. Should federal funds for science (grants, contracts, subsidies, and other support) be reduced substantially and diverted to the solution of our domestic problems?

Library Exploration

1. For another view of this subject, read C. P. Snow's essay "The Two Cultures" (on page 334 of this text), and investigate the debate between Snow and F. R. Leavis over the ideas advocated by the former.
2. Three books related to Chase's topic are: *Race to Oblivion*, by Herbert York; *The Technological Society*, by Jacques Ellul; and *Chronicle of a Generation*, by Raymond Fosdick.

Vocabulary

(1) MILIEU   environment; setting

(2) IRREPARABLE   beyond repair

(10) ULTERIOR   hidden

(11) IN TOTO   completely; in its entirety

(14) AFFLUENCE   wealth

(30) OBSOLESCENCE   state of being outmoded

This article examines the scientist's responsibility for war and peace, and suggests a new role for science: creating values for modern man.

JACOB BRONOWSKI

Science, the Destroyer or Creator

1 We all know the story of the sorcerer's apprentice; or *Frankenstein* which Mary Shelley wrote in competition with her husband and Byron; or some other story of the same kind out of the macabre invention of the nineteenth century. In these stories, someone who has special powers over nature conjures or creates a stick or a machine to do his work for him; and then finds that he cannot take back the life he has given it. The mindless monster overwhelms him; and what began as an invention to do the housework ends by destroying the master with the house.

2   These stories have become the epitome of our own fears. We have been inventing machines at a growing pace now for about three hundred years. This is a short span even in our recorded history, and it is not a thousandth part of our history as men. In that short moment of time we have found a remarkable insight into the workings of nature. We have used it to make ourselves far more flexible in our adaptation to the outside world than any other animal has ever been. We can survive in climates which even germs find difficult. We can grow our own food and meat. We can travel overland and we can tunnel and swim and fly, all in the one body. More important than any of these, we have come nearest to the dream which Lamarck had, that animals might inherit the skills which their parents learnt. We have discovered the means to record our experience so that others may live it again.

3   The history of other animal species shows that the most successful in struggle for survival have been those which were most adaptable to changes in their world. We have made ourselves by means of our tools beyond all measure more adaptable than any other species, living or extinct; and we continue to do so with gathering speed. Yet today we are afraid of our own shadow in the nine o'clock news; and we wonder whether we shall survive so over-specialised a creature as the Pekinese.

II

4   Everyone likes to blame his sense of defeat on someone else; and for some time scientists have been a favourite scapegoat. I want to look at their responsibility, and for that matter at everybody's, rather more closely. They do have a special responsibility; do not let us argue that out of existence; but it is a complicated one, and it is not the whole responsibility. For example, science obviously is not responsible for the readiness of people, who do not take their private quarrels beyond the stage of insult, to carry their public quarrels to the point of war. Many animals fight for their needs, and some for their mere greeds, to the point of death. Bucks fight for females, and birds fight for their territories. The fighting habits of man are odd because he displays them only in groups. But they were not supplied by scientists. On the contrary, science has helped to end several kinds of group murder, such as witch hunting and the taboos of the early nineteenth century against disinfecting hospitals.

5   Neither is science responsible for the existence of groups which believe themselves to be in competition: for the existence above all of nations. And the threat of war today is always a national threat. Some bone of contention and competition is identified with a national need: Fiume or the Polish corridor or the dignity of the Austrian Empire; and in the end nations are willing to organise and to invite the death of citizens on both sides in order to reach these collective aims. Science did not create the nations; on the contrary, it has helped to soften those strong national idiosyncrasies which it seems necessary to exploit if war is to be made with enthusiasm. And wars are not made by *any* traditional groups: they are made by highly organized societies, they are made by nations. Most of us have seen Yorkshiremen invade Old Trafford, and a bloody nose or two if the day was thirsty. But no

Yorkshireman would have grown pale if he had been told that Lancashire had the atomic bomb.

6   The sense of doom in us today is not a fear of science; it is a fear of war. And the causes of war were not created by science; they do not differ in kind from the known causes of the War of Jenkins' Ear or the War of Roses, which were carried on with only the most modest scientific aids. No, science has not invented war; but it has turned it into a very different thing. The people who distrust it are not wrong. The man in the pub who says "It'll wipe out the world," the woman in the queue who says "It isn't natural" — they do not express themselves very well; but what they are trying to say does make sense. Science has enlarged the mechanism of war, and it has distorted it. It has done this in at least two ways.

III

7   First, science has obviously multiplied the power of the warmakers. The weapons of the moment can kill more people more secretly and more unpleasantly than those of the past. This progress, as for want of another word I must call it — this progress has been going on for some time; and for some time it has been said, of each new weapon, that it is so destructive or so horrible that it will frighten people into their wits, and force the nations to give up war for lack of cannon fodder. This hope has never been fulfilled, and I know no one who takes refuge in it today. The acts of men and women are not dictated by such simple compulsions; and they themselves do not stand in any simple relation to the decisions of the nations which they compose. Grapeshot and TNT and gas have not helped to outlaw war; and I see no sign that the hydrogen bomb or a whiff of bacteria will be more successful in making men wise by compulsion.

8   Secondly, science at the same time has given the nations quite new occasions for falling out. I do not mean such simple objectives as someone else's uranium mine, or a Pacific Island which happens to be knee-deep in organic fertilizer. I do not even mean merely another nation's factories and her skilled population. These are all parts of the surplus above our simple needs which they themselves help to create and which gives our civilization its character. And war in our world battens on this surplus. This is the object of the greed of nations, and this also gives them the leisure to train and the means to arm for war. At bottom, we have remained individually too greedy to distribute our surplus, and collectively too stupid to pile it up in any more useful form than the traditional mountains of arms. Science can claim to have created the surplus in our societies, and we know from the working day and the working diet how greatly it has increased it in the last two hundred years. Science has created the surplus. Now put this year's budget beside the budget of 1750, anywhere in the world, and you will see what we are doing with it.

9   I myself think there is a third dimension which science has added to modern war. It has created war nerves and the war of nerves. I am not thinking about the technical conditions for a war of nerves: the camera man and the radio and the massed display of strength. I am thinking of the climate in which this stage lightning flickers and is made to seem

real. The last twenty years have given us a frightening show of these
mental states. There is a division in the mind of each of us, that has
become plain, between the man and the brute; and the rift can be
opened, the man submerged, with a cynical simplicity, with the mean-
est tools of envy and frustration, which in my boyhood would have
been thought inconceivable in a civilised society. I shall come back to
this cleavage in our minds, for it is much more than an item in a list of
war crimes. But it is an item. It helps to create the conditions for disaster. And I think that science has contributed to it. Science; the fact
that science is there, mysterious, powerful; the fact that most people
are impressed by it but ignorant and helpless — all this seems to me to
have contributed to the division in our minds. And scientists cannot
escape the responsibility for this. They have enjoyed acting the
mysterious stranger, the powerful voice without emotion, the expert
and the god. They have failed to make themselves comfortable in the
talk of people in the street; no one taught them the knack, of course,
but they were not keen to learn. And now they find the distance which
they enjoyed has turned to distrust, and the awe has turned to fear;
and people who are by no means fools really believe that we should
be better off without science.

IV

10   These are the indictments which scientists cannot escape. Of course,
they are often badly phrased, so that scientists can side-step them with
generalities about the common responsibility, and who voted the cred-
its for atomic research anyway; which are perfectly just, but not at all
relevant. That is not the heart of the matter; and the people in queues
and pubs are humbly groping for the heart. They are not good at saying things and they do not give model answers to interviewers. But
when they say "We've forgotten what's right," when they say "We're
not fit to handle such things," what is in their minds is perfectly true.
Science and society are out of joint. Science has given to no one in
particular a power which no one in particular knows how to use. Why
do not scientists invent something sensible? Wives say it every time
they stub their toe on the waste bin, and husbands say it whenever a
fuse blows. Why is it the business of no one in particular to stop fitting
science for death and to begin fitting it into our lives? We will agree
that warlike science is no more than a by-product of a warlike society.
Science has merely provided the means, for good or for bad; and society has seized it for bad. But what are we going to do about it?

11   The first thing to do, it seems to me, is to treat this as a scientific
question: by which I mean as a practical and sensible question, which
deserves a factual approach and a reasoned answer. Now that I have
apologised on behalf of scientists, and this on a scale which some of
them will certainly think too ample, let us cut out what usually happens
to the argument at this point, the rush of recriminations. The scientists
are conscious of their mistakes; and I do not want to discuss the mistakes of non-scientists — although they have made a great many —
except those which we all must begin to make good.

12   I have said that a scientific answer must be practical as well as sensible. This really rules out at once the panaceas which also tend to run

the argument into a blind alley at this stage; the panaceas which say summarily "Get rid of them." Naturally, it does not seem to me to be sensible to get rid of scientists; but in any case, it plainly is not practical. And whatever we do with our own scientists, it very plainly is not practical to get rid of the scientists of rival nations; because if there existed the conditions for agreement among nations on this far-reaching scheme, then the conditions for war would already have disappeared. If there existed the conditions for international agreement, say to suspend all scientific research, or to abandon warlike research, or in any other way to forgo science as an instrument of nationalism — if such agreements could be reached, then they would already be superfluous; because the conditions for war would already have disappeared. So, however we might sigh for Samuel Butler's panacea in *Erewhon,* simply to give up all machines, there is no point in talking about it. I believe it would be a disaster for mankind like the coming of the Dark Ages. But there is no point in arguing this. It just is not practical, nationally or internationally.

13   There are no panaceas at all; and we had better face that. There is nothing that we can do overnight, in a week or a month, which can straighten by a laying on of hands the ancient distortion of our society. Do not let us fancy that any one of us out of the blue will concoct that stirring letter to *The Times* which will change the black mood of history — and the instructions to diplomats. Putting scientists in the Cabinet will not do that, and women in the War Office will not, nor will bishops in the Privy Council. There are no panaceas. We are the heirs to a tradition which has left science and society out of step. The man in the street is right: we have never learnt to handle such things. Nothing will do but that we learn. But learning is not done in a year. Our ultimate survival is in our own hands. Our survival while we are learning is a much chancier thing. We had better be realistic about that.

14   Meanwhile we had better settle down to work for our ultimate survival; and we had better start now. We have seen that the diagnosis has turned out to be not very difficult. Science and our social habits are out of step. And the cure is no deeper either. We must learn to match them. And there is no way of learning this unless we learn to understand *both.*

V

15 Of the two, of course, the one which is strange is science. I have already blamed the scientist for that. He has been the monk of our age, timid, thwarted, anxious to be asked to help; and with a secret ambition to play the Grey Eminence. Through the years of childhood poverty he dreamt of this. Scientific skill was a blue door beckoning to him, which would open into the society of dignitaries of state. But the private motives of scientists are not the trend of science. The trend of science is made by the needs of society: navigation before the eighteenth century, manufacture thereafter; and in our age I believe the liberation of personality. Whatever the part which scientists like to act, or for that matter which painters like to dress, science shares the aims of our society just as art does. The difficulties of understanding either are not fundamental; they are difficulties only of language. To

grow familiar with the large ideas of science calls for patience and an effort of attention; and I hope I have shown that it repays them.

16   For two hundred years, these ideas have been applied to technical needs; and they have made our world anew, triumphantly, from top to toe. Our shoes are tanned and stitched, our clothes are spun and dyed and woven, we are lighted and carried and doctored by means which were unknown to neat Mr. Pope at Twickenham in 1740. We may not think it recompenses us for the absence of any Mr. Pope from Twickenham today; we may even hold it responsible. It is certainly not a spiritual achievement. But it has not yet tried to be. It has applied its ideas monotonously to shoe leather and bicycle bells. And it has made a superb job of them. Compare its record in its own field with that of any other ideas of the same age: Burke's ideas of the imagination, or Bentham's on government, or Adam Smith's on political economy. If any ideas have a claim to be called creative, because they have created something, then certainly it is the ideas of science.

17   We may think that all that science has created is comfort; and it certainly has done that—the very word "comfortable" in the modern sense dates from the Industrial Revolution. But have we always stopped to think what science has done not to our mode of living but to our life? We talk about research for death, the threat of war and the number of civilians who get killed. But have we always weighed this against the increase in our own life span? Let us do a small sum. The number of people killed in Great Britain in six years of war by German bombs, flying bombs, and V2's was sixty thousand. They were an average lot of people, which means that on an average they lost half their expectation of life. Quite an easy long division shows that the effect of this in our population of fifty million people was to shorten the average span of life by less than one tenth of one per cent. This is considerably less than a fortnight. Put this on the debit side. And on the credit side, we know that in the last hundred years the average span of life in England has increased by twenty years. That is the price of science, take it or leave it—a fortnight for twenty years of life. And these twenty years have been created by applying to daily life, to clothing and bedding, to hygiene and infection, to birth and death, the simple ideas of science—the fundamental ideas I have been talking about: order, cause, and chance. If any ideas have a claim to be called creative, because they have created life, it is the ideas of science.

VI

18   We have not neglected these ideas altogether in our social organisation. But it is a point I have made several times—we have got hopelessly behind with them. The idea of order is now old enough to have reached at least our filing cabinets. The idea of cause and effect has entered our habits, until it has become the new *a priori* in the making of administrative plans. The difficulty is to dislodge it, now that it is hardening into a scholastic formula. For the idea which has given a new vigour to science in our generation is larger than the machinery of cause and effect. It stipulates no special mechanism between the present and the future. It is content to predict the future, without in-

sisting that the computation must follow the steps of causal law. I have called this the idea of chance, because its method is statistical, and because it recognises that every prediction carries with it its own measurable uncertainty. A good prediction is one which defines its area of uncertainty; a bad prediction ignores it. And at bottom this is no more than the return to the essentially empirical, the experimental nature of science. Science is a great many things, and I have called them a great many names; but in the end they all return to this: science is the acceptance of what works and the rejection of what does not. That needs more courage than we might think.

19   It needs more courage than we have ever found when we have faced our worldly problems. This is how society has lost touch with science: because it has hesitated to judge itself by the same impersonal code of what works and what does not. We have clung to Adam Smith and Burke, or we have agitated for Plato and Aquinas, through wars and famine, through rising and falling birth-rates, and through libraries of learned argument. And in the end, our eyes have always wandered from the birth-rate to the argument: from the birth-rate to what we have wanted to believe. Here is the crux of what I have been saying. Here is our ultimate hope of saving ourselves from extinction. We must learn to understand that the content of all knowledge is empirical; that its test is whether it works; and we must learn to act on that understanding in the world as well as in the laboratory.

20   This is the message of science: our ideas must be realistic, flexible, unbigoted — they must be human, they must create their own authority. If any ideas have a claim to be called creative, because they have liberated that creative impulse, it is the ideas of science.

VII

21   This is not only a material code. On the contrary, my hope is that it may heal the spiritual cleft which two wars have uncovered. I have seen in my lifetime an abyss open in the human mind: a gulf between the endeavor to be man, and the relish in being brute. The scientist has indeed had a hand in this, and every other specialist too, with his prim detachment and his oracular airs. But of course, the large strain which has opened this fault is social. We have made men live in two halves, a Sunday half and a workday one. We have ordered them to love their neighbour and to turn the other cheek, in a society which has constantly compelled them to shoulder their neighbour aside and to turn their backs. So we have created a savage sense of failure which, as we know now to our cost, can be tapped with an ease which is frightening; and which can thrust up, with explosive force, a symbol to repeat to an unhappy people its most degrading dream.

22   Can science heal that neurotic flaw in us? If science cannot, then nothing can. Let us stop pretending. There is no cure in high moral precepts. We have preached them too long to men who are forced to live how they can: *that* makes the strain which they have not been able to bear. We need an ethic which is moral *and* which works. It is often said that science has destroyed our values and put nothing in their place. What has really happened of course is that science has

shown in harsh relief the division between our values and our world. We have not begun to let science get into our heads; where then was it supposed to create these values? We have used it as a machine without will, the conjured spirit to do the chores. I believe that science can create values: and will create them precisely as literature does, by looking into the human personality; by discovering what divides it and what cements it. That is how great writers have explored man, and this whether they themselves as men have been driven by the anguish in *Gulliver's Travels* or the sympathy in *Moll Flanders*. The insight of science is not different from that of the arts. Science will create values, I believe, and discover virtues, when it looks into man; when it explores what makes him man and not an animal, and what makes his societies human and not animal packs.

23   I believe that we can reach this unity in our culture. . . . Nations in their great ages have not been great in art or science, but in art and science. Rembrandt was the contemporary of Huygens and Spinoza. At that very time, Isaac Newton walked with Dryden and Christopher Wren. We know that ours is a remarkable age of science. It is for us to use it to broaden and to liberate our culture. These are the marks of science: that it is open for all to hear, and all are free to speak their minds in it. They are marks of the world at its best, and the human spirit at its most challenging.

Discussion of Theme

1. In paragraph 7 Bronowski dismisses the argument that nations might be forced to "give up war for lack of cannon fodder. This hope has never been fulfilled, . . ." Was the present resistance to the draft and to wars a sign that the argument has been dismissed prematurely?
2. What support does the author give for his statement that "Science has enlarged the mechanism of war, and it has distorted it"?
3. Who, according to Bronowski, bears the basic responsibility for the weapons used to wage modern warfare? Does he excuse the scientist entirely?
4. According to Bronowski, what are the causes of war?
5. Describe the "spiritual cleft which two wars have uncovered."

Discussion of Rhetoric

1. Why does the author divide the article into sections? Is there different focus on the thesis in each section?
2. What is the relation between the opening anecdote and the central idea of this selection?
3. In what paragraph does Bronowski state his central theme? How does he prepare the reader for his thesis?
4. What is the purpose of the references in paragraphs 5 and 6? In paragraph 23?

5. How does Bronowski avoid alienating his nonscientific reader?
6. In paragraph 7 the author uses the phrase "frighten people into their wits." What is the force of such an alteration of a cliché?

Writing Assignments

1. In the long run, has science done more to support life than to destroy it? Give specific illustrations.
2. Analyze the responsibility of the scientist during war. Does he have the right to refuse to work on the development of weapons?
3. The medieval period is known as the Age of Faith; it has been said that the twentieth century will be known as the Age of Science. State your observations on this idea.
4. The English scientist and novelist C. P. Snow says that our age is breaking up into two cultures — the arts and the sciences. Give some arguments for this view.

Library Exploration

1. What was the SALT conference? What has it accomplished? What nations now possess the H-bomb? Does this increase the possibility of war?
2. Investigate the deliberations that led to the decision to drop the atom bomb in World War II.
3. If you are not familiar with the following references, look them up: Lamarck, Fiume, and the Polish Corridor.

Vocabulary

(1) MACABRE gruesome
(1) CONJURES summons as if by magic
(2) EPITOME embodiment; ideal expression
(3) EXTINCT died out; vanished (said of a species)
(4) SCAPEGOAT whipping boy; someone to blame
(5) IDIOSYNCRASIES peculiarities
(6) QUEUE waiting line
(6) DISTORTED twisted; perverted
(8) BATTENS fattens; grows prosperous
(9) CLEAVAGE split
(10) INDICTMENTS accusations; formal charges
(11) RECRIMINATIONS counter-charges
(12) PANACEAS cure-alls
(13) CONCOCT devise; fabricate
(15) GREY EMINENCE a person who exercises power behind the scenes
(16) RECOMPENSES makes up for; pays back
(17) FORTNIGHT a period of fourteen nights, or two weeks
(18) A PRIORI something that is true or false by definition or convention alone
(19) EMPIRICAL based on observation or experience
(20) UNBIGOTED unprejudiced
(21) ORACULAR pronouncing divine wisdom
(22) ETHIC code of behavior

C. P. Snow (1905–   ) is a distinguished English scientist and novelist. At the beginning of the Second World War he left his teaching post at Cambridge University to administer scientific programs for the British government. Since 1940 he has published eight novels in a series known by the title of the first novel, "Strangers and Brothers."

His general audience probably knows Snow best for his theory that the intellectuals are divided into two distinct "cultures": the literary and the scientific. Here he argues for closing the cultural gap.

C. P. SNOW

The Two Cultures

1   It is about three years since I made a sketch in print of a problem which had been on my mind for some time.[1] It was a problem I could not avoid just because of the circumstances of my life. The only credentials I had to ruminate on the subject at all came through those circumstances, through nothing more than a set of chances. Anyone with similar experience would have seen much the same things and I think made very much the same comments about them. It just happened to be an unusual experience. By training I was a scientist: by vocation I was a writer. That was all. It was a piece of luck, if you like, that arose through coming from a poor home.

2   But my personal history isn't the point now. All that I need say is that I came to Cambridge and did a bit of research here at a time of major scientific activity. I was privileged to have a ringside view of one of the most wonderful creative periods in all physics. And it

[1]"The Two Cultures," *New Statesman*, 6 October 1956.

happened through the flukes of war—including meeting W. L. Bragg in the buffet on Kettering station on a very cold morning in 1939, which had a determining influence on my practical life—that I was able, and indeed morally forced, to keep that ringside view ever since. So for thirty years I have had to be in touch with scientists not only out of curiosity, but as part of a working existence. During the same thirty years I was trying to shape the books I wanted to write which in due course took me among writers.

3   There had been plenty of days when I have spent the working hours with scientists and then gone off at night with some literary colleagues. I mean that literally. I have had, of course, intimate friends among both scientists and writers. It was through living among these groups and much more, I think, through moving regularly from one to the other and back again that I got occupied with the problem of what, long before I put it on paper, I christened to myself as the "two cultures." For constantly I felt I was moving among two groups—comparable in intelligence, identical in race, not grossly different in social origin, earning about the same incomes, who had almost ceased to communicate at all, who in intellectual, moral and psychological climate had so little in common that instead of going from Burlington House or South Kensington to Chelsea, one might have crossed an ocean.

4   In fact, one had traveled much further than across an ocean—because after a few thousand Atlantic miles, one found Greenwich Village talking precisely the same language as Chelsea, and both having about as much communication with M.I.T. as though the scientists spoke nothing but Tibetan. For this is not just our problem; owing to some of our educational and social idiosyncrasies, it is slightly exaggerated here; owing to another English social peculiarity it is slightly minimised; by and large this is a problem of the entire West.

5   By this I intend something serious. I am not thinking of the pleasant story of how one of the more convivial Oxford great dons—I have heard the story attributed to A. L. Smith—came over to Cambridge to dine. The date is perhaps the 1890's. I think it must have been at St. John's, or possibly Trinity. Anyway, Smith was sitting at the right hand of the President—or Vice-Master—and he was a man who liked to include all round him in the conversation, although he was not immediately encouraged by the expressions of his neighbours. He addressed some cheerful Oxonian chit-chat at the one opposite to him, and got a grunt. He then tried the man on his own right hand and got another grunt. Then, rather to his surprise, one looked at the other and said, "Do you know what he's talking about?" "I haven't the least idea." At this, even Smith was getting out of his depth. But the President, acting as a social emollient, put him at his ease, by saying, "Oh, those are mathematicians! We never talk to *them*."

6   No, I intend something serious. I believe the intellectual life of the western society is increasingly being split into two polar groups. When I say the intellectual life, I mean to include also a large part of our practical life, because I should be the last person to suggest the two can at the deepest level be distinguished. I shall come back to the

practical life a little later. Two polar groups: at one pole we have the literary intellectuals, who incidentally while no one was looking took to referring to themselves as "intellectuals" as though there were no others. I remember G. H. Hardy once remarking to me in mild puzzlement, some time in the 1930's: "Have you noticed how the word 'intellectual' is used nowadays? There seems to be a new definition which certainly doesn't include Rutherford or Eddington or Dirac or Adrian or me. It does seem rather odd, don't y' know."[2]

7   Literary intellectuals at one pole — at the other scientists, and as the most representative, the physical scientists. Between the two a gulf of mutual incomprehension — sometimes (particularly among the young) hostility and dislike, but most of all lack of understanding. They have a curious distorted image of each other. Their attitudes are so different that, even on the level of emotion, they can't find much common ground. Non-scientists tend to think of scientists as brash and boastful. They hear Mr. T. S. Eliot, who just for these illustrations we can take as an archetypal figure, saying about his attempts to revive verse-drama, that we can hope for very little, but that he would feel content if he and his co-workers could prepare the ground for a new Kyd or a new Greene. That is the one, restricted and constrained, with which literary intellectuals are at home: it is the subdued voice of their culture. Then they hear a much louder voice, that of another archetypal figure, Rutherford, trumpeting: "This is the heroic age of science! This is the Elizabethan age!" Many of us heard that, and a good many other statements beside which that was mild; and we weren't left in any doubt whom Rutherford was casting for the role of Shakespeare. What is hard for the literary intellectuals to understand, imaginatively or intellectually, is that he was absolutely right.

8   And compare "this is the way the world ends, not with a bang but a whimper" — incidentally, one of the least likely scientific prophecies ever made — compare that with Rutherford's famous repartee, "Lucky fellow, Rutherford, always on the crest of the wave." "Well, I made the wave, didn't I?"

9   The non-scientists have a rooted impression that the scientists are shallowly optimistic, unaware of man's condition. On the other hand, the scientists believe that the literary intellectuals are totally lacking in foresight, peculiarly unconcerned with their brother man, in a deep sense anti-intellectual, anxious to restrict both art and thought to the existential moment. And so on. Anyone with a mild talent for invective could produce plenty of this kind of subterranean back-chat. On each side there is some of it which is not entirely baseless. It is all destructive. Much of it rests on misinterpretations which are dangerous. I should like to deal with two of the most profound of these now, one on each side.

10   First, about the scientists' optimism. This is an accusation which has

---

[2]This lecture was delivered to a Cambridge audience, and so I used some points of reference which I did not need to explain. G. H. Hardy, 1877–1947, was one of the most distinguished pure mathematicians of his time, and a picturesque figure in Cambridge both as a young don and on his return in 1931 to the Sadleirian Chair of Mathematics.

been made so often that it has become a platitude. It has been made by some of the acutest nonscientific minds of the day. But it depends upon a confusion between the individual experience and the social experience, between the individual condition of man and his social condition. Most of the scientists I have known well have felt—just as deeply as the non-scientists I have known well—that the individual condition of each of us is tragic. Each of us is alone: sometimes we escape from solitariness, through love or affection or perhaps creative moments, but those triumphs of life are pools of light we make for ourselves while the edge of the road is black; each of us dies alone. Some scientists I have known have had faith in revealed religion. Perhaps with them the sense of the tragic condition is not so strong. I don't know. With most people of deep feeling, however high-spirited and happy they are, sometimes most with those who are happiest and most high-spirited, it seems to be right in the fibres, part of the weight of life. That is as true of the scientists I have known best as of anyone at all.

11 But nearly all of them—and this is where the colour of hope genuinely comes in—would see no reason why, just because the individual condition is tragic, so must the social condition be. Each of us is solitary: each of us dies alone: all right, that's a fate against which we can't struggle—but there is plenty in our condition which is not fate, and against which we are less than human unless we do struggle.

12 Most of our fellow human beings, for instance, are underfed and die before their time. In the crudest terms, *that* is the social condition. There is a moral trap which comes through the insight into man's loneliness: it tempts one to sit back, complacent in one's unique tragedy, and let the others go without a meal.

13 As a group, the scientists fall into that trap less than others. They are inclined to be impatient to see if something can be done: and inclined to think that it can be done, until it's proved otherwise. That is their real optimism, and it's an optimism that the rest of us badly need.

14 In reverse, the same spirit, tough and good and determined to fight it out at the side of their brother man, has made scientists regard the other culture's social attitudes as contemptible. That is too facile: some of them are, but they are a temporary phase and not to be taken as representative.

15 I remember being cross-examined by a scientist of distinction. "Why do most writers take on social opinions which would have been thought distinctly uncivilised and démodé at the time of the Plantagenets? Wasn't that true of most of the famous twentieth-century writers? Yeats, Pound, Wyndham Lewis, nine out of ten of those who have dominated literary sensibility in our time—weren't they not only politically silly, but politically wicked? Didn't the influence of all they represent bring Auschwitz that much nearer?"

16 I thought at the time, and I still think, that the correct answer was not to defend the indefensible. It was no use saying that Yeats, according to friends whose judgment I trust, was a man of singular magnanimity of character, as well as a great poet. It was no use denying the facts, which are broadly true. The honest answer was that there is, in fact, a connection, which literary persons were culpably slow to see,

between some kinds of early twentieth-century art and the most imbecile expressions of anti-social feeling.[3] That was one reason, among many, why some of us turned our backs on the art and tried to hack out a new or different way for ourselves.[4]

17   But though many of those writers dominated literary sensibility for a generation, that is no longer so, or at least to nothing like the same extent. Literature changes more slowly than science. It hasn't the same automatic corrective, and so its misguided periods are longer. But it is ill-considered of scientists to judge writers on the evidence of the period 1914–50.

18   Those are two of the misunderstandings between the two cultures. I should say, since I began to talk about them—the two cultures, that is—I have had some criticism. Most of my scientific acquaintances think that there is something in it, and so do most of the practising artists I know. But I have been argued with by non-scientists of strong down-to-earth interests. Their view is that it is an over-simplification, and that if one is going to talk in these terms there ought to be at least three cultures. They argue that, though they are not scientists themselves, they would share a good deal of the scientific feeling. They would have as little use—perhaps, since they knew more about it, even less use—for the recent literary culture as the scientists themselves. J. H. Plumb, Alan Bullock and some of my American sociological friends have said that they vigorously refuse to be corralled in a cultural box with people they wouldn't be seen dead with, or to be regarded as helping to produce a climate which would not permit of social hope.

19   I respect those arguments. The number 2 is a very dangerous number: that is why the dialectic is a dangerous process. Attempts to divide anything into two ought to be regarded with much suspicion. I have thought a long time about going in for further refinements: but in the end I have decided against. I was searching for something a little more than a dashing metaphor, a good deal less than a cultural map: and for those purposes the two cultures is about right, and subtilising any more would bring more disadvantages than it's worth.

20   At one pole, the scientific culture really is a culture, not only in an intellectual but also in an anthropological sense. That is, its members need not, and of course often do not, always completely understand each other; biologists more often than not will have a pretty hazy idea of contemporary physics; but there are common attitudes, common standards and patterns of behaviour, common approaches and assumptions. This goes surprisingly wide and deep. It cuts across other mental patterns, such as those of religion or politics or class.

21   Statistically, I suppose slightly more scientists are in religious terms unbelievers, compared with the rest of the intellectual world—though there are plenty who are religious, and that seems to be increasingly

[3] I said a little more about this connection in *The Times Literary Supplement,* "Challenge to the Intellect," 15 August 1958. I hope some day to carry the analysis further.

[4] It would be more accurate to say that, for literary reasons, we felt the prevailing literary modes were useless to us. We were, however, reinforced in that feeling when it occurred to us that those prevailing modes went hand in hand with social attitudes either wicked, or absurd, or both.

so among the young. Statistically also, slightly more scientists are on the Left in open politics — though again, plenty always have called themselves conservatives, and that also seems to be more common among the young. Compared with the rest of the intellectual world, considerably more scientists in this country and probably in the U.S. come from poor families.[5] Yet, over a whole range of thought and behaviour, none of that matters very much. In their working, and in much of their emotional life, their attitudes are closer to other scientists than to non-scientists who in religion or politics or class have the same labels as themselves. If I were to risk a piece of shorthand, I should say that naturally they had the future in their bones.

22   They may or may not like it, but they have it. That was as true of the conservatives J. J. Thomson and Lindemann as of the radicals Einstein or Blackett: as true of the Christian A. H. Compton as of the materialist Bernal: of the aristocrats Broglie or Russell as of the proletarian Faraday: of those born rich, like Thomas Merton or Victor Rothschild, as of Rutherford, who was the son of an odd-job handyman. Without thinking about it, they respond alike. That is what a culture means.

23   At the other pole, the spread of attitudes is wider. It is obvious that between the two, as one moves through intellectual society from the physicists to the literary intellectuals, there are all kinds of tones of feeling on the way. But I believe the pole of total incomprehension of science radiates its influences on all the rest. That total incomprehension gives, much more pervasively than we realise, living in it, an unscientific flavour to the whole "traditional" culture, and that unscientific flavour is often, much more than we admit, on the point of turning anti-scientific. The feelings of one pole become the anti-feelings of the other. If the scientists have the future in their bones, then the traditional culture responds by wishing the future did not exist.[6] It is the traditional culture, to an extent remarkably little diminished by the emergence of the scientific one, which manages the western world.

24   This polarisation is sheer loss to us all. To us as people, and to our society. It is at the same time a practical and intellectual and creative loss, and I repeat that it is false to imagine that those three considerations are clearly separable. But for a moment I want to concentrate on the intellectual loss.

25   The degree of incomprehension on both sides is the kind of joke which has gone sour. There are about fifty thousand working scientists in the country and about eighty thousand professional engineers or applied scientists. During the war and in the years since, my colleagues and I have had to interview somewhere between thirty to forty thousand of these — that is, about 25 per cent. The number is large enough to give us a fair sample, though of the men we talked to most would still be under forty. We were able to find out a certain amount of what they read and thought about. I confess that even I,

---

    [5]An analysis of the schools from which Fellows of the Royal Society come tells its own story. The distribution is markedly different from that of, for example, members of the Foreign Service or Queen's Counsel.
    [6]Compare George Orwell's *1984*, which is the strongest possible wish that the future should not exist, with J. D. Bernal's *World without War*.

who am fond of them and respect them, was a bit shaken. We hadn't quite expected that the links with the traditional culture should be so tenuous, nothing more than a formal touch of the cap.

26   As one would expect, some of the very best scientists had and have plenty of energy and interest to spare, and we came across several who had read everything that literary people talk about. But that's very rare. Most of the rest, when one tried to probe for what books they had read, would modestly confess, "Well, I've *tried* a bit of Dickens," rather as though Dickens were an extraordinarily esoteric, tangled and dubiously rewarding writer, something like Rainer Maria Rilke. In fact that is exactly how they do regard him: we thought that discovery, that Dickens had been transformed into the type-specimen of literary incomprehensibility, was one of the oddest results of the whole exercise.

27   But of course, in reading him, in reading almost any writer whom we should value, they are just touching their caps to the traditional culture. They have their own culture, intensive, rigorous, and constantly in action. This culture contains a great deal of argument, usually much more rigorous, and almost always at a higher conceptual level, than literary persons' arguments — even though the scientists do cheerfully use words in senses which literary persons don't recognise, the senses are exact ones, and when they talk about "subjective," "objective," "philosophy" or "progressive,"[7] they know what they mean, even though it isn't what one is accustomed to expect.

28   Remember, these are very intelligent men. Their culture is in many ways an exacting and admirable one. It doesn't contain much art, with the exception, an important exception, of music. Verbal exchange, insistent argument. Long-playing records. Colour-photography. The ear, to some extent the eye. Books, very little, though perhaps not many would go so far as one hero, who perhaps I should admit was further down the scientific ladder than the people I've been talking about — who when asked what books he read, replied firmly and confidently: "Books? I prefer to use my books as tools." It was very hard not to let the mind wander — what sort of tool would a book make? Perhaps a hammer? A primitive digging instrument?

29   Of books, though, very little. And of the books which to most literary persons are bread and butter, novels, history, poetry, plays, almost nothing at all. It isn't that they're not interested in the psychological or moral or social life. In the social life, they certainly are, more than most of us. In the moral, they are by and large the soundest group of intellectuals we have; there is a moral component right in the grain of science itself, and almost all scientists form their own judgments of the moral life. In the psychological they have as much interest as most of us, though occasionally I fancy they come to it rather late. It isn't that they lack the interests. It is much more that the whole literature of the traditional culture doesn't seem to them relevant to those interests.

_____
    [7] *Subjective,* in contemporary technological jargon, means "divided according to subjects." *Objective* means "directed towards an object." *Philosophy* means "general intellectual approach or attitude" (for example, a scientist's "philosophy of guided weapons" might lead him to propose certain kinds of "objective research"). A "progressive" job means one with possibilities of promotion.

They are, of course, dead wrong. As a result, their imaginative under-standing is less than it could be. They are self-impoverished.

30   But what about the other side? They are impoverished too — per-haps more seriously, because they are vainer about it. They still like to pretend that the traditional culture is the whole of "culture," as though the natural order didn't exist. As though the exploration of the natural order was of no interest either in its own value or its conse-quences. As though the scientific edifice of the physical world was not, in its intellectual depth, complexity and articulation, the most beauti-ful and wonderful collective work of the mind of man. Yet most non-scientists have no conception of that edifice at all. Even if they want to have it, they can't. It is rather as though, over an immense range of intellectual experience, a whole group was tone-deaf. Except that this tone-deafness doesn't come by nature, but by training, or rather the absence of training.

31   As with the tone-deaf, they don't know what they miss. They give a pitying chuckle at the news of scientists who have never read a major work of English literature. They dismiss them as ignorant specialists. Yet their own ignorance and their own specialisation is just as start-ling. A good many times I have been present at gatherings of people who, by the standards of the traditional culture, are thought highly educated and who have with considerable gusto been expressing their incredulity at the illiteracy of scientists. Once or twice I have been provoked and have asked the company how many of them could describe the Second Law of Thermodynamics. The response was cold: it was also negative. Yet I was asking something which is about the scientific equivalent of: *Have you read a work of Shakespeare's?*

32   I now believe that if I had asked an even simpler question — such as, What do you mean by mass, or acceleration, which is the scientific equivalent of saying, *Can you read?* — not more than one in ten of the highly educated would have felt that I was speaking the same lan-guage. So the great edifice of modern physics goes up, and the ma-jority of the cleverest people in the western world have about as much insight into it as their neolithic ancestors would have had.

33   Just one more of those questions, that my non-scientific friends re-gard as being in the worst of taste. Cambridge is a university where scientists and non-scientists meet every night at dinner.[8] About two years ago, one of the most astonishing experiments in the whole his-tory of science was brought off. I don't mean the sputnik — that was admirable for quite different reasons, as a feat of organisation and a triumphant use of existing knowledge. No, I mean the experiment at Columbia by Yang and Lee. It is an experiment of the greatest beauty and originality, but the result is so startling that one forgets how beau-tiful the experiment is. It makes us think again about some of the fun-damentals of the physical world. Intuition, common sense — they are neatly stood on their heads. The result is usually known as the con-tradiction of parity. If there were any serious communication between the two cultures, this experiment would have been talked about at

---

[8]Almost all college High Tables contain Fellows in both scientific and non-scientific subjects.

every High Table in Cambridge. Was it? I wasn't here: but I should like to ask the question.

34   There seems then to be no place where the cultures meet. I am not going to waste time saying that this is a pity. It is much worse than that. Soon I shall come to some practical consequences. But at the heart of thought and creation we are letting some of our best chances go by default. The clashing point of two subjects, two disciplines, two cultures—of two galaxies, so far as that goes—ought to produce creative chances. In the history of mental activity that has been where some of the breakthroughs came. The chances are there now. But they are there, as it were, in a vacuum, because those in the two cultures can't talk to each other. It is bizarre how very little of twentieth-century science has been assimilated into twentieth-century art. Now and then one used to find poets conscientiously using scientific expressions, and getting them wrong—there was a time when "refraction" kept cropping up in verse in a mystifying fashion, and when "polarised light" was used as though writers were under the illusion that it was a specially admirable kind of light.

35   Of course, that isn't the way that science could be any good to art. It has got to be assimilated along with, and as part and parcel of, the whole of our mental experience, and used as naturally as the rest.

36   I said earlier that this cultural divide is not just an English phenomenon: it exists all over the western world. But it probably seems at its sharpest in England, for two reasons. One is our fanatical belief in educational specialisation, which is much more deeply ingrained in us than in any country in the world, east or west. The other is our tendency to let our social forms crystallise. This tendency appears to get stronger, not weaker, the more we iron out economic inequalities: and this is specially true in education. It means that once anything like a cultural divide gets established, all the social forces operate to make it not less rigid, but more so.

37   The two cultures were already dangerously separate sixty years ago; but a prime minister like Lord Salisbury could have his own laboratory at Hatfield, and Arthur Balfour had a somewhat more than amateur interest in natural science. John Anderson did some research in organic chemistry in Würzburg before passing first into the Civil Service, and incidentally took a spread of subjects which is now impossible.[9] None of that degree of interchange at the top of the Establishment is likely, or indeed thinkable, now.[10]

38   In fact, the separation between the scientists and non-scientists is much less bridgeable among the young than it was even thirty years ago. Thirty years ago the cultures had long ceased to speak to each other: but at least they managed a kind of frozen smile across the gulf. Now the politeness has gone, and they just make faces. It is not only

[9] He took the examination in 1905.

[10] It is, however, true to say that the compact nature of the managerial layers of English society—the fact that "everyone knows everyone else"—means that scientists and non-scientists do in fact know each other as people more easily than in most countries. It is also true that a good many leading politicians and administrators keep up lively intellectual and artistic interests to a much greater extent, so far as I can judge, than is the case in the U.S. These are both among our assets.

that the young scientists now feel that they are part of a culture on the rise while the other is in retreat. It is also, to be brutal, that the young scientists know that with an indifferent degree they'll get a comfortable job, while their contemporaries and counterparts in English or History will be lucky to earn 60 per cent as much. No young scientist of any talent would feel that he isn't wanted or that his work is ridiculous, as did the hero of *Lucky Jim*, and in fact, some of the disgruntlement of Amis and his associates is the disgruntlement of the underemployed arts graduate.

39   There is only one way out of all this: it is, of course, by rethinking our education. In this country, for the two reasons I have given, that is more difficult than in any other. Nearly everyone will agree that our school education is too specialised. But nearly everyone feels that it is outside the will of man to alter it. Other countries are as dissatisfied with their education as we are, but are not so resigned.

40   The U.S. teach out of proportion more children up to eighteen than we do: they teach them far more widely, but nothing like so rigorously. They know that: they are hoping to take the problem in hand within ten years, though they may not have all that time to spare. The U.S.S.R. also teach out of proportion more children than we do: they also teach far more widely than we do (it is an absurd western myth that their school education is specialised) but much too rigorously.[11] They know that—and they are beating about to get it right. The Scandinavians, in particular the Swedes, who would make a more sensible job of it than any of us, are handicapped by their practical need to devote an inordinate amount of time to foreign languages. But they too are seized of the problem.

41   Are we? Have we crystallised so far that we are no longer flexible at all?

42   Talk to schoolmasters, and they say that our intense specialisation, like nothing else on earth, is dictated by the Oxford and Cambridge scholarship examinations. If that is so, one would have thought it not utterly impracticable to change the Oxford and Cambridge scholarship examinations. Yet one would underestimate the national capacity for the intricate defensive to believe that that was easy. All the lessons of our educational history suggest we are only capable of increasing specialisation, not decreasing it.

43   Somehow we have set ourselves the task of producing a tiny *élite*— far smaller proportionately than in any comparable country—educated in one academic skill. For a hundred and fifty years in Cambridge it was mathematics: then it was mathematics or classics: then natural science was allowed in. But still the choice had to be a single one.

44   It may well be that this process has gone too far to be reversible. I have given reasons why I think it is a disastrous process, for the purpose of a living culture. I am going on to give reasons why I think it is fatal, if we're to perform our practical tasks in the world. But I can think of only one example, in the whole of English educational history,

[11] I tried to compare American, Soviet and English education in "New Minds for the New World," *New Statesman*, 6 September 1956.

where our pursuit of specialised mental exercises was resisted with success.

45   It was done here in Cambridge, fifty years ago, when the old order-of-merit in the Mathematical Tripos was abolished. For over a hundred years, the nature of the Tripos had been crystallising. The competition for the top places had got fiercer, and careers hung on them. In most colleges, certainly in my own, if one managed to come out as Senior or Second Wrangler, one was elected a Fellow out of hand. A whole apparatus of coaching had grown up. Men of the quality of Hardy, Littlewood, Russell, Eddington, Jeans, Keynes, went in for two or three years' training for an examination which was intensely competitive and intensely difficult. Most people in Cambridge were very proud of it, with a similar pride to that which almost anyone in England always has for our existing educational institutions, whatever they happen to be. If you study the fly-sheets of the time, you will find the passionate arguments for keeping the examination precisely as it was to all eternity: it was the only way to keep up standards, it was the only fair test of merit, indeed, the only seriously objective test in the world. The arguments, in fact, were almost exactly those which are used today with precisely the same passionate sincerity if anyone suggests that the scholarship examinations might conceivably not be immune from change.

46   In every respect but one, in fact, the old Mathematical Tripos seemed perfect. The one exception, however, appeared to some to be rather important. It was simply — so the young creative mathematicians, such as Hardy and Littlewood, kept saying — that the training had no intellectual merit at all. They went a little further, and said that the Tripos had killed serious mathematics in England stone dead for a hundred years. Well, even in academic controversy, that took some skirting round, and they got their way. But I have an impression that Cambridge was a good deal more flexible between 1850 and 1914 than it has been in our time. If we had had the old Mathematical Tripos firmly planted among us, should we have ever managed to abolish it?

Discussion of Theme

1. Do you believe, as Snow apparently does, that a gulf exists between young scientists and nonscientists in part because the former know "they'll get a comfortable job, while their contemporaries and counterparts in English or History will be lucky to earn 60 percent as much"? Is this a purely British attitude, or does it also exist in America?
2. What charges does Snow bring against scientists? Against literary people?
3. Why should the two cultures understand each other?
4. Does Snow suggest that the gap between the scientist and the literary scholar is a recent phenomenon, or one that dates from earliest times?

Discussion of Rhetoric

1. Note the poetry quoted in the first line of paragraph 8. What does it mean? In what poem do you find it? Why is this particular line so frequently quoted?
2. This essay is developed through comparison and contrast. How does this method determine the organization of the author's ideas?
3. How does Snow establish his authority in the opening paragraphs?
4. What is the purpose of the anecdote in paragraph 5?
5. What kinds of words does Snow use to connect paragraphs 10, 11, 13, and 14?

Writing Assignments

1. In paragraph 15 Snow reports a conversation with a fellow scientist who believes that writers, because of their "uncivilized" social opinions, are responsible for wars. How valid is his argument?
2. What is your concept of an intellectual? Describe the general attributes of such a person, and offer illustrations from either real life or from literature.
3. Give your definition of an educated man (500 words).
4. Examine some of the ways that American education can help close the cultural gap.

Library Exploration

1. An excellent introduction to Snow as a novelist is *The Masters*. Read and report on this or another of his novels.
2. Investigate the controversy between F. R. Leavis, the English literary critic, and Snow.

Vocabulary

(1) RUMINATE   reflect
(2) FLUKES   chances; strokes of luck
(5) CONVIVIAL   sociable; jovial
(5) EMOLLIENT   soothing salve
(7) INCOMPREHENSION   lack of understanding
(7) ARCHETYPAL   model; pattern-setting
(8) REPARTEE   clever response
(9) INVECTIVE   verbal attack or abuse
(10) PLATITUDE   trite remark
(10) ACUTEST   sharpest

(12) COMPLACENT   smug
(14) FACILE   easy; slick
(15) DÉMODÉ   out of style
(16) CULPABLY   in a manner deserving blame or censure
(19) SUBTILISING   refining
(23) PERVASIVELY   spread throughout
(26) ESOTERIC   understood only by a chosen few
(31) INCREDULITY   disbelief
(34) BIZARRE   weird; peculiar
(40) INORDINATE   excessive; immoderate

Loren Eiseley (1907–   ) is one of America's most distinguished anthropologists. Born in Nebraska, he received degrees from the University of Nebraska and the University of Pennsylvania, where he is now professor of anthropology and the history of science. The possessor of a distinct and readable literary style, he has gained a wide audience from his books, articles, and poetry. Among his books are "The Mind as Nature" (1962) and "The Unexpected Universe" (1969).

This essay is a reflection on man's uncompleted journey through time. The "cosmic orphan" of the title is man himself.

LOREN EISELEY

The Cosmic Orphan

1   When I was a young lad of that indefinite but important age when one begins to ask, Who am I? Why am I here? What is the nature of my kind? What is growing up? What is the world? How long shall I live in it? Where shall I go? I found myself walking with a small companion over a high railroad trestle that spanned a stream, a country bridge, and a road. One could look fearfully down, between the ties, at the shallows and ripples in the shining water some fifty feet below. One was also doing a forbidden thing, against which our parents constantly warned. One must not be caught on the black bridge by a train. Something terrible might happen, a thing called death.

2   From the abutment of the bridge we gazed down upon the water and saw among the pebbles the shape of an animal we knew only from picture books—a turtle, a very large, dark mahogany-colored turtle. We scrambled down the embankment to observe him more closely. From the little bridge a few feet above the stream, I saw that the

turtle, whose beautiful markings shone in the afternoon sun, was not alive and that his flippers waved aimlessly in the rushing water. The reason for his death was plain. Not too long before we had come upon the trestle, someone engaged in idle practice with a repeating rifle had stitched a row of bullet holes across the turtle's carapace and sauntered on.

3   My father had once explained to me that it took a long time to make a big turtle, years really, in the sunlight and the water and the mud. I turned the ancient creature over and fingered the etched shell with its forlorn flippers flopping grotesquely. The question rose up unbidden. Why did the man have to kill something living that could never be replaced? I laid the turtle down in the water and gave it a little shove. It entered the current and began to drift away. "Let's go home," I said to my companion. From that moment, I think, I began to grow up.

4   "Papa," I said in the evening by the oil lamp in our kitchen. "Tell me how men got here." Papa paused. Like many fathers of that time, he was worn from long hours, he was not highly educated, but he had a beautiful resonant voice and he had been born on a frontier homestead. He knew the ritual way the Plains Indians opened a story.

5   "Son," he said, taking the pattern of another people for our own, "once there was a poor orphan." He said it in such a way that I sat down at his feet. Once there was a poor orphan with no one to teach him either his way or his manners. Sometimes animals helped him, sometimes supernatural beings. But above all, one thing was evident. Unlike other occupants of earth he had to be helped. He did not know his place; he had to find it. Sometimes he was arrogant and had to learn humility; sometimes he was a coward and had to be taught bravery. Sometimes he did not understand his Mother Earth and suffered for it. The old ones who starved and sought visions on hilltops had known these things. They were all gone now, and the magic had departed with them. The orphan was alone; he had to learn by himself; it was a hard school.

6   My father tousled my head; he gently touched my heart. "You will learn in time there is much pain here," he said. "Men will give it to you; time will give it to you; and you must learn to bear it all, not bear it alone, but be better for the wisdom that may come to you if you watch and listen and learn. Do not forget the turtle, nor the ways of men. They are all orphans and they go astray; they do wrong things. Try to see better."

7   "Yes, Papa," I said, and that was how I believe I came to study men, not the men of written history but the ancestors beyond, beyond all writing, beyond time as we know it, beyond human form as it is known today. Papa was right when he told me men were orphans, eternal seekers. They had little in the way of instinct to instruct them, they had come a strange far road in the universe, passed more than one black, threatening bridge. There were even more to pass, and each one became more dangerous as our knowledge grew. Because man was truly an orphan and confined to no single way of life, he was, in essence, a prison breaker. But in ignorance his very knowledge sometimes led from one terrible prison to another. Was the final

problem, then, to escape himself, or, if not that, to reconcile his devastating intellect with his heart? All of the knowledge set down in great books directly or indirectly affects this problem. It is the problem of every man, for even the indifferent man is making, unknown to himself, his own callous judgment.

8   Long ago, however, in one of the Dead Sea Scrolls hidden in the Judean Desert, an unknown scribe had written: "None there be, can rehearse the whole tale." That phrase, too, contains the warning that man is an orphan of uncertain beginnings and an indefinite ending. All that the archaeological and anthropological sciences can do is to place a somewhat flawed crystal before man and say: "This is the way you came; these are your present dangers; somewhere, seen dimly beyond, lies your destiny. God help you, you are a cosmic orphan, a symbol-shifting magician, mostly immature and inattentive to your own dangers. Read, think, study, but do not expect this to save you without humility of heart." This the old ones knew long ago in the great deserts under the stars. This they sought to learn and pass on. It is the only hope of men.

9   What have we observed that might be buried as the Dead Sea Scrolls were buried for 2000 years and be broken out of a jar for human benefit, brief words that might be encompassed on a copper scroll or a ragged sheet of vellum? Only these thoughts, I think, we might reasonably set down as true, now and hereafter. For a long time, for many, many centuries, Western man believed in what we might call the existent world of nature; form as form was seen as constant in both animal and human guise. He believed in the instantaneous creation of his world by the Deity; he believed its duration to be very short, a stage upon which the short drama of a human fall from divine estate and a redemption was in progress.

10   Worldly time was a small parenthesis in eternity. Man lived with that belief, his cosmos small and man-centered. Then, beginning about 350 years ago, thoughts unventured upon since the time of the Greek philosophers began to enter the human consciousness. They may be summed up in Francis Bacon's dictum: "This is the foundation of all. We are not to imagine or suppose, but to *discover,* what nature does or may be made to do."

11   When, in following years, scientific experiment and observation became current, a vast change began to pass over Western thought. Man's conception of himself and his world began to alter beyond recall. " 'Tis all in pieces, all coherence gone," exclaimed the poet John Donne, Bacon's contemporary. The existing world was crumbling at the edges. It was cracking apart like an ill-nailed raft in a torrent—a torrent of incredible time. It was, in effect, a new nature comprising a past embedded in the present and a future yet to be.

12   First, Bacon discerned a *mundus alter,* another separate world that could be drawn out of nature by human intervention—the world that surrounds and troubles us today. Then, by degrees, time depths of tremendous magnitude began, in the late eighteenth century, to replace the Christian calendar. Space, from a surrounding candelabrum of stars, began to widen to infinity. The earth was recognized as a mere speck drifting in the wake of a minor star, itself rotating around

an immense galaxy composed of innumerable suns. Beyond and beyond, into billions of light years, other galaxies glowed through clouds of wandering gas and interstellar dust. Finally, and perhaps the most shocking blow of all, the natural world of the moment proved to be an illusion, a phantom of man's short lifetime. Organic novelty lay revealed in the strata of the earth. Man had not always been here. He had been preceded, in the 4 billion years of the planet's history, by floating mollusks, strange ferm forests, huge dinosaurs, flying lizards, giant mammals whose bones lay under the dropped boulders of vanished continental ice sheets.

13   The Orphan cried out in protest, as the cold of naked space entered his bones, "Who am I?" And once more science answered. "You are a changeling. You are linked by a genetic chain to all the vertebrates. The thing that is you bears the still-aching wounds of evolution in body and in brain. Your hands are madeover fins, your lungs come from a creature gasping in a swamp, your femur has been twisted upright. Your foot is a reworked climbing pad. You are a rag doll resewn from the skins of extinct animals. Long ago, two million years perhaps, you were smaller; your brain was not so large. We are not confident that you could speak. Seventy million years before that you were an even smaller climbing creature known as a tupaiid. You were the size of a rat. You ate insects. Now you fly to the moon."

14   "This is a fairy tale," protested the Orphan. "I am here, I will look in the mirror."

15   "Of course it is a fairy tale," said the scientists, "but so is the world and so is life. That is what makes it true. Life is indefinite departure. That is why we are all orphans. That is why you must find your own way. Life is not stable. Everything alive is slipping through cracks and crevices in time, changing as it goes. Other creatures, however, have instincts that provide for them, holes in which to hide. They cannot ask questions. A fox is a fox, a wolf is a wolf, even if this, too, is illusion. You have learned to ask questions. That is why you are an orphan. *You are the only creature in the universe who knows what it has been.* Now you must go on asking questions while all the time you are changing. You will ask what you are to become. The world will no longer satisfy you. You must find your way, your own true self."

16   "But how can I?" wept the Orphan, hiding his head. "This is magic. I do not know what I am. I have been too many things."

17   "You have indeed," said all the scientists together. "Your body and your nerves have been dragged about and twisted in the long effort of your ancestors to stay alive, but now, small orphan that you are, you must know a secret, a secret magic that nature has given to you. No other creature on the planet possesses it. You use language. You are a symbol-shifter. All this is hidden in your brain and transmitted from one generation to another. You are a time-binder; in your head the symbols that mean things in the world outside can fly about untrammeled. You can combine them differently into a new world of thought, or you can also hold them tenaciously throughout a lifetime and pass them on to others."

18   Thus out of words, a puff of air, really, is made all that is uniquely human, all that is new from one human generation to another. But

remember what was said of the wounds of evolution. The brain, parts of it at least, is very old, the parts laid down in sequence like geological strata. Buried deep beneath the brain with which we reason are ancient defense centers quick to anger, quick to aggression, quick to violence, over which the neocortex, the new brain, strives to exert control. Thus there are times when the Orphan is a divided being striving against himself. Evil men know this. Sometimes they can play upon it for their own political advantage. Men crowded together, subjected to the same stimuli, are quick to respond to emotion that in the quiet of their own homes they might analyze more cautiously.

19   Scientists have found that the very symbols that crowd our brains may possess their own dangers. It is convenient for the thinker to classify an idea with a word. This can sometimes lead to a process called hypostatization or reification. Take the word *Man,* for example. There are times when it is useful to categorize the creature briefly, his history, his embracing characteristics. From this, if we are not careful of our meanings, it becomes easy to speak of all men as though they were one person. In reality men have been seeking this unreal man for thousands of years. They have found him bathed in blood, they have found him in the hermit's cell, he has been glimpsed among innumerable messiahs, or in meditation under the sacred bo tree; he has been found in the physician's study or lit by the satanic fires of the first atomic explosion.

20   In reality he has never been found at all. The reason is very simple: Men have been seeking Man capitalized, an imaginary creature constructed out of disparate parts in the laboratory of the human imagination. Some men may thus perceive him and see him as either totally beneficent or wholly evil. They would be wrong. They are wrong so long as they have vitalized this creation and call it **Man.** There is no Man; there are only men: good, evil, inconceivable mixtures marred by their genetic makeup, scarred or improved by their societal surroundings. So long as they live, they are *men,* multitudinous and unspent potential for action. Men are great objects of study, but the moment we say *Man* we are in danger of wandering into a swamp of abstraction.

21   Surveying our fossil history, perhaps we are not even justified as yet in calling ourselves true men. The word carries subtle implications that extend beyond us into the time stream. If a remote half-human ancestor, barely able to speak, had had a word for his kind, as very likely he did, and just supposing it had been *Man,* would we approve the usage, the shape-freezing quality of it, now? I think not. Perhaps no true Orphan would wish to call himself anything but a traveler. Man in a cosmic, timeless sense may not be here.

22   The point is particularly apparent in the light of a recent and portentous discovery. In 1953 James D. Watson and Francis H. C. Crick discovered the structure of the chemical alphabet out of which all that lives is constituted. It was a strange spiral ladder within the cell, far more organized and complicated than nineteenth-century biologists had imagined; the tiny building blocks constantly reshuffled in every mating had both an amazing stability and, paradoxically, over long time periods, a power to alter the living structure of a species beyond

recall. The thing called man had once been a tree shrew on a forest branch; now it manipulates in its brain abstract symbols from which skyscrapers rise, bridges span the horizon, disease is conquered, the moon is visited.

23   Molecular biologists have begun to consider whether the marvelous living alphabet that lies at the root of evolution can be manipulated for human benefit. Varieties of domesticated plants and animals have been improved. Now at last man has begun to eye his own possible road into the future. By delicate excisions and intrusions could the mysterious alphabet we carry in our bodies be made to hasten our advancement into the future? Already our urban concentrations, with all their aberrations and faults, are future-oriented. Why not ourselves? Is it in our power to perpetuate great minds ad infinitum? But who is to judge? Who is to select this future man? There is the problem. Which of us poor orphans by the roadside, even those peering learnedly through the electron microscope, can be confident of the way into the future? Could the fish unaided by nature have found the road to the reptile, the reptile to mammal, the mammal to man? And how was man endowed with speech? *Could* men choose their way? Suddenly before us towers the blackest, most formidable bridge of our experience. Across what chasm does it run?

24   Biologists tell us that in the fullness of time over 90 percent of the world's past species have perished. The mammalian ones in particular are not noted for longevity. If the scalpel, the excising laser ray in the laboratory, were placed in the hands of some one man, some one poor orphan, what would he do? If assured, would he reproduce himself alone? If cruel, would he by indirection succeed in abolishing the living world? If doubtful of the road, would he reproduce the doubt? "Nothing is more shameful than assertion without knowledge," a great Roman, Cicero, once pronounced as though he had foreseen this final bridge of human pride—the pride of a god without foresight.

25   After the disasters of the Second World War when the dream of perpetual progress died from men's minds, an orphan of this violent century wrote a poem about the great extinctions revealed in the rocks of the planet. It concludes as follows:

26   I am not sure I love
                    the cruelties found in our blood
                    from some lost evil in our beginnings.
               May the powers forgive and seal us deep
                    when we lie down,
               May harmless dormice creep and red
                    leaves fall
               —over the prisons where we wreaked
                    our will—
               Dachau, Auschwitz, those places
                    everywhere.
               If I could pray, I would pray long for this.*

---

*From Mr. Eiseley's book *The Innocent Assassins*, published in 1973 by Charles Scribner's Sons.

27 One may conclude that the poet was a man of doubt. He did not regret man; he was confident that leaves, rabbits, and songbirds would continue life, as, long ago, a tree shrew had happily forgotten the ruling reptiles. The poet was an orphan in shabby circumstances, pausing by the roadside to pray, for he did pray despite his denial; God forgive us all. He was a man in doubt upon the way. He was the eternal orphan of my father's story. Let us then, as similar orphans who have come this long way through time, be willing to assume the risks of the uncompleted journey. We must know, as that forlorn band of men in Judea knew when they buried the jar, that man's road is to be sought beyond himself. *No man there is who can tell the whole tale.* After the small passage of 2000 years who would deny this truth?

Discussion of Theme

1. Why does the author object to grouping all of humanity into the single category of *man*? Why is such an abstraction dangerous?
2. Why does Eiseley call man an orphan?
3. Is the author attempting to bridge the gap between science and metaphysics? Is he successful?
4. Do you feel humans are closer to answering the question "Who am I?" than ever before? Discuss.
5. What are some of the ways humans have tried to reconcile the conflict between the intellect and emotions?

Discussion of Rhetoric

1. The author uses many rhetorical devices, such as the alliteration in paragraph 3. Why are these devices appropriate to his theme, and what is their effect?
2. Paraphrase the central thesis. Where does it first appear?
3. Why does the author personify science?
4. What techniques does the author use to make complex ideas comprehensible to the reader?
5. The author uses two key quotations (paragraphs 8 and 24). How do they relate to the theme and to each other?
6. Explain the following (paragraph 15): "Of course it is a fairy tale," said the scientists, "but so is the world and so is life. That is what makes it true."

Writing Assignments

1. How did you feel after reading this essay? Write your personal reactions in an essay.
2. In an essay, speculate on the questions posed in paragraph 24.

3. Write an imaginative essay based on the idea suggested in paragraph 21, that "Man in a cosmic, timeless sense may not be here." Consider the questions, "If man is yet to come, what are we?" and "How will Man be different from us?"

Library Exploration

1. Research and report on the Dead Sea scrolls.
2. Read some of the poetry of John Donne. How are the upheaval of beliefs and scientific discoveries reflected in his work?
3. Contrast and compare various creation myths of other cultures.
4. Research the origin and meaning of the word *man*.
5. Read Eiseley's book, *The Innocent Assassins*.

Vocabulary

(2) CARAPACE shell covering

(4) RESONANT deep and full; resounding

(9) VELLUM a sheet of calfskin prepared as parchment

(10) DICTUM an authoritative pronouncement

(19) HYPOSTATIZATION treatment of something as a distinct substance or reality

(19) REIFICATION the process of converting or regarding something as concrete

(20) VITALIZED gave life to

(20) MULTITUDINOUS very numerous

(23) EXCISIONS cuttings from something

(23) INTRUSIONS added or forced extraneous matter

(23) ABERRATIONS deviation from truth or morality

The author of over twenty
books, Philip Wylie (1902–71)
also wrote for films, newspapers, and for "The New Yorker."
He was well known for his unre-
lenting and often controversial
attacks on American manners
and morals. The book he is perhaps best known for, and which
is still widely read, is "A Generation of Vipers," published in
1942.

This article is typical of Wylie's
approach to social questions. It
is assuredly more than an amusing complaint about supper; it is
also a warning about the direction our civilization is taking.

PHILIP WYLIE

Science Has Spoiled My Supper

1   I am a fan for Science. My education is scientific and I have, in one
field, contributed a monograph to a scientific journal. Science, to my
mind, is applied honesty, the one reliable means we have to find out
truth. That is why, when error is committed in the name of Science, I
feel the way a man would if his favorite uncle had taken to drink.

2   Over the years, I have come to feel that way about what science has
done to food. I agree that America can set as good a table as any nation in the world. I agree that our food is nutritious and that the diet of
most of us is well-balanced. What America eats is handsomely pack-
aged; it is usually clean and pure; it is excellently preserved. The only
trouble with it is this: year by year it grows less good to eat. It appeals
increasingly to the eye. But who eats with his eyes? Almost everything
used to taste better when I was a kid. For quite a long time I thought
that observation was merely another index of advancing age. But

some years ago I married a girl whose mother is an expert cook of the kind called "old-fashioned." This gifted woman's daughter (my wife) was taught her mother's venerable skills. The mother lives in the country and still plants an old-fashioned garden. She still buys dairy products from the neighbors and, insofar as possible, she uses the same materials her mother and grandmother did — to prepare meals that are superior. They are just as good, in this Year of Grace, as I recall them from my courtship. After eating for a while at the table of my mother-in-law, it is sad to go back to eating with my friends — even the alleged "good cooks" among them. And it is a gruesome experience to have meals at the best big-city restaurants.

3   Take cheese, for instance. Here and there, in big cities, small stores and delicatessens specialize in cheese. At such places, one can buy at least some of the first-rate cheeses that we used to eat — such as those we had with pie and in macaroni. The latter were sharp but not too sharp. They were a little crumbly. We called them American cheeses, or even rat cheese; actually, they were Cheddars. Long ago, this cheese began to be supplanted by a material call "cheese foods." Some cheese foods and "processed" cheese are fairly edible; but not one comes within miles of the old kinds — for flavor.

4   A grocer used to be very fussy about his cheese. Cheddar was made and sold by hundreds of little factories. Representatives of the factories had particular customers, and cheese was prepared by hand to suit the grocers, who knew precisely what their patrons wanted in rat cheese, pie cheese, American and other cheeses. Some liked them sharper; some liked them yellower; some liked anise seeds in cheese, or caraway.

5   What happened? Science — or what is called science — stepped in. The old-fashioned cheeses didn't ship well enough. They crumbled, became moldy, dried out. "Scientific" tests disclosed that a great majority of the people will buy a less-good-tasting cheese if that's all they can get. "Scientific marketing" then took effect. Its motto is "Give the people the least quality they'll stand for." In food, as in many other things, the "scientific marketers" regard quality as secondary so long as they can sell most persons anyhow; what they are after is "durability" or "shippability."

6   It is not possible to make the very best cheese in vast quantities at a low average cost. "Scientific sampling" got in its statistically nasty work. It was found that the largest number of people will buy something that is bland and rather tasteless. Those who prefer a product of a pronounced and individualistic flavor have a variety of preferences. Nobody is altogether pleased by bland foodstuff, in other words; but nobody is very violently put off. The result is that a "reason" has been found for turning out zillions of packages of something that will "do" for nearly all and isn't even imagined to be superlatively good by a single soul!

7   Economics entered. It is possible to turn out in quantity a bland, impersonal, practically imperishable substance more or less resembling, say, cheese — at lower cost than cheese. Chain groceries shut out the independent stores and "standardization" became a principal means of cutting costs.

8   Imitations also came into the cheese business. There are American duplications of most of the celebrated European cheeses, mass-produced and cheaper by far than the imports. They would cause European food-lovers to gag or guffaw—but generally the limitations are all that's available in the supermarkets. People buy them and eat them.

9   Perhaps you don't like cheese—so the fact that decent cheese is hardly ever served in America any more, or used in cooking, doesn't matter to you. Well, take bread. There has been (and still is) something of a hullabaloo about bread. In fact, in the last few years, a few big bakeries have taken to making a fairly good imitation of real bread. It costs much more than what is nowadays called bread, but it is edible. Most persons, however, now eat as "bread" a substance so full of chemicals and so barren of cereals that it approaches a synthetic.

10   Most bakers are interested mainly in how a loaf of bread looks. They are concerned with how little stuff they can put in it—to get how much money. They are deeply interested in using chemicals that will keep the bread from molding, make it seem "fresh" for the longest possible time, and so render it marketable and shippable. They have been at this monkeyshine for a generation. Today a loaf of "bread" looks deceptively real; but it is made from heaven knows what and it resembles, as food, a solidified bubble bath. Some months ago I bought a loaf of the stuff and, experimentally, began pressing it together, like an accordion. With a little effort, I squeezed the whole loaf to a length of about one inch!

11   Yesterday, at the home of my mother-in-law, I ate with country-churned butter and home-canned wild strawberry jam several slices of actual bread, the same thing we used to have every day at home. People who have eaten actual bread will know what I mean. They will know that the material commonly called bread is not even related to real bread, except in name.

12   For years, I couldn't figure out what had happened to vegetables. I knew, of course, that most vegetables, to be enjoyed in their full deliciousness, must be picked fresh and cooked at once. I knew that vegetables cannot be overcooked and remain even edible, in the best sense. They cannot stand on the stove. That set of facts makes it impossible, of course, for any American restaurant—or, indeed, any city-dweller separated from supply by more than a few hours—to have decent fresh vegetables. The Parisians managed by getting their vegetables picked at dawn and rushed in farmers' carts to market, where no middleman or marketman delays produce on its way to the pot.

13   Our vegetables, however, come to us through a long chain of command. There are merchants of several sorts—wholesalers before the retailers, commission men, and so on—with the result that what were once edible products become, in transit, mere wilted leaves and withered tubers.

14   Homes and restaurants do what they can with this stuff—which my mother-in-law would discard on the spot. I have long thought that the famed blindfold test for cigarettes should be applied to city vegetables. For I am sure that if you puréed them and ate them blindfolded, you

couldn't tell the beans from the peas, the turnips from the squash, the Brussels sprouts from the broccoli.

15   It is only lately that I have found how much science has had to do with this reduction of noble victuals to pottage. Here the science of genetics is involved. Agronomists and the like have taken to breeding all sorts of vegetables and fruits — changing their original nature. This sounds wonderful and often is insane. For the scientists have not as a rule taken any interest whatsoever in the taste of the things they've tampered with!

16   What they've done is to develop "improved" strains of things for every purpose but eating. They work out, say, peas that will ripen all at once. The farmer can then harvest his peas and thresh them and be done with them. It is extremely profitable because it is efficient. What matter if such peas taste like boiled paper wads?

17   Geneticists have gone crazy over such "opportunities." They've developed string beans that are straight instead of curved, and all one length. This makes them easier to pack in cans, even if, when eating them, you can't tell them from tender string. Ripening time and identity of size and shape are, nowadays, more important in carrots than the fact that they taste like carrots. Personally, I don't care if they hybridize onions till they are big as your head and come up through the snow; but, in doing so, they are producing onions that only vaguely and feebly remind you of onions. We are getting some varieties, in fact, that have less flavor than the water off last week's leeks. Yet, if people don't eat onions because they taste like onions, what in the name of Luther Burbank do they eat them for?

18   The women's magazines are about one third dedicated to clothes, one third to mild comment on sex, and the other third to recipes and pictures of handsome salads, desserts, and main courses. "Institutes" exist to experiment and tell housewives how to cook attractive meals and how to turn leftovers into works of art. The food thus pictured looks like famous paintings of still life. The only trouble is it's tasteless. It leaves appetite unquenched and merely serves to stave off famine.

19   I wonder if this blandness of our diet doesn't explain why so many of us are overweight and even dangerously so. When things had flavor, we knew what we were eating all the while — and it satisfied us. A teaspoonful of my mother-in-law's wild strawberry jam will not just provide a gastronome's ecstasy: it will entirely satisfy your jam desire. But, of the average tinned or glass-packed strawberry jam, you need half a cupful to get the idea of what you're eating. A slice of my mother-in-law's apple pie will satiate you far better than a whole bakery pie.

20   That thought is worthy of investigation — of genuine scientific investigation. It is merely a hypothesis, so far, and my own. But people — and their ancestors — have been eating according to flavor for upwards of a billion years. The need to satisfy the sense of taste may be innate and important. When food is merely a pretty cascade of viands, with the texture of boiled cardboard and the flavor of library paste, it may be the instinct of *genus homo* to go on eating in the unconscious hope of finally satisfying the ageless craving of the frustrated taste buds. In

the days when good-tasting food was the rule in the American home, obesity wasn't such a national curse.

21   How can you feel you've eaten if you haven't tasted, and fully enjoyed tasting? Why (since science is ever so ready to answer the beck and call of mankind) don't people who want to reduce merely give up eating and get the nourishment they must have in measured doses shot into their arms at hospitals? One ready answer to that question suggests that my theory of overeating is sound: people like to taste! In eating, they try to satisfy that like.

22   The scientific war against deliciousness has been stepped up enormously in the last decade. Some infernal genius found a way to make biscuit batter keep. Housewives began to buy this premixed stuff. It saved work, of course. But any normally intelligent person can learn, in a short period, how to prepare superb baking powder biscuits. I can make better biscuits, myself, than can be made from patent batters. Yet soon after this fiasco became an American staple, it was discovered that a half-baked substitute for all sorts of breads, pastries, rolls, and the like could be mass-manufactured, frozen—and sold for polishing off in the home oven. None of these two-stage creations is as good as even a fair sample of the thing it imitates. A man of taste, who had eaten one of my wife's cinnamon buns, might use the premixed sort to throw at starlings—but not to eat! Cake mixes, too, come ready-prepared—like cement and not much better-tasting compared with true cake.

23   It is, however, "deep-freezing" that has really rung down the curtain on American cookery. Nothing is improved by the process. I have yet to taste a deep-frozen victual that measures up, in flavor, to the fresh, unfrosted original. And most foods, cooked or uncooked, are destroyed in the deep freeze for all people of sense and sensibility. Vegetables with crisp and crackling texture emerge as mush, slippery and stringy as hair nets simmered in Vaseline. The essential oils that make peas peas—and cabbage cabbage—must undergo fission and fusion in freezers. Anyhow, they vanish. Some meats turn to leather. Others to wood pulp. Everything, pretty much, tastes like the mosses of tundra, dug up in midwinter. Even the appearance changes, oftentimes. Handsome comestibles you put down in the summer come out looking very much like the corpses of wooly mammoths recovered from the last Ice Age.

24   Of course, all this scientific "food handling" tends to save money. It certainly preserves food longer. It reduces work at home. But these facts, and especially the last, imply that the first purpose of living is to avoid work—at home, anyhow.

25   Without thinking, we are making an important confession about ourselves as a nation. We are abandoning quality—even, to some extent, the quality of people. The "best" is becoming too good for us. We are suckling ourselves on machine-made mediocrity. It is bad for our souls, our minds, and our digestion. It is the way our wiser and calmer forebears fed, not people, but hogs: as much as possible and as fast as possible, with no standard of quality.

26   The Germans say, "*Mann ist was er isst*—Man is what he eats." If

this be true, the people of the U.S.A. are well on their way to becoming a faceless mob of mediocrities, of robots. And if we apply to other attributes the criteria we apply these days to appetite, that is what would happen! We would not want bright children any more; we'd merely want them to look bright — and get through school fast. We wouldn't be interested in beautiful women — just a good paint job. And we'd be opposed to the most precious quality of man: his individuality, his differentness from the mob.

27   There are some people — sociologists and psychologists among them — who say that is exactly what we Americans are doing, are becoming. Mass man, they say, is on the increase. Conformity, standardization, similarity — all on a cheap and vulgar level — are replacing the great American ideas of colorful liberty and dignified individualism. If this is so, the process may well begin, like most human behavior, in the home — in those homes where a good meal has been replaced by something-to-eat-in-a-hurry. By something not very good to eat, prepared by a mother without very much to do, for a family that doesn't feel it amounts to much anyhow.

28   I call, here, for rebellion.

Discussion of Theme

1. What is meant by "man is what he eats"?
2. Wylie wrote this article in 1954. Are we eating, in the 1970s, more of the sort of foods that Wylie complains about?
3. Does Wylie exaggerate in seeing a connection between standardized foods and a loss of "the great American ideas of colorful liberty and dignified individualism"?
4. Wylie's complaints about his food serve as a springboard for a larger attack. What is this main theme?
5. Do you agree with Wylie that many people are overweight because of the blandness of their diet? The author implies that fewer people were overweight in the past. Is this likely?
6. Wylie's mother-in-law serves an important function in this argument. How would you describe it?

Discussion of Rhetoric

1. Analyze the humor in the phrase "the scientific war against deliciousness." Are there any other examples of witty phrasing?
2. How does the last sentence in paragraph 1 set the tone of this essay?
3. Wylie develops his theme by a series of examples. What are some of them? How does he succeed in introducing each one smoothly?
4. This essay can be divided into three sections: paragraphs 1–18, 19–25, and 26–28. What is the thesis or central idea in each section? How are they linked to form a unified whole?
5. In order to avoid saying simply "it tastes bad," Wylie uses a number

of similes. In paragraph 16, for example, he says that peas taste like "boiled paper wads." Find other similes in the essay. How do they heighten his emphasis?

Writing Assignments

1. If you patronize health-food stores instead of supermarkets, explain your preference for organically grown foods or foods free of artificial supplements and chemical preservatives.
2. Attack Wylie's thesis by showing the benefits of scientific developments in food.
3. Wylie would probably agree with the observation that many products other than food are being produced with emphasis on appearance rather than quality. Describe some of these products.

Library Exploration

1. What are the duties of the Food & Drug Administration? Why is it unable to bring more than a small percentage of violations to court?
2. For a detailed treatment of the techniques used by food processors to make the products mentioned by Wylie more attractive, read Vance Packard's *The Hidden Persuaders*.
3. What actually happens to foods when they are dried or frozen? What structural or chemical changes take place?

Vocabulary

(1) MONOGRAPH a detailed article on one subject
(2) VENERABLE ancient and respected
(2) GRUESOME grisly; ghastly
(6) BLAND mild; flavorless
(13) IN TRANSIT on the way
(13) TUBERS roots
(14) PURÉED mashed
(15) VICTUALS foods
(15) POTTAGE thick soup
(15) AGRONOMISTS specialists in crop and soil management
(17) HYBRIDIZE crossbreed
(17) LEEKS vegetables related to the onion
(18) STAVE OFF ward off; keep away
(19) GASTRONOME one who likes good food and drink
(19) TINNED canned
(19) SATIATE satisfy; fill
(20) INNATE inborn
(20) VIANDS foods
(20) GENUS HOMO the race of man
(21) BECK summons
(22) FIASCO utter and ridiculous failure
(23) TUNDRA frozen wasteland
(23) COMESTIBLES edibles; foods

Rachel Carson (1907–65) received a number of awards for her work as a marine biologist and author. She was a rare combination of scientist, writer, and passionate member of the human society. In addition to "The Sea Around Us" (1951), she wrote about the marine world in "Under the Sea Wind" (1952) and "The Edge of the Sea" (1955). Two years before her death she swept into national prominence—and controversy—with her study of insecticides, "Silent Spring" (1962).

This excerpt explains something about the movement of the seas. Despite the technical nature of her subject, Miss Carson's style is lucid and often poetic.

RACHEL CARSON

The Shape of Ancient Seas

Till the slow sea rise and the sheer cliff crumble,
Till terrace and meadow the deep gulfs drink.
Swinburne

1 We live in an age of rising seas. Along all the coasts of the United States a continuing rise of sea level has been perceptible on the tide gauges of the Coast and Geodetic Survey since 1930. For the thousand-mile stretch from Massachusetts to Florida, and on the coast of the Gulf of Mexico, the rise amounted to about a third of a foot between 1930 and 1948. The water is also rising (but more slowly) along the Pacific shores. These records of the tide gauges do not include the transient advances and retreats of the water caused by winds and storms, but signify a steady, continuing advance of the sea upon the land.

2   This evidence of a rising sea is an interesting and even an exciting thing because it is rare that, in the short span of human life, we can actually observe and measure the progress of one of the great earth rhythms. What is happening is nothing new. Over the long span of geologic time, the ocean waters have come in over North America many times and have again retreated into their basins. For the boundary between sea and land is the most fleeting and transitory feature of the earth, and the sea is forever repeating its encroachments upon the continents. It rises and falls like a great tide, sometimes engulfing half a continent in its flood, reluctant in its ebb, moving in a rhythm mysterious and infinitely deliberate.

3   Now once again the ocean is overfull. It is spilling over the rims of its basins. It fills the shallow seas that border the continents, like the Barents, Bering, and China seas. Here and there it has advanced into the interior and lies in such inland seas as Hudson Bay, the St. Lawrence embayment, the Baltic, and the Sunda Sea. On the Atlantic coast of the United States the mouths of many rivers, like the Hudson and the Susquehanna, have been drowned by the advancing flood; the old, submerged channels are hidden under bays like the Chesapeake and the Delaware.

4   The advance noted so clearly on the tide gauges may be part of a long rise that began thousands of years ago—perhaps when the glaciers of the most recent Ice Age began to melt. But it is only within recent decades that there have been instruments to measure it in any part of the world. Even now the gauges are few and scattered, considering the world as a whole. Because of the scarcity of world records, it is not known whether the rise observed in the United States since 1930 is being duplicated on all other continents.

5   Where and when the ocean will halt its present advance and begin again its slow retreat into its basin, no one can say. If the rise over the continent of North America should amount to a hundred feet (and there is more than enough water now frozen in land ice to provide such a rise) most of the Atlantic seaboard, with its cities and towns, would be submerged. The surf would break against the foothills of the Appalachians. The coastal plain of the Gulf of Mexico would lie under water; the lower part of the Mississippi Valley would be submerged.

6   If, however, the rise should be as much as 600 feet, large areas in the eastern half of the continent would disappear under the waters. The Appalachians would become a chain of mountainous islands. The Gulf of Mexico would creep north, finally meeting in mid-continent with the flood that had entered from the Atlantic into the Great Lakes, through the valley of the St. Lawrence. Much of northern Canada would be covered by water from the Arctic Ocean and Hudson Bay.

7   All of this would seem to us extraordinary and catastrophic, but the truth is that North America and most other continents have known even more extensive invasions by the sea than the one we have just imagined. Probably the greatest submergence in the history of the earth took place in the Cretaceous period, about 100 million years ago. Then the ocean waters advanced upon North America from the north, south, and east, finally forming an inland sea about 1000 miles wide that extended from the Arctic to the Gulf of Mexico, and then spread

eastward to cover the coastal plain from the Gulf to New Jersey. At the height of the Cretaceous flood about half of North America was submerged. All over the world the seas rose. They covered most of the British Isles, except for scattered outcroppings of ancient rocks. In southern Europe only the old, rocky highlands stood above the sea, which intruded in long bays and gulfs even into the central highlands of the continent. The ocean moved into Africa and laid down deposits of sandstones; later weathering of these rocks provided the desert sands of the Sahara. From a drowned Sweden, an inland sea flowed across Russia, covered the Caspian Sea, and extended to the Himalayas. Parts of India were submerged, and of Australia, Japan, and Siberia. On the South American continent, the area where later the Andes were to rise was covered by sea.

8   With variations of extent and detail, these events have been repeated again and again. The very ancient Ordovician seas, some 400 million years ago, submerged more than half of North America, leaving only a few large islands marking the borderlands of the continent, and a scattering of smaller ones rising out of the inland sea. The marine transgressions of Devonian and Silurian time were almost as extensive. But each time the pattern of invasion was a little different, and it is doubtful that there is any part of the continent that at some time has not lain at the bottom of one of these shallow seas.

9   You do not have to travel to find the sea, for the traces of its ancient stands are everywhere about. Though you may be a thousand miles inland, you can easily find reminders that will reconstruct for the eye and ear of the mind the processions of its ghostly waves and the roar of its surf, far back in time. So, on a mountain top in Pennsylvania, I have sat on rocks of whitened limestone, fashioned of the shells of billions upon billions of minute sea creatures. Once they had lived and died in an arm of the ocean that overlay this place, and their limy remains had settled to the bottom. There, after eons of time, they had become compacted into rock and the sea had receded; after yet more eons the rock had been uplifted by bucklings of the earth's crust and now it formed the backbone of a long mountain range.

10   Far in the interior of the Florida Everglades I have wondered at the feeling of the sea that came to me — wondered until I realized that here were the same flatness, the same immense spaces, the same dominance of the sky and its moving, changing clouds; wondered until I remembered that the hard rocky floor on which I stood, its flatness interrupted by upthrust masses of jagged coral rock, had been only recently constructed by the busy architects of the coral reefs under a warm sea. Now the rock is thinly covered with grass and water; but everywhere is the feeling that the land has formed only the thinnest veneer over the underlying platform of the sea, that at any moment the process might be reversed and the sea reclaim its own.

11   So in all lands we may sense the former presence of the sea. There are outcroppings of marine limestone in the Himalayas, now at an elevation of 20,000 feet. These rocks are reminders of a warm, clear sea that lay over southern Europe and northern Africa and extended into southwestern Asia. This was some 50 million years ago. Immense numbers of a large protozoan known as nummulites swarmed

in this sea and each, in death, contributed to the building of a thick layer of nummulitic limestone. Eons later, the ancient Egyptians were to carve their Sphinx from a mass of this rock; other deposits of the same stone they quarried to obtain material to build their pyramids.

12 The famous white cliffs of Dover are composed of chalk deposited by the seas of the Cretaceous period, during that great inundation we have spoken of. The chalk extends from Ireland through Denmark and Germany, and forms its thickest beds in south Russia. It consists of shells of those minute sea creatures called foraminifera, the shells being cemented together with a fine-textured deposit of calcium carbonate. In contrast to the foraminiferal ooze that covers large areas of ocean bottom at moderate depths, the chalk seems to be a shallow-water deposit, but it is so pure in texture that the surrounding lands must have been low deserts, from which little material was carried seaward. Grains of windborne quartz sand, which frequently occur in the chalk, support this view. At certain levels the chalk contains nodules of flint. Stone Age men mined the flint for weapons and tools and also used this relic of the Cretaceous sea to light their fires.

13 Many of the natural wonders of the earth owe their existence to the fact that once the sea crept over the land, laid down its deposits of sediments, and then withdrew. There is Mammoth Cave in Kentucky, for example, where one may wander through miles of underground passages and enter rooms with ceilings 250 feet overhead. Caves and passageways have been dissolved by ground water out of an immense thickness of limestone, deposited by a Paleozoic sea. In the same way, the story of Niagara Falls goes back to Silurian time, when a vast embayment of the Arctic Sea crept southward over the continent. Its waters were clear, for the borderlands were low and little sediment or silt was carried into the inland sea. It deposited large beds of the hard rock called dolomite, and in time they formed a long escarpment near the present border between Canada and the United States. Millions of years later, floods of water released from melting glaciers poured over this cliff, cutting away the soft shales that underlay the dolomite, and causing mass after mass of the undercut rock to break away. In this fashion Niagara Falls and its gorge were created.

14 Some of these inland seas were immense and important features of their world, although all of them were shallow compared with the central basin where, since earliest time, the bulk of the ocean waters have resided. Some may have been as much as 600 feet deep, about the same as the depths over the outer edge of the continental shelf. No one knows the pattern of their currents, but often they must have carried the warmth of the tropics into far northern lands. During the Cretaceous period, for example, breadfruit, cinnamon, laurel, and fig trees grew in Greenland. When the continents were reduced to groups of islands there must have been few places that possessed a continental type of climate with its harsh extremes of heat and cold; mild oceanic climates must rather have been the rule.

15 Geologists say that each of the grander divisions of earth history consists of three phases: in the first the continents are high, erosion is active, and the seas are largely confined to their basins; in the second the continents are lowest and the seas have invaded them broadly; in

the third the continents have begun once more to rise. According to the late Charles Schuchert, who devoted much of his distinguished career as a geologist to mapping the ancient seas and lands: "Today we are living in the beginning of a new cycle, when the continents are largest, highest, and scenically grandest. The oceans, however, have begun another invasion upon North America."

16   What brings the ocean out of its deep basins, where it has been contained for eons of time, to invade the lands? Probably there has always been not one alone, but a combination of causes.

17   The mobility of the earth's crust is inseparably linked with the changing relations of sea and land — the warping upward or downward of that surprisingly plastic substance which forms the outer covering of our earth. The crustal movements affect both land and sea bottom but are most marked near the continental margins. They may involve one or both shores of an ocean, one or all coasts of a continent. They proceed in a slow and mysterious cycle, one phase of which may require millions of years for its completion. Each downward movement of the continental crust is accompanied by a slow flooding of the land by the sea, each upward buckling by the retreat of the water.

18   But the movements of the earth's crust are not alone responsible for the invading seas. There are other important causes. Certainly one of them is the displacement of ocean water by land sediments. Every grain of sand or silt carried out by the rivers and deposited at sea displaces a corresponding amount of water. Disintegration of the land and the seaward freighting of its substance have gone on without interruption since the beginning of geologic time. It might be thought that the sea level would have been rising continuously, but the matter is not so simple. As they lose substance the continents tend to rise higher, like a ship relieved of part of its cargo. The ocean floor, to which the sediments are transferred, sags under its load. The exact combination of all these conditions that will result in a rising ocean level is a very complex matter, not easily recognized or predicted.

19   Then there is the growth of the great submarine volcanoes, which build up immense lava cones on the floor of the ocean. Some geologists believe these may have an important effect on the changing level of the sea. The bulk of some of these volcanoes is impressive. Bermuda is one of the smallest, but its volume beneath the surface is about 2500 cubic miles. The Hawaiian chain of volcanic islands extends for nearly 2000 miles across the Pacific and contains several islands of great size; its total displacement of water must be tremendous. Perhaps it is more than coincidence that this chain arose in Cretaceous time, when the greatest flood the world has ever seen advanced upon the continents.

20   For the past million years, all other causes of marine transgressions have been dwarfed by the dominating role of the glaciers. The Pleistocene period was marked by alternating advances and retreats of a great ice sheet. Four times the ice caps formed and grew deep over the land, pressing southward into the valleys and over the plains. And four times the ice melted and shrank and withdrew from the lands it had covered. We live now in the last stages of this fourth withdrawal. About half the ice formed in the last Pleistocene glaciation

remains in the ice caps of Greenland and Antarctica and the scattered glaciers of certain mountains.

21 Each time the ice sheet thickened and expanded with the unmelted snows of winter after winter, its growth meant a corresponding lowering of the ocean level. For directly or indirectly, the moisture that falls on the earth's surface as rain or snow has been withdrawn from the reservoir of the sea. Ordinarily, the withdrawal is a temporary one, the water being returned via the normal runoff of rain and melting snow. But in the glacial period the summers were cool, and the snows of any winter did not melt entirely but were carried over to the succeeding winter, when the new snows found and covered them. So little by little the level of the sea dropped as the glaciers robbed it of its water, and at the climax of each of the major glaciations the oceans all over the world stood at a very low level.

22 Today, if you look in the right places, you will see the evidences of some of these old stands of the sea. Of course the strand marks left by the extreme low levels are now deeply covered by water and may be discovered only indirectly by sounding. But where, in past ages, the water level stood higher than it does today you can find its traces. In Samoa, at the foot of a cliff wall now 15 feet above the present level of the sea, you can find benches cut in the rocks by waves. You will find the same thing on other Pacific islands, and on St. Helena in the South Atlantic, on islands of the Indian Ocean, in the West Indies, and around the Cape of Good Hope.

23 Sea caves in cliffs now high above the battering assault and the flung spray of the waves that cut them are eloquent of the changed relation of sea and land. You will find such caves widely scattered over the world. On the west coast of Norway there is a remarkable, wave-cut tunnel. Out of the hard granite of the island of Torghatten, the pounding surf of a flooding interglacial sea cut a passageway through the island, a distance of about 530 feet, and in so doing removed nearly five million cubic feet of rock. The tunnel now stands 400 feet above the sea. Its elevation is due in part to the elastic, upward rebound of the crust after the melting of the ice.

24 During the other half of the cycle, when the seas sank lower and lower as the glaciers grew in thickness, the world's shorelines were undergoing changes even more far-reaching and dramatic. Every river felt the effect of the lowering sea; its waters were speeded in their course to the ocean and given new strength for the deepening and cutting of its channel. Following the downward-moving shorelines, the rivers extended their courses over the drying sands and muds of what only recently had been the sloping sea bottom. Here the rushing torrents — swollen with melting glacier water — picked up great quantities of loose mud and sand and rolled into the sea as a turgid flood.

25 During one or more of the Pleistocene lowerings of sea level, the floor of the North Sea was drained of its water and for a time became dry land. The rivers of northern Europe and of the British Isles followed the retreating waters seaward. Eventually the Rhine captured the whole drainage system of the Thames. The Elbe and the Weser

became one river. The Seine rolled through what is now the English Channel and cut itself a trough out across the continental shelf — perhaps the same drowned channel now discernible by soundings beyond Lands End.

26   The greatest of all Pleistocene glaciations came rather late in the period — probably only about 200 thousand years ago, and well within the time of man. The tremendous lowering of sea level must have affected the life of Paleolithic man. Certainly he was able, at more than one period, to walk across a wide bridge at Bering Strait, which became dry land when the level of the ocean dropped below this shallow shelf. There were other land bridges, created in the same way. As the ocean receded from the coast of India, a long submarine bank became a shoal, then finally emerged, and primitive man walked across "Adam's Bridge"[1] to the island of Ceylon.

27   Many of the settlements of ancient man must have been located on the seacoast or near the great deltas of the rivers, and relics of his civilization may lie in caves long since covered by the rising ocean. Our meager knowledge of Paleolithic man might be increased by searching along these old drowned shorelines. One archeologist has recommended searching shallow portions of the Adriatic Sea, with "submarine boats casting strong electric lights" or even with glass-bottomed boats and artificial light in the hope of discovering the out-lines of shell heaps — the kitchen middens of the early men who once lived here. Professor R. A. Daly has pointed out:

> The last Glacial stage was the Reindeer Age of French history. Men then lived in the famous caves overlooking the channels of the French rivers, and hunted the reindeer which throve on the cool plains of France south of the ice border. The Late-Glacial rise of general sea level was necessarily accompanied by a rise of the river waters downstream. Hence the lowest caves are likely to have been partly or wholly drowned . . . . There the search for more relics of Paleolithic man should be pursued.[2]

28   Some of our Stone Age ancestors must have known the rigors of life near the glaciers. While men as well as plants and animals moved southward before the ice, some must have remained within sight and sound of the great frozen wall. To these the world was a place of storm and blizzard, with bitter winds roaring down out of the blue mountain of ice that dominated the horizon and reached upward into gray skies, all filled with the roaring tumult of the advancing glacier, and with the thunder of moving tons of ice breaking away and plung-ing into the sea.

29   But those who lived half the earth away, on some sunny coast of the Indian Ocean, walked and hunted on dry land over which the sea, only recently, had rolled deeply. These men knew nothing of the distant glaciers, nor did they understand that they walked and hunted

---

[1]A thirty-mile chain of sandbanks between Ceylon and India, the remainder of an earlier continuous isthmus.

[2]Author's Note: From *The Changing World of the Ice Age*, 1934 edition, Yale University Press, p. 210.

where they did because quantities of ocean water were frozen as ice and snow in a distant land.

30   In any imaginative reconstruction of the world of the Ice Age, we are plagued by one tantalizing uncertainty: how low did the ocean level fall during the period of greatest spread of the glaciers, when unknown quantities of water were frozen in the ice? Was it only a moderate fall of 200 or 300 feet—a change paralleled many times in geologic history in the ebb and flow of the epicontinental seas? Or was it a dramatic drawing down of the ocean by 2000, even 3000 feet?

31   Each of these various levels has been suggested as an actual possibility by one or more geologists. Perhaps it is not surprising that there should be such radical disagreement. It has been only about a century since Louis Agassiz gave the world its first understanding of the moving mountains of ice and their dominating effect on the Pleistocene world. Since then, men in all parts of the earth have been patiently accumulating the facts and reconstructing the events of those four successive advances and retreats of the ice. Only the present generation of scientists, led by such daring thinkers as Daly, have understood that each thickening of the ice sheets meant a corresponding lowering of the ocean, and that with each retreat of the melting ice a returning flood of water raised the sea level.

32   Of this "alternate robbery and restitution" most geologists have taken a conservative view and said that the greatest lowering of the sea level could not have amounted to more than 400 feet, possibly only half as much. Most of those who argue that the drawing down was much greater base their reasoning upon the submarine canyons, those deep gorges cut in the continental slopes. The deeper canyons lie a mile or more below the present level of the sea. Geologists who maintain that at least the upper parts of the canyons were stream-cut say that the sea level must have fallen enough to permit this during the Pleistocene glaciation.

33   This question of the farthest retreat of the sea into its basins must await further searchings into the mysteries of the ocean. We seem on the verge of exciting new discoveries. Now oceanographers and geologists have better instruments than ever before to probe the depths of the sea, to sample its rocks and deeply layered sediments, and to read with greater clarity the dim pages of past history.

34   Meanwhile, the sea ebbs and flows in these grander tides of earth, whose stages are measurable not in hours but in millennia—tides so vast they are invisible and uncomprehended by the senses of man. Their ultimate cause, should it ever be discovered, may be found to be deep within the fiery center of the earth, or it may lie somewhere in the dark spaces of the universe.

Discussion of Theme

1. In this day of vast storage of data it seems curious that there is so little information on the rising level of the oceans. What reasons does Rachel Carson give for this?

2. What evidence does the author give that "in all lands we may sense the former presence of the sea"? How, for example, could a farmer in Nebraska sense the sea?
3. What has modern science contributed to our understanding of the rise and fall of the oceans?

Discussion of Rhetoric

1. Rachel Carson never lost her sense of wonder about the world. Does she arouse a sense of wonder in you? How?
2. Comment on the imagery in paragraph 28. Where else does the author produce pictures with her words?
3. In this essay Carson attempted to present a technical, scientific subject to laymen. Does she succeed? How?
4. Parallel structure is a device used by writers to give sentences greater clarity, force, and rhythm. Find several examples of parallel structure in this essay.
5. Carson cites many familiar names in her opening paragraphs. What is the impact of these names, in view of her subject?
6. What is distinctive about the tone of the writing in paragraphs 5 and 6? What is the effect of this kind of writing? Do you suppose it was intentional? Is it particularly forceful?

Writing Assignments

1. Write a paper in which you attack the dumping of raw sewage and debris into the oceans. How does this practice affect both health and recreation?
2. What philosophical thoughts does this article stimulate in you? Does it make you see man and his world from a new perspective? Do you have a different feeling about the ocean and other natural elements? Does religion enter into your thinking? Write a thoughtful, personal reaction to this article.
3. Describe some aspect of terrestrial evolution that parallels what happened in the oceans over a period of millions of years.

Library Exploration

1. Read the biography of Alexander von Humboldt, after whom the Humboldt Current was named. What features of this current are remarkable?
2. If you enjoyed Carson's essay, you will probably find her books rewarding. *Silent Spring,* for example, points out the dangers of the indiscriminate use of insect and weed killers.

3. Although oceanography is one of the most important sciences today, the average layman still knows relatively little about it. Choose some aspect of the study — such as the coral reefs, ocean currents — and report on the latest findings.

Vocabulary

(1) TRANSIENT temporary; passing

(2) ENCROACHMENTS intrusions

(3) EMBAYMENT bay

(7) SUBMERGENCE covering with water

(9) EONS ages

(10) VENEER coating; layer

(11) PROTOZOAN one-celled animal

(12) NODULES knots; rounded lumps

(13) ESCARPMENT steep slope

(14) BREADFRUIT tropical fruit

(15) EROSION wearing away

(23) INTERGLACIAL formed between two glacial epochs

(24) TURGID swollen

(28) TUMULT violent and noisy commotion

(33) SEDIMENTS materials deposited by water

(34) MILLENNIA thousands of years

The Antic Muse

Woody Allen (1935–   ) is a well-known movie, Broadway, and television comedian. In recent years, besides films, he has written humorous essays for "Playboy," "The New Yorker" magazine, and the "New York Times," from which this selection is taken.

This humorous essay is a satire of the techniques and behavior of protestors, dissenters, and the civil-disobedience movement.

WOODY ALLEN

A Brief, Yet Helpful, Guide to Civil Disobedience

1   In perpetrating a revolution, there are two requirements; someone or something to revolt against and someone to actually show up and do the revolting. Dress is usually casual and both parties may be flexible about time and place, but if either faction fails to attend, the whole enterprise is likely to come off badly. In the Chinese Revolution of 1650 neither party showed up and the deposit on the hall was forfeited.

2   The people or parties revolted against are called the "oppressors" and are easily recognized as they seem to be the ones having all the fun. The "oppressors" generally get to wear suits, own land, and play their radios late at night without being yelled at. Their job is to maintain the "status quo," a condition where everything remains the same although they may be willing to paint every two years.

3   When the "oppressors" become too strict, we have what is known as a police state wherein all dissent is forbidden as is chuckling, showing up in a bow tie, or referring to the mayor as "Fats." Civil liberties are greatly curtailed in a police state and freedom of speech is unheard of although one is allowed to mime to a record. Opinions critical of the government are not tolerated, particularly about their dancing. Freedom of the press is

also curtailed and the ruling party "manages" the news, permitting the citizens to hear only acceptable political ideas and ball scores that will not cause unrest.

4   The groups who revolt are called the "oppressed" and can generally be seen milling about and grumbling or claiming to have headaches. (It should be noted that the oppressors never revolt and attempt to become the oppressed as that would entail a change of underwear.)

5   Some famous examples of revolutions are:

6   *The French Revolution,* in which the peasants seized power by force and quickly changed all locks on the palace doors so the nobles could not get back in. Then they had a large party and gorged themselves. When the nobles finally recaptured the palace they were forced to clean up and found many stains and cigarette burns.

7   *The Russian Revolution,* which simmered for years and suddenly erupted when the serfs finally realized that the Czar and the Tsar were the same person.

8   It should be noted that after a revolution is over, the "oppressed" frequently take over and begin acting like the "oppressors." Of course by then it is very hard to get them on the phone and money lent for cigarettes and gum during the fighting may as well be forgotten about.

9   Methods of Civil disobedience:

10   *Hunger strike.* Here the oppressed goes without food until his demands are met. Insidious politicians will often leave biscuits within easy reach or perhaps some cheddar cheese, but they must be resisted. If the party in power can get the striker to eat, they usually have little trouble putting down the insurrection. If they can get him to eat and also lift the check, they have won for sure. In Pakistan, a hunger strike was broken when the Government produced an exceptionally fine veal cordon bleu which the masses found was too appealing to turn down, but such gourmet dishes are rare.

11   The problem with the hunger strike is that after several days one can get quite hungry, particularly since sound-trucks are paid to go through the street saying, "Um . . . what nice chicken—umm . . . some peas . . . umm. . . ."

12   A modified form of the Hunger Strike for those whose political convictions are not quite so radical is giving up chives. This small gesture, when used properly, can greatly influence a government, and it is well known that Mahatma Gandhi's insistence on eating his salads untossed shamed the British Government into many concessions. Other things besides food one can give up are: whist, smiling, and standing on one foot and imitating a crane.

13   *Sit-down Strike.* Proceed to a designated spot and then sit down, but sit all the way down. Otherwise you are squatting, a position that makes no political point unless the government is also squatting. (This is rare, although a government will occasionally crouch in cold weather.) The trick is to remain seated until concessions are made, but as in the Hunger Strike, the government will try subtle means of making the striker rise. They may say, "Okay, everybody up, we're closing." Or, "Can you get up for a minute, we'd just like to see how tall you are?"

14 *Demonstration and Marches*. The key point about a demonstration is that it must be seen. Hence the term, "demonstration." If a person demonstrates privately in his own home, this is not technically a demonstration but merely "acting silly," or "behaving like an ass."

15 A fine example of a demonstration was The Boston Tea Party, where outraged Americans disguised as Indians dumped British tea into the harbor. Later, Indians disguised as outraged Americans dumped actual British into the harbor. Following that, the British disguised as tea, dumped each other into the harbor. Finally, German mercenaries clad only in costumes from "The Trojan Women" leapt into the harbor for no apparent reason.

16 When demonstrating, it is good to carry a placard stating one's position. Some suggested positions are: (1) lower taxes, (2) raise taxes, and (3) stop grinning at Persians.

17 Miscellaneous methods of Civil Disobedience:

18 Standing in front of City Hall and chanting the word "pudding" until one's demands are met.

19 Tying up traffic by leading a flock of sheep into the shopping area.

20 Phoning members of "the establishment" and singing "Bess, You Is My Woman, Now" into the phone.

21 Dressing as a policeman and then skipping.

22 Pretending to be an artichoke but punching people as they pass.

Discussion of Theme

1. Is Allen making a serious statement about revolution? What is it?
2. Does such a "put-on" reveal some basic truths? What are they?
3. What is civil disobedience? Is it more than an abstraction?

Discussion of Rhetoric

1. While this essay is amusing, how would you describe the tone? What is the effect of a pseudo-serious approach to humor?
2. Do all of Allen's jokes have a point? For example, what does the item in paragraph 20 *mean*? Why is it funny?
3. Might the response to paragraph 20 be much the same as the response to a "sight gag"?

Writing Assignments

1. Do you think young people are losing their sense of humor? Why might this be so?
2. Compare and contrast the jokes being told today with some of the jokes your parents told when they were in school. What do the differences reflect about changes in attitudes and society?
3. Write an essay in which you analyze the humor of a social comedian like Lenny Bruce.

Library Exploration

1. Allen once again deals with the subject of revolution in his 1971 film, "Bananas." Read and report on reviews of this film.
2. For a famous example of a serious essay written in a sardonic tone (and which was taken seriously by many), read Jonathan Swift's "A Modest Proposal."
3. If you enjoy Allen's humor, you might want to read his books *Don't Drink the Water,* 1967 and *Getting Even,* 1971.

Max Shulman, the American humorist, is best known for his novel, "The Many Loves of Dobie Gillis."

With tongue in cheek, Shulman claims that the following essay demonstrates ". . . that logic, far from being a dry, pedantic discipline, is a living, breathing thing, full of beauty, passion, and trauma."

MAX SHULMAN

Love Is a Fallacy

1. Cool was I and logical. Keen, calculating, perspicacious, acute and astute—I was all of these. My brain was as powerful as a dynamo, as precise as a chemist's scales, as penetrating as a scalpel. And—think of it!—I was only eighteen.

2   It is not often that one so young has such a giant intellect. Take, for example, Petey Burch, my roommate at the University of Minnesota. Same age, same background, but dumb as an ox. A nice enough fellow, you understand, but nothing upstairs. Emotional type. Unstable. Impressionable. Worst of all, a faddist. Fads, I submit, are the very negation of reason. To be swept up in every new craze that comes along, to surrender yourself to idiocy just because everybody else is doing it—this, to me, is the acme of mindlessness. Not, however, to Petey.

3   One afternoon I found Petey lying on his bed with an expression of such distress on his face that I immediately diagnosed appendicitis. "Don't move," I said. "Don't take a laxative. I'll get a doctor."

    "Raccoon," he mumbled thickly.

5   "Raccoon?" I said, pausing in my flight.

    "I want a raccoon coat," he wailed.

    I perceived that his trouble was not physical, but mental. "Why do you want a raccoon coat?"

8   "I should have known it," he cried, pounding his temples. "I should

have known they'd come back when the Charleston came back. Like a fool I spent all my money for textbooks, and now I can't get a raccoon coat."

"Can you mean," I said incredulously, "that people are actually wearing raccoon coats again?"

10   "All the Big Men on Campus are wearing them. Where've you been?"

"In the library," I said, naming a place not frequented by Big Men on Campus.

He leaped from the bed and paced the room. "I've got to have a raccoon coat," he said passionately. "I've got to!"

"Petey, why? Look at it rationally. Raccoon coats are unsanitary. They shed. They smell bad. They weigh too much. They're unsightly. They—"

"You don't understand," he interrupted impatiently. "It's the thing to do. Don't you want to be in the swim?"

"No," I said truthfully.

"Well, I do," he declared. "I'd give anything for a raccoon coat. Anything!"

My brain, that precision instrument, slipped into high gear. "Anything?" I asked, looking at him narrowly.

"Anything," he affirmed in ringing tones.

19   I stroked my chin thoughtfully. It so happened that I knew where to get my hands on a raccoon coat. My father had had one in his undergraduate days; it lay now in a trunk in the attic back home. It also happened that Petey had something I wanted. He didn't *have* it exactly, but at least he had first rights on it. I refer to his girl, Polly Espy.

20   I had long coveted Polly Espy. Let me emphasize that my desire for this young woman was not emotional in nature. She was, to be sure, a girl who excited the emotions, but I was not one to let my heart rule my head. I wanted Polly for a shrewdly calculated, entirely cerebral reason.

21   I was a freshman in law school. In a few years I would be out in practice. I was well aware of the importance of the right kind of wife in furthering a lawyer's career. The successful lawyers I had observed were, almost without exception, married to beautiful, gracious, intelligent women. With one omission, Polly fitted these specifications perfectly.

22   Beautiful she was. She was not yet of pin-up proportions, but I felt sure that time would supply the lack. She already had the makings.

23   Gracious she was. By gracious I mean full of graces. She had an erectness of carriage, an ease of bearing, a poise that clearly indicated the best of breeding. At table her manners were exquisite. I had seen her at the Kozy Kampus Korner eating the specialty of the house—a sandwich that contained scraps of pot roast, gravy, chopped nuts, and a dipper of sauerkraut—without even getting her fingers moist.

24   Intelligent she was not. In fact, she veered in the opposite direction. But I believed that under my guidance she would smarten up. At any rate, it was worth a try. It is, after all, easier to make a beautiful dumb girl smart than to make an ugly smart girl beautiful.

25 "Petey," I said, "are you in love with Polly Espy?"

"I think she's a keen kid," he replied, "but I don't know if you'd call it love. Why?"

"Do you," I asked, "have any kind of formal arrangement with her? I mean are you going steady or anything like that?"

"No. We see each other quite a bit, but we both have other dates. Why?"

"Is there," I asked, "any other man for whom she has a particular fondness?"

30 "Not that I know of. Why?"

I nodded with satisfaction. "In other words, if you were out of the picture, the field would be open. Is that right?"

"I guess so. What are you getting at?"

"Nothing, nothing," I said innocently, and took my suitcase out of the closet.

"Where are you going?" asked Petey.

35 "Home for the weekend." I threw a few things into the bag.

"Listen," he said, clutching my arm eagerly, "while you're home, you couldn't get some money from your old man, could you, and lend it to me so I can buy a raccoon coat?"

"I may do better than that," I said with a mysterious wink and closed my bag and left.

"Look," I said to Petey when I got back Monday morning. I threw open the suitcase and revealed the huge, hairy, gamy object that my father had worn in his Stutz Bearcat in 1925.

"Holy Toledo!" said Petey reverently. He plunged his hands into the raccoon coat and then his face. "Holy Toledo!" he repeated fifteen or twenty times.

40 "Would you like it?" I asked.

"Oh yes!" he cried, clutching the greasy pelt to him. Then a canny look came into his eyes. "What do you want for it?"

"Your girl," I said, mincing no words.

"Polly?" he said in a horrified whisper. "You want Polly?"

"That's right."

45 He flung the coat from him. "Never," he said stoutly.

I shrugged. "Okay. If you don't want to be in the swim, I guess it's your business."

47 I sat down in a chair and pretended to read a book, but out of the corner of my eye I kept watching Petey. He was a torn man. First he looked at the coat with the expression of a waif at a bakery window. Then he turned away and set his jaw resolutely. Then he looked back at the coat, with even more longing in his face. Then he turned away, but with not so much resolution this time. Back and forth his head swiveled, desire waxing, resolution waning. Finally he didn't turn away at all; he just stood and stared with mad lust at the coat.

48 "It isn't as though I was in love with Polly," he said thickly. "Or going steady or anything like that."

"That's right," I murmured.

50 "What's Polly to me, or me to Polly?"

"Not a thing," said I.

"It's just been a casual kick—just a few laughs, that's all."

"Try on the coat," said I.

54   He complied. The coat bunched high over his ears and dropped all the way down to his shoe tops. He looked like a mound of dead raccoons. "Fits fine," he said happily.

55   I rose from my chair. "Is it a deal?" I asked, extending my hand.

56   He swallowed. "It's a deal," he said and shook my hand.

57   I had my first date with Polly the following evening. This was in the nature of a survey; I wanted to find out just how much work I had to do to get her mind up to the standard I required. I took her first to dinner. "Gee, that was a delish dinner," she said as we left the restaurant. Then I took her to a movie. "Gee, that was a marvy movie," she said as we left the theater. And then I took her home. "Gee, I had a sensaysh time," she said as she bade me good night.

58   I went back to my room with a heavy heart. I had gravely underestimated the size of my task. This girl's lack of information was terrifying. Nor would it be enough merely to supply her with information. First she had to be taught to *think*. This loomed as a project of no small dimensions, and at first I was tempted to give her back to Petey. But then I got to thinking about her abundant physical charms and about the way she entered a room and the way she handled a knife and fork, and I decided to make an effort.

59   I went about it, as in all things, systematically. I gave her a course in logic. It happened that I, as a law student, was taking a course in logic myself, so I had all the facts at my finger tips. "Polly," I said to her when I picked her up on our next date, "tonight we are going over to the Knoll and talk."

60   "Oo, terrif," she replied. One thing I will say for this girl: you would go far to find another so agreeable.

    We went to the Knoll, the campus trysting place, and we sat down under an old oak, and she looked at me expectantly. "What are we going to talk about?" she asked.

    "Logic."

    She thought this over for a minute and decided she liked it. "Magnif," she said.

    "Logic," I said, clearing my throat, "is the science of thinking. Before we can think correctly, we must first learn to recognize the common fallacies of logic. These we will take up tonight."

65   "Wow-dow!" she cried, clapping her hands delightedly.

    I winced, but went bravely on. "First let us examine the fallacy called Dicto Simpliciter."

    "By all means," she urged, batting her lashes eagerly.

    "Dicto Simpliciter means an argument based on an unqualified generalization. For example: Exercise is good. Therefore everybody should exercise."

    "I agree," said Polly earnestly. "I mean exercise is wonderful. I mean it builds the body and everything."

70   "Polly," I said gently, "the argument is a fallacy. *Exercise is good* is an unqualified generalization. For instance, if you have heart disease, exercise is bad, not good. Many people are ordered by their doctors *not* to exercise. You must *qualify* the generalization. You must say exercise is *usually* good, or exercise is good *for most people*. Otherwise you have committed a Dicto Simpliciter. Do you see?"

71   "No," she confessed. "But this is marvy. Do more! Do more!"

72   "It will be better if you stop tugging at my sleeve," I told her, and when she desisted, I continued. "Next we take up a fallacy called Hasty Generalization. Listen carefully: You can't speak French. I can't speak French. Petey Burch can't speak French. I must therefore conclude that nobody at the University of Minnesota can speak French."

73   "Really?" said Polly, amazed. *"Nobody?"*

74   I hid my exasperation. "Polly, it's a fallacy. The generalization is reached too hastily. There are two few instances to support such a conclusion."

75   "Know any more fallacies?" she asked breathlessly. "This is more fun than dancing even."

76   I fought off a wave of despair. I was getting nowhere with this girl, absolutely nowhere. Still, I am nothing if not persistent. I continued. "Next comes Post Hoc. Listen to this: Let's not take Bill on our picnic. Every time we take him out with us, it rains."

77   "I know somebody just like that," she exclaimed. "A girl back home—Eula Becker, her name is. It never fails. Every single time we take her on a picnic—"

78   "Polly," I said sharply, "it's a fallacy. Eula Becker doesn't *cause* the rain. She has no connection with the rain. You are guilty of Post Hoc if you blame Eula Becker."

79   "I'll never do it again," she promised contritely. "Are you mad at me?"

80   I sighed deeply. "No, Polly, I'm not mad."

"Then tell me some more fallacies."

"All right. Let's try Contradictory Premises."

"Yes, let's," she chirped, blinking her eyes happily.

I frowned, but plunged ahead. "Here's an example of Contradictory Premises: If God can do anything, can He make a stone so heavy that He won't be able to lift it?"

85   "Of course," she replied promptly.

"But if He can do anything, He can lift the stone," I pointed out.

"Yeah," she said thoughtfully. "Well, then I guess He can't make the stone."

"But He can do anything," I reminded her.

She scratched her pretty, empty head. "I'm all confused," she admitted.

90   "Of course you are. Because when the premises of an argument contradict each other, there can be no argument. If there is an irresistible force, there can be no immovable object. If there is an immovable object, there can be no irresistible force. Get it?"

91   "Tell me some more of this keen stuff," she said eagerly.

92   I consulted my watch. "I think we'd better call it a night. I'll take you home now, and you go over all the things you've learned. We'll have another session tomorrow night."

93   I deposited her at the girls' dormitory, where she assured me that she had had a perfectly terrif evening, and I went glumly home to my room. Petey lay snoring in his bed, the raccoon coat huddled like a great hairy beast at his feet. For a moment I considered waking him

and telling him that he could have his girl back. It seemed clear that my project was doomed to failure. The girl simply had a logic-proof head.

94   But then I reconsidered. I had wasted one evening; I might as well waste another. Who knew? Maybe somewhere in the extinct crater of her mind, a few embers still smoldered. Maybe somehow I could fan them into flame. Admittedly it was not a prospect fraught with hope, but I decided to give it one more try.

95   Seated under the oak the next evening I said, "Our first fallacy tonight is called Ad Misericordiam."

96   She quivered with delight.

97   "Listen closely," I said. "A man applies for a job. When the boss asks him what his qualifications are, he replies that he has a wife and six children at home, the wife is a helpless cripple, the children have nothing to eat, no clothes to wear, no shoes on their feet, there are no beds in the house, no coal in the cellar, and winter is coming."

98   A tear rolled down each of Polly's pink cheeks. "Oh, this is awful, awful," she sobbed.

99   "Yes, it's awful," I agreed, "but it's no argument. The man never answered the boss's question about his qualifications. Instead he appealed to the boss's sympathy. He committed the fallacy of Ad Misericordiam. Do you understand?"

100   "Have you got a handkerchief?" she blubbered.

101   I handed her a handkerchief and tried to keep from screaming while she wiped her eyes. "Next," I said in a carefully controlled tone, "we will discuss False Analogy. Here is an example: Students should be allowed to look at their textbooks during examinations. After all, surgeons have X-rays to guide them during an operation, lawyers have briefs to guide them during a trial, carpenters have blueprints to guide them when they are building a house. Why, then, shouldn't students be allowed to look at their textbooks during an examination?"

102   "There now," she said enthusiastically, "is the most marvy idea I've heard in years."

103   "Polly," I said testily, "the argument is all wrong. Doctors, lawyers, and carpenters aren't taking a test to see how much they have learned, but students are. The situations are altogether different, and you can't make an analogy between them."

     "I still think it's a good idea," said Polly.

105   "Nuts," I muttered. Doggedly I pressed on. "Next we'll try Hypothesis Contrary to Fact."

     "Sounds yummy," was Polly's reaction.

     "Listen: If Madame Curie had not happened to leave a photographic plate in a drawer with a chunk of pitchblende, the world today would not know about radium."

     "True, true," said Polly, nodding her head. "Did you see the movie? Oh, it just knocked me out. That Walter Pidgeon is so dreamy. I mean he fractures me."

109   "If you can forget Mr. Pidgeon for a moment," I said coldly, "I would like to point out that the statement is a fallacy. Maybe Madame Curie would have discovered radium at some later date.

Maybe somebody else would have discovered it. Maybe any number of things would have happened. You can't start with a hypothesis that is not true and then draw any supportable conclusions from it."

110 "They ought to put Walter Pidgeon in more pictures," said Polly. "I hardly ever see him any more."

111 One more chance, I decided. But just one more. There is a limit to what flesh and blood can bear. "The next fallacy is called Poisoning the Well."

112 "How cute!" she gurgled.

113 "Two men are having a debate. The first one gets up and says, 'My opponent is a notorious liar. You can't believe a word that he is going to say.' . . . Now, Polly, think. Think hard. What's wrong?"

114 I watched her closely as she knit her creamy brow in concentration. Suddenly a glimmer of intelligence—the first I had seen—came into her eyes. "It's not fair," she said with indignation. "It's not a bit fair. What chance has the second man got if the first man calls him a liar before he even begins talking?"

115 "Right!" I cried exultantly. "One hundred percent right. It's not fair. The first man has *poisoned the well* before anybody could drink from it. He has hamstrung his opponent before he could even start. . . . Polly, I'm proud of you."

116 "Pshaw," she murmured, blushing with pleasure.

117 "You see, my dear, these things aren't so hard. All you have to do is concentrate. Think—examine—evaluate. Come now, let's review everything we have learned."

118 "Fire away," she said with an airy wave of her hand.

119 Heartened by the knowledge that Polly was not altogether a cretin, I began a long, patient review of all I had told her. Over and over and over again I cited instances, pointed out flaws, kept hammering away without letup. It was like digging a tunnel. At first everything was work, sweat, and darkness. I had no idea when I would reach the light, or even *if* I would. But I persisted. I pounded and clawed and scraped, and finally I was rewarded. I saw a chink of light. And then the chink got bigger and the sun came pouring in and all was bright.

120 Five grueling nights this took, but it was worth it. I had made a logician out of Polly; I had taught her to think. My job was done. She was worthy of me at last. She was a fit wife for me, a proper hostess for my many mansions, a suitable mother for my well-heeled children.

121 It must not be thought that I was without love for this girl. Quite the contrary. Just as Pygmalion loved the perfect woman he had fashioned, so I loved mine. I determined to acquaint her with my feelings at our very next meeting. The time had come to change our relationship from academic to romantic.

122 "Polly," I said when next we sat beneath our oak, "tonight we will not discuss fallacies."

123 "Aw, gee," she said, disappointed.

124 "My dear," I said, favoring her with a smile, "we have now spent five evenings together. We have gotten along splendidly. It is clear that we are well matched."

125 "Hasty Generalization," said Polly brightly.

126 "I beg your pardon," said I.

"Hasty Generalization," she repeated. "How can you say that we are well matched on the basis of only five dates?"

128 I chuckled with amusement. The dear child had learned her lessons well. "My dear," I said, patting her hand in a tolerant manner, "five dates is plenty. After all, you don't have to eat a whole cake to know that it's good."

"False Analogy," said Polly promptly. "I'm not a cake. I'm a girl."

130 I chuckled with somewhat less amusement. The dear child had learned her lessons perhaps too well. I decided to change tactics. Obviously the best approach was a simple, strong, direct declaration of love. I paused for a moment while my massive brain chose the proper words. Then I began:

131 "Polly, I love you. You are the whole world to me, and the moon and the stars and the constellations of outer space. Please, my darling, say that you will go steady with me, for if you will not, life will be meaningless. I will languish. I will refuse my meals. I will wander the face of the earth, a shambling, hollow-eyed hulk."

There, I thought, folding my arms, that ought to do it.

"Ad Misericordiam," said Polly.

I ground my teeth. I was not Pygmalion; I was Frankenstein, and my monster had me by the throat. Frantically I fought back the tide of panic surging through me. At all costs I had to keep cool.

135 "Well, Polly," I said, forcing a smile, "you certainly have learned your fallacies."

"You're darn right," she said with a vigorous nod.

"And who taught them to you, Polly?"

"You did."

"That's right. So you do owe me something, don't you, my dear? If I hadn't come along you never would have learned about fallacies."

140 "Hypothesis Contrary to Fact," she said instantly.

I dashed perspiration from my brow. "Polly," I croaked, "you mustn't take all these things so literally. I mean this is just classroom stuff. You know that the things you learn in school don't have anything to do with life."

"Dicto Simpliciter," she said, wagging her finger at me playfully.

That did it. I leaped to my feet, bellowing like a bull. "Will you or will you not go steady with me?"

"I will not," she replied.

145 "Why not?" I demanded.

"Because this afternoon I promised Petey Burch that I would go steady with him."

I reeled back, overcome with the infamy of it. After he promised, after he made a deal, after he shook my hand! "The rat!" I shrieked, kicking up great chunks of turf. "You can't go with him, Polly. He's a liar. He's a cheat. He's a rat."

"Poisoning the Well," said Polly, "and stop shouting. I think shouting must be a fallacy too."

149 With an immense effort of will, I modulated my voice. "All right," I said. "You're a logician. Let's look at this thing logically. How could you choose Petey Burch over me? Look at me—a brilliant student, a

tremendous intellectual, a man with an assured future. Look at
Petey—a knothead, a jitterbug, a guy who'll never know where his
next meal is coming from. Can you give me one logical reason why
you should go steady with Petey Burch?"
150 "I certainly can," declared Polly. "He's got a raccoon coat."

Discussion of Theme

1. Do people really look for husbands or wives with such cold logic?
   Should they?
2. Is it really possible (or even desirable) for a person to think logically during times of great emotional stress?
3. Do you think the study of logic should be a basic college requirement?

Discussion of Rhetoric

1. What tone is established at the beginning of the essay? Does it
   change? Why?
2. What is wrong with this sentence from paragraph 39? "He plunged
   his hands into the raccoon coat and then his face." Is this a weakness or a deliberate device?
3. Identify the figure of speech used in paragraph 94 and explain its
   meaning.

Writing Assignments

1. Listen to a political speech or read newspaper editorials and identify logical fallacies. Write a report on your findings.
2. Write a humorous essay about a personal experience in which the
   use of logic either solved or complicated a problem.

Library Exploration

1. You may enjoy reading some other work of Max Shulman, such as
   Barefoot Boy with Cheek and *The Feather Merchants*.

Vocabulary

(2) ACME   the highest   (119) CRETIN   an idiot
    point

Humor is a most effective, yet frequently neglected, means of handling the difficult situations in our lives, as the anecdotes in this article make clear.

WILLIAM D. ELLIS

Solve That Problem— with Humor

1 A lot of us lose life's tougher confrontations by mounting a frontal attack—when a touch of humor might well enable us to chalk up a win. Consider the case of a young friend of mine, who hit a traffic jam en route to work shortly after receiving an ultimatum about being late on the job. Although there was a good reason for Sam's chronic tardiness—serious illness at home—he decided that this by-now-familiar excuse wouldn't work any longer. His supervisor was probably already pacing up and down with a dismissal speech rehearsed.

2 He was. Sam entered the office at 9:35. The place was as quiet as a loser's locker room; everyone was hard at work. Sam's supervisor approached him. Suddenly, Sam forced a grin and shoved out his hand. "How do you do!" he said. "I'm Sam Maynard. I'm applying for a job I understand became available just 35 minutes ago. Does the early bird get the worm?"

3 The room exploded in laughter. The supervisor clamped off a smile and walked back to his office. Sam Maynard had saved his job—with the only tool that could win, a laugh.

4 Humor is a most effective, yet frequently neglected, means of handling the difficult situations in our lives. It can be used for patching up differences, apologizing, saying "no," criticizing, getting the other fellow to do what you want without his losing face. For some jobs, it's the *only* tool that can succeed. It is a way to discuss subjects so sensitive that serious dialogue may start a riot. For example, many believe that comedians on television are doing more today for racial and religious tolerance than are people in any other forum.

5 Humor is often the best way to keep a small misunderstanding from escalating into a big deal. Recently a neighbor of mine had a squabble with his wife as she drove him to the airport. Airborne, he felt miserable, and he knew she did, too. Two hours after she returned home,

she received a long-distance phone call. "Person-to-person for Mrs. I. A. Pologize," intoned the operator. "That's spelled 'P' as in. . . ." In a twinkling, the whole day changed from grim to lovely at both ends of the wire.

6   An English hostess with a quick wit was giving a formal dinner for eight distinguished guests whom she hoped to enlist in a major charity drive. Austerity was *de rigueur* in England at the time, and she had drafted her children to serve the meal. She knew that anything could happen—and it did, just as her son, with the studied concentration of a tightrope walker, brought in a large roast turkey. He successfully elbowed the swinging dining-room door, but the backswing deplattered the bird onto the dining-room floor.

7   The boy stood rooted: guests stared at their plates. Moving only her head, the hostess smiled at her son. "No harm, Daniel," she said. "Just pick him up and take him back to the kitchen"—she enunciated clearly so he would think about what she was saying—"and bring in the *other* one."

8   A wink and a one-liner instantly changed the dinner from a red-faced embarrassment to a conspiracy of fun.

9   The power of humor to dissolve a hostile confrontation often lies in its unspoken promise: "You let me off the hook, my friend, and I'll let you off." The trick is to assign friendly motives to your opponent, to smile just a little—but not too much. Canada's Governor-General Roland Michener, master of the technique, was about to inspect a public school when he was faced with a truculent picket line of striking maintenance personnel. If he backed away from the line, he would seriously diminish his office's image; if he crossed it, he might put the government smack into a hot labor issue.

10   While he pondered the matter, more strikers gathered across his path. Suddenly, the graying pencil-line mustache on Michener's weathered face stretched a little in Cheshirean complicity. "How very nice of you all to turn out to see me!" he boomed. "Thank you. Shall we go in?" The line parted and, by the time the pickets began to chuckle, the governor-general was striding briskly up the school steps.

11   Next time you find yourself in an ethnically awkward situation, take a lesson from the diplomatic delegates to Europe's Common Market. In the course of history, nearly every member nation has been invaded or betrayed by at least one of the others, and the Market's harmony must be constantly buttressed. One method is the laugh based on national caricatures. Recently, a new arrival at Market headquarters in Brussels introduced himself as a minister for the Swiss navy. Everybody laughed. The Swiss delegate retorted, "Well, why not? Italy has a minister of finance."

12   Of course, humor is often more than a laughing matter. In its more potent guises, it has a Trojan-horse nature: no one goes on guard against a gag; we let it in because it looks like a little wooden toy. Once inside, however, it can turn a city to reform, to rebellion, to resistance. Some believe, for instance, that, next to the heroic British RAF, British humor did the most to fend off German takeover in World War II. One sample will suffice: that famous story of the

woman who was finally extracted from the rubble of her house during the London blitz. Asked, "Where is your husband?" she brushed brick dust off her head and arms and answered, "Fighting in Libya, the bloody coward!"

13   Similarly, whenever we Americans start taking ourselves a bit too seriously, a grassroots humor seems to rise and strew banana peels in our path. The movement is usually led by professionals: Mark Twain penlancing the boils of pomposity ("Man was made at the end of the week's work, when God was tired."); Will Rogers deflating our lawmakers ("The oldest boy became a Congressman, and the second son turned out no good, too."); Bill Mauldin needling fatuous officers (One 2nd lieutenant to another, on observing a beautiful sunset: "Is there one for enlisted men, too?"). Such masters of comic deflation restore the balance. They bring us back to ourselves.

14   When life has us in a tight corner, one of the first questions we might ask is, "Can I solve this with a laugh?" Men with giant responsibilities have frequently used this approach to solve giant problems—often with sweeping effect. As Gen. George C. Marshall, U.S. Army Chief of Staff, labored to prepare this then-unready nation to enter World War II, he met stiff opposition from his commander-in-chief regarding the elements that called for the most bolstering. Marshall felt that what we needed most were highly developed ground forces. President Roosevelt was a Navy man who believed that our principal need was for a powerful navy, plus a large air force. In increasingly tense debates with the President, Marshall pushed his argument so hard that he began to foster ever stronger resistance. Finally, during a particularly hot session, the usually stonefaced Marshall forced a grin. "At least, Mr. President," he said, "you might stop referring to the Navy as 'us' and the Army as 'them.'"

15   Roosevelt studied Marshall over his glasses, then unlipped a great show of teeth and laughter. Shortly thereafter, he made a more objective study of Marshall's recommendations and eventually bought the ground-force concept.

16   Occasionally, humor goes beyond saving arguments, saving face or saving jobs; it can save life itself. Viktor E. Frankl was a psychiatrist imprisoned in a German concentration camp during World War II. As the shrinking number of surviving prisoners descended to new depths of hell, Frankl and his closest prisoner friend sought desperately for ways to keep from dying. Piled on top of malnutrition, exhaustion and disease, suicidal despair was the big killer in these citadels of degradation.

17   As a psychiatrist, Frankl knew that humor was one of the soul's best survival weapons, since it can create, if only for moments, aloofness from horror. Therefore, Frankl made a rule that once each day he and his friend must invent and tell an amusing anecdote, specifically about something which could happen after their liberation.

18   Others were caught up in the contagion of defiant laughter. One starving prisoner forecast that in the future he might be at a prestigious formal dinner, and when the soup was being served, he would shatter protocol by imploring the hostess, "Ladle it from the *bottom!*"

19   Frankl tells of another prisoner, who nodded toward one of the most despised *capos*—favored prisoners who acted as guards and became as arrogant as the SS men. "Imagine!" he quipped. I knew him when he was only the president of a bank!"

20   If humor can be used successfully against such odds, what can't you and I do with it in daily life?

Discussion of Theme

1. Do you think that the author is being a bit simplistic? How can one, in times of extreme tension, stop and ask oneself, "Can I solve this with a laugh?"
2. According to the author, what are some of the practical values in humor?

Discussion of Rhetoric

1. What figure of speech is used in paragraph 2? Is it appropriate? Find other figures of speech used by the author and identify them.
2. What is the author's main method of development?
3. Does the author use any humor of his own in this essay? Where?

Writing Assignments

1. Report on a comedian who has effectively used his humor for social criticism.
2. Write an essay about how you handled a delicate situation with humor.
3. Write a short piece about your favorite joke, analyzing why it is funny to you.

Library Exploration

1. Research and report on the jokes that have arisen out of certain situations, such as the hippie and feminist movements, the economy, Watergate, or so on.

Vocabulary

(6) DE RIGUEUR   characterized by extreme strictness

(11) BUTTRESSED   supported

(13) POMPOSITY   ostentatious parade of dignity

(13) FATUOUS   foolish or silly; trite

(16) CITADELS   strongholds

Religion and Philosophy: Diverse Views

Loren Eiseley (1907–   ) is one of America's most distinguished anthropologists. Born in Nebraska, he received degrees from the University of Nebraska and the University of Pennsylvania, where he is now professor of anthropology and the history of science. The possessor of a distinct and readable literary style, he has gained a wide audience from his books, articles, and poetry. Among his books are "The Mind as Nature" (1962) and "The Unexpected Universe" (1969).

Significant truths are sometimes revealed to us by a hidden teacher, according to Professor Eiseley. His own casual encounter with a spider – described in the following article – led to a profound insight.

LOREN EISELEY

The Hidden Teacher

Sometimes the best teacher teaches only once to a single child or to a grownup past hope.

— ANONYMOUS

1   The putting of formidable riddles did not arise with today's philosophers. In fact, there is a sense in which the experimental method of science might be said merely to have widened the area of man's homelessness. Over two thousand years ago, a man named Job, crouching in the Judean desert, was moved to challenge what he felt to be the injustice of his God. The voice in the whirlwind, in turn, volleyed pitiless questions upon the supplicant – questions that have, in truth, precisely the ring of modern science. For the Lord asked of Job by

whose wisdom the hawk soars, and who had fathered the rain, or entered the storehouses of the snow.

2   A youth standing by, one Elihu, also played a role in this drama, for he ventured diffidently to his protesting elder that it was not true that God failed to manifest Himself. He may speak in one way or another, though men do not perceive it. In consequence of this remark perhaps it would be well, whatever our individual beliefs, to consider what may be called the hidden teacher, lest we become too much concerned with the formalities of only one aspect of the education by which we learn.

3   We think we learn from teachers, and we sometimes do. But the teachers are not always to be found in school or in great laboratories. Sometimes what we learn depends upon our own powers of insight. Moreover, our teachers may be hidden, even the greatest teacher. And it was the young man Elihu who observed that if the old are not always wise, neither can the teacher's way be ordered by the young whom he would teach.

4   For example, I once received an unexpected lesson from a spider.

5   It happened far away on a rainy morning in the West. I had come up a long gulch looking for fossils, and there, just at eye level, lurked a huge yellow-and-black orb spider, whose web was moored to the tall spears of buffalo grass at the edge of the arroyo. It was her universe, and her senses did not extend beyond the lines and spokes of the great wheel she inhabited. Her extended claws could feel every vibration throughout that delicate structure. She knew the tug of wind, the fall of a raindrop, the flutter of a trapped moth's wing. Down one spoke of the web ran a stout ribbon of gassamer on which she could hurry out to investigate her prey.

6   Curious, I took a pencil from my pocket and touched a strand of the web. Immediately there was a response. The web, plucked by its menacing occupant, began to vibrate until it was a blur. Anything that had brushed claw or wing against that amazing snare would be thoroughly entrapped. As the vibrations slowed, I could see the owner fingering her guidelines for signs of struggle. A pencil point was an intrusion into this universe for which no precedent existed. Spider was circumscribed by spider ideas; its universe was spider universe. All outside was irrational, extraneous, at best, raw material for spider. As I proceeded on my way along the gully, like a vast impossible shadow, I realized that in the world of spider I did not exist.

7   Moreover, I considered, as I tramped along, that to the phagocytes, the white blood cells, clambering even now with some kind of elementary intelligence amid the thin pipes and tubing of my body—creatures without whose ministrations I could not exist—the conscious "I" of which I was aware had no significance to these amoeboid beings. I was, instead, a kind of chemical web that brought meaningful messages to them, a natural environment seemingly immortal if they could have thought about it, since generations of them had lived and perished, and would continue to so live and die, in that odd fabric which contained my intelligence—a misty light that was beginning to seem floating and tenuous even to me.

8   I began to see that among the many universes in which the world of living creatures existed, some were large, some small, but that all, including man's, were in some way limited or finite. We were creatures of many different dimensions passing through each other's lives like ghosts through doors.

9   In the years since, my mind has many times returned to that far moment of my encounter with the orb spider. A message has arisen only now from the misty shreds of that webbed universe. What was it that had so troubled me about the incident? Was it that spidery indifference to the human triumph?

10   If so, that triumph was very real and could not be denied. I saw, had many times seen, both mentally and in the seams of exposed strata, the long backward stretch of time whose recovery is one of the great feats of modern science. I saw the drifting cells of the early seas from which all life, including our own, has arisen. The salt of those ancient seas is in our blood, its lime is in our bones. Every time we walk along a beach some ancient urge disturbs us so that we find ourselves shedding shoes and garments, or scavenging among seaweed and whitened timbers like the homesick refugees of a long war.

11   And war it has been indeed—the long war of life against its inhospitable environment, a war that has lasted for perhaps three billion years. It began with strange chemicals seething under a sky lacking in oxygen; it was waged through long ages until the first green plants learned to harness the light of the nearest star, our sun. The human brain, so frail, so perishable, so full of inexhaustible dreams and hungers, burns by the power of the leaf.

12   The hurrying blood cells charged with oxygen carry more of that element to the human brain than to any other part of the body. A few moments' loss of vital air and the phenomenon we know as consciousness goes down into the black night of inorganic things. The human body is a magical vessel, but its life is linked with an element it cannot produce. Only the green plant knows the secret of transforming the light that comes to us across the far reaches of space. There is no better illustration of the intricacy of man's relationship with other living things.

13   The student of fossil life would be forced to tell us that if we take the past into consideration the vast majority of earth's creatures—perhaps over ninety per cent—have vanished. Forms that flourished for a far longer time than man has existed upon earth have become either extinct or so transformed that their descendants are scarcely recognizable. The specialized perish with the environment that created them, the tooth of the tiger fails at last, the lances of men strike down the last mammoth.

14   In three billion years of slow change and groping effort only one living creature has succeeded in escaping the trap of specialization that has led in time to so much death and wasted endeavor. It is man, but the word should be uttered softly, for his story is not yet done.

15   With the rise of the human brain, with the appearance of a creature whose upright body enabled two limbs to be freed for the exploration and manipulation of his environment, there had at last emerged a

creature with a specialization—the brain—that, paradoxically, offered escape from specialization. Many animals driven into the nooks and crannies of nature have achieved momentary survival only at the cost of later extinction.

16   Was it this that troubled me and brought my mind back to a tiny universe among the grass-blades, a spider's universe concerned with spider thought?

17   Perhaps.

18   The mind that once visualized animals on a cave wall is now engaged in a vast ramification of itself through time and space. Man has broken through the boundaries that control all other life. I saw, at last, the reason for my recollection of that great spider on the arroyo's rim, fingering its universe against the sky.

19   The spider was a symbol of man in miniature. The wheel of the web brought the analogy home clearly. Man, too, lies at the heart of a web, a web extending through the starry reaches of sidereal space, as well as backward into the dark realm of prehistory. His great eye upon Mount Palomar looks into a distance of millions of light-years, his radio ear hears the whisper of even more remote galaxies, he peers through the electron microscope upon the minute particles of his own being. It is a web no creature of earth has ever spun before. Like the orb spider, man lies at the heart of it, listening. Knowledge has given him the memory of earth's history beyond the time of his emergence. Like the spider's claw, a part of him touches a world he will never enter in the flesh. Even now, one can see him reaching forward into time with new machines, computing, analyzing, until elements of the shadowy future will also compose part of the invisible web he fingers.

20   Yet still my spider lingers in memory against the sunset sky. Spider thoughts in a spider universe—sensitive to raindrop and moth flutter, nothing beyond, nothing allowed for the unexpected, the inserted pencil from the world outside.

21   Is man at heart any different from the spider, I wonder: man thoughts, as limited as spider thoughts, contemplating now the nearest star with the threat of bringing with him the fungus rot from earth, wars, violence, the burden of a population he refuses to control, cherishing again his dream of the Adamic Eden he had pursued and lost in the green forests of America. Now it beckons again like a mirage from beyond the moon. Let man spin his web, I thought further; it is his nature. But I considered also the work of the phagocytes swarming in the rivers of my body, the unresting cells in their mortal universe. What is it we are a part of that we do not see, as the spider was not gifted to discern my face, or my little probe into her world?

22   We are too content with our sensory extensions, with the fulfillment of that ice age mind that began its journey amidst the cold of vast tundras and that pauses only briefly before its leap into space. It is no longer enough to see as a man sees—even to the ends of the universe. It is not enough to hold nuclear energy in one's hand like a spear, as a man would hold it, or to see the lightning, or times past, or time to come, as a man would see it. If we continue to do this, the great brain —the human brain—will be only a new version of the old trap, and nature is full of traps for the beast that cannot learn.

23   It is not sufficient any longer to listen at the end of a wire to the rustlings of galaxies; it is not enough even to examine the great coil of DNA in which is coded the very alphabet of life. These are our extended perceptions. But beyond lies the great darkness of the ultimate Dreamer, who dreamed the light and the galaxies. Before act was, or substance existed, imagination grew in the dark. Man partakes of that ultimate wonder and creativeness. As we turn from the galaxies to the swarming cells of our own being, which toil for something, some entity beyond their grasp, let us remember man, the self-fabricator who came across an ice age to look into the mirrors and the magic of science. Surely he did not come to see himself or his wild visage only. He came because he is at heart a listener and a searcher for some transcendent realm beyond himself. This he has worshiped by many names, even in the dismal caves of his beginning. Man, the self-fabricator, is so by reason of gifts he had no part in devising — and so he searches as the single living cell in the beginning must have sought the ghostly creature it was to serve.

Discussion of Theme

1. In what way has "the experimental method of science . . . widened the area of man's homelessness"?
2. In what sense can a teacher be "hidden"? What does this imply about the learning process?
3. How does Eiseley show the relationship of man with other life?
4. According to the author, what characteristics have helped man to survive? Is he certain of man's continuing survival?
5. Explain the anecdote concerning the spider. What was the unexpected lesson (paragraph 4)?

Discussion of Rhetoric

1. How does Eiseley relate the anecdote of Job to his thesis?
2. The author uses analogies to explain or illustrate his central idea. Examine carefully one or two of these, and determine whether they help to clarify his thesis.
3. Note the author's use of specific details in various passages. Find such a passage and examine Eiseley's skillful use of diction and "picture-making."
4. How does this selection differ from most scientific writing? How does it resemble poetry?

Writing Assignments

1. Develop the following statement: "Sometimes the best teacher teaches only once to a single child or to a grownup past hope."
2. Select an experience from your own life that was comparable in

significance to that of Eiseley's with the spider. Describe the experience, showing what you learned from it.

3. In a paper, apply Eiseley's ideas on teachers and learning to higher education today. What reforms or changes would you propose?

Library Exploration

1. *The Unexpected Universe* (1969), from which this selection was taken, contains a fuller treatment of the miracle of man and his world.
2. Investigate one of the following: carbon 14; DNA; fossils; radio telescopes; electron microscopes.

Vocabulary

(1) SUPPLICANT   one who makes a request humbly and earnestly

(5) ARROYO   a small steep gulch

(5) GOSSAMER   something light, delicate, or tenuous

(6) CIRCUMSCRIBED   encircled

(6) EXTRANEOUS   external; foreign

(7) MINISTRATIONS   aid; assistance

(7) TENUOUS   slight; unsubstantial

(23) VISAGE   face

(23) TRANSCENDENT   going beyond the universe or material existence

Albert Camus (1913–60) was born and educated in Algiers, then under French rule. He was himself a rebel, a member of the French Resistance in World War II and, like so many of his comrades, a contributor to the intellectualism of postwar France. He was an associate of Jean-Paul Sartre but did not claim to be an existentialist. His serious writing began after the war in Europe, and his main ideas can be found in "The Stranger" (1946), "The Plague" (1948), and "The Myth of Sisyphus" (1955). He also wrote a considerable number of plays and short stories. He was awarded the Nobel Prize in Literature in 1957.

In this selection Camus defines the rebel and analyzes some of the philosophical ideas of rebellion.

ALBERT CAMUS

What Is a Rebel?

1 What is a rebel? A man who says no: but whose refusal does not imply a renunciation. He is also a man who says yes as soon as he begins to think for himself. A slave who has taken orders all his life, suddenly decides that he cannot obey some new command. What does he mean by saying "no"?

2   He means, for instance, that "this has been going on too long," "so far but no farther," "you are going too far," or again "There are certain limits beyond which you shall not go." In other words, his "no" affirms the existence of a borderline. You find the same conception in the rebel's opinion that the other person is "exaggerating," that he is exerting his authority beyond a limit where he infringes on the right of

others. He rebels because he categorically refuses to submit to conditions that he considers intolerable and also because he is confusedly convinced that his position is justified, or rather, because in his own mind he thinks that he "has the right to. . . ." Rebellion cannot exist without the feeling that somewhere, in some way, you are justified. It is in this way that the rebel slave says yes and no at the same time. He affirms that there are limits and also that he suspects — and wishes to preserve — the existence of certain things beyond those limits. He stubbornly insists that there are certain things in him which "are worth while . . ." and which must be taken into consideration.

3   In every act of rebellion, the man concerned experiences not only a feeling of revulsion at the infringement of his rights but also a complete and spontaneous loyalty to certain aspects of himself. Thus he implicitly brings into play a standard of values so far from being false that he is willing to preserve them at all costs. Up to this point he has, at least, kept quiet and, in despair, has accepted a condition to which he submits even though he considers it unjust. To keep quiet is to allow yourself to believe that you have no opinions, that you want nothing, and in certain cases it amounts to really wanting nothing. Despair, like Absurdism, prefers to consider everything in general and nothing in particular. Silence expresses this attitude very satisfactorily. But from the moment that the rebel finds his voice — even though he has nothing to say but no — he begins to consider things in particular. In the etymological sense, the rebel is a turn-coat. He acted under the lash of his master's whip. Suddenly he turns and faces him. He chooses what is preferable to what is not. Not every value leads to rebellion, but every rebellion tacitly invokes a value. Or is it really a question of values?

4   An awakening of conscience, no matter how confused it may be, develops from any act of rebellion and is represented by the sudden realization that something exists with which the rebel can identify himself — even if only for a moment. Up to now this identification was never fully realized. Previous to his insurrection, the slave accepted all the demands made upon him. He even very often took orders, without reacting against them, which were considerably more offensive to him than the one at which he balked. He was patient and though, perhaps, he protested inwardly, he was obviously more careful of his own immediate interests — in that he kept quiet — than aware of his own rights. But with loss of patience — with impatience — begins a reaction which can extend to everything that he accepted up to this moment, and which is almost retroactive. Immediately the slave refuses to obey the humiliating orders of his master, he rejects the condition of slavery. The act of rebellion carries him beyond the point he reached by simply refusing. He exceeds the bounds that he established for his antagonist and demands that he should now be treated as an equal. What was, originally, an obstinate resistance on the part of the rebel, becomes the rebel personified. He proceeds to put self-respect above everything else and proclaims that it is preferable to life itself. It becomes, for him, the supreme blessing. Having previously been willing to compromise, the slave suddenly adopts an

attitude of All or Nothing. Knowledge is born and conscience awakened.

5   But it is obvious that the knowledge he gains is of an "All" that is still rather obscure and of a "Nothing" that proclaims the possibility of sacrificing the rebel to this "All." The rebel himself wants to be "All" — to identify himself completely with this blessing of which he has suddenly become aware and of which he wishes to be recognized and proclaimed as the incarnation — or "Nothing" which means to be completely destroyed by the power that governs him. As a last resort he is willing to accept the final defeat, which is death, rather than be deprived of the last sacrament which he would call, for example, freedom. Better to die on one's feet than to live on one's knees.

6   Values, according to the best authorities, "usually represent a transition from facts to rights, from what is desired to what is desirable (usually through the medium of what is generally considered desirable)." The transition from facts to rights is manifest, as we have seen, in the act of rebellion, as is the transition from "this is how things should be" to "this is how I want things to be," and still more, perhaps, the conception of the submission of the individual to the common good. The appearance of the conception of "All or Nothing" demonstrates that rebellion, contrary to present opinion and despite the fact that it springs from everything that is most strictly individualistic in man, undermines the very conception of the individual. If an individual actually consents to die, and, when the occasion arises, accepts death as a consequence of his rebellion, he demonstrates that he is willing to sacrifice himself for the sake of a common good which he considers more important than his own destiny. If he prefers the risk of death to a denial of the rights that he defends, it is because he considers that the latter are more important than he is. He acts, therefore, in the name of certain values which are still indeterminate but which he feels are common to himself and to all men. We see that the affirmation implicit in each act of revolt is extended to something which transcends the individual insofar as it removes him from his supposed solitude and supplies him with a reason to act. But it is worth noting that the conception of values as pre-existent to any kind of action runs counter to the purely historical schools of philosophy in which values are established (if they are ever established) by action itself. An analysis of rebellion leads us to the suspicion that, contrary to the postulates of contemporary thought, a human nature does exist, as the Greeks believed. Why rebel if there is nothing worth preserving in oneself? The slave asserts himself for the sake of everyone in the world when he comes to the conclusion that a command has infringed on something inside him that does not belong to him alone, but which he has in common with other men — even with the man who insults and oppresses him.

7   Two observations will support this argument. First we can see that an act of rebellion is not, essentially, an egotistic act. Undoubtedly it can have egotistic aims. But you can rebel equally well against a lie as against oppression. Furthermore the rebel — at the moment of his greatest impetus and no matter what his aims — keeps nothing in re-

serve and commits himself completely. Undoubtedly he demands respect for himself, but only insofar as he identifies himself with humanity in general.

8   Then we note that revolt does not occur only amongst the oppressed but that it can also break out at the mere spectacle of oppression of which someone else is the victim. In such cases there is a feeling of identification with other individuals. And it must be made clear that it is not a question of psychological identification — a mere subterfuge by which the individual contrives to feel that it is he who has been oppressed. It can even happen that we cannot countenance other people being insulted in a manner that we ourselves have accepted without rebelling. The suicides of the Russian terrorists in Siberia, as a protest against their comrades being whipped, is a case in point. Nor is it a question of a community of interests. Injustices done to men whom we consider enemies can, actually, be profoundly repugnant to us. Our reaction is only an identification of destinies and a choice of sides. Therefore the individual is not, in himself, an embodiment of the values he wishes to defend. It needs at least all humanity to comprise them. When he rebels, a man identifies himself with other men and, from this point of view, human solidarity is metaphysical. But for the moment we are only dealing with the kind of solidarity that is born in chains.

9   It would be possible for us to define the positive aspect of the values implicit in every act of rebellion by comparing them to a completely negative conception like that of resentment as defined by Scheler. Actually, rebellion is more than an act of revenge, in the strongest sense of the word. Resentment is very well defined by Scheler as an auto-intoxication — the evil secretion, in a sealed vessel, of prolonged impotence. Rebellion, on the other hand, removes the seal and allows the whole being to come into play. It liberates stagnant waters and turns them into a raging torrent. Scheler himself emphasizes the passive aspect of resentment, and remarks on the prominent position it occupies in the psychology of women whose main preoccupations are desire and possession. The mainspring of revolt, on the other hand, is the principle of superabundant activity and energy. Scheler is also right in saying that resentment is always highly flavored with envy. But we envy what we do not possess while the rebel defends what he has. He does not only claim some benefit which he does not possess or of which he was deprived. His aim is to claim recognition for something which he has and which has already been recognized by him, in almost every case, as more important than anything of which he could be envious. Rebellion is not realistic. According to Scheler, resentment always turns into either unscrupulous ambition or bitterness, depending on whether it flourishes in a weak mind or a strong one. But in both cases it is always a question of wanting to be something other than what one is. Resentment is always resentment against oneself. The rebel, on the other hand, from his very first step, refuses to allow anyone to touch what he is. He is fighting for the integrity of one part of his being. At first he does not try to conquer, but simply to impose.

10   Finally, it would seem that resentment takes a delight, in advance, in the pain that it would like the object of its envy to feel. Nietzsche and Scheler are right in seeing an excellent illustration of this feeling in the passage where Tertullian informs his readers that one of the greatest sources of happiness in heaven will be the spectacle of the Roman emperors consumed in the fires of hell. This kind of happiness is also experienced by all the decent people who go to watch executions. The rebel, on principle, persistently refuses to be humiliated without asking that others should be. He will even accept pain provided that his integrity is respected.

11   It is hard to understand why Scheler absolutely identifies the spirit of revolt with resentment. His critique of resentment as a part of humanitarianism (which he considers as the non-Christian form of human love) could perhaps be applied to certain vague forms of humanitarian idealism, or to certain techniques of terror. But it is false in so far as a man's rebellion against his condition is concerned and equally false about the impulse that enlists individuals in the defense of a dignity common to all men. Scheler wants to prove that humanitarian feelings are always accompanied by misanthropy. Humanity is loved in general in order to avoid loving anybody in particular. In some cases this is correct and it is easier to understand Scheler when we realize that for him humanitarianism is represented by Bentham and Rousseau. But man's love for man can be born of other things than an arithmetic calculation of interests or a theoretical confidence in human nature. Despite what the utilitarians say, there exists, for example, the type of logic, embodied by Dostoievski in Ivan Karamazov, that begins with an act of rebellion and ends in metaphysical insurrection. Scheler is aware of this and sums up the conception in the following manner: "There is not enough love in the world to be able to squander it on anything else but the human race." Even if this proposition were true, the profound despair that it implies would merit any other reaction but contempt. Actually, it misinterprets the tortured nature of Karamozov's rebellion. Ivan's drama, on the contrary, arises from the fact that there is too much love without an object. The existence of God being denied, love becomes redundant and then he decides to lavish it on the human race as a generous act of complicity.

12   Nevertheless, in the act of revolt as we have envisaged it up to now, we do not choose an abstract ideal through lack of feeling or for sterile reasons of revenge. We demand that that part of man which cannot be confined to the realm of ideas should be taken into consideration—the passionate side of his nature that serves no other purpose but to help him to live. Does that imply that no act of rebellion is motivated by resentment? No, and we know this from the bitter experience of centuries. But we must consider the idea of revolt in its widest sense— and in its widest sense it goes far beyond resentment. When Heathcliff, in *Wuthering Heights,* says that he puts his love above God and would willingly go to Hell in order to be reunited with the woman he loves, he is prompted not only by his youth and his humiliation but by the consuming experience of a whole lifetime. The same emotion causes Eckart, in a surprising fit of heresy, to say that he prefers Hell

with Jesus to Heaven without Him. This is the very essence of love. Contrary to what Scheler thinks, it would be impossible to over-emphasize the passionate affirmation that underlies the fact of revolt and which distinguishes it from resentment. Rebellion, though apparently negative since it creates nothing, is profoundly positive in that it reveals the part of man which must always be defended.

13   But finally, are not rebellion and the values that it calls into play, interdependent? Reasons for rebellion seem, in fact, to change with the times. It is obvious that a Hindu pariah, an Inca warrior, a primitive native of Central Africa and a member of one of the first Christian communities had quite different conceptions about rebellion. We could even assert, with considerable assurance, that the idea of rebellion has no meaning in those actual cases. However, a Greek slave, a serf, a condottiere of the Renaissance, a Parisian bourgeois during the Regency, and a Russian intellectual at the beginning of the nineteenth century would undoubtedly agree that rebellion is legitimate, even if they differed about the reasons. In other words, the problem of rebellion only seems to assume a precise meaning within the confines of Western thought. It is possible to be even more explicit by saying, like Scheler, that the spirit of rebellion finds few means of expression in societies where inequalities are very great (the Hindu caste system) or, again, in those where there is absolute equality (certain primitive societies). The spirit of revolt can only exist in a society where a theoretic equality conceals great factual inequalities. The problem of revolt, therefore, has no meaning outside our Occidental society. It would be tempting to say that it was relative to the development of individualism if the preceding remarks had not put us on guard against this conclusion.

14   On the basis of the evidence, the only conclusion we can draw from Scheler's remark is that, thanks to the theory of political freedom, there is, in the very heart of our society, an extension of the conception of the rights of man and a corresponding dissatisfaction caused by the application of this theory of freedom. Actual freedom has not increased in proportion to man's awareness of it. We can only deduce, from this observation, that rebellion is the act of an educated man who is aware of his rights. But we cannot say that it is only a question of individual rights. Because of the sense of solidarity that we have already pointed out, it would rather seem that what is at stake is humanity's gradually increasing awareness of itself as it pursues its adventurous course. In fact, for the Inca and the pariah the problem of revolt never arises, because for them it has been solved by tradition before they had time to raise it—the answer being that tradition is sacrosanct. If, in the sacrosanct world, the problem of revolt does not arise, it is because no real problems are to be found in it—all the answers having been given simultaneously. Metaphysic is replaced by myth. But before man accepts the sacrosanct and in order for him to be able to accept it—or before he escapes from it and in order for him to be able to escape from it—there is always a period of soul-searching and revolt. The rebel is a man who is on the point of accepting or rejecting the sacrosanct and determined on creating a human situa-

tion where all the answers are human or, rather, formulated in terms of reason. From this moment every question, every word, is an act of rebellion, while in the sacrosanct world every word is an act of grace. It would be possible to demonstrate in this manner that only two possible worlds can exist for the human mind, the sacrosanct (or, to speak in Christian terms, the world of Grace)[1] or the rebel world. The disappearance of the one is equivalent to the appearance of the other, and this appearance can take place in disconcerting forms. There again we find the attitude of *All or Nothing*. The pressing aspect of the problem of rebellion depends only on the fact that nowadays whole societies have wanted to re-examine their position in regard to the sacrosanct. We live in an unsacrosanct period. Insurrection is certainly not the sum-total of human experience. But the controversial aspect of contemporary history compels us to say that rebellion is one of man's essential dimensions. It is our historical reality. Unless we ignore reality, we must find out values in it. Is it possible to find a rule of conduct outside the realm of religion and of absolute values? That is the question raised by revolt.

15   We have already noted the confused standard of values that are called into play by incipient revolt. Now we must inquire if these values are to be found in contemporary forms of rebellious thought and action and, if they do exist, we must specify their content. But, before going any farther, let us note that the basis of these values is rebellion itself. Man's solidarity is founded upon rebellion, and rebellion can only be justified by this solidarity. We then have authority to say that any type of rebellion which claims the right to deny or destroy this solidarity simultaneously loses the right to be called rebellion and actually becomes an accomplice to murder. In the same way, this solidarity, except in so far as religion is concerned, only comes to life on the level of rebellion. And so the real drama of revolutionary thought is revealed. In order to exist, man must rebel, but rebellion must respect the limits that it discovers in itself—limits where minds meet, and in meeting, begin to exist. Revolutionary thought, therefore, cannot dispense with memory: it is in a perpetual state of tension. In contemplating the results of an act of rebellion, we shall have to say, each time, whether it remains faithful to its first noble promise or whether, through lassitude or folly, it forgets its purpose and plunges into a mire of tyranny or servitude.

16   Meanwhile, we can sum up the initial progress that the spirit of rebellion accomplishes in a process of thought that is already convinced of the absurdity and apparent sterility of the world. In absurdist experience suffering is individual. But from the moment that a movement of rebellion begins, suffering is seen as a collective experience—as the experience of everyone. Therefore the first step for a mind overwhelmed by the strangeness of things is to realize that this feeling of strangeness is shared with all men and that the entire human race

---

[1] There is, of course, an act of metaphysical rebellion at the beginning of Christianity, but the resurrection of Christ and the annunciation of the Kingdom of Heaven interpreted as a promise of eternal life are the answers that render it futile.

suffers from the division between itself and the rest of the world. The unhappiness experienced by a single man becomes collective unhappiness. In our daily trials, rebellion plays the same role as does the "cogito" in the category of thought: it is the first clue. But this clue lures the individual from his solitude. Rebellion is the common ground on which every man bases his first values. I *rebel*—therefore we *exist*.

Discussion of Theme

1. Could Camus's observations in paragraph 4 apply to blacks in contemporary society?
2. Camus says that "reasons for rebellion seem to change with the times." Are there, nevertheless, basic principles underlying rebellion through the ages?
3. Do you derive comfort from Camus's theory that suffering is not solitary but is experienced in common with the entire human race?
4. Do you agree with the last sentence in paragraph 12? Explain.
5. Is it accurate to say that the rebel is actually asserting himself on behalf of all men?

Discussion of Rhetoric

1. How appropriate is Scheler's analogy, paragraph 9?
2. Would Camus's references to Scheler be more meaningful if he identified the man?
3. Is Camus's approach primarily objective or subjective? Support your view with evidence from the selection.
4. Is this piece a definition, or does it attempt to be persuasive as well?

Writing Assignments

1. What have you submitted to that you considered unjust? Do you intend to go on doing so?
2. Analyze the statement, "I rebel—therefore we exist."
3. Describe an act of rebellion in your life that you feel was necessary.

Library Exploration

1. Report on the work of Scheler, who is mentioned several times in this selection.
2. Report on one of Camus's novels.

Vocabulary

(2) INFRINGES trespasses on; violates

(2) CATEGORICALLY absolutely; positively

(3) REVULSION strong aversion

(3) ETYMOLOGICAL pertaining to the evolution of words

(3) TACITLY implicitly, that is, implied but not actually spoken or expressed

(4) INSURRECTION uprising; rebellion

(4) RETROACTIVE affecting previous events

(4) ANTAGONIST opponent; adversary

(6) POSTULATES basic principles; axioms

(7) EGOISTIC affecting only oneself

(7) IMPETUS driving force; impulse

(8) SUBTERFUGE evasion; deception

(8) CONTRIVES manages

(8) REPUGNANT revolting; nauseating

(8) METAPHYSICAL beyond the physical

(9) UNSCRUPULOUS without principles

(11) MISANTHROPY dislike of people

(11) REDUNDANT unnecessarily repetitious

(11) COMPLICITY partnership or involvement in wrongdoing or evil

(12) ENVISAGED visualized; seen

(13) PARIAH member of the lowest caste in India; outcast

(13) CONDOTTIERE mercenary; hired soldier

(14) SACROSANCT sacred; untouchable

(15) INCIPIENT just beginning

(15) LASSITUDE lethargy; torpor

(15) MIRE swamp; thick mud

Gordon E. Bigelow (1919–   )
received his Ph.D. from Johns
Hopkins University and has
been a professor of English at
the University of Kentucky and
the University of Florida. He is
the coauthor of "The U.S.A.:
Readings in English as a Second Language" (1960) and contributes articles to scholarly
journals including "College English," from which the following
is taken.

In defining six general characteristics of existentialism, Bigelow discusses the similarities
between the "godly" and "ungodly" existentialists.

GORDON E. BIGELOW

A Primer of Existentialism

1 For some years I fought the word by irritably looking the other way
whenever I stumbled across it, hoping that like dadaism and some of
the other "isms" of the French *avant garde* it would go away if I
ignored it. But existentialism was apparently more than the picture it
evoked of uncombed beards, smoky basement cafes, and French
beatniks regaling one another between sips of absinthe with brilliant
variations on the theme of despair. It turned out to be of major importance to literature and the arts, to philosophy and theology, and of increasing importance to the social sciences. To learn more about it, I
read several of the self-styled introductions to the subject, with the
baffled sensation of a man who reads a critical introduction to a novel
only to find that he must read the novel before he can understand the
introduction. Therefore, I should like to provide here something most
discussions of existentialism take for granted, a simple statement of
its basic characteristics. This is a reckless thing to do because there are
several kinds of existentialism and what one says of one kind may not
be true of another, but there is an area of agreement, and it is this common ground that I should like to set forth here. We should not run into

trouble so long as we understand from the outset that the six major themes outlined below will apply in varying degrees to particular existentialists. A reader should be able to go from here to the existentialists themselves, to the more specialized critiques of them, or be able to recognize an existentialist theme or coloration in literature when he sees it.

2   A word first about the kinds of existentialism. Like transcendentalism of the last century, there are almost as many varieties of this *ism* as there are individual writers to whom the word is applied (not all of them claim it). But without being facetious we might group them into two main kinds, the *ungodly* and the *godly*. To take the ungodly or atheistic first, we would list as the chief spokesmen among many others Jean-Paul Sartre, Albert Camus, and Simone de Beauvoir. Several of this important group of French writers had rigorous and significant experience in the Resistance during the Nazi occupation of France in World War II. Out of the despair which came with the collapse of their nation during those terrible years they found unexpected strength in the single indomitable human spirit, which even under severe torture could maintain the spirit of resistance, the unextinguishable ability to say "No." From the irreducible core in the human spirit, they erected after the war a philosophy which was a twentieth-century variation of the philosophy of Descartes. But instead of saying "I think, therefore I am," they said "I can say No, therefore I exist." As we shall presently see, the use of the word "exist" is of prime significance. This group is chiefly responsible for giving existentialism its status in the popular mind as a literary-philosophical cult.

3   Of the godly or theistic existentialists we should mention first a mid-nineteenth-century Danish writer, Soren Kierkegaard; two contemporary French Roman Catholics, Gabriel Marcel and Jacques Maritain; two Protestant theologians, Paul Tillich and Nicholas Berdyaev; and Martin Buber, an important contemporary Jewish theologian. Taken together, their writings constitute one of the most significant developments in modern theology. Behind both groups of existentialists stand other important figures, chiefly philosophers, who exert powerful influence upon the movement — Blaise Pascal, Friedrich Nietzsche, Henri Bergson, Martin Heidegger, Karl Jaspers, among others. Several literary figures, notably Tolstoy and Dostoievski, are frequently cited because existentialist attitudes and themes are prominent in their writings. The electic nature of this movement should already be sufficiently clear and the danger of applying too rigidly to any particular figure the general characteristics of the movement which I now make bold to describe:

4   1. EXISTENCE BEFORE ESSENCE. Existentialism gets its name from an insistence that human life is understandable only in terms of an individual man's existence, his particular experience of life. It says that a man *lives* (has existence) rather than *is* (has being or essence), and that every man's experience of life is unique, radically different from everyone else's and can be understood truly only in terms of his involvement in life or commitment to it. It strenuously shuns that view which assumes an ideal of Man or Mankind, a universal of human nature of which each man is only one example. It eschews the question

of Greek philosophy, *"What is mankind?"* which suggests that man can be defined if he is ranged in his proper place in the order of nature; it asks instead the question of Job and St. Augustine, *"Who am I?"* with its suggestion of the uniqueness and mystery of each human life and its emphasis upon the subjective or personal rather than the objective or impersonal. From the outside a man appears to be just another natural creature; from the inside he is an entire universe, the center of infinity. The existentialist insists upon this latter radically subjective view, and from this grows much of the rest of existentialism.

5   2. REASON IS IMPOTENT TO DEAL WITH THE DEPTHS OF HUMAN LIFE. There are two parts to this proposition — first, that human reason is relatively weak and imperfect, and second, that there are dark places in human life which are "nonreason" and to which reason scarcely penetrates. Since Plato, Western civilization has usually assumed a separation of reason from the rest of the human psyche, and has glorified reason as suited to command the nonrational part. The classic statement of this separation appears in the *Phaedrus,* where Plato describes the psyche in the myth of the chariot which is drawn by the white steeds of the emotions and the black unruly steeds of the appetites. The driver of the chariot is Reason who holds the reins which control the horses and the whip to subdue the surging black steeds of passion. Only the driver, the rational nature, is given human form; the rest of the psyche, the nonrational part, is given a lower, animal form. This separation and exaltation of reason is carried further in the allegory of the cave in *The Republic.* You recall the sombre picture of human life with which the story begins: men are chained in the dark in a cave, with their backs to a flickering firelight, able to see only uncertain shadows moving on the wall before them, able to hear only confused echoes of sounds. One of the men, breaking free from his chains, is able to turn and look upon the objects themselves and the light which casts the shadows; even, at last, he is able to work his way entirely out of the cave into the sunlight beyond. All this he is able to do through his reason; he escapes from the bondage of error, from time and change, from death itself, into the realm of changeless eternal ideas or Truth, and the lower nature which had chained him in darkness is left behind.

6   Existentialism in our time, and this is one of its most important characteristics, insists upon reuniting the "lower" or irrational parts of the psyche with the "higher." It insists that man must be taken in his wholeness and not in some divided state, that whole man contains not only intellect but also anxiety, guilt, and the will to power — which modify and sometimes overwhelm the reason. A man seen in this light is fundamentally ambiguous, if not mysterious, full of contradictions and tensions which cannot be dissolved simply by taking thought. "Human life," said Berdyaev, "is permeated by underground streams." One is reminded of D. H. Lawrence's outburst against Franklin and his rational attempt to achieve moral perfection: "The Perfectability of Man! . . . The perfectability of which man? I am many men. Which of them are you going to perfect? I am not a mechanical contrivance. . . . It's a queer thing is a man's soul. It is the whole of him. Which means it is the unknown as well as the known. . . . The soul

of man is a dark vast forest, with wild life in it." The emphasis in existentialism is not on idea but upon the thinker who has the idea. It accepts not only his power of thought, but his contingency and fallibility, his frailty, his body, blood, and bones, and above all his death. Kierkegaard emphasized the distinction between *subjective* truth (what a person *is*) and *objective* truth (what the person *knows*), and said that we encounter the true self not in the detachment of thought but in the involvement and agony of choice and in the pathos of commitment to our choice. This distrust of rational systems helps to explain why many existential writers in their own expression are paradoxical or prophetic or gnomic, why their works often belong more to literature than to philosophy.

7   3. ALIENATION OR ESTRANGEMENT. One major result of the dissociation of reason from the rest of the psyche has been the growth of science, which has become one of the hallmarks of Western civilization, and an ever-increasing rational ordering of men in society. As the existentialists view them, the main forces of history since the Renaissance have progressively separated man from concrete earthy existence, have forced him to live at ever higher levels of abstraction, have collectivized individual man out of existence, have driven God from the heavens, or what is the same thing, from the hearts of men. They are convinced that modern man lives in a four-fold condition of alienation: from God, from nature, from other men, from his own true self.

8   The estrangement from God is most shockingly expressed by Nietzsche's anguished cry, "God is dead," a cry which has continuously echoed through the writings of the existentialists, particularly the French. This theme of spiritual barrenness is a commonplace in literature of this century, from Eliot's "Hollow Man" to the novels of Dos Passos, Hemingway, and Faulkner. It often appears in writers not commonly associated with the existentialists as in this remarkable passage from *A Story-Teller's Story,* where Sherwood Anderson describes his own awakening to his spiritual emptiness. He tells of walking alone late at night along a moonlit road when,

> I had suddenly an odd, and to my own seeming, a ridiculous desire to abase myself before something not human and so stepping into the moonlit road, I knelt in the dust. Having no God, the gods having been taken from me by the life about me, as a personal God has been taken from all modern men by a force within that man himself does not understand but that is called the intellect, I kept smiling at the figure I cut in my own eyes as I knelt in the road. . . .
> There was no God in the sky, no God in myself, no conviction in myself that I had the power to believe in a God, and so I merely knelt in the dust in silence and no words came to my lips.

In another passage Anderson wondered if the giving of itself by an entire generation to mechanical things was not really making all men impotent, if the desire for a greater navy, a greater army, taller public buildings, was not a sign of growing impotence. He felt that Puritanism and the industrialism which was its offspring had sterilized modern life, and proposed that men return to a healthful animal vigor by renewed contact with simple things of the earth, among them untrammeled sexual expression. One is reminded of the unkempt and delectable raffishness of Steinbeck's *Cannery Row* or of D. H. Lawrence's quasi-religious doctrine of sex, "blood-consciousness" and the "divine otherness" of animal existence.

9   Man's estrangement from nature has been a major theme in literature at least since Rousseau and the Romantic movement, and can hardly be said to be the property of existentialists. But this group nevertheless adds its own insistence that one of modern man's most urgent dangers is that he builds ever higher the brick and steel walls of technology which shut him away from a health-giving life according to "nature." Their treatment of this theme is most commonly expressed as part of a broader insistence that modern man needs to shun abstraction and return to "concreteness" or "wholeness."

10   A third estrangement has occurred at the social level and its sign is a growing dismay at man's helplessness before the great machine-like colossus of industrialized society. This is another major theme of Western literature, and here again, though they hardly discovered the danger or began the protest, the existentialists in our time renew the protest against any pattern or force which would stifle the unique and spontaneous in individual life. The crowding of men into cities, the subdivision of labor which submerges the man in his economic function, the burgeoning of centralized government, the growth of advertising, propaganda, and mass media of entertainment and communication—all the things which force men into Riesman's "Lonely Crowd"—these same things drive men asunder by destroying their individuality and making them live on the surface of life, content to deal with things rather than people. "Exteriorization," says Berdyaev, "is the source of slavery, whereas freedom is interiorization. Slavery always indicates alienation, the ejection of human nature into the external." This kind of alienation is exemplified by Zero, in Elmer Rice's play "The Adding Machine." Zero's twenty-five years as a bookkeeper in a department store have dried up his humanity, making him incapable of love, of friendship, of any deeply felt, freely expressed emotion. Such estrangement is often given as the reason for man's inhumanity to man, the explanation for injustice in modern society. In Camus' short novel, aptly called *The Stranger,* a young man is convicted by a court of murder. This is a homicide which he has actually committed under extenuating circumstances. But the court never listens to any of the relevant evidence, seems never to hear anything that pertains to the crime itself; it convicts the young man on wholly irrelevant grounds—because he had behaved in an unconventional way at his mother's funeral the day before the homicide. In this book one feels the same dream-like distortion of reality as in the trial scene in *Alice in Wonderland*, a suffocating sense of being enclosed by events which are irrational or absurd but also inexorable. Most disturbing of all is the young man's aloneness, the impermeable membrane of estrangement which surrounds him and prevents anyone else from penetrating to his experience of life or sympathizing with it.

11   The fourth kind of alienation, man's estrangement from his own true self, especially as his nature is distorted by an exaltation of reason, is another theme having an extensive history as a major part of the Romantic revolt. Of the many writers who treat the theme, Hawthorne

comes particularly close to the emphasis of contemporary existentialists. His Ethan Brand, Dr. Rappaccini, and Roger Chillingworth are a recurrent figure who represents the dislocation in human nature which results when an overdeveloped or misapplied intellect severs "the magnetic chain of human sympathy." Hawthorne is thoroughly existential in his concern for the sanctity of the individual human soul, as well as in his preoccupation with sin and the dark side of human nature, which must be seen in part as his attempt to build back some fullness to the flattened image of man bequeathed to him by the Enlightenment. Whitman was trying to do this when he added flesh and bone and a sexual nature to the spiritualized image of man he inherited from Emerson, though his image remains diffused and attenuated by the same cosmic optimism. Many of the nineteenth-century depictions of man represent him as a figure of power or of potential power, sometimes as daimonic, like Melville's Ahab, but after World War I the power is gone; man is not merely distorted or truncated, he is hollow, powerless, faceless. At the time when his command over natural forces seems to be unlimited, man is pictured as weak, ridden with nameless dread. This brings us to another of the major themes of existentialism.

12   4. "FEAR AND TREMBLING," ANXIETY. At Stockholm when he accepted the Nobel Prize, William Faulkner said that "Our tragedy today is a general and universal physical fear so long sustained by now that we can even bear it. There are no longer problems of the spirit. There is only one question: When will I be blown up?" The optimistic vision of the Enlightenment which saw man, through reason and its extensions in science, conquering all nature and solving all social and political problems in a continuous upward spiral of Progress, cracked open like a melon on the rock of World War I. The theories which held such high hopes died in that sickening and unimaginable butchery. Here was a concrete fact of human nature and society which the theories could not contain. The Great Depression and World War II deepened the sense of dismay which the loss of these ideals brought, but only with the atomic bomb did this become an unbearable terror, a threat of instant annihilation which confronted all men, even those most insulated by the thick crust of material goods and services. Now the most unthinking person could sense that each advance in mechanical technique carried not only a chromium and plush promise of comfort but a threat as well.

13   Sartre, following Kierkegaard, speaks of another kind of anxiety which oppresses modern man — "the anguish of Abraham" — the necessity which is laid upon him to make moral choices on his own responsibility. A military officer in wartime knows the agony of choice which forces him to sacrifice part of his army to preserve the rest, as does a man in high political office, who must make decisions affecting the lives of millions. The existentialists claim that each of us must make moral decisions in our own lives which involve the same anguish. Kierkegaard finds that this necessity is one thing which makes each life unique, which makes it impossible to speculate or generalize about human life, because each man's case is irretrievably his own, something in which he is personally and passionately involved. His book

Fear and Trembling is an elaborate and fascinating commentary on the Old Testament story of Abraham, who was commanded by God to sacrifice his beloved son Isaac. Abraham thus becomes the emblem of man who must make a harrowing choice, in this case between love for his son and love for God, between the universal moral law which says categorically, "thou shalt not kill," and the unique inner demand of his religious faith. Abraham's decision, which is to violate the abstract and collective moral law, has to be made not in arrogance but in fear and trembling, one of the inferences being that sometimes one must make an exception to the general law because he is (existentially) an exception, a concrete being whose existence can never be completely subsumed under any universal.

14   5. THE ENCOUNTER WITH NOTHINGNESS. For the man alienated from God, from nature, from his fellow man and from himself, what is left at last but Nothingness? The testimony of the existentialists is that this is where modern man now finds himself, not on the highway of upward Progress toward a radiant Utopia but on the brink of a catastrophic precipice, below which yawns the absolute void, an uncompromised black Nothingness. In one sense this is Eliot's Wasteland inhabited by his Hollow Man, who is

> Shape without form, shade without color
> Paralyzed force, gesture without motion.

This is what moves E. A. Robinson's Richard Cory, the man who is everything that might make us wish that we were in his place, to go home one calm summer night and put a bullet through his head.

15   One of the most convincing statements of the encounter with Nothingness is made by Leo Tolstoy in "My Confession." He tells how in good health, in the prime of life, when he had everything that a man could desire — wealth, fame, aristocratic social position, a beautiful wife and children, a brilliant mind and great artistic talent in the height of their powers — he nevertheless was seized with a growing uneasiness, a nameless discontent which he could not shake or alleviate. His experience was like that of a man who falls sick, with symptoms which he disregards as insignificant; but the symptoms return again and again until they merge into a continuous suffering. And the patient suddenly is confronted with the overwhelming fact that what he took for mere indisposition is more important to him than anything else on earth, that it is death! "I felt the ground on which I stood was crumbling, that there was nothing for me to stand on, that what I had been living for was nothing, that I had no reason for living. . . . To stop was impossible, to go back was impossible; and it was impossible to shut my eyes so as to see that there was nothing before me but suffering and actual death, absolute annihilation." This is the "Sickness Unto Death" of Kierkegaard, the despair in which one wishes to die but cannot. Hemingway's short story, "A Clean, Well-Lighted Place," gives an unforgettable expression of this theme. At the end of the story, the old waiter climbs into bed late at night saying to himself, "What did he fear? It was not fear or dread. It was nothing which he knew too well. It was all a nothing and a man was nothing too. . . . Nada y pues nada, y nada y pues nada." And then because he has

experienced the death of God he goes on to recite the Lord's Prayer in blasphemous despair: "Our Nothing who are in Nothing, nothing be thy nothing. . . ." This is stark, even for Hemingway, but the old waiter does no more than name the void felt by most people in the early Hemingway novels, a hunger they seek to assuage with alcohol, sex, and violence in an aimless progress from bar to bed to bull-ring. It goes without saying that much of the despair and pessimism in other contemporary authors springs from a similar sense of the void in modern life.

16   6. FREEDOM. Sooner or later, as a theme that includes all the others, the existentialist writings bear upon freedom. The themes we have outlined above describe either some loss of man's freedom or some threat to it, and all existentialists of whatever sort are concerned to enlarge the range of human freedom.

17   For the avowed atheists like Sartre freedom means human autonomy. In a purposeless universe man is *condemned* to freedom because he is the only creature who is "self-surpassing," who can become something other than he is. Precisely because there is no God to give purpose to the universe, each man must accept individual responsibility for his own becoming, a burden made heavier by the fact that in choosing for himself he chooses for all men "the image of man as he ought to be." A man *is* the sum total of the acts that make up his life—no more, no less—and though the coward has made himself cowardly, it is always possible for him to change and make himself heroic. In Sartre's novel, *The Age of Reason,* one of the least likable of the characters, almost overwhelmed by despair and self-disgust at his homosexual tendencies, is on the point of solving his problem by mutilating himself with a razor, when in an effort of will he throws the instrument down, and we are given to understand that from this moment he will have mastery over his aberrant drive. Thus in the daily course of ordinary life must men shape their becoming in Sartre's world.

18   The religious existentialists interpret man's freedom differently. They use much the same language as Sartre, develop the same themes concerning the predicament of man, but always include God as a radical factor. They stress the man of faith rather than the man of will. They interpret man's existential condition as a state of alienation from his essential nature which is God-like, the problem of his life being to heal the chasm between the two, that is, to find salvation. The mystery and ambiguity of man's existence they attribute to his being the intersection of two realms. "Man bears within himself," writes Berdyaev, "the image which is both the image of man and the image of God, and is the image of man as far as the image of God is actualized." Tillich describes salvation as "the act in which the cleavage between the essential being and the existential situation is overcome." Freedom here, as for Sartre, involves an acceptance of responsibility for choice and a *commitment* to one's choice. This is the meaning of faith, a faith like Abraham's, the commitment which is an agonizing sacrifice of one's own desire and will and dearest treasure to God's will.

19   A final word. Just as one should not expect to find in a particular writer all of the characteristics of existentialism as we have described

them, he should also be aware that some of the most striking expressions of existentialism in literature and the arts come to us by indirection, often through symbols or through innovations in conventional form. Take the preoccupation of contemporary writers with time. In *The Sound and the Fury,* Faulkner both collapses and expands normal clock time, or by juxtapositions of past and present blurs time into a single amorphous pool. He does this by using various forms of "stream of consciousness" or other techniques which see life in terms of unique, subjective experience—that is, existentially. The conventional view of externalized life, a rational orderly progression cut into uniform segments by the hands of a clock, he rejects in favor of a view which sees life as opaque, ambiguous, and irrational—that is, as the existentialist sees it. Graham Greene does something like this in *The Power and the Glory.* He creates a scene isolated in time and cut off from the rest of the world, steamy and suffocating as if a bell jar had been placed over it. Through this atmosphere fetid with impending death and human suffering, stumbles the whiskey priest, lonely and confused, pursued by a police lieutenant who has experienced the void and death of God.

20   Such expressions in literature do not mean necessarily that the authors are conscious existentialist theorizers, or even that they know the writings of such theorizers. Faulkner may never have read Heidegger—or St. Augustine—both of whom attempt to demonstrate that time is more within a man and subject to his unique experience of it than it is outside him. But it is legitimate to call Faulkner's views of time and life "existential" in this novel because in recent years existentialist theorizers have given such views a local habitation and a name. One of the attractions, and one of the dangers, of existential themes is that they become like Sir Thomas Browne's quincunx: once one begins to look for them, he sees them everywhere. But if one applies restraint and discrimination, he will find that they illuminate much of contemporary literature and sometimes the literature of the past as well.

Discussion of Theme

1. Can a concept like existentialism be adequately defined?
2. Do you believe that each man's life is unique?
3. Do you view man as alienated from his fellows?
4. Is modern man more beset by anxiety and anguish than nineteenth-century man? How is the analogy concerning the anguish of Abraham meaningful to us?

Discussion of Rhetoric

1. What does Bigelow state as his purpose for writing the article? Has he succeeded?
2. Bigelow is apparently not an existentialist. What tone does he adopt toward the philosophy? How does he achieve it?

3. Find the thesis in paragraph 1 and show how it is developed throughout the selection.
4. Of what value are the numbered subheadings in this essay?

Writing Assignments

1. If you disagree that "reason is impotent to deal with the depths of human life," present an argument to refute this position.
2. In recent years the statement "I don't (or didn't) want to get in-volved" has been offered as a reason for standing by and allowing unjust acts — sometimes even murder — to be committed. Does man have a moral obligation to the rest of humanity? What are the re-sults of people's failure to become involved? Discuss this in terms of one social issue or several.
3. Interpret the existentialist belief that a man creates himself by taking action.

Library Exploration

1. *The Existential Imagination,* edited by Frederick R. Karl and Leo Hamalian, is an anthology of stories and selections (from Shake-speare to Beckett) that exemplifies and illustrates existentialism in literature.
2. *Waiting for Godot*, by Samuel Beckett, is the classic existentialist drama.
3. Jean-Paul Sartre's *The Flies* is an existentialist version of the Ores-teian story.
4. Report on one of the following: Jean-Paul Sartre, Albert Camus, Paul Tillich, or Soren Kierkegaard. Pay particular attention to the factors that contributed to his becoming an existentialist.

Vocabulary

(1) AVANT GARDE   the few who lead

(2) FACETIOUS   jocular; flip-pant

(2) INDOMITABLE   unconquer-able

(3) ECLECTIC   composed of elements drawn from many sources

(6) AMBIGUOUS   of doubtful or uncertain nature

(6) CONTINGENCY   dependence on something else

(6) FALLIBILITY   tendency to err

(6) PATHOS   sadness; sorrow

(6) PARADOXICAL   apparently contradictory

(6) GNOMIC   characterized by short pithy statements of general truth

(8) IMPOTENT   lacking in power, strength, or vigor

(8) UNTRAMMELED   unhin-dered; free

(8) DELECTABLE   delightful; tasty

(10) BURGEONING   rapid growth

(10) INEXORABLE   unalterable

(10) IMPERMEABLE impenetrable; not permitting passage

(11) RECURRENT returning again and again

(11) ATTENUATED weakened; lessened

(11) DAIMONIC driven by an inner spirit; possessed

(11) TRUNCATED cut down in size

(13) IRRETRIEVABLY beyond recall

(13) SUBSUMED classified within a larger category

(14) PRECIPICE steep cliff; crag

(15) ALLEVIATE relieve; lighten

(17) ABERRANT abnormal

(19) AMORPHOUS shapeless; vague

(19) FETID stinking

(20) QUINCUNX arrangement in a square of five objects, one at each corner and one in the middle

Plato (428–348 B.C.), Socrates's most famous pupil, founded a philosophical school, the
Academy, in 387 B.C. in Athens,
where he lectured and wrote.
He is considered by many the
most important Western philosopher. Among his significant
works are "The Republic,"
"Symposium," and "Timaeus."

This is a concise statement of
Plato's unending argument for
the triumph of reason over
doubt and ignorance.

PLATO

The Allegory
of the Cave

1 And now, I said, let me show in a figure how far our nature is enlightened or unenlightened: Behold! human beings living in an underground den, which has a mouth open toward the light and reaching
all along the den; here they have been from their childhood, and have
their legs and necks chained so that they cannot move, and can only
see before them, being prevented by the chains from turning around
their heads. Above and behind them a fire is blazing at a distance; and
between the fire and the prisoners there is a raised way; and you will
see, if you look, a low wall built along the way, like a screen which
marionette players have in front of them, over which they show the
puppets.

2 I see.

3 And do you see, I said, men passing along the wall carrying all sorts
of vessels, and statues and figures of animals made of wood and stone
and various materials, which appear over the wall? Some of them are
talking, others silent.

4 You have shown me a strange image, and they are strange prisoners.

5 Like ourselves, I replied; and they see only their own shadows, or
the shadows of one another, which the fire throws on the opposite
wall of the cave?

6 True, he said; how could they see anything but the shadows if they
were never allowed to move their heads?

7   And of the objects which are being carried in like manner they would only see the shadows?

8   Yes, he said.

9   And if they were able to converse with one another, would they not suppose that they were naming what was actually before them?[1]

10   Very true.

11   And suppose further that the prison had an echo which came from the other side, would they not be sure to fancy when one of the passers-by spoke that the voice which they heard came from the passing shadow?

12   No question, he replied.

13   To them, I said, the truth would be literally nothing but the shadows of the images.

14   That is certain.

15   And now look again, and see what will naturally follow if the prisoners are released and disabused of their error. At first, when any of them is liberated and compelled suddenly to stand up and turn his neck round and walk and look toward the light, he will suffer sharp pains; the glare will distress him, and he will be unable to see the realities of which in his former state he had seen the shadows; and then conceive some one saying to him, that what he saw before was an illusion, but that now, when he is approaching nearer to being and his eye is turned toward more real existence, he has a clearer vision— what will be his reply? And you may further imagine that his instructor is pointing to the objects as they pass and requiring him to name them—will he not be perplexed? Will he not fancy that the shadows which he formerly saw are truer than the objects which are now shown to him?

16   Far truer.

17   And if he is compelled to look straight at the light, will he not have a pain in his eyes which will make him turn away to take refuge in the objects of vision which he can see, and which he will conceive to be in reality clearer than the things which are now being shown to him?

18   True, he said.

19   And suppose once more, that he is reluctantly dragged up a steep and rugged ascent, and held fast until he is forced into the presence of the sun himself, is he not likely to be pained and irritated? When he approaches the light his eyes will be dazzled, and he will not be able to see anything at all of what are now called realities.

20   Not all in a moment, he said.

21   He will require to grow accustomed to the sight of the upper world. And first he will see the shadows best, next the reflections of men and other objects in the water, and then the objects themselves; then he will gaze upon the light of the moon and the stars and the spangled heaven; and he will see the sky and the stars by night better than the sun or the light of the sun by day?

22   Certainly.

---

[1] The text is uncertain. Probably the meaning is that in naming the shadows before them the prisoners suppose they see the real things.

23   Last of all he will be able to see the sun, and not mere reflections of
him in the water, but he will see him in his own proper place, and not in
another; and he will contemplate him as he is.

24   Certainly.

25   He will then proceed to argue that this is he who gives the season
and the years, and is the guardian of all that is in the visible world, and
in a certain way the cause of all things which he and his fellows have
been accustomed to behold?

26   Clearly, he said, he would first see the sun and then reason about
him.

27   And when he remembered his old habitation, and the wisdom of the
den and his fellow-prisoners, do you not suppose that he would felicitate himself on the change, and pity them?

28   Certainly, he would.

29   And if they were in the habit of conferring honours among themselves on those who were the quickest to observe the passing shadows
and to remark which of them went before, and which followed after,
and which were together; and who were therefore best able to draw
conclusions as to the future, do you think that he would care for such
honours and glories, or envy the possessors of them? Would he not say
with Homer,

> Better to be the poor servant of a poor master,

and to endure anything, rather than think as they do and live after
their manner?

30   Yes, he said, I think that he would rather suffer anything than enter-
tain these false notions and live in this miserable manner.

31   Imagine once more, I said, such a one coming suddenly out of the
sun to be replaced in his old situation; would he not be certain to have
his eyes full of darkness?

32   To be sure, he said.

33   And if there were a contest, and he had to compete in measuring the
shadows with the prisoners who had never moved out of the den, while
his sight was still weak, and before his eyes had become steady (and
the time which would be needed to acquire this new habit of sight
might be very considerable), would he not be ridiculous? Men would
say of him that up he went and down he came without his eyes; and
that it was better not even to think of ascending; and if any one tried
to loose another and lead him up to the light, let them only catch the
offender, and they would put him to death.

34   No question, he said.

35   This entire allegory, I said, you may now append, dear Glaucon, to
the previous argument; the prison-house is the world of sight, the light
of the fire is the sun, and you will not misapprehend me if you interpret the journey upward to be the ascent of the soul into the intellectual world according to my poor belief, which at your desire, I have
expressed — whether rightly or wrongly God knows. But, whether true
or false, my opinion is that in the world of knowledge the idea of good
appears last of all, and is seen only with effort; and, when seen, is also
inferred to be the universal author of all things beautiful and right,

parent of light and of the lord of light in this visible world, and the immediate source of reason and truth in the intellectual; and that this is the power upon which he who would act rationally either in public or private life must have his eye fixed.

Discussion of Theme

1. What is meant by "the truth shall make you free"? Do you believe this?
2. Plato says that "he who would act rationally either in public or private life" must be truthful. By Plato's standard, do many of our public personages act rationally? Have standards of rational behavior changed through the years?
3. Why is the concept of truth so difficult to grasp? Why do men in all stations of life attempt to define it?
4. In what areas of his existence is man still in a cave?
5. Explain the allegory of the cave in your own words.

Discussion of Rhetoric

1. Does an allegory actually make it easier or more difficult to grasp an abstraction?
2. Would you understand the allegory without paragraph 35?
3. Plato is painstaking in his development of the allegory. Is this necessary? Would it have been improved if he had condensed it somewhat?
4. What are the strengths and weaknesses of allegory, particularly this one?
5. Glaucon doesn't contribute much. Would straight exposition have been more effective here than dialogue form?

Writing Assignments

1. Plato's allegory suggests the brainwashing of political prisoners. How is brainwashing accomplished? Do societies, in effect, brainwash their citizens? To what extent and by what means?
2. Write an allegory dramatizing a specific condition of man—for example, his anxiety or his humility.
3. Analyze the appeal of Plato to modern thinkers.
4. Suggest what you think Plato would have us stress in our colleges today.
5. Write an imaginary Platonic dialogue in which you deal with one of the following topics—love and marriage, war, friendship, the good life.

Library Exploration

1. You might be interested in Plato's most famous pupil, Aristotle, who differed with Plato in many significant respects.
2. Investigate the use of the dialogue and the criticisms of this form of dialect.

Vocabulary

(1) MARIONETTE   puppet

(15) DISABUSED   set free from error or mistakes in reasoning

(27) FELICITATE   congratulate

Rufus M. Jones (1863–1948) was a professor of philosophy at Haverford College for thirty years. He was born in Maine and educated at Haverford, the University of Heidelberg, and Harvard. He wrote voluminously on the Quakers and their religion. Among his works are "Practical Christianity" (1899), "A Service of Love in Wartime" (1920), and "A Call to What Is Vital" (1948).

As nearly as words can convey it, this is a description of what a mystical experience accomplishes.

RUFUS M. JONES

The Mystic's Experience of God

1 According to those who have been there, the experience that we call mystical is charged with the conviction of real, direct contact and commerce with God. It is the almost universal testimony of those who are mystics that they find God through their experience. John Tauler says that in his best moments of "devout prayer and the uplifting of the mind to God," he experiences "the pure presence of God" in his own soul; but he adds that all he can tell others about the experience is "as poor and unlike it as the point of a needle is to the heavens above us."

2 There are many different degrees of intensity, concentration, and conviction in the experiences of different individual mystics, and also in the various experiences of the same individual from time to time. There has been a tendency in most studies of mysticism to regard the state of ecstasy as *par excellence* mystical experience. That is, however, a grave mistake. The calmer, more meditative, less emotional, less ecstatic experiences of God possess greater constructive value for life and character than do ecstatic experiences which presuppose a peculiar psychical frame and disposition. The seasoned Quaker, in the

corporate hush and stillness of a silent meeting, is far removed from ecstasy, but he is not the less convinced that he is meeting with God.

3   The more normal, expansive mystical experiences come apparently when the personal self is at its best. Its power and capacities are raised to an unusual unity and fused together. The whole being, with its accumulated submerged life, *finds itself*. The process of preparing for any high achievement is a severe and laborious one; but nothing seems easier in the moment of success than is the accomplishment for which the life has been prepared. There comes to be formed within the person what Aristotle called "a dexterity of soul," so that the person does with ease what he has become skilled to do. A mystic of the fourteenth century stated the principle in these words: "It is my aim to be to the Eternal God what a man's hand is to a man."

4   There are many human experiences which carry a man up to levels where he has not usually been before, and where he finds himself possessed of insight and energies that he had hardly suspected were his until that moment. One leaps to his full height when the right inner spring is reached. We are quite familiar with the way in which instinctive tendencies in us, and emotions both egoistic and social, become organized under a group of ideas and ideals into a single system, which we call a sentiment, such as love, or patriotism, or devotion to truth. It forms slowly, and one hardly realizes that it has formed until some occasion unexpectedly brings it into full operation and we find ourselves able with perfect ease to overcome the most powerful inhibitory and opposing instincts and habits, which until then had usually controlled us. Literary and artistic geniuses supply us with many instances in which, in a sudden flash, the crude material at hand is shot through with vision, and the complicated plot of a drama, the full significance of a character, or the complete glory of a statue stands revealed, as if, to use R. L. Stevenson's illustration, a jinni had brought it on a golden tray as a gift from another world. Abraham Lincoln, striking off in a few intense minutes his Gettysburg address, as beautiful in style and perfect in form as anything in human literature, is as good an illustration as we need of the way in which a highly organized person, by a kindling flash, has at his hand all the moral and spiritual gains of a lifetime.

5   We come now to the central question of our consideration: Do mystical experiences settle anything? Are they purely subjective and one-sided, or do they prove to have objective reference and so to be two-sided? Do they take the experiment across the chasm that separates "self" from "other"?

6   The most striking effect of such experience is not new fact-knowledge, not new items of empirical information, but new moral energy, heightened conviction, increased caloric quality, enlarged spiritual vision, an unusual radiant power of life. In short, the whole personality, in the case of the constructive mystics, appears to be raised to a new level of life and to have gained from somewhere many calories of life-feeding, spiritual substance, We are quite familiar with the way in which adrenalin suddenly flushes into the physical system and adds a new and incalculable power to brain and muscle. Under its stimulus a man can carry out a piano when the house is on fire. May not, perhaps,

some energy, from some Source with which our spirits are allied, flush our inner being with forces and powers by which we can be fortified to stand the universe and more than stand it?

7   I believe that mystical experiences do, in the long run, expand our knowledge of God, and do succeed in verifying themselves. Mysticism is a sort of spiritual protoplasm which underlies, as a basic substance, much that is best in religion, in ethics, and in life itself. It has generally been the mystic, the prophet, the seer, who have spotted out new ways forward in the jungle of our world or lifted our race to new spiritual levels. Their experiences have in some way equipped them for unusual tasks, have given supplies of energy to them which their neighbors did not have, and have apparently brought them into vital correspondence with dimensions and regions of reality that others miss. The proof that they have found God, or at least a domain of spiritual reality, is to be seen rather in the moral and spiritual fruits which test out and verify the experience.

8   Consciousness of beauty or of truth or of goodness baffles analysis as much as consciousness of God does. These values have no objective standing ground in current psychology. They are not things in the world of space. They submit to no adequate causal explanation. They have their ground of being in some other kind of world than that of the mechanical order, a world composed of quantitative masses of matter in motion. These experiences of value, which are as real for experience as stone walls are, make very clear the fact that there are depths and capacities in the nature of the normal human mind which we do not usually recognize, and of which we have scant and imperfect accounts in our textbooks. Our minds taken in their full range, in other words, have some sort of contact and relationship with an eternal nature of things far deeper than atoms and molecules.

9   Only very slowly and gradually has the race learned, through finite symbols and temporal forms, to interpret beauty and truth and goodness, which, in their essence, are as ineffable and indescribable as is the mystic's experience of God. Plato often speaks as if he had high moments of experience when he rose to the naked vision of beauty — beauty "alone, separate, and eternal," as he says. But, as a matter of fact, however exalted heavenly and enduring beauty may be in its essence, we know *what it is* only as it appears in fair forms of objects, of body, of soul, of actions; in harmonious blending of sounds or colors; in well-ordered or happily combined groupings of many aspects in one unity, which is as it ought to be. Truth and moral goodness always transcend our attainments, and we sometimes feel that the very end and goal of life is the pursuit of that truth or that goodness which eye hath not seen nor ear heard. But whatever truth we do attain, or whatever goodness we do achieve, is always concrete. Truth is just this one more added fact that resists all attempt to doubt it. Goodness is just this simple everyday deed that reveals a heroic spirit and a brave venture of faith in the midst of difficulties.

10   So, too, the mystic knowledge of God is not some esoteric communication, supplied through trance or ecstasy; it is an intuitive personal touch with God, felt to be the essentially real, the bursting forth of an

intense love for Him, which heightens all the capacities and activities of life, followed by the slow laboratory effects which verify it. "All I could never be" now *is*. It seems possible to stand the universe — even to do something toward the transformation of it. And if the experience does not prove that the soul has found God, it at least does this: it makes the soul feel that proofs of God are wholly unnecessary.

Discussion of Theme

1. After reading the essay, are you persuaded that there is a thing such as a mystical experience? Why (not)?
2. Do you think that the "literary and artistic geniuses" referred to in paragraph 4 may have been exaggerating the ease with which "crude material" was transformed? What might have accounted for the supposed transformation?
3. What practical value does the author believe a mystical experience has for an individual?
4. Do you receive the impression that Jones has undergone what he conceives of as a mystical experience? If so, why do you think this?
5. Can one's faith change physical events?
6. How do you regard the claims of users of hallucinatory drugs concerning their mystical experiences?

Discussion of Rhetoric

1. To what extent are Jones's views based on metaphysical claims? Does he use evaluative statements to support his belief?
2. What figurative language is embodied in the final sentence of paragraph 3?
3. The author raises a question in paragraph 6 but does not answer it. Why?
4. Would paragraph 7 be stronger if the author had used examples?
5. Note the use of analogy in paragraph 7. Find other examples.

Writing Assignments

1. Agree or disagree with Jones's statement that "It has generally been the mystic, the prophet, the seer, who have spotted out new ways forward in the jungle of our world or lifted our age to new spiritual levels." Illustrate with specific individuals.
2. Explain: "[W]hatever truth we do attain or whatever goodness we do achieve is always concrete."
3. Define *mysticism*.
4. Analyze a personal experience that might be labeled mystical.

Rufus M. Jones
428

Library Exploration

1. For an account of religious mysticism, read the biographies of St. John of the Cross and St. Theresa of Avila.
2. For a modern view of mysticism, read C. S. Lewis and Paul Tillich.

Vocabulary

(2) ECSTASY rapturous delight

(2) PSYCHICAL beyond physical knowledge

(3) EXPANSIVE broad; comprehensive

(4) EGOISTIC relating to self-interest

(4) INHIBITORY restraining

(6) INCALCULABLE immeasurable

(9) INEFFABLE inexpressible

(9) TRANSCEND go above and beyond

(10) ESOTERIC understood only by a chosen few

(10) INTUITIVE perceived without conscious reasoning

Clive Staples Lewis (1898–
1963) was a professor at Oxford, a scholar in medieval and
Renaissance English literature,
and a writer of novels, religious
works, and children's books.
"The Screwtape Letters," published in book form in 1942, is
one of literature's most famous
examples of sustained irony.

Screwtape, Lewis's personification of a devil, writes to his
ignorant nephew Wormwood,
who is in training to become a
devil himself.

C. S. LEWIS

Screwtape Letters 8 and 9

8

My dear Wormwood,

1 So you "have great hopes that the patient's religious phase is dying away," have you? I always thought the Training College had gone to pieces since they put old Slubgob at the head of it, and now I am sure. Has no one ever told you about the law of Undulation?

2   Humans are amphibians — half spirit and half animal. (The Enemy's determination to produce such a revolting hybrid was one of the things that determined Our Father to withdraw his support from Him.) As spirits they belong to the eternal world, but as animals they inhabit time. This means that while their spirit can be directed to an eternal object, their bodies, passions, and imaginations are in continual change, for to be in time means to change. Their nearest approach to constancy, therefore, is undulation — the repeated return to a level from which they repeatedly fall back, a series of troughs and peaks. If you had watched your patient carefully you would have seen this un-dulation in every department of his life — his interest in his work, his affection for his friends, his physical appetites, all go up and down. As long as he lives on earth periods of emotional and bodily richness and liveliness will alternate with periods of numbness and poverty. The

dryness and dullness through which your patient is now going are not, as you fondly suppose, your workmanship; they are merely a natural phenomenon which will do us no good unless you make a good use of it.

3   To decide what the best use of it is, you must ask what use the Enemy wants to make of it, and then do the opposite. Now it may surprise you to learn that in His efforts to get permanent possession of a soul, He relies on the troughs even more than on the peaks; some of His special favourites have gone through longer and deeper troughs than anyone else. The reason is this. To us a human is primarily food; our aim is the absorption of its will into ours, the increase of our own area of selfhood at its expense. But the obedience which the Enemy demands of men is quite a different thing. One must face the fact that all the talk about His love for men, and His service being perfect freedom, is not (as one would gladly believe) mere propaganda, but an appalling truth. He really *does* want to fill the universe with a lot of loathsome little replicas of Himself — creatures whose life, on its miniature scale, will be qualitatively like His own, not because He has absorbed them but because their wills freely conform to His. We want cattle who can finally become food; He wants servants who can finally become sons. We want to suck in, He wants to give out. We are empty and would be filled; He is full and flows over. Our war aim is a world in which Our Father Below has drawn all other beings into himself: the Enemy wants a world full of beings united to Him but still distinct.

4   And that is where the troughs come in. You must have often wondered why the Enemy does not make more use of His power to be sensibly present to human souls in any degree He chooses and at any moment. But you now see that the Irresistible and the Indisputable are the two weapons which the very nature of His scheme forbids Him to use. Merely to over-ride a human will (as His felt presence in any but the faintest and most mitigated degree would certainly do) would be for Him useless. He cannot ravish. He can only woo. For His ignoble idea is to eat the cake and have it; the creatures are to be one with Him, but yet themselves; merely to cancel them, or assimilate them, will not serve. He is prepared to do a little over-riding at the beginning. He will set them off with communications of His presence which, though faint, seem great to them, with emotional sweetness, and easy conquest over temptation. But He never allows this state of affairs to last long. Sooner or later He withdraws, if not in fact, at least from their conscious experience, all those supports and incentives. He leaves the creature to stand up on its own legs — to carry out from the will alone duties which have lost all relish. It is during such trough periods, much more than during the peak periods, that it is growing into the sort of creature He wants it to be. Hence the prayers offered in the state of dryness are those which please Him best. We can drag our patients along by continual tempting, because we design them only for the table, and the more their will is interfered with the better. He cannot "tempt" to virtue as we do to vice. He wants them to learn to walk and must therefore take away His hand; and if only the will to walk is really here He is pleased even with their stumbles. Do not be deceived, Wormwood. Our case is never more in danger than

when a human, no longer desiring, but still intending, to do our Enemy's will, looks round upon a universe from which every trace of Him seems to have vanished, and asks why he has been forsaken, and still obeys.

5   But of course the troughs afford opportunities to our side also. Next week I will give you some hints on how to exploit them,

> *Your affectionate uncle*
> *Screwtape*

9

My dear Wormwood,

6 I hope my last letter has convinced you that the trough of dullness or "dryness" through which your patient is going at present will not, of itself, give you his soul, but needs to be properly exploited. What forms the exploitation should take I will now consider.

7   In the first place I have always found that the Trough periods of the human undulation provide excellent opportunity for all sensual temptations, particularly those of sex. This may surprise you, because, of course, there is more physical energy, and therefore more potential appetite, at the Peak periods; but you must remember that the powers of resistance are then also at their highest. The health and spirits which you want to use in reproducing lust can also, alas, be very easily used for work or play or thought or innocuous merriment. The attack has a much better chance of success when the man's whole inner world is drab and cold and empty. And it is also to be noted that the Trough sexuality is subtly different in quality from that of the Peak — much less likely to lead to the milk and water phenomenon which the humans call "being in love," much more easily drawn into perversions, much less contaminated by those generous and imaginative and even spiritual concomitants which often render human sexuality so disappointing. It is the same with other desires of the flesh. You are much more likely to make your man a sound drunkard by pressing drink on him as an anodyne when he is dull and weary than by encouraging him to use it as a means of merriment among his friends when he is happy and expansive. Never forget that when we are dealing with any pleasure in its healthy and normal and satisfying form, we are, in a sense, on the enemy's ground. I know we have won many a soul through pleasure. All the same, it is His invention, not ours. He made the pleasures: all our research so far has not enabled us to produce one. All we can do is to encourage the humans to take the pleasures which our Enemy has produced, at times, or in ways, or in degrees, which He has forbidden. Hence we always try to work away from the natural condition of any pleasure to that in which it is least natural, least redolent of its Maker, and least pleasurable. An ever increasing craving for an ever diminishing pleasure is the formula. It is more certain; and it's better *style*. To get the man's soul and give him *nothing* in return — that is what really gladdens Our Father's heart. And the troughs are the time for beginning the process.

8   But there is an even better way of exploiting the Trough; I mean through the patient's own thoughts about it. As always, the first step

is to keep knowledge out of his mind. Do not let him suspect the law of undulation. Let him assume that the first ardours of his conversion might have been expected to last, and ought to have lasted, forever, and that his present dryness is an equally permanent condition. Having once got this misconception well fixed in his head, you may then proceed in various ways. It all depends on whether your man is of the desponding type who can be tempted to despair, or of the wishful-thinking type who can be assured that all is well. The former type is getting rare among the humans. If your patient should happen to belong to it, everything is easy. You have only got to keep him out of the way of experienced Christians (an easy task now-a-days), to direct his attention to the appropriate passages in scripture, and then set him to work on the desperate design of recovering his old feelings by sheer will-power, and the game is ours. If he is of the more hopeful type your job is to make him acquiesce in the present low temperature of his spirit and gradually become content with it, persuading himself that it is not so low after all. In a week or two you will be making him doubt whether the first days of his Christianity were not, perhaps, a little excessive. Talk to him about "moderation in all things." If you can once get him to the point of thinking that "religion is all very well up to a point," you can feel quite happy about his soul. A moderated religion is as good for us as no religion at all—and more amusing.

9 Another possibility is that of direct attack on his faith. When you have caused him to assume that the trough is permanent, can you not persuade him that "his religious phase" is just going to die away like all his previous phases? Of course there is no conceivable way of getting by reason from the proposition "I am losing interest in this" to the proposition "This is false." But, as I said before, it is jargon, not reason, you must rely on. The mere word *phase* will very likely do the trick. I assume that the creature has been through several of them before—they all have—and that he feels superior and patronising to the ones he has emerged from, not because he has really criticized them but simply because they are in the past. (You keep him well fed on hazy ideas of Progress and Development and the Historical Point of View, I trust, and give him lots of modern Biographies to read? The people in them are always emerging from Phases, aren't they?)

10 You see the idea? Keep his mind off the plain antithesis between True and False. Nice shadowy expressions—"It was a phase"—"I've been through that"—and don't forget the blessed word "Adolescent,"

Your affectionate uncle
Screwtape

Discussion of Theme

1. Does Lewis's version of the devil and of his relationship with God differ basically, or only in details, from the conventional version?
2. Can you enjoy these letters whether or not you have an interest in theological questions?

3. What is Lewis's meaning in the final sentence of paragraph 5? How would the concept be changed if "and still obeys" were left out? Why is this important?
4. Do you agree with Lewis's opinion of when it is easiest to cause a man to succumb to "sensual temptations"? Could the opposite be true just as often?

Discussion of Rhetoric

1. What is Lewis's purpose in capitalizing certain words? Does he overdo this?
2. Why are letters frequently a more effective way than essays to express personal beliefs?
3. Why does he say, "It is jargon, not reason, you must rely on"?
4. Find examples of irony in Letter 9.

Writing Assignments

1. If you disagree with the views expressed in these letters, write a letter to Screwtape explaining your own views on the matter.
2. Considering the Screwtape Letters in light of modern social attitudes, are the religious views Lewis expressed outmoded? Specify which and explain why.
3. Assume the same position as Screwtape and write some advice to a nephew about conformity.

Library Exploration

1. One of Lewis's most popular books on this theme is *Mere Christianity* (1952).
2. Another unusual treatment of the theme of heaven and hell is *Heavenly Discourse,* by Charles Erskine Scott Wood (1927).

Vocabulary

(1) UNDULATION wavelike movement
(2) AMPHIBIANS animals who live part of their life in water, part on land
(2) HYBRID product of cross-
(2) PHENOMENON observable fact or event
(4) MITIGATED moderated
(4) INCENTIVES inducements
(6) EXPLOITED used for one's own advantage

(7) INNOCUOUS harmless; ineffective
(7) CONCOMITANTS accompanying things
(7) ANODYNE pain reliever
(7) REDOLENT reeking; smelling
(8) ARDOURS enthusiasms
(8) ACQUIESCE accept passively
(10) ANTITHESIS opposite; contrast

John C. Bennett (1902–   ),
Canadian-born president of
Union Theological Seminary, is
a leading Protestant theologian.
He was educated at Oxford and
at Union and has taught religion
at several colleges and universities. Among his many books
are "Social Salvation" (1935),
"Christian Ethics and Social
Policy" (1946), and "Christians
and the State" (1958). He
edited "Nuclear Weapons and
the Conflict of Conscience"
(1962).

In the current debate on the
death of God some theologians
have countered with reaffirma-
tions of their faith. Here is what
one prominent Christian thinker
sees as indications that God is
still very much alive.

JOHN C. BENNETT

In Defense
of God

1   This Easter [1966] many Christians are puzzled and some are deeply
disturbed by strange voices within the church proclaiming, "God is
dead."
2   I do not think we should exaggerate the importance of this movement. But it would be unwise to ignore the conditions — and the
doubts — that have attracted listeners and followers.
3   Some people seem to feel that the theologians who belong to the
"death of God" school of thought are merely atheists who have blun-
dered into the church, but this is not true. These men are spokesmen
for a faith, however inadequate that faith may seem to those who do
not share it. They mean to be Christian, to be loyal followers of Jesus.
4   Statements by two spokesmen, which appeared in *The Christian
Century,* will indicate the broad outlines of this new doctrine:

5   "Theology itself is coming to confess that ours is a time in which God is dead," Thomas J. J. Altizer has written. And then he tells what this startling sentence means: "First we must acknowledge that we are not simply saying that modern man is incapable of believing in God, or that modern culture is an idolatrous flight from the presence of God, or even that we exist in a time in which God has chosen to be silent. . . . A theological statement that proclaims the death of God must mean that God is not present in the Word of faith. . . . He is truly absent, he is not simply hidden from view, and therefore he is truly dead."

6   Altizer's thought is extremely complicated and confusing. In place of the God of traditional theology, he has substituted a world view more akin to Buddhist mysticism than to a secularist atheism, and influenced by aspects of Christian teaching about Word and Spirit. The world he portrays is unlike that pictured by others who believe in a godless universe.

7   William Hamilton emphasizes the conviction shared by the leaders of this new theology that the death of God does not mean the end of Christianity, but actually points to a great emphasis on Jesus as the Lord and center of history.

8   "I insist that the time of the death of God is also the time of obedience to Jesus," he says. "This entails a claim that the New Testament Jesus can in fact be known, that a figure of sufficient clarity is available to us so that discipleship to him—to his life, his words and his death—is a possible center for Christian faith and life."

9   Hamilton does not find the new faith bleak and forbidding. He seems to be convinced that its tenets will remove a burden from the shoulders of many Christians who have felt similar doubts, but have not felt free to proclaim them:

10   "The death of God, obedience to Jesus and a new optimism—these are three of the themes I see emerging in the new radical movement in theology today. This movement involves a very small group which is not likely to be influential, but it is buoyant and full of spirit, for it is really excited by the direction in which it is having to move. And at its most euphoric, it really is convinced that it can work out a new way for men to be Christian in the kind of world we live in today."

11   The third theologian generally associated with this school is Paul M. van Buren. He is a more restrained and systematic thinker than the others. He does not emphasize the death of God, but develops a theology that, while centered in Jesus and the Resurrection, has no place for the word "God." For him, this word is too ambiguous to use, and he regards the usual Christian affirmations about God the Father as vetoed by the latest word in philosophy.

12   These three theologians have dramatized a crisis of belief present both inside and outside the church. They have, I believe, blurted out ideas quite widely held, even though they are not ordinarily fully acknowledged. When Hamilton asserts, "We are not talking about the absence of the experience of God, but about the experience of the absence of God," are not those words a confession that might be made by many of our most thoughtful contemporaries?

13   The great theologian Dietrich Bonhoeffer, who provided stimulus for this frank rejection of the presence of God, would himself have been horrified by the use now made of a few paragraphs in his writings. Bonhoeffer wrote about the world that had "come of age" and said, "It is becoming evident that everything gets along without God, and just as well as before. As in the scientific field, so in human affairs generally, what we call 'God' is being more and more edged out of life, losing more and more ground."

14   Even though he wrote from a Nazi prison at a time of historical catastrophe, Bonhoeffer did not revise his idea that man had come of age and that it was not necessary to invoke God to fill gaps in knowledge or to provide support in crises in personal life or in history. But I think that Bonhoeffer's theological self-denying ordinance is now being carried too far. He believed passionately that God as revealed in Christ was at the center of this world of men who had come of age. All that he says needs to be understood in the light of such words as these: "The God who makes us live in this world without using Him as a working hypothesis is the God before whom we are ever standing. Before God and with Him we live without God. God allows himself to be edged out of the world and onto the Cross."

15   There is a baffling paradox here, but it would be false to Bonhoeffer to break the paradox and leave us with a suffering Jesus apart from the God of the world.

16   Many of the questions these thinkers raise I can understand. However, the thought of each of them falls apart as a version of Christianity. The main problem is suggested by the title which *The Christian Century* gave to a review by Hamilton of a book by van Buren: "There is no God and Jesus is His Son"—an echo of a familiar characterization of Santayana's thought. The double cry: "God is dead. Long live Jesus" is more than a paradox. If there is no God, Jesus cannot be the guide for our ultimate beliefs.

17   There are at least three factors in our experience that cause sensitive and honest men to doubt the existence of God or to proclaim the absence of God. In some form, these factors have appeared in many times and places, but they now press upon us more than ever.

18   The first is that God seems to be crowded out of the world most of us experience. We see everywhere many agents at work that are not God, and naturally, most of us ask for signs of His activity.

19   If, however, we are among those who believe all visible agents are God at work, how can the word "God" have meaning of its own? Or, if we try to make a distinction between what God does and what is done by other agents, how can we tell one from the other?

20   The growth of scientific knowledge of nature and human behavior and the historical understanding of the context of events and the web of technological culture all seem to narrow the possible area of any distinctively *divine* action. To some people, this area appears to have vanished altogether. As Altizer puts it: "Surely it is not possible for any responsible person to think that we can any longer know or experience God in nature, in history, in the economic or political arenas, in the laboratory, or in anything which is genuinely modern, whether in

thought or in experience. Wherever we turn in our experience, we experience the eclipse or the silence of God."

21   A second difficulty is the conflict between our recognition of the vast evil in the world in contrast to the Biblical vision of the love of God. In Camus's *The Plague,* a character cries: "I refuse to love a scheme of things in which children are put to torture." We have seen a new universe of horror in which masses of people are victims of gas chambers or bombs. The catastrophes of a nation, a civilization, a generation are perhaps the greatest obstacle to faith in God.

22   Evil and suffering have completely different effects upon different people. For some, they destroy faith in God. For others, they destroy the substitutes for faith in God, and thus lead people into a deeper awareness of God's presence. The Christian community has the Cross, an instrument of torture and punishment, as its central symbol. But unless there are signs of resurrection somewhere in the same context, unless we see some hope that so stark an evil will be overcome, evil and suffering may easily lead to atheism. How can we live so close to the possibility of the annihilation of humanity and observe the apparent frustration of divine purposes? It is not surprising that atheism flourishes in the face of the possibility of such an end of human history, an end caused less by depravity than by the absurd actions of the "righteous."

23   There is a third ground for atheism, and that is a need that some men have felt to emancipate themselves from a God who may seem to threaten their freedom and their dignity. How can man be a free being if he lives under the sovereignty of the God of theism?

24   Does not God overwhelm man by his power? This is a major *motif* in contemporary atheism. The revolt of Karl Marx against God—as he understood the Christian teaching about Him—was basically a revolt in behalf of the humanity of man. This was based upon a profound misunderstanding of God as revealed in Christ, but it was a misunderstanding for which Christians were partly responsible.

25   One reason for the appearance of this new Christian atheism at this juncture in the life of Protestantism is that it follows after a powerful theological movement that affirmed the God of revelation and discarded all intimations of God apart from revelation. For some decades, an absolutely Christocentric approach to God won the minds of many Christian thinkers, including van Buren and Hamilton. The way from God to man and from man to God through Christ alone seemed clear for a time to some theologians, and then this faith lost the power to convince many of them. The negative judgments of philosophers about the arguments for God had confirmed the negative judgments of theologians.

26   I believe that there is a way of reopening the whole question. We must begin by accepting the view that there are no proofs of God and that there is no metaphysical system that can, on its own, provide the basis for belief. We must also recognize the precariousness of the absolutely independent and unsupported revelation of God that comes only through the person of Jesus Christ.

27   Instead, we may say that while there are no proofs of God, there are

intimations that the world of our experience is not self-sufficient without Him. There are pointers to God that will not of themselves convince the unbeliever, but may at least prepare the way for the vision of God made possible by revelation. What are they?

28   The world of our experience is neither a monotonous succession of disconnected sights and sounds nor is it without structures of moral and aesthetic values. The memories and imaginations of men grasp ideas and visions endlessly, and there is at least a partial organization of the ideas and visions of large communities of men.

29   What is the relationship of this organized world of experience to the cosmos as a whole and to all of the vistas of time and space that it reveals? Is our world merely an island of meaning in a sea of meaninglessness so far as value is concerned? Or do we in our experience touch something that is universal, something that gives unifying meaning to the totality of existence?

30   "It is remarkable . . . that men communicate with each other, form lasting and profound friendships, sometimes sacrifice themselves for one another, respect other persons quite differently from things, value creativity, build universities, and are incurably attracted by the ideal of fidelity to understanding," Michael Novak writes. "These facts are odd if the world of which these intelligent subjects are a part is so radically absurd. It seems that in an absurd world there would be neither fruitfulness nor honor in being faithful to understanding. If the real is absurd, man's nobility doubles the absurdity by his failing to grasp the irrelevance of nobility and honesty. If man can make nobility and honesty relevant, the real is not quite as absurd as it seems."

31   When I imagine the possible temporal end of this world, perhaps through some cosmic accident or nuclear annihilation, I ask: Would there remain *anywhere* any awareness that this world had ever existed? Perhaps on other planets there are other worlds of meaning, but what has taken place in our history is not known to them. Given the catastrophe that I project, we are left, if there is no God, with no memory anywhere that human history, with all of its greatness and its misery, its goodness and its depravity, had ever taken place. To me, the test of the credibility of atheism is to be able to live with this prospect, to be able to believe that this world of our experience is an island that may be lost forever, remembered by none. This may be the case, but to believe it taxes my credulity more than faith in God.

32   Harvey Cox, who must not be confused with the death of God theologians, though his thought has contributed to the current ferment on this subject, supports this position. He says: "Despite the efforts of some modern theologians to sidestep it, whether God exists or not is a desperately serious issue. . . . It is the question the Spanish philosopher Miguel Unamuno rightly felt overshadows all other questions man asks: 'Is man alone in the universe or not?'"

33   A second intimation is the sense of absolute obligation that we sometimes experience. This is no mere holdover from a Puritan conscience, for it has an ancient history. Wherever men have felt that it was better, as Plato said, to suffer injustice than to do injustice, prophetic spirits were willing to die rather than to say "yes" falsely to the powers of the world. Much of the moral experience of men can be explained as the

result of the necessities of social survival pressing upon the individual. But it is not possible in this way to explain the conscience of the individual who chooses to oppose the society that surrounds him at cost to himself. In the prophetic tradition, to seek justice has been to know God.

34   A third intimation of God comes from man's impulse to worship, to give himself in devotion and in sacrifice to something beyond himself. There is a logic of worship that reveals itself historically as men find themselves making idols. Today, there is a conflict of opinion between those who say that all men have gods of some kind, gods that become false religious absolutes unless they are overcome by the true God, and those who say that modern men who have come of age can now dispense with all deities, that modern men need no religious devotion of any kind.

35   I think the assumption that all men have a god of some kind is probably false; there are those who are genuinely neutral and detached. But surely, in the case of most men, passionate loyalties involving political fanaticism are likely to fill any vacuum created by atheism. Marxist atheism left room for the Communists' worship of state, party, ideology, program and future utopian goal. Already there are signs in some Communist societies that this is eroding. It may be followed by disillusionment and detachment from ideological commitment. The vacuum that remains may be filled by an absolute scientism, a fervent nationalism. There is also the possibility that as they lose their idols, men will find God again. The God of righteousness and love, who transcends in His being and purpose every human ideal and community and power and scheme of salvation, may deflate the idols and dispel the demons. Worship may be restored to its proper object, and thus sustain and liberate man.

36   The fourth intimation of God is the actual experience of healing, of what may be called grace in the midst of our common experience. Persons in deepest need, victims of estrangement, may actually find themselves blessed by a healing power. As Paul Tillich has said, they may find themselves recipients of grace without knowing what this power is or whence the grace comes. This experience does not provide a proof that any idea of God is true. It is no more than a hint of something that transcends our closed systems of thought and expectation.

37   I try to avoid all false claims for what can be inferred from these intimations of God. I do not regard them as a "natural theology" or a "philosophy of religion" that proves God exists. Much of the religious scepticism that opens the door to atheism in our time stems from a valid rejection of false claims. But that need not leave us in a world with no signs that point to God.

38   The signs I have presented make more sense if there is truth in the full revelation of God that has come to us through the Bible—especially through the life and death and resurrection of Jesus, allowing for much freedom of interpretation of what such words as "resurrection" mean. If this revelation is the bearer of truth, many more of the pieces of our life fit together than if this is not the case.

39   The vision of God as the transcendent Creator who in love identifies himself with His finite and sinful creatures is anything but obvious. It

must be revealed to be believed, but once revealed, it may remain a norm for the divine that has its own persuasive power. Christians see God in this way most clearly in Christ. But there are intimations of this understanding of God in the Old Testament. Is there not a gospel before the Gospel in the words of Isaiah: "For thus says the high and lofty One who inhabits eternity: I dwell in the high and holy place, and also with him who is of a contrite and humble spirit."

40   Often, radical critics make the doctrine of the Trinity one of their major targets. While it is easy to show the inadequacy of all formulations of this doctrine, the doctrine itself has been the way in which two aspects of God have been held together in Christian thought. The God who is the ultimate being is the same God who is *with us*. The critics are right in saying that the threeness of God is less clear than the contrast between the first person of the Trinity on the one hand and the second and third persons on the other. But arguments on this issue should be regarded as marginal. The great affirmation that has been expressed through this doctrine, and that may be expressed in simpler terms, is the faith that the transcendent Creator and Lord of all worlds is *with* His creatures. The ultimate or the holy is joined with love. How this can be is indeed a mystery, but it is better to live with this mystery than it is to cast it aside for a clearer and simpler model of the divine being. Is it not possible that when once we have had this vision of the union of the divine greatness and the divine humility, any other model of greatness may seem less great?

41   The God we encounter in the Bible respects the freedom of man. He is no arbitrary despot whose power prevents men from being themselves. Indeed, God is strangely patient with man. He seeks to persuade rather than to compel. It is true that one of the instruments of His persuasion is the judgment that men bring upon themselves when they persist in resisting Him, but they remain free to resist Him. Today, men, though they may have come of age in some respects, play recklessly with the means of their own annihilation.

42   One of the themes of Christian theology that needs great emphasis today, as the death of God is proclaimed partly to make room for man to be himself, is the reaffirmation of a Christian humanism. All teaching about God that by implication denies the freedom of man or downgrades him, and especially all teaching about God that downgrades some men, leaving them a less than human role, must be renounced. Often in the past, God has been seen as the great preserver of the status quo, which was organized for the benefit of the few at the expense of the many. But today, God is with the revolutionary efforts to raise the many to a position of human dignity and hope.

43   A great theologian of our time, Karl Barth, has often been accused of exalting God at the expense of man. In his earlier thought, he seemed to level all men down because of their sin. But in recent decades, he has leveled all men up because of Christ — whether they had had a conscious relationship to Christ or not. Barth says: "It is thought that the grace of God will be magnified if man is represented as a blotted or at best an empty page. . . . This representation cannot be sustained. Man cannot be depicted as a blotted or empty page." He goes on to chide the church for addressing man as though he were not

human, and he says: "He will rightly defend himself against what he is told. He will not be convicted of sin if he is uncharitably and falsely addressed concerning his humanity."

44   God does not threaten the humanity of man. On the contrary, the humanity of man can be threatened if the final word is that he is alone, that he is unknown to any being other than his fellows, that he is responsible to no authority above the state or the other powers of the world that claim his allegiance. The deepest source of his freedom may still be that he knows that he must "obey God rather than men."

Discussion of Theme

1. Why do you suppose people are so fascinated by the subject of whether or not there is a God?
2. Explain the difference between "the absence of the experience of God" and "the experience of the absence of God." Are you intimate with either?
3. If you believe in God, what do you consider the best evidence of his existence? If you don't, how do you answer Bennett?
4. Do you think that believers such as Altizer and Hamilton add to serious dialogue on the subject of God's existence?
5. Is the sense of absolute obligation a universal experience? Explain your answer.

Discussion of Rhetoric

1. Why does Bennett capitalize *God,* but not *godless?*
2. What tone does the author use in discussing theologians who disagree with him?
3. Are Bennett's arguments familiar ones that have been enlivened by commanding rhetoric, or does he introduce fresh reasoning to a much debated subject? If both, specify examples of each.
4. Notice the way Bennett deals first with the con argument and then with the pro argument. What effect has this on the organization of the essay?
5. One reason for the short paragraphs is the fact that the essay first appeared in *Look* magazine. Should paragraphs be this short for a book? Why?
6. In paragraph 22 the author repeats an idea introduced in paragraph 21. Is this a good transition?

Writing Assignments

1. Describe an experience that either strengthened or weakened (or possibly destroyed) your faith in God.
2. Explain your concept of God.
3. Can religion answer the needs of an individual who has used drugs as a means of solace in our society?

4. Has there been more harm than good done in the name of God?
5. Describe the most important religious decision you ever made.
6. Defend or attack one of Bennett's intimations of the existence of God.

Library Exploration

1. Look up reports on the Dead Sea scrolls and see if any of the information contained in the scrolls is relevant to Bennett's thesis.
2. Check on Bonhoeffer and see if you think he would have been "horrified" at the interpretations Altizer and others are making of his writings.

Vocabulary

(6) SECULARIST worldly; irreligious

(9) TENETS basic principles

(10) EUPHORIC elated

(11) AMBIGUOUS vague; unclear

(22) ANNIHILATION destruction; wiping out

(23) EMANCIPATE free

(23) SOVEREIGNTY power; authority

(24) MOTIF repeated theme

(25) INTIMATIONS hints

(25) CHRISTOCENTRIC Christ-centered

(26) PRECARIOUSNESS riskiness

(29) COSMOS universe

(31) CREDIBILITY believability

The Lively Arts

Yehudi Menuhin (1916–) is one of the leading violin virtuosos of this century. Born in New York City, but now a resident of London, he is president of the International Music Council of UNESCO.

Man the individual is the creative personality. Man as artist must dominate man as political animal. If he can divert his combative drives, he may survive.

YEHUDI MENUHIN

Art as Hope for Humanity

1 I look upon great works of art not only as isolated gifts and benefactions from heaven but also as high points of emerging from a continuing living process. It is upon this view that I base my belief in art as hope for humanity.

2   When we consider the great violin makers, we realize that their expertise evolved gradually and continuously from centuries of song and string playing, both in the folk and cultivated forms. Their tradition has roots in a musical, literate culture that is rich in composers and instrumentalists. Our Gothic churches evolved from the yearning of entire populations to reach up to God in prayer. Worship, dedication, love—these are qualities that must reside in the living, thinking, dreaming moments of the population at large before a genius can crystallize a total environment through his own eyes, ears, and hands and thus hold up a mirror, inspiring and moving, to his fellowmen.

3   Rhythm in music, proportion and movement in other arts—these are the assurances of continuity, of direction, and of design or logic in everyday life. Without these assurances life must often seem to the bewildered individual and innocent sufferer a "buzzing, booming confusion," without rhyme or reason. Thus not only the creative artist and poet, the musician and painter, but also the humblest craftsman serves his society. You will find that you can trust a good shoemaker and a botanist, perhaps even a violinist, in a way you cannot always

trust a politician, a lawyer, and a financier. The manipulators of men should learn first to use their hands, to manipulate clay and stone and to handle the good earth with gratitude and respect. Our mothers should sing to their children, and our children should sing together. Perhaps no other activity is so wholesome, for it engages completely our inner mobility—breath and circulation—our lungs and heart. Our spirit and sense of community are immeasurably enhanced by this exercise: the compelling and total discipline of rhythm and pitch further the sense of union and communal solidarity. When one thinks of the pathetic Balilla Mussolini's marching eight-year-olds, one could cry. And where did it bring them? Fortunately for the children, no Italian can take that kind of rubbish seriously. Marching is the very opposite of choral singing.

4   Art is, as I see it, a representation—an *intensification*—of life, much as a chess game is a minuscule representation of the ebb and flow of battle. In art, as in life, the elements of predictability and surprise are delicately balanced. Of course, predictability in rhythm and proportion must precede surprise. Spontaneity, surprise improvisation, are only inspiring and liberating when they occur upon the secure foundation of a base rhythm or a projected order of proportion or both. It is the wobble in the potter's wheel that accounts for the slight irregularity of a vase—the imperfection is deeply touching, for its testifies to the fallibility of a particular pair of hands. The great artist allows his inspiration a certain free rein, which, emerging from his supreme discipline, is a reminder of a human abandon, impulse, and surrender.

5   We are today surrounded—indeed, fenced in—by right angles set along interminable lines: In the United States a national north-south and east-west grid accounts for the streets and buildings of most cities. Americans are the first to recognize the asymmetrical, free-form beauty of Venice, old Bologna, Mykonos, or old Paris. Venice looks no different in reality than it does in the paintings of Canaletto, Guardi, and Turner. Art holds out a hope for the future if we will allow our cities to be designed by artists instead of by engineers—if we will take into our calculations the artist's conception of space and line and the musician's conception of time and melody. Thus, before we can allow ourselves hope, we must have faith and charity.

6   Perhaps one day the artist in man will dominate man the political animal. Let us never forget that the bigger units of administration only serve to organize, apply, and develop what man alone, the individual in the unique cultural environment, creates. It is the smaller and smallest unit that has vision and that creates, the larger that applies but cannot create. Ultimately, it is upon the individual we depend. Perhaps it is thinking very far ahead to say so, but eventually the nation-state must cede part of its autonomy both to the larger world unit and to the smaller neighborhood-community. On one hand, there must be international cooperation in various fields—food, pollution, space, resources. On the other hand, the nations must encourage regional autonomy—languages, dialects, art, music, theater, dress, diet, way of life, and all human, humane, and cultural activities.

7   Man's seemingly natural aggressive, combative, competing, and dominating instincts can find ample outlets and expression on other levels than those of the nation-state. We can do without emasculated deliberations conducted in committee rooms, deliberations that are divorced from human pain or pleasure. Let men play the violin, play chess, fence, go to the moon, play Ping-Pong, and write poetry. Let them vie with each other on individual, regional, and world levels. But let them not degenerate into dumb automatons, robots of the nation-state, manipulated physically, spiritually, and morally by the abuse of all their gifts and by the debasement of all their faculties.

8   I do not doubt for a moment that humankind will find creative alternatives to rigidity, and I do not doubt that art will play a functional, pragmatic role in our salvation. This is, at any rate, my faith—a faith strongly grounded in the traditions that have bequeathed us Michelangelo's *Moses,* Rembrandt's *Night Watch,* Chartres's Cathedral, and Bach's *B Minor Mass*—or Henry Moore's *King and Queen,* Picasso's *Pierrot,* the Sydney Opera House in Australia, and Bartok's string quartets.

Discussion of Theme

1. According to Yehudi Menuhin, why is art the great hope for humanity?
2. In what ways does art bring meaning to life?
3. The author suggests that there is something of the artist in everyone. Do you agree? Explain.
4. How would the quality of human life change if the author's hope became a reality?

Discussion of Rhetoric

1. Find examples of the author's use of illustrative material to make his abstractions specific.
2. Is this essay in any way persuasive? Is it meant to be?
3. Does the final paragraph "tie it all together," or could it be improved? How?

Writing Assignments

1. It has become a cliché to complain that the day of the craftsman is past—that everything is machinemade. Yet, in the last few years we have seen a great resurgence of crafts such as wood and leather work, stained glass, tie-dying, and many people now earn their livings by their craftmanship. Report on the possible reason for this occurrence.
2. Many artists give up their art or become Sunday artists because of economic reasons. In your opinion, should the government act as a

great patron and subsidize artists so that they can concentrate on their arts? Would this benefit society in practical ways?
3. Write a short essay expressing your opinion as to the function and purpose of art.

Library Exploration

1. Write a research paper on the topic, "Art as Propaganda in America."
2. Read Franz Kafka's short story, "The Hunger Artist," in which fasting is an art form.

Vocabulary

(1) BENEFACTIONS gifts
(2) GOTHIC a style of architecture originating in France around the twelfth century
(4) MINUSCULE small
(4) FALLIBILITY liable to make an error

(5) ASYMMETRICAL irregular in form
(6) CEDE yield
(7) DEBASEMENT a reduction in quality or value

Edmund Carpenter, professor of anthropology at Fordham University, has written studies of the effects of modern technology on man.

To an extent unrealized by most of us, we become what we behold. Our technology, Carpenter insists, has sculpted our bodies, programmed our senses, and modified sexual differences among us.

EDMUND CARPENTER

They Became What They Beheld

THE ISLANDER

1 "We don't know who discovered water, but we're certain it wasn't a fish." *John Culkin.*

2   It's the outsider who sees the environment. The islander sees the outline of the distant mainland. When he goes ashore, he commands, for he alone sees form and process.

3   Yeats, Joyce, Shaw, from Ireland; Eliot, from Missouri; Pound from Idaho, were the innovators of 20th Century English. Beaverbrook, from the Maritimes; Luce, from a missionary family in China; Thomson, from the Ontario bush, became the giants of 20th Century publishing. Detachment and perspective permit pattern recognition.

4   "In the histories of most peoples, there occur long lapses during which they lie creatively fallow. Western European man was late by a millenium or so in adding anything to ancient culture; the Jews between the Dispersion and their emergence from the ghettos did nothing that a historian of art and thought could not cover in a long footnote. When they re-entered the world, the Jews, as though seeing for the first time the structure to whose piecemeal growth they had contributed almost nothing, produced within a century a series of epic innovators—Karl Marx, Sigmund Freud, Albert Einstein—and scores of hardly less original minds (Kafka, for example). The re-emergence

of the Islamic peoples, when complete, may give us the same kind of constellation." *A. J. Liebling.*

HAIR

5   Chief Long-hair, a Crow Indian, wound his hair with a strap and folded it into a container, which he carried under his arm. It was his sacred medicine and about ten feet long. As this long tress grew, he bound it at intervals with balls of pitch, and on rare occasions released it while galloping on horseback.

6   Taking a scalp meant acquiring an enemy's power.

7   Samson's great strength resided in his hair, but Delilah shaved off his seven shaggy locks, unshorn from childhood, thus robbing him of his supernatural strength and rendering him impotent.

8   In the East Indies, a criminal under torture persisted in denying his guilt until the court ordered his hair cut, at which point he immediately confessed. "One man," recounts *Golden Bough*'s James Frazer, "who was tried for murder, endured without flinching the utmost ingenuity of his torturers till he saw the surgeon standing with a pair of shears. On asking what this was for and being told it was to cut his hair, he begged they would not do it, and made a clean breast."

9   In most preliterate societies, ordinary consciousness is associated with the heart and chest, but the early "Indo-Europeans," according to Onians, "believed that the head contained a different factor, the procreative life-soul or spirit, which survives death, and the seed of new life." Among the reasons for thus honoring the head, he cites the analogy with the flower of fruit, seed pod, at the top or end of a plant; association of sexual experience with sensations and appearances in the head; relating the hair of the head, especially the beard, to pubic hair and to sexual power generally; and, finally, the association of life and strength with the cerebrospinal fluid and with the seed that seemed to flow from, and be part of, the latter.

10   Among the Norse, the hair of thralls was cut short. Among Arabs, what distinguished a freeman was the lock on his forehead, the slave's forehead being shaved. Many religious groups shaved their heads as a symbol of submission.

11   Jews, shorn and naked, entered gas chambers silently. Military inductees are first shorn: In one swift cut, self-identity is muted. Following the trial of the Chicago Seven, the prison warden cut the hair of the prisoners, then exhibited their pictures to a cheering Republican club. French women who slept with German soldiers were punished by having their heads shaved.

12   With literacy, breath, body odors and hair were dissociated from the self, which was sharply delimited. Short hair was required, especially of business and military men: The artist was exempt but never fully approved. Today, the tendency toward long hair is more than social weaponry; it reflects a new self-concept much closer to tribal beliefs. On the surface, the issue seems embarrassingly minor to generate such intense conflict; but in fact its premises are so basic, its emotional roots so deep, that identity itself is challenged.

TELEPHONE

13 "'Hello, Central. Give me Dr. Jazz.'" *Jelly Roll Morton.*

14 The telephone is said to be the only thing that can interrupt that most precious of all moments.

15 Aimee Semple McPherson was buried with a live telephone in her coffin.

16 I once observed a man walking alone past a public phone that rang just as he passed. He hesitated and then, after the second ring, answered it. The call couldn't possibly have been for him.

17 I called various public phones on streets and in terminals and, when someone answered, as almost invariably someone did, I asked why he had. Most said, "Because it rang."

18 On September 6, 1949, a psychotic veteran, Howard B. Unruh, in a mad rampage on the streets of Camden, New Jersey, killed 13 people and then returned home. Emergency police crews, bringing up machine guns, shotguns and tear-gas bombs, opened fire. At this point, an editor on the Camden Evening Courier looked up Unruh's name in the telephone directory and called him, Unruh stopped firing and answered.

19 "Hello."
"This Howard?"
"Yes . . . ."
"Why are you killing people?"

20 "I don't know. I can't answer that yet. I'll have to talk to you later. I'm too busy now."

IGNORING OLD AUDIENCES, CREATING NEW

21 Today's revolutionary movement began with an inspired use of the newly invented LP record. Black humorists, denied access to mass radio audiences, created LP audiences. Though some of these were large, they possessed a sense of intimacy, even conspiracy, totally lacking in radio audiences. When Mort Sahl and others later turned to TV, black humor died. Sahl attributed this to political changes, but I wonder if another factor wasn't involved: Restricting information makes it highly explosive, while widely disseminating information neutralizes its effects.

THEY BECAME WHAT THEY BEHELD

22 "Oh, what a beautiful baby!"

23 "That's nothing," replied the mother, "you should see his photograph."

24 All people imitate their creations. Javanese dancers imitate the jerky movements of Javanese puppets. Jazz singers imitate instruments: "I never sing anything I can't play," says Louis Armstrong, "and I never play anything I can't sing."

25 Victorians moved like steam engines: The *grande dame* coming

through an archway (her bustle a coal car) looked like a locomotive emerging from a tunnel.

26   Today's fashions imitate our principal creations, which are electronic. Women imitate light bulbs or TV sets: Their clothes flow; their hair is luminous. They radiate. They can be turned on or off.

27   Illumination comes from within. It has no visible source. It's not dependent upon outside energy. Today's women are cordless.

28   "Is it on?" asked a three-year-old holding a ballpoint pen.

29   Psychologists were recently called to aid a boy who couldn't move or speak unless an electric cord, attached to his body, was plugged in.

30   California hippie: "One couple I know rarely speak but share the same rhythms with tambourines and drums, as well as with their breathing. These rhythms are the same as the ones their electric fan and refrigerator make."

31   Rural children dream of lambs and bunnies; urban children dream of cars and trains. But acidheads have visions of electronic instruments and especially under the influence of "electric drugs," identify with TV sets.

32   "Daddy, are we live or on tape?" *Five-year-old boy.*

33   "It took me a long time to discover that the key thing in acting is honesty. Once you know how to fake that, you've got it made." *Actor in "Peyton Place."*

MATING MEDIA

34 In the 1968 elections, the McCarthy campaign staff was approached with a suggestion for crossing media. In the United States, no law prohibits the mating of radio and TV. In Southern California, for example, Spanish-speaking sports fans watch the picture on TV but listen to a Spanish-speaking sports broadcaster on radio. So it was proposed that the New York–New Jersey area be offered a night of radio sound and TV picture. Five commentators were to provide the audio: John Culkin, Jean Shepherd, Marshall McLuhan, myself and Tony Schwartz, who originated the idea and had a sound studio equipped to handle the project. A bank of small TV sets would offer simultaneous coverage of all principal TV stations in the area; each would be kept on its particular channel. From these the commentators would select programs shown on a master TV set and would direct their comments toward these programs. The plan was to announce in the New York–New Jersey newspapers that at seven P.M. on a certain night, a local radio station would provide that evening's TV audio. For example, the audio for a TV cigarette commercial would be one minute of coughing via radio. If there was a laugh show, it would be pointed out that the laugh tracks were copyrighted in 1935 and that most of the people one heard laughing had been dead for some time. Then listeners would be asked to turn to a channel showing Walter Cronkite, at which point they would hear a taped "countdown," first in English, followed by an A-blast; then in Russian, then Chinese, each followed by blasts and more blasts and in the end by only a child's cry. Finally, and this was the point of the whole project, listeners would be

encouraged to turn to a channel with Hubert Humphrey speaking. Instead of his speech, however, they would hear—on radio—the four letters he wrote to his draft board, gaining exemption from duty in World War Two—one letter citing two lectures he had delivered to an R.O.T.C. class, while in the background would be played Hitler's ranting, bombs and screams: then Humphrey's pro-Vietnam-war speeches—"a glorious adventure and great fun, isn't it?"—while in the background, the explosions and screams continued.

35 The McCarthy team, mostly literary men, saw something profoundly immoral in the suggestion. New forms always seem immoral or chaotic, since they are unconsciously judged by reference to consecrated forms. But a curious contradiction arises: New forms are condemned, but the information they disseminate is believed, while the old and valued aren't even seen.

SERVICE ENVIRONMENTS

36 The moment any service exceeds what any single individual can control, that service is environmental. When environmental services exceed the reach of the greatest private wealth, the society is communistic. In this sense, the United States has been communistic for some time, more fully than any other country. Only a bookkeeping smoke screen conceals this fact. America reached this state via technology, not propaganda or revolution.

37 Television is part of the only environment today's children have ever known. To punish a child by forbidding him to watch TV is as nonsensical as depriving him of heat.

38 To try to restrict this service environment to white adults or to regard its benefits as products of private labor is equally nonsensical. The unemployed Negro youth who demands admission into this environment understands its nature far better than the middle-class white who strives to exclude him.

39 The unskilled-uneducated-unemployed of 1830 London lacked even minimal resources to participate in the service environment. They lacked not only the penny to mail a letter, they lacked the literacy to write it. They lived in the midst of a service environment but could not participate in it. Their admission into it was the reform movement of that day. Today we face a similar challenge: expanding membership in the service environment.

40 Electronic media have made all the arts environmental. Everyone can avail himself of cultural riches beyond what any millionaire has ever known. Today no serious scholar limits himself to Morgan Library when the entire New York Public Library is open daily and paperbacks are everywhere at hand. No art lover restricts himself to Mellon's collection. LPs and magnetic tapes make environmental all recorded music from all times: Music, like a wild bird's song, now belongs to the environment.

41 Today in the United States there are no longer any significant areas of private wealth. The multibillion-dollar service environment of electric information is free for all. Knowledge industries are the only sig-

nificant ones now. Education, news, transportation, entertainment, medicine, arts, telephone are all environmental.

MEDIA AS CODIFIERS

42 "When [Robert] Kennedy's body was brought back to New York from Los Angeles, one of us was at the airport to see it arrive. Standing with a group of reporters, he noticed that they almost all watched the event on a specially rigged television screen. The actual coffin was passing behind their backs scarcely any farther away than the small-screen version. On these occasions, the tenuous connections between journalism, written or visual, and the real texture of events usually ruptures completely." *"An American Melodrama," by three British journalists.*

43   By "the real texture" is presumably meant the initial sensory experience devoid of all resonances and reflections. But why, on this occasion, the "connection" between that event and its image on TV was said to be "ruptured" escapes me. Any medium abstracts from the given and codifies in terms of that medium's grammar. It converts "given reality" into experienced reality. This is one of its functions. Without such structuring and classifying there could be no meaningful experience. The "real" is in no sense immediately given to us. What is given is too complex, too ambiguous, too raw. It must first be cooked. Instincts aid lower animals in selecting and responding to stimuli. Man has culture. Culture is his means of selecting — structuring — classifying reality, and media are his principal tools for this end.

44   We regard it as "natural" to think in verbal categories, but not in TV categories, yet language is as much a technology as TV.

45   In TV studios, idle employees watch programs on monitors, though the live shows are just as close. Billy Graham reports more converts from closed-circuit TV than from among those watching him live.

46   In New Guinea, when a village leader is ignored by his people, the Papuan government sometimes records his speech on tape, then releases it on radio, to be heard by now-respectful villagers, played to them by the village leader himself, probably on his own radio.

47   In the highlands of New Guinea, I saw men with photographs of themselves mounted on their foreheads, in front of their head feathers. Friends greeted them by examining the photographs.

EMPTINESS

48 Convinced that Americans fear emptiness more than fines, a justice of the peace in Battle Creek, Michigan, devised a remarkable sentence; he forced traffic violators to sit alone in empty rooms for three to five hours. Outraged citizens made him abandon this punishment, which was regarded as unnecessarily cruel.

49   When we have a free day, we look forward to how we will fill it. A person who is unemployed must explain: He is ill, retired, seeking work. To do nothing is indefensible. Millionaires expect their children to work during school vacations. Welfare workers are made uneasy by

Indians sitting in front of gas stations, and when we come upon an idle child, we say, "What, doing nothing? Do something!"

50   Literate man regards silence as empty of value. He calls radio silence "dead air" and condemns any cocktail party marked by long silences. Silence at concerts is usually interrupted by applause from someone who mistakenly thinks the piece is over. A Gilbert Stuart portrait of George Washington, its background unfinished, sells for far less than an identical portrait with background complete.

51   Dorothy Lee writes: "In Western thought—and I speak here of the view of the unsophisticated—space is empty and to be occupied with matter; time is empty and to be filled with activity. In both primitive and civilized non-Western cultures, on the other hand, free space and time have being and integrity. It was this conception of *nothingness* as *somethingness* that enabled the philosophers of India to perceive the integrity of nonbeing, to name the free space and give us the zero."

52   Writing of the Bedouin tribesmen, T. E. Lawrence tells how one of them took him through a deserted palace where each room had a different scent, and then called, "Come and smell the very sweetest scent of all," and led him to a gaping window, where the empty wind of the desert went throbbing past. "This," he told him, "is the best; it has no taste."

SENSORY PROGRAMMING

53   Isolating one sense from all others calls for enormous training and self-control and is probably never fully achieved. Test this yourself: Run water into the bath while switching the light on and off: The sound appears louder in the darkness.

54   A child learns to separate the senses when he learns, in class, to read silently. His legs twist; he bites his tongue; but by an enormous effort he learns to fragment his senses, to turn on one at a time and keep the others in neutral. And so he is indoctrinated into that literate world where readers seek silent solitude, concertgoers close their eyes and museum guards warn, "Don't touch!"

55   But all this is history. Today's students mix homework with radio and hi-fi, even TV and telephone, and experience little difficulty correlating such data, or at least having them coexist. California students get into their wrap-around sports cars (a form of clothing), kick off their sandals so they can feel the freeway coming up through the car, travel at 70 miles an hour with signs flashing past and the oncoming traffic passing at 140 mph; top down; sun and wind in their faces; radio on and every fourth telephone pole in sync with the beat; sharing breakfast with a coed: total sensory involvement. Then they enter class, turn off all senses, put on a tribal face and go numb.

REDISCOVERY OF THE BODY

56   Literate man valued the delimited, controlling self, which he equated with the rational mind. He portrayed this "I" as detached from the body and emotions and in control of both. He said, "*I* lift *my* foot,"

with the "I" controlling *me* and *my*. He excluded passions from the "I"; these lay below: I *lost* my temper, *fell* in love, *delved* into my unconscious, but I *exercised* my reason.

57 Early analysts were called "alienists." Alienation begins when one feels revulsion with one's body, and fears the sensate world. Trudie Shoop, the dancer, helped schizophrenics rediscover themselves by reteaching them the earliest movements of the child.

58 The story is told of a group of Jews, with downcast eyes, entering gas chambers. One girl, a dancer, was ordered by a guard to dance for his amusement. Naked, shorn of her hair, she had no identity. But as she danced, she rediscovered herself in the dance, in her body. This gave her the courage to act: In a magnificent gesture, she attacked her tormentor.

59 If you manipulate people, you must first control their environment. Pavlov couldn't make dogs salivate on signal until he put them in artificial, controlled environments. Literate man was easily manipulated. He lived in a centrally heated, air-conditioned, canned-food world, cut off from personal sensations. He was ashamed of his body. He avoided nudity, was obsessed by toilet etiquette, made sex a sin and gluttony close to it. He became aware of his body only in sports and sex, and sometimes not even then.

60 Today's youths have rediscovered the body. They rebel against controlled environments; they create personal sensory environments.

61 Sharp differences between sexes, which marked the past, today disappear. Sex is cooled down. Men and women dress more alike. They share hair styles. Men wear jewelry. They're interested in lotions, hair dyes, cosmetics. This disturbs older people, who keep saying, "You can't tell the difference," and guffaw. Obviously, that difference must have meant a great deal to them or they wouldn't be so hung up on this stale joke.

62 It's a difference that's meaningless to the young. Young men and women today share a common sensate world. Their feelings about themselves and about this world are much alike. They can talk together. Sex polarization at social gatherings — so "men can talk, women visit" — is meaningless to the young.

63 "And everybilly lived alove with everybiddy else."

VIOLENCE AND THE QUEST FOR IDENTITY

64 William James once wrote that no more fiendish torture could be devised than when you speak, no one answers; when you wave, no one turns; but everyone simply cuts you dead. Soon, he said, there wells up within you such hostility you attack those who ignore you and, if that fails to bring recognition, you turn your hostility inward, upon yourself, to prove you really do exist.

65 Violence offers immediate public recognition. This is especially true for "invisibles," who thereby become — instantly — very visible. In 1967, when armed Black Panthers entered the California Legislative Assembly, pandemonium occurred. Even the threat of violence is a powerful force in any quest for identity.

66   Detribalizing the African slave robbed him of all identity, creating great misery of psychic alienation. Racism brainwashed him of his past, leaving him "Wandering between two worlds, one dead/The other powerless to be born." He became an invisible stranger in a strange land.

67   Though an estimated one third of the post–Civil War American cowboys were black, on screen they all turned white. The black was erased from history, unseen in advertisements and admitted to radio and film only in comic form. He made his first appearance on TV.

68   Today's invisibles demand visible membership in a society that has hitherto ignored them. They want to participate in society from the inside and they want that society to be reconstituted to allow membership for all. Above all, they want to be acknowledged *publicly,* on their own terms.

69   Electronic media make possible this reconstitution of society. But this also leads to a corresponding loss of identity among those whose identity was defined by the old society. This upheaval generates great pain and identity loss. As man is tribally metamorphosed by electronic media, people scurry around frantically in search of their former identities and, in the process, they unleash tremendous violence.

BODY AS SCULPTURE

70 "In the native world," writes Alan Lomax, "painting lives on the body, sculpture is something you use or worship, architecture you do yourself, and literature you recite or dance."

71   Grooming and dress are primary arts. Few activities involve more effort. Yet people rarely think of themselves as sculptors or painters, no matter how much effort they devote to making themselves into living art.

72   In the electronic environment, everyone is constantly bombarded by light images emanating from the cathode tube — Joyce's *Charge of the Light Brigade* — playing on us, going inside us, making us all *Lord of the Flies,* engulfed by flickering images.

73   Asked what she had on when posing for calendar shots, Marilyn Monroe replied, "The radio."

74   We wear our media; they are our new clothes. TV clothes our bodies tattoo style. It writes on our skins. It clothes us in information. It programs us. Nudity ceases to have meaning. How natural that we would now write ads and headlines on nudes.

PUTTING ON THE DOG

75 Pets don't come in breeds or races; they come in styles. Styles match owners. Pet psychoanalysts counsel both pet and owner, on the assumption they share psychic problems.

76   "We train you to train your dog."

77   A pet cemetery in Washington, D.C., guarantees that pets owned by Negroes aren't acceptable.

SENSATE WORLD OF NATIVES

78 When natives talk about their world, they speak about how things smell, taste, feel, sound; toes gripping roots along a slippery bank; peppery food burning the rectum; "He became aware of gentle heat playing on his right cheek and a fine smoke teasing his nostrils, while on the left he heard an odd gurgling sound."

79 "It is pleasant," said a Vedda, "for us to feel the rain beating over our shoulders, and good to go out and dig yams, and come home wet, and see the fire burning in the cave, and sit around it."

80 An Eskimo woman, Uvanuk, delighting in the joy of simply being moved by nature, sang:

> The great sea
> Has sent me adrift,
> It moves me
> As the wind in a great river.
>
> Earth and the great weather
> Move me,
> Have carried me away
> And move my inward parts with joy

81 The phrase translated "moves me" also means "to be in a natural state"; to be moved by nature is to be in nature, to belong there. Emotions are expressed as physical responses: anger, *loosening bowels;* fear, *tightening sinews;* joy, *floating viscera.* Man is small, no more than a weed moved endlessly by the current, but intensely aware of forces acting upon him and delighting in even the most trivial.

82 Toothless Kuilasar, an elderly Eskimo, told of starvation, of children born and husbands lost, of new lands and faces, and concluded, "How happy I have been! How good life has been to me!" She hadn't conquered life, nor been rewarded by it, but life had acted upon her, spoken through her, and this was joy.

Discussion of Theme

1. According to Carpenter, what effect has literacy had on human sensibility and self-concept in Western cultures?
2. Are the examples cited in paragraphs 22-33 a genuine trend, or are they merely isolated and bizarre instances?
3. Carpenter makes a number of "probes" or striking statements — for example, that the United States is communistic. Do you agree? Find other similarly provoking statements.
4. In what ways does man's environment control him? What has been youth's response to this tendency?
5. Why does our society have a preoccupation with keeping busy with work? What might Carpenter's explanation be?

Discussion of Rhetoric

1. Is the thesis of this article stated explicitly, or is it implied? If the later, state the thesis in your own words.
2. What is the chief method of paragraph development used by Carpenter? Is it overworked?
3. Do the vast asides, anecdotes, and allusions create confusion in the reader's mind, or do they help him to follow the central idea?
4. How does Carpenter's essay exemplify his thesis?
5. Explain the purpose of the final paragraph with respect to the rest of the article.

Writing Assignments

1. Apply Carpenter's concepts of the "islander" and the "mainlander" (paragraph 2) to an experience of your own.
2. Analyze the "de-polarization" taking place between the sexes in our society. (Consider, for example, hair and dress styles.)
3. If you disagree with Carpenter, write a refutation.

Library Exploration

1. For an extended treatment of these ideas, read the works of Marshall McLuhan, as well as others by Carpenter.

Vocabulary

(3) INNOVATORS those who make changes

(10) THRALLS slaves

(42) TENUOUS slight; unsubstantial

(43) CODIFIES arranges systematically

(62) SENSATE perceived by the senses

(65) PANDEMONIUM uproar; chaos

(69) METAMORPHOSED transformed

Robert Frost (1874–1963), one of this country's best-known poets, achieved his fame after a variety of jobs, including working on a newspaper and teaching school.

What is the poet's secret? According to Frost, it is nothing more than "a lump in the throat," "a tantalizing vagueness," "a fresh listen," and "something of the tinker's art."

ELAINE BARRY

Robert Frost on Writing

1 My poems . . . are all set to trip the reader head foremost into the boundless. Ever since infancy I have had the habit of leaving my blocks carts chairs and such like ordinaries where people would be pretty sure to fall forward over them in the dark. Forward, you understand, *and* in the dark.

2 A poem is never a put-up job so to speak. It begins as a lump in the throat, a sense of wrong, a homesickness, a lovesickness. It is never a thought to begin with. It is at its best when it is a tantalizing vagueness. It finds its thought and succeeds, or doesn't find it and comes to nothing.

3 I have never been good at revising. I always thought I made things worse by recasting and retouching. I never knew what was meant by choice of words. It was one word or none. When I saw more than one possible way of saying a thing I knew I was fumbling and turned from writing. If I ever fussed a poem into shape I hated and distrusted it afterward. The great and pleasant memories are of poems that were single strokes (one stroke to the poem) carried through. I won't say I haven't learned with the years something of the tinker's art. I'm surprised to find sometimes how I have just missed the word. It wasn't that I was groping for meaning. I had that clear enough and I had thought I had said the word for it. But I hadn't said within a row of apple trees of it.

4   The artist's object is to tell people what they haven't as yet realized they were about to say themselves.

5   I never tire of being shown how the limited can make snug in the limitless.

6   In poetry and under emotion every word used is "moved" a little or much—moved from its old place, heightened, made, made new. See what Keats did to the word "alien" in the ode ["Ode on a Grecian Urn"]. But as he made it special in that place he made it his—and his only in that place. He could never have used it again with just that turn. It takes the little one horse poets to do that. . . . I want the un-made words to work with, not the familiar made ones that everybody exclaims Poetry! at.

7   There are no two things as important to us in life and art as being threatened and being saved. What are ideals of form for if we aren't going to be made to fear for them? All our ingenuity is lavished on getting into danger legitimately so that we may be genuinely rescued.

8   [On style:] it is the mind skating circles round itself as it moves forward.

9   Poetry is a fresh look and a fresh listen.

10   It is very very kind of [The Amherst] Student to be showing sympathy with me for my age. But 60 is only a pretty good age. It is not advanced enough. The great thing is to be advanced. Now 90 would be really well along and something to be given credit for.

11   I remember the pleasure with which [Ezra] Pound and I laughed over the fourth "thought" in [Miniver Cheevy by Edwin Arlington Robinson]: "Miniver thought, and thought, and thought,/And thought about it."

12   Three "thoughts" would have been "adequate" as the critical praise-word then was. There would have been nothing to complain of, if it had been left at three. The fourth made the intolerable touch of poetry. With the fourth, the fun began.

13   The figure a poem makes[:] It begins in delight and ends in wisdom. The figure is the same as for love. No one can really hold that the ecstasy should be static and stand still in one place. It begins in delight, it inclines to the impulse, it assumes direction with the first line laid down, it runs a course of lucky events, and ends in a clarification of life—not necessarily a great clarification, such as sects and cults are founded on, but in a momentary stay against confusion. It has denouement. It has an outcome that though unforeseen was pre-destined from the first image of the original mood—and indeed from the very mood. It is but a trick poem and no poem at all if the best of it was thought of first and saved for the last. It finds its own name as it goes and discovers the best waiting for it in some final phrase at once wise and sad—the happy-sad blend of the drinking song.

14   No tears in the writer, no tears in the reader. No surprise for the writer, no surprise for the reader. For me the initial delight is in the surprise of remembering something I didn't know I knew.

15   Like a piece of ice on a hot stove the poem must ride on its own melting. A poem may be worked over once it is in being, but may not be worried into being. Its most precious quality will remain its having run itself and carried away the poet with it. Read it a hundred times:

it will forever keep its freshness as a petal keeps its fragrance. It can never lose its sense of a meaning that once unfolded by surprise as it went.

16 Many a quatrain is salvaged from a sonnet that went agley.

17 We throw our arms wide with a gesture of religion to the universe; we close them around a person. We explore and adventure for a while and then we draw in to consolidate our gains. The breathless swing is between subject matter and form.

18 The heart sinks when robbed of the chance to see for itself what a poem is all about. Any immediate preface is like cramming the night before an examination. Too late, too late! Any footnote while the poem is going is too late. Any subsequent explanation is as dispiriting as the explanation of a joke.

19 A poem is best read in the light of all the other poems ever written. We read A the better to read B (we have to start somewhere; we may get very little out of A). We read B the better to read C, C the better to read D, D the better to go back and get something more out of A. Progress is not the aim, but circulation. The thing is to get among the poems where they hold each other apart in their places as the stars do.

Discussion of Theme

1. What does Frost mean by the "intolerable touch of poetry"?
2. What does he think about reading interpretations of poems before reading the poems themselves?
3. What does Frost say is the best way to get the most out of poetry?
4. Do Frost's statements create a desire in you to read and or write poetry? Why or why not?

Discussion of Rhetoric

1. Explain the meaning of paragraph 5.
2. Choose several metaphors used by Frost in this selection and analyze them in terms of how they clarify and illuminate ideas.
3. After reading this excerpt, how would you characterize Frost, the man? Frost, the poet?
4. Find examples of parallelism in this work.
5. What is "poetic quality"?

Writing Assignments

1. In an essay, respond to the following quote by Yeats: "It is so many years before one can believe enough in what one feels even to know what the feeling is."
2. In an essay, develop Jacob Boehme's idea that "all things are created out of the imagination."
3. Write a poem in which you present one of your strong beliefs.
4. Write an analysis of a Frost poem of your choice.

Library Exploration

1. Read Keats' "Ode" mentioned in paragraph 6 and relate it to Frost's statements.
2. Discover how different poets have defined poetry and art.
3. Read *Poetic Vision and the Psychedelic Experience*, by R. A. Durr.
4. Read some of the poems of Robert Frost.

Vocabulary

(13) DENOUEMENT   the outcome or disentangling of a plot

(16) QUATRAIN   a stanza of four lines

(16) AGLEY   awry; wrong

Clement Greenberg (1909–), a well-known art critic, has been an editor for such publications as the "Nation," "Commentary," and "Partisan Review." A collection of essays in 1961, "Art and Culture," was a popular critical work.

In this defense of "modernist art in general, or abstract art in particular," Greenberg admits that abstract art has been attacked as being pathological, but he shows that "no hard-and-fast line separates it from representational art. . . ."

CLEMENT GREENBERG

The Case for Abstract Art

1   Many people say that the kind of art our age produces is one of the major symptoms of what's wrong with the age. The disintegration and, finally, the disappearance of recognizable images in painting and sculpture, like the obscurity in advanced literature, are supposed to reflect a disintegration of values in society itself. Some people go further and say that abstract, nonrepresentational art is pathological art, crazy art, and that those who practice it and those who admire and buy it are either sick or silly. The kindest critics are those who say it's all a joke, a hoax, and a fad, and that modernist art in general, or abstract art in particular, will soon pass. This sort of thing is heard or read pretty constantly, but in some years more often than others.

2   There seems to be a certain rhythm in the advance in popularity of modernist art, and a certain rhythm in the counterattacks which try to stem it. More or less the same works or arguments are used in all the polemics, but the targets usually change. Once it was the impressionists who were a scandal, next it was Van Gogh and Cézanne, then it was Matisse, then it was cubism and Picasso, after that Mondrian, and now it is Jackson Pollock. The fact that Pollock was an American shows, in a backhanded way, how important American art has lately become.

3   Some of the same people who attack modernist art in general, or abstract art in particular, happen also to complain that our age has lost those habits of disinterested contemplation, and that capacity for enjoying things as ends in themselves and for their own sake, which former ages are supposed to have cultivated. This idea has been advanced often enough to convert it into a cliché. I hate to give assent to a cliché, for it is almost always an oversimplification, but I have to make an exception in this case. While I strongly doubt that disinterested contemplation was as unalloyed or as popular in ages past as is supposed, I do tend to agree that we could do with more of it in this time, and especially in this country.

4   I think a poor life is lived by anyone who doesn't regularly take time out to stand and gaze, or sit and listen, or touch, or smell, or brood, without any further end in mind, simply for the satisfaction gotten from that which is gazed at, listened to, touched, smelled or brooded upon. We all know, however, that the climate of Western life, and particularly of American life, is not conducive to this kind of thing; we are all too busy making a living. This is another cliché, of course. And still a third cliché says that we should learn from Oriental society how to give more of ourselves to the life of the spirit, to contemplation and meditation, and to the appreciation of what is satisfying or beautiful in its own sole right. This last is not only a cliché, but a fallacy, since most Orientals are even more preoccupied than we are with making a living. I hope that I myself am not making a gross and reductive simplification when I say that so much of Oriental contemplative and aesthetic discipline strikes me as a technique for keeping one's eyes averted from ugliness and misery.

5   Every civilization and every tradition of culture seem to possess capacities for self-cure and self-correction that go into operation automatically, unbidden. If the given tradition goes too far in one direction it will usually try to right itself by going equally far in the opposite one. There is no question but that our Western civilization, especially in its American variant, devotes more mental energy than any other to the production of material things and services; and that, more than any other, it puts stress on interested, purposeful activity in general. This is reflected in our art, which, as has been frequently observed, put such great emphasis on movement and development and resolution, on beginnings, middles, and endings—that is, on dynamics. Compare Western music with any other kind, or look at Western literature, for that matter, with its relatively great concern with plot and overall structure and its relatively small concern with tropes and figures and ornamental elaborations; think of how slow-moving Chinese and Japanese poetry is by comparison with ours, and how much it delights in static situations; and how uncertain the narrational logic of non-Western fiction tends to be. Think of how encrusted and convoluted Arabic poetry is by contrast even with our most euphuistic lyrical verse. And as for non-Western music, does it not almost always, and literally, strike us as more monotonous than ours?

6   Well, how does Western art compensate for, correct, or at least qualify its emphasis on the dynamic—an emphasis that may or may not be excessive? And how does Western life itself compensate for, correct, or

at least qualify its obsession with material production and purposeful activity? I shall not here attempt to answer the latter question. But in the realm of art an answer is beginning to emerge of its own accord, and the shape of part of that answer is abstract art.

7   Abstract decoration is almost universal, and Chinese and Japanese calligraphy is quasi-abstract—abstract to the extent that few occidentals can read the characters of Chinese or Japanese writing. But only in the West, and only in the last fifty years, have such things as abstract pictures and free-standing pieces of abstract sculpture appeared. What makes the big difference between these and abstract decoration is that they are, exactly, pictures and free-standing sculpture—solo works of art meant to be looked at for their own sake and with full attention, and not as the adjuncts, incidental aspects, or settings of things other than themselves. These abstract pictures and pieces of sculpture challenge our capacity for disinterested contemplation in a way that is more concentrated and, I daresay, more conscious than anything else I know of in art. Music is an essentially abstract art, but even at its most rarefied and abstract, whether it's Bach's or the middle-period Schoenberg's music, it does not offer this challenge in quite the same way or degree. Music tends from a beginning through a middle toward an ending. We wait to see how it "comes out"—which is what we also do with literature. Of course, the *total* experience of literature and music is completely disinterested, but it becomes that only at a further remove. While undergoing the experience we are caught up and expectant as well as detached—disinterested and at the same time interested in a way resembling that in which we are interested in how things turn out in real life. I exaggerate to make my point—aesthetic experience *has* to be disinterested, and when it is genuine it always is, even when bad works of art are involved—but the distinctions I've made and those I've still to make are valid nevertheless.

8   With representational painting it is something like what it is with literature. This has been said before, many times before, but usually in order to criticize representational painting in what I think is a wrong-headed when not downright silly way. What I mean when I say, in this context, that representational painting is like literature, is that it tends to involve us in the interested as well as the disinterested by presenting us with the images of things that are inconceivable outside time and action. This goes even for landscapes and flower pieces and still lifes. It is not simply that we sometimes tend to confuse the attractiveness of the things represented in a picture with the quality of the picture itself. And it is not only that attractiveness as such has nothing to do with the abiding success of a work of art. What is more fundamental is that the meaning—as distinct from the attractiveness—of what is represented becomes truly inseparable from the representation itself. That Rembrandt confined impasto—thick paint, that is—to his highlights, and that in his later portraits especially these coincide with the ridges of the noses of his subjects is important to the artistic effect of these portraits. And that the effectiveness of the impasto, as impasto—as an abstract element of technique—coincides with its

effectiveness as a means of showing just how a nose looks under a certain kind of light is also genuinely important. And that the lifelike delineation of the nose contributes to the evocation of the personality of the individual to whom the nose belongs is likewise important. And the manner and degree of insight into that individual's personality which Rembrandt exhibits in his portrait is important too. None of these factors can be, or ought to be, separated from the legitimate effect of the portrait as a picture pure and simple.

9   But once we have to do with personalities and lifelikeness we have to do with things from which we cannot keep as secure a distance for the sake of disinterestedness as we can, say, from abstract decoration. As it happens, the whole tendency of our Western painting, up until the later stages of impressionism, was to make distance and detachment on the part of the spectator as insecure as possible. It laid more of a stress than any other tradition on creating a sculpture-like, or photographic, illusion of the third dimension, on thrusting images at the eye with a lifelikeness that brought them as close as possible to their originals. Because of their sculptural vividness, Western paintings tend to be far less quiet, far more agitated and active — in short, far more explicitly dynamic — than most non-Western paintings do. And they involve the spectator to a much greater extent in the practical and actual aspects of the things they depict and represent.

10   We begin to wonder what we think of the people shown in Rembrandt's portraits, as people; whether or not we would like to walk through the terrain shown in a Corot landscape; about the life stories of the burghers we see in a Steen painting; we react in a less than disinterested way to the attractiveness of the models, real or ideal, of the personages in a Renaissance painting. And once we begin to do this we begin to participate in the work of art in a so-to-speak practical way. In itself this participation may not be improper, but it does become so when it begins to shut out all other factors. This it has done and does, all too often. Even though the connoisseurs have usually been able in the long run to prefer the picture of a dwarf by Velasquez to that of a pretty girl by Howard Chandler Christy, the enjoyment of pictorial and sculptural art in our society has tended, on every other level than that of professional connoisseurship, to be excessively "literary," and to center too much on merely technical feats of copying.

11   But, as I've said, every tradition of culture tends to try to correct one extreme by going to its opposite. And when our Western tradition of painting came up at last with reservations about its forthright naturalism, these quickly took the form of an equally forthright antinaturalism. These reservations started with late impressionism, and have now culminated in abstract art. I don't at all wish to be understood as saying that it all happened because some artist or artists decided it was time to curb the excesses of realistic painting, and that the main historical significance of abstract art lies in its function as an antidote to these. Nor do I wish to be understood as assuming that realistic or naturalistic art inherently needs, or ever needed, such a thing as an antidote. The motivations, conscious and unconscious, of the first modernist artists, and of present modernists as well, were and are

quite different. Impressionism itself started as an effort to push naturalism further than ever before. And all through the history of art — not
only in recent times — consequences have escaped intentions.

12   It is on a different, and more impersonal and far more general level
of meaning and history that our culture has generated abstract art as
an antidote. On that level this seemingly new kind of art has emerged
as an epitome of almost everything that disinterested contemplation
requires, and as both a challenge and a reproof to a society that exaggerates, not the necessity, but the intrinsic value of purposeful and
interested activity. Abstract art comes, on this level, as a relief, an
archexample of something that does not have to mean, or be useful
for, anything other than itself. And it seems fitting, too, that abstract
art should at present flourish most in this country. If American society
is indeed given over as no other society has been to purposeful
activity and material production, then it is right that it should be reminded, in extreme terms, of the essential nature of disinterested
activity.

13   Abstract art does this in very literal and also very imaginative ways.
First, it does not exhibit the illusion or semblance of things we are already familiar with in real life; it gives us no imaginary space through
which to walk with the mind's eye; no imaginary objects to desire or
not desire; no imaginary people to like or dislike. We are left alone with
shapes and colors. These may or may not remind us of real things; but
if they do, they usually do so incidentally or accidentally — on our own
responsibility as it were; and the genuine enjoyment of an abstract
picture does not ordinarily depend on such resemblances.

14   Second, pictorial art in its highest definition is static; it tries to overcome movement in space or time. This is not to say that the eye does
not wander over a painted surface, and thus travel in both space and
time. When a picture presents us with an illusion of real space, there
is all the more inducement for the eye to do such wandering. But
ideally the whole of a picture should be taken in at a glance; its unity
should be immediately evident, and the supreme quality of a picture,
the highest measure of its power to move and control the visual
imagination, should reside in its unity. And this is something to be
grasped only in an individual instant of time. No expectancy is involved in the true and pertinent experience of a painting; a picture,
I repeat, does not "come out" the way a story, or a poem, or a piece
of music does. It's all there at once, like a sudden revelation. This "at-
onceness" an abstract picture usually drives home to us with greater
singleness and clarity than a representational painting does. And to
apprehend this "at-onceness" demands a freedom of mind and untrammeledness of eye that constitute "at-onceness" in their own right.
Those who have grown capable of experiencing this know what I
mean. You are summoned and gathered into one point in the continuum of duration. The picture does this to you, willy-nilly, regardless
of whatever else is on your mind; a mere glance at it creates the attitude required for its appreciation, like a stimulus that elicits an automatic response. You become all attention, which means that you
become, for the moment, selfless and in a sense entirely identified
with the object of your attention.

15   The "at-onceness" which a picture or a piece of sculpture enforces on you is not, however, single or isolated. It can be repeated in a succession of instants, in each one remaining an "at-onceness," an instant all by itself. For the cultivated eye, the picture repeats its instantaneous unity like a mouth repeating a single word.

16   This pinpointing of the attention, this complete liberation and concentration of it, offers what is largely a new experience to most people in our sort of society. And it is, I think, a hunger for this particular kind of experience that helps account for the growing popularity of abstract art in this country: for the way it is taking over in the art schools, the galleries, and the museums. The fact that fad and fashion are also involved does not invalidate what I say. I know that abstract art of the latest variety—that originating with painters like Pollock and Georges Mathieu—has gotten associated with progressive jazz and its cultists; but what of it? That Wagner's music became associated with German ultranationalism, and that Wagner was Hitler's favorite composer, still doesn't detract from its sheer quality of music. That the present vogue for folk music started, back in the 1930s, among the Communists doesn't make our liking for it any the less genuine, or take anything away from folk music itself. Nor does the fact that so much gibberish gets talked and written about abstract art compromise it, just as the gibberish in which art criticism in general abounds, and abounds increasingly, doesn't compromise art in general.

17   One point, however, I want to make glaringly clear. Abstract art is not a special kind of art; no hard-and-fast line separates it from representational art; it is only the latest phase in the development of Western art as a whole, and almost every "technical" device of abstract painting is already to be found in the realistic painting that preceded it. Nor is it a superior kind of art. I still know of nothing in abstract painting, aside perhaps from some of the near-abstract cubist works that Picasso, Braque and Léger executed between 1910 and 1914, which matches the highest achievements of the old masters. Abstract painting may be a purer, more quintessential form of pictorial art than the representational kind, but this does not of itself confer quality upon an abstract picture. The ratio of bad abstract painting to good is actually much greater than the ratio of bad to good representational painting. Nonetheless, the very best painting, the major painting, of our age is almost exclusively abstract. Only on the middle and lower levels of quality, on the levels below the first-rate—which is, of course, where most of the art that gets produced places itself—only there is the better painting preponderantly representational.

18   On the plane of culture in general, the special, unique value of abstract art, I repeat, lies in the high degree of detached contemplativeness that its appreciation requires. Contemplativeness is demanded in greater or lesser degree for the appreciation of every kind of art, but abstract art tends to present this requirement in quintessential form, at its purest, least diluted, most immediate. If abstract art—as does happen nowadays—should chance to be the first kind of pictorial art we learn to appreciate, the chances are that when we go to other kinds of pictorial art—to the old masters, say, and I hope we all do go to the old masters eventually—we shall find ourselves all the better able to

enjoy them. That is, we shall be able to experience them with less intrusion of irrelevancies, therefore more fully and more intensely.

19   The old masters stand or fall, their pictures succeed or fail, on the same ultimate basis as do those of Mondrian or any other abstract artist. The abstract formal unity of a picture by Titian is more important to its quality than what the picture images. To return to what I said about Rembrandt's portraits, the whatness of what is imaged is not unimportant—far from it—and cannot be separated, really, from the formal qualities that result from the way it is imaged. But it is a fact, in my experience, that representational paintings are essentially and most fully appreciated when the identities of what they represent are only secondarily present to our consciousness. Baudelaire said he could grasp the quality of a painting by Delacroix when he was still too far away from it to make out the images it contained, when it was still only a blur of colors. I think it was really on this kind of evidence that critics and connoisseurs, though they were almost always unaware of it, discriminated between the good and the bad in the past. Put to it, they more or less unconsciously dismissed from their minds the connotations of Rubens' nudes when assessing and experiencing the final worth of his art. They may have remained aware of the pinkness as a *nude* pinkness, but it was a pinkness and a nudity devoid of most of their usual associations.

20   Abstract paintings do not confront us with such problems. Or at least the frequenting of abstract art can train us to relegate them automatically to their proper place; and in doing this we refine our eyes for the appreciation of non-abstract art. That has been my own experience. That it is still relatively rare can be explained perhaps by the fact that most people continue to come to painting through academic art—the kind of art they see in ads and in magazines—and when and if they discover abstract art it comes as such an overwhelming experience that they tend to forget everything produced before. This is to be deplored, but it does not negate the value, actual or potential, of abstract art as an introduction to the fine arts in general, and as an introduction, too, to habits of disinterested contemplation. In this respect, the value of abstract art will, I hope, prove far greater in the future than it has yet. Not only can it confirm instead of subverting tradition; it can teach us, by example, how valuable so much in life can be made without being invested with ulterior meanings. How many people I know who have hung abstract pictures on their walls and found themselves gazing at them endlessly, and then exclaiming, "I don't know what there is in that painting, but I can't take my eyes off it." This kind of bewilderment is salutary. It does us good not to be able to explain, either to ourselves or to others, what we enjoy or love; it expands our capacity for experience.

Discussion of Theme

1. Greenberg says that abstract art does not confront us with the problems presented by realistic art. What problems is he talking about?

Does abstract art confront us with other problems? If so, what?

2. Do you agree with Greenberg that appreciating abstract art can actually increase our understanding of traditional art? Or would it work the other way around?

3. Perhaps you and your friends have denounced abstract art as a joke, a hoax, or a fad. Does this essay properly answer this charge?

4. What are impressionism and cubism?

5. Why is the *total* experience of literature and music completely disinterested? See paragraph 7.

Discussion of Rhetoric

1. Greenberg refers several times to clichés. What is the difference between a simple truth and a cliché?

2. Is the simile in paragraph 15 appropriate? Does it create a mental image that is at odds with what Greenberg may be trying to convey about abstract art?

3. What technique does Greenberg use to draw us into his essay? Is this used simply to make us agree with him?

4. What is the effect on the piece as a whole of using such awkward combinations as *lifelikeness, connoisseurship, archexample, untrammeledness, at-onceness, contemplativeness, whatness?*

Writing Assignments

1. If you enjoy abstract art, but for reasons different from those that Greenberg presents, explain how you look at modern art and what you see in it.

2. Discuss the difference between art and literature as propaganda and as purely artistic or intellectual vehicles.

3. Explain why you admire a particular work of art—a painting, or a sculpture, or a collage.

4. Frequently there is great beauty either in a "found object," such as a piece of twisted metal in a weathered board, or in many natural objects. If you have been struck by the beauty in an object that was not conceived as art, describe it and explain what it is that gives you pleasure in it.

Library Exploration

1. To learn more about the difficulties faced by artists in their own lifetime, read a biography of Rembrandt or Van Gogh.

2. Fernand Léger's famous painting *Nude Descending a Staircase* provoked an intense reaction when it first appeared. Read about the furor that it aroused; then look at the picture and try to determine why the public became so enraged.

Vocabulary

(1) PATHOLOGICAL   sick; diseased

(2) POLEMICS   disputes; tirades

(3) DISINTERESTED   objective; unbiased

(3) UNALLOYED   pure; unmixed

(4) CONDUCIVE   contributive; helpful

(4) REDUCTIVE   tending to diminish

(5) CONVOLUTED   twisted; intertwined

(5) EUPHUISTIC   high-flown; affected

(7) CALLIGRAPHY   handwriting

(10) CONNOISSEURS   those with expert knowledge and discrimination

(11) CULMINATED   resulted in; reached

(11) ANTIDOTE   remedy

(12) EPITOME   typical or ideal representation

(12) ARCHEXAMPLE   chief example

(14) UNTRAMMELEDNESS   freedom

(14) CONTINUUM   unbroken whole

(17) QUINTESSENTIAL   perfect; ultimate

(17) PREPONDERANTLY   primarily

(20) RELEGATE   consign

(20) DEPLORED   lamented

(20) SUBVERTING   undermining; corrupting

(20) ULTERIOR   undisclosed; more remote

(20) SALUTARY   beneficial

Aaron Copland (1900–   ), born in Brooklyn, is one of the nation's leading composers and music authorities. He studied piano and composition with Ricardo Vines and Nadia Boulanger. He has written music for films, ballets, plays, and operas, and has conducted his own symphonic works throughout the world. Among his books are "What to Listen For in Music" (1939), "Music and Imagination" (1952), and "Copland on Music" (1960).

In order to discuss listening to music, the author tackles his subject on three separate planes, beginning with simple enjoyment.

AARON COPLAND

What to Listen For in Music

1 We all listen to music according to our separate capacities. But, for the sake of analysis, the whole listening process may become clearer if we break it up into its component parts, so to speak. In a certain sense we all listen to music on three separate planes. For lack of a better terminology, one might name these: (1) the sensuous plane, (2) the expressive plane, (3) the sheerly musical plane. The only advantage to be gained from mechanically splitting up the listening process into these hypothetical planes is the clearer view to be had of the way in which we listen.

2   The simplest way of listening to music is to listen for the sheer pleasure of the musical sound itself. That is the sensuous plane. It is the plane on which we hear music without thinking, without considering it in any way. One turns on the radio while doing something else and absentmindedly bathes in the sound. A kind of brainless but attractive state of mind is engendered by the mere sound appeal of the music.

3   You may be sitting in a room reading this book. Imagine one note struck on the piano. Immediately that one note is enough to change the atmosphere of the room — proving that the sound element in music is a powerful and mysterious agent, which it would be foolish to deride or belittle.

4   The surprising thing is that many people who consider themselves qualified music lovers abuse that plane in listening. They go to concerts in order to lose themselves. They use music as a consolation or an escape. They enter an ideal world where one doesn't have to think of the realities of everyday life. Of course they aren't thinking about the music either. Music allows them to leave it, and they go off to a place to dream, dreaming because of and apropos of the music yet never quite listening to it.

5   Yes, the sound appeal of music is a potent and primitive force, but you must not allow it to usurp a disproportionate share of your interest. The sensuous plane is an important one in music, a very important one, but it does not constitute the whole story.

6   There is no need to digress further on the sensuous plane. Its appeal to every normal human being is self-evident. There is, however, such a thing as becoming more sensitive to the different kinds of sound stuff as used by various composers. For all composers do not use that sound stuff in the same way. Don't get the idea that the value of music is commensurate with its sensuous appeal or that the loveliest sounding music is made by the greatest composer. If that were so, Ravel would be a greater creator than Beethoven. The point is that the sound element varies with each composer, that his usage of sound forms an integral part of his style and must be taken into account when listening. The reader can see, therefore, that a more conscious approach is valuable even on this primary plane of music listening.

7   The second plane on which music exists is what I have called the expressive one. Here, immediately, we tread on controversial ground. Composers have a way of shying away from any discussion of music's expressive side. Did not Stravinsky himself proclaim that his music was an "object," a "thing," with a life of its own, and with no other meaning than its own purely musical existence? This intransigent attitude of Stravinsky's may be due to the fact that so many people have tried to read different meanings into so many pieces. Heaven knows it is difficult enough to say precisely what it is that a piece of music means, to say it definitely, to say it finally so that everyone is satisfied with your explanation. But that should not lead one to the other extreme of denying to music the right to be "expressive."

8   My own belief is that all music has an expressive power, some more and some less, but that all music has a certain meaning behind the notes and that that meaning behind the notes constitutes, after all, what the piece is saying, what the piece is about. This whole problem can be stated quite simply by asking, "Is there a meaning to music?" My answer to that would be, "Yes." And "Can you state in so many words what the meaning is?" My answer to that would be, "No." Therein lies the difficulty.

9   Simple-minded souls will never be satisfied with the answer to the

second of these questions. They always want to have a meaning, and
the more concrete it is the better they like it. The more the music
reminds them of a train, a storm, a funeral, or any other familiar conception the more expressive it appears to be to them. This popular
idea of music's meaning—stimulated and abetted by the usual run
of musical commentator—should be discouraged wherever and whenever it is met. One timid lady once confessed to me that she suspected
something seriously lacking in her appreciation of music because
of her inability to connect it with anything definite. That is getting the
whole thing backward, of course.

10   Still, the question remains, How close should the intelligent music
lover wish to come to pinning a definite meaning to any particular
work? No closer than a general concept, I should say. Music expresses,
at different moments, serenity or exuberance, regret or triumph, fury
or delight. It expresses each of these moods, and many others, in a
numberless variety of subtle shadings and differences. It may even
express a state of meaning for which there exists no adequate word in
any language. In that case, musicians often like to say that it has only
a purely musical meaning. They sometimes go farther and say that
all music has only a purely musical meaning. What they really mean
is that no appropriate word can be found to express the music's meaning and that, even if it could, they do not feel the need of finding it.

11   But whatever the professional musician may hold, most musical
novices still search for specific words with which to pin down their
musical reactions. That is why they always find Tschaikovsky easier to
"understand" than Beethoven. In the first place, it is easier to pin a
meaning-word on a Tschaikovsky piece than on a Beethoven one.
Much easier. Moreover, with the Russian composer, every time you
come back to a piece of his it almost always says the same thing to you,
whereas with Beethoven it is often quite difficult to put your finger
right on what he is saying. And any musician will tell you that that is
why Beethoven is the greater composer. Because music which always
says the same thing to you will necessarily soon become dull music,
but music whose meaning is slightly different with each hearing has a
greater chance of remaining alive.

12   Listen, if you can, to the forty-eight fugue themes of Bach's *Well-
Tempered Clavichord*. Listen to each theme, one after another. You
will soon realize that each theme mirrors a different world of feeling.
You will also soon realize that the more beautiful a theme seems to you
the harder it is to find any word that will describe it to your complete
satisfaction. Yes, you will certainly know whether it is a gay theme or a
sad one. You will be able, in other words, in your own mind, to draw a
frame of emotional feeling around your theme. Now study the sad one
a little closer. Try to pin down the exact quality of its sadness. Is it
pessimistically sad or resignedly sad; is it fatefully sad or smilingly
sad?

13   Let us suppose that you are fortunate and can describe to your own
satisfaction in so many words the exact meaning of your chosen theme.
There is still no guarantee that anyone else will be satisfied. Nor need
they be. The important thing is that each one feel for himself the spe-

cific expressive quality of a theme or, similarly, an entire piece of music. And if it is a great work of art, don't expect it to mean exactly the same thing to you each time you return to it.

14   Themes or pieces need not express only one emotion, of course. Take such a theme as the first main one of the *Ninth Symphony,* for example. It is clearly made up of different elements. It does not say only one thing. Yet anyone hearing it immediately gets a feeling of strength, a feeling of power. It isn't a power that comes simply because the theme is played loudly. It is a power inherent in the theme itself. The extraordinary strength and vigor of the theme results in the listener's receiving an impression that a forceful statement has been made. But one should never try to boil it down to "the fateful hammer of life," etc. That is where the trouble begins. The musician, in his exasperation, says it means nothing but the notes themselves, whereas the nonprofessional is only too anxious to hang on to any explanation that gives him the illusion of getting closer to the music's meaning.

15   Now, perhaps, the reader will know better what I mean when I say that music does have an expressive meaning but that we cannot say in so many words what that meaning is.

16   The third plane on which music exists is the sheerly musical plane. Besides the pleasurable sound of music and the expressive feeling that it gives off, music does exist in terms of the notes themselves and of their manipulation. Most listeners are not sufficiently conscious of this third plane. . . .

17   Professional musicians, on the other hand, are, if anything, too conscious of the mere notes themselves. They often fall into the error of becoming so engrossed with their arpeggios and staccatos that they forget the deeper aspects of the music they are performing. But from the layman's standpoint, it is not so much a matter of getting over bad habits on the sheerly musical plane as of increasing one's awareness of what is going on, in so far as the notes are concerned.

18   When the man in the street listens to the "notes themselves" with any degree of concentration, he is most likely to make some mention of the melody. Either he hears a pretty melody or he does not, and he generally lets it go at that. Rhythm is likely to gain his attention next, particularly if it seems exciting. But harmony and tone color are generally taken for granted, if they are thought of consciously at all. As for music's having a definite form of some kind, that idea seems never to have occurred to him.

19   It is very important for all of us to become more alive to music on its sheerly musical plane. After all, an actual musical material is being used. The intelligent listener must be prepared to increase his awareness of the musical material and what happens to it. He must hear the melodies, the rhythms, the harmonies, the tone colors in a more conscious fashion. But above all he must, in order to follow the line of the composer's thought, know something of the principles of musical form. Listening to all of these elements is listening on the sheerly musical plane.

20   Let me repeat that I have split up mechanically the three separate planes on which we listen merely for the sake of greater clarity. Actually, we never listen to one or the other of these planes. What we do

is to correlate them — listening in all three ways at the same time. It takes no mental effort, for we do it instinctively.

21   Perhaps an analogy with what happens to us when we visit the theater will make this instinctive correlation clearer. In the theater, you are aware of the actors and actresses, costumes and sets, sounds and movements. All these give one the sense that the theater is a pleasant place to be in. They constitute the sensuous plane in our theatrical reactions.

22   The expressive plane in the theater would be derived from the feeling that you get from what is happening on the stage. You are moved to pity, excitement, or gaiety. It is this general feeling, generated aside from the particular words being spoken, a certain emotional something which exists on the stage, that is analogous to the expressive quality in music.

23   The plot and plot development is equivalent to our sheerly musical plane. The playwright creates and develops a character in just the same way that a composer creates and develops a theme. According to the degree of your awareness of the way in which the artist in either field handles his material will you become a more intelligent listener.

24   It is easy enough to see that the theatergoer never is conscious of any of these elements separately. He is aware of them all at the same time. The same is true of music listening. We simultaneously and without thinking listen on all three planes.

25   In a sense, the ideal listener is both inside and outside the music at the same moment, judging it and enjoying it, wishing it would go one way and watching it go another — almost like the composer at the moment he composes it; because in order to write his music, the composer must also be inside and outside his music, carried away by it and yet coldly critical of it. A subjective and objective attitude is implied in both creating and listening to music.

26   What the reader should strive for, then, is a more *active* kind of listening. Whether you listen to Mozart or Duke Ellington, you can deepen your understanding of music only by being a more conscious and aware listener — not someone who is just listening, but someone who is listening *for* something.

Discussion of Theme

1. What are the three separate planes on which we all listen to music? Does one of these dominate your listening habits? Which of these planes does Copland consider the simplest?
2. What is "expressive power" in music? Does all music express a certain meaning? Should it?
3. In what way does Copland compare Beethoven with Tschaikovsky? Which of the two composers do you prefer? Why?
4. Why does the author believe that it is important for the layman to "become more alive to music on its sheerly musical plane"? What shortcoming does he say that professional musicians have in relation to the notes themselves?

Discussion of Rhetoric

1. Copland relies heavily on the use of one sort of sentence structure. What is it? Would greater variety have improved his essay?
2. The author is sparing in his use of transitional devices. What quality does this lend his essay?
3. Although he is dealing with abstractions, Copland tries to make his discussion specific. Is he successful?
4. With what paragraph does the conclusion of the essay begin?

Writing Assignments

1. Copland is discussing classical music. Do his comments about planes apply to popular music as well? Illustrate with reference to specific musical compositions.
2. Apply the three planes of listening to a musical experience of your own.
3. Discuss some subject like drama or painting in terms of what you consider its divisions or parts.
4. Define good music.

Library Exploration

1. Describe the historical steps in a major musical development such as progressive jazz.
2. Report on the background and development of an opera by Copland.

Vocabulary

(1) SENSUOUS appealing to the senses
(4) APROPOS OF with regard to
(5) POTENT powerful
(5) USURP take over
(6) COMMENSURATE equal in measure
(6) INTEGRAL intrinsic; essential to completeness
(7) INTRANSIGENT unyielding

(9) ABETTED encouraged
(12) PESSIMISTICALLY darkly; despairingly
(17) ARPEGGIOS notes of a chord
(17) STACCATOS notes played sharply and abruptly
(21) ANALOGY comparison

Florence King, the author of thirty-seven erotic novels, writes the column "Advice to the Loveworn" in "Viva" magazine.

According to Ms. King, there is now a calculated psychology to country music, a "message" that promotes alienation and a spirit of testy readiness that is disturbing to hear.

FLORENCE KING

Red Necks, White Socks, and Blue Ribbon Fear

1 Nashville has not yet written "The Ballad of Richard Nixon," but chances are that it will, and the song will go something like this:

> *From out of California*
> *This grocer's son did come*
> *To rise up by his bootstraps*
> *In the light of freedom's sun.*
> *He married him a red-haired gal*
> *From out Nevada way.*
> *She stuck with him through thick*
> *   and thin*
> *Through the godless enemy's*
> *   fray.*
>
> *(Chorus)*
> *Here's the church and here's*
> *   the steeple!*
> *The son and daughter of the*
> *   people!*

2   Now that Richard Nixon has spun a Yo-Yo on the stage of the Grand Ole Opry, we can stop laughing at the picture of Calvin

Coolidge in an Indian war bonnet. There is a difference between these two examples of Presidential whimsy, however; Coolidge had a sense of humor, but Nixon's appearance in Nashville was as deadly serious as he himself is. In his speech, he waggled his lapel and said, "The peace of the world . . . is going to depend on our character, our belief in ourselves, our love of our country, our willingness to not only wear the flag but to stand up for the flag, and country music does that!" Another Nixonian either-or was forged, and the audience cheered wildly, as the White House strategists who cooked up the trip knew it would.

3   The mind of the country music fan tends to pounce on anything that resembles a good old-fashioned reductio ad absurdum. The Nashville audience translated the President's words thus: he who does not like country music does not stand up for the flag and, therefore, is not a good American.

4   Polarization is as American as apple pie; it does not need to be encouraged because it flourishes like the green bay tree anyway, particularly among the rural Southerners and urban working people who make up country music audiences. In his visit to the Grand Ole Opry, President Nixon laid his imprimatur on a polarization that country music itself instigated and encouraged fourteen years ago, when the policies of John F. Kennedy—combined with his polished urbanity and sophistication—drove the South up the wall.

5   I have listened to country music all my life. My grandmother, who finished the fifth grade between chores on a tobacco farm in Prince William County, Virginia, was a great fan of what is correctly called "bluegrass" music. One of my earliest memories is of being held in her arms while she danced the cakewalk to "Down Yonder." My father was a professional banjo player in the dance bands of the Twenties and a friend of Eddie Peabody's. Whenever Peabody was in Washington, he came by, and he and my father would have a session of "picking." I hovered near them in awe, and one night, during a rousing rendition of "Turkey in the Straw," my father broke a string. It flew back and came within a hair of hitting me in the eye.

6   I also remember the World War II radio broadcasts of the Grand Ole Opry. My family would not dream of missing them, and we particularly loved Cousin Minnie Pearl because she reminded us of several cousins of our own. At this time, the music was good-naturedly called "hillbilly," a term that now rouses aficionados to defensive rage.

7   Even during the war years, I heard only one patriotic song in the country repertoire—"There's a Star Spangled Banner Waving Somewhere"—but it was a very mild-mannered lyric, with nothing of the love-it-or-leave-it paranoia exemplified in the tuneful threats issued by Merle Haggard today. The Grand Ole Opry usually stayed well within the goodbye-l'il-darlin' range popularized by Gene Autry. The songs were more Western than Southern; the latter were taken care of by the bluegrass repertoire. In either case, the trademark was geniality and tolerance; the most violent song around was "The Wreck of the Old '97."

8   After the war and during the Fifties, the genre was taken over by Hank Williams and Eddy Arnold. Williams infused some wry humor into his songs, and gave an authentic Cajun touch to "Jambalaya." Arnold contributed some interesting things to musical history by reviving an 1873 song called "Molly Darling," my all-time favorite, and a nineteenth-century ballad, "The Letter Edged in Black." During this period, many country music hits such as "I Love You Because" proved good enough to enter the popular music field.

9   The turning point in country music came around 1960. A truculent true-blue note crept into it in reaction to the hippie/civil-rights movements, and we began to hear the first of those now-famous talking records of the whatever-happened-to-Nathan-Hale school, in which the recitation is backed by patriotic music, usually "America, the Beautiful," played in last-post time.

10   Because the Kennedys personified grace, glamour, elegance, and Harvard intellect, and because Mrs. Jacqueline Kennedy especially fell somewhat short of being just plain home folks, country music struck back with a feisty pride in commonness that was quite different in tone and intent from the lighthearted hayseed humor of Cousin Minnie Pearl, whose routine was merely the reverse side of George M. Cohan's teasing jabs at the Reubens of New Rochelle. One suspects that Cousin Minnie and Cohan would have liked each other, but the rural-conservative country music fan hated Kennedys and Kennedy urbanity with a visceral passion. Country music fans started picking up on the idea that sophistication was the mark of *all* "nigger-lovin' Commanists," and we began to hear songs attacking city-dwellers. This theme has always been present in country music, but in the Sixties it became more prevalent and more acrimonious. A favorite target was New York, home of freedom riders and worse. The first anti-city song I remember, from about 1962 [*sic*], was harmless and hilarious, but the seeds of polarization were there. It was a ballad about Lizzie Borden called "You Can't Chop Your Papa Up in Massachusetts 'Cause Massachusetts Isn't Little Old New York." A few years later came "I Wouldn't Live in New York City (If They Gave Me the Whole Dang Town)," which had a background of hectoring street noises, sirens, and explosions.

11   I continued to enjoy country music until around 1968, when the Chicago imbroglio, the election of Nixon, and the advent of the women's liberation movement seemed to make even greater changes in the genre and I began to be repelled, offended, and occasionally frightened by the music I had loved all my life.

12   I now listen to my local country music station in a spirit of compulsive masochistic curiosity, wondering for whom the bell would toll if the spirit of some of these songs should someday become flesh.

13   The typical radio station now sounds like an armed camp. In addition to the songs themselves, there are regular features such as Arthur Kennedy's *Profile of a Patriot* series, and a Georgetown University legal advice series called *Law for Laymen,* which defines things like the search-and-seizure rule, and which occasionally achieves a tone of "It's us against the world." These productions are educational,

but the undercurrent that flows through them bears a striking similarity to the famous fighting side of Merle Haggard. As Clifton Webb, playing Mr. Belvedere, asked a child in a toy store, "Little boy, do you expect to be attacked?"

14   Many of today's country music songs are hymns to the fear of change that is dividing America along strict political, social, and sexual lines, and encouraging all working people to emulate and identify with the very worst sort of Southern reactionaries. There is now a calculated psychology to country music, a "message" that promotes alienation and a spirit of testy readiness that is disturbing to hear.

15   A recent song that particularly sticks in my mind goes: "So when you pass me by with your head up high/ You ain't no better than me./ When the facts are known you're just flesh and bone./ You ain't no better than me." This is one of the now-vast category of Inferiority songs. More famous is "Born to Lose," written in 1944 but revived in the Sixties. Its renaissance was disturbing because I noticed that a number of the rougher sort of Southern men had affixed the title to their arms in homemade tattoos. When Richard Speck was arrested, he was found to be similarly decorated.

16   There is a grim pride in these loser songs, and a note of fond self-pity illustrated by the prevalence of the "Poor Lonesome" theme. We have had "Poor Lonesome Me," "The Last Word in Lonesome is Me," and "Little Ole Wine-Drinker, Me." The most recent contribution to the category is "What Made Milwaukee Famous Made a Loser Out of Me."

17   The sullen defensiveness aroused in listeners by Inferiority songs becomes social dynamite when combined with the aggression inherent in songs of the Down-Home Patriotism category. The newest of these is "Red Necks, White Socks, and Blue Ribbon Beer," a truculent hymn to the twice-turned jockstrap that could someday become America's "Horst Wessel." This song goes far beyond the 1960 elevation of mere commonness in exalting roughnecks.

18   The two most famous patriotic songs are both by Merle Haggard: "The Fightin' Side of Me," which speaks of squirrely draft-dodgers who don't believe in fighting, and "Okie from Muskogee," which recommends leather boots instead of Roman sandals for manly footwear.

19   Racist Southerners objected to protest folk songs of the Sixties because they felt such songs contained implicit threats. "If I Had a Hammer" was made up of nothing but conditional verbs, and "Blowin' in the Wind" was a collection of rhetorical questions. Understandably, this provoked rage and fear in certain Southern circles. These same circles are now relishing the fiats of patriotism, Nashville style.

20   There are also talking records, which have come a long way from the Green Beret sentimentality of the Sixties. The latest hit of this type is "Americans," by Byron MacGregor, a Canadian who declaims that he is sick of hearing America criticized. In boosterish rhetoric he says that we are still the biggest, the kindest, and the best country in the world, the one that rushes to the aid of others in need. During the San Francisco earthquake, he says, not one foreign nation offered to

help us. This is all very stirring to someone saturated in Milwaukee's finest, but the only trouble is, it's not true. All the major foreign governments offered help to San Francisco, but Theodore Roosevelt, obsessed, as usual, with *machismo,* declined their aid, saying that America was strong enough to take care of her own house.

21   Loudly trumpeted supermasculinity is now a trademark of many country songs. It was not always so; Gene Autry made a very mild-mannered Marlboro man when he sang "Back in the Saddle Again," and Roy Rogers refused to shoot anyone on screen. In World War II, "Praise the Lord and Pass the Ammunition" told the story of a man who tried his best *not* to resort to "manly" solutions. He was a chaplain who was prohibited from picking up a gun, and only under extreme duress did he finally consent to do so.

22   Supermasculinity has currently been combined with those old chestnuts, mother songs, to encourage a myth dear to the heart of the average country music fan: men are fighting stags, and women submissive does. In "Mama Tried," a man brags he "turned twenty-one in prison doin' life without parole." "No one could steer me right but Mama tried," i.e., no female can tame a real man.

23   The mother figure in recent country music is very much like the long-suffering Irish mother. Each matriarch is honored but ignored, and it is always implied that although she is the salt of the earth and the rock upon which the family is built, she can do nothing to stop male violence except huddle in her shawl and pray. The mother in "Don't Take Your Guns to Town" pleads with her fine and uncontrollable sons, but the dominant male refuses to listen and returns home on a slab, his pride intact. How different these mother songs are from that Grand Ole Opry radio hit of thirty years ago, "Mama Don't Allow." That mother was ignored, too, but her sons were merely mischievous when they broke her rules about smoking and dancing. Even so, she was a strong-minded, warpath type who called to mind nothing less than Marjorie Main playing Queen Boadicea, not a helpless biddy terrified of maleness.

24   It was inevitable that the women's liberation movement would threaten male country music fans, so it is not surprising that Tammy Wynette's "Don't Liberate Me (Love Me)" became a big hit. Country music believes that men are men and women are women, and God help anybody who suggests that this twain should meet. At this writing, the number-one hit on the country music circuit is "Country Bumpkin." It tells of a lanky hayseed who goes into a bar and meets a barmaid with "hard and knowing eyes" who makes fun of his countrified manner. In the second verse, the with-it heroine is found "in a bed of joyful tears and death-like pain," giving birth to another country bumpkin who is proudly described as a "boy-child." In the third verse, "forty years of hard work later," the former barmaid is dying in the same bed, with her husband and grown son, both apparently healthy, in worshipful attendance. Innate male purity and righteousness have triumphed over innate female wickedness; she was saved by the love of a good man who married her, soiled dove though she was, and made an honest woman of her.

25   As Betty MacDonald said in *The Egg and I*: "The more I was

shown of that side of the life of a farmer's good wife, the more I saw in the life of an old-fashioned mistress. . . . I luxuriated in breaking the old mountain tradition that a decent woman is in bed only between the hours of 7:00 P.M. and 4:00 A.M. unless she is in labor or dead."

26   Men and women don't get along very well in country music. For every song like "The Happiest Girl in the Whole U.S.A." there are hundreds that describe doomed, guilt-ridden relationships that barrel on in a rondo of attempted serial monogamy like a sexual house that Jack built. She's nobody's darlin' but mine, yet she's down at the honky-tonk tavern with Big Bad John, who brought along his guns, who robs other men's castles, who's sorry he made her cry, because she walked the floor and left tears on her pillow after somebody stole her darlin' when they played "The Tennessee Waltz," while she was slippin' around with me down at the honky-tonk tavern on the blue side of town.

27   Such a disruptive sex life is hard on the nerves, so it is no wonder that one of the most popular country music categories is Escape From Women. In these songs, the Greyhound bus stars as deus ex machina, and the lyrics read like timetables. The popularity of "By the Time I Get to Phoenix" is directly related to the average country music fan's urge to flee and become king of the road.

28   Many of them tried to prove their kingship of the road in the recent truck drivers' strike. Next to diesel fuel, the truck driver's most vital requirement is his country music tape deck. These men are saturated with country music for mile after endless mile. The inevitable tedium of such work increases the feelings of isolation and alienation prompted by the Poor-Lonesome-Me songs; the Superstud and Patriotic songs keep them by turns stirred up, challenged, threatened, angry, and over-confident in a cocky, defensive way. The Honky-Tonk Angel songs make them wonder about the wives they leave at home for such long periods of time, and the Inferiority songs such as "If I Had Johnny's Cash, Charley's Pride and You" provide them with painful reminders that the American Dream which they have long cherished has ceased to exist—except, ironically, for a country music star like Loretta Lynn, who has made an enormous fortune even though she can barely read and write.

29   Hard as it may be to believe, I am not an intellectual snob, nor even an intellectual. Except for literature, my tastes are thoroughly music-hall and, unfortunately, I love beer. Now that I can no longer enjoy country music, I tend toward *larme dans la voix* Irish tenors at their most mawkish—John McCormack's rendition of "Sweet Jessie, the Flower o' Dunblane," for instance. I am concerned with the subject of country music not out of a quest for some arbitrary standard of loftiness but out of concern for domestic tranquillity. It is not too far-fetched to say that the violence of the truckers' strike was fired in part by the provocations of the Nashville sound. If this music is creating, encouraging, and isolating a rootless proletariat, that ought to give pause to the composers and artists in this field who claim to love America so much more than the rest of us.

Discussion of Theme

1. How did the nature of country music change in the 60's, and what events precipitated the change?
2. Do you think the author exaggerates the importance and power of today's country music? Why or why not?
3. What connection is made between the truckers' strike and country music?
4. What does the author mean by the statement that "Polarization is as American as apple pie. . . ." in paragraph 4?

Discussion of Rhetoric

1. There are a number of shifts in tone in this essay. Find specific shifts and analyze them in terms of purpose and effect.
2. Why does the author wait until the end of the essay to state her thesis? How is the organization of this essay determined by this device?
3. The author makes use of many references to a number of areas such as film, literary terms, and conventions, books—even a nursery rhyme. What does this device add to the essay? Explain the references and how they illuminate ideas.
4. What is the purpose of the personal statement in the conclusion in paragraph 29 in which the author describes her tastes?

Writing Assignments

1. Write an essay in which you analyze rock music in terms of its influence on society (or your own life).
2. Write a personal essay about song lyrics that influenced you in some way.
3. Listen to some country music lyrics and write your own impressions in an essay.
4. Write an essay based on the theme, "Sexism in song lyrics."

Library Exploration

1. Research and report on the protest songs of the 60's.
2. Research and report on the influence of the English ballad on American country and folk music.
3. Do a biographical study of your favorite country singer.

Vocabulary

(3) REDUCTIO AD ABSURDUM   a reduction to absurdity

(4) IMPRIMATUR   an official approval

(6) AFICIONADOS   ardent devotees

(4) URBANITY   refinement in manner; polish

(10) ACRIMONIOUS   caustic, stinging; bitter

(11) IMBROGLIO   a complicated or difficult situation

(26) RONDO   a work or movement of music

The authors of the following brief articles have had an unrivaled impact on film making. Ingmar Bergman (1918–), the Swedish stage and film producer, is perhaps best known for "Wild Strawberries" and "The Seventh Seal." Alain Robbe-Grillet (1922–), a native of France, is the author of several novels; he is best known in the United States, however, as the writer of the film script for "Last Year at Marienbad." And Michelangelo Antonioni (1929–) was a film critic and maker of documentary films in his native Italy before he achieved fame with "Blow-up."

In the following selections three master craftsmen examine some aspects of the art of film making. Bergman reminds us that the producer is basically a conjurer. Robbe-Grillet tells us that a film is the product of collaboration between the director and his scriptwriter. Finally, Antonioni reminds us that the camera is the vehicle by which the writer's and producer's ideas are transmitted.

The Filmic Arts: A Symposium

THE CONJURER'S ART
Ingmar Bergman

1   When I was ten years old I received my first, rattling film projector, with its chimney and lamp. I found it both mystifying and fascinating. The first film I had was nine feet long and brown in color. It showed a

girl lying asleep in a meadow, who woke up and stretched out her arms, then disappeared to the right. That was all there was to it. The film was a great success and was projected every night until it broke and could not be mended any more.

2   This little rickety machine was my first conjuring set. And even today I remind myself with childish excitement that I am really a conjurer, since cinematography is based on deception of the human eye. I have worked it out that if I see a film which has a running time of one hour, I sit through twenty-seven minutes of complete darkness — the blankness between frames. When I show a film I am guilty of deceit. I use an apparatus which is constructed to take advantage of a certain human weakness, an apparatus with which I can sway my audience in a highly emotional manner — make them laugh, scream with fright, smile, believe in fairy stories, become indignant, feel shocked, charmed, deeply moved or perhaps yawn with boredom. Thus I am either an impostor or, when the audience is willing to be taken in, a conjurer. I perform conjuring tricks with [an] apparatus so expensive and so wonderful that any entertainer in history would have given anything to have it.

STORY AND SCRIPT   Alain Robbe-Grillet

1   The collaboration between a director and his script writer can take a wide variety of forms. One might almost say that there are as many different methods of work as there are films. Yet the one that seems most frequent in the traditional commercial cinema involves a more or less radical separation of scenario and image, story and style; in short, "content" and "form."

2   For instance, the author describes a conversation between two characters, providing the words they speak and a few details about the setting; if he is more precise, he specifies their gestures or facial expressions, but it is always the director who subsequently decides how the episode will be photographed, if the characters will be seen from a distance or if their faces will fill the whole screen, what movements the camera will make, how the scene will be cut, etc. Yet the scene as the audience sees it will assume quite different, sometimes even contradictory meanings, depending on whether the characters are looking toward the camera or away from it, or whether the shots cut back and forth between their faces in rapid succession. The camera may also concentrate on something entirely different during their conversation, perhaps merely the setting around them: the walls of the room they are in, the streets where they are walking, the waves that break in front of them. At its extreme, this method produces a scene whose words and gestures are quite ordinary and unmemorable, compared to the forms and movement of the image, which alone has any importance, which alone appears to have a meaning.

3   This is precisely what makes the cinema an art: it creates a reality
with forms. It is in its form that we must look for its true content. The
same is true of any work of art, of a novel, for instance: the choice of a
narrative style, of a grammatical tense, of a rhythm of phrasing, of a
vocabulary carries more weight than the actual story. What novelist
worthy of the name would be satisfied to hand his story over to a
"phraseologist" who would write out the final version of the text for
the reader? The initial idea for a novel involves both the story and its
style; often the latter actually comes first in the author's mind, as a
painter may conceive of a canvas entirely in terms of vertical lines
before deciding to depict a skyscraper group.

4   And no doubt the same is true for a film: conceiving of a screen story,
it seems to me, would mean already conceiving of it in images, with
all the detail this involves, not only with regard to gestures and settings, but to the camera's position and movement, as well as to the
sequence of shots in editing. Alain Resnais and I were able to collabo-
rate only because we saw the film in the same way from the start; and
not just in the same general way, but exactly, in the construction of the
least detail as in its total architecture. What I wrote might have been
what was already in his mind; what he added during the shooting was
what I might have written.

IMAGE   Michelangelo Antonioni

1 It is in this spirit that I try to shoot the scenes of my films. I do not
read what I am about to shoot each morning—I know the scenario by
heart; thus I do not need to study it every morning at my desk. When I
arrive at the studio, I ask everyone to leave for a quarter of an hour or
twenty minutes, the time required to try out the camera movements,
to soak myself in them, to run through the sequence from a technical
point of view. I do not shoot several times over, I do not change. I
have no doubts about the position of the camera. Obviously, there
are problems I set myself, but I resolve them at the beginning and
then do not change afterwards.

2   Naturally I cannot work out camera movements at my desk. I have
to think about them at the studio. . . . I always use a dolly, even
when I am going to shoot an important scene (besides, I prefer vertical rather than horizontal movements). I follow the characters with
the movements I have already worked out, and I correct them later
if need be. I compose my scenes from behind the camera. Certain
directors—for instance, René Clair—work in a different way. I do not
say that theirs is not a legitimate system, but I cannot understand how
they manage to shoot from little designs and plans they have drawn on
paper ahead of time. I feel that the composition is a plastic, figurative
element which ought to be seen in its exact dimensions.

Discussion of Theme

1. Which of these authors is most subjective and personal in his discussion of film making?
2. Explain Bergman's statement that he is "either an imposter or a conjurer." Would you agree?
3. According to Robbe-Grillet, what is the contribution of the director to a film?
4. In what way is cinema an art? A craft?

Discussion of Rhetoric

1. Which writer avoids, for the most part, emotional, evocative, or connotative language?
2. What is the purpose of Bergman's anecdote about his first film projector? How does he relate it to his central thesis?
3. "Story and Script" contains a number of transitional phrases that give the selection unity and coherence. Find several of these and determine the function of each.

Writing Assignments

1. Write a review (not merely a plot summary) of a movie that you have seen recently.
2. Should the film be regarded as an art form, or merely a technical product?
3. Develop the following title into a theme: "Movies Are Getting Better (or Worse)."

Library Exploration

For a further treatment of these writers' veiws, read one or more of the following: *Four Screenplays of Ingmar Bergman* (1960), by Ingmar Bergman; *Last Year at Marienbad* (1962), by Alain Robbe-Grillet; and *The World of Film: Michelangelo Antonioni* (1963), by Pierre Leprohon.

Karl Shapiro (1913–   ), former editor of "Poetry" magazine, has won the Pulitzer Prize for his poetry. Currently professor of English at the University of California at Davis, he has been acclaimed as one of America's greatest poets of the century. Among his books are "Selected Poems," "To Abolish Children," and "White-Haired Lover," all published in 1968.

In the following article a poet who also teaches college undergraduates denounces today's students as a generation of illiterates. They prefer "sweepings and swill," rather than works of genuine literary merit.

KARL SHAPIRO

Student Illiteracy

1 I am no Jeremiah and will leave the ranting to others. But as a teacher of reading and writing, as a reader and writer myself, I wish to report to you my version of the degeneration of the literary intelligence and its attendant confusions everywhere in our lives.

2 When a professor at a venerable university has his life's work destroyed by student vandals, society may well begin to tremble.

3 Who would have thought, at least since the defeat of Hitler, that American professors would begin to remove their notes and files from their offices and take them home; that they would begin to remove their best or their irreplaceable volumes; that libraries would begin the reduplication of indices as a safety measure; that specially trained police and guards and firemen would replace the old innocuous campus cop.

4 I apologize for invoking these commonplaces, and yet who, except Lewis Carroll perhaps, would have dreamed of students acquiring the power to fire faculties, presidents and chancellors, to determine curricula, and worst of all, to force personal political opinion and dogma upon the teaching community at large, and upon society itself.

5   My experience is relatively unusual, and I believe I have a perspective upon the degenerative process in literature which should be shared.

6   For example, I have been engaged in creative writing programs for 20-odd years, virtually from the beginning of this kind of teaching. These programs have corroded steadily and today have reached the point of futility. Students in such programs today, according to my experience all over the United States, can no longer spell, can no longer construct a simple English sentence, much less a paragraph, and cannot speak.

7   We have the most inarticulate generation of college students in our history, and this may well account for their mass outbreaks of violence. They have no more intelligent way to express themselves.

8   But what is really distressing is that this generation cannot and does not read. I am speaking of university students in what are supposed to be our best universities. Their illiteracy is staggering.

9   But of course they say they read. They may slam the professor's anthology on the floor but they will go to a bookshop to buy the innumerable paperback best sellers of their generation, which are almost always trashy rewrites of current sociological or philosophical fads.

10   The kitsch-camp-op-pop-absurdist-revolutionary sweepings and swill with which they fill their wordless minds are what they bring to class.

11   They do not want to read; they want to "experience." They do not want to learn; they want to "feel." They have become almost impossible to teach.

12   As far as I can tell the high school has now reached the level of the grade school; the college is at high school level; the graduate school at college level; and whatever reading and writing is being done is being done by professors, the people who are taking their libraries home.

13   It appears the modern student enters the university with a contempt for the university, a contempt for society, a contempt for literature, and a contempt for himself. Where did he learn this? Not from school; not from the library. I don't think so.

14   He learned it from what the new illiterates call the media: TV, radio, newspaper, phonograph, rock festival, magazine and paperback bookstore. He learned it from what the new illiterates call counter culture; he learned it from his contemporaries and the exploiters of cults.

15   For the first time in history the illiterates have a literature of their own. Armed to the teeth with this quasi-literature, it is little wonder they slam textbooks on the floor and stomp to their cars, barefooted.

16   I will now introduce the hero, or anti-hero, if you like. He is a real person, and all the information I am going to give you is true and accurate, except for his name. I have changed his name not for any legalistic reason but because I feel humiliated to have to bring up his name at all. Here then is Dylan MacGoon.

17   I first heard of Dylan MacGoon as I was checking out of a hotel in Milwaukee. The girl behind the desk, who must have seen in the local

paper that I was lecturing on poetry, asked me what I thought of the poetry of Dylan MacGoon. Who? I said.

18 That was just about a year ago but in the ensuing months the name began to come at me from all directions. In one university where I gave a poetry reading I was challenged by a student from the audience who wanted to know what I thought of MacGoon. I had seen some of his verses by then and answered that I didn't think anything of them; they were not even trash.

19 I then began to see big ads about MacGoon's three new books, one of which had been commissioned, no less, by one of the largest and most respected publishing houses in New York. What bothered me was that the publisher was my publisher, a company that had printed Robinson Jeffers, all the works of W. H. Auden, Stephen Spender, myself, and many others.

20 How could this be? I tried to put it out of my head. MacGoon however, would not go away.

21 One day I saw him interviewed by a top news commentator, the kind of reporter who is assigned only to prime ministers and field marshals. Mr. MacGoon, said the commentator in tones of authentic awe, you are the foremost best-selling poet in the United States (I think he said the world). And then the commentator asked about MacGoon's creative regimen.

22 MacGoon tried to answer as best he could (language is not his strong point) and succeeded, between the awe of the commentator and his own honest dissimulations, in presenting the image of the poet. His millions of readers and listeners, all under 19, I hope, must have been gladdened.

23 I went to the little public library in the little town I live in, hoping against hope that there would be no MacGoon. There was. Still, I said to myself, the library is next door to a high school, and MacGoon is better for the kids than marijuana. Then again, maybe he isn't.

24 In a desperate attempt to exorcise MacGoon, I finally succumbed to the public prints and reviewed one of his three best sellers in a weekly New York book review. The remarks, in part, went more or less as follows:

25 The downhill speed of American poetry in the last decade has been breathtaking, for those who watch the sport. Poetry plunged out of the classics, out of the modern masters, out of all standards, and plopped into the playpen.

26 There we are entertained with the carnival of the Naughties and the Uglies, who have their own magazines and publishing houses, and the love-torn alienates, nihilists, disaffiliates who croon or "rock" their way into the legitimate publishing establishment. MacGoon falls into the latter category.

27 What hidden message have we here? Is the Beatleization of American poetry becoming a reality? Are the negative values on the rise in poetry also? Will the bilge work its way up to the library and the graduate school and to the art of writing itself? The answer to all these questions is a dismal groan.

28 Publishers, even those who formerly prided themselves on the qual-

ity of their publications, are now miring in the dismal swamp of the adolescent revolution. They seem to drool at the sight of a rock festival, which attracts a quarter to a half million of the new humanoids. They cannot resist the temptation. They seek out MacGoon and pay his overhead.

29   The aftermath of my critique was typical. There were letters and telephone calls and a dressing down from a reporter in Los Angeles who called to ask me to explain myself. He had been assigned to interview MacGoon. The crooner, it seems, had also read my diatribe. When asked what he thought of it he answered: Who cares what he thinks?

30   And the weekly book review dropped me.

31   There are many MacGoons in the country, as well as in Liverpool, the chief ones being Dylan, Leonard Cohen, our hero, and so on. In one of the more literate anarchist magazines I notice a serious explanation of a poem(?) written by a poet (?) named Buffy Sainte-Marie.

32   Buffy's lines, "Little wheel spin and spin/Big wheel turn around and around," which resemble the speech of the mental defective and are the norm of the new poetry, are explicated thus: "In Buffy's song the medieval and Elizabethan image of the microcosm mirroring the macrocosm becomes saturated with historical and political content."

33   We are experiencing a literary breakdown which is unlike anything I know of in the history of letters. It is something new and something to be reckoned with. We have reached the level of mindlessness at which students and the literate public can no longer distinguish between poetry and gibberish.

34   When critics and university students can no longer tell the difference between rock lyrics and the songs of Shakespeare, teaching is no longer possible; standards of good and inferior disappear; discrimination dies: and the true artist goes into hiding.

35   We are in the time that Yeats predicted, and everyone is quoting his famous lines: "The best lack all conviction, while the worst/Are full of passionate intensity."

Discussion of Theme

1. What is taking place in our colleges that reminds Shapiro of the days of Hitler? Is he serious or merely exaggerating?
2. How does he relate violence to the writing skills of college students?
3. What is his opinion of the books that he says students are reading? Can you identify any of those alluded to in paragraph 10? Who is Dylan MacGoon?
4. At what level are today's poets and publishers aiming, according to Shapiro? Do you agree? Is his criticism of students and modern writers justified?

Discussion of Rhetoric

1. Describe the tone of this article. What contributes to it?
2. What was Shapiro's purpose: to irritate his reader, or to "convert" him? How do you know?
3. Is Shapiro's argument weakened by his failure to document his case with examples, details, or other evidence?
4. What is irony? Sarcasm? Does Shapiro employ either in his article?
5. Shapiro says he will "leave the ranting to others." Does he?

Writing Assignments

1. If you would like to defend one of the writers attacked by Shapiro, do so in a paper that clearly states your arguments.
2. Select one of the modern poets mentioned in paragraph 31. If you agree with Shapiro's opinion of the poet, write an analysis of his
3. style, showing why he is inferior.
   If you disagree with the author of this selection, write a rebuttal.

Library Exploration

1. Read the poetry of Rod McKuen. See if Shapiro's remarks are valid when applied to his work.
2. Select for further study one of the writers mentioned by Shapiro.

Vocabulary

(2) VENERABLE worthy of reverence, usually because of age

(4) DOGMA a system of principles or beliefs

(7) INARTICULATE incapable of speaking clearly, coherently, or effectively

(22) DISSIMULATIONS false pretenses

(26) NIHILISTS those who believe that existence is senseless or useless

(32) MICROCOSM the world in miniature

(32) MACROCOSM the world; universe

John Ciardi (1916–) is poetry editor of "Saturday Review." He was born in Boston and educated at Tufts University and the University of Michigan. He left his university teaching post "because I found my own papers more interesting to work on than those of my students, and because I thought of a tax problem as more interesting than planned poverty." He is the author of many volumes of poetry, including "Homeward to America" (1940), "From Time to Time" (1951), "How Does a Poem Mean?" (1959), and "You Read to Me, I'll Read to You" (1962).

What is the proper perspective of words like "reality," "humanity," and "poetry"? Ciardi says that poetry "teaches the man an enlargement of his own sense of possibility."

JOHN CIARDI

...an ulcer, gentlemen, is an unwritten poem

1   The poet in our times is a figure of estrangement and he knows it. He not only knows it, he has grown used to the fact and does not much mind it. The truth seems to be, for that matter, that the poet—outside those Golden Ages of folk-poetry now long gone—never did reach more than a few special people in any culture.

2   In the past, however, poets have managed to persuade themselves that they were some sort of social force. Elizabethan poets liked to claim that their sonnets conferred immortality on the ladies they wrote

about. The seventeenth-century satirists were especially fond of the idea that by "holding folly up to ridicule" they purified the intellect of their age. More recently Shelley found it possible to assert that "Poets are the unacknowledged legislators of the world." And even within the last twenty-five years, the social poets of the thirties may be cited as having seriously believed that their poems of social protest had a measurable effect on the government of nations.

3   Stephen Spender, looking back on the mood of poetry in the thirties from the vantage point of 1950, summarized the poet's then-sense of himself as very much a warrior of the practical world:

> It was still possible then to think of a poem as a palpable, overt, and effective anti-fascist action. Every poetic assertion of the dignity of the individual seemed to be a bullet fired in the war against human repression.

4   I know of no sane poet today who persuades himself that the action of his art and imagination has any significant consequence in the practical reality of Dow-Jones averages, election returns, and state-of-the-nation. Wherever the practical world may be, Auden has defined the position of poetry in our time:

> For poetry makes nothing happen: it survives
> In the valley of its saying where executives
> Would never want to tamper; it flows south
> From ranches of isolation and the busy griefs,
> Raw towns that we believe and die in; it survives,
> A way of happening, a mouth.

5   But now—perhaps to prove that poets are no prophets—the executives have wanted to tamper. Under the auspices of the College English Association a group of leading business executives have been meeting regularly with writers and teachers of the liberal arts; and from their problems in the practical world of business management, they seem to be asking seriously what meeting there can be between the arts and the practicalities of industry.

6   The answer to these questions may well be that the poets and the practical men would be mutually happier in leaving one another strictly alone, the poets on their ranches of isolation practising a way of happening, and the practical men in their cities of numbered and lettered glass doors busily pushing the buttons of the world.

7   For the gap that divides the poet from the practical man is real. Nor will it be measurably closed by pointing out that some men have functioned with distinction in both the poetical and the practical imagination. There was a director of public works named Chaucer, there was a bricklayer named Ben Jonson, there was a good soldier named Richard Lovelace—one could compile endlessly. But all that such a list would prove is that some men are ambidextrous: it would not eliminate the distinction between the right hand and the left.

8   A poem is a kind of human behavior. Plowing a field, running a chemical experiment, and analyzing the character of a job-applicant are also kinds of human behavior. The poem may, of course, be about any one of these human actions; but when the poem deals with them, it does so in nonpractical ways. The poet who writes about plowing a

field may find significance in the *idea* of plowing, or he may describe plowing so richly that the riches of the description become a self-pleasing idea in themselves. He does not, however, turn physical soil, plant an actual crop, and take it to the literal human diet by way of a negotiable cash market. In the same way, the poet may create a powerfully penetrating picture of the character of the man the business executive is interviewing for a job. But when the poet has finished his analysis, he has no need to make a payroll decision and to assign the man to a specific job in a specific department.

9   Poetry and practicality are in fact two different worlds with two different orders of experience and of imagination. The poet enters his world as an *as if*: he writes *as if* he were plowing a field, *as if* he were conducting a chemical experiment, *as if* he were analyzing a real man seated before him. He is free with a stroke of the pen to change the lineaments of the world he has imagined. The work-sheets of a poem by Karl Shapiro contain a monumental example of this freedom to *as if* at will.

10   Setting out to describe the (*as if*) dome of darkness that settles over a city at night, he writes in his first draft: "Under the fatherly dome of the universe and the town." Now "fatherly dome" cannot fail to imply a theological universe in the mind of God the Father. For reasons that need not be examined here, Shapiro, in his second draft, rephrased the idea "Under the dome of zero." Simply by changing one central word, Shapiro swung the universe itself from the theological concept of "father" to the scientific concept of "zero." And the poem continued to follow itself as if the process of reversing thirty centuries of human attitudes in a single word amounted to nothing whatever.

11   The practical man has no such large freedom. He enters a world called *is*. When he is at work, he *is* plowing a field, he *is* assembling chemical apparatus, he *is* interviewing an actual man whose name appears on the census listings and who *is* offering his services in return for real and taxable wages.

12   It is only natural, moreover, that men who give their attention to either of these two worlds should not be especially well disposed to the other. Poets tend to think very little of stockbrokers, and stockbrokers tend to think even less—if at all—of poets. And the fact is that some of the best poetry of our times has been written on what may be called an inverted sense of reality, an order of imagination that asserts openly or by implication that what the practical men do is meaningless and that only the *as if* of the vicarious imagination has a place in the final mind of man. So Wallace Stevens, in a poem significantly titled "Holiday in Reality," lists a series of things seen and says of them: "These are real only if I make them so," and concludes:

> Intangible arrows quiver and stick in the skin
> And I taste at the root of the tongue the unreal
> Of what is real.

13   It may be very much to the point that Wallace Stevens, in another part of his imagination, is a vice-president of the Hartford Accident

and Indemnity Company and a specialist in claims on surety bonds. Obviously, however, Wallace Stevens cannot look into his surety bond claims and send in a report that "These are real only if I make them so." That difference between the world of practical solutions and the world of the vicarious imagination must not be blinked away.

14   What must be borne in mind, rather, is the fact that no sane human being is exclusively a practical man. The plant manager may be the most mechanically efficient of calculators during his waking hours; and still his dreams or his nightmares will be human and impractical. What is his order of reality and of business efficiency when he first holds his newborn child? Or when, as some men must in time, he stands by his child's grave? What is his order of reality when he steps out of a late conference and finds a hurricane shaking the earth? Or his wife is ill and the telephone rings: In one ear he hears his assistant howling that the sub-contractor sent the wrong parts and that a rush order is delayed, while with the other he hears the doctor close the bedroom door and start down the stairs to tell him his wife will or will not recover. Which of these realities is more real than the other to live to?

15   The poem does not care and cannot care what happens to that rush order. The poem is of the humanity of the man. And despite the tendency . . . [to admire] only those men who "do things" and to scorn "dreamers," the fact is that no man can be wholly practical or wholly impractical, and that the humanity of any man's life requires some, at least, of both orders of the imagination.

16   There is no poetry for the practical man. There is poetry only for the mankind of the man who spends a certain amount of his life turning the mechanical wheel. But let him spend too much of his life at the mechanics of practicality and either he must become something less than a man, or his very mechanical efficiency will become impaired by the frustrations stored up in his irrational human personality. An ulcer, gentlemen, is an unkissed imagination taking its revenge for having been jilted. It is an unwritten poem, a neglected music, an unpainted watercolor, an undanced dance. It is declaration from the mankind of the man that a clear spring of joy has not been tapped, and that it must break through, muddily, on its own.

17   Poetry is one of the forms of joy, the most articulate, the most expanding, and, therefore, the most fulfilling form. It is no separation from the world; it is the mankind of the world, the most human language of man's uncertain romance with the universe.

18   Despite the slanders of high-minded schoolmarms and even of some of the poets themselves, poetry is not a moral thing. It is a life thing. It is like hunger, or sex-drive, or the pleasure of stretching one's muscles. It exists. It is of the liveness of the man. Because the man is various, it may be mixed in him with the moral or the amoral, with the lofty or the coarse, with the sententious or the foppish, with the brilliant or the trivial. But where the living gift of poetry is real, it survives all added characteristics. Whatever the situation of the poet's learning, morals, or psychic base, the stomach wrinkles, the glands secrete, the consciousness evolves, and the gift, if there is gift

in the man, answers to the rhythm of its own living. As natively as a child sways to music, as blindly as a mouth sucks, as darkly as the hand of the sleeping man reaches to touch the woman and rests resolved and assured when it has found her — just so the human being needs the motion and repose that a good poem is. And just so, the man who has not been estranged from himself by busy motions, not only needs, but knows he needs, these fulfillments.

19 The moralist to the contrary, the impulse to poetry is a play impulse. It will not do to call it anything more high-sounding than that. It is necessary, rather, to see that poetic play is of the very fiber of life and that it runs equally through child's prattle, the designer's pleasure in finding and following the shape of his idea, and the substance of all religious ritual.

20 Form, whether in rhythm (time) or in mass (space) is inseparable from our perception of the world. To respond to form and to take the inevitable next step, which is to re-imagine it, is inseparable from the act of sentience a human life is.

21 That act of imagination and of re-imagination is not easy. It is better than easy: it is joyous. It is what Robert Frost called "the pleasure of taking pains." Taking pains is inseparable from human satisfaction. Every game ever developed by mankind is a way of inventing a difficulty for the sake of overcoming it. The lines a child draws for hopscotch, the rules chess players agree upon, the hurdles a track man puts in his way, are deliberately selected ways of making things hard for oneself. It would be easier to play hopscotch without the lines, but it would be no fun.

22 Poets throughout history have been men who played their life's game against form. However painful the overt subject of the good poem, the dance of the form has been the same life-dance for joy. Keats' sonnet, "On First Looking into Chapman's Homer," is a poem on a happy subject. His sonnet, "When I have fears that I may cease to be," is overtly addressed to his unhappy certainty of his impending death. Keats even concludes his brooding with a statement that nothing in the world matters:

> —then on the shore
> Of the wide world I stand alone, and think
> Till love and fame to nothingness do sink.

But though love and fame and world and time might sink to nothing, the rhymes still fall carefully into place, the meter is kept, the images follow, and the form completes itself in an open performance of the joy and the significance of making the poem well. Even in writing of his death the poet dances his life. Whatever the subject of the poem may seem to be, its true subject is the play of form which asserts, shapes, and fulfills the need of the man. Keats thinking about his death was a tragic man. Keats finding the form of his imagination that could best express and hold his feelings about his death was a joyous man.

23 Now, if we ask what sort of human behavior a poem is, we may answer, "It is this dance." The practical-minded man may still object

that the dance accomplishes nothing: Keats was not spared his death, and nothing in the act of giving shape to his dark thoughts had any effect on the reality of his tubercular lung. True, the poem moved nothing in the physical world. But equally true—even more true—in the act of writing Keats became more alive to himself. And whatever may or may not be measured in foot-pounds, that which gives life to life is a human good.

24   But there is more than the basic dance of joy in the human action of Keats' poem. In essence, Keats has found an act of joy wherewith to express the fact of loss. "Grief brought to numbers cannot be so fierce." All life is attended by losses: an action that can convert those very losses to joys must certainly seem an indispensable human resource.

25   And the more sensitively alive a man is, the more certainly his life must scar him. But it is only the *is*-reality that scars. In the act of re-imagining that reality and of capturing it into the *as-if* of poetic form, the poem releases the mind from the bonds of body and situation. Because the poet is free to *as-if* as many realities as he likes, he can, by that much, see his life as part of all other realities. He can imagine himself from outside himself. And he can imagine himself into the mind and feeling of other men. He is ready to acquire both sympathy and understanding.

26   In shorter terms than these there is no good poetry. And no man who lives his life in shorter terms than these is sufficiently alive. The poet is a man at play, but in Robert Frost's phrase, "the work is play for mortal stakes." However sternly the moralist may frown at this emphasis on the play function of poetry, the supreme statements of man's passion on the planet have been made by those men who were most alive to this play.

27   For in the pursuit of form, one not only finds but enlarges himself. "Endure a change of imagination," says the good poem. It is a long thing to be a man. And it is nothing a man may accomplish unaided. Poetry, by storing the world's best imagination, not only transmits experiences from the past of the race, but teaches the man an enlargement of his own sense of possibility.

28   Imagine, for example, a Greek musician of the Golden Age stumbling out of a time machine into the presence of one of our great symphony orchestras just as Toscanini led it into a Beethoven symphony. However passionately that Greek had devoted himself to his lyre and his harp, he never could have imagined the possibility of such music even as he responds to it and is filled by it. It is unlikely in fact that he could begin to understand the music. When we listen to a symphony, we listen with part of the heritage of the race, with the history that has evolved the tradition of that music, and the imaginary Greek would be missing that memory. As in time, however, he acquired that memory, he would certainly be filled with new possibilities, possibilities he could never have imagined unaided.

29   In a very real sense, all of us are that Greek. Left to ourselves we could not hope to have accomplished enough of the imagination of the race to sense our own possibilities and our own humanity. The presence of a true work of art is always an expansion of the human sense.

30   None of these extensions of the human being, to be sure, are useful in tightening a bolt or in adding a column of figures. A man especially sensitive to this life-play may in fact be too variable in his imagination for mechanical and mathematical accuracy. But to define the practical man in terms as mechanical as bolts and adding machines is to define practically no man at all. What is more practical in world and time than a good human being? Let there be good men and the machine will not want.

Discussion of Theme

1. Why does Ciardi believe that poets and practical men should remain aloof from one another?
2. Are you satisfied with Ciardi's explanation (paragraph 7) of why some poets were also men of practical accomplishments? Does the information about these particular poets destroy Ciardi's argument that poets are basically different from nonpoets?
3. Explain the reasoning Ciardi uses to develop the thought expressed in his title. Do you agree with him?
4. Does Ciardi believe that practical men are inferior to creative ones? Does he want to regard them as insensitive?
5. What does it mean for a man to be "estranged," as Ciardi uses the term?

Discussion of Rhetoric

1. What is Ciardi's definition of a poem? Does he define it in more ways than one?
2. Do you find that some of what Ciardi says is not easily grasped or immediately clear to you? What sentences or phrases require extra thought?
3. Which portions of the article do you consider poetic? What contributes to this quality?
4. What purposes do the first seven paragraphs serve? Why does the author wait until paragraph 8 to define a poem?
5. How effective is Ciardi's frequent use of *but* and *and* to begin sentences?

Writing Assignments

1. If you believe that Ciardi overrates the significance of poetry for mankind, write a paper in which you explain why you feel as you do.
2. Ciardi says that the poet "never did reach more than a few special people in any culture." Explore possible reasons for this.

3. Can the lyrics of today's popular songs be regarded as true poetry? If you believe they can, explain why they communicate effectively with young people, whereas "real poetry" often fails.
4. Using Ciardi's informal diction, write a paper on the contributions of painters, sculptors, or musicians.
5. Use the idea in paragraph 28 of a Greek musician stepping into the twentieth century as the basis for a creative theme.

Library Exploration

1. You might be interested in some further advice on poetry by Ciardi. Check the *Saturday Review* poetry section.
2. Read some selections in *The Poem Itself*, by Stanley Burshaw, and report on suggestions made for understanding poetry.

Vocabulary

(1) ESTRANGEMENT separation; alienation

(2) SATIRISTS writers who use wit or irony to expose vice and folly

(3) PALPABLE capable of being touched or felt

(3) OVERT open to view; not concealed

(7) AMBIDEXTROUS able to use both hands equally well

(8) NEGOTIABLE convertible into cash or equivalent value

(9) LINEAMENTS features; outlines

(12) VICARIOUS experienced through imagined participation in someone else's experience

(12) INTANGIBLE immaterial; not capable of being touched

(18) SENTENTIOUS given to excessive moralizing

(18) FOPPISH vain; affected

(18) REPOSE rest

(20) SENTIENCE awareness

Robert Penn Warren (1905–) was educated at Vanderbilt, the University of California, Yale, and Oxford. He is a poet, essayist, short-story writer, and novelist as well as a major American literary critic. Among his many novels are "All the King's Men" (1946), "Circus in the Attic" (1948), "World Enough and Time" (1950), and "The Cave" (1959).

A person who reads fiction demands a story, an imagined situation, yet he is in reality looking for a meaning to life itself.

ROBERT PENN WARREN

Why Do We Read Fiction?

1 Why do we read fiction? The answer is simple. We read it because we like it. And we like it because fiction, as an image of life, stimulates and gratifies our interest in life. But whatever interests may be appealed to by fiction, the special and immediate interest that takes us to fiction is always our interest in a story.

2 A story is not merely an image of life, but of life in motion — specifically, the presentation of individual characters moving through their particular experiences to some end that we may accept as meaningful. And the experience that is characteristically presented in a story is that of facing a problem, a conflict. To put it bluntly: No conflict, no story.

3 It is no wonder that conflict should be at the center of fiction, for conflict is at the center of life. But why should we, who have the constant and often painful experience of conflict in life and who yearn for inner peace and harmonious relation with the outer world, turn to fiction, which is the image of conflict? The fact is that our attitude toward conflict is ambivalent. If we do find a totally satisfactory adjustment in life, we tend to sink into the drowse of the accustomed.

Only when our surroundings — or we ourselves — become problematic again do we wake up and feel that surge of energy which is life. And life more abundantly lived is what we seek.

4   So we, at the same time that we yearn for peace, yearn for the problematic. The adventurer, the sportsman, the gambler, the child playing hide-and-seek, the teenage boys choosing up sides for a game of sandlot baseball, the old grad cheering in the stadium — we all, in fact, seek out or create problematic situations of greater or lesser intensity. Such situations give us a sense of heightened energy, of life. And fiction, too, gives us that heightened awareness of life, with all the fresh, uninhibited opportunity to vent the rich emotional charge — tears, laughter, tenderness, sympathy, hate, love, and irony — that is stored up in us and short-circuited in the drowse of the accustomed. Furthermore, this heightened awareness can be more fully relished now, because what in actuality would be the threat of the problematic is here tamed to mere imagination, and because some kind of resolution of the problem is, owing to the very nature of fiction, promised.

5   The story promises us a resolution, and we wait in suspense to learn how things will come out. We are in suspense, not only about what will happen, but even more about what the event will mean. We are in suspense about the story in fiction because we are in suspense about another story far closer and more important to us — the story of our own life as we live it. We do not know how that story of our own life is going to come out. We do not know what it will mean. So, in that deepest suspense of life, which will be shadowed in the suspense we feel about the story in fiction, we turn to fiction for some slight hint about the story in the life we live. The relation of our life to the fictional life is what, in a fundamental sense, takes us to fiction.

6   Even when we read, as we say, to "escape," we seek to escape not from life but to life, to a life more satisfying than our own drab version. Fiction gives us an image of life — sometimes of a life we actually have and like to dwell on, but often and poignantly of one we have had but do not have now, or one we have never had and can never have. The ardent fisherman, when his rheumatism keeps him housebound, reads stories from *Field and Stream*. The baseball fan reads *You Know Me, Al*, by Ring Lardner. The little co-ed, worrying about her snub nose and her low mark in Sociology 2, dreams of being a debutante out of F. Scott Fitzgerald; and the thin-chested freshman, still troubled by acne, dreams of being a granite-jawed Neanderthal out of Mickey Spillane. When the Parthians in 53 B.C. beat Crassus, they found in the baggage of Roman officers some very juicy items called *Milesian Tales*, by a certain Aristides of Miletus; and I have a friend who in A.D. 1944, supplemented his income as a GI by reading aloud *Forever Amber*, by a certain Kathleen Winsor, to buddies who found that the struggle over three-syllable words somewhat impaired their dedication to that improbable daydream.

7   And that is what, for all of us, fiction, in one sense, is — a daydream. It is, in other words, an imaginative enactment. In it we find, in imagination, not only the pleasure of recognizing the world we know and of reliving our past, but also the pleasure of entering worlds we do not know and of experimenting with experiences which we deeply

crave but which the limitations of life, the fear of consequences, or the severity of our principles forbid us to do. Fiction can give us this pleasure without any painful consequences, for there is no price tag on the magic world of imaginative enactment. But fiction does not give us only what we want; more importantly, it may give us things we hadn't even known we wanted.

8   In this sense then, fiction painlessly makes up for the defects of reality. Long ago Francis Bacon said that poetry—which, in his meaning, would include our fiction—is "agreeable to the spirit of man" because it affords "a greater grandeur of things, a more perfect order, and a more beautiful variety" than can "anywhere be found in nature. . . ." More recently we find Freud putting it that the "meagre satisfactions" that man "can extract from reality leave him starving," and John Dewey saying that art "was born of need, lack, deprivation, incompleteness." But philosophers aside, we all know entirely too well how much we resemble poor Walter Mitty.

9   If fiction is—as it clearly is for some readers—merely a fantasy to redeem the liabilities of our private fate, it is flight from reality and therefore the enemy of growth, of the life process. But is it necessarily this? Let us look at the matter in another way.

10   The daydream which is fiction differs from the ordinary daydream in being publicly available. This fact leads to consequences. In the private daydream you remain yourself—though nobler, stronger, more fortunate, more beautiful than in life. But when the little freshman settles cozily with his thriller by Mickey Spillane, he finds that the granite-jawed hero is not named Slim Willett, after all—as poor Slim, with his thin chest, longs for it to be. And Slim's college instructor, settling down to *For Whom the Bell Tolls*, finds sadly that this other college instructor who is the hero of the famous tale of sleeping bags, bridge demolition, tragic love and lonely valor, is named Robert Jordan.

11   In other words, to enter into that publicly available daydream which fiction is, you have to accept the fact that the name of the hero will never be your own; you will have to surrender something of your own identity to him, have to let it be absorbed in him. But since that kind of daydream is not exquisitely custom-cut to the exact measure of your secret longings, the identification can never be complete. In fact, only a very naïve reader tries to make it thrillingly complete. The more sophisticated reader plays a deep double game with himself; one part of him is identified with a character—or with several in turn—while another part holds aloof to respond, interpret and judge. How often have we heard some sentimental old lady say of a book: "I just loved the heroine—I mean I just went through everything with her and I knew exactly how she felt. Then when she died I just cried." The sweet old lady, even if she isn't very sophisticated, is instinctively playing the double game too: She identifies herself with the heroine, but she survives the heroine's death to shed the delicious tears. So even the old lady knows how to make the most of what we shall call her role-taking. She knows that doubleness, in the very act of identification, is of the essence of role-taking: There is the taker of the role

and there is the role taken. And fiction is, in imaginative enactment, a role-taking.

12   For some people — those who fancy themselves hardheaded and realistic — the business of role-taking is as reprehensible as indulgence in a daydream. But in trying to understand our appetite for fiction, we can see that the process of role-taking not only stems from but also affirms the life process. It is an essential part of growth.

13   Role-taking is, for instance, at the very center of children's play. This is the beginning of the child's long process of adaptation to others, for only by feeling himself into another person's skin can the child predict behavior; and the stakes in the game are high, for only thus does he learn whether to expect the kiss or the cuff. In this process of role-taking we find, too, the roots of many of the massive intellectual structures we later rear — most obviously psychology and ethics, for it is only by role-taking that the child comes to know, to know "inwardly" in the only way that finally counts, that other people really exist and are, in fact, persons with needs, hopes, fears and even rights. So the role-taking of fiction, at the same time that it gratifies our deep need to extend and enrich our own experience, continues this long discipline in human sympathy. And this discipline in sympathy, through the imaginative enactment of role-taking, gratifies another need deep in us: our yearning to enter and feel at ease in the human community.

14   Play when we are children, and fiction when we are grown up, lead us, through role-taking, to an awareness of others. But all along the way role-taking leads us, by the same token, to an awareness of ourselves; it leads us, in fact, to the creation of the self. For the individual is not born with a self. He is born as a mysterious bundle of possibilities which, bit by bit, in a long process of trial and error, he sorts out until he gets some sort of unifying self, the ringmaster self, the official self.

15   The official self emerges, but the soul, as Plato long ago put it, remains full of "ten thousand opposites occurring at the same time," and modern psychology has said nothing to contradict him. All our submerged selves, the old desires and possibilities, are lurking deep in us, sleepless and eager to have another go. There is knife-fighting in the inner dark. The fact that most of the time we are not aware of trouble does not mean that trouble is any the less present and significant; and fiction, most often in subtly disguised forms, liberatingly reenacts for us such inner conflict. We feel the pleasure of liberation even when we cannot specify the source of the pleasure.

16   Fiction brings up from their dark oubliettes our shadowy, deprived selves and gives them an airing in, as it were, the prison yard. They get a chance to participate, each according to his nature, in the life which fiction presents. When in Thackeray's *Vanity Fair* the girl Becky Sharp, leaving school for good, tosses her copy of Doctor Johnson's *Dictionary* out of the carriage, something in our own heart leaps gaily up, just as something rejoices at her later sexual and pecuniary adventures in Victorian society, and suffers, against all our sense of moral justice, when she comes a cropper. When Holden

Caulfield, of Salinger's *Catcher in the Rye*, undertakes his gallant and absurd little crusade against the "phony" in our world, our own nighdoused idealism flares up again, for the moment without embarrassment. When in Faulkner's *Light in August* Percy Grimm pulls the trigger of the black, blunt-nosed automatic and puts that tight, pretty little pattern of slugs in the top of the overturned table behind which Joe Christmas cowers, our trigger finger tenses, even while, at the same time, with a strange joy of release and justice satisfied, we feel those same slugs in our heart. When we read Dostoevski's *Crime and Punishment*, something in our nature participates in the bloody deed, and later, something else in us experiences, with the murderer Raskolnikov, the bliss of repentance and reconciliation.

17   For among our deprived selves we must confront the redeemed as well as the damned, the saintly as well as the wicked; and strangely enough, either confrontation may be both humbling and strengthening. In having some awareness of the complexity of self we are better-prepared to deal with that self. As a matter of fact, our entering into the fictional process helps to redefine this dominant self — even, as it were, to recreate, on a sounder basis — sounder because better understood — that dominant self, the official "I." As Henri Bergson says, fiction "brings us back into our own presence" — the presence in which we must make our final terms with life and death.

18   The knowledge in such confrontations does not come to us with intellectual labels. We don't say, "Gosh, I've got 15 per cent of sadism in me" — or 13 percent of unsuspected human charity. No, the knowledge comes as an enactment; and as imaginative enactment, to use our old phrase, it comes as knowledge. It comes, rather, as a heightened sense of being, as the conflict in the story evokes the conflict in ourselves, evokes it with some hopeful sense of meaningful resolution, and with, therefore, an exhilarating sense of freedom.

19   Part of this sense of freedom derives, to repeat ourselves, from the mere fact that in imagination we are getting off scot-free with something which we, or society, would never permit in real life; from the fact that our paradoxical relation to experience presented in fiction — our involvement and noninvolvement at the same time — gives a glorious feeling of mastery over the game of life. But there is something more important that contributes to this sense of freedom, the expansion and release that knowledge always brings; and in fiction we are permitted to know in the deepest way, by imaginative participation, things we would otherwise never know — including ourselves. We are free from the Garden curse: We may eat of the Tree of Knowledge, and no angel with flaming sword will appear.

20   But in the process of imaginative enactment we have, in another way, that sense of freedom that comes from knowledge. The image that fiction presents is purged of the distractions, confusions and accidents of ordinary life. We can now gaze at the inner logic of things — of a personality, of the consequences of an act or a thought, of a social or historical situation, of a lived life. One of our deepest cravings is to find logic in experience, but in real life how little of our experience comes to us in such a manageable form!

21   We have all observed how a person who has had a profound shock needs to tell the story of the event over and over again, every detail. By telling it he objectifies it, disentagling himself, as it were, from the more intolerable effects. This objectifying depends, partly at least, on the fact that the telling is a way of groping for the logic of the event, an attempt to make the experience intellectually manageable. If a child — or a man — who is in a state of blind outrage at his fate can come to understand that the fate which had seemed random and gratuitous is really the result of his own previous behavior or is part of the general pattern of life, his emotional response is modified by that intellectual comprehension. What is intellectually manageable is, then, more likely to be emotionally manageable.

22   This fiction is a "telling" in which we as readers participate and is, therefore, an image of the process by which experience is made manageable. In this process experience is foreshortened, is taken out of the ruck of time, is put into an ideal time where we can scrutinize it, is given an interpretation. In other words, fiction shows, as we have said, a logical structure which implies a meaning. By showing a logical structure, it relieves us, for the moment at least, of what we sometimes feel as the greatest and most mysterious threat of life — the threat of the imminent but "unknowable," of the urgent but "unsayable." Insofar as a piece of fiction is original and not merely a conventional repetition of the known and predictable, it is a movement through the "unknowable" toward the "knowable" — the imaginatively knowable. It says the "unsayable."

23   This leads us, as a sort of aside, to the notion that fiction sometimes seems to be, for the individual or for society, prophetic. Now looking back we can clearly see how Melville, Dostoevski, James, Proust, Conrad and Kafka tried to deal with some of the tensions and problems which have become characteristic of our time. In this sense they foretold our world — and even more importantly, forefelt it. They even forefelt us.

24   Or let us remember that F. Scott Fitzgerald and Hemingway did not merely report a period, they predicted it in that they sensed a new mode of behavior and feeling. Fiction, by seizing on certain elements in its time and imaginatively pursuing them with the unswerving logic of projected enactment, may prophesy the next age. We know this from looking back on fiction of the past. More urgently we turn to fiction of our own time to help us envisage the time to come and our relation to it.

25   But let us turn to more specific instances of that inner logic which fiction may reveal. In *An American Tragedy* Dreiser shows us in what subtle and pitiful ways the materialism of America and the worship of what William James called the "bitch-goddess Success" can corrupt an ordinary young man and bring him to the death cell. In *Madame Bovary* Flaubert shows us the logic by which Emma's yearning for color and meaning in life leads to the moment when she gulps the poison. In both novels we sense this logic more deeply because we, as we have seen, are involved, are accomplices. We, too, worship the bitch-goddess — as did Dreiser. We, too, have yearnings like Emma's,

and we remember that Flaubert said that he himself was Emma Bovary.

26   We see the logic of the enacted process, and we also see the logic of the end. Not only do we have now, as readers, the freedom that leads to a knowledge of the springs of action; we have also the more difficult freedom that permits us to contemplate the consequences of action and the judgment that may be passed on it. For judgment, even punishment, is the end of the logic we perceive. In our own personal lives, as we well know from our endless secret monologues of extenuation and alibi, we long to escape from judgment; but here, where the price tag is only that of imaginative involvement, we can accept judgment. We are reconciled to the terrible necessity of judgment—upon our surrogate self in the story, our whipping boy and scapegoat. We find a moral freedom in this fact that we recognize a principle of justice, with also perhaps some gratification of the paradoxical desire to suffer.

27   It may be objected here that we speak as though all stories were stories of crime and punishment. No, but all stories, from the gayest farce to the grimmest tragedy, are stories of action and consequence —which amounts to the same thing. All stories, as we have said, are based on conflict; and the resolution of the fictional conflict is, in its implications, a judgment too, a judgment of values. In the end some shift of values has taken place. Some new awareness has dawned, some new possibility of attitude has been envisaged.

28   Not that the new value is necessarily "new" in a literal sense. The point, to come back to an old point, is that the reader has, by imaginative enactment, lived through the process by which the values become valuable. What might have been merely an abstraction has become vital, has been lived, and is, therefore, "new"—new because newly experienced. We can now rest in the value as experienced; we are reconciled in it, and that is what counts.

29   It is what counts, for in the successful piece of fiction, a comic novel by Peter de Vries or a gut-tearing work like Tolstoy's *War and Peace*, we feel, in the end, some sense of reconciliation with the world and with ourselves. And this process of moving through conflict to reconciliation is an echo of our own life process. The life process, as we know it from babyhood on, from our early relations with our parents on to our adult relation with the world, is a long process of conflict and reconciliation. This process of enriching and deepening experience is a pattern of oscillation—a pattern resembling that of the lovers' quarrel: When lovers quarrel, each asserts his special ego against that of the beloved and then in the moment of making up finds more keenly than before the joy of losing the self in the love of another. So in fiction we enter imaginatively a situation of difficulty and estrangement—a problematic situation that, as we said earlier, sharpens our awareness of life—and move through it to a reconciliation which seems fresh and sweet.

30   Reconciliation—that is what we all, in some depth of being, want. All religion, all philosophy, all psychiatry, all ethics involve this human fact. And so does fiction. If fiction begins in daydream, if it springs from the cramp of the world, if it relieves us from the burden of being

ourselves, it ends, if it is good fiction and we are good readers, by returning us to the world and to ourselves. It reconciles us with reality.

31 Let us pause to take stock. Thus far what we have said sounds as though fiction were a combination of opium addiction, religious conversion without tears, a home course in philosophy and the poor man's psychoanalysis. But it is not; it is fiction.

32 It is only itself, and that *itself* is not, in the end, a mere substitute for for anything else. It is an art—an image of experience formed in accordance with its own laws of imaginative enactment, laws which, as we have seen, conform to our deep needs. It is an "illusion of life" projected through language, and the language is that of some individual man projecting his own feeling of life.

33 The story, in the fictional sense, is not something that exists of and by itself, out in the world like a stone or a tree. The materials of stories —certain events or characters, for example—may exist out in the world, but they are not fictionally meaningful to us until a human mind has shaped them. We are, in other words, like the princess in one of Hans Christian Andersen's tales; she refuses her suitor when she discovers that the bird with a ravishing song which he has offered as a token of love is only a real bird after all. We, like the princess, want an artificial bird—an artificial bird with a real song. So we go to fiction because it is a *created* thing.

34 Because it is created by a man, it draws us, as human beings, by its human significance. To begin with, it is an utterance, in words. No words, no story. This seems a fact so obvious, and so trivial, as not to be worth the saying, but it is of fundamental importance in the appeal fiction has for us. We are creatures of words, and if we did not have words we would have no inner life. Only because we have words can we envisage and think about experience. We find our human nature through words. So in one sense we may say that insofar as the language of the story enters into the expressive whole of the story we find the deep satisfaction, conscious or unconscious, of a fulfillment of our very nature.

35 As an example of the relation of words, of style, to the expressive whole which is fiction, let us take Hemingway. We readily see how the stripped, laconic, monosyllabic style relates to the tight-lipped, stoical ethic, the cult of self-discipline, the physicality and the anti-intellectualism and the other such elements that enter into his characteristic view of the world. Imagine Henry James writing Hemingway's story *The Killers*. The complicated sentence structure of James, the deliberate and subtle rhythms, the careful parentheses—all these things express the delicate intellectual, social and aesthetic discriminations with which James concerned himself. But what in the Lord's name would they have to do with the shocking blankness of the moment when the gangsters enter the lunchroom, in their tight-buttoned identical blue overcoats, with gloves on their hands so as to leave no fingerprints when they kill the Swede?

36 The style of a writer represents his stance toward experience, toward the subject of his story; and it is also the very flesh of our experience of the story, for it is the flesh of our experience as we read. Only through his use of words does the story come to us. As with language, so with

the other aspects of a work of fiction. Everything there — the proportioning of plot, the relations among the characters, the logic of motivation, the speed or retardation of the movement — is formed by a human mind into what it is, into what, if the fiction is successful, is an expressive whole, a speaking pattern, a form. And in recognizing and participating in this form, we find a gratification, though often an unconscious one, as fundamental as any we have mentioned.

37   We get a hint of the fundamental nature of this gratification in the fact that among primitive peoples decorative patterns are developed long before the first attempts to portray the objects of nature, even those things on which the life of the tribe depended. The pattern images a rhythm of life and intensifies the tribesman's sense of life.

38   Or we find a similar piece of evidence in psychological studies made of the response of children to comic books. "It is not the details of development," the researchers tell us, "but rather the general aura which the child finds fascinating." What the child wants is the formula of the accelerating buildup of tension followed by the glorious release when the righteous Superman appears just in the nick of time. What the child wants, then, is a certain "shape" of experience. Is his want, at base, different from our own?

39   At base, no. But if the child is satisfied by a nearly abstract pattern for the feeings of tenderness and release, we demand much more. We, too, in the build and shape of experience, catch the echo of the basic rhythm of our life. But we know that the world is infinitely more complicated than the child thinks. We, unlike the child, must scrutinize the details of development, the contents of life and of fiction. So the shaping of experience to satisfy us must add to the simplicity that satisfies the child something of the variety, roughness, difficulty, subtlety and delight which belongs to the actual business of life and our response to it. We want the factual richness of life absorbed into the pattern so that content and form are indistinguishable in one expressive flowering in the process that John Dewey says takes "life and experience in all its uncertainties, mystery, doubt and half-knowledge and turns that experience upon itself to deepen and intensify its own qualities." Only then will it satisfy our deepest need — the need of feeling our life to be, in itself, significant.

Discussion of Theme

1. What does Warren say is the difference between our own daydreams and fiction? What is "the double game" that we play when we read?
2. How does role-taking as we read fiction lead us to an awareness of others? How does it enable us to understand ourselves better?
3. Do you believe that people can learn more about life and about other people by reading nonfiction instead of fiction?
4. Why do you read fiction? Is conflict really the center of life?
5. How can something made up from the imagination be a serious comment on the actual world?

Discussion of Rhetoric

1. Is the author dealing in stereotypes in paragraphs 6 and 10? Is this deliberate or only incidental to his purpose? Does "little freshman" (paragraph 10) imply a patronizing attitude on Warren's part? Why does he describe students in this way?
2. What is Warren's definition of a story?
3. What is the implication of "prison yard" in the first sentence of paragraph 16? Do you regard this as appropriate?
4. Explain the allusion in the final sentence of paragraph 19.
5. This is a well-organized essay; the opening of almost every paragraph is an example of good transition. Find several examples and comment on how Warren connects paragraphs.

Writing Assignments

1. What novel(s) have you read that clarified the meaning of your own life for you? How did the book(s) accomplish this?
2. If you enjoy daydreaming, describe some of your daydreams. What useful purpose do daydreams serve? What harm can excessive daydreaming do?
3. If you believe that people can learn more from films than from novels, explain your reasons.

Library Exploration

1. Read James Thurber's *The Secret Life of Walter Mitty*.
2. Read and report on one of Warren's novels.

Vocabulary

(3) AMBIVALENT having contradictory attitudes toward a person, object, or action
(3) DROWSE doze
(6) POIGNANTLY touchingly
(6) ARDENT passionate
(12) REPREHENSIBLE deserving of rebuke
(12) INDULGENCE yielding to a desire
(16) OUBLIETTES dungeons with only a trapdoor in the ceiling
(16) COMES A CROPPER falls headlong; fails disastrously
(16) NIGH-DOUSED nearly quenched
(18) CONFRONTATIONS encounters

(19) PARADOXICAL contradictory
(21) GRATUITOUS uncalled for (often unwanted)
(22) RUCK jumble
(22) IMMINENT about to happen
(26) EXTENUATION partial justification
(26) SURROGATE substitute
(29) OSCILLATION swinging back and forth
(35) LACONIC sparing of words
(35) STOICAL showing indifference to pleasure or pain
(36) RETARDATION slowing down
(38) AURA atmosphere

Other Peoples, Other Places

8

Eugene Burdick (1918–65) successfully combined two careers: professor of political theory at the University of California at Berkeley, and author and co-author of several best-selling novels. After receiving degrees from Stanford and Oxford universities, Burdick served in the U.S. Navy during World War II, earning the Navy-Marine Corps Cross. He was the author of television plays, motion picture scripts, and magazine articles. He received greatest acclaim, however, for "The Ugly American" (with William Lederer, 1958), and "Fail-Safe" (with Harvey Wheeler, 1962).

Burdick's essay, taken from "The Blue of Capricorn" (1961), will serve as an antidote to those who have a romanticized or idealized version of Polynesia.

EUGENE BURDICK

The Polynesian

1   There is one fragment of the Pacific the American believes he knows
well: Polynesia. He may not be quite certain of Sumatra and Min-
danao or the difference between a *prau* and a gin pahit, but Polynesia
he knows. This is the South Seas, Paradise, the Sunny Isles. It is a
place of soft winds, surfboards and outriggers, the pink bulk of the
Royal Hawaiian Hotel, the scent of flowers. It is a place where beachcombers, defiantly drunken but still white and superior, watch their
vahines swim in the waves. In some haunting subtle way a vision of
Polynesia creeps into the knowledge of all Americans, a vision flaw-
less and jeweled. In Polynesia the defects of America are magically
eliminated. The place is warm and sunny. It glows.

2   My first hint of Polynesia came when I was fourteen. I went to
a carnival in Los Angeles which had a side show called South Sea

Mysteries. A deeply tanned girl, wearing a grass skirt made of red cellophane, a flashy artificial lei around her neck and a sequined bra, stepped out through a canvas flap. On the canvas behind the girl were painted brilliant green coconut trees and a circle of nipa huts. As the barker began to talk the girl did the hula. I was mesmerized. I had never seen anything so softly carnal.

3   "Step right in and see the ancient love dance of the old Hawaiian chiefs," the barker chanted. "There was a time when the eyes of commoners were torn out if they saw this dance, and you can see it it for exactly two bits."

4   My attention swung back to the girl. As a hidden phonograph played "My Little Grass Shack," her hands formed a shack, fish swimming, a moon rising, lovers embracing. She was very good, although I did not know it at the time. Her head was level, her feet never left the floor, her haunches undulated. She was erotic but restrained. She gave the impression of being virginal, but also wanton, which was exactly her purpose. I ignored the fact that her tan began to dissolve under the harsh Los Angeles sun and ran down her face in brown drops.

5   That day I was hooked by the South Seas or Polynesia or whatever the barker and the girl and the cheap tent stood for. I had a neat, precise and colorful vision of what it was like. There would be tiny clean islands, ringed with white sand and blue surf, and the air would be warm. In this vision the people were somewhat vague, but they would be lithe, brown, carefree, and they would dance. I didn't know then that millions of other Americans were experiencing exactly the same emotion, as the hula craze and movies like *Bird of Paradise* and a few score Hawaiian bands spread the vision broad and wide.

6   A cold and ununderstanding world kept me from leaving at once for the South Seas, so I turned to the library. The vision grew deeper. In Melville's *Typee* I read for the first time of Fayaway, who became the model for endless South Sea heroines: abandonedly voluptuous, a skin "the color of *cafe au lait*," a magnificent figure, a slightly fey and doomed look about the eyes, possessed of a deep tribal wisdom that shone through her eyes. In all the books, this beautiful stereotype gave herself willingly to the white man although she knew it would end in tragedy.

7   Lord Byron, something of a connoisseur of women and of love, wrote a book called *The Island* and made it clear that natural passions could have full expression in these exotic islands. Diderot, the famous French encyclopedist, wrote a rhapsodic book on Polynesia and argued that the "natural" life was far superior to "civilization." I needed no persuading. I plowed through novels, scientific treatises, biographies of missionaries, good writing and bad writing. It was all like diamond dust against a dull jewel: it ground my vision to a lapidary brightness.

8   Later I was to learn that Melville knew more about whales than about women, that Byron had never been to the South Seas, that Diderot had blantantly fictionalized the voyages of Bougainville. I was also to encounter the numerous works of the professional, nerve-

less, hard-eyed debunkers of Polynesia. None of this made any difference to me, nor, apparently, does it make any difference to most
others who go to Polynesia. The rebuffs, the savage letdowns, the hard
surprises are many, but seldom is the original vision altered. Indeed,
in a strange way, the foreigner's vision of Polynesia has come to trans-
form the reality of the place.

9   Of the hard knocks and surprises which the innocent may expect in
Polynesia, first is the low-pressure shock of its simple vastness. Spread
out a Mercator map and draw a triangle with Hawaii, Easter Island
and New Zealand at the three points. The sides will measure 4500 and
4500 and 4800 miles. Polynesia means many islands, but they are
tiny fragments scattered through this Pacific immensity. All the islands
of southwest Polynesia, taken together whose archipelagoes like the
Marquesas and the Australs and the Cooks, have less land area than
the single island of Hawaii.

10   This is one of the great empty spaces of the world. The huge sea
plains stretch away endlessly, identical, heaving, changing color but
not shape. The heat is solid and uncompromising. When you come
upon an island, an unbelievable lost speck, you ache for it to be beautiful. It usually is although not always in the languorous white sand
and coral reef tradition. On Nukuhiva in the Marquesas, for example,
there are sheer cliffs at the water's edge which rise over a thousand
feet and there are also canyons with walls so steep that one must go
by sea from valley to valley. Moorea is beautiful in a monumental,
craggy, cold-blue manner. And there are some atolls which are bare
and ugly . . . but not many. The high islands are a surprise to the
Western eye, but a pleasant one.

11   Once ashore you will have a job finding a pure-blooded Polynesian.
When you do it will be a shock, especially if it is a woman. She has a
short jaw: her body is squat and turns to fat rather early. If she is a
fa'a Samoa type her feet will be big, callused and tough. It is true
that her hair is black and lustrous and her skin is close enough to café
au lait so that she can sunburn, but her body is designed for work, not
for dancing. There is something solid, down to earth, almost utilitarian
about the Polynesian woman and the tiare behind her ear and the
limpidity of her eyes cannot disguise it.

12   You are suddenly aware that you have seen this woman before — in
the pictures of Gauguin. He was ruthlessly realistic. The heavy-jawed,
squat, bent women of his pictures are not a trick of Impressionism,
they are simple reality. The kind of lithe, slim Fayaway beauty is
very rare among pure Polynesians.

13   There is another subtly disturbing thing about Polynesian anatomy.
I discovered it when I approached a Marquesan reef on which a group
of men and women were searching for shellfish. The sun, as always
in the tropics, went down abruptly but there was a moment of intense
purple light. The figures on the reef turned black — and sexless. I
could not tell women from men.

14   Later I learned this was a common experience among newcomers to
Polynesia. There is a softness of line, a blurring of body distinctions.
Both sexes have the same long swimmer's muscles, both walk in the

same way, there is an absence of the vigorous gestures we ascribe to males, and the women do not develop the protective mannerisms we associate with femininity.

15   This is not to imply that Polynesian women lack beauty. Their beauty is of a different kind: a blending of gait and proud bearing, an aura of autonomy, lips that can form into a pout or the most spontaneous of laughs, a body which somehow does not value sleekness but promises almost too much competence in love-making. Gauguin put it well when writing of one of his models and lovers: "She was not at all handsome according to our aesthetic rules. She was beautiful."

16   There is one word which, in all of its shades and meanings, catches the sense of the Old Way Polynesia and much of the Polynesia now conquered by The Beach. It is the word "simple." There is a great simplicity in the lust of Polynesians for gambling and the cunning with which they can make a gamble of almost anything. They do not gamble as Chinese or Americans gamble; they gamble with a wild plunging abandon, with no sense of probability or odds. Win or lose, they give the same grin. There is also simplicity in the quite unconscious cruelty which Polynesians display toward animals. They will run a horse to a lathering death. A dog with a fishhook caught in its foot will be an object of laughter. I do not recall ever having seen a Polynesian pet a dog or give it food. The dog scavenges for itself.

17   At the same time you can spend weeks in a crowded Polynesian village and not hear a child cry. When it does the closest woman will instantly sweep it up and comfort it. In many dialects the word for "mother" covers almost every female relative and the child will be treated by any of these women with the warmness that we reserve only for our own children.

18   In all of Polynesia there is almost no artistic inventiveness. Rather there is a simple repetition of old designs. Tapa cloths, pandanus mats and seashell necklaces are often done in beautiful patterns, but the patterns are ancient, the outgrowth of timeless trial and error. When asked to invent, to create, to experiment in color, the Polynesian is uncomprehending. When given the choice between a magnificiently muted tapa cloth and a garnish Manchester calico the Polynesian will take the calico and explain his choice: "I like the red. It is prettier. The tapa is dull." This is simplicity itself.

19   The only working artist I know of in Polynesia is Agnes Teepee, the *vahine* of Don Carlos García-Palacios, a Chilean of the most exquisite sensitivities. Agnes paints big bold abstract paintings which are usually suggestive of tropical plants or the reef or the underwater life. Other Tahitians study her work with the most profound boredom until they can spot something in the painting which is recognizable . . . a sea anemone, a tiare, the eye of a shark. Then they will walk away satisfied. They seem quite incapable of understanding an abstract notion. They are literal minded in an almost rigid sense.

20   There is also a vast simplicity in the way the Polynesian regards youth. The Westerner looks back on youth with a terrible urge to recapture it, to possess it, to imitate it. The Polynesian regards youth more kindly, more benignly. I have never heard a Polynesian express the desire to be young again. He folds gracefully into each phase of

life knowing it is inevitable. He remembers youth not as something lost but something he once enjoyed. An ancient will look at Polynesian youth with the languid tolerant eyes of a lion regarding a litter of frisking cubs. They arouse no envy, no curiosity, no puritanical impulse to inhibit or reform.

21   This simplicity extends to the sex act and explains a basic misunderstanding between the Westerner and the Polynesian. To the Westerner, sex is a dramatic, committing, involving, often frightening thing. For the Polynesian it is a simple matter; as simple as eating or swimor a prayer or an argument. It need not have consequences. It can be an isolated moment of pleasure. The moment remains discrete, holding no potential of guilt, no web of obligations, no need to murmur love words.

22   Bengt Danielsson, who has lived in Polynesia for many years, states that a casual meeting between a Tahitian boy or girl always leads to intercourse. Only two conditions need exist: a bit of privacy and sure knowledge that the boy and girl are not related. In fa'a Polynesia adolescents often spent their nights together in a separate building where the older children gave sexual instructions to the younger. The language of young children when translated literally would make the brain of even the most progressive parent reel. But the sexual words and phrases are used with no desire to shock and never as swear words. The missionaries have ended the common sex huts but have made almost no inroads into the casualness with which sex is treated.

23   There are some exceptions. In a few Polynesian societies virginity is highly prized and in the fa'a days it was always assumed that female aristocrats would marry as virgins. The deflowering was done publicly by one of the older chiefs from the bridegroom's clan. If blood did not flow the girl's father would smash in her head with a club. Today this kind of behavior is not expected of aristocrats.

24   There are still islands on which the wedding is celebrated by allowing all of the male guests that desire it to have intercourse with the bride. Many a popular bride comes through such an experience half dead from fatigue and takes weeks to recover.

25   One day my wife was sitting on a beach outside of Papeete while I was skin diving. A net fisherman, a big attractive man of about twenty-five, was working the water close to the shore. Perhaps my wife looked lonely. In any case she was alone. The fisherman walked over and said hello to her in French.

26   "Would you like to make love?" he asked, without any introductory remarks and in a very gentle voice. "I know a place just behind these trees."

27   My wife explained that she was waiting for me to come in from skin diving. He looked out toward the reef and then back at my wife.

28   "He may be out there for hours," he said simply.

29   My wife still declined. He was not the least offended. He pointed out the private place beyond the trees in case we should like to use it. Then he went back to his fishing.

30   During the nineteenth century a whole literature developed around the dewy-eyed and innocent South Seas maiden who was seduced by the white man and then abandoned to a life of misery and regret.

This was based on a misreading of Polynesian character. First, the girl was not abandoned; she had the family, the tribe, the island to return to. Secondly, she did not put as much into the affair as the white man imagined — she could not, it was a psychological impossibility. Sex does not mean this to the Polynesian. Thirdly, there was no misery to the situation as such. An individual white *tane* (man) might be miserable to live with but his Polynesian vahine could not be made miserable simply because she had lived with him. Once over, the affair continued only in the tortured imagination of the white man.

31   The girl can be rapt and devoted to a lover, her simplicity and dignity can even be exciting. But what disconcerts the Westerner is to learn that he may well be one of a series of lovers, that he has not bitten deep into her soul, that she does not and cannot see him as the "only" man.

32   After a time this knowledge, so directly counter to our puritanical, high-pitched and intense attitude toward sex, can make white men miserable. They long to make the relationship more tense and involved. For the Polynesian woman this is impossible. She does not know how to become involved and desperate. The act of love-making in Polynesia is much different from the elaborate love-making of Europe and America. There is very little kissing or caressing, very little concern for a simultaneous climax. It is what the Polynesians call "Maori love" as opposed to the white man's form of love. It is quick, silent and often brutal. At the climax a Polynesian couple will often scratch one another's faces and during one of the day-long feasts called *tamaaraa* a particularly attractive girl may go into the bushes with fifteen or twenty men and have welts on her face for days afterwards. The substitute for what white marriage counselors call "foreplay" is the dance. It is the most directly sexual dance in the world. There is no disguising its intention nor its effect. It is meant to be provocative and stimulating and it is.

33   Another facet of the Polynesian simplicity is recklessness. For example, every time a tidal wave strikes the Hawaiian Islands a number of lives are lost unnecessarily. The tidal wave is always preceeded by a powerful outward suck of the ocean which leaves reefs and harbor floors suddenly exposed, fish flopping widly, sandbars steaming in the sun. The Hawaiians cannot resist flocking out onto the reefs, laughing wildly, grabbing for free fish — although they know that in a few moments a wall of water will come sweeping in. When the horizon suddenly tilts skyward and a gray line rises suddenly, they turn and scramble for the beach, roaring with laughter. The silent inexorable rush of the vast wave always traps a few, but despite the keening and wailing for the lost ones, no one thinks of staying away when the next tidal wave comes.

34   Simplicity also embodies a thin red thread of cruelty, childlike indifference to pain in others. Polynesia is no exception. When Captain Cook's death was avenged by a savage bombardment of a Hawaiian town, the native girls on board clapped their hands with delight, shouted *maitai* — "very fine" — enjoyed the pyrotechnic display which was destroying their friends and families.

35   In fa'a Samoa, chiefs often ticked off a subject to be buried alive at the base of each corner post of a new royal residence. Records indicate that the victims grinned up wolfishly as the pole came crashing down on them, and that their families roared wildly and went on with the festivities. Prisoners were often bound tightly with tinder-dry coconut fronds and then set alight, and the whole village watched as the human torch ran desperately for the sea. If he made it, fine; if he did not, the first step in preparing the body for a feast had been taken.

36   In most of Polynesia, The Beach has won a solid victory over the Old Way. Indeed, the victory was won long ago and today it is almost impossible to find a pure Polynesian or an undiluted practice of the Old Way. In some islands the Old Way has virtually vanished, but somehow, in a way which is not clear to anyone, the flavor of the South Seas still comes through. Nowhere is the mystery more puzzling than in Honolulu. By any act of sympathetic interpretation it is not an especially attractive place. The outskirts are ringed with junkyards, used-car lots, small factories and warehouses. The center of the city is badly planned, crowded, noisy, spangled with neon lights. Tract housing crawls hideously up the green mountains and disappears into the perpetual fogs of the Pali. The hotels of Waikiki are international style — tall, sleek, concrete. Enormously tall and enormously profitable, they age quickly in the soft climate, but they will be there forever. The visitor could be in Miami or Dallas or Los Angeles. But somehow the magic of the place still works, and thousands of tourists return to the mainland with the glazed eyes of those who have seen Paradise. Nothing that land developers and commercial bad taste do can destroy two things: the trade winds and the Pacific. The place may be conventional and ordinary, but the soft warm wind and the sparkling sea are there. Apparently they are enough.

37   The "outer islands" of Hawaii, such as Maui and Kauai, and the Big Island are infinitely more attractive than Honolulu, but most tourists stay riveted to Waikiki. Eventually they will move to the outer islands, but right now they are content to gaze mesmerized at the rhythmic sweep of the waves, drink exotic mixtures of rum and fresh pineapple and floating orchids and enjoy the trades. Nowhere is the vision of Polynesia more distorted, stifled and lacquered. But enough is still there to satisfy the American urge to "see the South Seas."

38   Once the traveler leaves Honolulu and moves southward to the Marquesas or Tuamotus or Tahiti or Samoa, the victory of The Beach is less visible, but it is still substantial. There are no slick intercontinental hotels, but there are tin roofs among the coconut thatch. It is true that the most desired import is canned meat (followed by flour, sugar, tobacco and piece goods), but one can still eat a magnificent Old Way meal of broiled fish, a curry of shrimp and octopus and sea snail, breadfruit and a dessert of cool juicy fruits picked from nearby trees. Beachcombers are few and far between, but in Quinn's Bar in Tahiti, for a few francs, you can take a picture of Emile Gauguin, the fat and idle son of Paul Gauguin. It is true that many nipa huts will have a foot-operated Singer sewing machine and an old Victor phonograph, but they will also have the softly beautiful pandanus mats. You will also

see jeep springs used as coconut scrapers and watch native skin divers come up from the depths wearing American diving goggles. But push deeper into the bush, or sail to an island that is the least bit isolated, and at once the lacquer is gone. The mark of The Beach is there, but it is still blurred, still faint.

39   In many ways The Beach has made the reality of Polynesia more like a vision. Take the matter of feminine beauty. As the Polynesian began to intermarry with Chinese, Australians, Portuguese, Americans, Japanese and others, an odd change occurred. The pudgy, squat, waistless girl began to be replaced by a mestizo of more elegant features, a molded jaw, slimmer legs and slighter build. Today throughout Polynesia there is an amazing incidence of girls who possess the beauty invented by Melville's imagination. The fevered men who went to the South Seas inspired by the nineteenth-century vision were probably disappointed, but their visits guaranteed that future generations of Polynesian women would look hauntingly like Fayaway.

40   The vision which the white man took to Polynesia also worked wonders with the hula. In cold fact the hula of the Old Way was a shambling, dreary, and very boring dance which went on for hours, a low-grade folk dance performed to the beat of sticks on hollow logs. Even the missionaries found little to remark in it except its tedium. At the same time Polynesia had a courtship dance which was brutal, direct and highly erotic. It was danced infrequently, but few who witnessed it forgot it.

41   It was the genius or the curse or the bland ignorance of The Beach that it modified both these dances and blended them. The result is the modern Hawaiian hula, softly sexual but not violent. It is danced to steel guitars and ukuleles and almost any other kind of instrument. It is, by any standard, a great improvement over the original version, and perhaps more important, it is infinitely more compatible with the soft languorous version of the South Seas. But be prepared for the fact that outside of Hawaii the Hawaiian hula is regarded as a joke. In the Tuamotus and Marquesas and Tahiti the hula is danced the old way. The only time the tamed Hawaiian version is danced is to satirize it. The waving graceful hand motions of the Hawaiian hula will send a group of Polynesians into gales of laughter.

42   Some aspects of Polynesian life are so deeply rooted that The Beach has not affected them at all. One is always aware, for example, that these are an oceanic people. For Westerners the ocean has an ageless thin edge of danger to it. One sees this in the doleful faces of the wives of Portuguese fishermen and the resignation of seamen shipping out of San Francisco. For us the sea is stern, possessed of Calvinistic finality.

43   The Polynesian regards the ocean differently. He loves it. He knows it can be dangerous, but the danger is Olympian, capricious, zestful. A man has a chance against it. The Polynesians will tease the sea, take enormous chances, challenge it to the very edge of impudence.

44   Even the Hawaiians, who have received the fiercest onslaught of softening Western ways, still possess this calculated recklessness. One place they show it is at Makapuu Beach on the windward side of Oahu. The entrance to the beach is flanked by signs which say, "Dan-

ger. Heavy Under-Tow. Off-Limits to Service Personnel." On storm days the wave trains come in with an awesome, towering regularity. They are gray and low at the horizon, but rise to enormous heights as the bottom shoals and turn a bitter green before they dissolve into smoky water. The crash of water is so solid that, standing on the beach, you can feel it as a tiny shock in your teeth.

45   I went body-surfing at Makapuu with two Hawaiian friends and it was not until we were past the surf line and treading water and waiting for a "big one" that I realized what they intended. Body-surfing is a much more intricate art than surfboarding, because you must catch the wave at exactly the right point, arch your shoulders exactly right, and if you know the art, shoot in to the beach with your body out well in front of the wave. Once mastered, it is not particularly dangerous. But what my companions proposed to do was to ride the storm waves directly toward an outcropping of rock and coral against which the waves shattered themselves into the maddest spume I had ever seen. The trick, they patiently explained, was to duck out of the wave just before it hit the rocks, dive deep to escape the turbulence and swim underwater back toward the surf line. It called for exquisite timing.

46   They demonstrated for me a few times. Just as the wave was about to shatter on the rocks I saw their feet flash into the air, their bottoms rolled forward and they disappeared. A half-minute later their heads popped to the surface just beyond the churning white water.

47   I could not do it. Technically I understood what had to be done, and I have surfed a good deal. But I did not view the ocean as they did. What they were doing struck me as a kind of insanity. To launch oneself at forty miles an hour, in the grip of a huge wave, directly at a wall of hard rock and coral was beyond my Westernized capacity. In the end I took the long safe glide into the sandy beach.

48   The Polynesian, on the other hand, has a highly developed skill at sliding neatly by those parts of white culture which bore, stifle or restrain him. He has only the slightest interest in politics. The Malay can become rigid with nationalistic excitement. Polynesians, with the exception of the Maoris, let politics alone. Nor does the Polynesian, merely because he goes to church, really accept the ethical stiffness and content of Western religion. He can understand a chief punishing someone for adultery as a *crime,* as something necessary to maintain a minimum of order. But he cannot see adultery as *sin.* The difference is important. All Polynesian gods are Olympic gods: puckish, capable of mistakes, possessed of human qualities, forgiving, occasionally drunk. The only part of Christian religion which Polynesians understand thoroughly are the Ten Commandments, because they sound very much like Ten Tabus.

49   This shrewd and protective selection of white attitudes is nowhere more obvious than at the movies. I once spent several nights at a hot, tin-roofed, overcrowded theater in Samoa. Each night I saw the same film. So did everyone else in the village. The place steamed with heat, and insects flew like crazy motes up and down the flickering light from the projector. The movie was an ancient Western with a classic cast of good guys, bad guys, fair damsels and wicked Indians.

50   The audience ignored every scene except those that involved shooting, drinking or kissing. In a long dull scene they called on the local
Don Juan to tell of his latest exploits. He was reluctant, but he was
persuaded. He stood in the aisle and did a bawdy hula and recited his
prowess. I was later told that he delicately left out the names of his
amours, but the audience gleefully chanted them out. In mid-gesture
an Indian appeared on the screen and the Samoan buck dropped into
his seat like a man shot. Every eye swung back to the movie, the sound
of the insects rose in the silence. At the end of the film, when the cow-
boy hero kissed his girl modestly on the cheek, the entire audience
rose and chanted out a piece of Samoan advice which described in
explicit detail what a man should do with a girl in such circumstances.

51   Other audiences in the Pacific will sit frozen in their seats, absorbing
every scene, never laughing, enraptured by the study of a life that
might be theirs in the future. The air is dense with thought, with a
sense of desire. They leave with a sigh. In Polynesia the audience is
irreverent, bawdy, Hogarthian, and there is not the slightest indication
of desire for "the American way of life."

52   The currents of Western thought are swirling over the vast sun-
drenched Pacific. In some places they have dissolved the Old Way
forever. In other places they have made only the slightest impression.
But wherever The Beach makes itself felt, it is also subtly transformed,
softened by the climate and the vast distances. One has the dim, but
sure, knowledge that the capacity of the Pacific to resist is nearly
infinite, like the reaches of its water.

E. B. White (1899–   ) is best known through the collections of his familiar essays. After his graduation from Cornell University, White began his career as a reporter; he later became contributing editor to "The New Yorker" and "Harper's." He is the author of "Is Sex Necessary?" (with James Thurber, 1929), "One Man's Meat" (1942), and "The Second Tree from the Corner" (1953), as well as children's stories ("Stuart Little" and "Charlotte's Web") and numerous essays.

At first reading, this is a nostalgic description of childhood vacations; yet the reader is left with the uneasy feeling that it is more than just that.

E. B. WHITE

Once More to the Lake

AUGUST, 1941

1   One summer, along about 1904, my father rented a camp on a lake in Maine and took us all there for the month of August. We all got ringworm from some kittens and had to rub Pond's Extract on our arms and legs night and morning, and my father rolled over in a canoe with all his clothes on; but outside of that the vacation was a success and from then on none of us ever thought there was any place in the world like that lake in Maine. We returned summer after summer — always on August first for one month. I have since become a salt-water man, but sometimes in summer there are days when the restlessness of the tides and the fearful cold of the sea water and the incessant wind which blows across the afternoon and into the evening make me wish for the placidity of a lake in the woods. A few weeks ago this feeling got so

strong I bought myself a couple of bass hooks and a spinner and returned to the lake where we used to go, for a week's fishing and to
revisit old haunts.

2   I took along my son, who had never had any fresh water up his nose
and who had seen lily pads only from train windows. On the journey
over to the lake I began to wonder what it would be like. I wondered
how time would have marred this unique, this holy spot—the coves
and streams, the hills that the sun set behind, the camps and the paths
behind the camps. I was sure that the tarred road would have found it
out and I wondered in what other ways it would be desolated. It is
strange how much you can remember about places like that once you
allow your mind to return into the grooves which lead back. You remember one thing, and that suddenly reminds you of another thing. I
guess I remember clearest of all the early mornings, when the lake was
cool and motionless, remembered how the bedroom smelled of the
lumber it was made of and of the wet woods whose scent entered
through the screen. The partitions in the camp were thin and did not
extend clear to the top of the rooms, and as I was always the first up I
would dress softly so as not to wake the others and sneak out into the
sweet outdoors and start out in the canoe, keeping close along the
shore in the long shadows of the pines. I remembered being very careful never to rub my paddle against the thwart for fear of disturbing the
stillness of the cathedral.

3   The lake had never been what you would call a wild lake. There
were cottages sprinkled around the shores, and it was in farming country although the shores of the lake were quite heavily wooded. Some
of the cottages were owned by nearby farmers, and you would live at
the shore and eat your meals at the farmhouse. That's what our family
did. But although it wasn't wild, it was a fairly large and undisturbed
lake and there were places in it which, to a child at least, seemed infinitely remote and primeval.

4   I was right about the tar: it led to within half a mile of the shore. But
when I got back there, with my boy, and we settled into a camp near a
farmhouse and into the kind of summertime I had known, I could tell
that it was going to be pretty much the same as it had been before—I
knew it, lying in bed the first morning, smelling the bedroom, and
hearing the boy sneak quietly out and go off along the shore in a boat.
I began to sustain the illusion that he was I, and therefore, by simple
transposition, that I was my father. This sensation persisted, kept cropping up all the time we were there. It was not an entirely new feeling,
but in this setting it grew much stronger. I seemed to be living a dual
existence. I would be in the middle of some simple act, I would be
picking up a bait box or laying down a table fork, or I would be saying
something, and suddenly it would be not I but my father who was saying the words or making the gesture. It gave me a creepy sensation.

5   We went fishing the first morning. I felt the same damp moss covering the worms in the bait can, and saw the dragonfly alight on the tip
of my rod as it hovered a few inches from the surface of the water. It
was the arrival of this fly that convinced me beyond any doubt that
everything was as it always had been, that the years were a mirage
and there had been no years. The small waves were the same, chuck-

ing the rowboat under the chin as we fished at anchor, and the boat was the same boat, the same color green and the ribs broken in the same places, and under the floorboards the same fresh-water leavings and debris—the dead helgramite, the wisps of moss, the rusty discarded fishhook, the dried blood from yesterday's catch. We stared silently at the tips of our rods, at the dragonflies that came and went. I lowered the tip of mine into the water, tentatively, pensively dislodging the fly, which darted two feet away, poised, darted two feet back, and came to rest again a little farther up the rod. There had been no years between the ducking of this dragonfly and the other one—the one that was part of memory. I looked at the boy, who was silently watching his fly, and it was my hands that held his rod, my eyes watching. I felt dizzy and didn't know which rod I was at the end of.

6   We caught two bass, hauling them in briskly as though they were mackerel, pulling them over the side of the boat in a businesslike manner without any landing net, and stunning them with a blow on the back of the head. When we got back for a swim before lunch, the lake was exactly where we had left it, the same number of inches from the dock, and there was only the merest suggestion of a breeze. This seemed an utterly enchanted sea, this lake you could leave to its own devices for a few hours and come back to, and find that it had not stirred, this constant and trustworthy body of water. In the shallows, the dark, water-soaked sticks and twigs, smooth and old, were undulating in clusters on the bottom against the clean ribbed sand, and the track of the mussel was plain. A school of minnows swam by, each minnow with its small individual shadow, doubling the attendance, so clear and sharp in the sunlight. Some of the other campers were in swimming, along the shore, one of them with a cake of soap, and the water felt thin and clear and unsubstantial. Over the years there had been this person with the cake of soap, this cultist, and here he was. There had been no years.

7   Up to the farmhouse to dinner through the teeming, dusty field, the road under our sneakers was only a two-track road. The middle track was missing, the one with the marks of the hooves and the splotches of dried, flaky manure. There had always been three tracks to choose from in choosing which track to walk in; now the choice was narrowed down to two. For a moment I missed terribly the middle alternative. But the way led past the tennis court, and something about the way it lay there in the sun reassured me; the tape had loosened along the backline, the alleys were green with plantains and other weeds, and the net (installed in June and removed in September) sagged in the dry noon, and the whole place steamed with midday heat and hunger and emptiness. There was a choice of pie for dessert, and one was blueberry and one was apple, and the waitresses were the same country girls, there having been no passage of time, only the illusion of it as in a dropped curtain—the waitresses were still fifteen; their hair had been washed, that was the only difference—they had been to the movies and seen the pretty girls with the clean hair.

8   Summertime, oh summertime, pattern of life indelible, the fade-proof lake, the woods unshatterable, the pasture with the sweet-fern and the juniper forever and ever, summer without end; this was the

background, and the life along the shore was the design, the cottages with their innocent and tranquil design, their tiny docks with the flag-pole and the American flag floating against the white clouds in the blue sky, the little paths over the roots of the trees leading from camp to camp and the paths leading back to the outhouses and the can of lime for sprinkling, and at the souvenir counters at the store the minia-ture birch-bark canoes and the post cards that showed things looking a little better than they looked. This was the American family at play, escaping the city heat, wondering whether the newcomers in the camp at the head of the cove were "common" or "nice," wondering whether it was true that the people who drove up for Sunday dinner at the farmhouse were turned away because there wasn't enough chicken.

9   It seemed to me, as I kept remembering all this, that those times and those summers had been infinitely precious and worth saving. There had been jollity and peace and goodness. The arriving (at the beginning of August) had been so big a business in itself, at the rail-way station the farm wagon drawn up, the first smell of the pine-laden air, the first glimpse of the smiling farmer, and the great importance of the trunks and your father's enormous authority in such matters, and the feel of the wagon under you for the long ten-mile haul, and at the top of the last long hill catching the first view of the lake after eleven months of not seeing this cherished body of water. The shouts and cries of the other campers when they saw you, and the trunks to be unpacked, to give up their rich burden. (Arriving was less exciting nowadays, when you sneaked up in your car and parked it under a tree near the camp and took out the bags and in five minutes it was all over, no fuss, no loud wonderful fuss about trunks.)

10   Peace and goodness and jollity. The only thing that was wrong now, really, was the sound of the place, an unfamiliar nervous sound of the outboard motors. This was the note that jarred, the one thing that would sometimes break the illusion and set the years moving. In those other summertimes, all the motors were inboard; and when they were at a little distance, the noise they made was a sedative, an ingredient of summer sleep. They were one-cylinder and two-cylinder engines, and some were make-and-break and some were jump-spark, but they all made a sleepy sound across the lake. The one-lungers throbbed and fluttered, and the twin-cylinder ones purred and purred, and that was a quiet sound too. But now the campers all had outboards. In the daytime, in the hot mornings, these motors made a petulant, irritable sound; at night, in the still evening when the afterglow lit the water, they whined about one's ears like mosquitoes. My boy loved our rented outboard, and his great desire was to achieve singlehanded mastery over it, and authority, and he soon learned the trick of choking it a little (but not too much), and the adjustment of the needle valve. Watching him I would remember the things you could do with the old one-cylinder engine with the heavy flywheel, how you could have it eating out of your hand if you got really close to it spiritually. Motor boats in those days didn't have clutches, and you made a landing by shutting off the motor at the proper time and coasting in with a dead rudder. But there was a way of reversing them, if you learned the trick, by cutting the switch and putting it on again exactly on the final dying

revolution of the flywheel, so that it would kick back against compression and begin reversing. Approaching a dock in a strong following breeze it was difficult to slow up sufficiently by the ordinary coasting method, and if a boy felt he had complete mastery over his motor, he was tempted to keep it running beyond its time and then reverse it a few feet from the dock. It took a cool nerve, because if you threw the switch a twentieth of a second too soon you would catch the flywheel when it still had speed enough to go up past center, and the boat would leap ahead, charging bull-fashion at the dock.

11   We had a good week at camp. The bass were biting well and the sun shone endlessly, day after day. We would be tired at night and lie down in the accumulated heat of the little bedrooms after the long hot day and the breeze would stir almost imperceptibly outside and the smell of the swamp drift in through the rusty screens. Sleep would come easily and in the morning the red squirrel would be on the roof, tapping out his gay routine. I kept remembering everything, lying in the bed in the morning — the small steamboat that had a long rounded stern like the lip of a Ubangi, and how quietly she ran on the moonlight sails, when the older boys played their mandolins and the girls sang and we ate doughnuts dipped in sugar, and how sweet the music was on the water in the shining night, and what it had felt like to think about girls then. After breakfast we would go up to the store and the things were in the same place — the minnows in a bottle, the plugs and spinners disarranged and pawed over by the youngsters from the boys' camp, the fig newtons and the Beeman's gum. Outside, the road was tarred and cars stood in front of the store. Inside, all was just as it had always been, except there was more Coca Cola and not so much Moxie and root beer and birch beer and sarsaparilla. We would walk out with a bottle of pop apiece and sometimes the pop would backfire up our noses and hurt. We explored the streams, quietly, where the turtles slid off the sunny logs and dug their way into the soft bottom; and we lay on the town wharf and fed worms to the tame bass. Everywhere we went I had trouble making out which was I, the one walking at my side, the one walking in my pants.

12   One afternoon while we were there at that lake a thunderstorm came up. It was like the revival of an old melodrama that I had seen long ago with childish awe. The second-act climax of the drama of the electrical disturbance over a lake in America had not changed in any important respect. This was the big scene, still the big scene. The whole thing was so familiar, the first feeling of oppression and heat and a general air around camp of not wanting to go very far away. In mid-afternoon (it was all the same) a curious darkening of the sky, and a lull in everything that had made life tick; and then the way the boats suddenly swung the other way at their moorings with the coming of a breeze out of the new quarter, and the premonitory rumble. Then the kettle drum, then the snare, then the bass drum and cymbals, then crackling light against the dark, and the gods grinning and licking their chops in the hills. Afterward the calm, the rain steadily rustling in the calm lake, the return of light and hope and spirits, and the campers running out in joy and relief to go swimming in the rain, their bright cries perpetuating the deathless joke about how they were getting

simply drenched, and the children screaming with delight at the new sensation of bathing in the rain, and the joke about getting drenched linking the generations in a strong indestructible chain. And the comedian who waded in carrying an umbrella.

13   When the others went swimming my son said he was going in too. He pulled his dripping trunks from the line where they had hung all through the shower, and wrung them out. Languidly, and with no thought of going in, I watched him, his hard little body, skinny and bare, saw him wince slightly as he pulled up around his vitals the small, soggy, icy garment. As he buckled the swollen belt suddenly my groin felt the chill of death.

Alexander H. Leighton (1908–
), professor of social psychiatry at Cornell University and
author of several articles and
textbooks in that field, received
his training at Princeton, Cambridge, and Johns Hopkins universities. He has done fieldwork
in anthropology among the
Navaho Indians and the Eski-
mos of Alaska.

The pain and horror of "that
day" at Hiroshima are re-cre-
ated by Leighton, who visited
Japan as a research leader of
the United States Strategic
Bombing Survey of Japan.

ALEXANDER H. LEIGHTON

That Day at Hiroshima

1   We approached Hiroshima a little after daybreak on a winter day,
driving in a jeep below a leaden sky and in the face of a cold, wet wind.
On either side of the road, black felt fields were turning green under
winter wheat. Here and there peasants worked, swinging spades or
grubbing in mud and water with blue hands. Some in black split-
toed shoes left tracks like cloven hoofs. To the north, looming close
over the level land, mountains thrust heavy summits of pine darkly
against the overcast. To the south and far away, the bay lay in dull
brightness under fitful rain.

2   "Hiroshima," said the driver, a GI from a Kansas farm, who had
been through the city many times, "don't look no different from any
other bombed town. You soon get used to it. You'll see little old mud
walls right in the middle of town that wasn't knocked down. They been
exaggerating about that bomb."

3   Within a few miles the fields along the road were replaced by houses
and shops that looked worn and dull yet intact. On the road itself
people straggled to work, some on bicycles, most of them on foot—

tattered and bandy-legged old men, girls with red cheeks and bright eyes, ancient women under towering bundles, middle-aged men looking stiff in Western business suits. In one place there were several Koreans together, the women easily distinguished from the Japanese by their white blouses and the full skirts that swung as they strode. At a bus stop a crowd stood waiting in a line long enough to fill a train. Half a mile farther on we passed the bus, small, battered, and gray, standing half obliterated by the cloud of smoke that came from the charcoal burner at the back while the driver stood working at its machinery.

4   Children of all ages waved, laughed, and shouted at us as had the children in other parts of Japan.

5   "Haro-goodabye! Haro-goodabye!"

6   "Jeepu! Jeeeepu!"

7   Like the children of Hamelin to the piper, they came rushing, at the sound of our approach, from doorways and alleyways and from behind houses, to line up by the road and cheer. One little fellow of about six threw himself into the air, his little body twisting and feet kicking in a fit of glee.

8   The adults gazed at us with solemn eyes or looked straight ahead. They were more subdued than those I had seen elsewhere in Japan. The children seemed different, possessed by some common animation denied their elders — an animation which impelled them toward the occupation forces, toward the strong and the new.

9   Presently a two-story trade school appeared, with boards instead of window glass, and then a factory in the same condition. Soon there were shops and houses all along the way with windows missing. A house came into view with its roof pressed down, tiles scattered, and walls bulging outward. A shop with no front, like an open mouth, showed its contents, public and private, clear to the rear window.

10   The road turned to the Ota River, where the tide was running out and boats lay heaved over on the beach. A bridge ended suddenly like a headless neck. Now every house and shop was damaged and lay with only one end or a corner standing.

11   Then all the buildings ceased and we came as if from a forest out on a plain, as if from tumult into silence. Imagine a city dump with its smells of wet ashes, mold, and things rotting, but that runs from your feet almost to the limits of vision. As is often the case with level and desolate places on the earth, the sky seemed close above it. The predominant colors were red and yellow, crumbles of stone, bricks, red earth, and rust. Low walls made rectangles that marked where houses had stood, like sites of prehistoric villages. Here and there in the middle distance, a few large buildings stood about, buttes in the rubble of the plain.

12   "You see them?" said the driver, as if it were a triumph for his side. "The bomb didn't knock *them* down."

13   Running like ruler lines through the waste were black roads surprisingly dotted with people, some on foot and some in carts of all sizes drawn by man, woman, horse, or cow. Clothing was old and tattered and of every combination from full European to full Japanese. People looked as if they had grabbed what they could from a rummage sale.

14   Occasionally, blending like protective coloration with the rubble were shacks built out of fragments of boards and iron. Around them were vegetable gardens, for the most part full of *daikon,* Japanese radish. A few more pretentious sheds were going up, shining bright yellow with new boards.

15   We slowed down to go around a piece of cornice that lay partly across the road like a glacial boulder, and from somewhere in a band of children who cheered and called to us came the gift of a tangerine that landed on the floor of the jeep. Wondering at them, I picked it up and put it in my pocket.

16   When crossing a bridge, we could see down through the swiftly running water to stone and shells on the bottom. This clearness gave a feeling of odd contrast to the disorder of the land. We passed a number of trees burned black but still holding up some leafless branches as if in perpetual winter.

17   The drive ended at a large building that was still standing, a former bank, now a police headquarters, where I had an appointment with the chief to arrange for office space and guides. The driver said, as he got out, "This is it."

II

18 One hears it said that, after all, Japanese cities were really a collection of tinderboxes, while American urban centers are made of stronger stuff. In Hiroshima there were many buildings of types common in the United States and some, prepared against earthquakes, far stronger. The engineers of the U.S. Strategic Bombing Survey concluded from their examination that "the overwhelming bulk of buildings in American cities would not stand up against an atomic bomb bursting at a mile or a mile and a half from them." To this must be added the realization that the bomb dropped at Hiroshima will be considered primitive by future standards.

19   The bank building which housed the police headquarters was a well-made structure of stone, three stories high. Through an imposing entrance my interpreter and I went past tall and solid metal doors that were bent inward like cardboard and no longer usable. The lobby was large and high, but dark because it had no window glass and the openings were boarded up to keep out the wind. Through poor light there loomed the white face of a clock up on one wall, its hands pointing to 8:10—the time it had stopped on August 6.

20   In the years when that clock had been going, Hiroshima had been a city, at first unknown to Europe and America, then a source of immigrants to the United States, and finally an enemy port. It lay on a delta between the seven mouths of the Ota and was traversed by canals and an ancient highway that connected Kyoto in the east with Shimonoseki in the west. Close around the city stood mountains covered with red pine, while before it stretched the bay, indented with headlands and spread with islands, in places narrow and steep like a fjord. In shallows near the shore, rows of poles stood as if in a bean patch, set in the sea to anchor oysters and to catch edible seaweed passing in the tide. In deeper water, fishing boats with hawkish prows

and planked with red pine were tending nets. A few fishermen used cormorants to make their catch.

21   Hiroshima had expanses of park, residences, gardens, orange and persimmon trees. Since there had been much traveling back and forth by relatives of immigrants to California, the influence of the United States was marked, On main streets there were movies and restaurants with facades that would have fitted into shopping districts of Bakersfield or San Diego.

22   But Hiroshima was also ancient. Its feudal castle raised a five-story keep that could be seen a long distance over the level land of the delta. There were three large temples and many smaller ones and the tombs of the Asano family and of the wife and son of the leader of the Forty-seven Ronin, Oishi-Yoshio. There were also Christian churches, whose bells mingled with the temple gongs and the honking of auto horns and the rattling of trolleys.

23   The people of the city had earned their living by buying and selling farm produce and fish, by making mountain pines into boats for the fishing fleet of the Inland Sea, by meat packing, rubber processing, and oil refining, by making textiles from the cocoons of wild silkworms, by brewing rice and grape wine, by manufacturing paper umbrellas, needles, *tabi* socks, small arms, metal castings, and by working in utilities and services such as electricity, transportation, schools, and hospitals.

24   During the war there was an increase of industrialization, and plants grew up, chiefly in the outskirts.

25   There was a famous gay district with little streets along which a person walking in the night could hear laughter, the twang of the *samisen*, and geishas singing.

26   The university had been an active cultural center but also stressed athletics, particularly swimming. There were sometimes mass aquatic exercises when hundreds of students would swim for miles, strung out in the bay in a long line with boats attending.

27   Although not a fortified town, Hiroshima was a major military command station, supply depot, and staging area because of its protected position and because of Ujina Harbor with access to the Pacific, the Sea of Japan, and the East China Sea. More than a third of the city's land was taken up with military installations, and from the harbor troopships left for Korea, Manchuria, China, and the southern regions. However, toward the end of hostilities, most of the shipping had ceased because of sinkings in the Inland Sea.

28   The population of Hiroshima was given as well over 300,000 before war, but this was reduced by evacuation, before the atomic bomb fell, probably to about 245,000. It is still not certain how many the bomb killed, but the best estimate is from 70,000 to 80,000.

III

29   About seven o'clock on the morning of August 6 there was an air-raid warning and three planes were reported in the vicinity. No one was much disturbed. For a long time B-29's flying over in small numbers had been a common sight. At some future date, Hiroshima might

suffer an incendiary raid from masses of planes such as had devastated other Japanese cities. With this possibility in mind there had been evacuations, and firebreaks were being prepared. But on this particular morning there could be no disaster from just three planes.

30 By 7:30 the "all clear" had sounded and people were thinking again of the day's plans, looking forward to their affairs and engagements of the morning and afternoon. The castle keep stood in the sun. Children bathed in the river. Farmers labored in the fields and fishermen on the water. City stores and factories got under way with their businesses.

31 In the heart of the city near the buildings of the Prefectural Government and at the intersection of the business streets, everybody had stopped and stood in a crowd gazing up at three parachutes floating down through the blue air.

32 The bomb exploded several hundred feet above their heads.

33 The people for miles around Hiroshima, in the fields, in the mountains, and on the bay, saw a light that was brilliant even in the sun, and felt heat. A countrywoman was going out to her farm when suddenly, "I saw a light reflected on the mountain and then a streak just like lightning came."

34 A town official was crossing a bridge on his bicycle about ten miles from the heart of the city when he felt the right side of his face seared, and thinking that he had sunstroke, he jumped to the ground.

35 A woman who was washing dishes noticed that she felt "very warm on the side of my face next the wall. I looked out the window toward the city and saw something like a sun in bright color."

36 At a slower pace, after the flash, came the sound of the explosion, which some people have no recollection of hearing, while others described it as an earth-shaking roar, like thunder or a big wind. A black smoky mass, lit up with color, ascended into the sky and impressed beholders with its beauty. Red, gold, blue, orange, and many other shades mingled with the black.

37 Nearer to the city and at its edges, the explosion made a more direct and individual impact on people. Almost everyone thought that an ordinary bomb had landed very close to him, and only later realized the extent of the damage.

38 A man who was oiling the machinery in a factory saw the lights go out and thought that something must be wrong with the electricity. "But when the roof started crumbling down, I was in a daze, wondering what was happening. Then I noticed my hands and feet were bleeding. I don't know how I hurt myself."

39 Another, who was putting points on needles, was knocked unconscious, and when he came to, found "all my surroundings burned to the ground and flames raging here and there. I ran home for my family without knowing I was burned around my head. When I arrived home, our house was devastated and destroyed by flames. I ran to the neighbors and inquired about my family and learned that they had all been taken to safety across the river."

40 An invalid who was drinking tea said, "The tin roof sidings came swirling into my room and everything was black. Rubble and glass and everything you can think of was blasted into my house."

41   Said a woman, "I was in the back of the house doing the washing. All of a sudden, the bomb exploded. My clothes were burned off and I received burns on my legs, arms, and back. The skin was just hanging loose. The first thing I did was run in the air-raid shelter and lie there exhausted. Then I thought of my baby in the house and ran back to it. The whole house was knocked down and was burning. My mother and father came crawling out of the debris, their faces and arms just black. I heard the baby crying, and crawled in and dug it out from under the burning embers. It was pretty badly burned. My mother carried it to the shelter."

42   In the heart of the city death prevailed and few were left to tell us about it. That part of the picture has to be reconstructed, as in archeology, from the remains.

43   The crowd that stood gazing upward at the parachutes went down withered and black, like a burned-out patch of weeds. Flames shot out of the castle keep. Trolleys bulging with passengers stopped, and all died at once, leaving burned figures still standing supporting each other and fingers fused to the straps. The military at their barracks and offices were wiped out. So too were factories full of workers, including students from schools, volunteers from neighboring towns working on the firebreaks, children scavenging for wood, the Mayor's staff, and the units for air-raid precaution, fire, welfare, and relief. The larger war industries, since they were on the fringe of the city, were for the most part not seriously damaged. Most of the personnel in the Prefectural Government offices were killed, though the Governor himself happened to be in Tokyo. In hospitals and clinics, patients, doctors, and nurses all died together, as did the priests and pastors of the temples and the churches. Of 1780 nurses, 1654 were killed, and 90 per cent of the doctors in Hiroshima were casualties.

44   People who were in buildings that sheltered them from the instantaneous effects that accompanied the flash were moments later decapitated or cut to ribbons by flying glass. Others were crushed as walls and floors gave way even in buildings that maintained their outer shells erect. In the thousands of houses that fell, people were pinned below the wreckage, not killed in many cases, but held there till the fire that swept the city caught up with them and put an end to their screams.

45   A police chief said that he was in his back yard when the bomb went off. He was knocked down and a concrete wall fell over him, but he was able to dig himself out and go at once toward the police station in the bank. "When I arrived at the office, I found ten policemen, some severely wounded. These were evacuated to a place of safety where they could get aid. We tried to clean up the glass from the windows, but fire was spreading and a hot southerly wind was blowing. We used a hose with water from a hydrant and also formed a bucket brigade. At noon the water in the hydrants gave out, but in this building we were lucky because we could pump water from a well. We carried buckets up from the basement to the roof and threw water down over the building. People on the road were fainting from the heat and we threw water on them too and carried them into the one room in the building that had not been affected by the bomb. We applied oil and

ointment to those who had burns.

46   "About 1:00 P.M. we began to apply first aid to the people outside, since the fire seemed under control as far as this building was concerned. A doctor came to help. He himself was wounded in one leg. By night this place was covered by a mass of people. One doctor applied all the first aid."

47   A doctor who was at a military hospital outside Hiroshima said that about an hour after the bomb went off, "many, many people came rushing to my clinic. They were rushing in all directions of the compass from the city. Many were stretcher cases. Some had their hair burned off, were injured in the back, had broken legs, arms, and thighs. The majority of the cases were those injured from glass; many had glass imbedded in the body. Next to the glass injuries, the most frequent were those who had their faces and hands burned, and also the chest and back. Most of the people arrived barefooted; many had their clothes burned off. Women were wearing men's clothing and men were wearing women's. They had put on anything they could pick up along the way.

48   "On the first day about 250 came, who were so injured they had to stay in the hospital, and we also attended about 500 others. Of all of these about 100 died."

49   A talkative man in a newspaper office said that the most severely burned people looked like red shrimps. Some had "skin which still burned sagging from the face and body with a reddish-white skin underneath showing."

50   A reporter who was outside the city at the time of the explosion, but came in immediately afterward, noticed among the dead a mother with a baby held tightly in her arms. He saw several women running around nude, red from burns, and without hair. Many people climbed into the water tanks kept for putting out fires and there died. "The most pathetic cases were the small children looking for their parents. There was one child of about eleven with a four-year-old on his back, looking, looking for his mother in vain."

51   Shortly after the bomb fell, there was a high wind, or "fire storm" engendered by the heat, that tore up trees and, whirling over the river, made water spouts. In some areas rain fell.

52   The severly burned woman who had been washing when the bomb fell said that she went down to the river, where "there were many people just dripping from their burns. Many of them were so badly burned that you could see the meat. By this time it was raining pretty badly. I could not walk or lie down or do anything. Water poured into the shelter and I received water blisters as well as blisters from the burns. It rained a lot right after the bomb."

53   Although the fire burned for days, the major destruction did not take very long. A fisherman out on the bay said, "I saw suddenly a flash of light. I thought something burned my face. I hid in the boat face down. When I looked up later, Hiroshima was completely burned."

IV

54   Hiroshima, of course, never had been prepared for a disaster of the magnitude which overtook it, but in addition the organized sources of

aid that did exist were decimated along with everything else. As a result, rescue had to come from surrounding areas, and soon trucks and trains were picking up the wounded, while hospitals, schools, temples, assembly halls, and tents were preparing to receive them. However, the suburbs and surrounding areas were overwhelmed by the rush of immediate survivors out of the bombed region and so, for about a day, help did not penetrate far into the city. This, together with the fact that survivors who were physically uninjured were stunned and bewildered, resulted in great numbers of the wounded dying from lack of aid.

55   The vice-mayor of a neighboring town that began receiving the wounded about 11:30 in the morning said, "Everybody looked alike. The eyes appeared to be a mass of melted flesh. The lips were split up and also looked like a mass of molten flesh. Only the nose appeared the same as before. The death scene was awful. The patient would turn blue and when we touched the body the skin would stick to our hands."

56   Those who ventured into Hiroshima were greeted by sights they were reluctant to describe. A businessman reported: "The bodies of half-dead people lay on the roadside, on the bridges, in the water, in the gardens, and everywhere. It was a sight no one wants to see. Practically all of these people were nude. Their color was brownish blackish and some of their bodies were dripping. There was a fellow whose head was half burned so that I thought he was wearing a hat." Another man said, "The bodies of the dead were so burned that we could not distinguish men from women."

57   In the public parks great numbers of both wounded and dead were congregated. There were cries for aid and cries for water and there were places where unidentifiable shapes merely stirred.

58   In the late afternoon, aid began to come farther into the city from the outer edges. Rice balls and other food were brought. From their mission up the valley a number of Jesuits came, and one of them, Father Siemes, gave a vivid and careful description of what he had seen, when he was later interviewed by members of the Bombing Survey in Tokyo. He said, "Beneath the wreckage of the houses along the way many had been trapped and they screamed to be rescued from the oncoming flames. They had to be left to their fate."

59   On a bridge, he encountered a procession of soldiers "dragging themselves along with the help of staves or carried by their less severely injured comrades. Abandoned on the bridge there stood with sunken heads a number of horses with large burns on their flanks.

60   "Fukai, the secretary of the mission, was completely out of his mind. He did not want to leave the house when the fires were burning closer, and explained that he did not want to survive the destruction of his fatherland." He had to be carried away by force.

61   After dark, the priests helped pull from the river two children who suffered chills and then died. There was a sand-spit in the river, covered with wounded, who cried for help and who were afraid that the rising tide would drown them. After midnight, "only occasionally did we hear calls for help."

62   Many patients were brought to an open field right behind Hiro-shima station, and tents were set up for them. Doctors came in from the neighboring prefectures and from near-by towns such as Yama-guchi, Okayama, and Shimane. The Army also took part in relief measures, and all available military facilities and units were mobilized to that end.

63   A fisherman who came to Hiroshima to see what had happened said, "I cannot describe the situation in words, it was so pitiful. To see so many people dead was a terrible sight. Their clothes were shredded and their bodies puffed up, some with tongues hanging out. They were dead in all shapes."

64   As late as the second day the priests noted that among cadavers there were still many wounded alive. "Frightfully injured forms beck-oned to us and then collapsed."

65   They carried some to the hospitals, but "we could not move every-body who lay exposed to the sun." It did not make much difference, anyway, for in the hospitals there was little that could be done. They just lay in the corridors, row on row, and died.

66   A businessman came into Hiroshima on the third day. "I went to my brother's house in the suburbs and found that all were wounded but none killed. They were stunned and could hardly speak. The next day, one of the four children died. She got black and blue in the face, just as if you had mashed your finger, and died fifteen minutes after that. In another half hour, her sister did the same thing and she died also."

67   The wife of a soldier who had been with the Hiroshima troops said, "My husband was a soldier and so he was to die, but when it actually happened, I wondered why we did not all go with him. They called me and I went to see. I was to find him in the heap, but I decided against looking at the bodies. I want to remember him as he was— big and healthy, not some horribly charred body. If I saw that, it would remain forever in my eyes."

68   A police chief told how the dead were collected and burned. "Many could not be identified. In cases where it was possible, the corpses or the ashes were given to the immediate family. Mostly, the cremation was done by the police or the soldiers, and the identified ashes were given to the family. The ashes of those not identified were turned over to the City Hall. There still are boxes in the City Hall. Occasionally even now one is identified, or is supposed to be identified, and is claimed."

69   The destroyed heart of Hiroshima consisted of 4.7 square miles, and the best estimates indicate that the mortality rate was 15,000 to the square mile. For many days funeral processions moved along the roads and through the towns and villages all around Hiroshima. The winds were pervaded by the smell of death and cremation. At night the skies were lit with the flames of funeral pyres.

V

70 Very few of the people we interviewed at Hiroshima attempted to make a play for sympathy or to make us feel guilty. The general man-ner was one which might be interpreted as due either to lingering

apathy and absence of feeling consequent on shock, or to reserve which masked hate. It was probably a mixture of both, in varying degrees in different people. But on the surface everyone appeared willing to cooperate and oblige.

71   An official of a near-by small town thought that "if America had such a weapon, there was no use to go on. Many high school students in Hiroshima who were wounded in the raid spoke incoherently on their deathbeds saying, 'Please avenge that raid for us somehow.' However, most of the people felt that since it was war, it was just *shikata ga nai,* could not be helped. But we were unified in the idea that we had to win the war."

72   A newspaper reporter said that after the bomb fell, some felt that this was the end, while others wanted to go on regardless. "Those who had actually experienced the bomb were the ones who wanted to quit, while those who had not, wanted to go on."

73   The wife of a soldier killed in the blast said, "Though many are resentful against America, I feel no animosity. It was an understood war and the use of weapons was fair. I only wonder why they didn't let the people know about this bomb and give us a chance, before bombing us, to give up."

74   A police chief believed that the general reaction among the people was one of surprise and a feeling that "we have taken the worst beating, we have been the goats." He said, "They felt that America had done a terrible thing and were very bitter, but after the surrender they turned on the Japanese military. They felt they had been fooled, and wondered if the military knew that the bomb was coming and why they did not take steps. The bomb made no difference in the fighting spirit of the people: it drew them together and made them more cooperative. My eldest son was killed, but I felt that it was destiny that ruled. When I see people who got away without any injury, I feel a little pang of envy naturally, but I don't feel bitter toward them."

75   Poking in the ruins one day, I came on the stone figure of a dog, one of that grinning type derived from China which commonly guards the entrances to temples. It was tilted on its pedestal but undamaged, and the grin gleamed out as if it were hailing me. Its rakish air and its look of fiendish satisfaction with all that lay around drew me on to inspect it more closely. It was then apparent that the look was not directed at me, but out somewhere beyond. It was, of course, only a piece of stone, and it displayed no particular artistic merit; yet in looking at it I felt that I was a clod, while it had a higher, sentient wisdom locked within.

76   The look and the feeling it inspired were familiar and I groped to remember where I had seen it before other than on temple dogs. The eyes were creased in a fashion that did not exactly connotate mirth, and the lips were drawn far back in a smile that seemed to blend bitterness, glee, and compassion. The word "sardonic" came to mind, and this led to recognition and a realization of terrible appropriateness.

77   All who have acquaintance with the dead know the curious smile that may creep over the human face as *rigor mortis* sets in, a smile of special quality called by doctors *risus sardonicus.* The dog had this

look, and it seemed to me probable that some ancient Oriental sculptor, in seeking an expression for temple guardians that would drive off evil spirits, had taken this death grin as his model, and thus it had come down through hundreds of years to this beast looking out on Hiroshima.

78   Many a soldier has seen this face looking up at him from the field of battle, before he himself was wearing it, and many a priest and doctor has found himself alone with it in a darkened room. As with the dog, at first the look seems at you, and then beyond you, as if there lay at last behind it knowledge of the huge joke of life which the rest of us feel vaguely but cannot comprehend. And there is that tinge of compassion that is as dreadful as it is unknowable.

79   As I continued to study this stone face, it began to appear that the grin was not directed at the waste and the destruction around, at the red and yellow and the smells, any more than it was at me. It was not so much a face looking at Hiroshima as it was the face of Hiroshima. The carved eyes gazed beyond the rubble, beyond the gardens of radishes and fields of winter wheat, beyond the toiling adults and the rippling children with their tangerines and shouts of "Haro-good-abye!" surging up with new life like flowers and weeds spreading over devastation, beyond the mountains with red pines in the blue sky, beyond all these, over the whole broad shoulder of the world to where, in cities and towns, watches on wrists and clocks on towers still ticked and moved. The face seemed to be smiling and waiting for the harvest of the wind that had been sown.

80   There was one woman in Hiroshima who said, "If there are such things as ghosts, why don't they haunt the Americans?"

81   Perhaps they do.

The assassination of John F. Kennedy (1917–63) left the world, and particularly the youth of the United States, in a state of shock. He was the youngest man and the first Roman Catholic to be elected president. His tremendous personal appeal and his energy won over millions, and he fired their imagination with his wit and intelligence. His administration took as its slogan "The New Frontier," an accurate description of his approach to the presidency.

Kennedy describes the heroism of a little-known figure of American history and points out that Ross's act of conscience required as much bravery as any deeds on the battlefield.

JOHN F. KENNEDY

I Looked Down into My Open Grave

1 In a lonely grave, forgotten and unknown, lies "the man who saved a President," and who as a result may well have preserved for ourselves and posterity constitutional government in the United States —the man who performed in 1868 what one historian has called "the most heroic act in American history, incomparably more difficult than any deed of valor upon the field of battle"—but a United States Senator whose name no one recalls: Edmund G. Ross of Kansas.

2 The impeachment of President Andrew Johnson, the event in which the obscure Ross was to play such a dramatic role, was the sensational climax to the bitter struggle between the President, de-

termined to carry out Abraham Lincoln's policies of reconciliation with the defeated South, and the more radical Republican leaders in Congress, who sought to administer the downtrodden Southern states as conquered provinces which had forfeited their rights under the Constitution. It was, moreover, a struggle between Executive and Legislative authority. Andrew Johnson, the courageous if untactful Tennessean who had been the only Southern Member of Congress to refuse to secede with his state, had committed himself to the policies of the Great Emancipator to whose high station he had succeeded only by the course of an assassin's bullet. He knew that Lincoln prior to his death had already clashed with the extremists in Congress, who had opposed his approach to reconstruction in a constitutional and charitable manner and sought to make the Legislative Branch of the government supreme. And his own belligerent temperament soon destroyed any hope that Congress might now join hands in carrying out Lincoln's policies of permitting the South to resume its place in the Union with as little delay and controversy as possible.

3   By 1866, when Edmund Ross first came to the Senate, the two branches of the government were already at each other's throats, snarling and bristling with anger. Bill after bill was vetoed by the President on the grounds that they were unconstitutional, too harsh in their treatment of the South, an unnecessary prolongation of military rule in peacetime or undue interference with the authority of the Executive Branch. And for the first time in our nation's history, important public measures were passed over a President's veto and became law without his support.

4   But not all of Andrew Johnson's vetoes were overturned; and the "Radical" Republicans of the Congress promptly realized that one final step was necessary before they could crush their despised foe (and in the heat of political battle their vengeance was turned upon their President far more than their former military enemies of the South). That one remaining step was the assurance of a two-thirds majority in the Senate—for under the Constitution, such a majority was necessary to override a Presidential veto. And more important, such a majority was constitutionally required to accomplish their major ambition, now an ill-kept secret, conviction of the President under an impeachment and his dismissal from office!

5   The temporary and unstable two-thirds majority which had enabled the Senate Radical Republicans on several occasions to enact legislation over the President's veto was, they knew, insufficiently reliable for an impeachment conviction. To solidify this bloc became the paramount goal of Congress, expressly or impliedly governing its decisions on other issues—particularly the admission of new states, the readmission of Southern states and the determination of senatorial credentials. By extremely dubious methods a pro-Johnson Senator was denied his seat. Over the President's veto Nebraska was admitted to the Union, seating two more anti-administration Senators. Although the last minute maneuvers failed to admit Colorado over the President's veto (sparsely populated Colorado had rejected statehood in a referendum) an unexpected tragedy brought false tears and fresh hopes for a new vote, in Kansas.

6   Senator Jim Lane of Kansas had been a "conservative" Republican
sympathetic to Johnson's plans to carry out Lincoln's reconstruction
policies. But his frontier state was one of the most "radical" in the
Union. When Lane voted to uphold Johnson's veto of the Civil Rights
Bill of 1866 and introduced the administration's bill for recognition of
the new state government of Arkansas, Kansas had arisen in outraged
heat. A mass meeting at Lawrence had vilified the Senator and speed-
ily reported resolutions sharply condemning his position. Humiliated,
mentally ailing, broken in health and laboring under charges of financial irregularities, Jim Lane took his life on July 1, 1866.

7   With this thorn in their side removed, the Radical Republicans in
Washington looked anxiously toward Kansas and the selection of
Lane's successor. Their fondest hopes were realized, for the new
Senator from Kansas turned out to be Edmund G. Ross, the very man
who had introduced the resolutions attacking Lane at Lawrence.

8   There could be no doubt as to where Ross's sympathies lay, for his
entire career was one of determined opposition to the slave states of
the South, their practices and their friends. In 1854, when only
twenty-eight, he had taken part in the mob rescue of a fugitive slave
in Milwaukee. In 1856, he had joined the flood of antislavery immigrants to "bleeding" Kansas who intended to keep it a free territory.
Disgusted with the Democratic party of his youth, he had left that
party, and volunteered in the Kansas Free State Army to drive back
a force of proslavery men invading the territory. In 1862, he had
given up his newspaper work to enlist in the Union Army, from which
he emerged a Major. His leading role in the condemnation of Lane at
Lawrence convinced the Radical Republican leaders in Congress that
in Edmund G. Ross they had a solid member of that vital two-thirds.

9   The stage was now set for the final scene—the removal of Johnson.
Early in 1867, Congress enacted over the President's veto the
Tenure-of-Office Bill which prevented the President from removing
without the consent of the Senate all new officeholders whose appointment required confirmation by that body. At the time nothing
more than the cry for more patronage was involved, Cabinet Members having originally been specifically exempt.

10   On August 5, 1867, President Johnson—convinced that the Secretary of War, whom he had inherited from Lincoln, Edward M. Stanton, was the surreptitious tool of the Radical Republicans and was
seeking to become the almighty dictator of the conquered South
—asked for his immediate resignation; and Stanton arrogantly fired
back the reply that he declined to resign before the next meeting of
Congress. Not one to cower before this kind of effrontery, the President one week later suspended Stanton, and appointed in his place
the one man whom Stanton did not dare resist, General Grant. On
January 13, 1868, an angry Senate notified the President and Grant
that it did not concur in the suspension of Stanton, and Grant vacated
the office upon Stanton's return. But the situation was intolerable.
The Secretary of War was unable to attend Cabinet meetings or associate with his colleagues in the administration; and on February 21,
President Johnson, anxious to obtain a court test of the act he be-

lieved obviously unconstitutional, again notified Stanton that he had been summarily removed from the office of Secretary of War.

11   While Stanton, refusing to yield possession, barricaded himself in his office, public opinion in the nation ran heavily against the President. He had intentionally broken the law and dictatorially thwarted the will of Congress! Although previous resolutions of impeachment had been defeated in the House, both in committee and on the floor, a new resolution was swiftly reported and adopted on February 24 by a tremendous vote. Every single Republican voted in the affirmative, and Thaddeus Stevens of Pennsylvania—the crippled, fanatical personification of the extremes of the Radical Republican movement, master of the House of Representatives, with a mouth like the thin edge of an ax—warned both Houses of the Congress coldly: "Let me see the recreant who would vote to let such a criminal escape. Point me to the one who will dare do it and I will show you one who will dare the infamy of posterity."

12   With the President impeached—in effect, indicted—by the House, the frenzied trial for his conviction or acquittal under the Articles of Impeachment began on March 5 in the Senate, presided over by the Chief Justice. It was a trial to rank with all the great trials in history—Charles I before the High Court of Justice, Louis XVI before the French Convention, and Warren Hastings before the House of Lords. Two great elements of drama were missing: the actual cause for which the President was being tried was not fundamental to the welfare of the nation; and the defendant himself was at all times absent.

13   But every other element of the highest courtroom drama was present. To each Senator the Chief Justice administered an oath "to do impartial justice" (including even the hotheaded Radical Senator from Ohio, Benjamin Wade, who as President Pro Tempore of the Senate was next in line for the Presidency). The chief prosecutor for the House was General Benjamin F. Butler, the "butcher of New Orleans," a talented but coarse and demagogic Congressman from Massachusetts. (When he lost his seat in 1874, he was so hated by his own party as well as his opponents that one Republican wired concerning the Democratic sweep, "Butler defeated, everything else lost.") Some one thousand tickets were printed for admission to the Senate galleries during the trial, and every conceivable device was used to obtain one of the four tickets allotted each Senator.

14   From the fifth of March to the sixteenth of May, the drama continued. Of the eleven Articles of Impeachment adopted by the House, the first eight were based upon the removal of Stanton and the appointment of a new Secretary of War in violation of the Tenure-of-Office Act; the ninth related to Johnson's conversation with a general which was said to induce violations of the Army Appropriations Act; the tenth recited that Johnson had delivered "intemperate, inflammatory and scandalous harangues . . . as well against Congress as the laws of the United States"; and the eleventh was a deliberately obscure conglomeration of all the charges in the preceding articles, which had been designed by Thaddeus Stevens to furnish a common ground

for those who favored conviction but were unwilling to identify themselves on basic issues. In opposition to Butler's inflammatory arguments in support of this hastily drawn indictment, Johnson's able and learned counsel replied with considerable effectiveness. They insisted that the Tenure-of-Office Act was null and void as a clear violation of the Constitution; that even if it were valid, it would not apply to Stanton, for the reasons previously mentioned; and that the only way that a judicial test of the law could be obtained was for Stanton to be dismissed and sue for his rights in the courts.

15   But as the trial progressed, it became increasingly apparent that the impatient Republicans did not intend to give the President a fair trial on the formal issues upon which the impeachment was drawn, but intended instead to depose him from the White House on any grounds, real or imagined, for refusing to accept their policies. Telling evidence in the President's favor was arbitrarily excluded. Prejudgment on the part of most Senators was brazenly announced. Attempted bribery and other forms of pressure were rampant. The chief interest was not in the trial or the evidence, but in the tallying of votes necessary for conviction.

16   Twenty-seven states (excluding the unrecognized Southern states) in the Union meant fifty-four members of the Senate, and thirty-six votes were required to constitute the two-thirds majority necessary for conviction. All twelve Democratic votes were obviously lost, and the forty-two Republicans knew that they could afford to lose only six of their own members if Johnson were to be ousted. To their dismay, at a preliminary Republican caucus, six courageous Republicans indicated that the evidence so far introduced was not in their opinion sufficient to convict Johnson under the Articles of Impeachment. "Infamy!" cried the Philadelphia *Press*. The Republic has "been betrayed in the house of its friends!"

17   But if the remaining thirty-six Republicans would hold, there would be no doubt as to the outcome. All must stand together! But one Republican Senator would not announce his verdict in the preliminary poll—Edmund G. Ross of Kansas. The Radicals were outraged that a Senator from such an anti-Johnson stronghold as Kansas could be doubtful. "It was a very clear case," Senator Sumner of Massachusetts fumed, "especially for a Kansas man. I did not think that a Kansas man could quibble against his country."

18   From the very time Ross had taken his seat, the Radical leaders had been confident of his vote. His entire background, as already indicated, was one of firm support of their cause. One of his first acts in the Senate had been to read a declaration of his adherence to Radical Republican policy, and he had silently voted for all of their measures. He had made it clear that he was not in sympathy with Andrew Johnson personally or politically; and after the removal of Stanton, he had voted with the majority in adopting a resolution declaring such removal unlawful. His colleague from Kansas, Senator Pomeroy, was one of the most Radical leaders of the anti-Johnson group. The Republicans insisted that Ross' crucial vote was rightfully theirs, and they were determined to get it by whatever means available. As stated by DeWitt in his memorable *Impeachment of Andrew*

Johnson, "The full brunt of the struggle turned at last on the one remaining doubtful Senator, Edmund G. Ross."

19   When the impeachment resolution had passed the House, Senator Ross had casually remarked to Senator Sprague of Rhode Island, "Well, Sprague, the thing is here; and so far as I am concerned, though a Republican and opposed to Mr. Johnson and his policy, he shall have as fair a trial as an accused man ever had on this earth." Immediately the word spread that "Ross was shaky." "From that hour," he later wrote, "not a day passed that did not bring me, by mail and telegraph and in personal intercourse, appeals to stand fast for impeachment, and not a few were the admonitions of condign visitations upon any indication even of lukewarmness."

20   Throughout the country, and in all walks of life, as indicated by the correspondence of Members of the Senate, the condition of the public mind was not unlike that preceding a great battle. The dominant party of the nation seemed to occupy the position of public prosecutor, and it was scarcely in the mood to brook delay for trial or to hear defense. Washington had become during the trial the central point of the politically dissatisfied and swarmed with representatives of every state of the Union, demanding in a practically united voice the deposition of the President. The footsteps of the anti-impeaching Republicans were dogged from the day's beginning to its end and far into the night, with entreaties, considerations, and threats. The newspapers came daily filled with not a few threats of violence upon their return to their constituents.

21   Ross and his fellow doubtful Republicans were daily pestered, spied upon and subjected to every form of pressure. Their residences were carefully watched, their social circles suspiciously scrutinized, and their every move and companions secretly marked in special notebooks. They were warned in the party press, harangued by their constituents, and sent dire warnings threatening political ostracism and even assassination. Stanton himself, from his barricaded headquarters in the War Department, worked day and night to bring to bear upon the doubtful Senators all the weight of his impressive military associations. The Philadelphia *Press* reported "a fearful avalanche of telegrams from every section of the country," a great surge of public opinion from the "common people" who had given their money and lives to the country and would not "willingly or unavenged see their great sacrifice made naught."

22   The New York *Tribune* reported that Edmund Ross in particular was "mercilessly dragged this way and that by both sides, hunted like a fox night and day and badgered by his own colleagues, like the bridge at Arcola now trod upon by one Army and now trampled by the other." His background and life were investigated from top to bottom, and his constituents and colleagues pursued him throughout Washington to gain some inkling of his opinion. He was the target of every eye, his name was on every mouth and his intentions were discussed in every newspaper. Although there is evidence that he gave some hint of agreement to each side, and each attempted to claim him publicly, he actually kept both sides in a state of complete suspense by his judicial silence.

23   But with no experience in political turmoil, no reputation in the
Senate, no independent income and the most radical state in the
Union to deal with, Ross was judged to be the most sensitive to criticism and the most certain to be swayed by expert tactics. A committee of Congressmen and Senators sent to Kansas, and to the states of
the other doubtful Republicans, this telegram: "Great danger to the
peace of the country and the Republican cause if impeachment fails.
Send to your Senators public opinion by resolutions, letters, and del-
egations." A member of the Kansas legislature called upon Ross at
the Capitol. A general urged on by Stanton remained at his lodge
until four o'clock in the morning determined to see him. His brother
received a letter offering $20,000 for revelation of the Senator's in-
tentions. Gruff Ben Butler exclaimed of Ross, "There is a bushel of
money! How much does the damned scoundrel want?" The night before the Senate was to take its first vote for the conviction or acquittal
of Johnson, Ross received this telegram from home:

> Kansas has heard the evidence and demands the conviction of the Pres-
> ident.
>
> [signed] D. R. Anthony and 1,000 Others

And on that fateful morning of May 16 Ross replied:

> To D. R. Anthony and 1,000 Others: I do not recognize your right to
> demand that I vote either for or against conviction. I have taken an oath to
> do impartial justice according to the Constitution and laws, and trust that I
> shall have the courage to vote according to the dictates of my judgment
> and for the highest good of the country.
>
> [signed] E. G. Ross

24   That morning spies traced Ross to his breakfast; and ten minutes
before the vote was taken his Kansas colleague warned him in the
presence of Thaddeus Stevens that a vote for acquittal would mean
trumped up charges and his political death.

25   But now the fateful hour was at hand. Neither escape, delay or
indecision was possible. As Ross himself later described it: "The galleries were packed. Tickets of admission were at an enormous premium. The House had adjourned and all of its members were in the
Senate chamber. Every chair on the Senate floor was filled with a
Senator, a Cabinet Officer, a member of the President's counsel or a
member of the House." Every Senator was in his seat, the desperately ill Grimes of Iowa being literally carried in.

26   It had been decided to take the first vote under that broad
Eleventh Article of Impeachment, believed to command the widest
support. As the Chief Justice announced the voting would begin, he
reminded "the citizens and strangers in the galleries that absolute silence and perfect order are required." But already a deathlike stillness enveloped the Senate chamber. A Congressman later recalled
that "Some of the members of the House near me grew pale and sick
under the burden of suspense"; and Ross noted that there was even

"a subsidence of the shuffling of feet, the rustling of silks, the fluttering of fans, and of conversation."

27 The voting tensely commenced. By the time the Chief Justice reached the name of Edmund Ross twenty-four "guilties" had been pronounced. Ten more were certain and one other practically certain. Only Ross's vote was needed to obtain the thirty-six votes necessary to convict the President. But not a single person in the room knew how this young Kansan would vote. Unable to conceal the suspense and emotion in his voice, the Chief Justice put the question to him: "Mr. Senator Ross, how say you? Is the respondent Andrew Johnson guilty or not guilty of a high misdemeanor as charged in this Article?" Every voice was still; every eye was upon the freshman Senator from Kansas. The hopes and fears, the hatred and bitterness of past decades were centered upon this one man.

28 As Ross himself later described it, his "powers of hearing and seeing seemed developed in an abnormal degree."

29   "Every individual in that great audience seemed distinctly visible, some with lips apart and bending forward in anxious expectancy, others with hand uplifted as if to ward off an apprehended blow . . . and each peering with an intensity that was almost tragic upon the face of him who was about to cast the fateful vote. . . . Every fan was folded, not a foot moved, not the rustle of a garment, not a whisper was heard. . . . Hope and fear seemed blended in every face, instantaneously alternating, some with revengeful hate . . . others lighted with hope . . . The Senators in their seats leaned over their desks, many with hand to ear. . . . It was a tremendous responsibility, and it was not strange that he upon whom it had been imposed by a fateful combination of conditions should have sought to avoid it, to put it away from him as one shuns, or tries to fight off, a nightmare. . . . I almost literally looked down into my open grave. Friendships, position, fortune, everything that makes life desirable to an ambitious man were about to be swept away by the breath of my mouth, perhaps forever. It is not strange that my answer carried waveringly over the air and failed to reach the limits of the audience, or that repetition was called for by distant Senators on the opposite side of the Chamber."

30 Then came the answer again in a voice that could not be misunderstood—full, final, definite, unhesitating and unmistakable: "Not guilty." The deed was done, the President saved, the trial as good as over and the conviction lost. The remainder of the roll call was unimportant, conviction had failed by the margin of a single vote and a general rumbling filled the chamber until the Chief Justice proclaimed that "on this Article thirty-five Senators having voted guilty and nineteen not guilty, a two-thirds majority not having voted for conviction, the President is, therefore, acquitted under this Article."

31 A ten-day recess followed, ten turbulent days to change votes on the remaining Articles. An attempt was made to rush through bills to readmit six Southern states, whose twelve Senators were guaranteed to vote for conviction. But this could not be accomplished in time. Again Ross was the only one uncommitted on the other Articles, the only one whose vote could not be predicted in advance. And again he

was subjected to terrible pressure. From "D. R. Anthony and others," he received a wire informing him that "Kansas repudiates you as she does all perjurers and skunks." Every incident in his life was examined and distorted. Professional witnesses were found by Senator Pomeroy to testify before a special House committee that Ross had indicated a willingness to change his vote for a consideration. (Unfortunately this witness was so delighted in his exciting role that he also swore that Senator Pomeroy had made an offer to produce three votes for acquittal for $40,000.) When Ross, in his capacity as a Committee Chairman, took several bills to the President, James G. Blaine remarked: "There goes the rascal to get his pay." (Long afterward Blaine was to admit: "In the exaggerated denunciation caused by the anger and chagrin of the moment, great injustice was done to statesmen of spotless character.")

32 Again the wild rumors spread that Ross had been won over on the remaining Articles of Impeachment. As the Senate reassembled, he was the only one of the seven "renegade" Republicans to vote with the majority on preliminary procedural matters. But when the second and third Articles of Impeachment were read, and the name of Ross was reached again with the same intense suspense of ten days earlier, again came the calm answer "Not guilty."

33 Why did Ross, whose dislike for Johnson continued, vote "Not guilty"? His motives appear clearly from his own writings on the subject years later in articles contributed to *Scribner's* and *Forum* magazines:

34 "In a large sense, the independence of the executive office as a coordinate branch of the government was on trial. ... If ... the President must step down ... a disgraced man and a political outcast ... upon insufficient proofs and from partisan considerations, the office of President would be degraded, cease to be a coordinate branch of the government, and ever after subordinated to the legislative will. It would practically have revolutionized our splendid political fabric into a partisan Congressional autocracy. ... This government had never faced so insidious a danger ... control by the worst element of American politics. ... If Andrew Johnson were acquitted by a nonpartisan vote ... America would pass the danger point of partisan rule and that intolerance which so often characterizes the sway of great majorities and makes them dangerous."

35 The "open grave" which Edmund Ross had foreseen was hardly an exaggeration. A Justice of the Kansas Supreme Court telegraphed him that "the rope with which Judas Iscariot hanged himself is lost, but Jim Lane's pistol is at your service." An editorial in a Kansas newspaper screamed:

36 "On Saturday last Edmund G. Ross, United States Senator from Kansas, sold himself, and betrayed his constituents; stultified his own record, basely lied to his friends, shamefully violated his solemn pledge ... and to the utmost of his poor ability signed the death warrant of his country's liberty. This act was done deliberately, because the traitor, like Benedict Arnold, loved money better than he did principle, friends, honor and his

country, all combined. Poor, pitiful, shriveled wretch, with a soul so small that a little pelf would outweigh all things else that dignify or ennoble manhood."

37   Ross's political career was ended. To the new New York *Tribune,* he was nothing but "a miserable poltroon and traitor." The Philadelphia *Press* said that in Ross "littleness" had "simply borne its legitimate fruit," and that he and his fellow recalcitrant Republicans had "plunged from a precipice of fame into the groveling depths of infamy and death." The Philadelphia *Inquirer* said that "They had tried, convicted and sentenced themselves." For them there could be "no allowance, no clemency."

38   Comparative peace returned to Washington as Stanton relinquished his office and Johnson served out the rest of his term, later—unlike his Republican defenders—to return triumphantly to the Senate as Senator from Tennessee. But no one paid attention when Ross tried unsuccessfully to explain his vote, and denounced the falsehoods of Ben Butler's investigating committee, recalling that the General's "well known grovelling instincts and proneness to slime and uncleanness" had led "the public to insult the brute creation by dubbing him 'the beast.' " He clung unhappily to his seat in the Senate until the expiration of his term, frequently referred to as "the traitor Ross," and complaining that his fellow Congressmen, as well as citizens on the street, considered association with him "disreputable and scandalous," and passed him by as if he were "a leper, with averted face and every indication of hatred and disgust."

39   Neither Ross nor any other Republican who had voted for the acquittal of Johnson was ever re-elected to the Senate, not a one of them retaining the support of their party's organization. When he returned to Kansas in 1871, he and his family suffered social ostracism, physical attack, and near poverty.

40   Who was Edmund G. Ross? Practically nobody. Not a single public law bears his name, not a single history book includes his picture, not a single list of Senate "greats" mentions his service. His one heroic deed has been all but forgotten. But who might Edmund G. Ross have been? That is the question—for Ross, a man with an excellent command of words, an excellent background for politics and an excellent future in the Senate, might have well outstripped his colleagues in prestige and power throughout a long Senate career. Instead, he chose to throw all of this away for one act of conscience.

41   But the twisting course of human events eventually upheld the faith he expressed to his wife shortly after the trial: "Millions of men cursing me today will bless me tomorrow for having saved the country from the greatest peril through which it has ever passed, though none but God can ever know the struggle it has cost me." For twenty years later Congress repealed the Tenure-of-Office Act, to which every President after Johnson, regardless of party, had objected; and still later the Supreme Court, referring to "the extremes of that episode in our government," held it to be unconstitutional. Ross moved to New Mexico, where in his later years he was to be appointed Territorial

Governor. Just prior to his death when he was awarded a special pension by Congress for his service in the Civil War, the press and the country took the opportunity to pay tribute to his fidelity to principle in a trying hour and his courage in saving his government from a devastating reign of terror. They now agreed with Ross's earlier judgment that his vote had "saved the country from . . . a strain that would have wrecked any other form of government." Those Kansas newspapers and political leaders who had bitterly denounced him in earlier years praised Ross for his stand against legislative mob rule: "By the firmness and courage of Senator Ross," it was said, "the country was saved from calamity greater than war, while it consigned him to political martyrdom, the most cruel in our history. . . . Ross was the victim of a wild flame of intolerance which swept everything before it. He did his duty knowing that it meant his political death. . . . It was a brave thing for Ross to do, but Ross did it. He acted for his conscience and with a lofty patriotism, regardless of what he knew must be the ruinous consequences to himself. He acted right."

D. H. Lawrence (1885–1930) has been called the great high priest of sex in contemporary English literature. Such a judgment is unfair, however, and stems chiefly from his authorship of "Lady Chatterley's Lover," which caused a sensation when it appeared in 1928. Born in Nottingham of lower-class parents, Lawrence taught school for several years upon graduation from college. His novels express his conviction that a new world should be created in which men could live unhampered by notions of racial or religious superiority. His most signficant novels, in addition to "Lady Chatterley's Lover," are "Sons and Lovers" (1913), "Women in Love" (1921), and "The Plumed Serpent" (1926).

It is market day in a Mexican village. Notice that the tempo and tone of the writing match the leisurely pace of the Indians as they plod to the marketplace.

D. H. Lawrence

Market Day

1   This is the last Saturday before Christmas. The next year will be momentous, one feels. This year is nearly gone. Dawn was windy, shaking the leaves, and the rising sun shone under a gap of yellow cloud. But at once it touched the yellow flowers that rise above the *patio* wall, and the swaying, glowing magenta of the bougainvillea, and the fierce red outbursts of the poinsettia. The poinsettia is very splendid, the flowers very big, and of a sure stainless red. They call them Noche Buenas, flowers of Christmas Eve. These tufts throw out their scarlet sharply, like red birds ruffling in the wind of dawn as if going to bathe,

all their feathers alert. This for Christmas, instead of holly-berries. Christmas seems to need a red herald.

2   The Yucca is tall, higher than the house. It is, too, in flower, hanging an arm's-length of soft creamy bells, like a yard-long grape-cluster of foam. And the waxy bells break on their stems in the wind, fall noiselessly from the long creamy bunch, that hardly sways.

3   The coffee-berries are turning red. The hibiscus flowers, rose-coloured, sway at the tips of the thin branches, in rosettes of soft red.

4   In the second *patio,* there is a tall tree of the flimsy acacia sort. Above itself it puts up whitish fingers of flowers, naked on the blue sky. And in the wind these fingers of flowers in the bare blue sky sway with the reeling, roundward motion of tree-tips in a wind.

5   A restless morning, with clouds lower down, moving also with a larger roundward motion. Everything moving. Best to go out in motion too, the slow roundward motion like the hawks.

6   Everything seems slowly to circle and hover toward a central point, the clouds, the mountains round the valley, the dust that rises, the big, beautiful white-barred hawks, *gabilanes,* and even the snow-white flakes of flowers upon the dim palo blanco tree. Even the organ cactus, rising in stock-straight clumps, and the candelabrum cactus, seem to be slowly wheeling and pivoting upon a centre, close upon it.

7   Strange that we should think in straight lines, when there are none, and talk of straight courses, when every course, sooner or later, is seen to be making the sweep round, swooping upon the centre. When space is curved, and the cosmos is sphere within sphere, and the way from any one point to any other point is round the bend of the inevitable, that turns as the tips of the broad wings of the hawk turn upward, leaning upon the air like the invisible half of the ellipse. If I have a way to go, it will be round the swoop of a bend impinging centripetal toward the centre. The straight course is hacked out in rounds, against the will of the world.

8   Yet the dust advances like a ghost along the road, down the valley plain. The dry turf of the valley-bed gleams like soft skin, sunlit and pinkish ochre, spreading wide between the mountains that seem to emit their own darkness, a dark-blue vapor translucent, sombering them from the humped crests downward. The many-pleated, noiseless mountains of Mexico.

9   And away on the footslope lie the white specks of Huayapa, among its lake of trees. It is Saturday, and the white dots of men are threading down the trail over the bare humps to the plain, following the dark twinkle-movement of asses, the dark nodding of the woman's head as she rides between the baskets. Saturday and marketday, and morning, so the white specks of men, like sea-gulls on plough-land, come ebbing like sparks from the palo blanco, over the fawn undulating of the valley slope.

10   They are dressed in snow-white cotton, and they lift their knees in the Indian trot, following the ass where the woman sits perched between the huge baskets, her child tight in the rebozo, at the brown breast. And girls in long, full, soiled cotton skirts running, trotting, ebbing along after the twinkle-movement of the ass. Down they come

in families, in clusters, in solitary ones, threading with ebbing, running, barefoot movement noiseless toward the town, that blows the bubbles of its church-domes above the stagnant green of trees, away under the opposite fawn-skin hills.

11   But down the valley middle comes the big road, almost straight. You will know it by the tall walking of the dust, that hastens also toward the town, overtaking, overpassing everybody. Overpassing all the dark little figures and the white specks that thread tinily, in a sort of under-world, to the town.

12   From the valley villages and from the mountains the peasants and the Indians are coming in with supplies, the road is like a pilgrimage, with the dust in greatest haste, dashing for town. Dark-eared asses and running men, running women, running girls, running lads, twink-ling donkeys ambling on fine little feet, under twin great baskets with tomatoes and gourds, twin great nets of bubble-shaped jars, twin bundles of neat-cut faggots of wood, neat as bunches of cigarettes, and twin net-sacks of charcoal. Donkeys, mules, on they come, great pan-nier baskets making a rhythm under the perched woman, great bun-dles bouncing against the sides of the slim-footed animals. A baby donkey trotting naked after its piled-up dam, a white, sandal-footed man following with the silent Indian haste, and a girl running again on light feet.

13   Onward, on a strange current of haste. And slowly rowing among the foot-travel, the ox-wagons rolling solid wheels below the high net of the body. Slow oxen, with heads pressed down nosing to the earth, swaying, swaying their great horns as a snake sways itself, the shovel-shaped collar of solid wood pressing down on their necks like a scoop. On, on between the burnt-up turf and the solid, monumental green of the organ cactus. Past the rocks and the floating palo blanco flowers, past the towsled dust of the mesquite bushes. While the dust once more, in a greater haste than anyone, comes tall and rapid down the road, overpowering and obscuring all the little people, as in a cata-clysm.

14   They are mostly small people, of the Zapotec race: small men with lifted chests and quick, lifted knees, advancing with heavy energy in the midst of dust. And quiet, small, round-headed women running barefoot, tightening their blue rebozos round their shoulders, so often with a baby in the fold. The white cotton clothes of the men so white that their faces are invisible places of darkness under their big hats. Clothed darkness, faces of night, quickly, silently, with inexhaustible energy advancing to the town.

15   And many of the Serranos, the Indians from the hills, wearing their little conical black felt hats, seem capped with night, above the straight white shoulders. Some have come far, walking all yesterday in their little black hats and black-sheathed sandals. Tomorrow they will walk back. And their eyes will be just the same, black and bright and wild, in the dark faces. They have no goal, any more than the hawks in the air, and no course to run, any more than the clouds.

16   The market is a huge roofed-in place. Most extraordinary is the noise that comes out, as you pass along the adjacent street. It is a huge

noise, yet you may never notice it. It sounds as if all the ghosts in the world were talking to one another, in ghost-voices, within the darkness of the market structure. It is a noise something like rain, or banana leaves in a wind. The market, full of Indians, dark-faced, silent-footed, hush-spoken, but pressing in in countless numbers. The queer hissing murmurs of the Zapotec *idioma,* among the sounds of Spanish, the quiet, aside-voices of the Mixtecas.

17   To buy and to sell, but above all, to commingle. In the old world, men make themselves two great excuses for coming together to a centre, and commingling freely in a mixed, unsuspicious host. Market and religion. These alone bring men, unarmed, together since time began. A little load of firewood, a woven blanket, a few eggs and tomatoes are excuse enough for men, women, and children to cross the foot-weary miles of valley and mountain, To buy, to sell, to barter, to exchange. To exchange, above all things, human contact.

18   That is why they like you to bargain, even if it's only the difference of a centavo. Round the centre of the covered market, where there is a basin of water, are the flowers: red, white, pink roses in heaps, many-coloured little carnations, poppies, bits of larkspur, lemon and orange marigolds, buds of madonna lilies, pansies, a few forget-me-nots. They don't bring the tropical flowers. Only the lilies come wild from the hills, and the mauve red orchids.

19   "How much this bunch of cherry-pie heliotrope?"
20   "Fifteen centavos."
      "Ten."
      "Fifteen."
      You put back the cherry-pie, and depart. But the woman is quite content. The contact, so short even, brisked her up.
      "Pinks?"
25   "The red ones, Señorita? Thirty centavos."
      "No. I don't want red ones. The mixed."
      "Ah!" The woman seizes a handful of little carnations of all colours, carefully puts them together. "Look Señorita! No more?"
      "No, no more. How much?"
      "The same. Thirty centavos."
30   "It is much."
      "No, Señorita, it is not much. Look at this little bunch. It is eight centavos."—Displays a scrappy little bunch. "Come then, twenty-five."
      "No! Twenty-two."
      "Look!" She gathers up three or four more flowers, and claps them to the bunch. "Two *reales,* Señorita."
34   It is a bargain. Off you go with multicoloured pinks, and the woman has had one more moment of contact, with a stranger, a perfect stranger. An intermingling of voices, a threading together of different wills. It is life. The centavos are an excuse.

GLOSSARY

Abstract Words   words that refer to feelings, generalities, or ideas (love, fear, philosophy, patriotism) rather than to things or objects. Because they allude to referents that cannot be easily visualized, abstract words are often less forceful than concrete words.

Allusion   a hint or *indirect* reference to a person, object, or action.

Analogy   a comparison of two things or situations that are not exactly alike but still resemble each other in certain ways. Analogy is often used for argument or explanation.

Analysis   the technique of dividing a topic into basic parts or divisions, showing their relationship and function.

Argumentation   traditionally, one of the four basic kinds of discourse. (The others are *Description, Exposition,* and *Narration.*) The purpose of argumentation is to convince the reader of the truth or relevance of the author's position, to persuade him to adopt that point of view, or take the action recommended. The means used should be objective evidence and logic.

Balanced Sentence   a balanced sentence is one in which similar or opposing thoughts are arranged in parallel structure. See *Parallelism.*

Beginning   an effective beginning introduces the subject to be discussed and catches the reader's interest. Some ways to begin: with a statement of fact, a question, an anecdote, or a short, startling statement.

Cause and Effect   a common method of development that examines events and their causes.

Chronological Order   a method of development commonly used in narrative writing in which events are presented in the order they happen in time.

Classification   a grouping of persons, objects, or ideas into categories on the basis of similarities or common qualities.

Cliché   an overworked or trite expression or phrase.

Coherence   a paragraph or an essay has coherence when its various parts (sentences or paragraphs, respectively) fit together to form an integrated whole. See *Unity.*

Comparison and Contrast   a method of paragraph and theme development in which the similarities and differences between two or more objects or ideas are pointed out.

Conclusion   effective conclusions bring into focus the main point. The paragraph making the last important point, or the climactic point, may be a thoroughly adequate conclusion. Avoid stopping in the middle of things, rambling, and repetition.

Concrete Words   words that refer to things or objects and thus bring exactness and suggestiveness to writing.

Connotation and Denotation   the denotation of a word is its literal, dictionary meaning; its connotation is the meaning it conveys because of the context in which it is used or the particular associations it has for the reader.

Contrast   See *Comparison and Contrast.*

Deduction   a method of reasoning in which the conclusion follows necessarily from the premises presented. The pattern of development proceeds from the general to the specific. See also *Induction.*

Definition   in logic, placing a term in a general class and then showing how it differs from others within that class. In rhetoric, definition is a method of development in which the meaning of a term is shown by various techniques: description, example, synonyms, origin, history, or comparison and contrast.

Denotation   See *Connotation and Denotation.*

Description   traditionally, one of the four basic kinds of discourse. (The others are *Argumentation, Exposition,* and *Narration.*) Description conveys a sensory impression of a person, object, feeling, or event.

Diction   in rhetoric, diction refers to choice of words in speaking or writing. The skillful writer chooses words that are clear, effective, and appropriate.

Ending   your themes should not merely stop; they should end with an effective conclusion. Some ways to end your essay: summarize your major ideas, conclude with a restatement of your thesis, draw a logical conclusion from the facts you have presented.

Equivocation   a fallacy in which the same term is used with different meanings. In writing, equivocation occurs when abstract words like *democracy* or *freedom* are used in one way at the beginning of a paper and in another way later on.

Euphemism   an indirect reference or softening expression that refers to unpleasant or embarrassing things. Examples: "passed on" for "died," "expecting" for "pregnant."

Exemplification   the use of examples to explain or clarify a subject. Examples may be used either as evidence to support the author's thesis or as illustrations in a deductive pattern.

Exposition   traditionally, one of the four basic kinds of discourse. (See also *Argumentation, Description,* and *Narration.*) The purpose of exposition is to inform, illustrate, or explain. Most textbooks depend heavily on exposition, especially in mathematics.

Figurative Language   the broad category for language that goes beyond the literal meaning of the words or phrases. (See also *Hyperbole, Litotes, Metaphor, Metonymy, Oxymoron, Personification,* and *Simile.*)

Generalization   a general statement, idea, or principle based on specific instances. Writers often use generalizations to introduce the topic or thesis.

Hyperbole   the use of extravagant exaggeration for emphasis or intensification (a figure of speech): "He must have been thirty feet tall!"

Idiom   an expression in a language that either does not conform to conventional rules of grammar or has a meaning that cannot be derived from the literal meaning of the words involved. Common expressions such as to "strike a bargain" and "catch a cold" are idioms. (As idioms wear, they often turn into clichés.)

Illustration   a method of developing a generalization through the use of examples that illustrate the subject or thesis.

Imagery   language that conveys sensory impressions. In writing, images tell us about the feelings, sounds, smells, tastes, and sights of life.

Induction   a method of reasoning in which a conclusion is reached by observing a number of specific examples. The pattern of development proceeds from the specific to the general. See also *Deduction.*

Irony   the expression of a meaning that is different from, and sometimes the exact opposite of, the literal meaning of the words themselves; an incongruity. In other words, irony says one thing but means another. (Compare *Paradox.*)

Litotes, or Understatement   a figure of speech that affirms an idea by denying its opposite. For example: "This is no small change you have suggested."

Loose Sentence   a sentence with the main element or idea at the beginning and subordinate elements following.

Metaphor   strictly speaking, a figure of speech that implies a likeness between two otherwise unlike objects; for example: "Tommy wolfed down his dinner" or "He was a tornado." (Compare *Simile.*)

Metonymy and Synecdoche   metonymy is the use of one name for something closely related to it, as when we say "The White House (actually, a representative of the executive branch of the government) announced the appointment of a new Secretary of the Interior this morning."

Synecdoche is the use of the part to signify the whole, or vice versa. ("He asked for the girl's hand in marriage.") Some authorities make a distinction between these two figures of speech; others use metonymy to cover both.

Mood   the dominant emotional state or feeling of a literary work.

Narration   the recounting of action over a period of time. Narration is one of the four basic kinds of discourse. (The others are *Argumentation, Description,* and *Exposition.*)

Non Sequitur   an instance in which the conclusion drawn does not follow from the evidence or claims already made.

Onomatopoeia   words whose names are derived from the sounds they describe: for example, "the boom of the cannon," "the buzzing of the bees."

Oxymoron   a paradoxical combination of seemingly contradictory words in one figure of speech. For example: "friendly enemy," "eloquent silence," "mournful optimist."

Paradox   a statement that seems to contradict itself. As a rhetorical device, paradox can be used to attract attention or to create emphasis.

Parallelism   the arrangement of syntactically similar words, phrases, or clauses in equal or parallel structures.

Parody   a literary work that closely imitates the style of another work or author for purposes of humor or ridicule.

Periodic Sentence   a sentence in which main elements and ideas are placed at the end rather than the beginning.

Personification   a figure of speech in which human feelings or characteristics are ascribed to nonhuman creatures, objects, or abstract ideas: "the courageous tree," "the sighing of the sand."

Plagiarism   stealing someone's ideas and passing them off as one's own, particularly in term papers and other documented research.

Précis   A formal summary or abridgement that retains the order, language, and style of the original work.

Premise   a specific proposition in logical writing. In certain kinds of logical organization, the premise precedes the conclusion.

Proposition   in scholarly writing, it refers to the kind of statement that is being affirmed or denied in an argument.

Pun   a play on the meaning or sounds of words. For instance, "He learned to drive by accidents," "Working with oil colors can be a "paint" in the neck."

Rhetoric   the study of the principles of composition. Included in the study of rhetoric: usage, coherence, unity, logic, and persuasion.

Rhetorical Question   a question to which no answer is expected or required. This device is used by writers to dramatize a situation or to make a comment.

Rhythm   the notion that the way a sentence "sounds" is important in writing. Such matters as alliteration and kinds of sentences add to rhythm.

Satire   any use of derisive wit to attack human follies or vices by making them appear ridiculous, contemptible, or foolish.

Semantics   the study of language, especially the relationship of signs and symbols. Also, the study of the way sentences work and the effect they have on the reader.

Sentence Variety   variation in the length, type, or structure of sentences. There are certain pitfalls to overcome: a series of short, choppy sentences; rambling, directionless long ones; a series of sentences beginning only with the subject, rather than an occasional modifier; a series of periodic sentences with main ideas buried and a resultant lack of emphasis.

Simile   a figure of speech in which two essentially unlike things are explicitly compared; usually introduced by *like, as,* or *than.* (Compare *Metaphor.*)

Slang   the nonstandard vocabulary of a given culture, subculture, or group, often characterized by raciness and spontaneity. Some slang words are colorful or specific and eventually become respectable; others are trite, flat, or vague in meaning.

Style   the distinctive characteristics or qualities of a writer's work.

Support   in argumentative writing, evidence furnished to prove the author's thesis. Support often consists of observation, personal experience, validated facts, or reliable authority.

Symbolism   a device in which one thing is used to represent another because of association, resemblance, or convention. The moon, for example, is often used as a symbol for romance or distance.

Synecdoche   See *Metonymy.*

Syntax   the arrangement of words into phrases and sentences. This term is generally used in commenting on the structure of a literary work.

Thesis   the central topic or idea in a composition; the sentence containing such a statement.

Tone   the author's attitude toward his topic or his audience as reflected in his writing. Tone can vary from neutral or objective to pompous, sentimental, arrogant, cynical, ironic, or sarcastic. It is determined by diction, as well as by selection and arrangement of facts.

Transition   the way in which an author moves from one topic—or aspect of a topic—to another. Transition is usually accomplished by recognizable linguistic devices, such as repetition of words and phrases, restatement of sentences, indirect references or words like *thus, therefore, in conclusion,* or *to summarize,* and so on. In a great deal of contemporary writing, mechanical devices such as stars, subheads, or a series of centered periods (called bullets) are used to show transitions.

Understatement   See *Litotes.*

Unity   the development of one subject or theme at a time. A paragraph or composition that has unity contains only those sentences and ideas that develop its central or guiding purpose. (See also *Coherence.*)

GUIDE TO RHETORIC

In the process of analyzing the essays in this text, we annotated each one, marking certain paragraphs for strong and good use of various rhetorical devices. We thought that this information might be helpful to others who are studying the essays from a rhetorical point of view. The following list is by no means exhaustive, but it does offer specific examples of effective usage of eighteen rhetorical principles and devices.

INDEX

ACKNOWLEDGMENTS *Continued*

THE LANGUAGE OF SOUL copyright © 1968 by Claude Brown. Reprinted by permission of The Sterling Lord Agency, Inc.

CUSTER DIED FOR YOUR SINS reprinted with permission of The Macmillan Company from *Custer Died for Your Sins* by Vine Deloria, Jr. Copyright © 1969 by Vine Deloria Jr.

THE CHICANA AND THE WOMEN'S RIGHTS MOVEMENT reprinted from "The Chicana & the Women's Rights Movement" by Consuelo Nieto in *Civil Rights Digest,* Spring 1974. Used by permission of the author.

JESUS VIEWED AS A WOMAN'S LIBERATIONIST reprinted by permission of The Associated Press.

UNLIBERATED, BUT BORN FREE copyright 1970, Los Angeles Times. Reprinted by permission.

THE SEXUAL REVOLUTION from an article by Arnold Toynbee in *Realities,* February 1971. Reprinted by permission.

HOW AMERICANS CHOOSE THEIR HEROES reprinted by permission of Charles Scribner's Sons from *The Hero in America* by Dixon Wecter. Copyright 1941 Charles Scribner's Sons; renewal copyright © 1969 Elizabeth Farrar Wecter.

THE DECLINE OF HEROES reprinted by permission of the author from The Saturday Evening Post. November 1, 1958.

AENEAS: THE ROMAN HERO reprinted by permission of Macmillan & Co. Ltd. from C. M. Bowra's *From Virgil to Milton.*

LET'S STOP ENFORCING THE POT LAWS reprinted by permission of the author.

A MODEST PROPOSAL reprinted by permission from High Fidelity Magazine, June 1970. Copyright 1970.

PESSIMISM AND OPTIMISM from *Out of My Life and Thought* by Albert Schweitzer. Translated by C. T. Campion. Copyright 1933, 1949, © 1961 by Holt, Rinehart and Winston, Inc., and George Allen & Unwin, Ltd., London.

ELEPHANTS ARE DIFFERENT TO DIFFERENT PEOPLE: from *Home Front Memo,* copyright, 1943, by Carl Sandburg; renewed, 1971, by Lillian Steichen Sandburg. Reprinted by permission of Harcourt Brace Jovanovich, Inc.

NOBEL PRIZE ACCEPTANCE SPEECH reprinted from *The Faulkner Reader,* by William Faulkner. Copyright 1954 by William Faulkner. Reprinted by permission of Random House, Inc., and Chatto & Windus Ltd., London.

THE PERILS OF OBEDIENCE as it appeared in *Harper's Magazine.* Abridged and adapted from *Obedience To Authority* by Stanley Milgram. Copyright © 1974 by Stanley Milgram. Permission of Harper & Row, Publishers, Inc. and Tavistock Publishers Ltd.

JACKALS AND ARABS reprinted by permission of Schocken Books, Inc., and Martin Secker & Warburg Limited, from *The Penal Colony,* by Franz Kafka. Copyright © 1948 by Schocken Books, Inc.

A FABLE FOR OUR TIMES reprinted by permission of the author from the Sierra Club Bulletin, July 1970. Copyright 1970, James E. Ramsey.

CO-EXISTENCE OR NO EXISTENCE reprinted by permission from The Nation, June 18, 1955.

THE MOST CHEERFUL GRAVEYARD IN THE WORLD copyright © 1958 by Paul Jacobs. Reprinted by permission of Cyrilly Abels, Literary Agent.

MONSTER IN A MASON JAR copyright © 1973 by Annie Dillard. Published in *Harper's Magazine* August, 1973. Drawn from *Pilgrim at Tinker Creek.* Reprinted by permission of the author and her agent Blanche C. Gregory, Inc.

TWO CHEERS FOR TECHNOLOGY reprinted by permission of the author and publisher from THE SATURDAY REVIEW, February 20, 1971. Copyright 1971, Saturday Review, Inc.

SCIENCE, THE DESTROYER OR CREATOR reprinted by permission of Harvard University Press, and Heinemann Educational Books Ltd., from Jacob Bronowski, *The Common Sense of Science* (Harvard University Press, 1953).

THE TWO CULTURES reprinted by permission of the Cambridge University Press from *The Two Cultures* and *The Scientific Revolution*, by C. P. Snow.

THE COSMIC ORPHAN reprinted by permission of the author and *The Encyclopedia Britannica*.

WHY DID THEY GO? reprinted by permission of Charles Scribner's Sons, from "Why Did They Go?" from *The Innocent Assassins* by Loren Eiseley. Copyright © 1973 Loren Eiseley. Also reprinted by permission of Garnstone Press.

SCIENCE HAS SPOILED MY SUPPER copyright 1954 by The Atlantic Monthly Company, Boston, Mass. 02116. Reprinted by permission of Harold Ober Associates Inc.

THE SHAPE OF ANCIENT SEAS from *The Sea Around Us,* by Rachel L. Carson. Copyright 1950, 1951, 1961 by Rachel L. Carson. Reprinted by permission of Oxford University Press, Inc., and Marie Rodell.

A BRIEF GUIDE TO CIVIL DISOBEDIENCE © 1972–1974 by The New York Times Company. Reprinted by permission.

LOVE IS A FALLACY copyright 1951 by Max Shulman, reprinted by permission of Harold Matson Co. Inc.

SOLVE THAT PROBLEM—WITH HUMOR reprinted with permission from the May 1973 *Reader's Digest,* copyright 1973 by The Reader's Digest Assn., Inc. Condensed from *Christian Herald.*

THE HIDDEN TEACHER from "The Hidden Teacher," © 1964, 1969, by Loren Eiseley. Reprinted from his volume, *The Unexpected Universe,* by permission of Harcourt Brace Jovanovich, Inc., and Victor Gollanctz Ltd.

WHAT IS A REBEL? from *The Rebel* by Albert Camus, translated by Anthony Bower. Copyright © 1956 by Alfred A. Knopf, Inc. Reprinted by permission of Alfred A. Knopf, Inc., and Hamish Hamilton, Ltd.

A PRIMER OF EXISTENTIALISM from an article by Gordon Bigelow in College English, December 1961. Copyright © 1961 by The National Council of Teachers of English. Reprinted by permission of the publisher and Gordon Bigelow.

THE MYSTIC'S EXPERIENCE OF GOD reprinted by permission of the estate of the author from *The Atlantic Monthly,* November 1921. Copyright 1921, 1942, The Atlantic Monthly Company, Boston, Massachusetts 02116.

SCREWTAPE LETTERS 8 AND 9 from *The Screwtape Letters* and *Screwtape Proposes a Toast,* by C. S. Lewis. Copyright 1942 by C. S. Lewis. Reprinted by permission of The Macmillan Company and Curtis Brown Ltd.

IN DEFENSE OF GOD reprinted by permission from *Look,* April 19, 1966. Copyright 1966 by Cowles Communications, Inc.

ART AS HOPE FOR HUMANITY reprinted by permission of *Saturday Review.*

THEY BECAME WHAT THEY BEHELD originally appeared in *Playboy* magazine. Copyright © 1970 by Ken Heyman and Edmund Carpenter. Reprinted by permission of Outerbridge & Dienstfrey.

Selections Appearing in ROBERT FROST ON WRITING, are taken from the following sources: SELECTED PROSE OF ROBERT FROST, edited by Hyde Cox and Edward Connery Lathem. Copyright 1939, 1954, © 1966, 1967 by Holt, Rinehart and Winston, Inc. Copyright 1946, © 1959, by Robert Frost. Copyright © 1956 by The Estate of Robert Frost. Reprinted by permission of Holt, Rinehart and Winston, Publishers and Jonathan Cape, Ltd.

Grateful acknowledgment is made to the Esate of Robert Frost. Copyright © 1973 by The Estate of Robert Frost. Reprinted by permission of the Estate of Robert Frost and Granada Publishing, Ltd.

Edited by   James C. Budd
Designed by   Judy Olson
Sponsoring Editor   Gerald Richardson

The text copy for *Reading, Writing, and Rhetoric, Third Edition,* is set in Book-
man and Trade Gothic Bold Extended; display type is Typositor, Eurostile Bold
Extended, set by Graphic Typesetting Service. Unit openers are by Patricia
Hinley; cover art is by Naomi Takigawa. The book was printed by Kingsport Press.